Business Ethics: A European Perspective

business
ethics

A EUROPEAN PERSPECTIVE

Managing Corporate Citizenship and Sustainability
in the Age of Globalization

ANDREW CRANE and
DIRK MATTEN

OXFORD
UNIVERSITY PRESS

OXFORD
UNIVERSITY PRESS

Great Clarendon Street, Oxford OX2 6DP

Oxford University Press is a department of the University of Oxford.
It furthers the University's objective of excellence in research, scholarship,
and education by publishing worldwide in

Oxford New York
Auckland Bangkok Buenos Aires
Cape Town Chennai Dar es Salaam Delhi Hong Kong Istanbul
Karachi Kolkata Kuala Lumpur Madrid Melbourne Mexico City Mumbai
Nairobi São Paulo Taipei Tokyo Toronto

Oxford is a registered trade mark of Oxford University Press
in the UK and in certain other countries

Published in the United States
by Oxford University Press Inc., New York

British Library Cataloguing in Publication Data
Data available

Library of Congress Cataloging in Publication Data
Data available

ISBN 0-19-925515-6

10 9 8 7 6 5 4 3

Typeset by Graphicraft Limited, Hong Kong
Printed in Great Britain by Antony Rowe Ltd, Chippenham

■ ACKNOWLEDGEMENTS

We gratefully acknowledge the help of numerous people who have provided assistance in writing this book. First, we would like to mention the little army of anonymous OUP reviewers whose invaluable comments contributed much to the development and sharpening of the text. We would also thank Isabelle Maignan for her comments and input into early drafts of the proposal. Geir Andreassen, Robert Caruana, Paula Mullins, Rohit Sharma, and Ceri Thomas: thank you for your research on the case material for this book. We would also like to thank our secretary Elaine Ellard for her valued help at various stages of the book. We would also like to offer thanks to our editor at OUP, Patrick Brindle, for his support, encouragement, and funny emails throughout the development of the manuscript. Since his departure, we have been more than ably supported by Katie Allan, Laura Hodgson, and Amaryllis Roy in the OUP offices. Finally, thank you to everyone at Nottingham, Cardiff, and Swansea Universities who provided comments and encouragement, but mostly just left us alone to do what we had to do.

A. C.
D. M.

■ CONTENTS

PART I
Understanding Business Ethics   5

1 Introducing Business Ethics   7

**PART II
Contextualizing Business Ethics: The Corporate Citizen
and its Stakeholders**

Introduction to Part II

6   Shareholders and Business Ethics

7   Employees and Business Ethics   223

8 Consumers and Business Ethics

10 Civil Society and Business Ethics

■ LIST OF FIGURES

■ LIST OF BOXES

■ INTRODUCTION

Given the respectable number of texts on business ethics that are already on the market, there must be some very good reasons for authors to come forward with yet another one. Although a number of very good books are certainly available, when preparing modules on business ethics over the years, we found ourselves increasingly frustrated with a number of features of existing books. Our main irritation was that whilst we were teaching primarily in Europe, we could only do so either with American books or with rather dated European texts. The American bias was a problem for a variety of reasons, including the different legal context, and different approaches to business ethics evident on either side of the Atlantic. Consequently, the first aim of this book was to provide a student-friendly, comprehensive overview of business ethics from a distinctly European perspective. This does not only include the choice of cases, illustrations, and examples, but also includes the theoretical and conceptual angle. Europe in this sense is treated as more than just another geographical region, since we also honour its different cultural, intellectual, and political legacy.

Next to the European focus, this book is built around three core themes that all represent topical new developments in the field, but which are rarely a feature of other texts on the market. These are globalization, sustainability, and corporate citizenship.

Many texts in business ethics mention *globalization*, but usually as a separate chapter or sub-issue. As we do not think that this mirrors the business reality of contemporary economic life, or for that matter of our students, this book treats globalization as a central topic that pertains to every aspect of business ethics. However, in seeking to avoid the trap of using the 'G-word' as just another fashionable buzzword, we carefully ground our views in recent theoretical developments about the concept and its meaning.

Another major element of this book is *sustainability*. This again is one of the most commonly used (and misused) terms in the current discourse on business ethics, but rarely gets much of an airing in business ethics textbooks. Once more, our intention has been to treat sustainability as a key concept throughout the entire book, whilst at the same time enabling readers to access the topic from a critical perspective.

The third central concept is the notion of *corporate citizenship*, again a popular way of framing certain ethical issues in business practice at the moment, especially by business people. We are, once more, not uncritical of this terminology and its usage, and in fact we hope to show that a critical perspective on corporate citizenship can help us to examine some of the major social, economic, and political challenges that arise in contemporary business practice.

Overall, then, the book is scholarly, but with a strong emphasis on making the text interesting, readable, and accessible to students and practising managers (such as those doing executive courses). This applied approach means that examples and illustrations are used throughout the book in order to illuminate and test out theoretical insights and concepts. In addition, we provide in each chapter the following features:

Part I: Understanding Business Ethics

Chapter 1:
Introducing Business Ethics

Chapter 2: Framing Business Ethics	**Chapter 3:** Evaluating Business Ethics	**Chapter 4:** Making Decisions in Business Ethics	**Chapter 5:** Managing Business Ethics
Corporate Responsibility, Stakeholders, and Citizenship	Normative Ethical Theories	Descriptive Ethical Theories	Tools and Techniques of Business Ethics Management

Part II: Contextualizing Business Ethics—The Corporate Citizen and its Stakeholders

Chapter 6: Shareholders	**Chapter 7:** Employees	**Chapter 8:** Consumers	**Chapter 9:** Suppliers and Competitors	**Chapter 10:** Civil Society	**Chapter 11:** Government and Regulation
Shareholders as Stakeholders	Employees as Stakeholders	Consumers as Stakeholders	Suppl. and Comp. as Stakeholders	Civil Society as Stakeholders	Government as Stakeholders
Ethical Issues	Ethical Issues	Ethical Issues	Ethical Issues	Ethical Issues	Ethical Issues
Shareholders & Globalization	Employees & Globalization	Consumers & Globalization	Suppl. and Comp. & Globalization	Civil Society & Globalization	Government & Globalization
Shareholders & Citizenship	Employees & Citizenship	Consumers & Citizenship	Suppl. and Comp. & Citizenship	Civil Society & Citizenship	Government & Citizenship
Shareholders & Sustainability	Employees & Sustainability	Consumers & Sustainability	Suppl. and Comp. & Sustainability	Civil Society & Sustainability	Government & Sustainability

Chapter 12: Conclusions and Future Perspectives

Figure A. Structure of the book

- Two extended 'Ethics in Action' examples based on current dilemmas faced by industry, leading-edge initiatives, or high-profile ethics cases that have hit the national press.

- One hypothetical 'Ethical Dilemma' relevant to the chapter content. These describe an ethical scenario and provide you with the opportunity to think about what you would do in a typical business ethics situation.

- One end of chapter 'Case study' that describes in some detail the events surrounding high-profile business ethics problems or decisions faced in Europe by leading companies (or industries) such as BMW, Elf, Ericsson, McDonald's, Nestlé, and Shell.

- A liberal sprinkling of invitations to 'Think theory', providing you with the opportunity to apply theoretical material to the practical issues and real-world examples discussed in the chapters.

- A series of end of chapter 'Study questions' and a 'Research exercise' that provide the opportunity to test your knowledge and understanding of the material covered, and encourage you to apply your knowledge to other cases and examples from the real world.

Structure of the book

The book consists of two parts, as shown in Figure A. In the initial section, *Part I*, the key conceptual foundations of the book are presented, enabling you to gain a thorough understanding of business ethics in theory and practice. In the second section, *Part II*, of the book, this material will be used to examine business ethics in different contexts. Each chapter will focus on an individual stakeholder group, and will explore the ethical issues and challenges typically encountered by the corporation in dealing with these constituencies.

Chapter 1 provides a basic introduction to the concept of business ethics, and its importance both at an academic level, and in terms of practical management in organizations. As well as explaining the European focus adopted in the book, this chapter introduces two of the main themes of the book, namely globalization and sustainability.

Chapter 2 introduces ways of framing business ethics in the context of the corporation being part of a wider society. The chapter provides a concise overview of concepts such as corporate social responsibility and stakeholder theory, and leads on to an analysis of key contemporary concepts such as corporate accountability and corporate citizenship. Although as yet relatively under-theorized, we identify corporate citizenship in particular as offering important conceptual space for understanding business ethics beyond its traditional boundaries.

Chapter 3 sets out the key normative ethical theories that can be applied to business ethics problems, in terms of both traditional and contemporary theoretical approaches. Our main intention is to identify a pragmatic approach to theory application.

Chapter 4 provides an alternative way of addressing these questions of ethical decision-making by looking at how decisions are actually made in business ethics, and by assessing the various descriptive theories in the literature. The main focus is on revealing the different influences on how (and whether) business people recognize and deal with ethical problems.

Chapter 5 provides a critical examination of proposals for managing business ethics through specific tools, techniques, practices, and processes. We do so by looking at the importance of, and problems in, attempting to manage business ethics in the global economy, and the development over time of different ethics tools and techniques.

Part II of the book takes these foundations and applies them to individual stakeholder groups. The structure of each chapter therefore breaks down into five main parts: (*a*) the nature of the stake held by the particular group; (*b*) the main ethical issues arising in the firm's relation to this group; (*c*) a deepening discussion of those issues in the light of the challenges of globalization; (*d*) an analysis from the viewpoint of corporate citizenship thinking; and (*e*) an assessment of the challenges of sustainability for the specific stakeholder group.

Chapter 6 sets out the rights and responsibilities of *shareholders*, emphasizing the changing nature of ownership and governance in the global economy. It highlights also specific changes in the role of shareholders as initiators of ethical change in the corporation.

Chapter 7 examines ethical issues in relation to *employees*. It discusses the various rights and duties of this stakeholder group. It also sets out the specific context of European models of employee relations, and enlarges the perspectives to employee constituencies in the developing world.

Chapter 8 considers the ethical issues arising in the context of *consumers*. We address problems both old and new, and ultimately question the divergence in interests between marketers, consumers, and society.

Chapter 9 explores the ethical issues arising in relation to firms' *suppliers* and *competitors*. In so doing, we discuss a group of stakeholders that has not been discussed in business ethics very intensively so far, but which is crucial for an understanding of the broad context of business relations.

Chapter 10 considers the relationships between businesses and *civil society organizations* (CSOs), addressing the changing patterns of relationship between these traditionally adversarial institutions. This stakeholder group is certainly one of the fastest growing in relevance, posing a fundamental challenge to business organizations in the age of globalization.

Chapter 11 covers *government* and *regulation*. Government as a stakeholder is a very multifaceted group, which we unpack at various levels, functions, and areas. The chapter also examines the shifting relationships between regulation, government, and business, stressing the increasingly important role played by corporations in the politics of the global economy.

Chapter 12 finally provides a review of the previous chapters and assesses the major topics of the book (citizenship, sustainability, globalization, European focus, etc.) and draws conclusions about the future relevance of the issues discussed throughout the book.

PART I

Understanding Business Ethics

Introducing Business Ethics

In this chapter we will:

• Provide a basic introduction and definition of business ethics;

• Outline the relationship between business ethics and the law;

• Distinguish between ethics, morality, and ethical theory;

• Discuss the importance of business ethics both at an academic level and in terms of practical management in organizations;

• Present globalization as an important, yet contested concept, which represents a critical new context for business ethics;

• Present the 'triple bottom line' of sustainability as a potential new goal for business ethics;

• Critically examine the argument that there is a distinctive European perspective on business ethics.

What is business ethics?

'A book on business ethics? Well that won't take long to read!'

'You're taking a course on business ethics? So what do you do in the afternoon?'

'Business ethics? I didn't think there were any!'

These are not very good jokes. Still, that does not seem to have stopped a lot of people from responding with such comments (and others like them) whenever students of business ethics start talking about what they are doing. And even if they are not particularly funny things to say, nor even very original, they do immediately raise an important problem with the subject of business ethics: some people cannot even believe that it exists!

Business ethics, it has been claimed, is an oxymoron (Collins 1994). By an oxymoron, we mean the bringing together of two apparently contradictory concepts, such as in 'a cheerful pessimist' or 'a deafening silence'. To say that business ethics is an oxymoron suggests that there are not, or cannot be, ethics in business: that business is in some way unethical (i.e. that business is inherently bad), or that it is, at best, amoral (i.e. outside of our normal moral considerations). For example, in the latter case, Albert Carr (1968) notoriously argued in his article 'Is business bluffing ethical' that the 'game' of business was not subject to the same moral standards as the rest of society, but should be regarded as analogous to a game of poker where deception and lying were perfectly permissible.

To some extent, it is not surprising that some people think this way. Various scandals concerning undesirable business activities, such as the despoiling of rivers with industrial pollutants, the exploitation of sweatshop workers, the payment of bribes to government officials, and the deception of unwary consumers, have highlighted the unethical way in which some firms have gone about their business. However, just because such malpractices take place, this does not mean that there are not some kinds of values or principles driving such decisions. After all, even what we might think of as 'bad' ethics is still ethics of a sort. And clearly it makes sense to try and understand why those decisions get made in the first place, and indeed to try and discover whether more acceptable business decisions and approaches can be developed.

Certainly, then, the revelations of corporate malpractice should not be interpreted to mean that thinking about ethics in business situations is entirely redundant. After all, as various writers have shown, many everyday business activities require the maintenance of basic ethical standards, such as honesty, trustworthiness, and co-operation (Collins 1994; Watson 1994). Business activity would be impossible if corporate directors always lied; if buyers and sellers never trusted each other; or if employees refused to ever help each other.

Similarly, it would be wrong to infer that scandals involving corporate wrongdoing mean that the *subject* of business ethics is in some way naive or idealistic. Indeed, on the contrary, it can be argued that the subject of business ethics primarily exists in order to provide us with some answers as to *why* certain decisions should be evaluated as ethical or unethical, or right or wrong. Without systematic study, how are we able to offer anything more than vague opinions or hunches about whether particular business activities are acceptable?

Whichever way one looks at it, then, there appears to be good reason to suggest that business ethics as a phenomenon, and as a subject, is not an oxymoron. Whilst there will inevitably be disagreements about what exactly constitutes 'ethical' business activity, it is possible at least to offer a fairly uncontroversial definition of the subject itself. So, in a nutshell, here is what we regard the subject of business ethics as:

> Business ethics is the study of business situations, activities, and decisions where issues of right and wrong are addressed.

It is worth stressing that by 'right' and 'wrong' we mean morally right and wrong as opposed to, for example, commercially, strategically, or financially right or wrong. Moreover, by 'business' ethics, we do not mean only commercial businesses, but also government organizations, pressure groups, not-for-profit businesses, charities, and other organizations. For example, questions about how to manage employees fairly, or what constitutes deception in advertising, are equally as important for organizations such as Greenpeace, the University of Stockholm, or the German Christian Democrat Party as they are for Shell, Volvo, or Deutsche Bank. However, given the high profile of ethical issues in relation to commercial businesses, it is on these types of businesses that we shall predominantly focus in this book.

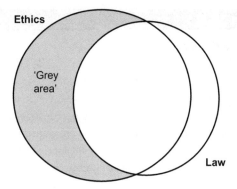

Figure 1.1. The relationship between ethics and the law

Business ethics and the law

Having defined business ethics in terms of issues of right and wrong, one might quite naturally question whether this is in any way distinct from the law. Surely the law is also about issues of right and wrong? This is true, and there is indeed considerable overlap between ethics and the law. In fact, the law is essentially an institutionalization or codification of ethics into specific social rules, regulations, and proscriptions. Nonetheless, the two are not equivalent. Perhaps the best the way of thinking about ethics and the law is in terms of two intersecting domains (see **Figure 1.1**). The law might be said to be a definition of the minimum acceptable standards of behaviour. However, many morally contestable issues, whether in business or elsewhere, are not explicitly covered by the law. For example, just as there is no law preventing you from being unfaithful to your girlfriend or boyfriend (although this is perceived by many to be unethical), so there is no law in many European countries preventing businesses from testing their products on animals, selling landmines to oppressive regimes, or preventing their employees from joining a union—again, issues which many feel very strongly about. Similarly, it is possible to think of issues that are covered by the law, but which are not really about ethics. For example, the law prescribes whether we should drive on the right or the left side of the road. Although this prevents chaos on the roads, the decision about which side we should drive is not an ethical decision as such.

In one sense, then, business ethics can be said to begin where the law ends. Business ethics is primarily concerned with those issues not covered by the law, or where there is no definite consensus on whether something is right or wrong. Discussion about the ethics of particular business practices may eventually *lead* to legislation once some kind of consensus is reached, but for most of the issues of interest to business ethics, the law typically does not currently provide us with guidance. For this reason, it is often said that business ethics is about the 'grey areas' of business, or where, as Treviño and Nelson (1999: 4) put it, 'values are in conflict'. **Ethical Dilemma 1** presents one such situation that you might face where values are in conflict. Read through this and have a go at answering the questions at the end.

As we shall see many times over in this book, the problem of trying to make decisions in the grey areas of business ethics, or where values may be in conflict, means that many

Ethical Dilemma 1

No such thing as a free drink?

A good friend of yours who studies at the same university has been complaining for some time to you that he never has any money. He decides that he needs to go out and find a job, and after searching for a while, he is offered a job as a bartender in the student bar at your university. He gladly accepts and begins working three nights a week. You too are pleased, not only because it means that your friend will have more money, but also because the fact is that you often go to student bar anyway and so will continue to see him quite frequently despite him having the new job.

The extra money is indeed much welcomed by your friend (especially as he has less time to spend it now too), and initially he seems to enjoy the work. You are also rather pleased with developments since you notice that whenever you go up to the bar, your friend always serves you first regardless of how many people are waiting at the time.

After a while though, it becomes apparent that your friend is enjoying the job rather less. Whenever you see him, he always seems to have a new story of mild, but annoying treatment at the hands of the bar manager, such as getting the worst shifts, being repeatedly chosen to do the least popular jobs, and being reprimanded for the kind of minor blunders which go uncensured for the rest of the staff.

This goes on for a short while, and then one day, when you are in the bar having a drink with some of your other friends, your friend the bartender does something that you are not quite sure how to react to. When you go up to pay for a round of four beers for you and your other friends, he discreetly only charges you for one. Whilst you are slightly uncomfortable with this, you certainly don't want to get your friend into any kind of trouble by mentioning it. And when you tell your friends about it, they of course think it is very funny and congratulate you for the cheap round of drinks! In fact, when the next one of your friends goes up to pay for some drinks, he turns around and asks you to take his money, so that you can do the same trick for him. Although you tell him to get his own drinks, your friend the bartender continues to undercharge you whenever it is your turn to go to the bar. In fact this goes on for a number of visits, until you resolve to at least say something to him when no one else behind the bar is listening. However, when you do end up raising the subject he just laughs it off and says, 'Yeah, it's great isn't it? They'll never notice and you get a cheap night out. Besides, it's only what this place deserves after the way I've been treated.'

Questions

1 Who is wrong in this situation—your friend for undercharging you, you for accepting it, or neither of you?

2 Confronted by this situation, how would you handle it? Would you ask your friend to stop undercharging you? If so, what if he refused?

3 To what extent do you think that being deliberately undercharged is different from other forms of preferential treatment, such as serving you in front of other waiting customers?

4 Does the fact that your friend feels aggrieved at the treatment he receives from his boss condone his behaviour at all? Does it help to explain either his or your actions?

of the questions posed are *equivocal*. There simply may not be a definitive 'right' answer to many business ethics problems. And as is the case with issues such as the animal testing of products, executive pay, persuasive sales techniques, or child labour, business ethics problems also tend to be very controversial and open to widely different points of view. In this sense business ethics is not like subjects such as accounting, finance, engineering, or business law where you are supposed to learn specific procedures and facts in order to make objectively correct decisions. Studying business ethics should help you to make *better* decisions, but this is not the same as making unequivocally *right* decisions.

Defining morality, ethics, and ethical theory

Some of the controversy regarding business ethics is no doubt due to different understandings of what constitutes morality or ethics in the first place. Before we continue, then, it is important for us to sort out some of the terminology we are using.

In common usage, the terms 'ethics' and 'morality' are often used interchangeably. In many ways, it is probably true to say that this does not pose many real problems for most of us in terms of communicating and understanding things about business ethics. However, in order to clarify certain arguments, many academic writers have proposed clear differences between the two terms (e.g. Crane 2000; M. Parker 1998). Unfortunately though, different writers have sometimes offered somewhat different distinctions, thereby serving more to confuse us than clarify our understanding.[1] Nonetheless, we do agree that there are certain advantages in making a distinction between 'ethics' and 'morality', and following what we feel is the most common and useful way of distinguishing them, we offer this distinction:

> Morality is concerned with the norms, values, and beliefs embedded in social processes which define right and wrong for an individual or a community.

> Ethics is concerned with the study of morality and the application of reason to elucidate specific rules and principles that determine right and wrong for any given situation. These rules and principles are called ethical theories.

In this way of thinking, then, morality precedes ethics, which in turn precedes ethical theory (see **Figure 1.2**). All individuals and communities have morality, a basic sense of right or wrong in relation to particular activities. Ethics represents an attempt to systematize and rationalize morality into generalized normative rules that supposedly offer a solution to all situations of moral uncertainty.[2] The outcomes of the codification of these

---

[1] For example, Kelemen and Peltonen (2001) analyse the different usage of the concepts of 'ethics' and 'morality' in the writings of Michel Foucault and Zygmunt Bauman, two leading authors in the area of postmodern business ethics. They reveal strikingly different distinctions that in fact virtually provide a direct contradiction to one another.

[2] The emergence of the formal study of ethics is therefore aligned by several authors such as Bauman (1993), Johnson and Smith (1999), and M. Parker (1998) with the modernist Enlightenment project, and the idea that moral uncertainty can be 'solved' with recourse to human rationality and abstract reasoning. As we shall show in Chapters 3 and 4, this has come under increasing attack from a number of quarters including feminists and postmodernists.

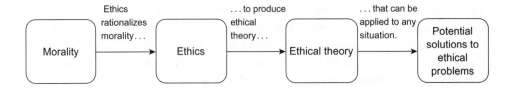

Figure 1.2. The relationship between morality, ethics, and ethical theory

rules are ethical theories, such as rights theory or justice theory. The importance of this distinction will hopefully therefore become clearer, and will certainly become more pertinent, as we start to examine these and other theories (in Chapter 3), as well as assessing how they feed into ethical decision-making in business (in Chapter 4). Indeed, contributing to the enhancement of ethical decision-making is one of the primary aims of this book, and of the subject of business ethics more generally. In the next section, we shall briefly review this and some of the other reasons why studying business ethics is becoming increasingly important today in Europe and beyond.

Why is business ethics important?

Business ethics is currently a very prominent business topic, and the debates and dilemmas surrounding business ethics have tended to attract an enormous amount of attention from various quarters. For a start, consumers and pressure groups appear to be increasingly demanding that firms should seek out more ethical and ecologically sounder ways of doing business. The media also constantly seems to be keeping the spotlight on corporate abuses and malpractices. And even firms themselves appear to be increasingly recognizing that being ethical (or at the very least being seen to be ethical) may actually be good for business. In recent years, we have even seen protesters of all kinds in the streets of Seattle, Stockholm, Genoa, London, and elsewhere actually challenging the very nature of capitalism and questioning the impact of global corporations on society.

There are therefore many reasons why business ethics might be regarded as an increasingly important area of study, whether for students interested in evaluating business activities, or for managers seeking to improve their decision-making skills. Here then are the main reasons why we think that a strong understanding of business ethics is important:

1. The power and influence of business in society is greater than ever before. Evidence suggests that many members of the public are uneasy with such developments (Bernstein 2000). Business ethics helps us to understand why this is happening, what its implications might be, and how we might address this situation.

2. Business malpractices have the potential to inflict enormous harm on individuals, on communities, and on the environment. Through helping us to understand more about the causes and consequences of these malpractices, business ethics seeks, as

the founding editor of the *Journal of Business Ethics* has suggested (Michalos 1988), 'to improve the human condition'.[3]

3. The demands being placed on business to be ethical by its various stakeholders are constantly becoming more complex and more challenging. Business ethics provides the means to appreciate and understand these challenges more clearly, in order that firms can meet these ethical expectations more effectively.

4. Few business people in Europe and elsewhere have received formal business ethics education or training. Business ethics can help to improve ethical decision-making by providing managers with the appropriate knowledge and tools that allow them to correctly identify, diagnose, analyse, and provide solutions to the ethical problems and dilemmas they are confronted with.

5. Ethical infractions continue to occur in business. Ferrell et al. (2000: 13), for example, cite a survey revealing that 48 per cent of US employees claimed to have done something unethical or illegal in the previous year. Business ethics provides us with a way of looking at the reasons behind this, and the ways in which such problems might be dealt with by managers, regulators, and others interested in improving business ethics.

6. Business ethics can provide us with the ability to assess the benefits and problems associated with different ways of managing ethics in organizations.   )

7. Finally, business ethics is also extremely interesting in that it supplies us with knowledge that transcends the traditional framework of business studies and confronts us with some of the most important questions faced by society. The subject can therefore be richly rewarding to study because it provides us with knowledge and skills which are not simply helpful for doing business, but rather, by helping us to understand modern societies in a more systematic way, can advance our ability to address life situations far beyond the classroom or the office desk.

This is not to say there are not problems with the subject of business ethics, and these have prompted writers such as Andrew Stark (1994) to pose the question 'what's the matter with business ethics?' and Tom Sorrell (1998) to pronounce on the 'strange state of business ethics'. After all, despite many years of business ethics being researched and taught in colleges and universities, ethics problems persist and the public remains sceptical of the ethics of business. However, in the main these concerns are focused on how theories of business ethics have been developed and applied, rather than questioning the importance of business ethics as a subject *per se*.

Indeed, there does seem to be a growing consensus regarding the importance of business ethics, whether by students, by academics, by governments, by consumers, or of course by businesses. There are now modules in business ethics being run in universities across Europe; there has been an outpouring of journal and newspaper articles on the subject; and one recent review reported finding over 20,000 web pages and nearly 1,200

---

[3] For a summary and assessment of the contribution to this endeavour of the first eighteen volumes of the *Journal of Business Ethics* (i.e. 1982–99), see Collins (2000).

books on business ethics (Kelemen and Peltonen 2001). Similarly, the last few years have witnessed significant growth in what might be regarded as the business ethics 'industry', i.e. corporate ethics officers, independent ethics consultants, ethical investment trusts, and activities associated with ethics auditing, monitoring, and reporting (as have been recently developed by the likes of KPMG, McKinsey, PriceWaterhouseCoopers, and others).

What is clear then is that business ethics has not only been recognized as increasingly important, but has also undergone rapid changes and developments during the past decade or so. In this book, we are concerned with addressing what we see as the two most fundamental challenges facing business ethics in Europe at this time: the new context provided by the phenomenon of globalization; and the new goals represented by the concept of sustainability.

Globalization: a new context for business ethics?

Globalization has become one of the most prominent buzzwords of recent times. Whether in newspaper articles, politicians' speeches, or business leaders' press conferences, the 'G-word' is frequently identified as one of the most important issues in contemporary society. In the business community in particular there has been considerable enthusiasm about globalization. For instance, the chairman of Goldman Sachs has talked of 'the gospel of globalization' and has praised the increasingly interconnected world economy and its benefits for economic growth, global welfare, democracy, and world peace (Paulson 2001).

But globalization is not unanimously viewed as a positive development. Similar to the anti-nuclear power movement back in the 1970s, we have witnessed the rise of a new worldwide culture of 'anti-globalization' campaigners. Like a consecutive global festival, they turn up at every meeting of the WTO, the IMF, the World Bank, or the summits of G8 or EU leaders and articulate their profound criticism and often violent protest against the 'global world order', 'global capitalism', the 'dictate of the multinationals', and so on. Riots in Seattle, Davos, Prague, and Genoa have made the public aware of the fact that globalization is a highly contested and controversial topic on the public agenda.

In the context of business ethics, this controversy over globalization plays a crucial role. After all, corporations—most notably multinational corporations (MNCs)—are at the centre of the public's criticism on globalization. They are accused of exploiting workers in less developed countries (LDCs), destroying the environment, and, by abusing their economic power, engaging less developed countries in a so-called 'race to the bottom'. This term describes a process whereby MNCs pitch LDCs against each other by allocating their investment to those countries which offer them the most favourable conditions in terms of low tax rates, low level of environmental regulation, and restricted workers' rights. However true these accusations are in practice, there is no doubt that globalization is the most current and demanding arena in which corporations have to define and legitimize the 'right or wrong' of their behaviour.

What is globalization?

Globalization is not only a very controversial topic in the public debate, it is also a very contested term in academic discourse.[4] Apart from the fact that—mirroring the public debate—the camp seems to be divided into supporters and critics, there is growing concern about whether globalization is a fact at all. So, for example, some argue that there is nothing like a 'global' economy, because roughly 90 per cent of world trade only takes part between the three great economic blocks of the EU, North America, and Japan, leaving out all other major parts of the globe (Rugman 2000). Obviously, we have to examine the 'globalization' buzzword more carefully and to develop a more precise definition if we want to understand its character and its implications for business ethics.

What globalization is not

Using the work of Jan Aart Scholte (2000), we will try to bring some order into the chaos of 'global blurb' by examining various definitions which are often used, but which do not really identify the central and new character of globalization. These redundant concepts of globalization, which are especially popular among authors in business studies, are characterized by Scholte (2000: 44–6) as follows:

- Globalization as *internationalization*: many see the recent increase in cross-border transactions as the new defining element of globalization. However, this has not been a new development. This phenomenon was already well established in ancient history, and even at the end of the nineteenth century, the percentage of cross-border transactions worldwide was not considerably lower than at the end of the twentieth century (Moore and Lewis 1999).

- Globalization as *liberalization*: the recent globalization debate coincides with an increase in trade liberalization and various kinds of deregulation. Nevertheless, this phenomenon is much older and does not justify the invention and use of the term 'globalization' to describe it.

- Globalization as *universalization*: an aspect of globalization is the fact that it leads to an increasing global spread of products, lifestyles, and ideas. However, this is not a new phenomenon either: throughout the last 2,000 years, for example, world religions such as Christianity or Islam have spread over large parts of the globe with the same unifying power and assimilating effects on people's lives. Therefore a new term such as 'globalization' is not needed to describe this old phenomenon.

- Globalization as *westernization*: much of the criticism on globalization focuses on the fact that it results in the export of western culture to other, culturally different world regions. Again, this is not a new phenomenon at all: the era of colonization in the nineteenth century resulted in the export of various facets of western culture to the colonized countries, evidenced for example by the British legacy in countries such as India, the Spanish legacy in South America, and the French legacy in Africa.

---

[4] There is a wide range of literature addressing globalization and its meaning. Good introductions are provided by Beck (1999), Giddens (1999), and Held and McGrew (2000).

What globalization is

All of these views of globalization describe some of the more visible features of globaliza-tion. They are certainly important issues, but as Scholte (2000) shows, they do not char-acterize the significantly *new* aspects of globalization. If we want to get a grasp on the decisive features of globalization, he suggests we can start by looking at the way social connections traditionally took place. These connections, be it personal relations to family members or friends, or economic relations such as shopping or working, took place within a certain territory. People had their family and friends in a certain village, they had their work and business relations within a certain town or even country. Social interaction traditionally needed a certain geographical space to take place. However, this link between social con-nections and a certain territory has been continuously weakened, mainly by two develop-ments during the last few decades.

The first development is *technological* in nature. Modern communication technology, from the telephone, to radio and television, and now the internet, opens up the possibility of connecting and interacting with people despite the fact that there are large geographical distances between them. Furthermore, the rapid development of global transportation technologies allows people to easily connect with other people all over the globe. While Marco Polo had to travel many months to finally arrive in China, people today can step on a plane and, after a passable meal and a short sleep, arrive some time later on the other side of the globe. Territorial distances play a less and less important role today. The people we do business with, or who are our friends, no longer necessarily have to be in the same place as we are.

The second development is *political* in nature. Territorial borders have been the main obstacles to worldwide connections between people. Only fifteen years ago it was still largely impossible to enter the countries in the eastern bloc without lengthy visa pro-cedures, and even then, interactions between people from the two sides were very limited and restricted. With the fall of the Iron Curtain, but also with the huge liberalization efforts for instance within the EU, national borders have been eroded and, in many cases, have even been abolished. In Europe you can drive from Lapland to Sicily without neces-sarily stopping at a single national border.

These two developments mainly account for the massive proliferation and spread in supraterritorial connections. These connections may not always necessarily have a global spread in the literal sense of worldwide spread. The new thing though about these connections is that they no longer need a geographical territory to take place and they are not restricted by territorial distances and borders any more. Scholte (2000: 46–61) thus characterizes glob-alization as *deterritorialization*, suggesting that we can define globalization as follows:

> Globalization is the progressive eroding of the relevance of territorial bases for social, economic, and political activities, processes, and relations.

Let us have a look at some examples of globalization according to this definition:

- Due to the modern communication infrastructure, many of us actually witnessed the crumbling of the World Trade Centre towers on 11 September 2001 live on TV—regardless of where we were located at that time. This event was global not in the sense that it actually happened all over the world, but in the sense that billions of people saw it, and to some extent took part in it, regardless of whether they were standing in Manhattan, Manchester, or Manila.

- We can potentially drink the same Heineken beer, drive the same model of Toyota car, or buy the same expensive Rolex watch almost wherever we are in the world—we do not have to be in Amsterdam, Tokyo, or Geneva. Certain global products are available all over the world and going for a 'Chinese', 'Mexican', or 'French' meal indicates certain tastes and styles rather than a trip to a certain geographical territory.

- We no longer tend to worry about where our bank stores our money and if their 'safes' really deserve that name. We can quite easily have a credit card which allows us to withdraw money all over the world, we can pay our bills at home in Europe via internet banking while sitting in an internet café in India, or even order our Swiss private banking broker to buy an option on halved pigs at the Chicago exchange without even moving our feet from the sofa.

Global communications, global products, and global financial systems and capital markets are only the most striking examples of deterritorialization in the world economy. There are many other areas where globalization in this sense is a significant social, economic, and political process. As we shall now see, globalization also has significant implications for business ethics.

The relevance of globalization for business ethics

Globalization as defined in terms of the deterritorialization of economic activities is particularly relevant for business ethics, and this is evident in three main areas—culture, law, and accountability.

Cultural issues

As business becomes less fixed territorially, so corporations increasingly engage in overseas markets, suddenly finding themselves confronted with new and diverse, sometimes even contradicting ethical demands. Moral values which were taken for granted in the home market may get questioned as soon as corporations enter foreign markets (Donaldson 1996). For example, attitudes to racial and gender diversity in Europe may differ significantly from those in Middle Eastern countries. Similarly, Chinese people might regard it as more unethical to sack employees in times of economic downturns than would be typical in Europe. Again, whilst Europeans tend to regard child labour as strictly unethical, some Asian countries might have a more moderate approach (for further examples see Kumar and Steinmann 1998). **Ethics in Action 1.1** discusses the issues faced by the British clothing retailer French Connection in using its provocative advertising campaign overseas.

■ **Think theory**

Think about the idea of globalization as 'deterritorialization'. What aspects of deterritorialization would you say are evident in the example of FCUK?

Ethics in Action 1.1

FCUK goes international

....

The UK fashion retail chain French Connection experienced considerable commercial success in the highly competitive UK high street during the late 1990s and early 2000s. As founder and CEO Steven Matts has claimed, one of the keys to its success in the UK has lain in the firm's aggressive advertising campaign, establishing the acronym *fcuk* and its connotative meaning at the core of their slogans. The *fcuk* slogan appears to appeal to French Connection's target audience of young consumers and the repeated criticism of their advertising campaigns by the Advertising Standards Authority (ASA) in the UK has only boosted the 'naughty' image of the brand. In the course of 2001, French Connection not only expanded its product range into cosmetics and drinks, but also made a further move towards expanding its international business.

One of the main target markets for French Connection has been the USA. In their effort to establish a global brand, the company has used the same marketing campaigns used in the UK—and faced considerable problems. Even in more liberal places such as New York, San Francisco, or Los Angeles, public outrage was stirred up by the *fcuk* campaigns. So, for instance, some of New York's taxi drivers refused to have the advertisement on their cabs. Earlier on, the company had met similar reactions in Singapore, where public outcry caused the local bus company to ask the company to change their ads showing the letters *fcuk* in black and white on their buses. In the USA, the controversy was even boosted by the fact that many Americans use the word 'fcuk' in place of the direct expletive 'fuck' on the internet in order to avoid filters.

Steve Rabosky, the chief creative officer of the advertising firm Saatchi & Saatchi in Los Angeles, said of the issue: 'The problem over here [in the USA] is it is going to get a lot of censorship. This society is not as open as the UK. If *fcuk* goes outside New York and San Francisco it could run into problems. Things are very politically correct over here right now. The entertainment industry is being pressured to cut back on violence and nudity, and advertising is part of that.'

The risks of this provocative campaign are also boosted by the different legal frameworks in the UK and the USA. Whereas French Connection only faces one central authority, the ASA, in the UK, censorship of advertising in the USA is the responsibility of local authorities. Although in the initial stages of the campaign they had no conflicts with such bodies in New York or San Francisco, expanding their business to Salt Lake City or Atlanta could provoke different reactions.

The *fcuk* case shows that moral values and cultural norms differ significantly across the globe and that corporations have to be very careful in toning their communications to the local specifics. In the event, French Connection decided to run their provocative TV campaigns only on selected US stations such as MTV, which directly focuses on their target audience of young consumers.

SOURCES

BBC (2000). 'Fcuk slogan "not funny" '. BBC News On-line, 5 July, **http://news.bbc.co.uk**.
Benady, D. (2001). 'Fcuk America'. *Marketing Week*, 22 Mar.: 26–9.
Duckers, J. (2001). 'French Connection still confident in the US'. *Financial Times*, 20 Sept.

....

The reason why there is potential for such problems is that whilst globalization results in the deterritorialization of some processes and activities, in many cases there is still a close connection between the local culture, including moral values, and a certain geographical region. For example, Europeans largely disapprove of capital punishment, whilst many Americans appear to regard it as morally acceptable. Women can freely sunbathe topless on most European beaches, yet in some states of America they can get fined for doing so—and in Pakistan would be expected to cover up much more. This is one of the contradictions of globalization: on the one hand, globalization makes regional difference less important since it brings regions together and encourages a more uniform 'global culture'. On the other hand, in eroding the divisions of geographical distances, globalization reveals economic, political, and cultural differences and confronts people with them. This dialectical effect has been a growing subject for research in recent years (see Child 2000; Sorge 2000).

Legal issues

A second aspect is closely linked to our previous observation about the relation between ethics and law. The more economic transactions lose their connection to a certain regional territory, the more they escape the control of the respective national governments. The power of a government has traditionally been confined to a certain territory, for example: French laws are only binding on French territory, UK laws on UK territory, and so on. As soon as a company leaves its home territory and moves part of its production chain to, for example, a third world country, the legal framework becomes very different. Consequently, managers can no longer simply rely on the legal framework when deciding on the right or wrong of certain business practices. If, as we said earlier (see 9), business ethics largely begins where the law ends, then deterritorialization increases the demand for business ethics because deterritorialized economic activities are beyond the control of national (territorial) governments. For example, global financial markets are beyond the control of any national government, and the constant struggle of governments against issues such as child pornography on the internet shows the enormous difficulties in enforcing national laws in deterritorialized spaces.

Accountability issues

Taking a closer look at global activities, one can easily identify corporations as the dominant actors on the global stage: MNCs own the mass media which determines much of our information and entertainment intake, they supply global products, they pay people's salaries, and they pay (directly or indirectly) much of the taxes that keep governments running. Furthermore, one could argue that MNCs are economically more powerful than many governments. For example, the GDP of Denmark is about the same as the turnover of General Motors. However, whereas the Danish government has to be accountable to the Danish people and must face elections on a regular basis, the managers of General Motors are formally accountable only to the relatively small group of people who own shares in the company. The communities in the USA, Brazil, or Germany that depend directly on General Motors' investment decisions however have next to no influence on the company and, unlike a regional or national government, General Motors at least in principle is not accountable to these constituencies.

Stakeholders	Impacts of globalization
Shareholders	Lack of regulation of global capital markets, leading to financial risks and instability
Employees	Corporations outsource production to LDCs in order to reduce costs in global marketplace; raised potential for exploitation of employees with different cultural backgrounds and divergent moral standards
Consumers	Global products face protests about cultural imperialism and westernization. Vulnerable consumers in LDCs face possibility of exploitation by MNCs
Suppliers and competitors	Suppliers in LDCs face regulation from MNCs through supply chain management. Small-scale indigenous competitors exposed to powerful global players
Civil society (pressure groups, NGOs, local communities)	Global business activities bring the company in direct interaction with local communities with possibility for erosion of traditional community life; globally active pressure groups emerge with aim to 'police' the corporation in countries where governments are weak and tolerant
Government and regulation	Globalization weakens governments and increases the corporate responsibility for jobs, welfare, maintenance of ethical standards, etc.

Figure 1.3. Examples of the impact of globalization on different stakeholder groups

What this means is that the more economic activities get deterritorialized, the less governments can control them, and the less they are open to democratic control of the affected people. Consequently, the call for direct (democratic) accountability of MNCs has become increasingly louder during the last few years, evidenced for example by the aforementioned anti-globalization protests. Put simply, globalization leads to a growing demand for *corporate accountability*. We shall examine this argument fully in the next chapter, but clearly it is exactly here where business ethics is increasingly in demand since it offers the potential for corporations to examine and respond to the claims made on them by various stakeholders. Indeed, globalization can be seen to affect *all* stakeholders of the corporation, as we shall discuss in Part II of the book. Some examples of these impacts are presented in **Figure 1.3**.

Sustainability: a new goal for business ethics?

At the same time that these new challenges raised by the context of globalization have been emerging, considerable interest has also been directed towards the development of new ways of addressing the diverse impacts of business in society. Many of these impacts are far-reaching and profound. To mention just a few, one only needs to think of impacts such as:

• The environmental pollution caused by the production, transportation, and use of products such as cars, refrigerators, or newspapers;

• The ever-increasing problems of waste disposal and management as a result of excessive product packaging and the dominance of 'throwaway culture';

Company	Sustainability statement	Source
BP	'We are committed to respond to the challenges posed by the objective of sustainable development. In our view sustainable development is a long term strategic issue that will involve business in considerations beyond its normal responsibilities.'	*Environmental and Social Review*, 2000.
Carlsberg Breweries	'Carlsberg Breweries seeks to meet the needs of its consumers, customers, and employees in an environmentally sound and sustainable manner.'	*Environmental Report*, 1998–2000.
Nokia	'Global industries are moving towards operating by social and ethical principles, such as environmentally sustainable practices. We wholeheartedly support this development and also participate actively in the global initiatives that support it.'	**www.nokia.com.**
Shell	'Shell companies are committed to contribute to sustainable development.'	*People, Planets and Profits: The Shell Report*, 2000.
Volvo	'Volvo's environmental programmes shall be characterised by a holistic view, continuous improvement, technical development and resource efficiency. Volvo shall, by these means, gain competitive advantage and contribute to a sustainable development.'	*Environmental Report*, 2000.

Figure 1.4. Corporate commitments to sustainability

- The devastating consequences for individuals and communities as a result of plant closures and 'downsizing' as experienced throughout Europe, from south Wales in the UK to the Lorraine in France and the Ruhr in Germany;
- The erosion of local cultures and environments due to the influx of mass tourism in places as diverse as Mallorcan fishing villages, Swiss alpine communities, or ancient Roman monuments.

Faced with such problems (and many more besides), it has been widely suggested that the goals and consequences of business require radical rethinking. Following the Rio Earth Summit of 1992, one concept in particular appears to have been widely promoted (though not universally accepted) as the essential new conceptual frame for assessing not only business activities specifically, but industrial and social development more generally. That concept is *sustainability*.

Sustainability has become an increasingly common term in the rhetoric surrounding business ethics, and has been widely used by corporations, governments, consultants, pressure groups, and academics alike. **Figure 1.4** provides some examples of sustainability being used in the corporate reports and other business communications of some major European firms.

Despite this widespread use, sustainability is a term that has been utilized and interpreted in substantially different ways (Dobson 1996). Probably the most common usage of sustainability, however, is in relation to *sustainable development*, which is typically defined as follows:

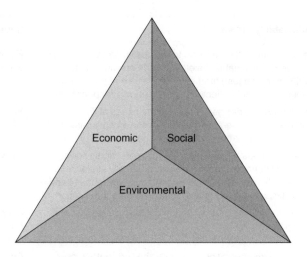

Figure 1.5. The three components of sustainability

> Sustainable development is development that meets the needs of the present without compromising the ability of future generations to meet their own needs.
>
> (World Commission on Environment and Development 1987)

This, however, is only the core idea of an elusive and widely contested concept—and one that has also been subject to a vast array of different conceptualizations and definitions (Gladwin et al. 1995). So whilst we would caution against an unreserved acceptance of any particular interpretation, at a very basic level, sustainability appears to be primarily about system maintenance, as in ensuring that our actions do not impact upon the system —for example the earth or the biosphere—in such a way that its long-term viability is threatened. By focusing sustainable development on the potential for future generations to satisfy their needs, sustainability also surfaces considerations of *intergenerational equity*, i.e. equality between one generation and another.

With its roots in environmental management and analysis, for a long time sustainability as a concept was largely synonymous with environmental sustainability. More recently, though, the concept of sustainability has been broadened to include not only environmental considerations, but also economic and social considerations (Elkington 1999). This is shown in **Figure 1.5**.

This extension of the sustainability concept arose primarily because it is not only impractical, but even sometimes impossible, to address the sustainability of the natural environment without also considering the social and economic aspects of relevant communities and their activities. For example, whilst environmentalists have opposed road-building programmes on account of the detrimental impact of such schemes on the environment, others have pointed to the benefits for local communities of lower congestion in their towns and extra jobs for their citizens. **Ethics in Action 1.2** looks at this problem of trade-offs between environmental, social, and economic criteria as faced by the UK airlines British Airways and Virgin Atlantic in the wake of their plans to expand airline capacity in the UK. Another argument for this extension is the consideration that

Ethics in Action 1.2

Freedom to Fly?

After the much publicized 'dirty tricks' allegations of the 1990s, where British Airways were convicted of unscrupulous activities in their competitive battle against bitter rivals Virgin Atlantic, many people would not have expected the two airlines to enter into a friendly partnership. However, on 14 January 2001, that is exactly what happened when Sir Richard Branson, the charismatic chairman of Virgin, and Rod Eddington, the chief executive of BA, joined forces with airports, business groups, and trade unions to launch the Freedom to Fly campaign in the UK.

A broad-based coalition of interest groups, the Freedom to Fly launch represented a major new move to campaign for more air capacity in the UK. With over 180 million passengers using UK airports in 2000, government forecasts were predicting a doubling of demand in the next twenty years. The coalition thus sought to avert a crisis in capacity over the next few decades by campaigning for major investment into building new terminals and runways. At the launch, coalition members argued that without expansion, the travelling public would face restrictions in their freedom to fly as well as have to put up with more delays, higher prices, and less choice. Jobs, business, tourism, and the economy would also be likely to suffer, claimed the coalition.

While the move was welcomed by business, environmental groups and anti-noise campaigners opposed the initiative. Expansion in air travel ordinarily translates into substantial increases in the emission of the greenhouse gases that lead to climate change. Similarly, more communities tend to be affected, and affected to a greater degree, by the additional noise pollution resulting from extra air traffic. As the chairman of one anti-noise campaigning group said in response to the launch: 'What this new lobby group fails to address is the effect that an expansion of aviation will have on the people living under the flight paths to airports and the damage aviation is doing to our wider environment. Our members are more concerned about the freedom to sleep than the freedom to fly.'

The Freedom to Fly campaign thus illustrates one of the key problems faced in relation to sustainability: how to reconcile the inevitable trade-offs between social, economic, and environmental considerations.

SOURCES

BBC (2002). 'UK air industry looks to expand'. BBC News On-line, 14 Jan., **http://news.bbc.co.uk**.
Macalister, T. (2002). 'Virgin flies back to Atlantic business'. *Guardian*, 15 Jan.: 23.

■ **Think theory**

Think about the example of the Freedom to Fly campaign in terms of the triple bottom line of sustainability. Which aspects of sustainability are raised here?

---

if equity is to be extended to future generations, then logically it should also be extended to all those in the current generation. Hence, one of the WCED's primary espoused aims was the eradication of world poverty and inequity.

As we see it then, sustainability can be regarded as comprising three components—environmental, economic, and social. This suggests the following definition:

> Sustainability refers to the long-term maintenance of systems according to environmental, economic, and social considerations.

Whilst we regard this definition as sufficient for determining the essential content of the sustainability concept, it is evident that sustainability as a phenomenon also represents a specific goal to be achieved. The framing of sustainability as a goal for business is encapsulated most completely in the notion of a 'triple bottom line' (Figure 1.5).

The triple bottom line

The triple bottom line (TBL) is a term coined by, and vigorously advocated by, John Elkington, the director of the SustainAbility strategy consultancy and author of a number of influential books on corporate environmentalism. His view of the TBL is that it represents the idea that business does not have just one single goal—namely adding economic value—but that it has an extended goal set which necessitates adding environmental and social value too (Elkington 1999). From this perspective, it should be clear why we have highlighted sustainability as a potentially important new goal for business ethics. However, in order to develop a clearer picture of just what the three components of sustainability actually represent in terms of a new goal for business ethics, we shall have to examine each of them in turn.

Environmental perspectives

As we mentioned briefly above, the concept of sustainability is generally regarded as having emerged from the environmental perspective, most notably in forestry management and then later in other areas of resource management (Hediger 1999). Indeed, it would probably be true to say that, at the present moment, there is still a fairly widespread conception within business (though we believe a mistaken one) that sustainability is a purely environmental concept.

The basic principles of sustainability in the environmental perspective concern the effective management of physical resources so that they are conserved for the future. All biosystems are regarded as having finite resources and finite capacity, and hence sustainable human activity must operate at a level that does not threaten the health of those systems. Even at the most basic level, these concerns suggest a need to address a number of critical business problems, such as the impacts of industrialization on biodiversity, the continued use of non-renewable resources such as oil, steel, and coal, as well as the production of damaging environmental pollutants like greenhouse gases and CFCs from industrial plants and consumer products. At a more fundamental level, though, these concerns also raise the problem of economic growth itself, and the vexed question of whether future generations can really enjoy the same living standards as us without a reversal of the trend towards ever more production and consumption.

Economic perspectives

The economic perspective on sustainability initially emerged from economic growth models that assessed the limits imposed by the carrying capacity of the earth (see Meadows et al. 1974). The recognition that continued growth in population, industrial activity, resource use, and pollution could mean that standards of living would eventually decline, led to the emergence of sustainability as a way of thinking about ensuring that future generations would not be disadvantaged by the activities and choices of the present generation. Economists such as Kenneth Arrow (Arrow and Hurwicz 1977), Herman Daly (Daly 1991; Daly and Cobb 1989), and David Pearce (1999) have since been highly influential in advancing the agenda for macroeconomic understanding of sustainability.

The implications for business ethics of such thinking occur on different levels. A narrow concept of economic sustainability focuses on the economic performance of the corporation itself: the responsibility of management is to develop, produce, and market those products that secure long-term economic performance for the corporation. This includes a focus on those strategies which, for example, lead to a long-term rise in share price, revenues, and market share rather than short-term 'explosions' of profits at the expense of long-term viability of success. An example of an unsustainable approach in this perspective would be the 'dot.com bubble' at the beginning of this century. A broader concept of economic sustainability would include the company's attitude towards and impacts upon the economic framework in which it is embedded. Paying bribes or building cartels, for instance, could be regarded as economically unsustainable because these activities undermine the long-term functioning of markets. Corporations which attempt to avoid paying corporate taxes through subtle accounting tricks might be said to behave in an unsustainable way: if they are not willing to fund the political-institutional environment (such as schools, hospitals, the police, and the justice system) they erode one of the key institutional bases of their corporate success.

Social perspectives

The development of the social perspective on sustainability has tended to trail behind that of the environmental and economic perspectives (Scott et al. 2000) and remains a relatively new development. The explicit integration of social concerns into the business discourse around sustainability can be seen to have emerged during the 1990s, primarily, it would seem, in response to concerns regarding the impact of business activities on indigenous communities in less developed countries and regions. It would be wrong to assume though that this means that, until this time, local community claims on business (and other social issues) went entirely unheard by business, or unexamined by business ethics scholars. Indeed, in Chapter 2 we shall be tracing a quite impressive literature dealing with such issues. However, the inclusion of social considerations such as these within the specific domain of sustainability marked a significant shift in the way that notions of sustainability were conceptualized.

The key issue in the social perspective on sustainability is that of *social justice*. Despite the impressive advances in standards of living that many of us have enjoyed, the UN

2001 *Report on the World Social Situation* (UN 2001) identified growing disparities in income and wealth within many countries, including much of Latin America, Eastern Europe, and almost two-thirds of OECD countries. Similarly, the report identified a continued widening in the distance between richer and poorer countries. The UN also identified general under-provision and widespread deterioration of basic services in many countries, coupled with an inability to keep pace with even basic needs. As one of the main engines of economic development, business is increasingly bound up in such debates. Therefore a more just and equitable world, whether between rich consumers in the west and poor workers in developing countries, between the urban rich and the rural poor, or between men and women, remains the central concern in the social perspective on sustainability.

Implications of sustainability for business ethics

Given this extended set of expectations placed on business according to the triple bottom line of sustainability, there are clearly significant implications for how we should look at business ethics. Issues of an ethical nature, be they plant closures, questionable market-ing techniques, or industrial pollution, demand that we consider a diverse and complex range of considerations and concerns. However, to achieve genuine sustainability in any of the three areas, still more in *all* of them, is perhaps expecting too much at the present time. After all, there are few if any products, businesses, or industries that can confidently claim to be sustainable in the full sense of the word. However, with the notion of sustain-ability widely promoted by governments, businesses, NGOs, and academia, it is clearly vital that we understand its full implications and evaluate business ethics practices at least according to their *potential* to contribute to sustainability. As Elkington (1999) sug-gests, the TBL is less about establishing accounting techniques and performance metrics for achievements in the three dimensions (which we shall look at in Chapter 5), and more about revolutionizing the way that companies think about and act in their business. It is these challenges, as they are framed according to each of the corporation's stakeholders, that we shall be examining in the second part of the book.

Europe: a new perspective for business ethics?

Having addressed the challenges for business ethics represented by globalization, as well as the goals proposed by sustainability, we come now to the final part of this introductory chapter where we examine the question of whether there is a distinctly European perspective on business ethics.

Whilst ethical and unethical business practices have long been the subject of public debate in Europe, the formal academic subject of business ethics is largely an American inven-tion and has most of its roots and a large part of its traditions on the other side of the Atlantic. The reception of business ethics in Europe however is fairly young, and only became visible from the beginning of the 1980s (van Luijk 2001). In presenting a European text we believe that although many of these original ideas have been, and still are, very useful in the European context, there are definite limits to the transfer of North American approaches into the European business context. The European context poses some distinctly different questions, which are not necessarily on the agenda from an American perspective (Spence 2002). Likewise, Europe has quite a distinct historical, philosophical, and religious legacy, giving rise to a different approach to the study, as well as the practice, of business ethics in Europe (von Weltzien Hoivik 2002).

What is Europe?

When talking about Europe the immediate question normally would be: what exactly is meant by the term Europe? In simple geographic terms, one could think of the territory between Ireland and Portugal in the west and the Urals and the Bosporus in the east, and from Lapland in the north to Sicily in the south. However, in terms of economic conditions and business activities, this is an extremely heterogeneous entity, which would easily require different books about these different 'Europes'. Therefore, moving on from these merely geographical framings, there can be no doubt that for our purposes, Europe is better defined by a common intellectual and cultural heritage (Morin 1987).

For practical reasons, we will use the term 'Europe' in the sense that it includes the members of the European Union as well as its new and prospective new member states in the east, and including countries such as Norway and Switzerland, which are not as yet members of the EU. We are aware that this is still a bit delicate, given the heterogeneity of the cultural heritage amongst these countries. For example, one might argue that the UK shares a more substantial cultural heritage with the USA than with the rest of Europe, whilst continental Europe in many aspects differs quite significantly from the UK in the areas that are relevant to the topic of this book. However, given the long history of international relations within Europe, as well as increasing integration in recent years, as exemplified by the EU and the euro currency, one might reasonably argue that Europe as a whole represents a distinct world block that is differentiated from that of North America, from where much of the literature on business ethics has originated. This, as we shall now see, has a number of important implications for how we shall be approaching the subject of business ethics.

European and American approaches to business ethics

Authors such as Henk van Luijk (1990), David Vogel (1992; 1998), and Georges Enderle (1996) have claimed that there are certain fundamental differences in the way in which business ethics is practised and studied in Europe compared to the USA. We shall look at these differences in relation to six key questions (summarized in **Figure 1.6**).

• Who is responsible for ethical conduct in business?

The USA exhibits a strong culture of individualism, suggesting that individuals are responsible for their own success. Hence, if there is demand for solving ethical questions, it is the individual who is usually expected to be responsible for making the right choices.

	United States	Europe
Who is responsible for ethical conduct in business?	The individual	Social control by the collective
Who is the key actor in business ethics?	The corporation	Government, trade unions, corporate associations
What are the key guidelines for ethical behaviour?	Corporate codes of ethics	Negotiated legal framework of business
What are the key issues in business ethics?	Misconduct and immorality in single decision situations	Social issues in organizing the framework of business
What is the dominant stakeholder management approach?	Focus on shareholder value	Multiple stakeholder approach

Figure 1.6. Differences between Europe and the United States from a business ethics perspective

There is an impressive literature dealing with individual ethical decision-making emanating from the USA (as we shall discuss in Chapter 4), and many US textbooks focus on decision-making at this level (e.g. Ferrell et al. 2002; Treviño and Nelson 1999). In Europe, however, it has traditionally been thought that it is not the individual business person, nor even the single company, that is primarily expected to be responsible for solving ethical dilemmas in business. Rather, it is a collective and overarching institution, usually the state. European business ethics has therefore tended to focus more on the choice *of* constraints compared with the US approach of focusing on choice *within* constraints (Enderle 1996).

• **Who is the key actor in business ethics?**

The result of this is that in most European countries there is quite a dense network of regulation on most of the ethically important issues for business. Workers' rights, social and medical care, and environmental issues are only a few examples where European companies could be said to have traditionally not had to consider so very much the moral values which should guide their decisions. These questions have, at least in principle, been tackled by the government in setting up a tight institutional framework for businesses. Examples range from the Scandinavian welfare state, to the German cohabitation system, and the strong position of trade unions and workers' rights in France.

In Europe, governments, trade unions, and corporate associations have therefore been key actors in business ethics. In most (but not all) areas, the institutional framework of business ethics in the USA has been significantly looser, and so the key actor has tended to be the corporation. This at least partly explains the more practical altitude to business ethics evident in the US approach (Enderle 1996). Similarly, given that business ethics is particularly important when the law has not yet codified the 'right' or 'wrong' of a certain action, this would also seem to partially explain the longer legacy of the subject in the USA. However, the identification of the corporation as the key actor in the USA also means that corporate misconduct tends to face greater enforcement and harsher penalties (Vogel 1992).

● **What are the key guidelines for ethical behaviour?**

This differing character and extent of the legal framework in Europe and the USA to some degree necessitates different approaches to business ethics on each side of the Atlantic (as we will see in more detail in the second part of the book). Similarly, it also suggests that whereas the key guidelines for ethical behaviour in Europe tend to be codified in the negotiated legal framework of business, in the USA, guidelines tend to come from businesses themselves, in the form of corporate codes of ethics and internal compliance programmes (Enderle 1996). However, these are often put in place to avoid the potentially hefty fines that accompany breaches of the US federal sentencing guidelines (Vogel 1992).

● **What are the key issues in business ethics?**

This contrast is manifested in the types of issues deemed important within business ethics on the two sides of the Atlantic. This becomes evident when looking at contemporary US business ethics textbooks, since they tend to accord considerable amount of space to issues such as privacy, workers' rights, salary issues, and whistleblowing, just to name a few. These are deemed to be the responsibility of the individual company, since the state, in principle, does not take on full responsibility for regulating these issues. The European approach, in contrast, has tended to focus more on social issues in organizing the frame-work of business. Hence, European business ethics textbooks have tended to also include greater consideration of subjects such as the ethics of capitalism and economic rationality (Enderle 1996).

● **What is the most dominant stakeholder management approach?**

Another important aspect that follows from the above is the different character of European and US corporations (Whitley 1992). European corporations in general are smaller, and see multiple stakeholders as opposed to simply shareholders as the focus of corporate activity. European models of capitalism are not so dominated by the drive for shareholder value maximization compared with American companies. European com-panies are often managed by large executive and supervisory boards, with considerable amount of interlocking ownership structures between companies and close bank rela-tions (van Luijk 1990).

Sources of difference between Europe and America

From where have such differences emerged? Thinking in terms of Europe as a shared cul-tural and intellectual heritage, we can see that many of these differences are rooted in the differing cultural, economic, and religious histories of the USA and Europe. For example, even though today we tend to talk about much of Europe and the USA as secularized countries, there are significant differences in the religious legacies of the two regions. One argument here is that the influence of the Catholic and Lutheran Protestant religions in Europe led to a collective approach to organizing economic life whereas the individual focus

of the Calvinist Protestant religion in the USA led to the rise of a distinctly different, capitalist (in the original sense) economic system (Weber 1905).[5]

Georges Enderle (1996) suggests that the interest in broader macro issues of business
ethics in Europe can also be partly traced to the need to rebuild institutions after the
Second World War and in the aftermath of economic and political restructuring in Eastern
Europe. Moreover, Vogel (1992) argues further that the focus on individual action and codes
of conduct in the USA has been substantially driven by the impact of widely publicized
corporate scandals which have focused attention on the need to avoid ethical violation
at the firm level. As we can see, then, there are a number of reasons that can be advanced
to explain these differences. But does this mean the differences are becoming more or less
distinct?

Globalization and assimilation between Europe and America

Finally, then, we might ask whether these culturally rooted differences in business ethics
between Europe and the USA are likely to be sustained given ongoing processes of globalization. Certainly, globalization has quite significantly reduced and mitigated some of the
peculiarities of the European business system and the European firm (Whittington and Mayer
2002). Therefore, however important it is to see the differences between Europe and the
USA, there is a clear tendency of assimilation in the different business systems. In Europe,
this has been manifested in a decrease in importance of (especially national) governmental
regulation for business. Globalization has resulted in a rapid and comprehensive move
towards deregulation of business activities which increasingly puts businesses in contexts
similar to the American version of capitalism (van Luijk 2001). This is even more the case
if we focus on Eastern Europe: economies in transition are typically characterized by a weak
state, and a deficit in law enforcement, which together leave a growing amount of ethical
issues to be tackled by businesses (Lang 2001). Therefore this book, while keeping a distinct focus on the European corporation and its experience of globalization, will also
integrate and discuss contributions from the American business ethics school, as there is
still a considerable (even growing) overlap in issues, problems, and agendas.

---

[5] In a nutshell, this argument suggests that Catholicism sees people as sinners, who depend on the Church to
help them and to lead them on the right way throughout their life, so that they reach heaven and salvation once
their life on earth comes to an end. Man is born into this world, receives salvation through baptism in the
Church as a baby, becomes a member of the Church as a child, receives various sacraments such as marriage or
the regular pardon of sins after confession, and, upon death, the priest is there to administer the 'last rites'. This
has supposedly then led to an approach to organizing social and economic life where the collective, chiefly the
state, has the main responsibility. The individual's well-being is more of a public issue rather than a result of the
individual's personal struggle for wealth, success, and happiness. Calvinism on the contrary is said to see man as
a responsible being with an individual responsibility to work for his or her own salvation. People are sinners, but
they are able to achieve salvation by leading a godly and pious life. To attain salvation is one's individual responsibility
and, most notably, is beyond the authority of the Church or any other superior authority. It is argued that this
religious approach has led to a very different approach: if the individual is in charge of their own future success,
there should be the least amount of hindrances to do so. The individual's success is the dominant focus of the
economic system, and the rules and institutions in society should be tailored in such a way that every person is
able to succeed in the most effective manner.

Specifically, we shall provide the following balance between the two traditional positions on each of the main differences in business ethics evident in Europe and the USA:

- Rather than selecting either one or the other, we will consider *both* the individual decision-maker and the corporation itself as responsible for ethical conduct. Although it is clearly individuals in organizations who ultimately make business ethics decisions, the European tradition suggests that we also have to look at the context that shapes those decisions. Moreover, most of us quite naturally regard corporations as significant actors in business ethics. If there is an incident of industrial pollution or it is revealed that children are being used in an overseas factory, it is usually the company as a whole that we criticize rather than any specific manager(s);

- We will focus on the corporation in its *relations* with other key actors such as government, pressure groups, and trade unions;

- We will provide a critical perspective on *both* individual level ethical guidelines, such as codes of conduct, *and* broader forces shaping ethical decision-making such as product and financial markets, supply chains, civil society, and systems of governance;

- The morality of single business situations will be considered in the *context* of the organizing framework of business;

- A multiple stakeholder approach that *includes* shareholders as a particularly important constituency will be taken. As we will outline in Chapter 2, this assumes some intrinsic rights for stakeholders rather than focusing only on their role in affecting shareholder value.

Summary

In this chapter we have defined business ethics, and set it within a number of significant currents of thinking. First, we have shown the importance of business ethics to current business theory and practice, suggesting that knowledge of business ethics is vital in the contemporary business environment. Second, we have argued that business ethics has been fundamentally recontextualized by the forces of globalization, necessitating a distinctly global view of ethical problems and practices in business. Third, we have identified sustainability as a crucial concept that helps to determine and frame the goals of business activities from an ethical perspective. Finally, we have made the case for a distinctly European perspective on business ethics, given both the specific intellectual and commercial heritage in Europe, as well as the need to understand current developments insofar as they are likely to affect European business and society. In the rest of the book we shall revisit these themes of globalization, sustainability, and Europe many more times in order to expand, refine, and contextualize the initial arguments put forward here. In the next chapter, though, we shall move on to consider specifically the social role and responsibilities of the corporation, and examine the emerging concept of corporate citizenship.

STUDY QUESTIONS

1 How would you define business ethics? Do you agree with the definition given in this chapter?
2 Critically evaluate the proposition that business ethics is an oxymoron.
3 What is the relation between business ethics and the law?
4 What is globalization? Select one multinational corporation based in your home country and set out the different ways in which globalization might have reframed business ethics for that corporation.
5 What is sustainability? To what extent do you think it is possible for corporations in the following industries to be sustainable:
    (a) Tobacco industry
    (b) Oil industry
    (c) Car industry
    Explain your answers.
6 In what ways do you think that the context of the country you are currently studying in differs in the way that business ethics is thought about and practised compared with:
    (a) The USA
    (b) Other European countries

RESEARCH EXERCISE

Conduct some research on the ethical issues and criticisms that accompanied the Enron accounting scandal in 2002.

1 What were the main issues and criticisms in this case?
2 To what extent is it possible to classify these as ethical as opposed to legal violations?
3 What influence do you think this scandal had on the general public's view of business ethics?
4 To what extent do you think the problems at Enron were related to its US context? Could similar problems arise in Europe? Explain your answer.

CASE 1

McEurope: McDonald's faces ethical criticism in Europe

This case examines campaigns against the US fast food chain McDonald's in Europe, focusing on the McLibel trial in the UK, and the farmers' protests led by Jose Bové in France. The criticisms faced by McDonald's have covered many of the key issues around globalization and sustainability that we have discussed in Chapter 1, and the case offers a chance to explore the specifically European context of these issues.

McDonald's is truly a multinational corporation. By 2002, the firm was operating some 29,000 restaurants in 121 countries, serving an incredible 46 million customers a day. The market leader in its industry, and one of the most vigorous exponents of a global business approach, McDonalds has pioneered an innovative business model that has since been widely imitated, in the fast food industry and beyond.

However, there are many who are not so positive about the corporation's approach, and protests against McDonald's have been a common feature of the past two decades. Nowhere has this been more evident than in Europe, where since the corporation first entered the region in the 1970s, the rapid inroads it has made into European markets have been paralleled with growing numbers of anti-McDonald's attacks. The two phenomena that perhaps most exemplify the issues arising in Europe, as well as the approach that McDonald's has taken in response to its critics in the region, are the McLibel trial in the UK, and the farmers' protests led by Jose Bové in France.

McLibel: McDonald's goes to court in the UK

Whilst McDonald's business achievements have been many, the company probably did not anticipate gaining the distinction of being the subject of England's longest ever trial. But that is exactly what happened following the corporation's decision in 1990 to take two activists, Helen Steel and Dave Morris, to court for distributing a leaflet headed 'What's Wrong with McDonald's?' The leaflet attacked McDonald's on a wide range of issues, including the promotion of unhealthy food, ill treatment of animals, exploitation of staff, environmental damage, economic imperialism, exploitation of children, and the destruction of rainforests.

This was certainly not the first time that McDonald's had taken to the courts to defend its reputation. However, in the past, it had usually found that the mere threat of legal action was sufficient to force retractions from its critics. According to the *Guardian* newspaper, in the UK alone McDonald's had threatened legal action against more than ninety organizations since the early 1980s, including the BBC, Channel 4, the Vegetarian Society, the *Guardian*, and even a children's theatre group. All had been forced to make apologies rather than face the enormous risks of going to trial. For McDonald's, then, the strategy of responding to criticism through immediate legal threat had been a successful one, at least in terms of denying public voice to their critics. In the case of Steel and Morris, however, the resulting McLibel trial produced a rather different result.

The McLibel trial was an epic case. There were twenty-eight pre-trial hearings before the case even got to court. Then, from June 1994 to December 1996, over 313 days in the court, every one of the accusations made in the 'What's Wrong with McDonald's?' leaflet was meticulously examined and contested. With 180 witnesses called to court, including environmentalists, nutritionists, former employees, and trade unionists, and 40,000 pages of documents and witness statements admitted, almost every aspect of the multinational's vast business empire came under scrutiny. As the case dragged on, the modern-day David and Goliath story of the community gardener (Steel) and the unemployed postal worker (Morris) who defended themselves (without lawyers or legal aid) against the corporate giant attracted massive international publicity.

The McSpotlight website was set up in 1996 in support of the defendants and immediately made a wealth of information critical of McDonald's available to an international audience. Versions of the very leaflets that were at issue in the court battle began to be far more widely distributed than the defendants could ever have dreamed of. Hosted in the Netherlands (in the belief that any efforts by McDonald's to close the site down would be greatly resisted there) McSpotlight gained immediate international media coverage and recorded millions of hits—including 1,700 visits from McDonald's itself in the first week alone! The site carried transcripts and statements from the trial, and revelled in some embarrassing comments from senior McDonald's figures. For example, David Green, the Senior Vice-President of Marketing, suggested that Coca-Cola was 'nutritious' because it was 'providing water, and I think that is part of a balanced diet'. Ed Oakley, the UK Chief

Purchasing Officer, even claimed that the dumping of waste was 'a benefit, otherwise you will end up with lots of vast, empty gravel pits all over the country'!

When the judge finally delivered his verdict in June 1997, it represented a partial victory for both sides. Steel and Morris were ruled to have not proved their allegations against the multinational on issues of rainforest destruction, heart disease and cancer, food poisoning, starvation in the third world, and bad working conditions. However, they were adjudged to have proven their claims that McDonald's 'exploits children' with its advertising; is 'culpably responsible' for cruelty to animals; is 'strongly antipathetic' to unions; pays its workers low wages; falsely advertises its food as nutritious; and risks the health of its most regular, long-term customers. The defendants were ordered to pay £60,000 in damages (reduced to £40,000 on appeal in 1999), which Steel and Morris immediately said they would not pay and which McDonald's has never tried to collect. The verdict was met with a day of action of leafleting and protests outside McDonald's restaurants across the world.

The trial became the subject of an acclaimed book, a TV programme, a documentary film, and numerous media articles. McDonald's has since decided not to apply for an injunction to halt any further dissemination of the original leaflet, which has now been translated into twenty-six languages and is freely available on McSpotlight and elsewhere.

Jose Bové: France's farm crusader takes on McDonald's

As it was recovering from the public relations disaster of the McLibel trial in the UK, McDonald's immediately found itself caught up in further tribulations across the channel. In August 1999, in the town of Millau in southern France, up to 300 protesters stormed a building site and wrecked a half-built McDonald's restaurant. Jose Bové and nine other members of his radical farmers' union, the Confédération Paysanne, were subsequently accused. Bové argued that the attack was in protest against US trade restrictions on French delicacies, such as Roquefort cheese, which is produced in the region around Millau. The restrictions had been put in place by the USA following an EU ban on unlabelled hormone-injected American beef.

Bové, a sheep farmer and union leader, immediately became a folk hero in France for his defence of small, local producers. With his large moustache, the French media likened him to the cartoon character Astérix, the indomitable Gaul who fights against the might of the Roman Empire. Bové also became heavily involved in the fight against genetically modified crops, and subsequently led Brazilian farmers on a mission to destroy trial fields of GM crops. Hailed as a 'McHero' for his exploits, these crusades against the injustices of the world trade system led to him being taken up as a figurehead for anti-globalization protesters.

His trial for the McDonald's attack took place in July 2000 and saw thousands of protesters take to the streets of the tiny market town of Millau. The carnival atmosphere saw streets covered in banners and filled with stalls selling local produce and distributing anti-globalization and anti-McDonald's leaflets. Bové was eventually given a three-month jail sentence for the attack, whilst eight of the his nine accomplices were also convicted and handed lesser sentences.

Two years after the first McDonald's attack, Bové returned to the now completed Millau restaurant in August 2001. In a peaceful demonstration, Bové and several thousand protesters barred access to the restaurant claiming that McDonald's exemplified 'la malbouffe americaine' (crap American food), and the inexorable march of multinationals and their threats to the small producer. Said Bové: 'For me, malbouffe means both the standardisation of food—the same taste from one end of the world to the other—and the choice of food associated with the use of hormones and GMOs.' The Millau restaurant manager defended McDonald's against Bove's attacks, saying: 'We work as partners with French agriculture. We buy French, and serve one million meals a day.'

The next chapter in the story was yet more symbolic. In December 2001, McDonald's announced that from January 2002 the international icon Ronald McDonald would be replaced in French TV adverts by none other than Astérix the Gaul. Regularly identified as France's favourite cartoon character, the drafting in of Astérix appeared to be an attempt by McDonald's to appease anti-American feeling and counter the anti-globalization backlash that had centred upon the US multinational.

Questions

1 Set out the main criticisms that have been levelled at McDonald's. Are these criticisms specific to the corporation, or are there other more general issues at stake? If so, what are they?

2 Describe and evaluate the tactics used by McDonald's in responding to their critics in the UK and France.

3 How could McDonald's seek to avoid similar problems in the future?

Sources

BBC (2001a). 'Bové appeals over McDonald's rampage'. BBC News On-line, 15 Feb.
—— (2001b). ' "McHero" cheered at anti-Davos meeting'. BBC News On-line, 30 Jan.
Donson, F. (2000). *Legal Intimidation: A SLAPP in the Face of Democracy*. London: Free Association Books.
Duffy, J. (2002). 'How Ronald got le boot'. BBC News On-line, 22 Jan.
Jeffries, S. (2001). 'Bové relishes a second bite'. *Observer*, 12 Aug.: 22.
Vidal, J. (1997). *McLibel*. London: Macmillan.

2

Framing Business Ethics
Corporate Responsibility, Stakeholders, and Citizenship

In this chapter we will:

- Analyse the notion of responsibility for corporations;

- Distinguish the various notions of corporate social responsibility;

- Present the stakeholder theory of the firm as a powerful concept of business–society relations;

- Develop the concept of corporate accountability, and establish its importance in understanding the political role of the firm in society;

- Critically examine the newly emerging notion of corporate citizenship and assess its contribution to the framing of business ethics;

- Discuss throughout the chapter the specific European implication of these—mostly US-born—concepts

Towards a framework for business ethics

In Chapter 1 we defined the subject of business ethics as 'the study of business situations, activities, and decisions where issues of right and wrong are addressed'. In order to address issues of right and wrong, the crucial starting point is the question of whether companies are actors who have to make decisions beyond simply producing goods and services on a profitable basis. It is the definition and justification of these potentially wider responsibilities that is the subject of this chapter. We begin by addressing the fundamental nature of the modern corporation in order to answer the question of whether corporations can have a moral responsibility in the same way as individual persons responsible for the right and the wrong of their actions do. We then proceed to discuss key themes in the literature on the social role of business, namely corporate social responsibility, stakeholder theory, and corporate accountability. We finish the chapter by exploring the notion of corporate citizenship. We argue that although this is a new concept to have emerged from the literature, and can be interpreted in a number of different ways, in its fullest sense, it can be extremely useful for framing many of the problems of business ethics in the global economy raised in Chapter 1.

What is a corporation?

It may seem like an obvious question, but the practical and legal identification of a corporation within any given society has significant implications for how, and indeed whether, certain types of responsibility can be assigned to such a body. Corporations are clearly not the same as individual people, and before we can decide what responsibilities they might have, we need to define exactly what they are, and why they exist in the first place.

The corporation is by far the dominant form of business entity in the modern global economy. Although not all businesses (such as sole traders) are corporations, and many corporations (such as charities and universities) are not-for-profit businesses, we shall be primarily concentrating on business in the corporate form.

Key features of a corporation

So what is it then that defines a corporation? A corporation is essentially defined in terms of *legal status* and the *ownership of assets*. Legally, corporations are typically regarded as independent from those who work in them, manage them, invest in them, or receive products or services from them. Corporations are separate entities in their own right. For this reason, corporations are regarded as having perpetual succession, i.e. as an entity they can survive the death of any individual investors, employees, or customers—they simply need to find new ones.

This legal status leads on to the second key defining feature of corporations. Rather than shareholders or managers owning the assets associated with a corporation, *the corporation itself* usually owns those assets. The factories, offices, computers, machines, and other assets operated by, say, the Anglo-Dutch consumer products giant Unilever are the property of Unilever, not of its shareholders. Shareholders simply own a share in the company that entitles them to a dividend and some say in certain decisions affecting the company. They could not, for instance, arrive at Unilever's HQ and try to remove a computer or a desk and take it home, because it is Unilever that owns that computer or desk, not the shareholder. Similarly, employees, customers, suppliers, etc. deal with, and agree contracts with, the corporation, not with shareholders.

The implications of this situation are extremely significant for our understanding of the responsibilities of corporations:

- **Corporations are typically regarded as 'artificial persons' in the eyes of the law.** That is, they have certain rights and responsibilities in society, just as an individual citizen might.

- **Corporations are notionally 'owned' by shareholders, but exist independently of them.** The corporation holds its own assets, and shareholders are not responsible for the debts or damages caused by the corporation (they have limited liability).

- **Managers and directors have a 'fiduciary' responsibility to protect the investment of share-holders.** This means that senior management is expected to hold shareholders' investment in trust and to act in their best interests. As we will see in Chapter 6, the exact nature of the duty this imposes on managers and how it is legally structured actually varies across Europe and across other parts of the world.

This establishes a legal framework for corporations to be opened up to questions of responsibility. However, this is not quite the same as assigning a *moral* responsibility to corporations. After all, it is one thing to say that a person feels a sense of moral responsibility for their actions, and can feel pride or shame in doing the right or wrong thing, but clearly we cannot claim the same for inanimate entities such as corporations. Hence we need to look a little more closely at the specific nature and responsibilities of corporations.

Can a corporation have social responsibilities?

In 1970, just after the first big wave in the business ethics movement in the USA, the Nobel Prize winning economist Milton Friedman published an article that has since become a classic among those who question the alleged social role of corporations. Under the provocative title 'The social responsibility of business is to increase its profits' he vigorously protested against the notion of social responsibilities for corporations. He based his argument on three main premisses:

- **Only human beings have a moral responsibility for their actions.** His first substantial point was that corporations are not human beings and therefore cannot assume true moral responsibility for their actions. Since corporations are set up by individual human beings, it is those human beings who are then individually responsible for the actions of the corporation.

- **It is managers' responsibility to act solely in the interests of shareholders.** His second point was that as long as a corporation abides by the legal framework society has set up for business, the only responsibility of the managers of the corporation is to make profit, because it is for this task that the firm has been set up and the managers have been employed. Acting for any other purpose constitutes a betrayal of their special responsibility to shareholders and thus essentially represents a 'theft' from shareholders' pockets.

- **Social issues and problems are the proper province of the state rather than corporate managers.** Friedman's third main point was that managers should not, and cannot, decide what is in society's best interests. This is the job of government. Corporate managers are neither trained to set and achieve social goals, nor (unlike politicians) are they democratically elected to do so.

We will deal with the second and third points shortly. First, however, we will examine the proposition that a company cannot be morally responsible for what it does, since its decisions are essentially those of individual people.

Can a corporation be morally responsible for its actions?

Is a corporation just a collection of individuals who work together under the same roof, or is the corporation not only a *legal* entity in its own right, but also a *moral* one? Can a corporation actually assume moral responsibility for the right and wrong of its actions? The debate regarding the assignation of moral responsibilities to corporations is a long and complex one,[1] but there is general support from the literature for some degree of responsibility to be accredited to corporations. Nevertheless, this is not the same as, and probably weaker than, the moral responsibility of individuals.

These arguments are primarily based on the idea that in order to assign responsibility to corporations, it is necessary to show that in addition to legal independence from their members (as discussed above), they also have *agency* independent of their members (Moore 1999a). There are two main arguments in support of this point. The first argument looks at the fact that apart from individuals taking decisions within companies, every organization has a **corporate internal decision structure** which directs corporate decisions in line with predetermined goals (French 1979). Such an internal decision structure gets manifest in various elements which, acting together, result in a situation whereby the majority of corporate actions cannot be assigned to any individual's decisions—and therefore responsibility—alone. The corporate internal decision structure is manifest in the organization chart as well as in the established corporate policies that determine the company's actions far beyond any individual's contribution. This view does not exclude the fact that individuals still act independently within the corporation and that there are still quite a number of decisions that can be directly traced back to individual actors. The crucial point is that corporations normally have an organized framework of decision-making that, by establishing an explicit or implicit *purpose* for decisions, clearly transcends the individual's framework of responsibility.

A second argument supporting the moral dimension of corporate responsibility is the fact that all companies not only have an organized corporate internal decision structure, but furthermore manifest a set of beliefs and values that lay out what is generally regarded as right or wrong in the corporation—namely, the **organizational culture** (Moore 1999a). As we shall see in Chapter 4, these values and beliefs are widely believed to be a strong influence on the individual's ethical decision-making and behaviour. Hence, many of the issues discussed in this book for which corporations receive either praise or blame can be traced back to the company's culture. For example, many commentators have attributed Levi Strauss & Co.'s progressive response to child labour and other human rights problems in developing countries to the firm's ethical beliefs and espoused core values (see Donaldson 1996: 54).

---

[1] There are numerous authors who have argued for and against the assignation of moral responsibility to corporations—see Moore (1999a) for a review.

We therefore can conclude that corporations do indeed have some le~
responsibility that is more than the responsibility of the individuals cor
corporation. Not only does the legal framework of most developed cour
corporation as a 'legal' or 'artificial' person which has a legal responsibilit'
but the corporation also appears to have moral agency of sorts which sha~
made by those in the corporation.

In the following sections we will take a closer look at the second argument forward by Friedman (and many of his followers). This questions any social responsibilities a corporate manager might have beyond those which are based on the duty to produce profits for shareholders. In order to do so, we shall primarily discuss probably the two most influential concepts to have arisen from the business ethics literature to date: corporate social responsibility and stakeholder theory.

Corporate social responsibility

The systematic reasoning about a conceptual framework for corporate social responsibility (CSR) started in the USA half a century ago (Carroll 1999). During this time many different concepts and principles have been aired and debated in relation to CSR. Such debates have focused on two key questions:

- Why might it be argued that corporations have social as well as financial responsibilities?

- What is the nature of these social responsibilities?

Let us look at each of these two questions in turn.

Why do corporations have social responsibilities?

This first question has raised enormous amounts of controversy in the past, but it is by now fairly widely accepted that businesses do indeed have responsibilities beyond simply making a profit. This is based on a number of distinct but related arguments,[2] many of which tend to be couched in terms of **enlightened self-interest**, i.e. the corporation takes on social responsibilities insofar as doing so promotes its own self-interest. For example:

- Corporations perceived as being socially responsible might be rewarded with extra and/ or more satisfied customers, whilst perceived irresponsibility may result in boycotts or other undesirable consumer actions. For example, in 2001 oil giant ExxonMobil experienced a consumer boycott in many European countries in response to the corporation's refusal to sign up to (and active lobbying against) the Kyoto global warming protocol.

- Similarly, employees might be attracted to work for, and even be more committed to, corporations perceived as being socially responsible (Greening and Turban 2000).

- Voluntarily committing to social actions and programmes may forestall legislation and ensure greater corporate independence from government.

[2] These arguments have been widely presented in the CSR literature, but are largely derived from the work of Davis (1973) and Mintzberg (1983).

- Making a positive contribution to society might be regarded as a long-term investment in a safer, better-educated, and more equitable community, which subsequently benefits the corporation by creating an improved and stable context in which to do business.

These are primarily good *business* reasons why it might be advantageous for the corporation to act in a socially responsible manner. In arguing against CSR, Friedman (1970) in fact does not dispute the validity of such actions, but rather says that when they are carried out for reasons of self-interest, they are not CSR at all, but merely profit maximization 'under the cloak of social responsibility'. This may well be true, and to a large extent depends on the *primary motivations* of the decision-maker (Bowie 1991). It is not so much a matter of whether profit subsequently arises from social actions, but whether profit or altruism was the main reason for the action in the first place. However, corporate motives are difficult, sometimes impossible, to determine. Moreover, despite numerous academic studies, a direct relationship between social responsibility and profitability has been almost impossible to unambiguously 'prove'.[3] Even though the overall weight of evidence seems to suggest some kind of positive relationship, there is still the issue of causality. When successful companies are seen to be operating CSR programmes, it is just as reasonable to suggest that CSR does not contribute to the success, but rather the financial success frees the company to indulge in the 'luxury' of CSR.

Hence, in addition to these business arguments for CSR, it is also important to consider further *moral* arguments for CSR:

- Corporations cause social problems and hence have a responsibility to solve those they have caused and to prevent further social problems arising;

- As powerful social actors, with recourse to substantial resources, corporations should use their power and resources responsibly in society;

- All corporate activities have social impacts of one sort or another, whether through the provision of products and services, the employment of workers, or some other corporate activity. Hence, corporations cannot escape responsibility for those impacts, whether they are positive, negative, or neutral;

- Corporations rely on the contribution of a much wider set of constituencies, or stakeholders in society (such as consumers, suppliers, local communities), rather than just shareholders, and hence have a duty to take into account the interests and goals of these stakeholders as well as those of shareholders (see 50–55);

Given this range of moral and business arguments for CSR, the case for CSR is on a reasonably secure footing, although, as we shall discuss later in the chapter, there are also problems with this, particularly in terms of the accountability of corporations (55–61). Our next question, though, is, if corporations have some type of social responsibility, what form does that responsibility take?

---

[3] This relationship has been examined at least since the early 1970s, with interest apparently unabated despite (or perhaps because of) the somewhat equivocal findings so far. Good overviews of this literature are provided in the articles by Griffin and Mahon (1997), McWilliams and Siegel (2000), and Waddock and Graves (1997).

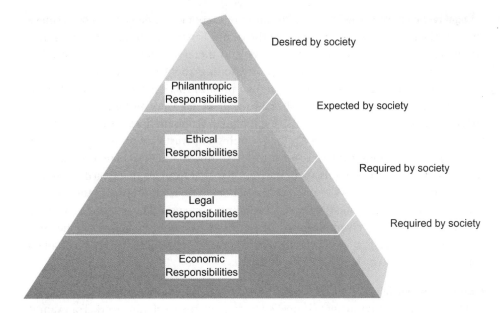

Figure 2.1. Carroll's four-part model of corporate social responsibility

Source: Carroll (1991).

What is the nature of corporate social responsibilities?

Probably the most established and accepted model of CSR which addresses our second question is the 'Four-Part Model of Corporate Social Responsibility' as initially proposed by Archie Carroll (1979), and subsequently refined in later publications (e.g. Carroll 1991; Carroll and Buchholtz 2000: 27–62). This model is depicted in **Figure 2.1**.

Carroll regards CSR as a multi-layered concept, which can be differentiated into four interrelated aspects—economic, legal, ethical, and philanthropic responsibilities. He presents these different responsibilities as consecutive layers within a pyramid, such that 'true' social responsibility requires the meeting of all four levels consecutively. Hence, Carroll and Buchholtz (2000: 35) offer the following definition:

> Corporate social responsibility encompasses the economic, legal, ethical, and philanthropic expectations placed on organizations by society at a given point in time.

• **Economic responsibility.** Companies have shareholders who demand a reasonable return on their investments, they have employees who want safe and fairly paid jobs, they have customers who demand good-quality products at a fair price, etc. This is by definition the reason why businesses are set up in society and so the first responsibility of business is to be a properly functioning economic unit and to stay in business. This first layer of CSR is the basis for all the subsequent responsibilities, which rest on this (ideally) solid basis. According to Carroll (1991), the satisfaction of economic responsibilities is thus *required* of all corporations.

• **Legal responsibility.** The legal responsibility of corporations demands that businesses abide by the law and 'play by the rules of the game'. Laws, as we have seen in Chapter 1, are the codification of society's moral views, and therefore abiding by these standards is a necessary prerequisite for any further reasoning about social responsibilities. For example, in the last few years a number of high-profile firms have been convicted of anti-competitive behaviour as a result of illegal strategies aimed at maintaining market share and profitability (i.e. focusing excessively on their economic responsibilities). The US software giant Microsoft has faced a long-running antitrust case for abusing its mono-polistic position to disadvantage competitors, resulting in tough settlements against the company. Similarly, revelations about the price-fixing conspiracy that rigged the art mar-ket during much of the 1990s resulted in convictions of senior executives at the venerated Sotheby's and Christie's auction houses, including a one-year jail term and a €8.5m fine for the former Sotheby's chairman Alfred Taubman. As with economic responsibilities, then, Carroll (1991) suggests that the satisfaction of legal responsibilities is *required* of all cor-porations seeking to be socially responsible.

• **Ethical responsibility.** These responsibilities oblige corporations to do what is right, just, and fair even when they are not compelled to do so by the legal framework. For example, when Shell sought to dispose of the Brent Spar oil platform at sea in 1995, it had the full agreement of the law and the British government to do so, yet still fell victim to a vigor-ous campaign against the action by Greenpeace as well as a consumer boycott. As a result, the *legal* decision to dispose of the platform at sea was eventually reversed since the firm had failed to take account of society's (or at least the protesters') wider *ethical* expectations (see end of chapter Case 5 176–180 for more discussion of this case). Carroll (1991) argues that ethical responsibilities therefore consist of what is generally *expected* by society over and above economic and legal requirements.

• **Philanthropic responsibility.** Lastly, at the tip of the pyramid, the fourth level of CSR looks at the philanthropic responsibilities of corporations. The Greek word 'philanthropy' means literally 'the love of the fellow human' and by using this idea in a business context, the model includes all those issues that are within the corporation's discretion to improve the quality of life of employees, local communities, and ultimately society in general. This aspect of CSR addresses a great variety of issues, including things such as charitable donations, the building of recreation facilities for employees and their families, support for local schools, or sponsoring of art and sports events. According to Carroll (1991: 42), philanthropic responsibilities are therefore merely *desired* of corporations without being expected or required, making them 'less important than the other three categories'.

The *benefit* of the four-part model of CSR is that it structures the various social responsib-ilities into different dimensions, yet does not seek to explain social responsibility without acknowledging the very real demands placed on the firm to be profitable and legal. In this sense, it is fairly pragmatic.

However, its main *limitation* is that it does not adequately address the problem of what should happen when two or more responsibilities are in conflict. For example, the threat of plant closures often raises the problem of balancing economic responsibilities

Ethics in Action 2.1

Free drugs for developing countries

....

In the late 1980s, the American multinational Merck set an example for a practice that has become increasingly common throughout the last decade: pharmaceutical companies giving away medicines in developing countries. In 1987, Merck committed itself to donate for free its Mectizan drug, which is used in the treatment of onchocerciasis (more commonly known as 'river blindness') —the world's second-leading cause of infectious blindness. The donation programme, which operates in Africa, Latin America, and Yemen, involves collaboration with the World Health Organization, the World Bank, UNICEF, and various national ministries of health. It recently dispensed its 250 millionth treatment, marking a major achievement in the eradication of river blindness amongst those most in need, but least able to afford medicines.

Similarly, in 1998 the UK firm SmithKline Beecham (now GlaxoSmithKline) launched a scheme to provide free drugs to help in eradicating the tropical disease Lymphatic Filariasis (commonly known as elephantiasis) by 2020. The disease, which causes a swelling of the limbs and genitals by up to three times their normal size, affects 120 million people a year and poses a threat to a fifth of the world's population. In launching the scheme, the company explained that it 'was donating the drug as part of its corporate philosophy to help communities in which it worked and traded'. This particular programme costs the company some £500m (€750m) to produce the drug and another £500m in distribution. The *Financial Times* hailed the decision as 'the single biggest act of corporate philanthropy in any industry'.

Philanthropy, however, is not always as easy as simply donating drugs—as SmithKline Beecham's future merger partner Glaxo Wellcome had discovered two years earlier. At the time, pharmaceutical giant Glaxo had just taken over Wellcome, a smaller manufacturer with a tradition of developing drugs for tropical diseases. The new owners discovered that Wellcome had just developed Malaron, a very effective drug against malaria, a disease that still kills around 1 million people in Africa every year. However, as one Glaxo manager put it, 'malaria simply isn't a commercial opportunity for a big research-based company'. The costs of developing and producing Malaron were astronomical, while the potential market in Africa accounted for just 1 per cent of global pharmaceutical sales. Like Merck before them, Glaxo therefore decided not to market Malaron, but to donate it for free.

After three years, though, instead of handing out the proposed one million doses, they had just given away about a hundred! There were several reasons. First, health authorities in African countries were very suspicious of such a 'donation' and saw it as part of an experiment, or as a trick to hook them on the substance and then to introduce a fee at a later stage. Second, it proved to be extremely difficult to integrate such an expensive drug into a health system of a poor country, let alone tackle the risk of theft and black market trade. Third, a global donation of one million doses put the World Health Organization (Glaxo's partner in the scheme) into a serious distribution problem: what was the most just and efficient way of distributing the drugs, when even one million treatments were not enough for all affected people?

Although they applaud individual initiatives to provide free drugs in the developing world, health organizations can be rather critical of the approach in general. For them, the main issue is that because of the lack of purchasing power in the developing world, research and development at major drug companies rarely targets the diseases typically encountered there. Moreover, there is little progress from corporations in developing appropriate support and distribution systems for drugs and healthcare. As a result, most of the major diseases afflicting the world's poorest regions remain unaddressed, and do not feature prominently on the radar screens of the pharmaceutical companies. Hence, critics argue that while drug donations are laudable in themselves they often represent more of a 'PR tonic' for corporations than a viable alternative to a comprehensive healthcare system.

SOURCES

Garrett, A. (1998). 'Charities: free drugs for the poor give donors a PR tonic'. *Observer*, 1 Feb.: 8.
Mihill, C. (1998). 'Drug firm donates £1bn to defeat tropical disease'. *Guardian*, 27 Jan.: 9.
Pilling, D. (1999). 'The drug they couldn't give away'. *Financial Times* (Weekend FT), 13 Nov.: 1.
www.merck.com.
www.gsk.com.

> ■ **Think theory**
>
> Think about the case of drug donations to developing countries in terms of Carroll's four levels of corporate social responsibility. Which levels of responsibility would you say that the pharmaceutical companies discharge with free drug donations?

(of remaining efficient and profitable) with ethical responsibilities to provide secure jobs to employees. Hence, when the French car manufacturer Renault announced its decision to close its Belgian factory at a cost of 3,100 jobs, the Belgian government denounced the move as 'brutal' yet Renault saw its share price immediately jump by 13 per cent (Buckley and Owen 1997). **Ethics in Action 2.1**, which describes the free donation of drugs by pharmaceutical companies in developing countries, illustrates further some of the trade-offs involved. A second problem with the model, and indeed with much of the CSR literature, is that it is strongly biased towards the US context, as we shall now discuss.

CSR in a European context

CSR as a view of business responsibility in society has been particularly strong as a concept in the USA, from where much of the authors, literature, and conceptualizations have emerged. In Europe, however, the concept of CSR has never been quite as influential. The reasons for this lie in some of the differences we discussed in Chapter 1. Generally, one could argue that all levels of CSR play a role in Europe, but they have different significance, and furthermore are interlinked in a somewhat different manner.

- The aspect of *economic* responsibility in the USA is strongly focused on profitability of companies and thus chiefly looks at the responsibility to shareholders. As we shall explain in more detail in Chapter 6, the dominating model of capitalism in much of continental Europe has traditionally been somewhat different. This model tends to define this economic responsibility far more widely and focus, at least to the same extent (if not more), on the economic responsibility of corporations to employees and local communities as well (Hunt 2000). For example, many German companies, such as the engineering conglomerate Thyssen, keep running their unprofitable operations in eastern Germany. The reason for this is that at present 'abandoning' the east of Germany with its stumbling economy is regarded as socially unacceptable and would result in serious problems for the public image of the corporations.

- The element of *legal* responsibility is often regarded as the basis of every other social responsibility in Europe, particularly given the prominent role of the state in regulating corporate practice. Continental European thinking tends to see the state in the role of enforcing the accepted rules of the game whereas, in the Anglo-American worldview, governmental rules are more likely to be regarded as an interference with private liberty.

- Most of the social issues on the corporate agenda in Europe are actually located in the area of *ethical* responsibility. It has been found that Europeans tend to exhibit far greater mistrust of modern corporations (Wootliff and Deri 2001).[4] Hence, a general disquiet about corporations, even if they are running properly in economic terms and comply with the law, suggests the need for constant reaffirmation of their social legitimacy. Thus, nuclear power, genetic engineering, and animal testing have always been issues far higher up on the public-corporate agenda in Europe than in other parts of the world. For example, public outcry regarding the issue of GM food (and its labelling) became a major issue for European corporations to deal with in 1999, yet had little impact in the USA.

- With regard to *philanthropic* responsibility, this aspect in Europe has mostly been implemented not via discretionary acts of successful companies or rich capitalists such as Bill Gates (as in the USA), but compulsorily via the legal framework. Since income and corporate taxes in Europe are generally higher than in the USA, funding of art, higher education, or local community services—just to name a few examples—has never been so much a task for corporations as for government (Reingold 1993). Similarly, labour laws in Europe have tended to grant social benefits to workers and their families, rather than this being a responsibility of 'philanthropic' corporations.

As we can see then, whilst the four levels of responsibility are still largely valid in a European context, they take on different nuances, and may be accorded different significance. For example, Maignan (2001) has found that while US consumers stress the economic responsibilities of companies, their French and German counterparts tend to be far more concerned about companies complying with social norms and laws relating to social performance. Thus, CSR, even if neatly defined along the lines of Carroll's model, still remains a relatively vague and in many aspects arbitrary construct. This has led to the demand to reframe CSR as a more strategic concept of *corporate social responsiveness*.

---

[4] To some extent it can be argued that this is rooted in first-hand experience with the 'industrialized' killing of millions of Jews during the Holocaust (Bauman 1989), often with the active involvement of corporations (Dingwall 1999).

CSR and strategy: corporate social responsiveness

The idea of corporate social responsiveness conceptualizes the more strategic and pro-cessual aspects of CSR, as in how corporations actively respond to social concerns and expectations. It has often been presented as the action phase of CSR (Carroll 1979; Wood 1991). Frederick (1994) thus defines corporate social responsiveness in the following way:

> Corporate social responsiveness refers to the capacity of a corporation to respond to social pressures.

Again, Archie Carroll has been very influential in setting out modes of social responsiveness and his delineation of four 'philosophies' or strategies of social responsiveness (Carroll 1979) have been widely cited.[5] These are:

• **Reaction**—the corporation denies any responsibility for social issues, for example by claim-ing that they are the responsibility of government, or by arguing that the corporation is not to blame;

• **Defence**—the corporation admits responsibility but fights it, doing the very least that seems to be required. Hence, the corporation may adopt an approach based mainly on superficial public relations rather than positive action;

• **Accommodation**—the corporation accepts responsibility and does what is demanded of it by relevant groups;

• **Proaction**—the corporation seeks to go beyond industry norms and anticipates future expectations by doing more than is expected.

Many corporations appear to have a shifting strategy of social responsiveness. For example, in the past, tobacco companies have denied outright a link between smoking and health problems such as lung cancer (reaction). Once the health link had been publicly accepted, however, tobacco firms still fought anti-tobacco campaigners by allegedly denying knowledge of the addictive properties of nicotine, lobbying against further government regulation, and delaying litigation cases (defence). More recently, the weight of evidence against the industry has arguably led to a more accommodative stance, with firms such as BAT now admitting they are in a 'controversial' industry marketing 'risky' products, and Phillip Morris proclaiming a youth smoking prevention programme. Some suggestion of a more proactive strategy might even be said to be emerging. BAT for example claim that they are changing some of the ways they address issues of concern by introducing 'stake-holder dialogue' and producing a social report. However, given their poor strategies of responsiveness of the past, it is perhaps not surprising that such moves are still often interpreted as defensive tactics by their critics.[6]

---

[5] Carroll's (1979) four modes of social responsiveness were in fact derived from the work of Ian Wilson. They have subsequently been applied by Wartick and Cochran (1985) and Clarkson (1995) among others. Wood (1991), in contrast, provides a critique of this typology, and develops a different categorization based on specific processes, namely: environmental assessment, stakeholder management, and issues management.

[6] For more argument from both sides on these issues, you may want to visit the websites of ASH (www.ash.org.uk) and BAT (www.bat.com).

Such difficulties in identifying clear-cut strategies of social responsiveness have led to the development of ways of conceptualizing observable outcomes of business commitment to CSR, namely *corporate social performance*.

Outcomes of CSR: corporate social performance

If we are able to measure, rate, and classify companies on their economic performance, why should it not be possible to do the same with their 'societal' performances as well? The answer to this question has been given by the idea of *corporate social performance* (CSP) and again, the debate about adequate constructs has been long and varied in output. Donna Wood (1991) has presented a model which is regarded by many as the state-of-the-art concept and has been extensively cited in the CSR literature. Following her model, corporate social performance can be observed as the *principles* of CSR, the *processes* of social responsiveness, and the *outcomes* of corporate behaviour. These *outcomes* are delineated in three concrete areas:

- **Social policies**—explicit and pronounced corporate social policies stating the company's values, beliefs, and goals with regard to its social environment. For example, most major firms now explicitly include social objectives in their mission statements and other corporate policies. Some corporations also have more explicit goals and targets in relation to social issues, such as Royal Dutch/Shell's commitment to reduce greenhouse gas emissions by 10 per cent below 1990 levels by 2002.

- **Social programmes**—specific social programmes of activities, measures, and instruments implemented to achieve social policies. For example, many firms have implemented programmes to manage their environmental impacts based around environmental management systems such as ISO 14000/1 and EMAS that include measures and instruments that facilitate the auditing of environmental performance.

- **Social impacts**—social impacts can be traced by looking at concrete changes the corporation has achieved through the programmes implemented in any period. Obviously this is frequently the most difficult to achieve, since much data on social impacts is 'soft' (i.e. difficult to collect and quantify objectively), and the specific impact of the corporation cannot be easily isolated from other factors. Nevertheless, some impacts can be reasonably well estimated. For example: policies aimed at benefiting local schools can examine literacy rates and exam grades; environmental policies can be evaluated with pollution data; employee welfare policies can be assessed with employee satisfaction questionnaires; and equal opportunity programmes can be evaluated by monitoring the composition of the workforce and benchmarking against comparable organizations.

Clearly then, whilst the outcomes of CSR in the form of CSP is an important consideration, the actual measurement of social performance remains a complex task. We shall be discussing some of the potential tools and techniques for achieving this in more detail in Chapter 5. A more immediate problem, however, is to define not only *what* the corporation is responsible for, but *who* it is responsible to. This is the task of stakeholder theory.

Stakeholder theory of the firm

The stakeholder theory of the firm is probably the most popular and influential theory to emerge from business ethics (Stark 1994). Whilst the term 'stakeholder' was first recorded in the 1960s, the theoretical approach was in the main developed and brought forward by Edward Freeman (1984) in the 1980s. Unlike the CSR approach, which strongly focuses on the corporation and its responsibilities, the stakeholder approach starts by looking at various groups to which the corporation has a responsibility. The main starting point is the claim that corporations are not simply managed in the interests of their shareholders alone but that there is a whole range of groups, or *stakeholders*, that have a legitimate interest in the corporation as well.

Although there are numerous different definitions as to who or what constitutes a stakeholder,[7] Freeman's (1984: 46) original definition is perhaps the most widely used:

> A stakeholder in an organization is . . . any group or individual who can affect, or is affected by, the achievement of the organization's objectives.

But what do we mean here by 'affects' and 'affected by'? To provide a more precise definition, Evan and Freeman (1993) suggest we can apply two simple principles. The first is the **principle of corporate rights**, which demands that the corporation has the obligation not to violate the rights of others. The second, the **principle of corporate effect**, says that companies are responsible for the effects of their actions on others. In the light of these two basic principles we can define a stakeholder in the following slightly more precise way:

> A stakeholder of a corporation is an individual or group which either:
>
> • is harmed by, or benefits from, the corporation;
>
> *or*
>
> • whose rights can be violated, or have to be respected, by the corporation.

This definition makes clear that the range of stakeholders differs from company to company, and even for the same company in different situations, tasks, or projects. Using this definition, then, it is not possible to identify a definitive group of relevant stakeholders for any given corporation in any given situation. However, a typical representation is given in Figure 2.2.

Figure 2.2 (*a*) shows the traditional model of managerial capitalism, where the company is seen as only related to four groups. Suppliers, employees, and shareholders provide the basic resources for the corporation, which then uses these to provide products for consumers. The shareholders are the 'owners' of the firm and they consequently are the dominant group, in whose interest the firm should be run.

In Figure 2.2 (*b*) we find the stakeholder view of the firm, where the shareholders are one group among several others. The company has obligations not only to one group but also

---

[7] See Mitchell et al. (1997) for a comprehensive review of stakeholder definitions.

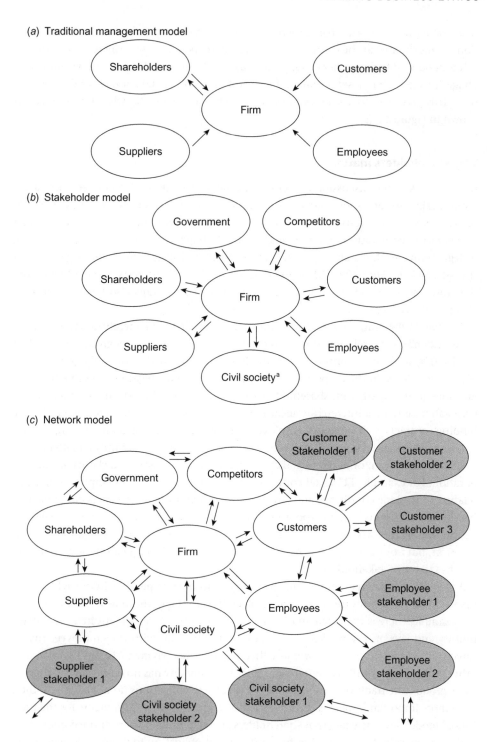

Figure 2.2. Stakeholder theory of the firm

[a] By civil society, we mean pressure groups, local communities, non-government organizations, etc.

to a whole variety of other constituencies that are affected by its activities. The corporation is thus situated at the centre of a series of interdependent two-way relationships.

It is important to remember though that stakeholder groups also might have duties and obligations to their *own* set of stakeholders, and to the other stakeholders of the corporation. This gives rise to a *network model* of stakeholder theory (Rowley 1997), which is shown in Figure 2.2 (*c*).

Why stakeholders matter

If we go back to our discussion earlier in the chapter regarding Milton Friedman's arguments against social responsibility, his second main objection was that businesses should only be run in the interests of their owners. This correlates with the traditional stockholder model of the corporation, where managers' only obligation is to shareholders. Indeed, in legal terms, we have already seen that in most developed nations, managers have a special *fiduciary relationship* with shareholders to act in their interests. Stakeholder theory therefore has to provide a compelling reason why other groups also have a legitimate claim on the corporation.

Freeman (1984) himself gives two main arguments. First, on a merely descriptive level, if one examines the relationship between the firm and the various groups to which it is related by all sorts of contracts, it is simply not true to say that the only group with a legitimate interest in the corporation is shareholders. From a **legal perspective** there are far more groups apart from shareholders that appear to hold a legitimate 'stake' in the corporation since their interests are already protected in some way. There are not only legally binding contracts with suppliers, employees, or customers but also an increasingly dense network of laws and regulation enforced by society which make it simply a matter of fact that a large spectrum of different stakeholders have certain rights and claims on the corporation. For example, EU social contract legislation protects certain employee rights in relation to working conditions and pay, suggesting that, from an ethical point of view, it has already been agreed that corporations have certain obligations toward employees. Of course, among this broader set of obligations and rights, there are also obligations toward investors, but from a legal perspective this does not remove the obligation the corporation also has to other stakeholders.

A second group of arguments comes from an **economic perspective**. In the light of new institutional economics there are further objections to the traditional stockholder view. For example, there is the problem of *externalities*: if a firm closes a plant in a small community and lays off the workers, it is not only the relation with the employees that is directly affected—shop owners will lose their business, tax payments to fund schools and other public services will also suffer—but since the company has no *contractual* relation to these groups, the traditional model suggests that these obligations do not exist. Another, even more important aspect is the *agency problem*: one of the key arguments for the traditional model lies in the fact that shareholders are seen as the owners of the corporation, and consequently the corporation has its dominant obligation to them. This view, however, only reflects the reality of shareholders' interests in a very limited number of cases. The majority of shareholders invest in shares not predominantly to 'own' a company (or parts of it), nor do they necessarily seek for the firm to maximize its long-term profitability. In the first place, shareholders often buy shares for speculative reasons, and it is the development of the share price that is their predominant interest—and not 'ownership' in a physical corporation. Hence, it is not evident why the highly speculative and mostly short-term interests of shareowners should prevail over the often long-term interests of other groups such as customers, employees, or suppliers.

A new role for management

According to Freeman, this broader view of responsibility towards multiple stakeholders assigns a new role to management. Rather than being simply agents of shareholders, management has to take into account the rights and interests of all legitimate stakeholders. Whilst they still have a fiduciary responsibility to look after shareholders' interests, managers must balance this with the competing interests of other stakeholders for the long-term survival of the corporation, rather than maximizing the interests of just one group at a time. We shall look at some of the ways in which managers can achieve this in Chapter 5. Furthermore, though, since the company is obliged to respect the rights of *all* stakeholders, this automatically implies that, to a certain extent, stakeholders should be able to take part in those managerial decisions that substantially affect their welfare and their rights. In a more developed form, Freeman has argued in favour of **stakeholder democracy** where every corporation has a stakeholder board of directors giving stakeholders the opportunity to influence and control corporate decisions. This also includes the idea of a model or a legally binding code of **corporate governance**, which codifies and regulates the various rights of the stakeholder groups. This, as we shall now see, appears to be more developed in Europe than it is in the USA, where stakeholder theory originated.

Stakeholder thinking in a European context

Stakeholder theory is a very simple, straightforward approach to the modern corporation. Therefore, in the second part of the book we will have a detailed look at major stakeholders of the company and provide an in-depth analysis of the company's obligations and managerial approaches towards these different stakeholders. Nevertheless it is important to frame stakeholder thinking from a European perspective. As we indicated above, the shareholder domination of the model of managerial capitalism has never been as strongly developed in continental Europe and Scandinavia as it has in the Anglo-American tradition. Therefore, a general 'shift' towards other stakeholders has not particularly been seen as so much of a necessity. Furthermore, with state influence—even ownership—still playing a considerable role in large parts of Europe, one of the major 'shareholders' automatically represents a large variety of 'stakeholders', with the result that the rights of social groups other than the direct contractual partners of the firm have traditionally been fairly well respected anyway. This applies traditionally to France, Germany, and Italy, but to a smaller degree to all major countries in Europe. It applies as well to most countries of Eastern Europe where the large state-owned industrial entities always had a strong commitment to all sorts of groups other than their owners—a pattern which still survived quite significantly the recent phase of privatization (Edwards and Lawrence 2000).

In a certain sense then, one could argue that although the *terminology* of stakeholder theory is relatively new in Europe, the general principles have actually been *practised* for some time. Let's just consider two examples:

- Freeman's vision of a stakeholder democracy reads as something of a blueprint for the German model of industrial relations: on the supervisory board of large public shareholder-owned corporations at least one-third of the board members have to be representatives of the employees—and in some branches they even have up to 50 per cent of the votes. Furthermore, there is a very dense 'corporate law' of governance that codifies far-reaching rights of codetermination within the company. Although one might argue that this is focusing on just one stakeholder group, namely employees, this example is representative of a generally broader orientation of corporations towards stakeholders in many European countries.

- In the early 1990s, the Netherlands introduced the instrument of 'covenants' into environmental legislation (Immerzeel-Brand 2002). In order to improve the environmental performance of industry, the Dutch government gave targets to thirteen sectors while the responsibility for meeting these targets was an issue of self-regulation for companies within these sectors. Companies were thus treated as partners by the government, and rather than reacting to imposed standards, corporate actors in the Netherlands embarked on a long negotiation process with regulators, competitors, suppliers, local authorities, and a number of other stakeholders in order to find a mutually satisfactory solution for all groups.

We will look at further aspects of stakeholder management, inclusion, and participation in the second part of the book when we move on to focusing on each stakeholder group individually. However, at this stage it is important to recognize that there are not only different ways in which a stakeholder approach can be implemented, but there are actually quite different *forms* of the theory itself.

Different forms of stakeholder theory

The popularity of stakeholder theory in the business ethics literature has meant that quite different forms of the theory have emerged, and it is important to be able to distinguish between them.[8] Thomas Donaldson and Lee Preston (1995) provide a convincing argument that there are in fact three forms of stakeholder theory:

- **Normative stakeholder theory**—this is theory which attempts to provide a reason why corporations *should* take into account stakeholder interests.

- **Descriptive stakeholder theory**—this is theory which attempts to ascertain whether (and how) corporations *actually do* take into account stakeholder interests.

---

[8] There are a number of excellent papers which offer reviews of stakeholder theory, in particular Donaldson and Preston (1995) and Stoney and Winstanley (2001).

- **Instrumental stakeholder theory**—this is theory which attempts to answer the question of whether it is *beneficial for the corporation* to take into account stakeholder interests.

In the preceding discussion, we have mainly used the first two types of argument to present the case for a stakeholder approach—that managers should and indeed do (at least to some extent) take into consideration interests beyond narrow shareholder concerns. However, we will develop a deeper normative basis for our arguments regarding specific stakeholder groups in Part II of the book. The instrumental argument—that considering the interests of stakeholders is in the best interests of the corporation—is largely akin to the argument for enlightened self-interest that we presented on pp. 41–42.

By now, it should be fairly evident that Friedman's (1970) first and second arguments against the social role and responsibilities of the corporation face considerable dissent from those advocating a CSR and/or stakeholder position. However, there is still one final aspect of his argument that we have not yet addressed. This is the issue of corporate accountability.

Corporate accountability: the firm as a 'political' actor

In Friedman's view, corporations should not undertake social policies and programmes because this is the task of government; and since corporate managers are acting on behalf of shareholders rather than being elected by the general public, their accountability is primarily to shareholders, not to the public. It is important that we make it clear what we mean by accountability in this context. Hence, for our purposes:

> Corporate accountability refers to whether a corporation is answerable in some way for the consequences of its actions.

In arguing against the inclusion of a social role in corporate activity, Friedman was therefore suggesting that corporations should only be involved in commercial activities and hence should, and indeed could, only be answerable to their shareholders. Although it could potentially be argued that Friedman's argument was defensible when his article was published, more recently the question of corporate accountability has become far more vexed. This is because it has been increasingly recognized that despite this apparent lack of accountability with respect to their social consequences, corporations *have* begun to be involved in numerous social activities and have actually taken up many of the functions previously undertaken by government. Firms have thus begun to take on the role of 'political' actors.

During the late 1980s and 1990s, we witnessed a growing tendency toward the privatization of many political functions and processes formerly assigned to governments. There were two major reasons for this development:

- Governmental failure;
- Increasing power and influence of corporations.

Both developments assign to business a considerably widened array of political responsibilities, which in turn result in a growing demand for corporate accountability with regard to the use of this power. Whilst we shall refrain from an extended discussion of the specific relations between business and government at this stage (this is the subject of Chapter 11), it is important to briefly set out these two underlying processes that are driving demands for greater corporate accountability.

Governmental failure: 'risk society' and the institutional failure of politics

In 1986 the German sociologist Ulrich Beck published a book under the title of *Risk Society*[9] which, in close co-operation with British authors such as Anthony Giddens, has laid the basis for a new view on industrial societies in the late twentieth and early twenty-first centuries. Beck starts by describing the way that various threats to the survival of mankind and its natural environment are becoming increasingly dominant on the public agenda. Examples are the risks of nuclear power, the risks of global warming, the risks of industrial agriculture, and the risks inherent in new technologies such as genetic engineering, just to name a few. In Europe such risks certainly came dramatically to the attention of the general public with the landmark experience of the nuclear accident in Chernobyl in 1986, followed by the BSE crisis, the foot and mouth outbreak, and various other industrial catastrophes.

Normally, these problems are the classic tasks for governments and politicians to deal with, causing them to issue laws that regulate these phenomena and protect citizens. However, the crucial point in these cases is that governments have been largely unable to protect their citizens; on the contrary, most of these risks and catastrophes happened with the government either being equally affected, or, as the BSE case shows, being one of the main actors responsible for the problem. Beck and Giddens in their theory then conclude that this leads us to a general problem of modern societies: as well as providing their citizens with an abundance of goods and services, modern industrial societies also confront their citizens with severe risks to their health, their environment, even to the survival of mankind as such on the planet. At the same time, we see that the political institutions of modern societies are not able to protect their citizens from these self-imposed consequences of industrialization.

Why do governments fail?

There are numerous reasons why governments are not able to do their job here. Sometimes, as already indicated, they are too much part of the problem to be able to be part of the solution. More often, tackling these issues would result in severe changes in the lifestyle of modern society and in a decrease of public welfare—something politicians are quite reluctant to impose on their electorate. Sometimes even these risks are beyond the control of a single government, as the example of Chernobyl or the risk of global warming shows. Beck talks of an 'organized irresponsibility' in this context and analyses some other ways of coping with these hazards that have started to emerge as a consequence.

---

[9] Published 1992 in English translation—see Beck (1992).

In particular, Beck suggests that in many important areas politics is obviously no longer a task carried out *exclusively* by politicians. In the case of numerous social and environmental issues, non-governmental organizations (NGOs) such as Greenpeace or Friends of the Earth, or else protest groups and campaigners such as anti-road protesters, have also been important political actors (see Chapter 10 for more discussion of the role of such groups). Beck speaks of a new political arena, which he calls 'subpolitics', meaning political action that is taken by actors, as it were, 'below' the level of traditional governmental politics. The example of Shell's Brent Spar platform is worth returning to here. The implications of this incident were that the effective political regulation of this issue was not brought about by governmental institutions (since the UK government and the EU environmental ministers were expressly in favour of the deep sea disposal option), but rather with Greenpeace highlighting the problem and consumers all across Europe boycotting Shell, the issue was effectively regulated by 'sub-political' actors.

We could find numerous other examples that would show us that governments in many aspects have lost some of their traditional capability to solve major issues in modern industrial societies. Crucially though, at the same time as we have witnessed a *weakened state*, we have also witnessed a parallel development which has seen a massive *rise in corporate power and influence*.

Corporate power on the rise

The rise in corporate power and influence over the past twenty years or so has been receiving growing attention from academics and the general public alike. We have seen various street demonstrations against growing corporate power, as well as targeted attacks on specific corporations such as McDonald's (see Case 1) and Shell (Case 5). Moreover a number of influential books such as David Korten's (1995) *When Corporations Rule the World*, Noreena Hertz's (2001b) *The Silent Takeover*, and Naomi Klein's (2000) best-selling *No Logo* have argued that the 'big brand bullies' have increasingly exercised more and more influence and control over society. There is however considerable controversy in the literature about this thesis: whilst this growing body of work sees a problem in the extended power residing in the corporate sector, some mainstream business writers still contend that even large MNCs are considerably weak and politically dependent on national governments (e.g. Rugman 2000).

The crucial point in the critical view is the argument that across the globe people's lives are increasingly controlled and shaped no longer by governments but by corporations. Let us have a look at some examples:

- The liberalization and deregulation of markets and industries during the rule of centre-right governments throughout the 1980s and the early 1990s (as exemplified by 'Thatcherism' and 'Reaganomics') has given more influence, liberty, and choice to private actors. The more strongly the market dominates economic life, the weaker governmental intervention and influence is.

- The same period has resulted in a huge privatization of major public services and formerly public-owned companies. Major industries such as media, telecommunications, transport, and utilities are now dominated by private actors.

Ethical Dilemma 2

When good results are bad results?

Professor Ballistico is scratching his head. Looking at the results of last month's series of experiments makes him feel a bit uneasy. He has been sitting in his office for hours now trying to analyse the spread-sheets from every possible angle—but without success. He even had an argument with his three research assistants accusing them of having not measured the results properly—but they had been right this time.

Not that Ballistico is particularly unhappy about his project. It is actually quite a successful piece of research looking at the various side effects of food additives in frozen food. The two-year project has already resulted in some very good publications; he has even been invited several times to give interviews on the television and in the press about the results. However, this time round he has a strange feeling. What actually causes him trouble is the fact that according to the results of the latest tests, two substances involved in the study, called 'longlife' and 'rotnever', appear to quite significantly increase the risk of human allergies for long-time consumers of the additives. And however he turns and interprets the results, his assistants really seem to have delivered solid work on this occasion.

Normally such surprising results would be good news. Solid results of this kind would make for sensational presentations at the next conference of the World Food Scientist Federation. On top of that, 'longlife' and 'rotnever' are very common additives in the products of the large food multinational Foodcorp, which is the market leader in frozen food in his country. His results could really make big headlines.

There is one little problem though: Professor Ballistico is director of the Foodcorp Centre for Food Science at BigCity University. Three years ago, the food company donated €2.3m to BigCity University in order to set up the research centre and to fund its activities. The company felt that as 'a good corporate citizen we should give something back to society by funding academic research and teaching, to the benefit of future generations'. They also signalled that they saw this as a continuous engagement over time, and the decision about the next €2m funding will be imminent three months from now.

Professor Ballistico is only too aware of the dilemma: if he publishes his results, Foodcorp might get into serious trouble. He also knows that this will be quite embarrassing at the next meeting with his sponsor, and it will most certainly influence the company's decision to further fund the centre. And he hardly dares to think of his next meeting with the vice-chancellor, who is always so proud of BigCity having such excellent ties to companies and scoring highest in the country in terms of its ability to secure external funding. Should he therefore just tell Foodcorp privately about his results so that they can take appropriate action to deal with rotnever and longlife?

Questions

1 What are the main ethical issues for Professor Ballistico here?
2 What options are open to him? How would you assess these options?
3 How should Ballistico proceed, and what can he realistically do to prevent similar problems arising in the future?

4 What are the wider ethical concerns regarding corporate involvement in funding universities and other public institutions?

5 In the light of this case, give a critical assessment of the potential, as well as the limits, of corporations stepping into roles formerly assigned to governments.

- Most industrialized countries have to varying degrees struggled with unemployment. Although governments are made responsible for this, at the same time they have less and less possibility of influencing these figures, since the decisions over employment, relocation, or lay-offs are taken by corporations (see Case 2 on BMW and Rover, pp. 71–4).

- Globalization facilitates relocation and makes companies able to engage governments in a 'race to the bottom', i.e. corporations have tended to relocate to 'low-cost' regions where they are faced by only limited regulation (or at least enforcement) of pay and working conditions, environmental protection, and corporate taxation.

- Since many of the new risks emergent in industrial society (as discussed above) are complex and far-reaching (often beyond the scope of individual countries), they would require very intricate laws, which in turn would be very difficult to implement and monitor. Hence, corporations have increasingly been set the task of regulating themselves rather than facing direct government regulation (see Chapter 11 for more detailed discussion). For example, in various legislative projects the European Union has set incentives for companies or industries to come up with self-regulation and self-commitments rather than imposing a law upon them from above. Consequently, companies—or bodies of organized corporate interests—are increasingly assuming the role of a political actor in the sphere of social and environmental issues.

We could easily add to this list and will come back to these issues throughout the book. **Ethical Dilemma 2**, for example, describes another situation where business might be involved in taking over previously governmental functions, namely the funding of universities.

The central problem behind these trends, however, is clearly visible: the idea of democracy is to give people control over the basic conditions of their lives and the possibility to choose those policies that they regard as desirable. However, since many such decisions are no longer taken by governments (and hence, indirectly by individual citizens) but by corporations (who are not subject to democratic election), the problem of democratic accountability becomes crucial.

The problem of democratic accountability

The central point here is the question as to **who controls corporations** and **to whom are corporations accountable**. There are those like Friedman, as discussed above, who see it as a given that corporations are only accountable to their shareholders, and, furthermore, are accountable to obey and comply with the laws of the countries in which they do business. But there are also good arguments for the view that since corporations now shape and influence so much of public and private life in modern societies, since in effect they are political actors, they have to become more accountable to society.

One argument, offered by Hertz (2001a) and others, is that given the power of big corporations, there is more democratic power in an individual's choice as a consumer (for or against certain products) than in their choice at the ballot box. As Smith (1990) contends, consumption choices are to some extent 'purchase votes' in the social control of corporations. However, as we shall discuss in more detail in Chapter 8 when we cover business relations with consumers, one should also recognize the limitations of the individual's power to affect corporate policy through purchase choices. There is little guarantee that consumers' social choices will be reflected in their consumer choices, nor that such social choices will be even recognized, never mind acted on, by corporations. After all, not only do corporations benefit from a massive power imbalance compared to individual consumers, but consumers are also constrained in executing their voting rights by the choices offered by the market. Perhaps most importantly, consumers are just one of the multiple stakeholders that corporations might be expected to be accountable to.

This has led to further questions regarding how corporations can be made more accountable for their actions to the broad range of relevant stakeholders. One important stream of literature has examined the possibility for corporations to audit and report on their social, ethical, and environmental performance through new accounting procedures, such as environmental accounting and social reporting (e.g. Gray et al. 1997; Livesey 2002a; Zadek et al. 1997). Another important stream of literature has looked at broader issues of communication with stakeholders, and development of stakeholder dialogue and stakeholder partnerships (e.g. Bendell 2000a; Crane and Livesey 2003). We shall look at these developments, which have been largely pioneered by European academics, institutions, and corporations, in more detail later in the book, most notably in Chapters 5 and 10. However, the key issue here is that in order to enhance corporate accountability, corporate social activity and performance should be made more visible to those with a stake in the corporation. The term usually applied to this is **transparency**.

Although transparency can relate to any aspect of the corporation, demands for transparency usually relate primarily to *social* as opposed to *commercial* concerns, since traditionally corporations have claimed that much of their data is commercially confidential. However, it is evident that many social issues cannot be easily separated from commercial decisions. For example, Nike long claimed that the identity and location of their suppliers could not be revealed because it was commercially sensitive information that their competitors could exploit. However, concerns over working conditions in these factories led to demands for Nike to make the information public, which to some extent they have eventually agreed to do. Similarly, manufacturers and retailers of cars, CDs, and other consumer products have traditionally kept a close guard on information relating to costs. However, in the face of accusations regarding consumer exploitation as a result of collusion amongst competitors to produce artificially inflated prices (particularly in the UK), pressure has been put on firms in these industries to make their cost structures more transparent (Piercy 1999: 122–46).

Clearly then, we need to take a fairly broad view of transparency in this regard, giving rise to the following definition:

> Transparency is the degree to which corporate decisions, policies, activities and impacts are acknowledged and made visible to relevant stakeholders.

The tenor of current demands for greater corporate accountability and transparency, particularly as exemplified by the protest movement against global capitalism, MNCs, and global background institutions such as the IMF or the World Bank, suggests that these developments might no longer be an option for corporations. Increasingly, corporate accountability and transparency are being presented as necessities, not only from a normative point of view, but also with regard to the practical aspects of effectively doing business and maintaining public legitimacy. In the face of such developments, we have witnessed increasing emphasis being placed on the notion of *corporate citizenship*—a relatively new, but potentially important addition to the lexicon of business ethics. In the last main section of the chapter then, we shall examine this new term and assess its significance for the conceptualization of the social role of the corporation.

Corporate citizenship

Towards the middle of the 1990s, the term 'corporate citizenship' (CC) emerged as a new way of addressing the social role of the corporation. Initially favoured primarily by practitioners (Altman and Vidaver-Cohen 2000), corporate citizenship has also increasingly been introduced into the academic literature. Though again the shift in terminology largely started in the USA, numerous companies in Europe have since committed themselves to CC (see **Figure 2.3**), and various consultancies and research centres based around the concept of CC have been founded in Europe as well as elsewhere across the globe.

Why a new term?

One might first ask why this new label of *corporate citizenship* emerged, and indeed why the existing terms of 'corporate social responsibility', or 'corporate social responsiveness' and 'corporate social performance', not to mention 'business ethics', were apparently perceived as inappropriate. Apart from the fact that CC potentially has some substantial new elements to add to the traditional views of corporations in society (as we will see shortly), there are a few possible reasons why business might be argued to be happy to embrace this new terminology.

- As van Luijk (2001) has pointed out, industry has never been completely happy with the language used in business ethics. To start with, the very notion of business *ethics* might be seen as somewhat suspicious as it implies that 'ethics' is something that is not originally present in business, or, even worse, something which is opposed to business; 'ethics' as such for many practitioners has already quite an elitist, even patronizing slant to it.

- A similar argument can be made for corporate social *responsibility*: this, from a business point of view, could be seen to suggest a very admonishing and even reproachful

Company	Corporate citizenship statement	Source
Ford	'Corporate citizenship has become an integral part of every decision and action we take. We believe corporate citizenship is demonstrated in who we are as a company, how we conduct our business and how we take care of our employees, as well as in how we interact with the world at large.'	**www.ford.com.**
GlaxoSmithKline	'GlaxoSmithKline makes substantial investments in its community and corporate citizenship programmes with the aim of enabling people to enjoy a better, healthier, more fulfilling lifestyle.'	**www.gsk.com.**
Nokia	'Our goal is to be a good corporate citizen wherever we operate, as a responsible and contributing member of society.'	**www.nokia.com**
Novartis	'For Novartis, the Policy on Corporate Citizenship sums up its societal and environmental values and commitments.'	*Corporate Citizenship at Novartis Report*, 2001–2
Siemens	'In a time of such wide-ranging challenges, dialogue with society and responsible corporate citizenship are more vital than ever before. In the words of our Corporate Principles, "Our knowledge and our solutions help create a better world." And we are convinced that every company—as an integral part of society—has a corresponding obligation to contribute to the common good.'	*Corporate Citizenship Report*, 2001.

Figure 2.3. Commitments to corporate citizenship

connotation, apart from the fact that it was used by many proponents in the sense of reminding business of something *additional* they should do.

- It is also worth noting that most of the existing terms were initially introduced into the debate by academics, making it more difficult to establish legitimacy and a lasting place in the business world.

- 'Citizenship', on the other hand, has a rather different connotation for business. Not only was CC initially coined by practitioners, but it can be said to highlight the fact that the corporation sees—or recaptures—its rightful place in society, next to other 'citizens', with whom the corporation forms a community. Citizenship then focuses on rights and responsibilities of all members of the community, who are mutually interlinked and dependent on each other (Waddell 2000).

In Europe, this choice of phrasing for the new corporate commitment to social responsibility coincides with, and is fuelled by, three further developments:

- In the course of the ongoing unification process in Europe, the debate about the notion of citizenship has been rekindled (Van Parijs 2000). One might question what it means to be part of this new entity, and what rights and duties of citizenship are linked to our part within it.

- In Eastern Europe, most of the newly founded, reorganized, or taken-over states are only little older than a decade. After the communist legacy, questions surrounding the role of business and government in society, as well as the political organization of new communities, values, duties, rights, and responsibilities, remain in a process of redefinition and reallocation.

- Globalization has also substantially eroded the unifying power of the notion of citizenship. For example, being a Swedish citizen entitles one to various rights granted by the Swedish state. The power of states however is territorially confined. The more that social interaction is deterritorialized (see Chapter 1), the more interrelations are taking place beyond the control of the nation state, and the more the notion of (national) citizenship is weakened (Hettne 2000). This has raised the question of what citizenship means on the global level. With corporations counting among the key actors at this level, debates about global citizenship have tended to be conflated with debates about the meaning of global *corporate* citizenship.

A recent landmark in this process has been a joint statement on 'Global Corporate Citizenship—The Leadership Challenge for CEOs and Boards', signed during the World Economic Forum in New York in January 2002 by CEOs from thirty-four of the world's largest MNCs, among them major European companies such as ABB, Deutsche Bank, Diageo, Philips, Renault, and UBS (World Economic Forum 2002). Given such emphasis being placed on CC, we need to be clear about what exactly it means. This task, however, is complicated by the different meanings implied by those employing the term, as we shall now see.

Defining corporate citizenship: three perspectives

As we have already seen, CC is currently an extremely prominent term in key debates about business ethics in Europe, the USA, and elsewhere. In business practice in particular, CC is beginning to dominate ways of thinking and talking about the social role of the corporation. As such, much of the discussion in this book is therefore framed around the concept of CC. However, as the literature on CC is relatively new, and a widely accepted definition of CC has yet to be established, we will first of all need to develop a working definition of CC that can be used in the subsequent chapters of the book. In order to do so, we will first have to delineate our definition of CC within other definitions typically employed either explicitly or implicitly elsewhere. Currently, the literature on CC reveals three different perspectives (Matten et al. 2003):

- **A limited view of CC**—this essentially equates CC with corporate philanthropy

- **An equivalent view of CC**—this essentially equates CC with CSR

- **An extended view of CC**—this acknowledges the extended political role of the corporation in society

We shall briefly discuss each of these three perspectives. **Figure 2.4** provides an overview of the three views of CC. However, it will soon become evident that although the first two views are by far the most common in popular usage, only the extended view of CC

	Limited view	Equivalent view	Extended view
Initiation	Voluntary	Partly voluntary, partly obligatory	Partly voluntary, partly imposed
Focus	Philanthropy, focused on projects, limited scope	All areas of CSR	Citizenship: social, political, and civil rights
Role of the company	Active, strategic focus	Rather passive, living up to demands of society	Active political; stepping in for governmental failure
Main stakeholder group	Local communities, employees	Broad range of stakeholders; society in general	Broad range of stakeholders; society in general
Role of self-interest	Dominant	Tolerated, but not the primary motivation	Mixture of self-interest and responsible attitude towards society
View of capitalism	Endorsing; social engagement is part of the business interest	Critical; threatening to neoclassical views of capitalisms	Accepting; though using CC as a disguise for corporate power
Motivation	Economic	Ethical and legal	Economic and political
Moral grounding	No particular; 'tit for tat' appeals to economic rationality	Liberal or socialist orientation, strong reference to ethical reasoning and grounding	Grounding is not moral, but comes from changes in the political arena

Figure 2.4. Three views of corporate citizenship

actually offers anything genuinely new to the terms and concepts already discussed in this chapter. The extended view is also, we suggest, probably the most significant and appropriate way of employing CC from a *descriptive* perspective—that is, in terms of framing how things actually are. Hence, in the remainder of the book, we shall mainly use the term CC in the context of the extended view.

Limited view of CC

Initially, CC was, and in many instances still is, used to identify the philanthropic role and responsibilities the firm voluntarily undertakes in the local community, such as charitable donations. The limited view of CC tends to focus nearly completely on the direct physical environment of the company, resulting in a strong focus on local communities as the main stakeholder of the firm (Altman 1998). Carroll (1991) for example identifies 'being a good corporate citizen' with his fourth level of CSR, namely philanthropic responsibilities. Accordingly, Carroll (1991) places CC at the top level of his CSR pyramid, suggesting that it is a discretionary activity beyond that which is expected of business.

Citizenship in this respect is essentially about putting something back into the community, and is based on the corporation receiving from society with the one hand and giving to society with the other. **Ethics in Action 2.2**, which discusses the UK organization Business

```
Ethics in Action 2.2
```

Business in the Community—developing corporate citizenship

In July 2002, 'Business in the Community' (BITC), a prominent, and in some ways remarkable, institution within the European business community, had its twentieth birthday. BITC is a British organization with around 700 member companies that was established in order to improve companies' relations with their local communities and to help them to assume responsibility for improving the quality of life among their local stakeholders.

BITC was founded in the early 1980s 'against a backdrop of enormously high levels of unemployment and urban rioting' (**www.bitc.org.uk**). Since corporations might be adversely affected by urban decay, escalations in criminality, and deteriorating standards in education of potential staff (to name just a few aspects), the aim of the initiative was to improve the immediate local environment of companies. What began as a spreading of an 'uncertain message' (bitc.org.uk) is today an established institution in British industry—so much so that Prince Charles has been its president since 1997.

BITC has four main areas of involvement:

- Improving the environmental impact of corporations
- Cause-related marketing
- Investment in a diverse workplace
- Building healthy communities

With regard to the starting points of involvement in local communities BITC is quite outspoken about its self-interest on the one hand and governmental failure on the other:

Companies need healthy, well-educated and skilled employees in order to keep their competitive edge. Employed and healthy people are also customers, so it is in the interests of the business to operate in communities where there are good schools and where people live in a healthy, sustaining environment. The needs of some communities present problems, which cannot be solved by governments alone. The skills and resources of the private sector can provide the impetus to help many of these communities. (**www.bitc.org.uk**)

A good example is their involvement in cause-related marketing, defined as a commercial activity in which businesses and charities form a partnership with each other to market an image, product, or service for mutual benefit. BITC clearly encourages its members to engage in these issues because research has shown that cause-related marketing has significantly improved customer retention and a positive perception of the brand.

The twentieth anniversary was celebrated by setting up various awards for outstanding projects of member companies. Some ventures of the finalists are typical of BITC's projects:

- The Bank of Scotland's co-operation with the *Big Issue*, a magazine run by homeless people, in order to overcome the obstacles homeless people face in setting up a bank account;
- British Airways, together with UNICEF and the local borough, turned parts of their new headquarters in London into a Community Learning Centre for the use of local community organizations;

- In a deprived part of the north of England, the supermarket chain Tesco worked with various stake-holders to offer training and jobs to unemployed people from disadvantaged backgrounds.

Apart from these bigger projects, the focus of much of BITC's work is on smaller-scale initiatives, such as pro-bono consulting for charities and local community bodies. A typical example would be a senior executive of a business mentoring a head teacher in how to manage budgets and motivate staff. A strong focus of initiatives actually lies on projects that benefit the staff of companies, such as GlaxoSmithKline, which runs a special hygiene education scheme in some of its central African subsidiaries to stop diarrhoeal disease, a major factor for child mortality in these countries.

The assessment of BITC's twenty years of community involvement is overall very positive. The member corporations judge their involvement as good for their business, either in qualitative out-comes such as brand perception or in quantitative terms such as KPMG's estimated savings in annual operating costs of £250,000 through environmental measures. A recent survey among the 1,019 schools, community organizations, health centres, and training groups working with BITC brought the response that more than half of the organizations regard business support as crucial to their organization. However, this research surfaced certain shortcomings of the involvement: many BITC initiatives are one-offs while a constant and committed engagement would be more helpful in order to achieve long-term results. Furthermore, even though (or maybe because?) BITC has always focused on the business case for corporate citizenship, it still seems rather difficult to persuade a larger number of businesses to become active members.

SOURCES

David, R. (ed.) (2000). *Business in the Community: BITC Awards Year 2000 (Financial Times Guide)*. London: Financial Times.
Financial Times (2002a). 'Good imprint on the environment'. *Financial Times*, 19 June: 17.
——— (2002b). 'Benefits for the young and old'. *Financial Times*, 19 June: 17.
Maitland, A. (2002). 'Involvement by companies produces a ripple effect'. *Financial Times*, 19 June: 17.
www.bitc.org.uk (visited in June 2002).

in the Community, shows an example of how this 'tit-for-tat' rationale might work in concrete projects and environments.

> ■ **Think theory**
>
> Think about the experiences of Business in the Community in terms of the firm as a political actor. To what extent are the issues dealt with by the organization a result of either governmental failure or increasing corporate power?

Although academics and managers discussing corporate citizenship often imply this meaning, we might question whether the limited view of CC really justifies the invention and usage of a new terminology. There is little that is genuinely new here and only very poor reference to the usage of the term 'citizenship'.

Equivalent view of CC

The second common understanding of CC consists in a somewhat updated label for CSR (or sometimes stakeholder management), without attempting to define any new role or responsibilities for the corporation. The most striking example for this use of CC is probably Carroll himself who, in a paper entitled 'The four faces of corporate citizenship' (Carroll 1998), defines CC exactly the same way as he initially defined CSR two decades ago! Similarly, Isabelle Maignan and her colleagues (e.g. Maignan and Ferrell 2000, 2001; Maignan et al. 1999) have defined CC as 'the extent to which businesses meet the economic, legal, ethical and discretionary responsibilities imposed on them by their stakeholders'—essentially a repackaging of Carroll's (1991) definition of CSR.

Clearly, this is a very common way of employing the terminology of CC, but given that it creates quite a bit of conceptual confusion, it is not particularly helpful from an academic point of view. However, it is perhaps understandable given that CC is a concept that is mainly used and understood by practitioners, and hence academics, consultants, and others seeking to influence corporations might expect their ideas to be better understood and received in the corporate world by framing them in recognized practitioner terminology. Nonetheless, a significantly new conception of the social role and responsibilities of corporations can be discerned within the emerging debate on corporate citizenship, and it is to this that we shall now turn.

An extended view of CC

Whilst there has been only very limited discussion of an extended view of CC, it has been alluded to in a number of recent articles (e.g. van Luijk 2001; Wood and Logsdon 2001; Windsor 2001) and has been more fully set out in Matten et al. (2003).

The extended view takes as its starting point the notion of 'citizenship'. The current understanding of citizenship that is dominant in most industrialized societies is based on the liberal tradition, where citizenship is defined as a set of individual rights (Faulks 2000: 55–82). Following the still widely accepted categorization by T. H. Marshall (1965), liberal citizenship comprises three different aspects of entitlement:

- **Social rights**—these provide the individual with the *freedom to* participate in society, such as the right to education, healthcare, or various aspects of welfare. These are sometimes called 'positive' rights since they are entitlements towards third parties.

- **Civil rights**—these provide *freedom from* abuses and interference by third parties (most notably the government); among the most important ones are the rights to own property, to engage in 'free' markets, or freedom of speech. These are sometimes called 'negative' rights since they protect the individual against the interference of stronger powers

- **Political rights**—these include the right to vote or the right to hold office and, generally speaking, enable the individual to take part in the process of collective will formation beyond the sphere of his or her own privacy.

The key actor for these rights is the government, which upholds these rights for individual citizens. Thus, at first glance, it is somewhat hard to make any sense of something like 'corporate citizenship' at all, since social and political rights in particular cannot be regarded as an entitlement for a corporation. Wood and Logsdon (2001), however, suggest that corporations enter the picture not because they have an entitlement to certain rights as a 'real' citizen would, but as powerful public actors which have a responsibility to respect those 'real' citizens' rights. Similarly, as we have discussed above in relation to corporate accountability, the failure of governments to fulfil some of their traditional functions, coupled with the rise in corporate power, has meant that corporations have increasingly taken on a political role in society. Hence, corporations enter the arena of citizenship at the point where traditional governmental actors start to fail to be the only 'counterpart' of citizenship. Quite simply, they can be said to partly take over those functions with regard to the protection, facilitation, and enabling of citizens' rights—formerly an expectation placed solely on the government. Let us consider some examples:

- **Social rights.** Ethics in Action 2.2 illustrated how the UK organization Business in the Community pursues initiatives formerly within the province of the welfare state: feeding homeless people, helping headmasters in managing school budgets, or improving deprived neighbourhoods. Similarly, in developing countries where governments simply cannot (and very often do not want to) afford a welfare state, the task of improving working conditions in sweatshops, ensuring employees a living wage, providing schools, medical centres, and roads, or even providing financial support for the schooling of child labourers are all activities in which corporations such as Shell, Nike, Levi Strauss, and others have engaged under the label of CC.

- **Civil rights.** Governmental failure again becomes particularly visible in developing or transforming countries. Drastic examples, such as the role of Shell in Nigeria and its apparent role in the restriction of the civil rights of the Ogoni people (see Boele et al. 2000), show that corporations might play a crucial role in either discouraging (as Shell) or encouraging governments to live up to their responsibility in this arena of citizenship. A positive example for the latter might be General Motors and other corporations in South Africa during the apartheid period, who, after being pressurized by their own stakeholders, eventually exerted some pressure of their own on the South African government to desist from violating the civil rights of black South Africans.

- **Political rights.** Voter apathy in national elections has been widely identified in many industrialized countries, yet there appears to be a growing willingness on the part of individuals to participate in political action *aimed at corporations rather than at governments* (Hertz 2001a). Whether through single-issue campaigns, anti-corporate protests, consumer boycotts, or other forms of sub-political action, individual citizens have increasingly sought to effect political change by leveraging the power, and to some extent vulnerability, of corporations. Returning to the McEurope example in Case 1 (32–5), when the French peasant farm union leader Jose Bové, or the London Greenpeace activists Helen Steel and Dave Morris (the McLibel Two), sought to draw attention to various political issues such as import tariffs, cultural homogenization, environmental protection, and union rights, they achieved international coverage for their efforts not by tackling the French or the UK governments, but by attacking the McDonald's corporation.

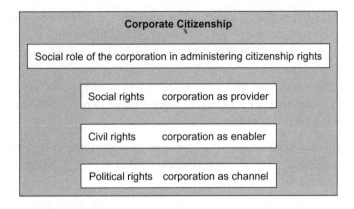

Figure 2.5. An extended view of corporate citizenship

Hence, given this emerging role for corporations in the administration of social, civil, and political rights, the extended view of CC suggests the following definition:

> Corporate citizenship describes the corporate function for administering citizenship rights for individuals.

These rights are administered by the corporation in different ways. With regard to social rights, the corporation basically either supplies or does not supply individuals with social services and hence largely takes on a *providing role*. In the case of civil rights, corporations either capacitate or constrain citizens' civil rights, and thus can be viewed as assuming more of an *enabling role*. Finally, in the realm of political rights, the corporation is essentially an additional conduit for the exercise of individuals' political rights—hence the corporation primarily assumes a *channelling role*. This extended conceptualization of corporate citizenship is shown in **Figure 2.5**.

It is evident that corporate citizenship may be the result either of a voluntary, self-interest driven corporate initiative, or of a compulsory, public pressure driven corporate reaction. Most firms actually claim not to want to take on such a political role in society, yet it seems that increasingly they do, either because of pressure from activists, or sometimes simply out of necessity. If an oil company needs to make sure its staff working out in a poor African community are healthy, it may need to build its own health centre because the local authorities may simply not have the resources to do so. The point is that we do not need to know the motivation to label something an act of 'extended' CC. This is because this view of CC is essentially a *descriptive* conceptualization of what does happen, rather than a *normative* conceptualization of what should happen.

Assessing corporate citizenship as a framework for business ethics

Having set out these three views of CC, we need to consider whether the concept of corporate citizenship really represents a useful new way of framing business ethics—or at least whether it offers us anything different or better compared with CSR, stakeholder theory, and the other concepts we have discussed in this chapter.

Our view is that CC as it is *typically* used by academics and managers—which is either in the 'limited' or the 'equivalent' sense—doesn't really add anything to our understanding of business ethics. Essentially it is just a new buzzword to describe existing ideas about business–society relations.

However, in the 'extended' view that we have described here, CC does seem to add something significant that helps us frame business ethics in new ways. There are a number of respects in which it does this:

• The extended view of CC helps us to see better the *political role* of the corporation and clarifies the demand for *corporate accountability* that is such a prominent feature of contemporary business ethics thinking;

• By providing us with a way of understanding business in relation to common rights of citizenship across cultures, CC in this sense also helps us to better understand some of the challenges presented by the new context of *globalization*;

• These rights of citizenship, which include rights to equality, participation, and a safe and clean environment, also have strong links to the new goal for business ethics of *sustainability*;

• Finally, although the notion of CSR has been widely adopted in Europe, the extended view of CC provides us with a more critical perspective on the social role of business that is more in keeping with the *European tradition* of business ethics.

Of course, the downside to the extended view of CC is that it is both new, and not widely accepted yet within the mainstream discourse of business ethics. Hence, in the remainder of the book, although we shall mainly refer to CC in this extended sense, we shall also where relevant refer to the other meanings that we have outlined here.

Summary

In this chapter, we have discussed business ethics in relation to the social role of the corporation. We outlined the nature of corporations and argued that confining corporations to their initial purpose of producing goods and services in a way that yields a maximal profit for the shareholders of the corporation is too limited. We subsequently discussed and analysed the different views and elements of CSR, stakeholder theory, and corporate accountability, and assessed their relevance in a European context. This was complemented with insights into recent changes in the political framework of European societies and how globalization results in assigning a political role to corporations. Finally, we highlighted the current debate in business ethics and discussed corporate citizenship as the latest paradigm in the field.

Our argument is that the shifts and changes in the global economy in recent years have surfaced the necessity for a new framing of business ethics. However, CC as used by practitioners and academics alike is at present still a rather messy concept. Our extended perspective on CC—which ultimately sees the corporation as a political actor administering the citizenship rights of individual stakeholders—helps to bring some much-needed definitional clarity to the CC debate. Perhaps more importantly though, it helps us to conceptualize the emerging role of corporations in the global economy, as well as to clarify the ethical expectations increasingly placed upon them.

STUDY QUESTIONS

1 What are the main implications of the *legal status* of corporations for notions of corporate social responsibility?

2 'Only human beings have a moral responsibility for their actions.' Critically assess this proposition in the context of attempts to ascribe a moral responsibility to corporations.

3 What is enlightened self-interest? Compare and evaluate arguments for corporate social responsibility based on enlightened self-interest with more explicitly moral arguments.

4 According to Archie Carroll, what are the four levels of corporate social responsibility? How relevant is this model in a European context?

5 Explain the difference between normative, descriptive, and instrumental versions of stakeholder theory. To what extent do stakeholders have intrinsic moral rights in relation to the management of the corporation?

6 Define the extended view of corporate citizenship. Give examples to illustrate the concept.

RESEARCH EXERCISE

Select one of the following companies:

(a) GlaxoSmithKline (**www.gsk.com**)

(b) Nokia (**www.nokia.com**)

(c) Volkswagen (**www.vw.com**)

Investigate the company's website and set out the main aspects of their corporate responsibility or corporate citizenship programmes. Which aspects of their programmes might be said to be formerly governmental responsibilities? What are the benefits and drawbacks of the corporation taking over these responsibilities?

CASE 2

The 'English Patient': BMW withdraws from Rover Longbridge

This case discusses the decision by the German automotive company BMW to pull out of a failing UK manufacturing plant in 2000 in the face of low productivity and spiralling losses. The potential closure of the Rover plant, located in the former heartland of British car manufacturing in the West Midlands, raised the prospects of massive job losses in an area suffering a major economic downturn. The case provides the opportunity to examine the nature of social responsibility, and to explore the relative responsibilities of governments and corporations for providing employment.

The name Longbridge stands for nearly a hundred years of British car manufacturing. The huge manufacturing site near Birmingham in the West Midlands area has been the stage for many of the peaks and troughs of automotive history in the UK. Once the birthplace of the sporty Austin Healy, the legendary Mini, and the practical Metro, the site has also been associated in the 1970s with industrial unrest and union militancy. More recently, the plant had started to become a virtual synonym for industrial downturn and decay, and the reversal in fortune of the British car industry.

It was a history with ups and downs, but the plant seemed to be in for a bright future when in 1994 BMW took Longbridge over from the British car manufacturer Rover. Despite suffering from under-investment, BMW saw the Rover takeover as a suitable means of expanding its range of models beyond the luxury segment that it had become famous for, into more medium-sized, family saloons that appealed to the mass market, particularly in the UK.

During the first five years of its involvement in Britain, BMW invested more than £2.5bn (€3.8bn) in Rover. The results though were somewhat uninspiring. While the development of new models went quite well, and led to the 1999 launch of the Rover 75, productivity in the ageing facilities at the Longbridge plant never really reached competitive levels: starting at an incredible 50 per cent of BMW's other plants, even after four years of massive investment, productivity was still languishing 30 per cent below German rates. In fact, in 1998, Longbridge workers produced roughly the same amount of cars as those at Škoda in the Czech Republic, but only a third of what Nissan put out at their UK plant at Sunderland.

BMW's problems were not only with Longbridge's productivity, though. The strength of the pound was another factor that made sales abroad difficult and inflated costs for supplies. And despite massive job cuts, and the introduction of more flexible work patterns, by 1999/2000 BMW was running up annual losses of £880m (€1,320m) on the Rover investment, more than £2m a day! Such losses had major impacts on BMW, as one of the smaller players in the international automotive industry. Under constant threat of hostile takeover bids itself, the company's management got clear signals from its shareholders and from the financial industry that it had to either cure 'the English patient' (as Rover was now known back at head office in Munich), or get rid of it.

With the prospect of BMW pulling out, though, serious trouble was looming. The potential closure of Longbridge would not only threaten more than 10,000 jobs at the plant, but would also have severe implications for up to 50,000 local jobs that depended on Rover's business. The West Midlands region where Longbridge was located had already been hit hard by the decline in British manufacturing, and the closure of the Rover plant would effectively mean that a large area of British industrial heartland would be devastated. It was therefore no wonder that the UK government was extremely keen on ensuring that BMW maintained its commitment to the plant and to the area, not least because twenty-three of twenty-seven parliamentary seats within a fifteen-mile radius of Longbridge were held by the (ruling) Labour Party.

By March 2000, BMW signalled that it was about to act. Amid uproar from unions, local communities, and the press, the Secretary of State for Trade and Industry, Steven Byers, engaged in frantic shuttle diplomacy between London, Longbridge, and Munich to try and stave off BMW's imminent withdrawal. However, despite offers of £150m (€230m) in government subsidies, BMW eventually announced it was going to 'pull the plug' on Rover, to the despair of workers and the embarrassment of the powerless government.

In what was claimed to be the largest industrial march for a decade, the reaction to BMW's announcement saw workers marching through Birmingham city protesting against the 'outrageous' behaviour of the BMW management. BMW dealerships were vandalized, and in the tabloid press, the German manufacturer was depicted as a symbol of cold, inhumane, global capitalism. Similarly, the UK government experienced a major rebuff in the manner of BMWs withdrawal, coming as it did after extended negotiations with the company, and a matter of days after the government had offered substantial financial aid. Moreover, with Jaguar and Peugeot as the other owners of larger car manufacturing plants in the West Midlands, much of the protest also reflected workers' fears of being completely dependent on decisions taken thousands of miles away in Detroit, Paris, or, in this case Munich.

The next crucial issue, however, was who the potential buyer of the discarded Rover businesses would be. There were several offers for the Longbridge business, from local millionaires who wanted to retain jobs in the region, to consortia of finance companies who were interested in buying the brand names and assets of Rover and then downsizing the operations by only producing niche-market sports cars. While the financially most lucrative deal for BMW was offered by one of these finance groups, the most plausible option that would actually lead to the survival of the majority of Longbridge jobs was that of the 'Phoenix' consortium headed by former Rover CEO John Towers.

Alerted to the public relations backlash, potential legal proceedings from car worker unions, and the need to maintain smooth relations for its remaining UK businesses, BMW looked for a quick deal and finally agreed to sell Longbridge to Towers's Phoenix group for a nominal £10 (€15)! BMW also took over all debts of Rover and provided the new consortium with an interest-free loan of £500m (€750m).

The upshot of BMW's disposals was that it kept the Mini brand (formerly belonging to Rover) for itself, and transferred production of this and several other models to another (retained) Rover plant. It also sold Land-Rover (another of Rover's businesses) to Ford for considerably more than the £10 it got for Longbridge!

As of writing, the Phoenix consortium has managed to keep Longbridge afloat with minimal job losses, though its future and the future of its employees still remains unsettled. Not too much though seems to have changed in BMW's fractious relationships with its remaining UK workers. In February 2003, in one of its Mini supply parts plants in Birmingham, workers allegedly threatened the company with sabotage following leaked reports that BMW was considering the future closure of the plant. In the same week, *Forbes Magazine* ranked BMW as the 'most admired' European company in the USA.

Questions

1 Set out the main stakeholders in this situation. How would you determine the relative importance of their stake in:
   (a) BMW
   (b) The Longbridge plant?

2 How would each of these stakeholders benefit/suffer from the different options open to BMW in this case?

3 What are the central dilemmas a company such as BMW finds itself in with respect to situations such as these?

4 Think about BMW's problem in terms of Carroll's pyramid of CSR—which responsibilities was it upholding, and how would you say it was ranking them? Do you think this is appropriate or inappropriate in this situation?

5 How would you define BMW's role in the context of the 'extended' view on corporate citizenship? What insights does this provide you with in analysing the case?

Sources

Anon. (2003). 'Europas meistgeschätztes Unternehmen ist deutsch'. *Spiegel Online*, 24. Feb., **www.spiegel.de**.

Morley, C. (2003). 'BMW plant plan fury'. *Birmingham Evening Mail*, 25 Feb.: 9.

Steele, J. (2000). 'Longbridge—the inside story'. *Guardian*, 1 Apr.: 4.

Stevens, R. (1998). 'BMW/Rover to axe thousands of auto jobs at Longbridge, England'. *World Socialist Web Site*, 27 Oct., **www.wsws.org**.

Wintour, P., and Ward, L. (2000). 'Byers hits back at BMW'. *Guardian*, 31 Mar.

3

Evaluating Business Ethics
Normative Ethical Theories

In this chapter we will:

• Locate the role of normative ethical theory for ethical decision-making in business;

• Highlight the European perspective on normative ethical theory;

• Provide a critical overview of traditional ethical theories, such as utilitarianism, ethics of duty, and rights and justice;

• Explore the potential of contemporary views on ethical theories for business, such as virtue ethics, feminist ethics, discourse ethics, and postmodernism;

• Suggest that the most appropriate usage of normative ethical theory is in a pragmatic and pluralistic fashion that contributes to, rather than dictates, ethical decision-making.

Introduction

In our everyday lives, we constantly come up against situations where values are in conflict and where we have to make a choice about what is right or wrong. Whether it is a question of whether to lie about something in order to protect a friend's feelings, driving over the speed limit when rushing to avoid being late for a date, or thinking about whether to report on a classmate you have seen cheating on their assignment, we all have some prior knowledge of what is right or wrong that helps us to decide what to do. Most of the situations like this that we are faced with in our personal lives are pretty much within the scope of what a typical person would be able to decide. In a business context, however, situations might become considerably more complex.

We could think, for example, of the situation of a multinational company intending to establish a subsidiary in a developing country: not only do we have to cope with a number of ethical problems at the same time—maybe paying bribes for planning permission, deciding on the wage level for the workers, or establishing a minimum age for workers, etc.—but we also face the problem that a variety of people will be involved, all of whom might have different views and attitudes towards these moral issues. Consequently, coming to an ethical conclusion in business situations is far more complex than in most of the situations where we as private individuals have to make ethical decisions.

Perhaps more importantly, in a business context there is often a need for these decisions to be based on a systematic, rational, and widely understandable argument so that they can be adequately defended, justified, and explained to relevant stakeholders. Similarly, if we believe that what an organization has done is wrong, we need some concrete basis from which to argue our case. After all, at what point can we say that a particular behaviour is more than just *different* from what we would have done, but in some way actually *wrong*? This is the point where normative ethical theories come into play. By normative, we mean ethical theories that propose to prescribe the morally correct way of acting. Such ethical theories, as we set out in Chapter 1, can be defined as follows:

> Ethical theories are the rules and principles that determine right and wrong for any given situation.

In this chapter we will take a look at the major ethical theories and analyse their value and potential for business ethics. To begin with, though, we first need to be clear about how exactly we shall be using ethical theory in the context of this chapter, and in the rest of the book that follows.

The role of ethical theory

In locating a place for ethical theory, Richard De George (1999: 33–54) suggests that two extreme positions can be imagined:

• **Ethical absolutism.** On the one side of the spectrum would be a position of ethical absolutism, which claims that there are eternal, universally applicable moral principles. According to this view, right and wrong are *objective* qualities that can be rationally determined.

• **Ethical relativism.** The other extreme would be a position of relativism, which claims that morality is context dependent and *subjective*. Relativists tend to believe that there are no universal right and wrongs that can be rationally determined—it simply depends on the person making the decision and the culture in which they are located. In its best-known form, the notion of relativism occurs in international business issues, where it is argued that since morality is culturally determined, a moral judgement about behaviour in another culture cannot be made from outside. Ethical relativism is different from **descriptive relativism**: whilst the latter merely suggests that different cultures *have* different ethics, the former proposes that both sets of beliefs can be equally *right*. Ethical relativism then is still a normative theory (De George 1999: 41).

Most *traditional* ethical theories tend to be absolutist in nature. They seek to set out universal rules or principles that can be applied to any situation to provide the answer as to what is right or wrong. More *contemporary* ethical theories often tend towards a more relativistic position. However, in the course of this chapter, we want to show that for the practical purposes of making effective decisions in business, both of these positions are not particularly useful.

Our position therefore is one of **pluralism**. This occupies something of a middle ground between absolutism and relativism. Pluralism accepts different moral convictions and backgrounds while at the same time suggesting that a consensus on basic principles and rules in a certain social context can, and should, be reached. Ethical theories, as we shall show, can help to clarify different moral presuppositions of the various parties involved in a decision—e.g. one person may tend to think in terms of one theory, whilst another might think in terms of a different theory. In making good business decisions, we need to understand this range of perspectives in order to establish a consensus on the solution to ethical problems (Kaler 1999*b*). Rather than establishing a single universal theory, in this chapter we will present the different theoretical frameworks as complementary resources or conceptual tools that help us make a practical, structured, and systematic assessment of the right and wrong in particular business decisions. Theory can help to clarify these situations, and each theory highlights different aspects that need to be considered.

This view rests on two basic things that Kaler (1999*b*) suggests we already know about morality before we even try to introduce ethical theory into it. First, morality is foremost a **social phenomenon**. We need morality because we constantly have to establish the rules and arrangements of our living together as social beings. It seems reasonable to accept the argument of *descriptive relativism*: that a diversity of moral convictions, be they religiously, philosophically, or otherwise ideologically grounded, is a given. Hence, even if there were one and only 'objectively' right moral conviction, it is simply a matter of fact that this is not widely agreed upon. It only needs a quick visit to the pub or café to listen in to the conversations around us to discover that people from the same street or place of work differ considerably in their moral views and convictions. From a business angle this gets even more important due to globalization, since this multiplies the relevant 'supply' of moralities by the sheer number of different cultural contexts playing a role in business decisions. As morality seeks to solve questions of right and wrong in organizing social life, we cannot realistically rely on an absolutist position, since empirically we see a variety of moral convictions. If we are to make good decisions that are acceptable to others, we obviously need to develop some knowledge of the different moralities that we are likely to be faced with.

The second of Kaler's (1999*b*) assumptions is that morality is all about **harm and benefit**. Right and wrong are largely about avoiding harm and providing benefits. After all, if we didn't dislike harm, or value benefits, there would simply be no need for morality. As we will see further on, 'benefit' and 'harm' are matters that are conceptualized differently by various ethical theories. Nevertheless, we argue that there is a certain consensus about the fact that morality should ultimately help a society to avoid harm and provide benefits for its members. Given this focus, it is possible to partly refute the position of the relativists and claim that morality is more than a subjective feeling or opinion since it is about actual harms and benefits that we need to address. Ultimately, the logic of relativism is that everything is just different and nothing is wrong (Donaldson 1996). This 'anything goes' approach to morality is not very helpful when we see genuine harm being inflicted on people.

However, as the relativists suggest, this second assumption also necessarily places ethical theories in a pragmatic context: even the most subtle theory is used by individuals in a concrete business situation where most people have a basic 'gut' feeling about the right and wrong of the situation based on the perceived harms and benefits (Treviño and Nelson 1999). Therefore, narrowly and rigidly applying one theory and treating the theory as the only authority in questions of right and wrong would give ethical theory a status that it will never actually have in practical business decisions. The immense value though of ethical theories lies in the fact that they help to rationalize—and by this understand—this gut feeling. Furthermore, they make it possible to engage in a rational discourse between individuals whose moral values are different from each other.

Normative ethical theories: a European perspective

In Chapter 1 (26–31) we argued that business ethics in America is quite different from European thinking in the area. This is particularly the case in the use of ethical theories. Most of the literature available in English is more or less dominated by an Anglo-American view, whereas many of the continental European approaches are less widely received since most of the literature is published in languages other than English. And although we find several continental European approaches also in American and British textbooks, the general use and the necessity for theory in business ethics is fairly different on both sides of the Atlantic. We believe it is helpful to highlight the following differences which are significant in the context of this chapter (see Palazzo 2000).

• **Individual versus institutional morality.** As we saw in Chapter 1, the US approach to studying business ethics tends to have a more individualistic perspective on morality than in Europe (where the focus is more on the economic system and the wider governing institutions). Therefore, normative ethical theories in America tend to be more applicable to *individual behaviour* whereas in Europe the *design of institutions* in the economic system seems to be the main influence in developing and applying theory.

• **Consequences versus duties.** Anglo-American business ethics seems to focus more on the consequences of actions and conceptualize moral status in terms of the *pleasure* or the *pain* of any of these outcomes. This is pretty much in line with the success orientation of the Protestant ethic that has dominated the American business climate (Jackall 1988). In Europe the focus often lies more on the *duties* of the economic actors, since they are generally conceptualized more as parts of a larger entity. This approach sees the individual as deeply embedded in a wider social and economic environment to which she or he is to contribute and which consequently makes certain normative demands on his or her actions.

• **Questioning versus accepting capitalism.** Most of the mainstream business ethics literature in America does not particularly question the existing framework of management but rather sees ethical problems occurring *within the capitalist system*, which it treats as a given. In Europe, relevant parts of business ethics focus on *questioning the ethical justification of capitalism*. Hence, considerable effort in business ethics theory has been dedicated to defending or refining the ethical legitimacy of capitalist economic thought. Although one has to say that not all of this work has been immediately helpful in solving day-to-day issues in business life, it nevertheless helps to develop a more critical and distanced approach to the institutions which govern and determine business decisions, and by this provide substantial help in understanding and theorizing a number of ethical dilemmas in business life, including corporate governance, employee rights, and stakeholder involvement.

• **Justifying versus applying moral norms.** Although some of the religious roots in both continents are still remarkably influential on the institutional fabric of economic life, substantial processes of secularization—that is, movement towards a *non-religious* form of organizing—have taken place. In Europe, most notably in the northern parts, this secularization process has opened the door to a variety of other ideological and philosophical approaches. In general, Sweden, Germany, and the Netherlands for example are characterized by a strong pluralism of moral convictions and values. Therefore, the challenge for business ethics on the theoretical level consists to a strong degree in the *justification and ethical legitimization of norms* for addressing ethical dilemmas in business situations. In America, however, judging by most American business ethics textbooks, these issues do not seem to take such a dominant position: apart from a section on normative theories in business, most textbooks seem to treat the question of moral values as a given and focus chiefly on the *application of morality* to business situations. American society—at least as far as the dominant white majority is concerned—seems to rest on a quite rigid set of mostly Christian-based values which are accepted as a given code of moral values and are therefore not put under further scrutiny. This seems to have been further reinforced by the recent rise of the evangelical far right and Christian conservative movements.

Notwithstanding these important differences, it is important to recognize that no single normative theory can be 'claimed' or attributed to any individual country or region. As we shall now see, most of the traditional theories routinely embraced by American authors are in fact originally European in origin.

Traditional ethical theories

Traditional ethical theories generally offer a certain rule or principle which one can apply to any given situation—hence they are *absolutist* in intention. These theories are normative because they start with an assumption about the nature of the world, and more specific assumptions about the nature of human beings. Consequently, the degree to which we can accept the theory and the outcome of its application to particular business situations depends chiefly on the degree to which we share their underlying assumptions. As they have a considerably well-defined rule of decision, the main advantage of these theories is the fact that they normally provide us with a fairly *unequivocal solution* to ethical problems.

These theories generally can be differentiated into two groups (see **Figure 3.1**). On the right side of Figure 3.1 we have theories that base moral judgements on the outcomes of

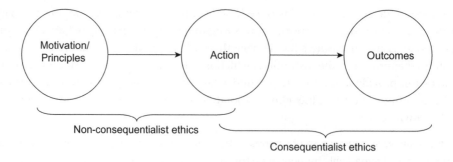

Figure 3.1. Consequentialist and non-consequentialist theories in business ethics

a certain action. If these outcomes are desirable then the action in question is morally right; if the outcomes of the action are not desirable, the action is morally wrong. The moral judgement in these **consequentialist theories** is thus based on the intended outcomes, the aims, or the goals of a certain action. Therefore, consequentialist ethics is often also referred to by the term '*teleological*', based on the Greek word for 'goal'.

On the other hand, we have those theories that base the moral judgement on the underlying principles of the decision-maker's motivation. An action is right or wrong, these theories suggest, not because we like the consequences it produces but because the underlying principles are morally right. These **non-consequentialist** approaches are quite closely linked to Judaeo-Christian thinking and start from reasoning about the individual's rights and duties. These philosophic theories, also called '*deontological*' (based on the Greek word for 'duty'), look at the desirability of principles, and, based on these principles, deduce a 'duty' to act accordingly in a given situation, regardless of the desirability of the consequences.

In the following we will have a closer look at both families of philosophic theories and analyse their potential for solving various business decisions. **Figure 3.2** gives a short

	Egoism	**Utilitarianism**	**Ethics of duties**	**Rights and justice**
Contributors	Adam Smith	Jeremy Bentham John Stuart Mill	Immanuel Kant	John Locke John Rawls
Focus	Individual desires or interests	Collective welfare	Duties	Rights
Rules	Maximization of desires/self-interest	Act/rule utilitarianism	Categorical imperative	Respect for human beings
Concept of human beings	Man is an actor with limited knowledge and objectives	Man is controlled by avoidance of pain and gain of pleasure ('hedonist')	Man is a rational moral actor	Man is a being that is distinguished by dignity
Type	Consequentialist	Consequentialist	Non-consequentialist	Non-consequentialist

Figure 3.2. Major normative theories in business ethics

overview of the relevant philosophical schools and the basic elements of their thinking. In explaining these theories we shall use them to reflect on a particular business problem, as presented in **Ethical Dilemma 3**. We suggest you read this before continuing with the chapter.

Consequentialist theories

Here we shall look at two main consequentialist theories:

- Egoism
- Utilitarianism

Whilst both of these theories address right and wrong according to the outcomes of a decision, we shall see that they address those outcomes in different ways—egoism by focusing on the outcomes for the *decision-maker*, utilitarianism by focusing on the wider *social outcomes within a community*.

Egoism

Egoism is one of the oldest philosophical ideas, and it was already well known and discussed by ancient Greek philosophers such as Plato. In the last three centuries it has been quite influential in modern economics, particularly in its espousal by Adam Smith (1723–90) in his design of liberalist economics. Egoism can be defined as follows:

> Following the theory of egoism an action is morally right if the decision-maker freely decides in order to pursue either their (short-term) desires or their (long-term) interests.

The justification for egoism lies in the underlying concept of man: as man has only limited insight into the consequences of his actions, the only suitable strategy to achieve a good life is to pursue his own desires or interests. Adam Smith (1793) argued that in the economic system, this pursuit of individual self-interest was acceptable because it produced a morally desirable outcome for society through the 'invisible hand' of the marketplace. Smith's argument may thus be summarized as saying that one is likely to find a moral outcome as the end-product of a system based on free competition and good information. For example, if a producer makes and sells shoddy or faulty products, then consumers may suffer in the short term as the result of the lack of fitness of the products that they have bought. However in the longer run, providing consumers know about alternative choices, the producer's trade will suffer as consumers turn to other producers. Hence, the producer will avoid producing shoddy goods for their own self-interest, thus producing a situation that is beneficial to all. Because of his aim to produce wider social benefits, some have likened Smith's theory to 'egoist practices for utilitarian results' (Beauchamp and Bowie 1997: 18). However, whatever the desired outcomes Smith might have had, the decision rule that is to be applied by individual decision-makers is certainly primarily an egoist one.

It is important to distinguish egoism based on desire from **selfishness**. Whereas the egoist can be moved by pity for others in seeking to remove his own distress caused by their plight, the selfish person is insensitive to the other. So, for example, a good deal of what we discussed as voluntary elements in the concept of corporate social responsibility

Ethical Dilemma 3

Producing toys—child's play?

You are the product manager of a chocolate company that includes small plastic toys together with their chocolates. Having met a potential Thai manufacturer of these toys at a trade fair in Europe you now visit the company in the north-eastern part of Thailand to finalize a two-year supply contract. Arriving there and talking to the sales manager you are able to arrange a deal which supplies you with the toys at a third of the cost currently charged by your Portuguese supplier, but with equivalent quality and supply arrangements.

In order to check the reliability of the manufacturing process you ask the manager to show you around the place. You are surprised to find out that there is no real workshop on the premises. Rather, the production process is organized in such a way that at 6 a.m. in the morning, about thirty men line up at the company's gate, load large boxes with the single parts of the toys on their little carts or motor-scooters and take the material to their homes.

Your future supplier then takes you to one of these places where you see a large family sitting in a garage-like barn assembling the toys. Not only are the mother and father doing the job, but also the couple's six children, aged 5 to 14, are working busily—and from what you see, very cheerfully —together with the parents, while the grandmother is looking after the food in an adjacent room. In the evening, at around 8 p.m., the day's work is done, the assembled toys are stored back in the boxes and taken to the workshop of the company, where the men receive the money for the delivered goods. At the end of the week the toys are shipped to the customers in Europe. As you have never come across such a pattern of manufacturing, your Thai partner explains to you that this is a very common and well-established practice in this part of the country, and one which guarantees a good level of quality. Satisfied, you tell the Thai manager that you will conclude the paperwork once you get back home, and you leave the company offices happy in the knowledge of the cost savings you're going to make, and quietly confident that it will result in a healthy bonus for you at the end of the year.

On your way back, while buying some souvenirs for your 5- and 7-year-old nieces at the airport, you suddenly start wondering if you would like to see them growing up in the same way as the 'workers' whom you have just employed with this great deal.

Read Chapter 3 carefully and make sure you understand how each theory applies to this dilemma.

Questions

1 Looking at all of the insights gained from using each theory, set out a list of the main ethical issues and considerations at stake in this case.
2 Prioritize this list of issues and considerations according to their importance from your perspective. According to what criteria would you say you have prioritized these issues?
3 Which theory or theories do you feel offers the best perspective(s) on this case? Why?
4 Having thought through the dilemma carefully, what would you now do?

or corporate citizenship in Chapter 2 can be perfectly in line with an egoistic philosophy as long as the company, or the rich philanthropist, chooses to donate to a worthy cause (because it makes them feel better or because it is for the ultimate benefit of the company) rather than voting themselves a pay rise.

Within moral philosophy, an important criticism of egoism based on desire is that it renders patently different approaches to life as being equivalent; thus in this view, the life of the student who just gets drunk every night in the Students' Union is as admirable as that of the student who works hard for a first-class degree, if both followed their desire. Therefore, within this school of philosophy, an egoism based on the pursuit of interests is the ultimate rendering of this concept (Graham 1990). The idea of interests based on the pursuit of one's long-term well-being enables one to distinguish between the life of the hard-drinking student and that of the hard-working student. In this formulation, a gap opens up between desire (or longing) and what is in one's ultimate interests, such that one can say that it is not in the interest of the drinking student to give in to immediate desires. An egoism based on interests therefore approaches the idea of objective value—i.e., that one way of acting is objectively better or 'more ethical' than another.

This leads to the notion of '**enlightened egoism**', which is quite frequently discussed in the context of business ethics. We have come across it already in Chapter 2 when discussing 'enlightened self-interest'. For example, corporations might invest in the social environment, such as supporting schools or sponsoring a new ambulance for the local health service, because an improved level of social services is in the interest of workforce retention and satisfaction.

If we apply this theory to Ethical Dilemma 3 we would have to look at the actors involved and analyse if they freely pursue their own desires or interests in engaging in the deal. This certainly applies to the manager and his Thai partner, and by the looks of the case, it could also apply to the parents of the family business. As for the children, it could be that they are quite happy to help the parents and just take it for granted that things work like this in their world. From this perspective, an egoistic look at the situation might consider the deal as morally right. One might however wonder if it is in the children's long-term interest to engage in this type of work: although one could argue that it prevents them from being forced into far less desirable forms of work, moral concerns arise when considering that this type of work prevents them from going to school and exposes them to fairly hard working hours, all of which casts some doubts on whether they really are able to freely pursue their own interests. The latter considerations then would rather suggest that, from an egoistic point of view, this action could be immoral.

It doesn't take much thought to discover certain weaknesses in egoist ethics. To begin with, this theory works fine if there is a mechanism in society that makes sure that no individual egoist pursues his or her own interests at other egoists' expense. In Adam Smith's thinking this mechanism would be the market. Although in a great number of cases we can see that the market works perfectly well, there are numerous situations where this does not seem to be the case, and where the egoism of single actors leads to unfavourable results. The current anti-globalization movement is largely fuelled by the fact that, on a global level, markets are not functioning perfectly and we thus witness a blatantly unequal distribution of wealth across the globe. Another example would be the sustainability debate: the victims of today's resource depletion are the future generation which are not yet present to take part in any kind of market. This clearly shows some initial limitations of egoist theory.

Utilitarianism

The philosophy of utilitarianism has been one of the most commonly accepted ethical theories in the Anglo-Saxon world. It is linked to the names of the British philosophers and economists Jeremy Bentham (1748–1832) and John Stuart Mill (1806–73) and has been influential in modern economics in general. The basic principle of utilitarianism could be defined as follows:

> According to utilitarianism, an action is morally right if it results in the greatest amount of good for the greatest amount of people affected by the action.

This principle, also called the '**greatest happiness principle**', is the ultimate consequentialist principle since it focuses solely on the consequences of an action, weighs the good results against the bad results, and finally encourages the action which results in the greatest amount of good for all people involved. Unlike egoism, it does not only look at each individual involved and ask whether their *individual* desires and interests are met, but it focuses on the *collective* welfare that is produced by a certain decision.

The underlying idea is the notion of utility, which Bentham sees as the ultimate goal in life. Man is seen as a hedonist, whose purpose in life is to maximize pleasure and minimize pain. In this hedonistic rendition of utilitarianism, utility is measured in terms of *pleasure and pain* (the 'hedonistic' view). Other interpretations of utility look at *happiness and unhappiness* (the 'eudemonistic' view) while others take a strongly extended view that includes in the equation not only pleasure or happiness but ultimately all *intrinsically valuable human goods* (the 'ideal' view). These goods then would typically include aspects such as friendship, love, trust, etc. The latter view in particular makes utilitarianism open to a great number of practical decision situations and prevents it from being rather narrowly focused on pleasure and pain only.

Utilitarianism has been very powerful since it puts at the centre of the moral decision a variable which is very commonly used in economics as a parameter which measures the (economic) value of actions: 'utility'. Since one can quantify this variable, the utilitarian analysis is highly compatible with the quantitative, mathematical methodology of economics. So, in analysing two possible actions in a single business decision, we just assign a certain utility to each consequence and each person involved, and the action with the highest aggregate utility is morally correct. Ultimately utilitarianism then comes close to what we know as **cost–benefit analysis**.

Typical situations where utilitarian analysis can be very helpful are situations such as animal testing for medical research: although this inflicts considerable pain on animals, utilitarianists argue that it is still morally right, as the pain of these animals has to be weighed against the fact that it prevents far greater pain on behalf of all those humans that profit from the tested drugs. Ultimately, utilitarian thinking has been used in very extreme situations: so, for example, the group of German generals who conspired to assassinate Hitler in 1944 justified their attempt on utilitarian grounds in that the murder (pain) of one person opened the way to reducing the pain of millions of other people.

	Action 1: doing the deal		Action 2: not doing the deal	
	Pleasure	Pain	Pleasure	Pain
Product manager	Success; bonus	Bad conscience	Good conscience	Loss of a good deal
Thai dealer	Good deal			Loss of a good deal Search for a new customer in Europe
Parents	Secure the family's income	Limited prospects for children		Search for other sources of income
Children	Feeling of being needed, being 'grown up'; approval of the parents;	Hard work; no chance of school education	No hard work; time to play and go to school	Potentially forced to do other, more painful work
Grandmother	Family is able to support her			Loss of economic support

Figure 3.3. Example of a utilitarian analysis

If we apply this theory to the situation described in Ethical Dilemma 3 we first of all have a look at all the actors involved and analyse their potential utility in terms of the pleasure and pain involved in different courses of action, say either going ahead with the deal (action one) or not doing the deal (action two). We could set up a simple balance sheet, such as that depicted in **Figure 3.3**.

After analysing all the good and bad effects for the persons involved one can now add up 'pleasure' and 'pain' for action one, and the result would be the *utility* of this action. After having done the same with action two, the moral decision is relatively easy to identify: the greatest utility of the respective actions is the morally right one. In our hypothetical case, the decision would probably go towards action one (doing the deal) as it involves the most pleasure for all parties involved whereas in action two (not doing the deal) the pain seems to dominate the analysis.

This example shows already some of the more complicated issues with utilitarian philosophy. The main **problems with utilitarianism** are:

• **Subjectivity.** Clearly when using this theory you have to think rather creatively, and assessing such consequences as pleasure or pain might depend heavily on the subjective perspective of the person that carries out the analysis;

• **Problems of quantification.** Similarly, it is quite difficult to assign costs and benefits to every situation. This might be quite easy in the example for the persons directly involved with the transaction, but it is certainly difficult to do so for the children involved, since their pleasure and pain is not quantifiable. Especially in these cases it might be quite difficult to weigh pleasure against pain: is losing a good contract really comparable to forcing children into labour? Similarly, under utilitarianism health and safety issues in the firm require 'values' of life and death to be quantified and calculated, without the possibility of acknowledging that they might have an intrinsic worth beyond calculation.

• **Distribution of utility.** Finally, it would appear that by assessing the greatest good for the greatest number, the interests of minorities are overlooked. In our example, a minority of children might suffer so that the majority might benefit from greater utility.

Of course, utilitarians were always aware of the limits of their theory. The problem of subjectivity for example led to a refinement of the theory, differentiating into what has been defined as 'act utilitarianism' versus 'rule utilitarianism':

> Act utilitarianism looks to single actions and bases the moral judgement on the amount of pleasure and the amount of pain this single action causes.

> Rule utilitarianism looks at classes of action and ask whether the underlying principles of an action produce more pleasure than pain for society in the long run.

Our utilitarian analysis of Ethical Dilemma 3 used the principle of **act utilitarianism** by asking whether just in that *single situation* the collective pleasure exceeded the pain inflicted. Given the specific circumstances of the case, this might result in the conclusion that it is morally right, because the children's pain is considerably small, given the fact, for instance, that they might have to work anyway or that school education might not be available to them. From the perspective of **rule utilitarianism**, however, one would have to ask whether child labour *in principle* produces more pleasure than pain. Here, the judgement might look considerably different, since it is not difficult to argue that the pains of child labour easily outweigh the (mainly) economic benefits of it. Rule utilitarianism then relieves us from examining right or wrong in every single situation and offers the possibility of establishing certain principles that we then can apply to all such situations.

Non-consequentialist theories

Here we shall look at the two main types of non-consequentialist ethical theories that have been traditionally applied to business ethics:

• Ethics of duties

• Ethics of rights and justice

These two approaches are very similar, stemming from assumptions about basic universal principles of right and wrong. However, whilst rights-based theories tend to start by assigning a right to one party and *then* advocating a corresponding duty on another party to protect that right, ethics of duties *begin* with the assignation of the duty to act in a certain way.

Ethics of duties

The shift from act towards rule utilitarianism is a good starting point for discussing ethics of duties. Its main contributor, the German philosopher Immanuel Kant (1724–1804), thought that morality and the decision about right and wrong action was not dependent on a particular situation, let alone on the consequences of the action. For Kant, morality was a question of certain eternal, abstract, and unchangeable principles that humans should apply to all ethical problems. In this, his theory is strongly in the tradition of

Judaeo-Christian morality, which starts from certain ('divine' or God-given) moral principles. As a key Enlightenment thinker, though, Kant was convinced that human beings did not need God, the Church, or some other superior authority to identify these principles. He saw humans as *rational* actors who could decide these principles for themselves. Hence, humans could also be regarded as independent *moral actors* who made their own rational decisions regarding right and wrong.

Kant subsequently developed a theoretical framework through which these principles could be derived, called the **'categorical imperative'**. By this he meant that this theoretical framework should be applied to *every* moral issue regardless of who is involved, who profits, and who is harmed by the principles once they have been applied in specific situations.

The categorical imperative consists of three parts (see De George 1999):

Maxim 1:   Act only according to that maxim by which you can at the same time will that it should become a universal law.

Maxim 2:   Act so that you treat humanity, whether in your own person or in that of another, always as an end and never as a means only.

Maxim 3:   Act only so that the will through its maxims could regard itself at the same time as universally lawgiving.

According to Kant, these three maxims can be used as tests for every possible action, and an action is to be regarded as morally right if it 'survives' all three tests. This suggests that morality is characterized by three important elements, each of which is tested by one of these maxims.

Maxim one checks whether the action could be performed by everyone and reflects the aspect of **consistency**: an action can only be right if everyone could follow the same underlying principle. So, for example, murder is an immoral action because if we allowed everybody to murder there would be no possibility of human life on earth; lying is immoral, because if everybody were allowed to lie, the entire notion of 'truth' would be impossible and an organized and stable human civilization would not be imaginable.

Maxim two focuses on Kant's view that humans deserve respect as autonomous, rational actors, and that this **human dignity** should never be ignored. We all use people as means, as soon as we employ them or pay them to provide us with goods or services. However, this does not mean we should *only* treat them as means to achieve what we want and just forget about their own needs and goals in life, and their expectations to make their own choices.

The third maxim scrutinizes the element of **universality**. I might come to the conclusion that a certain principle could be followed consistently by every human being; I could also come to the conclusion that in following that principle, I respect human dignity and do not just 'use' people as a means only. But then Kant wants us to check whether the principles of our actions would be acceptable for every human being. This test therefore tries to overcome specifically the risk of *subjectivity* inherent to the utilitarian analysis, since it asks us to check whether other rational actors would endorse our judgement of a certain situation as well. In other contexts this point has been referred to as the 'New York Times test' (Treviño and Nelson 1999: 89)—namely, if you would be uncomfortable if your actions were reported in the press, you can be fairly sure that they are of doubtful moral status.

If we apply Kant's moral 'test' to Ethical Dilemma 3, we get the following insights:

- According to *maxim one*, the first question would be to ask whether we would want everybody to act according to the principles of our action. Obviously, as the product manager you are already uncomfortable about applying the principle of exploiting child labour from a third world context to your own family back home in Europe. You probably would not like this to become a universal law, which would then suggest that this activity could be deemed immoral on the basis of inconsistency.

- Regarding *maxim two*, it is questionable whether the children have freely and autonomously decided to work. By making use of their labour you could be said to be largely treating them as cheap labour for your own ends rather than as 'ends in themselves', suggesting that their basic human dignity was not being fully recognized and respected.

- Looking at *maxim three*, there is also the question of whether you would like your friends and family to know about your decision. In other words, it would seem rather doubtful that every rational human being would universally come to the same conclusion that child labour is a principle that should be followed on a general basis.

Kant's theory is quite extensive, and for the purpose of this book we do not want to dig any deeper into it beyond these three basic principles. But already these can be quite helpful in practical situations and have had a considerable influence on business ethics thinking. For example, in Chapter 2 we discussed the *stakeholder concept* of the firm. Evan and Freeman (1993) argue that the ethical basis of this concept has been substantially derived from Kantian thinking. Hence, in order to treat employees, local communities, or suppliers not only as means, but also as constituencies with goals and priorities of their own, Evan and Freeman suggest that firms have a fundamental *duty* to allow these stakeholders some degree of influence on the corporation. By this, they would be enabled to act as free and autonomous human beings rather than being merely factors of production (employees), or sources of income (consumers), etc.

■ Think theory

Stakeholder theory has also been considered from other theoretical perspectives. How would you apply utilitarianism for instance to the concept of stakeholder theory?

There are, however, also **problems with ethics of duty**.

- **Undervaluing outcomes.** Obviously, one of these problems is that there is rather little consideration of the outcomes of one's actions in ethics of duty. Although Kant would argue that you can consider consequences providing you would agree that everyone should when faced with similar situations, it gives you no real way of assessing these outcomes, and they do not form a fundamental part of the theory itself. They *may* be incorporated, but then again they may not.

- **Complexity.** Secondly, Kant's categorical imperative could be quite complicated to apply in single situations. His principles-led way of checking a situation requires a certain amount of abstraction and it is this level of intellectual scrutiny that one could not take for granted in each and every case.

- **Misplaced optimism?** Furthermore, Kant's theory is quite optimistic: his view of man as a rational actor who acts consequently according to self-imposed duties seems more of an ideal than a reality with regard to business actors. In contrast, the strength of egoism is that it is a concept of humans that is generally quite well confirmed by the conventional pattern of business behaviour.

Ethics of rights and justice

In Chapter 2 we briefly discussed the notion of citizenship as defined in terms of a set of individual rights. Actually, this notion of rights goes back to an entire philosophical school initially linked to the British philosopher John Locke (1632–1714). He conceptualized the notion of 'natural rights', or moral claims, that humans were entitled to, and which should be respected and protected (at that time, primarily by the state). Among the most important rights conceived by Locke and subsequent rights theorists were *rights to life, freedom, and property*. These have since been extended to include rights to freedom of speech, conscience, consent, privacy, and the entitlement to a fair legal process, among others.

In terms of an ethical theory we could define rights along the following lines:

> Natural rights are certain basic, important, inalienable entitlements that should be respected and protected in every single action.

The general significance of the notion of rights in terms of an ethical theory lies in the fact that these rights result in the duty of other actors involved in a certain situation to respect them. In this aspect, rights are the equivalent to duties since the rights of one person result in a corresponding duty for other persons to respect, protect, or facilitate these rights. My right to property imposes a duty on others not to interfere with my property or take it away. My right to privacy imposes a duty on others to refrain from gathering personal information about my private life without my consent. Rights and duties are thus two sides of the same coin.

This link to corresponding duties makes the theory of rights similar to Kant's approach. The main difference is that it does not rely on a rather complex process of determining the duties by applying the categorical imperative. Rather, the notion of rights is based on a certain axiomatic claim about human nature that rests mostly on various philosophical approaches of the Enlightenment, often backed up by certain religious views, such as the approach of Catholic social thought. Natural rights, or human rights, as they are referred to mostly today, are based on a certain consensus of all human beings about the nature of *human dignity*.

Despite its lack of a complicated theoretical deduction—or maybe even just because of its rather simple and plausible viewpoint—the rights approach has been very powerful throughout history and has substantially shaped the constitutions of many modern states. This includes the Declaration of the Rights of Man that was influential during the period of the French Revolution (1789), and the American Constitution, which is largely based on notions of rights. These ideas have also led to the United Nations Charter of Human Rights, issued in 1948, which has been a powerful standard of worldwide enforcement of various rights. The most recent manifestation of this thinking is the Charter of Fundamental Human Rights for the European Union agreed as part of the Nice Treaty in 2000. Based on the original idea of 'natural rights', these entitlements have been broken down to many different areas of social, political, and economic life, leading to various civil, social, and political rights, which ultimately define the notion of modern (liberal) citizenship.

Today, basic human rights would include a right to life, liberty, justice, education, fair trial, fair wages, freedom of belief, association, and expression, to name just a few. It is this background that makes the entire notion of human rights one of the most common and important theoretical approaches to business ethics on a practical level. Corporations, especially multinationals, are increasingly judged with regard to their attitude to human rights and how far they respect and protect them.

The perspective of human rights certainly provides the most straightforward answer to An Ethical Dilemma 3. In using child labour, the product manager would certainly violate the right to education and furthermore the freedom of consent. Furthermore, a human rights perspective would cast doubt on the issue of fair wages in general as the deal appears to profit from the poverty evident in a rather deprived area of the developing world.

Ethical theories based on rights are very powerful because of their widely acknowledged basis in human rights. However, the theoretical basis is one of plausibility rather than a deep theoretical methodology. Moreover, maybe the most substantial limitation of this approach is that notions of rights are quite strongly based in a western view of morality. A considerable amount of friction might occur if these ideas are directly transferred to, if not imposed on, communities with a different cultural and religious legacy. **Ethics in Action 3.1** illustrates this with reference to the problem of Aboriginal 'land rights' in the context of the British mining company Rio Tinto.

The problem of justice

The approach of human rights to ethics has a particular relation to economic and business decisions. Whenever two parties enter an economic transaction there has to be agreement on a fair distribution of costs and benefits between the parties. This is what contracts are for, or, most commonly, this is achieved by means of the market. Problems of distribution, however, do not only occur in transactions, but on a wider scale as well:

- How should a company pay its shareholders, executives, and normal workers so that everybody gets a fair compensation for their input into the corporation?
- How should a company take into account the demands of local communities, employees, and shareholders when planning an investment with major impacts on the environment?
- How should a government allocate money for education so that every part of society gets a fair chance of a good education?

Ethics in Action 3.1

Rio Tinto and Aboriginal claims on mining land in Australia

The UK multinational Rio Tinto is probably not the best known for its products. Still, there are probably few people in the industrialized world who do not indirectly use one of its products almost every day. This is because Rio Tinto is the world's largest mining company, extracting a wide range of natural resources, from diamonds to uranium to bauxite. Among campaigners, though, the group is probably one of the best known, since it arguably counts among the companies with the most extensive record of protest regarding environmental and human rights issues.

Although the company has made the headlines in many parts of the world, recent conflicts have focused on its engagement in Northern and Western Australia. These regions are extremely rich in resources, and Rio Tinto with its subsidiaries is one of the main extracting companies in the area. Next to environmental issues—some mines are even located in national parks—the key issue has been the role of Australia's original inhabitants, the Aborigines.

Before the European settlers entered Australia 250 years ago, the Aborigines were living in these territories, mostly with a nomadic lifestyle. Their relation to these lands then was not so much characterized by what we would call 'property rights' which assign certain territories to certain tribes or families. The main relation of these communities to 'their' land is via sacred sites, so-called 'dreamtimes' or 'story places', which are important elements of Aboriginal beliefs and rituals. Some of them would also abandon houses where people died and would only enter them after a while when the spirits had vanished.

Many of the locations where Rio Tinto was extracting minerals, or intended to do so, during the last two decades originally 'belonged' to the Aborigines in this sense. The Australian law, based on the legal fiction of the 'principle of terra nullus', made this approach quite easy for the company. This principle basically assumes that Australia was uninhabited when the white settlers arrived, and therefore it largely disenfranchised the Aborigine people. Although this principle was overturned in 1992 by a high court ruling, this did not exactly solve the problem. Even when offered generous compensation, Aboriginal councils refused many of the proffered deals. The central issue for them was that 'we are not against mining but we must protect our sacred places', as one tribesman puts it. 'Our Aboriginal law tells us that; it is a law thousands of years old. The white man's law in Australia is only 250 years old.'

Over time, Rio Tinto has made considerable efforts to deal with the land rights problem in Australia. Regarding a new project in Northern Australia, the company's chairman stated the company's clear line on the issue at the 2002 Johannesburg summit: 'We won't develop it without their [Aboriginal] consent. Full Stop.' However, despite such victories for the Aborigine people, problems of property rights remain. For example, a couple of days prior to making the above statement, Rio Tinto won an Australian high court case that entirely denied the claims of the Miriuwung-Gajoerrong people on another of the company's mining operations in the remote north-west. Although conceding rights to land, the court stated that there is 'no native title right to minerals or petroleum' mined from that land. As a result, Rio Tinto had to share not a single cent of its £1.7bn annual profit (€2.5bn) with the tribe whose land it extracted its valuable resources from.

SOURCES

Anon. (1978). 'Australian uranium delayed again'. *The Economist*, 30 Sept.: 88.

—— (1980). 'Australia: sacred sites and an unholy row'. *The Economist*, 3 May: 95.

Brown, P. (2001). 'The world's largest mining company has been given a chance to prove its green credentials and save Aboriginal homelands'. *Guardian*, 14 Feb.: 8.

Fickling, D. (2002). 'Mining verdict damages Aboriginal land rights'. *Guardian*, 9 Aug.: 13.

Nisse, J. (2002). 'Aborigines halt Rio Tinto project'. *Independent on Sunday*, 15 Sept.: 3.

Pilkington, E. (1994). 'Dog fight for mine site'. *Guardian*, 5 Mar.: 25.

··

> **■ Think theory**
>
> Whose rights are in conflict in this case? What are the implications for an ethical theory based on rights and justice? Would you suggest other approaches to satisfactorily solve this conflict?

We could multiply these examples, but what becomes clear is that individual rights have to be realized in a certain social context in such a way that they are addressed and respected equally and justly. This is where the issue of justice arises.

> Justice can be defined as the simultaneously fair treatment of individuals in a given situation with the result that everybody gets what they deserve.

The crucial moral issue here however is the question of what exactly 'fairness' means in a situation, and by which standards we can decide what a person might reasonably deserve. According to Beauchamp and Bowie (1997: 42), theories of justice typically see fairness in two main ways:

• **Fair procedures.** Fairness is determined according to whether everyone has had an equal opportunity to achieve a just reward for his or her efforts. This is commonly referred to as *procedural justice*.

• **Fair outcomes.** Fairness is determined according to whether the consequences are distributed in a just manner. This is commonly referred to as *distributive justice*.

Most views of justice would ideally seek to achieve both types of fairness, but this is not always possible. Consider the case of access to higher education. Say it was discovered that certain ethnic groups were under-represented in your university's degree programmes. Given that ethnicity is not correlated with innate intelligence, we might seek to solve this problem by reserving a certain number of places for under-represented groups to make sure that educational rewards were *distributed* fairly amongst these different sections of society. However, this would impose a potentially unfair *procedure* on the university's admissions, since 'over-represented' groups would be excluded from applying for the reserved places.

Notions of justice have been widely applied in business ethics problems, notably in relation to employment practices and the question of discrimination. Justice has also been a key feature of debates about globalization and sustainability. Here, the main concern is about issues of social and economic justice—themes that have long pervaded reasoning about the ethics of economic systems.

This problem of a just distribution of wealth in and between societies has been addressed in numerous ways, although historically answers have tended to fall somewhere between two extreme positions: **egalitarianism** and **non-egalitarianism**.

The *egalitarian* approach claims that justice is the same as equality—burdens and rewards should be distributed equally and deviations from equality are unjust (Beauchamp and Bowie 1997). Revelations that 358 billionaires have as much wealth as the poorest 45 per cent of the world's entire population (McIntosh et al. 1998: 15) would therefore clearly be seen as unjust by an egalitarian. One obvious example of an attempt to develop an egalitarian approach to economic systems is communist regimes. Here, everybody had the same wage (roughly), was allowed to own the same amount of property (which meant that the state essentially owned everything), paid the same state-allocated prices, etc.

However, egalitarian approaches have problems with the fact that there are differences between people. For instance, should someone who works hard earn the same as a lazy person? Are all skills really worth the same? Egalitarian approaches also tend to be inefficient, since there are no incentives for innovation and greater efficiency as everyone is rewarded equally anyway. Furthermore they can lead to restrictions in individual freedom, since freedom to engage in economic transactions, for instance, could again lead to inequality among the actors involved, as the free market system clearly demonstrates.

The *non-egalitarian* approach, at the other end of the spectrum, would claim that justice in economic systems is ultimately a product of the fair process of free markets. Actors with certain needs would meet actors who can answer the needs, and if they agree on a transaction, justice is determined by the market forces of supply and demand. As discussed in Chapter 2 this approach was popular in the 1980s in many western countries. However, it has also been argued that it led to considerable inequality. The notion of the market presupposes fairly equal participants in the market in order to produce fair results. But insofar as people differ in income, ability, health, social and economic status, etc., markets can lead to results that some people would no longer regard as fair. On a global level, this has become visible when poor, underdeveloped countries have tried to compete with highly industrialized countries: it is as if in Formula 1 we would allow a bicycle to start next to a Ferrari: even with the fairest rules, the driver on the bicycle would be doomed to lose.

Obviously, the two extreme answers to the question of what exactly justice means in an economic context are unsatisfactory. The answer might well lie in between the two. A very popular approach to this problem has been proposed by the American John Rawls (1971). In his **'theory of justice'** he suggests two criteria, two 'tests' as it were, to decide whether an action could be called just. According to Rawls, justice is achieved when:

1. Each person is to have an equal right to the most extensive total system of basic liberties compatible with a similar system of liberty for all.
2. Social and economic inequalities are to be arranged so that they are both:
   (*a*) to the greatest benefit of the least advantaged; and
   (*b*) attached to offices and positions open to all under conditions of fair equality of opportunity.

The first principle is the most important one: before allowing for any inequalities we should ensure that the basic freedoms are realized to the same degree for everyone affected by the decision. The first condition thus looks to general human rights and requires their fulfilment before we would be able to proceed to the next step.

The second test is based on the assumption that inequalities are unavoidable in a free and competitive society. However, two conditions should be met. First, an arrangement is just when even the one who profits least from it is still better off than they would be without it. This for example would suggest that high salaries for corporate leaders might be acceptable providing that employees at the bottom of the corporate hierarchy were also better off as a result—say, because the high salary for the leader led to better corporate performance, which in turn could be translated into higher wages for all. The second condition, again following this example, would be met if not only a privileged few could ascend the corporate ladder, but everyone had a fair chance to do so, regardless of gender, race, appearance, etc.

There are, of course, a couple more considerations, conditions, and elements to Rawls's theory that we will not go into here. Even in this simplified form, though, we can usefully apply some of its basic findings to various business situations in order to determine 'just' treatment of stakeholders.

If we look to our example in Ethical Dilemma 3, the first test would be to ask if all people involved (including the product manager) were in possession of the same basic liberty. Apart from the cultural differences between Europe and Thailand this is certainly not the case for the children, since they are obviously not allowed to have even a basic education. The second principle could conceivably allow for a more tolerant approach to child labour: the first criterion for inequality would be to ask if the children are worse or better off with the arrangement. One might reasonably argue here that children are often forced into worse things in developing countries than assembling plastic toys. Prostitution, begging, and theft might be other alternatives, suggesting that the children would be better off if you concluded the deal. However, if concluding your deal meant that the children would miss schooling that they otherwise would have had, the arrangement is definitely not benefiting the least well off. The second criterion, though, poses even more of a problem, since without access to education the children do not have a realistic chance to achieve the position of the better parties such as yourself. Hence, they are definitely not 'under conditions of fair equality of opportunity'.

If we extend our view slightly more broadly, Rawls's view of justice can actually be used to justify multinationals' exploitation of low wages and poor conditions in less developed countries—at least under certain conditions. For example, some MNCs have taken it upon themselves to cater for school education or basic healthcare in less developed manufacturing locations. By this, MNCs still take advantage of lower wages in these countries, but by providing a 'system of basic liberties compatible with a similar system of liberty for all' and creating 'conditions of fair equality of opportunity' (at least on a local level), one might argue that the resulting inequalities are still 'to the greatest benefit of the least advantaged'. After all, without the manufacturing plant, local people would probably face greater poverty and less opportunity for development than they would with it.

Limits of traditional theories

If we look back to these major traditional ethical theories, we could argue that they present a quite comprehensive view of humans and society, and, based on various assumptions, they come up with actionable principles to answer ethical questions. In presenting such a closed 'model' of the world, these theories have the substantial advantage that they could come up with a solution to every possible situation. They have, however, the big disadvantage that their view of the world only presents one aspect of human life, while reality normally tends to be more complex than the simplified view of these ethical theories.

In the previous discussions we have outlined some of the main benefits and drawbacks of each of these main ethical theories. However, the very approach of *all* traditional theories is open to criticism. As largely absolutist theories based on objective reason, a number of drawbacks for approaching business ethics problems through theory of this sort can be identified.

The main criticisms of traditional ethical theories are:

• **Too abstract.** Stark (1994) suggests that traditional ethical theories are too theoretical and impractical for the pragmatic day-to-day concerns of managers. In real life, managers are unlikely to apply abstract principles derived from long-dead philosophers when dealing with the concrete problems of business. The business context has its own values and structures and practices that need to be taken into account (Furman 1990).

• **Too reductionist.** Kaler (1999*b*) argues that each theory tends to focus on one aspect of morality at the cost of all the rest of morality. Why choose consequences *or* duties *or* rights when *all* are important?

• **Too objective and elitist.** Parker (1998) suggests that ethical theories attempt to occupy a rarefied high ground, such that those specialist ethicists and philosophers who know and understand the theories can pronounce on the right and wrong of other people without any subjective experience of the situation they are faced with. Just because Crane and Matten know the difference between utilitarianism and justice why should that mean that we can decide whether a product manager in Thailand is doing the right thing?

• **Too impersonal.** By focusing on abstract principles, traditional ethical theories do not take account of the personal bonds and relationships which shape our thoughts and feelings about right and wrong (Gilligan 1982).

• **Too rational and codified.** Ethical theories try and distil right and wrong down to codified rational rules of behaviour. Bauman (1993) contends that this suppresses our moral autonomy and denigrates the importance of our moral feelings and emotions, all of which he claims are crucial for acting morally towards others.

Clearly then, there are certain problems associated with traditional theories. Many of these stem from their emphasis on the more absolutist approach to ethical theory. As a result there have been a number of more recent attempts to develop or resurrect ethical theories that emphasize greater flexibility, as well as including consideration of decision-makers, their context, and their relations with others as opposed to just abstract universal principles. Although these are also open to criticism, they help to enrich the choice of perspectives we could take on ethical issues in business.

Contemporary ethical theories

Contemporary ethical theories are those that have either been developed or brought to prominence in the business ethics field over the past decade or so. As such they much less commonly appear in business ethics texts, yet we would suggest that they offer an important alternative perspective which should not be ignored, and which, we would suspect, may become increasingly more influential in the business ethics literature. We shall be looking at four main contemporary ethical theories:

- Virtue ethics
- Feminist ethics
- Discourse ethics
- Postmodern ethics

Virtue ethics

Up to now we have chiefly looked at right and wrong according to the ethics of particular *actions*. Virtue ethics however starts from a different perspective: rather than checking every single action according to its outcomes, or its underlying principles, this approach looks to the character of the *decision-maker*. Essentially, the message of this theoretical view would roughly be 'good actions come from good persons'. We could therefore define it along the following lines:

> Virtue ethics contends that morally correct actions are those undertaken by actors with virtuous characters. Therefore, the formation of a virtuous character is the first step towards morally correct behaviour.

Virtues are a set of acquired traits of character that enable a person to lead a good life. Virtues can be differentiated into **intellectual virtues**—'wisdom' being the most prominent one—and **moral virtues**, which comprise a long list of possible characteristics such as honesty, courage, friendship, mercy, loyalty, modesty, patience, etc. All these virtues are manifested in actions that are a habitual pattern of behaviour of the virtuous person rather than just occurring once, or in one-off decisions. As these traits are not ours by birth, we acquire them by learning, and most notably, in business, by being in relationships with others in a community of practice (MacIntyre 1984).

Central to ethics of virtue is the notion of a 'good life'. For Aristotle, one of the original proponents of virtue ethics, this consists of happiness, not in a limited hedonistic, pleasure-oriented sense, but in a broader sense. This most notably includes virtuous behaviour as an integral part of the good life: a happy business person would not only be one who finally makes the most money, but one who does so by at the same time savouring the pleasures of a virtuous manner of achieving their success. In a business context, the 'good life' means far more than being a profitable company. Virtue ethics takes a much more holistic view by also looking at the way this profit is achieved, and, most notably, by claiming that economic success is just one part of the good business life—with satisfaction of employees, good relations among all members of the company, and harmonious relations with all stake-holders being equally important (Collier 1995).

From this point of view, the virtuous product manager in Ethical Dilemma 3 could take in different perspectives, depending on the community from which the notion of a virtuous manager was derived. On the one hand, you could be compassionate and con-siderate with the situation of the suppliers. Taking into account their need for work and money as well as the children's need for education, you perhaps would try to do business with them while at the same time assuming responsibility for the children's education. For instance, you could support a local school or pay sufficiently high wages to allow the family to send their children to school rather than making use of them as cheap labour. On the other hand, you might also think that the 'good life' in rural Thailand might in fact consist in an entire family working happily together and that western concepts of education, professionalization, and efficiency are a different concept of a 'good life' which does not necessarily have to be identical with the Thai approach to life. Typically, though, virtue ethics in a business context such as this would suggest that the solution to many of the problems faced by managers is located in the culture and tradition of the relevant community of practice. The product manager should determine what a 'virtuous' product manager would do from his or her professional code of conduct, from virtuous role models, or from professional training.

It doesn't take long to see what the main drawback of virtue ethics is: how do we deter-mine which community ideal of good practice to consult? And, in the absence of a clear code of conduct from our relevant communities, how do we translate ideas of virtuous traits into ethical action? Still, the relevance of virtue ethics for business ethics is that it reminds us that right and wrong cannot simply be resolved by applying a specific rule or principle, but that we need to cultivate our knowledge and judgement on ethical matters over time through experience and participation.

Feminist ethics

This eschewal of a principle-based approach to ethical problems has also been taken up by another more recent school of thought in business ethics. Feminist approaches to busi-ness ethics start from the assumption that men and women have fairly different attitudes towards organizing social life, with significant impact on the way ethical conflicts are handled (Gilligan 1982). In addressing ethical problems, traditional ethical theory has looked for rules and principles to be applied in a fair, objective, and consistent way. This approach has been almost exclusively established and promulgated by male philosophers and thinkers such as Kant, Locke, Bentham, Smith, and Mill. The 'ethics of rights', as this male view is sometimes called (Maier 1997), tries to establish legitimate grounds for claims and interests of individuals in situations of social conflict.

Feminist ethics, on the other hand, has a different approach that sees the individual deeply embedded in a network of interpersonal relations. Consequently, responsibility for the mem-bers of this network and maintenance of connectedness, rather than allegiance to abstract moral principles, is the predominant concern of feminist ethics. This approach, often therefore called an 'ethics of care', consequently results in significant differences in the view

	'Ethics of rights' (male approach)	'Ethics of care' (feminist ethics)
View of humans	Autonomous, separate, independent Bearer of a function in the group	Interdependent actors within a social web
Moral goal	Fairness and impartiality Maintenance of rules	Avoid harm Maintenance of relationships
Moral problem	Conflict of rights between individuals	Conflict of responsibilities in relationships
Values	Rights, duties, fairness, due process, equal protection	Harmony, empathy, community, caring, responsiveness, integration
Focus	Results	Processes
Driving social force	Competition, winning	Co-operation, compromise

Figure 3.4. Contrasting gender-based views of business ethics

Source: Based on Maier (1997: 949).

of ethical issues (Maier 1997; Rabouin 1997). Moral problems are conflicts of responsibilities in relationships rather than conflicts of rights between individuals. They therefore can only be solved by personal, subjective reasoning which particularly stresses the importance of intuition and feeling. Whilst male approaches would focus on 'fair' results, feminist perspectives stress social processes and particularly aim at the achievement of harmony, empathy, and integration with regard to ethical issues. The main goal is to avoid harm and maintain healthy relationships. Following this description, we might suggest the following definition:

> Feminist ethics is an approach that prioritizes empathy, harmonious and healthy social relationships, care for one another, and avoidance of harm above abstract principles.

Figure 3.4 shows relevant characteristics of feminist ethics and compares them to the male approach. It is important to remember, though, that, as an ethical theory, feminism does not argue that women are the *best* ethical actors. Feminism rather proposes a particular attitude toward ethical conflicts that is more within the framework of what women allegedly would do by intuition anyway. Consequently, an organization with feminist values and approaches is a business where men and women alike follow these principles and all employees regardless of their gender are educated and encouraged to embrace a 'feminine' approach to ethical issues.

Applying feminist theory to the case in Ethical Dilemma 3 would in a certain sense require far more knowledge about the case than we can acquire from just reading about it. A feminist perspective would cause the product manager to try to get a closer view of the family involved, and see if the children are really happy in this situation. It would also involve a better understanding of the social and economic constraints that cause the family to embark on this particular production pattern. Ironically, a feminist perspective would not necessarily argue categorically against any involvement of children in the process as long as the inter-familiar relationships are functioning well, and the children are not forced or exploited or compelled to work beyond their physical capacities. As the latter conditions might not be fulfilled, feminist perspectives would probably tend to object to child labour as well—not so much because it violates certain (western) principles, but because of the perceivable distress and suffering of the children. Furthermore, feminist theories would also look at the situation of the other actors involved and scrutinize, for example, the question of how the money earned by the assembling of toys is spent and how the income in the family is distributed, etc.

Discourse ethics

All the theoretical approaches we have discussed so far start from a certain perspective on humans, on the values or goals governing their decisions, and a few other assumptions that in essence are all normative in nature. By 'normative' remember we mean prescriptions of right and wrong action. Having said 'normative', however, we might step back for a minute and ask if this starting point is in fact a very handy way to solve ethical conflicts in business. After all, we cannot take it for granted in a given situation that everybody shares, for instance, the notion of humans being hedonistic, or of feminist values being the most appropriate ones to address ethical problems in business. This is already problematic in a group of relatively homogeneous people; say, the marketing department of a Swedish car company. But it gets even more complicated if there is a meeting of all marketing directors of the company worldwide, since this could conceivably include participants as diverse as evangelical fundamentalists from the USA, atheists from Russia, Muslims from Egypt, and Buddhists from Japan. In these situations, the most significant problems arise from the diverging normative perspectives that the different people might bring to the table.

It is at this point where discourse ethics comes into the picture. The philosophical underpinning of this theoretical approach is the argument that norms ultimately cannot be justified by rational arguments, but that they have to be generated and applied to solve ethical conflicts on a day-to-day basis (Preuss 1999). Steinmann and Löhr (1994), as the main proponents of a discourse approach to business ethics, argue that ethical reflection has to start from real-life experiences (rather than belief systems, which could be too diverse). They contend that the ultimate goal of ethical issues in business should be the **peaceful settlement of conflicts**.

With this goal in mind, different parties in a conflict should sit together and engage in a discourse about the settlement of the conflict, and ultimately provide a solution that is acceptable to all. This 'ideal discourse', as it is usually called, is more than an occasional chat or business meeting; it has to answer certain philosophical criteria such as impartiality, non-persuasiveness, non-coercion, and expertise of the participants (Habermas 1983). This would particularly include the injunction that those who are more powerful in a certain situation refrain from using this power to solve the ethical conflict according to their belief systems. Such a discourse then would lead to norms for a specific situation which are an expression of the rational consensus of all affected persons or represented parties. In establishing a rational 'ideal discourse' about specific problems, this approach is thus supposed to be *norm generating*.

Given this brief outline, we might usefully posit the following basic definition:

> Discourse ethics aims to solve ethical conflicts by providing a process of norm generation
> through rational reflection on the real-life experience of all relevant participants.

Discourse ethics then is more a recipe for practical conflict solution than an ethical theory comparable to those discussed above. In simple terms, the only condition for it to work is the assumption that all rational human beings share the experience, and that the norm of peaceful resolution of conflict is the best way to organize social interaction. It is based on rationality and requires a dialogue in which people are able and willing to exchange arguments and follow the 'non-coercive coercion of the best argumentation' (Habermas 1983). There are understandably certain practical limits to this approach, especially the considerable amount of time it involves, and the fairly optimistic assumptions about rational human behaviour in discourses. Nevertheless, discourse ethics has been the underlying concept for the settlement of numerous disputes about environmental impacts of corporate decisions, in which various stakeholders with completely divergent value systems had to come to a common decision on certain controversial projects (Renn et al. 1995). See **Ethics in Action 3.2**.

If we apply discourse ethics to Ethical Dilemma 3 it lies in the nature of the concept that we are not able to say whether this would influence in any way the resulting decision of the parties involved. It would however suggest that all parties involved, starting with the Thai trading company, the chocolate manufacturer, the parents, the children, but potentially also the consumers in Europe should meet together to enter a 'norm-generating' discourse on the topic. Apart from the fact that this shows some practical difficulties of the concept, the idea does open the way to a solution that could be closest to the interests of all parties involved.

Postmodern perspectives on business ethics

Postmodern perspectives on business ethics take up a point that we have already touched upon when discussing discourse ethics in the previous section. The postmodern school of thought fundamentally questions the link between rationality and morality that is inherent in all traditional ethical theories. These traditional theories have their origins in modernism, which emerged roughly during the eighteenth-century Enlightenment era. 'Modern' thinkers strove for a rational, scientific explanation of the world and aimed for comprehensive, inclusive, theoretically coherent theories of explaining nature, man, or society. In the area of the social sciences one of the results of this was various theories commonly in the form of certain '-isms', such as liberalism, communism, socialism, rationalism, capitalism, etc. Postmodern thinkers contend that these comprehensive theories, these 'grand narratives' of society (Lyotard 1984), are too ambitious, optimistic, and reductionist, ultimately failing to explain the complex reality of human existence.

While postmodernism tends to embrace a whole range of theoretical propositions and arguments, postmodern thinkers have been particularly influential in ethics, since they identify the specific danger of rational approaches to morality. Zygmunt Bauman (1993), one of the best-known proponents of postmodern ethics, argues that by codifying morality within specific rules and codes of behaviour (as, for example, exemplified in bureaucratic

Ethics in Action 3.2

Mediation as a peaceful form of conflict resolution in Ravensburg

Ravensburg is a small, sleepy town of 70,000 inhabitants in the deep south of Germany, basically in the middle of nowhere between Stuttgart and Lake Constance. In the late 1990s the Council of Ravensburg, together with the local chamber of commerce and other business representatives, came up with a project that was intended to boost the town's attractiveness to local and regional consumers as well as to investors from all over Europe. The idea was to redevelop the entire area around the Ravensburg railway station into what they called 'Bahnstadt' (meaning something like 'rail city'). The planned project would include a new shopping centre, office buildings, hotels, car parks, and leisure facilities with a view to reinvigorating the area around the station. The project would also include a substantial reorganization of the road network in central Ravensburg.

A project of this dimension however has some crucial implications for the neighbouring communities: an increase in noise was the main concern, but more pollution, the social and visual impact of new buildings, and other environmental aspects played a role as well. In order to prevent lengthy court proceedings and tedious administrative procedures caused by the anticipated protests from local community groups, the authorities chose a different trajectory to solve the looming conflict. They decided to organize a mediation project.

The German think tank 'Centre for Technology Assessment in Baden-Württemberg', which organized the mediation talks, had previously developed a tool that had already been successful in a number of other projects. It consisted of a three-step approach.

As a *first step* the affected citizens were invited into various focus groups in order to find out about their values, preferences, and objections with regard to the project.

The *second* and main stage of the project focused on a round table discussion where experts from the local council and representatives of local business, the police, the chamber of industry and commerce, and all other parties involved were present. Here representatives from the focus groups presented their values and preferences and discussed them with the other interest groups and experts. These discussions—or 'discourses', as they were properly called—had to answer some key criteria, including:

• All members have equal status and rights;

• Rational exchange of information and disclosure of arguments;

• Primary goal is consensus decisions—only if these are not feasible is compromise allowed;

• The results shall be binding for the local council.

Between October 1999 and May 2000, eight sessions took place during which representatives of sixteen interest groups exchanged arguments and views about the controversial project.

As a *third step*, the mediation group came up with a recommendation that ranked various measures to reduce the environmental impacts of the project according to performance, costs, political feasibility, and time. In 74 per cent of the discussed issues, the round table in fact was able to produce consensus between all involved parties. Only in 26 per cent of the issues did compromise have to be found and reached. Ultimately, the mediation process helped to resolve a conflict that might otherwise have resulted in costly delays and anxiety for all parties involved and was regarded as a success by all members.

SOURCES

Keck, G. 2001. *Öffentlichkeitsbeteiligung zur Lärmreduzierung in der Ravensburger 'Bahnstadt'—Ergebnisbericht*. Stuttgart: Akademie für Technikfolgenabschätzung in Baden-Württemberg. **www.stadt-ravensburg.de**.

> ■ **Think theory**
>
> To what extent do you think that discourse ethics as illustrated in Ravensburg is applicable to other business problems? What are the benefits and drawbacks of such an approach?

organizations), rational approaches deny the real source of morality which is rooted in a 'moral impulse' towards others. This is a subjective, emotional conviction of every human being about right and wrong, based on their experiences, sentiments, and instincts. Moral judgement then is a gut feeling more than anything else, but this is inevitably nullified when people enter organizations and become distanced from the people who are actually going to experience the consequences of their decisions, such as consumers, investors, suppliers, and others. These ideas lead us to the following definition:

> Postmodern ethics is an approach that locates morality beyond the sphere of rationality in an emotional 'moral impulse' towards others. It encourages individual actors to question everyday practices and rules, and to listen to and follow their emotions, inner convictions, and 'gut feelings' about what they think is right and wrong in a particular incident of decision-making.

Ultimately, postmodernists are rather sceptical about the entire venture of business ethics (ten Bos and Willmott 2001), since ethical theories aim at finding 'rules and principles that determine right or wrong' (our definition in Chapter 1). Postmodernists tend to suggest otherwise, such that 'the foolproof—universal and unshakably founded—ethical code will never be found'. A postmodern perspective on business ethics does not then provide us with any rule or principle, not even a 'recipe' for ethical decision-making such as discourse ethics. However, postmodern ethics has quite significant implications for ethical decisions in business. Gustafson (2000: 21), for example, suggests that postmodern business ethics emphasizes the following:

• **Holistic approach.** As morality is an inner conviction of individual actors there is no separation between the private and professional realm. Postmodernists argue that modernist theories of ethical behaviour lead to an abstract and distant view of ethical issues that ultimately causes actors to follow different standards in their professional and private lives. For business organizations, such a view of ethical decision-making could unleash quite a subversive potential to business ethics as it might question the beliefs and practices held by the organization (Bauman 1993).

- **Examples rather than principles.** As morality is not based on rational theories, ethical reasoning is not embodied in principles and rules. Rather, it is based on narratives of experience, relies on metaphors to explain inner convictions, and suggests persons as role models of certain virtues that the individual could point to as an embodiment of his or her 'moral instinct'. Of all theories discussed so far, virtue ethics therefore has the strongest affiliation to postmodern ethics (Shaw 1995).

- **'Think local, act local'.** Modernist theories and '-isms' are aimed at general principles that are applicable to each and every situation. Postmodernists think that ethical reasoning has to be far more modest: a realistic expectation towards ethics would be to come up with local rules applicable to single issues and situations. Rather than finding one principle for multiple situations, business ethics focuses on deciding one issue after the other. This does not mean that postmodernists do not take their decisions seriously and could decide on an issue in one way today and in another way tomorrow. It rather highlights the fact that no one situation is the same and that different actors, power relations, cultural antecedents, and emotional contexts might lead to different judgements in situations which superficially could be regarded as being in the same 'class' and subject to the same 'principles'.

- **Preliminary character.** Postmodern ethicists are more pessimistic than their modern counterparts. They know that ethical decisions are subject to non-rational processes, and thus less controllable and predictable. Ethical reasoning therefore is a constant learning process, an ongoing struggle and quest for certainty, an ongoing striving for solutions which have an even better fit, for reasoning that just makes more sense and works better than the approaches tried out so far.

From the nature of a postmodern view on business ethics it might already be clear that the notion of discussing the abstract case of Ethical Dilemma 3 is a nearly impossible venture. Indeed, postmodernist thinkers are sceptical of the vignette or hypothetical case method of learning about business ethics, preferring instead to engender moral commitment to others through real-life encounters (McPhail 2001). We would at best only be able to come up with some form of judgement if we travelled to Thailand, visited the site, talked to the people, and emphatically immersed ourselves in the real-life situation over there. We would then have a 'moral impulse' on what to feel about the situation and come up with what we think is the moral way to decide in this situation.

However, the example does gives us a few indications, and as good postmodernists, we would be well aware of the limitations of our present view on the issue and would try to suggest a preliminary view of what we would do in the situation of the product manager. We might for example at least suggest that we as the product manager have made the right first move in actually going to the site of production and facing those who will be affected by our decisions rather than staying at home and simply dismissing them as faceless 'suppliers'. We might also point to our attempt to make our own autonomous decision based on the situation faced in the specific culture of Thailand, rather than relying on a corporate code of ethics, particularly one which is intended to have universal application. However, postmodernists would also question the extent to which we as the product manager are so steeped in a corporate mentality that we immediately think in terms of costs and bonuses rather than people and their lives.

Ultimately, it lies in the nature of postmodernism that we are not able to finally decide on the situation for the manager, since we lack the contextual nuances of the situation and we are not aware of the extent to which a genuine 'moral impulse' is possible in this context.

Summary: towards a pragmatic use of ethical theory

The array of ethical theories discussed in this chapter provides us with a rich source of assistance in making morally informed decisions. However, the discussion of our case, An Ethical Dilemma 3, has surfaced quite a variety of different views and normative implications depending on the theoretical approach that has been chosen. Sometimes these views provide quite widely contradictory results.

As we have already indicated earlier in this chapter we will not suggest one theory or one approach as the best or true view of a moral dilemma. We would rather suggest that *all* these theoretical approaches throw light from different angles on one and the same problem and thus work in a complementary rather than a mutually excluding fashion. **Figure 3.5** elucidates this role of ethical theories: by viewing an ethical problem through the 'prism' of ethical theories we are provided with a variety of considerations and aspects pertinent to the moral assessment of the matter at hand. Based on this 'spectrum' of views the business actor then is able to fully comprehend the problem, its issues and dilemmas, and its possible solutions and justifications.

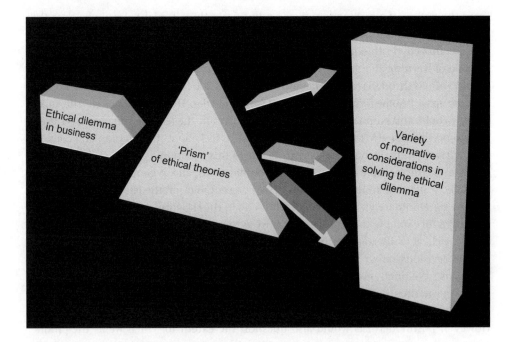

Figure 3.5. The value of ethical theories in solving ethical dilemmas in business

By using theory in this non-dogmatic way we not only take up the notion of pluralism as discussed earlier, but genuinely confront the issue that real business decisions normally involve multiple actors with a variety of ethical views and convictions which feed into the decision. Ethical theories help to articulate these views and pave the way to an intelligent and considered response to the problem. Furthermore, as we have already discussed in the context of contemporary theories, ethical decision-making does not only rely on rational considerations. Moral matters embrace human beings in their totality of reason, emotion, bodily existence, social embeddedness, and past experiences, just to name a few. Rather than looking only for universal principles to dogmatically apply to every situation, we suggest a pragmatic approach that allows all these aspects to play a role in business ethics.

Figure 3.6 provides a summary of the main consideration raised by each theory discussed in this chapter. Although we would draw short of advocating something akin to a 'ten-point

Consideration	Typical question you might ask yourself	Theory
One's own interests	Is this really in my, or my organization's, best long-term interests? Would it be acceptable and expected for me to think only of the consequences to myself in this situation?	Egoism
Social consequences	If I consider all of the possible consequences of my actions, for everyone that is affected, will we be better or worse off overall? How likely are these consequences and how significant are they?	Utilitarianism
Duties to others	Who do I have obligations to in this situation? What would happen if everybody acted in the same way as me? Am I treating people only to get what I want for myself (or my organization) or am I thinking also of what they might want too?	Ethics of duty
Entitlements of others	Whose rights do I need to consider here? Am I respecting fundamental human rights and people's need for dignity?	Ethics of rights
Fairness	Am I treating everyone fairly here? Have processes been set up to allow everyone an equal chance? Are there major disparities between the 'winners' and 'losers' that could be avoided?	Theories of justice
Moral character	Am I acting with integrity here? What would a decent, honest person do in the same situation?	Virtue ethics
Care for others and relationships	How do (or would) the other affected parties feel in this situation? Can I avoid doing harm to others? Which solution is most likely to preserve healthy and harmonious relationships among those involved?	Feminist ethics
Process of resolving conflicts	What norms can we work out together to provide a mutually acceptable solution to this problem? How can we achieve a peaceful settlement of this conflict that avoids 'railroading' by the most powerful player?	Discourse ethics
Moral impulse and emotions	Am I simply going along with the usual practice here, or slavishly following the organization's code, without questioning whether it really feels right to me? How can I get closer to those likely to be affected by my decision? What do my emotions or gut feelings tell me once I'm out of the office?	Postmodern ethics

Figure 3.6. Considerations in making ethical decisions: summary of key insights from ethical theories

plan' for ethical decision-making, you might want to use this figure as a checklist of potential ways of addressing business ethics problems and dilemmas.

In fact, there is actually a school of *ethical pragmatism* that is becoming more and more influential in business ethics thinking, and there is an ongoing debate in the literature about the necessity for opening up ethical decision-making to embrace not only rational theoretical reasoning, but a variety of individual and situational aspects of human existence (Rosenthal and Buchholz 2000). Without going to the postmodern extreme of denying the relevance of rationality for moral reasoning and locating these decisions mostly in the emotional sphere, there is a growing insight into the necessity of, for instance, combining reason and emotion in business ethics (ten Bos and Willmott 2001). The pragmatic approach we would like to advocate welcomes theoretical approaches in normative business ethics in their variety while at the same time accepting that they play a role alongside personal, cultural, psychological, cognitive, and context-related factors, all of which ultimately feed into a moral decision in business. Therefore in the next chapter we will focus more on these factors that shape how we *actually* make ethical decisions in organizations.

STUDY QUESTIONS

1 What are ethical theories?

2 Is ethical theory of any practical use to managers? Discuss using examples from current business practice.

3 Define ethical absolutism, ethical relativism, and ethical pluralism. To what extent is each perspective useful for studying and practising business ethics?

4 What are the two main families of traditional ethical theories? Explain the difference between these two approaches to ethical theory.

5 Which ethical theory do you think is most commonly used in business? Why do you think this is so?

6 Read the following case:

   You are the manager of FoodFile, a busy city centre restaurant catering mainly to local office workers at lunchtimes and an eclectic, fashionable crowd of professionals in the evenings. You are proud of your renowned food and excellent service. Most of your staff have been with you since you opened three years ago—unusual in an industry characterized by casual labour and high turnover. You consider this to be one of the key factors in your consistency and success. Now, your head chef has come to you and told you, in confidence, that she is HIV positive. She is very distressed and you want to reassure her. However, you are troubled about her continuing working in the kitchens and are concerned about the effect this news could have on the other staff, or even on your customers should they find out about her situation.

   (a) Set out the main ethical considerations that are suggested by each of the theories covered in this chapter

   (b) Which theories are most persuasive in dealing with this dilemma?

   (c) What would you do in this situation and why?

RESEARCH EXERCISE

Select a business ethics problem or dilemma that you have faced or which has arisen in an organization of which you have been part, either as an employee, a student, or a manager.

1 Briefly describe the basic details of the case, and identify and discuss the main business ethics issues involved.

2 Set out the main responses, solutions, or courses of action that *could* have been considered in relation to this problem.

3 Evaluate these options using theory discussed in this chapter.

4 What decision was finally made? To what extent do you believe that this was the best option, and why?

CASE 3

A bitter pill: the pharmaceutical industry and affordable AIDS drugs for Southern Africa

This case examines the dispute about AIDS medication for Southern African countries. It exposes the conflict between the needs of the world's poor and patent protection, which is needed to cover expensive development costs for new pharmaceutical products. The case provides a challenging opportunity to apply ethical theories to make a substantiated judgement in circumstances where a diversity of actors and a complexity of issues is involved.

South Africa has been in the headlines throughout most of the last decade for rather uplifting news. The end of apartheid and the relatively peaceful transition to a stable democratic society, represented by one of the most sympathetic and respected of all world statesmen, Nelson Mandela, gave hope and joy to many other nations across the globe. Although its flag counts among the best recognized in the world, another, rather sad side of the country has for long been ignored. While apartheid disadvantaged the black part of society through political means, it is the AIDS epidemic that 'is the new apartheid, the new enemy', as Archbishop Desmond Tutu put it in a recent interview.

HIV is currently expected to substantially devastate large swathes of the black population not only in South Africa, but also in most parts of the continent. In 2001, 70 per cent of the world's forty million people infected with AIDS lived in Africa, as did 2.3 million out of the 3 million who had died from the disease. In South Africa, where every ninth person is HIV positive, life expectancy is now a mere 47 years—without AIDS it would be 66. Even worse is the situation in other Southern African countries such as Mozambique or Swaziland, where the average life expectancy is well below 40. If things go on as they do, seven to ten million South Africans will have died of HIV/AIDS by 2010.

Apart from the humanitarian tragedy that hides behind these figures, there are of course also substantial economic and political aspects to this crisis. In 1999, for example, 860,000 schoolchildren in Sub-Saharan Africa lost their teachers. Often the disease kills exactly the people who in other circumstances could be a foundation of wealth and prosperity in such countries.

With recent progresses in pharmaceutical research, however, there is the theoretical chance of treating HIV-infected people. The HAART (highly active antiretroviral therapy) medication cocktails calm down the symptoms of the disease and lower infection rates, especially for mothers giving birth to children. The only problem is that such a therapy would cost between €10,000 and €15,000 per person per year—a sum completely out of the reach of governments that can hardly spend €10 on their citizens' health each year.

What should these countries then do to get hold of treatment? All the major drugs are produced by American and European multinationals, among which Merck, GlaxoSmithKline, and Boehringer are the most important ones. When the issues entered the political agenda in the mid-1990s these companies were reiterating the fact that they had to cover their enormous costs for developing the medications. With developing costs of €800m for each new drug released on the market, and an average twelve years' research time necessary to bring the drug from inception, the drug companies might be said to have quite a strong case for wanting to reap the benefits of their investment. In another vein, who else but these companies would be in a position to provide help for these appalling conditions in the other half of the globe?

One option for these countries was to resort to so-called generics. These are drugs produced according to the same recipe as those of the major companies, but marketed without the benefit of their brand identity. In the case of HIV drugs, these generics, mainly produced by companies in Brazil and India, are available for €300–400 per person per year. Obviously, this is a considerably cheaper option than the branded drugs, but still only affordable to the richer African countries.

A further problem, though, is that the import of generics represents a breach of the TRIPS (trade-related aspects of intellectual property rights) agreement of the WTO. Such a breach risks the consequence of sanctions, imposed for example by the USA, which is the home of many major pharmaceutical companies. While some countries such as Nigeria got away with ignoring the TRIPS agreement, the government of South Africa was taken to court by thirty-nine multinational pharmaceutical companies when it authorized the importation of generics in 1997.

During the court proceedings, which ultimately lasted four years, civil society groups managed successfully to mount public pressure on the companies involved. And when in 2001 the companies recognized the very real prospect of actually losing the case, they dropped their claim—a result that was widely considered to be a defeat for the industry. While prices for retroviral therapy had fallen by 80 per cent during the last years anyway, the prospect of a public relations disaster was probably considered by the companies as the most compelling reason to drop the case, especially when the poverty of the potential users meant that any 'win' would probably be more symbolic than financial.

Some companies, in the follow-up, then applied their own strategies. The UK firm GlaxoSmithKline granted a licence to a South African company to produce the cocktail and sell it below cost for around €1 per day per person. The US firm Merck even launched a programme to provide free retroviral drugs to Botswana. Other companies that have large operations in South Africa, such as the mining and extraction giants Anglo-American and DeBeers, launched projects to give away free treatment to their employees.

The issue, however, still remains on the agenda. After all, AIDS is just one of the epidemics that kill millions of people in the developed world every year. Other diseases such as tuberculosis and malaria are still waiting to be tackled. Only sixteen out of 1,400 drugs developed in the past twenty-five years have targeted tropical diseases. Apart from that, the main contributory factors to the spread of infection in Southern Africa are still poverty and lack of education. So, for example, AIDS medications only work together with decent intakes of food and a very organized, regular lifestyle.

Ultimately, the pharmaceutical industry, far from being converted to the cause of eliminating health problems in Southern Africa, seems rather warned by these developments. At the WTO conference on pharmaceutical patent rights in February 2003 in Geneva, the American representatives vetoed any loosening of patent rights. Critics suggested that the American pharmaceutical industry, which had just donated $US60m (€60m) to the Republican mid-term election campaign in the USA, had exerted its considerable influence to encourage the government to reject any changes. As one WTO official put it: 'it's payback time, the industry is calling in its favours.'

Questions

1 What are the main harms and benefits in this case for the different actors involved? How could that affect their ethical assessment of the situation?

2 Which moral principles, based on their duties to certain constituencies, would you suggest to the pharmaceutical companies involved?

3 What clashes of rights are involved in this case? Is it possible to rate the importance of the different rights involved?

4 How would an ethical assessment based on virtues differ from the assessments hitherto? Which 'moral community' could a pharmaceutical manager look to in order to determine a virtuous course of action?

5 Assess the potential of discourse and postmodern ethical theories in this case. Would you consider them to be helpful in any way?

Sources

Boseley, S., and Denny, C. (2003). 'Prescription for the world's poorest stays unwritten'. *Guardian*, 20 Feb.: 10.

Brennan, R., and Baines, P. (2002). 'Ethical aspects of drug pricing: GlaxoSmithKline and anti-retroviral drugs in South Africa'. Paper presented at the 2002 Academy of Marketing Annual Conference, Nottingham.

Denny, C. (2003). 'Gates's $200m gift to fight killer disease'. *Guardian*, 28 Jan.

Lamont, J. (2002). 'Merck seeks wider private-sector coalition on Aids'. *Financial Times*, 13 Sept.: 10.

—— and Williams, F. (2001). 'Campaigners attack drug companies on Aids patents'. *Financial Times*, 17 Oct.: 14.

McGreal, C. (2001). 'Defiant Nigeria to import cheap copies of HIV drugs: rejection of copyright will infuriate multinationals'. *Guardian*, 11 Dec.: 2.

Watkins, S. (2003). 'Where are all the new wonder drugs?' *Financial Mail on Sunday*, 5 Jan.: 6.

4

Making Decisions in Business Ethics
Descriptive Ethical Theories

In this chapter we will:

• Examine the question of why ethical and unethical decisions get made in the workplace;

• Review prominent ethical decision-making models and delineate key elements in terms of individual and situational influences on ethical decision-making;

• Discuss the importance of differences between individuals in shaping ethical decision-making, comparing demographic, cultural, experiential, cognitive, and imaginative aspects;

• Critically evaluate the importance of situational influences on ethical decision-making, delineating between issue-based and context-based factors;

• Identify points of leverage for managing and improving ethical decision-making in business, surfacing the concept of ethical culture as a prominent focus for such discussions.

Introduction

Why do some business people make what appear to be the right ethical choices, whilst some do things that are unscrupulous or even illegal? Are people who make these unethical decisions inherently bad, or are there other reasons that can explain the incidence of ethics problems in business? Do people have different ethical beliefs and values at work from those they have at home? This chapter provides a way of addressing these questions by examining what are called *descriptive* ethical theories.

> Descriptive business ethics theories seek to describe how ethics decisions are actually made in business, and what influences the process and outcomes of those decisions.

Descriptive ethical theories provide an important addition to the *normative* theories covered in the previous chapter: rather than telling us what business people *should* do (which is the intention of normative theory), descriptive theories seek to tell us what business people *actually* do—and, more importantly, *why* they do it.

Understanding the reasons why people make certain decisions is clearly important from a business ethics perspective, not least because it helps us to comprehend the factors which lead to ethical and unethical decisions. From a practical point of view, though, this is also useful for attempts to manage and improve business ethics. Obviously, we first need to know what shapes ethical decision-making before we can try and influence it. Therefore, descriptive theories can be said to provide a practical understanding of how the ethical theories covered in the previous chapter can be applied, as well as assisting in identifying points of leverage for managing business ethics, as will be discussed in the next chapter.

We begin by looking at the various models that have been put forward to explain the process of ethical decision-making in the workplace. This shows us that although ethical decision-making is very complex, extensive research over the years from psychologists, sociologists, management scholars, and others has provided us with a relatively clear picture of the important stages and influences that are central to understanding the ethical decision-making process. We proceed to summarize and evaluate current knowledge about these stages and influences, covering issues of the cognitive and emotional processes individuals go through in making ethical evaluations as well as the situational influences that shape the decisions and actions they actually come to make.

Models of ethical decision-making

If we think about times when we have been confronted with an ethical dilemma, we might well now be able to recognize what kind of normative principles we were employing—perhaps we were mainly concerned with possible consequences, or maybe we were thinking mainly about rights or relationships. However, we are probably less likely to know why we in fact thought about it in this way, or why we even saw it as an ethical issue in the first place. This, however, is the purpose of descriptive models of ethical decision-making. Various such models have been presented in the literature, and by far the most widely cited ones have been derived from the work of psychologists.

Many of the models most influential to business ethics have appeared in the mainstream management literature, and include those by Linda Treviño (1986) and Thomas Jones (1991). Important contributions have also been made in the marketing literature (which in itself is strongly influenced by psychology), such as the models by Hunt and Vitell (1986) and by O. C. Ferrell and colleagues (Ferrell and Gresham 1985; Ferrell et al. 1989). These models are not necessarily competing models, since they draw extensively upon one another and are often presented as 'extensions' to, or a 'synthesis' of, earlier models.

In general, all of these models primarily seek to represent two things:

- The different stages in decision-making people go through in responding to an ethics problem in a business context;
- The different influences on that process.

We shall briefly look at each of these two aspects in turn and link them together to form a framework for understanding ethical decision-making in business.

Stages in ethical decision-making

In a review of research on ethical decision-making in business, Loe et al. (2000: 186) suggest that the Jones (1991) model 'provides the most comprehensive synthesis model of ethical decision-making'. Jones bases his model on a four-stage process of ethical decision-making introduced by James Rest (1986). According to this model, individuals move through a process whereby they:

(i)   Recognize a moral issue;

(ii) Make some kind of moral judgement about that issue;

(iii) Establish an intention to act upon that judgement;

(iv) Finally actually act according to their intentions.

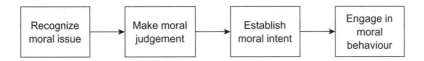

Figure 4.1. Ethical decision-making process

Source: Derived from Rest (1986), as depicted in Jones (1991).

This is shown in **Figure 4.1**. As Jones (1991) suggests, these stages are intended to be conceptually distinct, such that although one might reach one stage in the model, this does not mean that one will necessarily move on to the next stage. Hence, the model distinguishes between *knowing* what is the right thing to do and actually *doing* something about it; or between *wanting* to do the right thing, and actually *knowing* what the best course of action is. So, for example, even though a salesperson might know that lying to customers is wrong (a moral judgement), for one reason or another—such as needing to meet aggressive sales targets—they might not actually always tell the truth (a moral behaviour). Similarly, although a purchasing manager may realize that receiving personal gifts from suppliers is ethically questionable (a moral recognition), they may defer making a judgement about the problem (a moral judgement) until someone actually questions them about it.

Relationship with normative theory

The role of normative theory (which is the type of theory we discussed in the previous chapter) in these stages of ethical decision-making is primarily in relation to *moral judgement*. Moral judgements can be made according to considerations of rights, duty, consequences, etc. Whilst there has been very little research actually examining the types of normative theories used by managers and employees, there is some evidence to suggest that commercial managers continue to rely primarily on consequentialist thinking

(Premeaux and Mondy 1993). This is perhaps not surprising given that, as we saw in Chapter 3, much economic and business theory is itself largely predicated upon consequentialism (Desmond and Crane 2003). However, the issue of *whether* and *how* normative theory is used by an individual decision-maker depends on a range of different factors that influence the decision-making process, as we shall now see.

Influences on ethical decision-making

Models of ethical decision-making generally divide the factors which influence decisions into two broad categories: individual and situational (Ford and Richardson 1994).

• **Individual factors.** These are the unique characteristics of the individual actually making the relevant decision. These include factors which are given by birth (such as age and gender) and those acquired by experience and socialization (such as education, personality, and attitudes).

• **Situational factors.** These are the particular features of the context that influence whether the individual will make an ethical or an unethical decision. These include factors associated with the work context (such as reward systems, job roles, and organizational culture) and those associated with the issue itself (such as the intensity of the moral issue, or the ethical framing of the issue).

Many versions of the ethical decision-making models attempt to link certain influences to certain stages in the decision process. However, in categorizing the factors into our two broad categories, we feel that this is neither feasible, nor particularly necessary. Attempts to isolate influences to one stage or another are often very reductivist, whereas, taken broadly, the two groups of factors actually help to explain why certain business decisions get made, and why people behave in ethical and unethical ways in business situations. From our point of view, it matters less at which stage in someone's decision process an influence occurs (after all, sometimes a person can go through the process in a matter of seconds!), and more whether it occurs at all, and what can be done about it.

For our purposes, then, it is sufficient to present individual and situational factors as general influences on the ethical decision-making framework. This gives rise to the framework in **Figure 4.2**, which is the one that we shall use to structure our discussion in this chapter. During the rest of this chapter we will examine the two sets of factors in much more detail, with the intention of providing the basis for assessing their relative importance to ethical decision-making. Before we do, however, it is worth offering a brief word of warning about using a model such as this to structure our discussions.

Limitations of ethical decision-making models

As we have said, the model depicted in Figure 4.2 is very useful for structuring our discussion and for seeing clearly the different elements that come into play within ethical decision-making. However, such an approach is not without its problems, and as we go through the chapter, you might notice that it is not always particularly straightforward

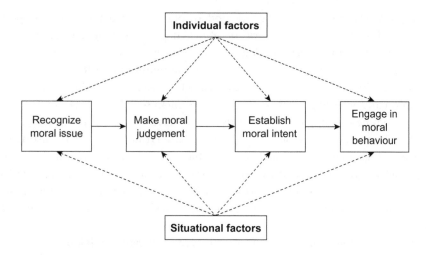

Figure 4.2. Framework for understanding ethical decision-making

(nor, some would argue, sensible) to break down these various elements into discrete units. Many of the various stages and influences are, to differing degrees, related, perhaps even interdependent. It can thus seem quite optimistic at times to separate out an individual factor and attempt to identify its unique role in the process of ethical decision-making. Nonetheless, these are criticisms that can be levelled at *all* models of this type, and we feel that as long as one is aware that the model is intended not as a definitive representation of ethical decision-making, but as a relatively simple way to present a complex process, such problems are not too serious. Finally, it is also worth mentioning that ethical decision-making models have largely originated in the USA, and this can sometimes give a national or cultural bias to the types of issues and considerations that might be included. Let us just briefly then review the European perspective before continuing.

European perspective on ethical decision-making

In Chapter 1 we discussed some of the differences in business ethics between America and Europe, and we will again meet some of these in this chapter about ethical decision-making. As we mentioned in Chapter 1, in America the central focus of the business ethics subject tends to be individual actors and their behaviour, whereas in Europe there is more interest in the design of economic institutions and how they function in a morally desirable way and/or encourage moral behaviour in business actors. This difference in perspective becomes quite visible with the topic of ethical decision-making since we could argue that research on *individual factors* influencing ethical decision-making has a strong US bias, whilst *situational factors*, on the other hand, have been subject to a lengthy debate principally originated and driven by European authors. The significance of this difference is that a focus on individual factors is consistent with the US focus on choice *within* constraints, whilst a focus on situational factors reflects the more European concern with the *constraints* themselves.

To begin with, the very founders of modern organizational theory in Europe have stressed the influence of *social contexts* on ethical decision-making. For example, in the nineteenth century, the French sociologist Émile Durkheim (1993) discussed the emergence of, and necessity for, new work-related moral communities due to the effects of the industrial revolution in eroding the traditional value systems that held societies together (Thompson and McHugh 2002). Similarly, the German sociologist Max Weber, to name another prominent example from the early twentieth century, shed a critical light on the ethical basis and influence of bureaucratic organizations (du Gay 2000). He distinguished between actions that were guided by an 'ethics of ultimate ends' and an 'ethics of responsibility'.[1] Whilst the first would represent an idealistic view of man, reflecting a person's real moral convictions rooted in social good, the latter is an ethics that sees responsibility for the pursuit of the organization's goals as the ultimate moral imperative (Parkin 1982).

We will discuss the influence of bureaucratic organizations on individual actors in more detail later in the chapter. However, along these lines, the Polish sociologist Zigmunt Bauman (1991) has more recently argued not only that there is an *influence* of bureaucratic organization on the morality of actors, but he regards the two as *mutually exclusive*. We have come across Bauman already in Chapter 3 as one of the key thinkers in postmodern ethics (100–103). As such, he contends that organizational dynamics act to neutralize the 'moral impulse' of the individual. Rational organizations require loyalty, discipline, and obedience, all of which, Bauman contends, stifle the personal and emotional aspects that are crucial for a sense of morality to exist (ten Bos and Willmott 2001). We will explore some of these organizational influences on ethical decision-making later on in this chapter. We will start, though, with an examination of key individual influences.

Individual influences on ethical decision-making

What is it about you or me that makes us act in a particular way when confronted by an ethical problem? Individual influences on ethical decision-making relate to these facets of the individual who is actually going through the decision-making process. Clearly all employees bring certain traits and characteristics with them into an organization, and these are likely to influence the way in which the employee thinks and behaves in response to ethical dilemmas. Although this could be taken to suggest that some people are simply more ethical than others, this is rather too simplistic a view. Individual factors can also account for why some people are perhaps more swayed than others into unethical conduct because of the influence of their colleagues. Similarly, individual factors can explain why some people perceive particular actions to be unethical whilst others do not. Hence, the issue is not so much about determining the reasons why people are more or less ethical, but is more concerned with the factors influencing us to think, feel, act, and perceive in certain ways

---

[1] The English translations are quite misleading, as 'ethics of responsibility' ('Verantwortungsethik') sounds more positive than in its original German rendition, whereas 'ethics of ultimate ends' ('Gesinnungsethik') seems rather narrow for Weber's argument.

Factor	Influence on ethical decision-making
Age and gender	Very mixed evidence leading to unclear associations with ethical decision-making.
National and cultural characteristics	Appear to have a significant effect on ethical beliefs, as well as views of what is deemed an acceptable approach to certain business issues.
Education and employment	Somewhat unclear, although some clear differences in ethical decision-making between those with different educational and professional experience seem to be present.
Psychological factors: Cognitive moral development Locus of control	Small but significant effect on ethical decision-making. At most a limited effect on decision-making, but can be important in predicting the apportioning of blame/approbation.
Personal integrity	Significant influence likely, but lack of inclusion in models and empirical tests.
Moral imagination	A new issue for inclusion with considerable explanatory potential.

Figure 4.3. Individual influences on ethical decision-making

that are relevant to ethical decision-making. Over the years, researchers have surfaced a number of important individual influences, as we shall now see. The factors and their likely influence on ethical decision-making are summarized in **Figure 4.3**.

Age and gender

Are men or women more ethical? This is no doubt an interesting question, and, according to Ford and Richardson (1994), gender has been the individual influence on ethical decision-making in business most often subjected to investigation. However, overall the results have been less than conclusive, with different studies offering contradictory results (Loe et al. 2000). For example, half of the studies reported by Ford and Richardson (1994) conclude that women are more ethical than men, whilst half suggest no difference.

Perhaps, though, the problem is more with the studies themselves and the questions they seek to answer (Loe et al. 2000). As we have said, it is rather simplistic to assume that some people are just more ethical than others, and even if this could be claimed, there seems no obvious reason why gender would be an important determinant. However, as we saw when discussing feminist ethics in the previous chapter (which we shall return to shortly below), there is evidence to suggest that the *ways* in which men and women think and act in response to ethical dilemmas might differ.

Another basic factor we might look at is whether age makes any difference to ethical decision-making. However, a similar problem is present with age as with gender. Empirical tests have tended to report very mixed results, with no clear picture emerging on the influence of age on ethical beliefs and action. Indeed, again it would seem to be too generalized to categorize certain age groups as 'more ethical' than others, although certain *experiences* might in themselves shape the way in which we recognize and respond to ethical problems.

National and cultural characteristics

When we meet people from different countries and cultures, either at home or overseas, it doesn't take long before we start to see certain differences in what they perceive as ethical or unethical, or how they might go about dealing with ethical issues. Issues of nationality, ethnicity, and religion have therefore been of increasing interest to researchers of ethical decision-making, as one might expect given the trends towards globalization identified in Chapter 1.

As we argued previously, people from different cultural backgrounds are still likely to have different beliefs about right and wrong, different values, etc. and this will inevitably lead to variations in ethical decision-making across nations, religions, and cultures. Whilst we will be addressing this in more detail in Chapter 7 (when we move on to focus on business ethics and employees), there is again a problem here with assuming that people from particular nations, religions, or ethnic groups can simply be deemed to be 'more ethical' or 'less ethical' in their decision-making than others. Research has, however, suggested that nationality can have a significant effect on ethical beliefs, as well as views of what is deemed an acceptable approach to certain business issues.[2] These differences have been noted not just in the somewhat obvious cases of managers from developed and from less developed countries, but also between those from different European countries and those from Europe and the USA.

Geert Hofstede's (1980; 1994) research has been extremely influential in shaping our understanding of these differences. Based on surveys completed by IBM employees throughout the world, Hofstede suggests that differences in cultural knowledge and beliefs across countries—our 'mental programming'—can be explained in terms of four dimensions:

• **Individualism/collectivism.** This represents the degree to which one is autonomous and driven primarily to act for the benefit of one's self, contrasted with a more social orientation that emphasizes group working and community goals.

• **Power distance.** This represents the extent to which the unequal distribution of hierarchical power and status are accepted and respected.

• **Uncertainty avoidance.** This measures the extent of one's preference for certainty, rules, and absolute truths.

• **Masculinity/femininity.** The extent to which an emphasis is placed on valuing money and things (masculinity) versus valuing people and relationships (femininity).

Hofstede's dimensions can be seen to explain certain differences in ethical decision-making. For example, someone from an individualist culture such as found in northern Europe and America might be more likely to reflect on ethical problems alone in order to make their own independent decision, whilst someone from a collectivist culture such as

---

[2] There are numerous studies which have examined this question, including Becker and Fritzsche's (1987) study of French, German, and US managers; Lysonski and Gaidis's (1991) study of US, Danish, and New Zealand business students; Nyaw and Ng's (1994) study of Canadian, Japanese, Hong Kong, and Taiwanese business students; Jackson and Artola's (1997) study of French and German managers; and Jackson's (2001) ten-country study across four continents.

found in southern Europe and Latin America might be more likely to consult with the wider group. Similarly, someone from a high power distance culture (i.e. one that respects and accepts stratification in power and status) like Japan or China might be less willing to question the orders given by their superiors, even if they felt they were being asked to do something ethically questionable. Empirical work has generally tended to support these sorts of relationships (e.g. Jackson 2001).

Clearly, though, with the eroding of the territorial basis for business activities—exemplified by rising international trade, frequent international business travel, and growth in expatriate employment—the robustness and consistency of beliefs and values inherited simply from our cultural origin is likely to be increasingly weakened. For example, a Greek IT consultant with an MBA from Manchester University and five years' experience working for an American bank in Frankfurt might be expected to differ significantly from a Greek IT manager who has always lived and worked in Athens. This suggests that education and employment might also play a significant role in shaping our ethical beliefs and values.

Education and employment

The type and quality of education received by individuals as well as their professional training and experience might also be considered to be important individual influences on ethical decision-making. For example, research reveals that business students not only rank lower in moral development than students in other subjects such as law, but are also more likely to engage in academic cheating, such as plagiarism (McCabe et al. 1991; McCabe and Treviño 1993)! Business students have also been found to be driven more by self-centred values than other students (McCabe et al. 1991).

Clearly, business education devoid of an ethics component can reinforce the 'myth of amoral business' (De George 1999)—the idea that business is not expected to be concerned with questions of morality. Hence, although some aspects of individual morality may be developed through upbringing and general education, there is also a place for ethics training in enhancing people's ability to recognize and deal with ethics problems in the workplace (Treviño and Nelson 1999). Overall, then, whilst the relationships between ethical decision-making and employment experience and education still remain somewhat unclear (Loe et al. 2000), some clear differences in ethical decision-making between those with different educational and professional experience seem to be present. Our hope is certainly that by studying business ethics in the critical and pluralistic fashion we advocate here you may expand and refine your analytical skills in dealing with ethical issues and problems.

Psychological factors

Psychological factors are concerned with cognitive processes, in other words, how people actually think. From an ethical decision-making point of view, knowing about the differences in the cognitive processes of individuals can clearly help us to improve our understanding of how people decide what is the morally right or wrong course of action.

Level	Stage	Explanation	Illustration
I Pre-conventional	1 Obedience and punishment	Individuals define right and wrong according to expected rewards and punishments from authority figures.	Whilst this type of moral reasoning is usually associated with small children, we can also see that business people frequently make unethical decisions because they think their company would either reward them or let them go unpunished (see Gellerman 1986).
	2 Instrumental purpose and exchange	Individuals are concerned with their own immediate interests and define right according to whether there is fairness in the exchanges or deals they make to achieve those interests.	An employee might cover for the absence of a co-worker so that their own absences might subsequently be covered for in return—a 'you scratch my back, I'll scratch yours' reciprocity (Treviño and Nelson 1999).
II Conventional	3 Interpersonal accord, conformity, and mutual expectations	Individuals live up to what is expected of them by their immediate peers and those close to them.	An employee might decide that using company resources such as the telephone, the internet, and email for personal use whilst at work is acceptable because everyone else in their office does it.
	4 Social accord and system maintenance	Individuals' consideration of the expectations of others broadens to social accord more generally, rather than just the specific people around them.	A factory manager may decide to provide employee benefits and salaries above the industry minimum in order to ensure that employees receive wages and conditions deemed acceptable by consumers, pressure groups, and other social groups.
III Post-conventional	5 Social contract and individual rights	Individuals go beyond identifying with others' expectations, and assess right and wrong according to the upholding of basic rights, values, and contracts of society.	The public affairs manager of a food manufacturer may decide to reveal which of the firm's products contain genetically modified ingredients out of respect for consumers' rights to know, even though they are not obliged to by law, and have not been pressurized by consumers or anyone else.
	6 Universal ethical principles	Individuals will make decisions autonomously based on self-chosen universal ethical principles, such as justice, equality, and rights, which they believe everyone should follow.	A purchasing manager may decide that it would be wrong to continue to buy products or ingredients that are tested on animals because he believes this doesn't respect animal rights to be free from suffering.

Figure 4.4. Stages of cognitive moral development

Source: Adapted from Ferrell et al. (2002); Kohlberg (1969); Treviño and Nelson (1999).

We shall look at two of the most prominent psychological factors: cognitive moral development and locus of control.

Cognitive moral development

The most common theory to have been utilized to explain these cognitive processes comes from the psychology discipline, namely Lawrence Kohlberg's (1969) theory of *cognitive moral development* (CMD). In fact, virtually all current models of ethical decision-making in business utilize this theory (Fraedrich et al. 1994).[3]

Kohlberg developed CMD theory to explain the different reasoning processes that individuals would use to make ethical judgements as they matured through childhood into adulthood. Hence:

> Cognitive moral development refers to the different levels of reasoning that an individual
> can apply to ethical issues and problems.

Kohlberg suggested that three broad levels of moral development could be discerned, namely:

• **Level one.** The individual exhibits a concern with self-interest and external rewards and punishments;

• **Level two.** The individual does what is expected of them by others;

• **Level three.** The individual is developing more autonomous decision-making based on principles of rights and justice rather than external influences.

Kohlberg identified two specific stages within each of the three levels, giving six stages of moral development altogether. **Figure 4.4** sets out these six stages, providing an illustration of how each stage might be manifested in business ethics decisions.

CMD theory proposes that as one advances through the different stages, one is moving to a 'higher' level of moral reasoning. The important thing to remember about CMD theory, however, is that it is not so much *what* is decided that is at issue, but *how* the decision is reached in terms of the individual's reasoning process. Two people at different levels could conceivably make the same decision, but as a result of different ways of thinking. All the same, Kohlberg argued that the higher the stage of moral reasoning, the more 'ethical' the decision.

Empirical research by Kohlberg and others[4] has led to the conclusion that most people tend to think with level two reasoning (hence its 'conventional' tag). Research into the cognitive schema of business managers has also tended to place them at level two (e.g. Weber 1990). This means that most of us decide what is right according to *what we perceive others to believe*, and according to *what is expected of us by others*. As Treviño and Nelson (1999: 107) suggest, '[Most] individuals aren't autonomous decision makers who strictly

---

[3] For example, CMD is included in ethical decision-making models by Ferrell et al. (1989; 2002), Jones (1991), Treviño (1986), and Treviño and Nelson (1999), among others.

[4] James Rest (1986), whose depiction of the stages of ethical decision-making we presented earlier in the chapter, has been a vigorous proponent of cognitive moral development and devised a widely used measuring instrument, called the Defining Issues Test. A summary of some the vast amount of empirical work carried out can be found in Rest (1986), some of which is also presented in Goolsby and Hunt (1992).

follow an internal moral compass. They look up and around to see what their superiors and their peers are doing and saying, and they use these cues as a guide to action.'

As we shall see shortly, this implies that the situational context in which employees might find themselves within their organization is likely to be very influential in shaping their ethical decision-making—although according to Kohlberg, this influence will vary according to whether employees are at stage three or four in moral development.

Although CMD theory has been very influential in the ethical decision-making literature, there have been numerous criticisms of the theory. It is worth remembering that the theory was initially developed in a non-business context, from interviews with young American males—hardly representative of the men and women employed in businesses across the globe! Hence, according to Fraedrich et al. (1994), the most notable criticisms of CMD are the following:

• **Gender bias.** Perhaps the best known of Kohlberg's critics is one of his former students, Carol Gilligan, who claimed that the theory was gender biased due to its emphasis on the abstract principles esteemed by Kohlberg and his male subjects. As we saw in Chapter 3 (97–9), Gilligan (1982) argued that women tended to use an 'ethic of care' in deciding what was morally right, emphasizing empathy, harmony, and the maintenance of interdependent relationships rather than abstract principles. This work was subsequently influential in shaping **feminist ethics**, an approach to ethical theory that we discussed in the previous chapter.

• **Implicit value judgements.** Derry (1987) and others have expanded Gilligan's criticism to suggest that CMD privileges rights and justice above numerous other bases of morality, such as those discussed in the previous chapter. Kohlberg has thus interjected his own value judgements regarding the 'most ethical' way of reasoning into what is essentially supposed to be a descriptive theory of how people *actually* think.

• **Invariance of stages.** Kohlberg's contention that we sequentially pass through discrete stages of moral development can be criticized if we observe that people either regress in CMD or, more importantly, use different moral reasoning strategies at different times and in different situations. Studies by Fraedrich and Ferrell (1992) and Weber (1990) for example both revealed cognitive inconsistency amongst managers across work and non-work situations when making ethical decisions. Essentially we don't always use the same reasoning when we are at work as we do at home or on the sports field. This is the reason why in this chapter we highlight the context dependency of business people's reasoning about ethical problems (Jones 1991; Thompson 1995).

Despite these criticisms, CMD appears to be widely accepted as an important element in the individual influences on ethical decision-making. Various empirical studies have suggested that it at least plays some role in the decision-making process (e.g. Treviño and Youngblood 1990; Goolsby and Hunt 1992), although its influence appears to be rather more limited than that proposed by Kohlberg.

Locus of control

The second psychological factor commonly identified as an influence on ethical thinking is *locus of control*.

An individual's locus of control determines the extent to which they believe that they have control over the events in their life.

So someone with a high *internal* locus of control believes that the events in their life can be shaped by their own efforts, whereas someone with a high *external* locus of control believes that events tend to be the result of the actions of others, or luck, or fate. You might think of this in terms of how you might respond if you received a grade for your business ethics exam that was lower than you expected. If you had an external locus of control you might automatically blame your professor for setting a difficult test, or you might blame Crane and Matten's book for not preparing you properly. If you had an internal locus of control, however, your first thoughts would probably be more along the lines of questioning whether you had really done enough preparation for the exam.

In terms of ethical decision-making, Treviño and Nelson (1999) suggest that those with a strong internal locus of control might be expected to be more likely to consider the consequences of their actions for others, and may take more responsibility for their actions. Internals may also be more likely to stick to their own beliefs, and thus be more resistant to peer group pressure to act in a way that violates those beliefs. However, there hasn't actually been a great deal of empirical research on the effects of locus of control on ethical decision-making in business. What research has been conducted, though, gives a generally mixed picture: whilst some studies have discerned no significant effect (e.g. Singhapakdi and Vitell 1990), others have identified a noticeable influence (e.g. Treviño and Youngblood 1990).

Overall, even among the individual factors, it would appear that locus of control has, at most, only a relatively limited effect on ethical decision-making. Nonetheless, understanding whether your co-workers have internal or external loci of control can be important for predicting how they will respond to business ethics problems, and particularly how they apportion blame or offer approbation when faced with the consequences of those decisions.

Personal integrity

One word that has increasingly surfaced in relation to ethical decision-making is *integrity*.

Integrity is defined as an adherence to moral principles or values.

The original meaning of the word is concerned with unity and wholeness, and we can see that an adherence to moral principles essentially means that one maintains a consistency or unity in one's beliefs and actions, regardless of any inducement or temptation to deviate from them.

For example, let us consider the issue of **whistleblowing**, a subject typically of interest to scholars and students of business ethics. Whistleblowing refers to acts by employees to expose their employers for perceived ethical violations. If, for instance, an engineer identifies a safety problem with one of her firm's products, she may decide to tell her work colleagues or her boss. As a result the engineer may be encouraged to ignore the problem or desist from taking any further action as her superiors have taken on responsibility for the issue. However, if the problem persists, even after further warnings from the engineer, she may choose to reveal the problem—or 'blow the whistle'—by approaching an industry regulator, a journalist, or some other outside agency. Although there are clearly various other factors involved, such acts of external whistleblowing often require the employee to maintain their personal integrity, or commitment to a set of principles, despite being confronted with numerous difficulties, obstacles, and opposition. This is especially the case since whistleblowers have often subsequently been faced with a range of negative consequences for their actions. This includes victimization by colleagues or superiors as a result of their 'betrayal'; being passed over for promotion; job loss; even 'blacklisting' to prevent them getting another job in the same field (Rothschild and Miethe 1999).

Ethics in Action 4.1 describes a true-life example of whistleblowing that you may have encountered at the movies, in the Oscar-nominated film *The Insider*. As the experiences of Jeffrey Wigand, as depicted in *The Insider*, attest, certain acts of ethical decision-making appear to be strongly influenced by the degree of personal integrity of the individual. Think for example of a situation where all of your work colleagues habitually steal small items of company property from the storeroom. A group can easily see this as 'acceptable' simply because 'everyone does it'. If this was something that you usually would not agree with, though, it might require some degree of integrity—that is, adherence to your moral principles—to register your disapproval with your colleagues, and may even need some courage to report it to a superior. Certainly, then, the exercising of integrity also often requires some level of protection from possible recriminations. Ethics in Action 4.1, for example, raises questions about whether Wigand's experiences would be similar in Europe, given the different legislative context surrounding whistleblowing in various European countries.

■ **Think theory**

Read Ethics in Action 4.1 and think about the decision faced by Jeffrey Wigand from the perspective of ethics of duty. Who did he have duties towards, and why did these duties arise? Is it possible to decide which of these duties is paramount, or are other theoretical approaches preferable to ethics of duty in this case?

Despite increasing attention to the importance of the issue of integrity (e.g. Solomon 1999), most descriptive models of ethical decision-making have not tended to include it as a factor influencing how we decide in business ethics matters. Whilst it would appear that this might be likely to change as we start to learn more about its role and effects, for the moment, business ethics scholars seem to be largely uncertain as to how and why personal integrity affects the process of ethical decision-making.

Moral imagination

Finally, another individual factor which has been accorded increasing attention in business ethics over the past few years is *moral imagination*. Moral imagination is concerned less with whether one has, or sticks to, a set of moral values, and more with whether one

The Insider: getting inside whistleblowing and its protection
....

The Insider (dir. Michael Mann) is based on the real-life events surrounding the decision by Jeffrey Wigand (played by Russell Crowe) to blow the whistle on the US tobacco giant Brown and Williamson. Released in 1999, the film chronicles the events of the mid-1990s when Wigand, who had been a senior vice-president of research at Brown and Williamson, was persuaded by Lowell Bergman (played by Al Pacino), the producer of the CBS TV programme *60 Minutes*, to make public highly sensitive inside information from the tobacco industry. Wigand was in a position to prove not only that cigarette company bosses had lied under oath before Congress (in claiming that they did not know that nicotine was addictive), but also that nicotine levels were manipulated by the firms to make cigarettes more addictive.

As a senior scientist, Wigand is shown to be deeply disturbed by the results of his studies at Brown and Williamson, which indicated that cigarettes were essentially 'a delivery device for nicotine'. In voicing his disagreement with company policy, however, Wigand was removed from the Brown and Williamson payroll in March 1993, ostensibly for 'poor communication skills'. On departure, he is pressurized into signing a confidentiality agreement with the firm which prevents him from making further disclosures in return for guarantees on his severance pay and continued medical coverage. If he goes public, therefore, he risks facing lawsuits as well as sacrificing his financial security.

The Pacino character, Bergman, eventually persuades Wigand to do an interview with *60 Minutes* —despite death threats and the very real possibility of losing his wife and going to jail. However, at the last moment, threats of legal action by Brown and Williamson prompt CBS to pull the interview before transmission, rather than risk a lucrative takeover that is due to earn CBS bosses millions of dollars in payoffs. Wigand is betrayed and Bergman's story is sacrificed for financial gain. Bergman, however, doesn't give up, and, through complex manipulation of the power of the media, eventually succeeds in airing the story some months later. In real life, Wigand's revelations eventually led to the $236bn settlement against the big tobacco firms in the USA.

The film vividly depicts the problems and dangers that can confront whistleblowers intent on maintaining their integrity. Ironically, the USA actually has some of the best legal protection for whistleblowers, particularly at the state level. In Europe, the picture is somewhat mixed. Whilst in many countries there is an institutional structure which facilitates free disclosure by employees (e.g. 'openness laws' in Sweden, and workers' councils in Germany), the UK has perhaps the strongest specific legal protection for whistleblowers of any country in the world (after the introduction of the Public Interest Disclosure at Work Act 1998). Few other countries actually have specific legislation which would have protected Wigand in his battle to expose the tobacco giants. However, there are signs that this is changing: the Netherlands (where whistleblowers are called 'bell ringers') is due to introduce a new whistleblowers law, and interest is also growing in Belgium, Germany, and elsewhere. Indeed, new OECD Guidelines for Multi-National Enterprises include whistleblower provisions, and the Council of Europe has requested its nations to pass whistleblower protection laws as part of their convention against corruption.

SOURCES

The Insider, Buena Vista Home Entertainment, 2002.
www.whistleblower.org.
www.pcaw.co.uk.

....

has 'a sense of the variety of possibilities and moral consequences of their decisions, the ability to imagine a wide range of possible issues, consequences, and solutions' (Werhane 1998: 76). This means that moral imagination is the creativity with which an individual is able to reflect about an ethical dilemma. Interest in moral imagination has been driven by the recognition that people often bracket their personal moralities and moral considerations whilst at work (Jackall 1988). According to Werhane (1998), higher levels of moral imagination can allow us to see beyond the rules of the game that seem to be operating in the workplace, and beyond the day-to-day supposed 'realities' of organizational life, so as to question prevailing ways of framing and addressing organizational problems. Thus, rather than accepting the usual organizational recipe for looking at, prioritizing, and dealing with things, those with greater moral imagination should be able to envisage a greater set of moral problems, perspectives, and outcomes.

■ **Think theory**

Think about the notion of moral imagination from the perspective of our three different approaches to normative ethical theory: absolutism, relativism, and pluralism. Would you say that moral imagination would be of help or hindrance to applying ethical theory in each of these approaches?

As with personal integrity, moral imagination has yet to be included in typical models of ethical decision-making, and has been subjected to little, if any, empirical testing. However, it holds significant potential for helping us to uncover why there is variation between individuals in the effect of work context on their ethical decision-making—a vital issue if we are to understand the relative influence of our two sets of factors, individual and situational. Hence, it would seem timely now to consider in more depth the second of our sets of factors, namely those dealing with the situation in which the decision is taking place.

Situational influences on decision-making

The preceding section sought to examine the influence of various differences between individuals in the judgements and decisions they make when faced with ethical problems. However, as we saw, the judgements and decisions that people make in businesses, and, perhaps more importantly, the things they actually do, cannot be successfully explained simply in terms of these individual traits. After all, many people appear to have 'multiple ethical selves' (Treviño and Nelson 1999: 149)—that is, they make different decisions in different situations. In fact, most evidence we have points to situational influences being at least equally, and probably *more* important, in shaping our ethical decision-making. **Ethical Dilemma 4** offers a typical situation which showcases a number of situational influences and constraints on ethical decision-making.

For a start, the decision process we go through will vary greatly according to what type of issue it is that we are dealing with. Some issues will be perceived as relatively unimportant, and will therefore prompt us into fairly limited ethical decision-making, whereas issues seen as more intense may well necessitate deeper, and perhaps somewhat different,

A Friday fix?

You have recently been appointed as a sales consultant working for a small manufacturing company producing office furniture. It is Friday afternoon and, having had a busy but productive week, you have made plans to go out for a few drinks after work with two of your new work colleagues in the administration office.

Towards the end of the afternoon, one of the other sales consultants approaches you and asks you for a favour. He has been having a long meeting with a corporate client from whom he had been hoping to negotiate a substantial order. He tells you that the talks have gone very well, with the result that the client has agreed to place a large order. As is common practice at the company in such circumstances, he has promised to take the client out for dinner after the meeting at the company's expense. The reason he has come to you is that he has just received a call from home about a domestic problem, which means that he will have to leave work straight away and will not be able to take the client out as promised. There are no other sales consultants in the office, and he asks you if you have any plans for the evening, and, if not, whether you would mind taking his place.

You mention about the planned night out with your work colleagues, at which the other sales consultant says, 'Oh that should be fine—why not bring them along and the four of you go somewhere together? You can claim it all on expenses anyway, so the other two won't complain will they?' Knowing the company's strict rules about expense claims for hospitality, you point out that under the rules you would only be allowed to claim expenses for yourself and the client—the rules specifically state that for each outside guest only one member of staff is eligible for expenses. The other sales consultant shrugs and says that providing the claim is within the €200 limit for hospitality claims, the firm doesn't lose out really. 'Why not go somewhere a little bit cheaper than normal and let everyone benefit a little? After all, that's what I usually do, and it keeps up a good relationship with the office staff. If I didn't take them out for a treat every now and then, no one else would. And besides it will be nice for the client to see everyone being together as a team. It can be a bit embarrassing if you're there trying to impress a client and then have to apologize to the others for not being able to pay for them too. Just get the restaurant to give you a bill which says there are two of you so that you can make the expense form look like it's OK and no one will be any the wiser.'

You say that you'll have to check with the others to see what they want to do. They are both happy to go along with you and the client, and confirm that the other sales consultant usually includes the office staff in his expense claims. In fact, they say, the rules always seemed a little unfair to them and they were glad that the other sales consultant was thoughtful enough to bend the rules a bit occasionally to keep a good team atmosphere going. Pondering on this, you return to your desk to give the other sales consultant your decision.

Questions

1 What are the ethical issues at stake in this situation?
2 Set out the main influences which could impact upon your decision-making here.
3 What would you say to the other consultant? What steps would you then take?
4 In what way would your actions change if:
   (a) the other consultant was your immediate superior;
   (b) rather than working in a company, you were working for a charity.
5 What do you think most people would do in this situation? Why?

Type of factor	Factor	Influence on ethical decision-making
Issue-related	Moral intensity	Reasonably new factor, but evidence suggests significant effect on ethical decision-making.
	Moral framing	Fairly limited evidence, but existing studies show strong influence on some aspects of the ethical decision-making process, most notably moral awareness.
Context-related	Rewards	Strong evidence of relationship between rewards/punishments and ethical behaviour, although other stages in ethical decision-making have been less investigated.
	Authority	Good general support for a significant influence from immediate superiors and top management on ethical decision-making of subordinates.
	Bureaucracy	Significant influence on ethical decision-making well documented, but actually exposed to only limited empirical research. Hence, specific consequences for ethical decision-making remain contested.
	Work roles	Some influence likely, but lack of empirical evidence to date.
	Organizational culture	Strong overall influence, although implications of relationship between culture and ethical decision-making remain contested.
	National context	Limited empirical investigation, but some shifts in influence likely.

Figure 4.5. Situational influences on ethical decision-making

moral reflection. For example, if you worked in a bar you might think rather more deeply about the morality of taking €20 out of the cash register for yourself than you would about pouring your friends a couple of unauthorized drinks 'on the house'. These are what we call **issue-related factors**.

At another level, we must also remember that we are, after all, 'social animals'. Hence (as Kohlberg would suggest of the majority of us at a conventional level of morality), our beliefs and actions are largely shaped by what we see around us: the group norms, expectations, and roles we are faced with; the nature of the climate in which we work; and the rewards and punishments that we can expect as a consequence of our actions. These are **context-related factors**.

Accordingly, we can identify two main types of situational influences:

- Issue-related factors
- Context-related factors

The principal factors in these two categories, and their likely influence on ethical decision-making, are presented in **Figure 4.5**, and are discussed in more detail in the following sections.

Issue-related factors

Although initially absent from many models of ethical decision-making, issue-related factors have been increasingly recognized as important influences on the decisions business people make when faced with ethical problems. At one level, we need to consider the nature of the ethical issue itself, and in particular its degree of **moral intensity**—that is, how important the issue is to the decision-maker. However, it is also evident that, regardless of the intensity of an issue, we need also to consider how that issue is actually represented within the organization, in that some issues will be presented as important ethical issues, whilst others may not. Hence, we need to also consider the issue's **moral framing**. Such issue-related factors have been shown to influence both whether an individual actually recognizes the moral nature of a problem in the first place (i.e. the moral recognition stage) and also the way that people actually think about and act upon the problem (the subsequent stages in the ethical decision-making process).

Moral intensity

The notion of moral intensity was initially proposed by Thomas Jones (1991) as a way of expanding ethical decision-making models to incorporate the idea that the relative importance of the ethical issue would itself have some bearing on the process that decision-makers go through when faced with ethical problems. Jones (1991: 374–8) proposes that the intensity of an issue will vary according to six factors:

- **Magnitude of consequences.** This is the expected sum of the harms (or benefits) for those impacted by the problem or action. Obviously, an issue will be felt more intensely if the consequences are significant, such as health problems or death as a result of a faulty product.

- **Social consensus.** This is the degree to which people are in agreement over the ethics of the problem or action. Moral intensity is likely to increase when it is certain that an act will be deemed unethical by others.

- **Probability of effect.** This refers to the likelihood that the harms (or benefits) are actually going to happen.

- **Temporal immediacy.** This is concerned with the speed with which the consequences are likely to occur. When outcomes are likely to take years to have much effect, decision-makers may perceive the moral intensity to be much lower—for example in the case of the long-term effects of smoking or other 'unhealthy' products.

- **Proximity.** This factor deals with the feeling of nearness (social, cultural, psychological, or physical) the decision-maker has for those impacted by his or her decision. For example poor working conditions in factories in one's own country might be experienced as a more intense moral issue than poor conditions in a developing world country.

- **Concentration of effect.** Here we are concerned with the extent to which the consequences of the action are concentrated heavily on a few, or lightly on many. For example, many people may feel that cheating a person out of a hundred Euros is much more morally intense than cheating the same sum out of a large multinational with millions of shareholders.

Jones's (1991) original formulation of moral intensity is theoretical (based largely on social psychology), but has subsequently been exposed to empirical testing, providing good support for his propositions (e.g. Morris and McDonald 1995; Frey 2000). However, we would suggest that the intensity of an issue is not necessarily an objective, factual variable, but rather depends on how the issue and its intensity is understood and made meaningful within the organization. This is where moral framing comes in.

Moral framing

Whilst it may be possible to determine the degree of intensity a moral issue should have to decision-makers according to Jones's (1991) six variables, it is clear that people in different organizational contexts are likely to perceive that intensity differently. The same problem or dilemma can be perceived very differently according to the way that the issue is framed. For example, imagine that a student talks about 'cutting and pasting some material from the internet' into their assignment. This may sound quite innocuous. But imagine that instead the student says, 'I plagiarized something I found on the internet', or even 'I stole someone's ideas and passed them off as my own'! This would give a very different impression, and would make us sense a deeper moral importance about the student's actions. The way in which moral issues are framed is therefore a key influence on ethical decision-making.

As we can see from the example above, probably the most important aspect of moral framing is the language in which moral issues are couched. As Treviño and Nelson (1999: 101) state: 'Using moral language (words like integrity, honesty, fairness, propriety—or lying, cheating, stealing) will more likely trigger moral thinking because these terms are attached to existing cognitive categories that have moral content.' The problem is that many people in business are reluctant to ascribe moral terms to their work, even if acting for moral reasons, or if their actions have obvious moral consequences. Bird and Waters (1989) describe this as **moral muteness**. In a widely cited research project based on interviews with managers, they found that groups of managers would tend to reframe moral actions and motives, and talk instead of doing things for reasons of practicality, organizational interests, and economic good sense. According to Bird and Waters (1989), managers would do this out of concerns regarding perceived threats to:

• **Harmony.** Managers tended to believe that moral talk would disturb organizational harmony by provoking confrontation, recrimination, and finger-pointing;

• **Efficiency.** Managers often felt that moral talk could cloud issues, making decision-making more difficult, time-consuming, and inflexible;

• **Image of power and effectiveness.** Managers also felt that their own image might suffer since being associated with ethics could be seen as idealistic and utopian, and lacking sufficient robustness for effective management.

These are very real concerns for people employed at all levels in companies, and the dangers not only of moral talk, but of being seen as overly involved in business ethics, can impact negatively on employees working in organizations where such issues are viewed with suspicion. Andrew Crane's (2001a) study of managers involved in environmental programmes highlights some of these concerns and problems, suggesting that fears of being marginalized can lead managers to engage in a process of **amoralization**. That is, they seek to distance themselves and their projects from being defined as ethically motivated or ethical in nature, and instead build a picture of corporate rationality suffused with justifications of corporate self-interest. Hence, even with ostensibly 'intense' ethical issues such as environmental protection, many workers remain distant and disengaged from the potential moral dimensions of their jobs.

Context-related factors

Our second group of situational influences is context-related factors. By context, we mean the organizational context in which an employee will be working—especially the expectations and demands placed on business people within the work environment that are likely to influence their perceptions of what is the morally right course of action to take. These factors appear to be especially important in shaping ethical decision-making within organizations. Perhaps more importantly for the management of business ethics, they are also, as we shall see, probably the main factors that can be addressed in order to *improve* ethical decision-making in the workplace.

Systems of reward

We tend to take it for granted that people are likely to do what they are rewarded for—for example, many organizations offer commission or bonuses for salespeople in order to motivate them to achieve greater numbers of sales—yet it is easy to forget that this has implications for ethical conduct too. For example, if an organization rewards its salespeople for the number of sales they make, then those salespeople may be tempted to compromise ethical standards in their dealings with customers in order to earn more commission. This would particularly be the case if the organization did not appear to punish those salespeople who were seen to behave unethically towards their customers, for example by exaggerating a product's benefits, or misleading customers about a competitor's products. Quite simply, ethical violations that go unpunished are likely to be repeated.

Similarly, adherence to ethical principles and standards stands less chance of being repeated and spread throughout a company when it goes unnoticed and unrewarded— or still worse, when it is actually punished, as we saw with the case of whistleblowing. Sometimes, however, the effects of rewards and punishments may not even be direct; employees may sense the prevailing approach to business ethics in their organization by looking at who gets promoted and who doesn't, or who seems to get the favour of the boss and who doesn't, and interpret 'correct' behaviour from the experiences of their more or less fortunate colleagues.

There is considerable evidence to suggest that employees' ethical decision-making is indeed influenced by the systems of reward they see operating in the workplace. We have already seen in the previous section how Crane's (2001a) research revealed that fears of marginalization and lack of progression could influence managers to avoid the explicit moral framing of problems and issues. Robert Jackall's (1988) extensive research into managers' rules for success in the workplace further reveals that what is regarded as 'right' in the workplace is often that which gets rewarded. For instance, he reports a former vice-president of a large firm saying: 'What is right in the corporation is not what is right in a man's home or in his church. *What is right in the corporation is what the guy above you wants from you.* That's what morality is in the corporation' (Jackall 1988: 6).

Tony Watson (1998) contends that managers are actually more likely to take a balanced approach, whereby pragmatic concerns and instrumental rewards are consciously inter-woven with moral considerations in management decision-making. Survey work, however, has certainly tended to support a strong relationship between rewards and ethical behaviour, with Loe et al. (2000) reporting that a majority of studies have revealed a significant correla-tion between the rewarding of unethical behaviour and the continuation of such behaviour.

Authority

This leads us to also consider the issue of authority. People don't just do what gets rewarded, they do what they are told to do—or, perhaps more correctly, what they *think* they're being told to do. Sometimes this can be a direct instruction from a superior to do something that the subordinate does not necessarily question or refuse to do because of their lower status in the hierarchy. At other times, the manager may not be directly instructing the employee to do something unethical, but their instructions to the employee may appear to leave little option but to act in a questionable manner. For example, a university professor may ask their Ph.D. student to grade 200 undergraduate exam scripts in two days, leaving the Ph.D. student insufficient time to even read all of the scripts, let alone mark them competently. As a result, the student might resort to grading the scripts in an arbitrary and unfair way.

Managers can also have an influence over their subordinates' ethical behaviour by setting a bad example. Many of us tend to look up to our superiors to determine what passes for ethical behaviour in the workplace. Significantly, however, employees often seem to perceive their superiors as lacking in ethical integrity. Posner and Schmidt's (1992) widely cited surveys of US managers suggested that more than a third of lower- and middle-ranking managers felt that managers in their companies often engaged in behaviour that they personally considered unethical. More recent evidence suggests that less than half of the employees of large and medium-sized organizations rate their leaders as having high personal integrity (see Ferrell et al. 2002: 135).

Finally, it is evident that those in authority can influence ethical decision-making by employees simply by looking the other way when confronted with potential problems. For example, in 1999, managers at Ford Motor Company's largest UK plant in Dagenham were accused of ignoring complaints, and allowing a culture of racial harassment to develop in the plant, leading to the victimization and bullying of Asian and other non-white workers. It took an employment tribunal, walkouts by workers, union condemnation, and the threat of an official inquiry by the Commission for Racial Equality before Ford managers accepted there was a problem and committed to tackle racial tensions at the plant.[5]

Bureaucracy

Underlying the influence of rewards, punishments, and authority is the degree of bureau-cracy in business organizations. Bureaucracy is a type of formal organization based on

---

[5] BBC News (**www.bbc.co.uk/news**): 'Warning to Ford over racism' (24 Aug. 2000); 'Ford race row meeting' (25 Oct. 2000); 'Ford workers walkout' (5 Oct. 2000).

rational principles, and characterized by detailed rules and procedures, impersonal hierarchical relations, and a fixed division of tasks.

Based on the work of Max Weber (1947) regarding the bureaucratic form, as well as later discussions of bureaucracy in relation to morality by Robert Jackall (1988), Zigmunt Bauman (1989; 1993), and more recently René ten Bos (1997), bureaucracy has been argued to have a number of effects on ethical decision-making:[6]

- **Suppression of moral autonomy.** Individual morality tends to be subjugated to the functionally specific rules and roles of the bureaucratic organization. Thus, effective bureaucracy essentially 'frees' the individual from moral reflection and decision-making since she or he needs only to follow the prescribed rules and procedures laid down to achieve organizational goals. This can cause employees to act as 'moral robots', simply following the rules rather than thinking about why they are there, or questioning their purpose.

- **Instrumental morality.** Bureaucracy focuses organization members' attentions on the efficient achievement of organizational goals. Hence, morality will be made meaningful only in terms of conformity to established rules for achieving those goals—i.e. instrumentalized—rather than focusing attention on the moral substance of the goals themselves. Accordingly, ethical decision-making will focus on whether 'correct' procedures have been taken to achieve certain goals rather than whether the goals themselves are morally beneficial. Thus, loyalty rather than integrity ultimately becomes the hallmark of bureaucratic morality.

- **Distancing.** Bureaucracy serves to further suppress our own morality by distancing us from the consequences of our actions—for example a supermarket purchasing manager in Lyon is rarely going to be faced with the effects of their supply negotiations on farm workers producing the supermarket's coffee beans in Columbia.

- **Denial of moral status.** Finally, bureaucracy has been argued to render moral objects, such as people or animals, as things, variables, or a collection of traits. Thus, employees become human 'resources' that are means to some organizational end; consumers are reduced to a collection of preferences on a marketing database; animals become units of production or output that can be processed in a factory. The point is that by dividing tasks and focusing on efficiency, the totality of individuals as moral beings is lost and they are ultimately denied true moral status.

■ **Think theory**

Think about the theory proposed here—that bureaucracy suppresses morality. Consider a bureaucratic organization that you have had personal experience of and try to relate the four effects highlighted here to that organization. Does the theory seem to have much validity in this instance?

---

[6] Bureaucracy bashing has been a popular pastime for organization scholars for a considerable time, and business ethics writers have also tended to offer largely negative evaluations of the effects of bureaucracy on ethical decision-making. However, for a powerful and eloquent critique of some of these ideas, see du Gay (2000).

Work roles

As we have seen, the bureaucratic organization of work assigns people into specific spe-cializations or tasks that represent work roles. These are patterns of behaviour expected by others from a person occupying a certain position in an organization (Buchanan and Huczynski 1997: 374). Work roles can be *functional*—e.g. the role of an accountant, an engineer, or a shop assistant—or they can be *hierarchical*—the role of a director, manager, or supervisor, for example. Roles can encapsulate a whole set of expectations about what to value, how to relate to others, and how to behave.

These expectations are built up during formal education, training, and through experience, and can have a strong influence on a person's behaviour. For example, think about when you are in the lecture theatre or seminar room of your university or college. Most of you prob-ably naturally adopt the role of 'student' in the classroom—listening, taking notes, asking and answering questions when prompted—and the person taking the class will probably naturally adopt the role of 'teacher'. But it wouldn't take much for us to refuse to adopt those roles: for the students to stand up and walk out, or for the teacher to sit down and say nothing. The main reason we do not is the fact that, as a rule, we all seem to know how we are supposed to act and we stick to it fairly faithfully. We simply adopt our prescribed roles.

In the business ethics context, prescribed work roles, and the concomitant expectations placed on the person adopting the role, would appear to be significant influences on decision-making. Our individual morality, the values and beliefs we might normally hold, can be stifled by our adoption of the values and beliefs embedded in our work role. Perhaps the most vivid illustration of this is the Stanford Prison Experiment, which is the subject of **Ethics in Action 4.2**. This is about as powerful an example as you can get of how work roles can have substantial impacts on how we behave. However, whilst there is con-siderable evidence supporting a significant impact for work roles on organizational behaviour *generally*, there has as yet been rather limited research that has specifically addressed the impact of roles on *ethical* decision-making and behaviour. Nonetheless, the important thing to remember is that many of us will adopt different roles in different contexts, reinfor-cing this idea of people having multiple ethical selves. For example, many people take on different roles when with their family compared to when they are at work, or with their friends, or in other social situations. Roles are therefore not constant traits or facets of our personality (as was the case with our individual factors) but are highly contextual influences on our decision-making and behaviour.

Organizational norms and culture

Another potentially powerful influence on ethical decision-making is the group norms which delineate acceptable standards of behaviour within the work community—be this at the level of a small team of workers, a department, or the entire organization. Group norms essentially express the way in which things are, or should be, done in a certain environ-ment, and may well conflict with the official rules or procedures laid down by the organ-ization. For example, a group of office workers may agree amongst themselves that illegally pirating licensed software from work for home use is perfectly acceptable as an unofficial 'perk' of the job, for instance because it helps compensate for what they as a group see as

Ethics in Action 4.2

The Stanford Prison Experiment

The Stanford Prison Experiment, co-ordinated by Dr Philip Zimbardo, took place in 1971. This experiment frequently features in discussions about human psychology, roles, and ethical behaviour —and has achieved an enduring place in popular culture: it has not only served as the inspiration for a recent BBC TV show called *The Experiment* and a German movie, *Das Experiment*, but has also given its name to an American punk band, the Stanford Prison Experiment. So what accounts for the classic status of Zimbardo's experiment?

Zimbardo's plan was to take twenty-four average, healthy, middle-class, male college students and randomly assign them into one of two groups to play either prisoners or prison guards for a two-week period. His intention was to examine the psychology of prison life. The 'prisoners' were rounded up unexpectedly in a police squad car, blindfolded, handcuffed, and then locked into stark cells in the 'jail' in the basement of the Stanford University Psychology building. While the prisoners were given smocks and nylon stocking caps to wear, the guards were given uniforms, reflector sunglasses, clubs, and handcuffs—all of which emphasized their roles, minimized their individuality, and reinforced the power differentials between the two groups. Prisoners had to refer to guards as 'Mr Correction Officer', and guards were given only minimal instructions in order to achieve their goal of 'maintaining law and order'. Although physical violence was forbidden, they were allowed to devise their own rules and ways of working.

Although planned to last two weeks, the experiment was dramatically halted after only six days. Some of the guards had begun to treat the prisoners with excessive aggression and clearly took pleasure in exercising their power and inflicting psychological cruelty. The prisoners quickly became servile, dependent, helpless, and depressed, thinking only of their own survival and their hatred of the guards. After only thirty-six hours, the first prisoner had to be released due to fits of rage, uncontrollable crying, and depression. More prisoners were released in the days that followed, suffering from similar symptoms.

Despite being randomly allocated into the two roles, the study's participants had almost immediately begun to think of themselves as their prisoner and guard roles. They rapidly adopted the ways of thinking and behaving associated with those roles, and the arbitrary rules of the new organizational environment into which they had been thrust were accepted as legitimate. The participants became so programmed to think of themselves as prisoners that they did not feel capable of just withdrawing from the experiment, and the researchers themselves even became so locked into their roles as prison authorities that the prisoners' deteriorating physical and mental conditions were initially interpreted as faked in order to 'con' their way out of the experiment! The distinction between the real self and the role had blurred to such an extent that nearly all aspects of the individual's thoughts, feelings, and behaviours, whether as participant or researcher, had experienced dramatic changes. Zimbardo concluded that the experiment supported the theory that individual behaviour is largely controlled by role and situation rather than personal characteristics and traits.

Although it is clear that most workplaces are quite different from the prison environment, the Stanford experiment does show us that people very easily adopt the roles they are assigned to, and may quite readily fall into attitudes and behaviours which conflict significantly with those they have in 'normal' life. As Zimbardo himself said of the guards: 'These guys were all peaceniks. They became like Nazis.'

SOURCES

www.prisonexp.org.

Brockes, E. (2001). 'The Experiment', *Guardian* (G2), 16 Oct.: 2–3.

Buchanan, D., and Huczynski, A. (1997). *Organizational Behaviour: An Introductory Text*. Hemel Hempstead: Prentice Hall: 380–1.

For more details, go to: **www.prisonexp.org**, which has a detailed description of the experiment, including a slide show and video clips. There are also links for further reading.

■ **Think theory**

Think about what this experiment says about roles and moral relativism. Is it reasonable to justify behaviour on these grounds?

low wages. Group norms might thus relate to ways of acting, talking, justifying, dressing, even thinking and evaluating. As a result, group norms tend to be included within an expanded range of factors, including shared values, beliefs, and behaviours, that are captured by the notion of *organizational culture*.

Whilst there are numerous, often conflicting definitions of what organizational culture actually is, at a basic level, we can say that it represents the overall environment or climate found within the organization (or certain parts of it). Culture is further said to constitute particular meanings, beliefs, and common-sense knowledge which are shared among the members of the organization, and which are represented in taken-for-granted assumptions, norms, and values. Organizational culture has been widely identified as a key issue in shaping ethical decision-making. Not only has it been frequently included in models of ethical decision-making (e.g. Ferrell et al. 1989), but it has also been widely examined in empirical investigations (Loe et al. 2000). This is not particularly surprising, for there is wide-ranging evidence, as well as strong conceptual support, for the proposition that culture and ethical decision-making are profoundly interwoven (e.g. Sinclair 1993; Dahler-Larsen 1994; Starkey 1998). Clearly, as employees become socialized into particular ways of seeing, interpreting, and acting, this will shape the kinds of decisions they make when confronted with ethical problems. Cultural expectations and values can provide a strong influence on what we think of as 'right' and 'wrong'. For example, the failed US energy giant Enron was accused of developing a culture of dishonesty that culminated in the misleading accounting which brought down the firm in 2001. Our cultural understandings and knowledge can thus act as both facilitators and barriers to ethical reflection and behaviour.

As a consequence of such reasoning, many authors, such as Treviño and Nelson (1999) and Ferrell et al. (2002), thus speak of the need for an 'ethical culture' to enhance and reinforce ethical decision-making. However, as we shall see in the next chapter (when we move on to discuss ways of managing business ethics), there is considerable disagreement about how this should be done, or indeed, whether it is even possible or desirable. Certainly it would appear that the deliberate management of culture is an extremely challenging undertaking, and one where many of the outcomes will be unpredictable. Nonetheless, even though it may be unclear how to deal with organizational culture's influence on ethical decision-making, the very fact that there is some kind of relationship between the two would appear almost irrefutable.

National and cultural context

Finally, just as the culture of the organization or work group may influence ethical decision-making, so might the country or culture in which the individual's organization is located. This factor varies from the national and cultural characteristics discussed on pp. 118–19 as individual influences: at that time we were looking at the *nationality* of the individual making the decision; now we are considering the *nation* in which the decision is actually taking place, regardless of the decision-maker's nationality. As we have discussed a number of times in the book so far, different cultures still to some extent maintain different views of what is right and wrong, and these differences have significant effects on whether a moral issue is recognized, and the kind of judgements and behaviours entered into by individuals. For example, a French office manager working in the USA may start to become sensitized to different perceptions of what constitutes sexual harassment compared to their colleagues back in France. Or a Danish human resource manager might consider the issue of employment conditions quite differently should she be working in Indonesia rather than at home. However, with globalization eroding some of these national cultural differences, we might expect to see shifts in the influence of this factor, perhaps with more complex effects and interactions emerging.

Whilst some models have incorporated factors relating to the social and cultural environment (e.g. Hunt and Vitell 1986; Ferrell et al. 1989), there has been little, if any, empirical research investigating the effect of this on ethical decision-making, prompting authors such as Thompson (1995) to argue for much greater emphasis to be placed on the culturally situated decision-maker.

Summary

In this chapter we have discussed the various stages of and influences on ethical decision-making in business, so that by now you should have a reasonably clear picture of the overall process and its most important elements. The basic model presented in the chapter can be used to provide a clear outline of how these elements fit together, although, as we mentioned earlier, this model should be regarded simply as an illustration of the relationships involved, not as a definitive causal model. Having outlined both individual and situational influences on ethical decision-making, we would suggest that some individual factors—such as cognitive moral development, nationality, and personal integrity—are clearly influential, particularly, it would appear, on the moral judgements made by individuals.

However, in terms of recognizing ethical problems and actually doing something in response to them, it is situational factors that appear to be the most influential. This is important because it means that it is situational factors that are likely to be the most promising levers for attempts to manage and improve ethical decision-making in organizations. In particular, the possibilities for addressing organizational culture as a route to managing ethics have been widely alluded to in the literature and will provide an important aspect of our discussions in the next chapter.

STUDY QUESTIONS

1 What is the difference between descriptive and normative ethical theories?

2 Set out the four stages in Rest's (1986) ethical decision-making process. What are the relationships between each stage?

3 Given that most business people are not inherently stupid or evil, how do you explain the continued prevalence of unethical behaviour within business? What are the implications of your answer for the management of business ethics?

4 Critically evaluate the contribution of Kohlberg's theory of cognitive moral development for our understanding of ethical decision-making in organizations.

5 What are the two main types of issue-related factors in ethical decision-making? What is the significance of these factors for managers seeking to prevent ethical violations in their organizations?

6 What are the main impacts of bureaucracy on ethical decision-making? How would you suggest that a highly bureaucratic organization could enhance its employees' ethical decision-making?

RESEARCH EXERCISE

Ethics in Action 4.1 described the events in the movie *The Insider*. If you can, get the movie out of the video store or library and watch it. Alternatively, select another movie that you know involves people having to make ethical or unethical decisions in organizations. Use the events in the movie to provide a critical appraisal of the ethical decision-making literature.

CASE 4

Rogue traders: scandals in the banking and finance industry

How and why can the actions of a single trader bring about financial scandals involving the loss of hundreds of millions of dollars? This case examines the circumstances surrounding two events that rocked the financial world—the collapse of Barings Bank in 1995 and the massive alleged fraud encountered by a US subsidiary of Allied Irish Bank (AIB) in 2002—both of which appear to have been the result of solo 'rogue traders' making unauthorized trades. The case provides the opportunity to examine some of the influences on ethical decision-making, as well as highlighting some of the challenges for organizations attempting to ensure ethical conduct of their employees in different cultural contexts.

In 1995, unauthorized trading at Barings Bank's Singapore office spectacularly spiralled into losses of an incredible €1,200m. Barings—a once venerable member of the British banking establishment —was unable to offset such enormous losses and went bust. Nick Leeson, the so-called 'rogue trader' at the centre of the collapse, went into hiding and was subsequently arrested at Frankfurt airport whilst attempting a return to Europe.

The shockwaves of the collapse of Barings were felt throughout the finance world. How could such a catastrophic loss have been allowed to happen? Why didn't established controls and risk man-agement systems prevent a lone rogue trader from exposing Barings to such a disastrously vulner-able position? Could such a scandal happen again? The answer to the last question, it seems, is yes. Just seven years later, it was revealed in February 2002 that another rogue trader, this time in Baltimore, USA, had brought disaster upon another redoubtable European financial institution, Allied Irish Bank (AIB). Fortunately, the unauthorized dealings by John Rusnak at AIB's US subsidiary Allfirst did not quite bring the bank to collapse. But with a whopping loss of almost €700m to deal with, AIB's profitability, reputation, and credibility took a severe blow, and several top managers were forced, or chose, to resign.

Whilst there were many parallels between this and the Barings case—not least the fact that neither Leeson nor Rusnak appeared to have run up the losses for direct personal gain but rather as failed attempts to cover earlier losses—perhaps the most interesting difference was that whilst Leeson was commonly depicted in the media as an arrogant, opportunistic, high-living city dealer from the wrong side of the tracks, Rusnak was widely reported to be a hard-working, religious family man who was a pillar of his local community. As many commentators asked at the time, how could such a seemingly decent and honest employee turn into a rogue trader guilty of losing his firm €700m? As we shall see, the stories of the rogue traders say as much about the influence of the context in which they worked as they do about the traders themselves.

Nick Leeson and the Barings Bank collapse

As part of a move away from its traditional and very conservative roots, Barings Bank had begun exploring opportunities for lucrative speculation in global stock markets. In 1992 Nick Leeson was posted to Singapore to set up a Barings trading office on the SIMEX (Singapore International Monetary Exchange). His goal was to make profits by 'arbitraging'—exploiting the price fluctuations between the SIMEX in Singapore and the Nikkei in Japan.

The problems started soon after Leeson's arrival. One of his inexperienced clerks entered a sale rather than a purchase on some stock that had been traded. Having neglected to correct the error immediately as he should have, market rises meant the cost of the mistake grew, prompting Leeson to set up an error account (numbered 8888), in which he could hide the loss until it could be offset with profitable transactions. To cover his tracks, Leeson created fake transactions so that the Barings head office and the Singapore Stock Exchange would not detect his sleight of hand. However, in the weeks and months that followed, more errors occurred, boosting the size of the account and leading Leeson to ever more daring ways of concealing the losses. Since Barings had taken the unusual decision at the Singapore office to place Leeson in charge of both the front office (which makes the trades) and the back office (which supervises the trading activities), his evasions did not come under immediate scrutiny. And the Barings' monthly audits could be misled by care-ful movement of funds between accounts whilst the audits were taking place.

The creation of error accounts is actually common practice in stock market trading, and any losses or gains are usually deducted from the trading office's end of year profits. It is these profits that then determine staff bonuses. By hiding account 8888, Leeson managed to maintain the false impression that his office was highly profitable. As the apparent profitability of his operation grew, so did Leeson's end of year bonuses. By 1995, he was rumoured to be in line for a £1m (€1.5m) bonus. Of course, with the losses in account 8888 increasing all the time, Leeson made constant attempts to reduce the shortfall. However, as the problem escalated, so did Leeson's willingness to gamble his firm's money on high-risk, unauthorized trades. As the Leeson character says in the film *Rogue Trader* which depicts the Barings events: 'That's all the market is: one giant casino.' However, too many of Leeson's gambles simply failed to pay off.

As time went on, not all of the increased risk could be hidden by Leeson. Speculation about the precarious position hedged by Barings circulated in the Singapore market. Barings' bosses, though, seemed willing to accept Leeson's frequent demands for additional funding to fuel his speculation without initiating any further investigations. With Leeson's office seemingly highly profitable, he experienced considerable goodwill from the London head office. The failure to impose adequate regulations however allowed Leeson's unauthorized trading to spiral out of control. This was accentuated by the slightly unreal world of the trading floor. As Leeson explains in his book: 'All the money we dealt with was unreal: abstract numbers which flashed across screens or jumped across the trading pit with a flurry of hands. Our clients made or lost thousands of pounds, we just made commission.'

In the end, though, Leeson and Barings would both suffer from the bank's failure to provide adequate supervision of the rogue trader. The 'abstract numbers' in account 8888 totalled an incredible £800m by the time of Leeson's arrest. Unable to withstand such a loss, Barings, once a pillar of the conservative British banking establishment, went bust and had to endure the ignominy of being sold to the Dutch ING Bank for a desultory £1 (about €1.50). Four senior executives, including the chairperson and his two deputies, were forced to resign. Leeson fared even worse. Extradited back to Singapore, he stood trial for deception and falsifying documents for which he was convicted and sentenced to six and half years in jail. Some commentators, though, saw Leeson as a convenient scapegoat for neglect higher up. For example, at a later trial in 2002 (of Barings' auditors Deloitte & Touche for negligence in not picking up the unauthorized trades), the former head of Barings' Singapore operations, James Bax, admitted that providing Leeson with millions of pounds of funding without proper questions merited '10 out of 10 for recklessness'.

For several years after the events of 1995, the 'banana skin survey'—an annual poll of executives by the UK's Centre for the Study of Financial Innovation—regularly reported that financial managers considered a rogue trader to be the second or third most likely cause of problems for a bank. However, as improved systems began to be introduced, rogue traders slipped down the agenda. By the 2001 poll, they were twenty-fourth on executive' list of concerns. Then came John Rusnak.

John Rusnak and the AIB Bank scandal

The case of John Rusnak revealed that it was still all too easy for a rogue trader to bring calamity upon his employer. Working at AIB's US subsidiary Allfirst, Rusnak also ran up a huge loss by unsuccessfully trying to trade his way out of earlier blunders. Again, the degree of risk that Rusnak exposed his employer to was hidden by subterfuge and bogus transactions. In fact, one of the more comical findings of the official report into the Rusnak case by Eugene Ludwig was that copies of the bogus documents used by Rusnak to cover his trail were stored on his PC in a file marked 'fake docs'!

Just as in Barings, then, the controls applied to Rusnak's trading were surprisingly lax, with poorly defined lines of authority and considerable confidence placed in the star trader by his superiors. Rusnak, as with Leeson, was engaged in a form of trading which although apparently profitable was not really fully understood by his supervisors. The need to diversify the bank's revenue stream meant that new areas of business had to be developed and Rusnak sold himself as an expert in a new, fairly esoteric area of trading. AIB's control systems were stretched by its rapid internationalization (which afforded the Allfirst subsidiary considerable autonomy) and the move into ever more complex areas of trading. This marked a significant departure from AIB's traditional banking base—a situation common in today's finance industry, and clearly also a contributory factor in the Barings case. As Professor Ray Kinsella, an expert in banking controls from University College Dublin, said at the time of the AIB revelations, this process had led to the inevitability of banks' vulnerability to rogue traders: 'What I'm saying in unequivocal terms', he said, 'is not only can it happen again, but it will happen again. The market is always changing in terms of products, complexity and vulnerability . . . The bottom line is internal controls are always playing catch-up.'

Even the internal controls that were in place at AIB were not stringently applied and clearly failed to pick up on Rusnak's escalating losses, despite the fact that concerns were raised about some of the positions he was holding as far back as 1998, a full five years before the scandal broke. However, the company obviously did not give the concerns a great deal of attention. For example, after notification by Citibank in 2000 about an unusually large account being administered by Rusnak (which allowed him to make bigger trades), the request by AIB bosses for 'discreet' enquiries into Rusnak's trading inevitably provided little in-depth investigation.

Other opportunities for stopping Rusnak were also missed. Reports from the American Securities Exchange Commission suggested that Rusnak was trading well beyond his brief. In fact, a staggering 95 per cent of Allfirst's foreign exchange options trade were conducted by Rusnak himself, yet a promised internal audit that might have revealed the extent of the problem simply did not happen. And again, as with Leeson, the back office that was supposed to supervise the traders failed to fully scrutinize his activities. Rusnak would resist interference by back office staff by exploiting his star trader status, and by making sure his bogus transactions were purportedly with Tokyo or Singapore branches so that transaction confirmations would have supposedly arrived in the middle of the night, giving him ample opportunity to avoid detection. He worked alone and even worked from his laptop whilst on holiday to avoid providing any occasion for direct scrutiny of his activities.

Despite earning substantial bonuses for his seemingly 'profitable' trading, few commentators have made Rusnak out to be anything other than a hard-working, community-spirited man who was simply trying to disguise from his employers the extent of his losses. As the 'fake docs' file suggests, he did not even seem to be particularly artful in his deception. As one reporter concluded: 'Rusnak was able to continue unhindered for five years not through genius but through an almost farcical laxity in controls and risk management.' Of course, one is bound to wonder what sort of person it is that can run up losses of almost €700m rather than confessing to their mistake before things got out of hand. Perhaps Nick Leeson will soon be able to tell us. Following his release from prison, and having recovered from colon cancer, he enrolled for a psychology degree at Middlesex University in London.

Questions

1 Set out the main factors that appear to have influenced Leeson and Rusnak to become rogue traders. Try and classify your factors according to the different types covered in the chapter.

2 Which of these factors appear to have been most important in causing the AIB and Barings scandals?

3 To what extent do you think it is possible to safeguard against further rogue traders? What factors or conditions in the finance industry might make such safeguards (a) more possible; and (b) less possible.

4 Who was ultimately responsible for the Barings and AIB disasters?

Sources

Bates, Adam (2002). 'It is still too easy for a rogue trader to operate'. *The Times* (Business), 4 Apr.

Darroch, Valerie (2002). 'How could it happen again?' *Sunday Herald*, 10 Feb.: 5.

Hargreaves, Deborah (2002). 'Disasters focus management on need for change'. *Financial Times* (Survey-Financial Training), 25 June: 5.

Kinsella, Ray (2002). 'Ludwig's lessons: the lack of controls at Allied Irish Banks could be found inside many institutions'. *Financial Times*, 15 Mar.: 19.

O'Connell, Dominic (2002). 'How AIB failed to account for Rusnak'. *Sunday Times* (Business), 17 Mar.

Tait, Nikki (2002). 'Barings "reckless in funding Leeson" '. *Financial Times*, 9 July.

5

Managing Business Ethics
Tools and Techniques of Business Ethics Management

In this chapter we will:

- Discuss the nature and evolution of business ethics management, stressing the emerging focus on managing the overall social role of the corporation rather than focusing primarily on managing employee behaviour;

- Provide a critical review of arguments and evidence relating to the usefulness of introducing codes of ethics in order to manage the ethical behaviour of employees;

- Examine current theory and practice regarding the management of stakeholder relationships and develop an understanding of the role of closer stakeholder collaboration on the management of business ethics;

- Describe the development of social, ethical, and environmental accounting, auditing, and reporting tools and analyse their contribution to managing and assessing ethical performance, and promoting corporate accountability;

- Examine different ways of organizing for the management of business ethics, and critically assess the role of organization culture and leadership;

- Question the extent to which the developments reported in the chapter represent genuine commitment to business ethics or simply reflect ever more sophisticated public relations.

Introduction

It is being increasingly recognized by academics, businesses, policy-makers, and others that business ethics in the global economy is simply too important to be merely left to chance. Global corporations such as McDonald's, Shell, Nike, Nestlé, and others have realized to their cost the threat that perceived ethical violations can pose to their zealously guarded reputations. Similarly, errant employees across the other side of the globe, such as John Rusnak at AIB subsidiary Allfirst Financial in Baltimore and Nick Leeson of Barings Bank in Singapore (see Case 4: 138–142), have dramatically shown the effect that unethical decision-making can have on the fortunes of once stable and successful companies.

As a result, there have been numerous attempts, both theoretical and practical, to develop a more systematic and comprehensive approach to *managing* business ethics. Indeed, this has given rise to a multi-million-euro international business ethics 'industry' of ethics managers, consultants, auditors, and other experts available to advise and implement ethics management policies and programmes in corporations across the globe.

But how can companies actually manage business ethics on a day-to-day basis across the various national and cultural contexts that they may be operating in? Is it possible to control the ethical behaviour of employees so that they make the right ethical decision every time? And what kinds of management programmes are necessary to produce the level of information and impacts that various stakeholders demand? These are the kinds of questions that we will deal with in this chapter. However, in this area in particular, there are as yet few definite answers, not least because many of the questions themselves have only fairly recently been addressed at any length. Indeed, much of the theory and practice covered in this chapter is at the very forefront of current business ethics debates.

What is business ethics management?

Before we proceed any further, it is necessary to first establish what exactly it is that we mean by managing business ethics. Obviously, managing any area of business, whether it is production, marketing, accounting, human resources, or any other function, constitutes a whole range of activities covering formal and informal means of planning, implementation, and control. For our purposes, though, the most relevant aspects of the management of business ethics are those that are clearly visible and directed specifically at resolving ethical problems and issues. Hence, we might offer the following definition:

> Business ethics management is the direct attempt to formally or informally manage ethical issues or problems through specific policies, practices, and programmes.

This, as we shall now show, covers a whole range of different elements, each of which may be applied individually, or in combination, to address ethical issues in business.

Components of business ethics management

There are numerous management activities that could be regarded as aspects of business ethics management, some of which, such as codes of ethics, are fairly well established, whilst others, such as social auditing, are still in relatively early stages of development and uptake. Without intending to be exhaustive, **Figure 5.1** sets out the main components currently in place today, at least within European and US corporations. These are all explained briefly below. The most important of these components are described

---

Typical components of business ethics management

- Mission or values statements
- Codes of ethics
- Reporting/advice channels
- Ethics managers, officers, and committees
- Ethics consultants
- Ethics education and training
- Auditing, accounting, and reporting

Figure 5.1. Business ethics management

in fuller detail later in the chapter when we look in depth at managing the ethical behaviour of employees, managing stakeholder relations, and managing and assessing ethical performance.

Mission or values statements

These are general statements of corporate aims, beliefs, and values. Such statements frequently include social goals of one kind or another (David 1989; Starkey 1998), and may often specify a commitment to operate in an ethical fashion. For example, the Swedish furniture giant IKEA suggests that its corporate vision is to 'create a better everyday life for everyone' whilst the British retailer Marks & Spencer aims to be 'the most trusted retailer wherever we trade by demonstrating a clear sense of social responsibility and consistency in our decision making and behaviour'. Whilst virtually all large, and many small and medium-sized organizations, now have a mission statement of some kind, there is little evidence to suggest that they have much impact on employee behaviour (Bart 1997).

Codes of ethics

These are explicit outlines of what type of conduct is desired and expected of employees from an ethical point of view within a certain organization, profession, or industry. As probably the most widespread, but also one of the most controversial approaches to managing business ethics, we shall discuss codes of ethics in more detail on pp. 148–156 below.

Reporting/advice channels

Gathering information on ethical matters is clearly an important input into effective management, and providing employees with appropriate channels for reporting or receiving advice regarding ethical dilemmas can be a vital means of identifying potential problems and resolving them before they escalate and/or become public. Some organizations have therefore introduced ethics hotlines or other forms of reporting channels specifically dedicated to providing a mechanism for employees to notify management of ethics abuses or problems and to seek help and guidance on solutions. One recent UK survey reported that something like 60 per cent of the firms it sampled had instituted channels of this kind (Arthur Andersen 2000).

Ethics managers, officers, and committees

In some organizations, specific individuals or groups are appointed to co-ordinate and/or take responsibility for managing ethics in their organization. Designated ethics officers (under various titles) are now fairly prevalent in the USA: according to a 1995 survey, a third of Fortune 1,000 firms reported having an ethics officer function (Weaver et al. 1999a), and an Ethics Officer Association, set up in 1992, had grown to a total of approximately 740 members by 2001 (Hoffman et al. 2001). In Europe and elsewhere, such positions are far less common, but in September 2001 the European Business Ethics Network (EBEN) launched The Ethics Practitioner Forum. Based on the US Ethics Officer Association, this is a European practitioner network dedicated to identifying and sharing best practices and resource information among business ethics managers (**www.eben.org**). Similarly, a growing number of large corporations now have an ethics committee, or a CSR committee, which oversees many aspects of the management of business ethics. For example, the pharmaceutical giant AstraZeneca has recently established a CSR committee with members from across a number of corporate functions. The responsibility of this committee is the implementation and review of the company's approach to CSR, the setting of priorities, and planning of future activities.

Ethics consultants

Business ethics consultants have also become a small, but firmly established fixture in the marketplace, and a wide range of companies have used external consultants rather than internal executives to manage certain areas of business ethics. The initial growth in this sector was driven by environmental consultants who tended to offer specialist technical advice, but as the social and ethical agenda facing companies has developed, the consultancy market has expanded to offer a broader portfolio of services including research, project management, strategic advice, social and environmental auditing and reporting, verification, stakeholder dialogue, and others. At present, whilst there are numerous small ethics consultancy firms, the overall market is still relatively limited in size and is dominated by large accountancy firms, such as KPMG and PriceWaterhouseCoopers, which offer ethics consultancy along with other consulting services.

Ethics education and training

With greater attention being given to business ethics, education and training in the subject has also been on the rise. Provision might be offered either in-house, or externally through ethics consultants, universities and colleges, or corporate training specialists. Again, formal corporate ethics training has tended to be more common in the USA than in Europe, as have been undergraduate, M.Sc., and MBA modules in business ethics. However, this appears to be changing. For example, a 1999 survey of large UK businesses revealed that ethics training was being conducted at 40 per cent of participating companies, a rise of more than 100 per cent in three years (Arthur Andersen 2000). Indeed, many academic writers have stressed the need for more ethics education among business people, not only in terms of providing them with the tools to solve ethical dilemmas, but also providing them with the ability to recognize and talk about ethical problems more accurately and easily (Thorne LeClair and Ferrell 2000). Diane Kirrane (1990) thus summarizes the goals for ethics training as: (*a*) identifying the situation where ethical decision-making is involved; (*b*) understanding the culture and values of the organization; and (*c*) evaluating the impact of the ethical decision on the organization.

Stakeholder consultation, dialogue, and partnership programmes

These are various means of including an organization's stakeholders more fully in corporate decision-making. Again, these are central activities in the promotion of corporate accountability. Just as importantly, though, it is evident that if 'good' business ethics is about doing the 'right' thing, then it is essential that organizations consult with relevant stakeholders in order to determine what other constituencies regard as 'right' in the first place. Either way, stakeholder consultation, dialogue, and partnership are increasingly becoming accepted—if still relatively new—ways of managing business ethics, and since they are issues that we will return to throughout the book, they will be afforded further elucidation later when we address the more general topic of managing stakeholder relations (156–162).

Auditing, accounting, and reporting

These are all very closely related activities that are concerned with measuring, evaluating, and communicating the organization's impacts and performance on a range of social, ethical, and environmental issues of interest to their stakeholders. Unlike most of the previous developments, these aspects of business ethics management have been pioneered in Europe, with companies such as BSO/Origin, Norsk Hydro, SbN Bank, Traidcraft, Body Shop, and Shell being at the forefront of innovation in this area. However, there is rapid development in this field across the globe, with one recent survey suggesting that 50 per cent of the world's largest companies now produce social and environmental reports (Line et al. 2002). This is further evident in programmes such as SA 8000 and the Global Reporting Initiative (GRI) that—as we shall discuss in more detail later—seek to provide internationally comparative standards for aspects of auditing, accounting, and reporting. Indeed, although these elements of management are still in relatively early periods of experimentation and development, they can play a crucial role in enhancing corporate accountability in the era of corporate citizenship as we suggested in Chapter 2. Accordingly, we will return to these developments in more detail below as part of our discussion about assessing ethical performance (162–170).

Evolution of business ethics management

Before proceeding to discuss some of the most common components in more detail, we should stress that few if any businesses are likely to have *all* of these tools and techniques in place, and many may not even have *any* of them. However, the take-up of different components does appear to be increasing. The UK survey reported by Arthur Andersen (2000: 12) for example reveals that: 'without exception, the use of all reviewed components has increased substantially compared to three years ago. This is a remarkable increase in activity during a period when organizations have had to find additional resources to address priorities such as the millennium bug and the launch of the Euro, and meet increasing demands for cost cutting.'

Also, over the last decade or so, there appears to have been a change in emphasis, particularly among European organizations (but also to a lesser extent among US organizations), concerning the purpose of business ethics management. Whereas previously, business ethics management (as pioneered in the USA) tended to focus primarily on *managing employee behaviour* (through codes etc.), there has been increasing attention (as pioneered in Europe) to developing and implementing tools and techniques associated with the *management of broader social responsibilities*. These more externally focused components have typically involved the consideration of other stakeholder demands and considerations, such as in the development of social accounting tools and techniques.

In the next three sections we shall take a look at the three main areas where the management of business ethics might be particularly relevant:

- **Setting standards of ethical behaviour.** Here we shall mainly examine the role of ethical codes and their implementation.

- **Managing stakeholder relations.** Here we shall look mainly at how to assess stakeholders, different ways of managing them, and the benefits and problems of doing so.

- **Assessing ethical performance.** Here we shall consider the role of social accounting in contributing to the management and assessment of business ethics.

Setting standards of ethical behaviour: designing and implementing codes of ethics

Over the past couple of decades many organizations have made efforts to set out specific standards of appropriate ethical conduct for their employees to follow. As we shall see later in the chapter, much of this standard setting might well be done informally or even implicitly, such as through the example set by leaders. However, most attention in business ethics theory and practice has focused on *codes of ethics* (also called codes of conduct).

> Codes of ethics are voluntary statements that commit organizations, industries, or professions to specific beliefs, values, and actions and/or set out appropriate ethical behaviour for employees.

There are four main types of ethical codes:

- **Organizational or corporate codes of ethics.** These are specific to a single organization. Sometimes they are called codes of conduct or codes of business principles, but basically these codes seek to identify and encourage ethical behaviour at the level of the individual organization.

- **Professional codes of ethics.** Professional groups also often have their own guidelines for appropriate conduct for their members. Whilst most traditional professions such as medicine, law, and accountancy have long-standing codes of conduct, it is now also increasingly common for other professions such as marketing, purchasing, or engineering to have their own codes of ethics.

• **Industry codes of ethics.** As well as specific professions, particular industries also sometimes have their own codes of ethics. For example, in many countries, the financial services industry will have a code of conduct for companies and/or employees operating in the industry. Similarly, at the international level, in 1997 the World Federation for the Sporting Goods Industry (WFSGI) developed a code of conduct for its members 'to ensure that member companies satisfy the highest ethical standards in the global marketplace' (see van Tulder and Kolk 2001).

• **Programme or group codes of ethics.** Finally, certain programmes, coalitions, or other sub-groupings of organizations also establish codes of ethics for those participating in the specific programmes. For example, a collaboration of various business leaders from Europe, the USA, and Japan resulted in the development of a global code of ethics for business called the CAUX Roundtable Principles for Business (**www.cauxroundtable.org**). Sometimes, conforming to a particular programme code is a prerequisite for using a particular label or mark of accreditation. For instance, companies wishing to market their products as 'fairly traded' will have to abide by the code established by the relevant fair trade body, such as the Fairtrade Foundation in the UK, or Max Havelaar in the Netherlands.

There has been a lot of research on codes of ethics over the past two decades, primarily focusing on four main issues:

• Prevalence of corporate codes of ethics;
• Content of codes of ethics;
• Effectiveness of codes of ethics;
• Possibilities for global codes of ethics.

Prevalence of codes of ethics

On the first point, codes of ethics are increasingly prevalent, with a substantial rise in their usage identified during the 1990s, particularly in large companies. Whilst studies have differed in their findings (usually due to different definitions of what constitutes a code of ethics), it is reasonable to conclude that something like two-thirds of large UK firms now have some kind of formal ethical code, whilst in the USA, it has been suggested almost all large firms have a code of ethics of some kind (Weaver et al. 1999a). Evidence on their prevalence elsewhere in Europe and in small and medium-sized enterprises (SMEs) is fairly scant, but the general indication is of a much lower figure (Spence and Lozano 2000).

Content of codes of ethics

In terms of content, codes of ethics typically attempt to do one or both of the following:

(a) Define principles or standards that the organization, profession, or industry believes in or wants to uphold;

Standard of Conduct: We conduct our operations with honesty, integrity and openness, and with respect for the human rights and interests of our employees. We shall similarly respect the legitimate interests of those with whom we have relationships.

Obeying the Law: Unilever companies are required to comply with the laws and regulations of the countries in which they operate.

Employees: Unilever is committed to diversity in a working environment where there is mutual trust and respect and where everyone feels responsible for the performance and reputation of our company. We will recruit, employ and promote employees on the sole basis of the qualifications and abilities needed for the work to be performed. We are committed to safe and healthy working conditions for all employees. We will not use any form of forced, compulsory or child labour. We are committed to working with employees to develop and enhance each individual's skills and capabilities. We respect the dignity of the individual and the right of employees to freedom of association. We will maintain good communications with employees through company based information and consultation procedures.

Consumers: Unilever is committed to providing branded products and services which consistently offer value in terms of price and quality, and which are safe for their intended use. Products and services will be accurately and properly labelled, advertised and communicated.

Shareholders: Unilever will conduct its operations in accordance with internationally accepted principles of good corporate governance. We will provide timely, regular and reliable information on our activities, structure, financial situation and performance to all shareholders.

Business Partners: Unilever is committed to establishing mutually beneficial relations with our suppliers, customers and business partners. In our business dealings we expect our partners to adhere to business principles consistent with our own.

Community Involvement: Unilever strives to be a trusted corporate citizen and, as an integral part of society, to fulfil our responsibilities to the societies and communities in which we operate.

Public Activities: Unilever companies are encouraged to promote and defend their legitimate business interests. Unilever will co-operate with governments and other organisations, both directly and through bodies such as trade associations, in the development of proposed legislation and other regulations which may affect legitimate business interests. Unilever neither supports political parties nor contributes to the funds of groups whose activities are calculated to promote party interests.

The Environment: Unilever is committed to making continuous improvements in the management of our environmental impact and to the longer-term goal of developing a sustainable business. Unilever will work in partnership with others to promote environmental care, increase understanding of environmental issues and disseminate good practice.

Innovation: In our scientific innovation to meet consumer needs we will respect the concerns of our consumers and of society. We will work on the basis of sound science, applying rigorous standards of product safety.

Competition: Unilever believes in vigorous yet fair competition and supports the development of appropriate competition laws. Unilever companies and employees will conduct their operations in accordance with the principles of fair competition and all applicable regulations.

Business Integrity: Unilever does not give or receive, whether directly or indirectly, bribes or other improper advantages for business or financial gain. No employee may offer, give or receive any gift or payment which is, or may be construed as being, a bribe. Any demand for, or offer of, a bribe must be rejected immediately and reported to management. Unilever accounting records and supporting documents must accurately describe and reflect the nature of the underlying transactions. No undisclosed or unrecorded account, fund or asset will be established or maintained.

Conflicts of Interests: All Unilever employees are expected to avoid personal activities and financial interests which could conflict with their responsibilities to the company. Unilever employees must not seek gain for themselves or others through misuse of their positions.

Figure 5.2. Unilever's Code of Business Principles

Source: **www.unilever.com/company/ourprinciples.**

Compliance—Monitoring—Reporting: Compliance with these principles is an essential element in our business success. The Unilever Board is responsible for ensuring these principles are communicated to, and understood and observed by, all employees. Day-to-day responsibility is delegated to the senior management of the regions and operating companies. They are responsible for implementing these principles, if necessary through more detailed guidance tailored to local needs. Assurance of compliance is given and monitored each year. Compliance with the Code is subject to review by the Board supported by the Audit Committee of the Board and the Corporate Risk Committee. Any breaches of the Code must be reported in accordance with the procedures specified by the Joint Secretaries. The Board of Unilever will not criticise management for any loss of business resulting from adherence to these principles and other mandatory policies and instructions. The Board of Unilever expects employees to bring to their attention, or to that of senior management, any breach or suspected breach of these principles. Provision has been made for employees to be able to report in confidence and no employee will suffer as a consequence of doing so.

In this Code the expressions 'Unilever' and 'Unilever companies' are used for convenience and mean the Unilever Group of companies comprising Unilever N.V., Unilever PLC and their respective subsidiary companies. The Board of Unilever means the Directors of Unilever N.V. and Unilever PLC.

Figure 5.2. (*continued*)

(*b*) Set out practical guidelines for employee behaviour, either generally or in specific situations (such as accepting gifts, treating customers, etc.).

Figure 5.2 shows the code of ethics developed by Unilever for its business operations across the globe. As you can see, this mainly focuses on *general* principles, such as 'Unilever believes in vigorous yet fair competition,' but also includes *specific* guidelines for behaviour in areas such as bribery. For instance, the code specifies that 'any demand for or offer of such bribe must be immediately rejected'.

According to Hoffman et al. (2001: 44), to be effective, codes should address *both* of these tasks: 'rules of conduct without a general values statement lack a framework of meaning and purpose; credos without rules of conduct lack specific content.' The question of exactly how codes can actually be crafted to achieve these ends is, however, a crucial one. Cassell et al. (1997) for example argue that whilst clarity is obviously important, the desire for clear prescriptions for employees in specific situations can clash with needs for flexibility and applicability to multiple and/or novel situations. As we shall discuss in more detail shortly, this is particularly pertinent in the context of multinationals where employees are likely to be exposed to new dilemmas and differing cultural expectations (Donaldson 1996). Similarly, given that many ethical dilemmas are characterized by a clash of values or by conflicting stakeholder demands, ethical codes might be expected to identify which values or groups should take precedence—yet the need to avoid offending particular stakeholder groups often results in rather generalized statements of obligation (Hosmer 1987).

Such ambiguousness has unsurprisingly led many commentators to conclude that codes of ethics are primarily a rhetorical PR device which firms can offer as evidence of ethical commitment in order to pacify critics whilst maintaining business as usual. Indeed, most evidence suggests that simply having a formal written code is neither sufficient nor even always necessary for ensuring ethical behaviour (Cleek and Leonard 1998; Schlegelmilch and Houston 1989).

Effectiveness of codes of ethics

In many respects, then, in terms of effectiveness, it is perhaps less important what a code says than how it is developed, implemented, and followed up. A code imposed on employees without clear communication about what it is trying to achieve and why might simply raise resentment. Similarly, a code that is written, launched, and then promptly forgotten is unlikely to promote enhanced ethical decision-making. Perhaps worst of all, a code that is introduced and then seen to be breached with impunity by senior managers or other members of staff is probably never going to achieve anything apart from raising employee cynicism.

So how to get the implementation right? Whilst there are few, if any, unequivocal answers to this question, a number of suggestions have been presented. Lisa Newton (1992) for example has stressed the importance of maximizing the *participation* of organization members in the development stage in order to encourage commitment and 'buy-in' to the principles and rules of the code. Simon Webley (2001) further contends that in order for codes to have credibility, companies must be willing to *discipline* employees found in breach of them. Similarly, Treviño et al.'s (1999) survey revealed that *follow-through* (such as detection of violations, follow-up on notification of violations, and consistency between the policy and action) tended to be much more influential on employee behaviour than the mere presence of a code, regardless of how familiar employees might be with it.

These are, almost certainly, eminently sensible suggestions and findings. However, clear research findings relating to the effect of codes and their implementation on employee decision-making and behaviour are still relatively limited (Cassell et al. 1997). Moreover, recent years have witnessed the emergence of a stream of literature more critical of ethical codes. Not only have codes been identified as questionable control mechanisms that potentially seek to exert influence over employee beliefs, values, and behaviours (Schwartz 2000), but, as we saw in Chapter 3, there is a growing interest from postmodernists, feminists, and others in the possibility for codified ethical rules and principles to 'suppress' individual moral instincts, emotions, and empathy in order to ensure bureaucratic conformity and consistency. In **Ethical Dilemma 5** you can work through some of these issues in the context of a specific example.

Global codes of ethics

Finally, the issue of global codes of ethics has also received increasing attention from business and academia over the past decade or so. Given the rise of multinational business, many organizations have found that codes of ethics developed for use in their home country may need to be revisited for their international operations. Are guidelines for domestic employees still relevant and applicable in overseas contexts? Can organizations devise one set of principles for all countries in which they operate? According to one review of the codes of multinationals conducted for the Institute of Business Ethics, the cross-cultural issues most commonly addressed are:[1]

---

[1] See Webley (1997).

Ethical Dilemma 5

Clear codes for grey zones?

It's another Monday morning and after a weekend of celebrating the birthday of one of your friends, you sit in your office and sort out your diary for the week. As the IT manager of a small credit card company you have to prepare for your staff meeting at 10 a.m. where all of your fifteen team members will be present. You are planning to discuss the launch of your new promotion scheme, which is due to begin at the end of the week. Fortunately, Paul, who is the main market analyst for the company, was ready to do some extra work at home over the weekend in order to make sure the forecasts were ready for the meeting.

While sipping your first cup of coffee, someone knocks at the door. It is Fred, the hardware manager. He looks a bit embarrassed, and after a little stilted small talk, he tells you that 'a problem' has come up. He has just checked in the laptop that Paul the market analyst had taken out of the company's pool and used at home over the weekend in order to finish the forecasts you had asked for. However when completing the routine check of the laptop, Fred tells you he noticed links to various pornography sites in the history file of the laptop's internet browser. He tells you that they must have been accessed over the weekend that Paul had the laptop—the access dates refer to the last two days, and, as is usual practice, the history file was emptied after the last person had borrowed it.

There is a strict company policy prohibiting employees from making personal use of company hardware, and access to sites containing 'material of an explicit nature' is tantamount to gross misconduct and may result in the immediate termination of the employee's contract. When your hardware manager leaves the office, you take a big breath and slowly finish your coffee.

After a few minutes thinking through the problem, you ask Paul to come into your office. You have a quick chat about his work and tell him that you are really pleased with the forecasts he put together over the weekend. Then, you bring up the problem with the laptop's history file. When you tell him what has surfaced in the history file, Paul is terribly embarrassed and assures you that he has absolutely no idea how this could have happened. After some thought, though, he tells you that he did allow 'a friend' to use the laptop a couple of times over the weekend to check his email. Although Paul says that this is the only possible explanation for the mystery files, he does not volunteer any more information on the friend involved. As it goes, this does not actually make you feel much better about the situation: the company's code of conduct also prohibits use of IT equipment by anyone other than employees.

While driving home that evening, you turn the issue over and over in your head. Yes, there is the corporate code of conduct with regard to web access and personal use of company resources. And in principle you agree on this—after all you were part of the committee that issued the code in the first place. A company like yours has to be able to have clarity on such issues, and there have to be controls on what the company's equipment is used for—no doubt about that. You can't help thinking that Paul has been pretty stupid in breaking the rules—whether he visited the sites himself or not.

On the other hand, you are also having a few problems with taking this further. Given the amount of embarrassment this has caused Paul already, isn't it likely to be just a one-off? Doesn't the company need Paul's experience and expertise, especially now with the big launch a few days off? Why make problems over the matter of a few websites? Couldn't you just forget about it for once?

As soon as you start thinking this, though, you remember that Fred already knows about the problem —and given his good connections throughout the firm you can imagine that the gossip has started circulating already. After all, two years ago, when the guidelines were freshly issued, a junior typist who had committed the same offence had been sacked on short notice. This looks set to be a tough call.

Questions

1 What are your main ethical problems in this case?
2 Set out the possible courses of action open to you.
3 Assess these alternatives according to the different moral considerations raised in Chapter 3—duties, consequences, rights, justice, etc.
4 What would you do, and why?
5 Based on your answer, what are the apparent benefits and limitations of the code of conduct in this example?

- Gifts (hospitality and bribes);
- Conflicts of interest;
- Insider dealing;
- Equal opportunities and discrimination;
- Protection of the environment.

The issue of gifts for example is often one where cultural context has a distinct bearing on what might be regarded as acceptable ethical behaviour. Whilst many European organizations have specific guidelines precluding the offer or acceptance of gifts and hospitality as part of their business operations, in some countries such as Japan, not only is the offering of gifts considered to be a perfectly acceptable business activity, but the refusal to accept such offerings can be regarded as offensive. Similarly, questions of equal opportunity are somewhat more equivocal in a multinational context. European or US organizations with codes of practice relating to equal opportunities may find that these run counter to cultural norms, and even legal statutes, overseas. For example, in many countries such as India there is a cultural expectation that people should show preference for their close friends and family over strangers, even in business contexts such as recruitment. In many Islamic countries, the equal treatment of men and women is viewed very differently from how it is in the west, with countries such as Saudi Arabia even banning women from working outside the home.

According to Thomas Donaldson (1996), one of the leading writers on international business ethics, the key question for those working overseas is: when is different just different and when is different wrong? As such, the question of how multinationals should address cultural differences in drafting their ethical codes returns us to the discussion of relativist versus absolutist positions on ethics that we introduced in Chapter 3 (76–8). A relativist would suggest that different codes should be developed for different contexts, whilst an absolutist would contend that one code can and should fit all. Donaldson's (1996) solution is to propose a middle ground between the two extremes whereby the organization should be guided by three principles:

(*a*) Respect for core human values, which determine an absolute moral threshold;

(*b*) Respect for local traditions;

(*c*) The belief that context matters when deciding what is right and wrong.

What this means is that global codes should define minimum ethical standards according to core human values shared across countries, religions, and cultures, such as the need to respect human dignity and basic human rights. Beyond this, though, codes should also respect cultural or contextual difference in setting out appropriate behaviour in areas such as bribery or gift giving.

The search for core values or universal ethical principles as a basis for global business codes of ethics has given rise to a number of important initiatives:[2]

- In 1994, business and government leaders, theologians, and academics representing three religions—Christian, Jewish, and Islamic—devised the **Interfaith Declaration: A Code of Ethics on International Business for Christians, Muslims, and Jews.** This sought to identify key principles shared by the three faiths that could guide international business behaviour. These principles are justice, mutual respect, stewardship, and honesty.

- The **CAUX Roundtable**, an international network of senior business leaders from Europe, the USA, and Japan, launched its own set of principles in 1994. These are guided by two broad ethical ideals—human dignity and kyosei (a belief of living and working together for the good of all). The CAUX principles promote similar values to the Interfaith Declaration, namely: shared prosperity, justice, and civic responsibility.

- More recently, in 1999 the United Nations Secretary-General Kofi Annan proposed the **UN Global Compact**, a set of nine 'globally acknowledged' principles concerned with human rights, labour, and the environment. By 2002, several hundred companies from all regions of the world had signed up to the compact, including major multinationals such as BASF, Bayer, Du Pont, Ericsson, Kikkoman, Nike, Pearson, Rio Tinto, and Volvo. For an extended discussion of the Global Compact see Ethics in Action 11.2 in Chapter 11 (424–5).

Whilst the necessity of developing globally acceptable and relevant principles means that such codes tend to be rather general in nature, these developments do at least show that some level of international agreement on appropriate standards of business behaviour is possible. Ultimately, however, it is important to realize that the drive for codes of ethics, whether national or international, is never going to 'solve' the management of business

---

[2] For more information on these initiatives, there are further details on these (and other similar) programmes at the websites of the CAUX Roundtable (**www.cauxroundtable.org**) and the Global Compact (**www.unglobalcompact.org**).

ethics. As we saw in the previous chapter, there are a vast array of influences on individual decision-makers within the organization, of which a written code is but one aspect. A code can rarely do more than set out the *minimum expectations* placed on organizations and their members, and cannot be expected to be a substitute for organizational contexts supportive of ethical reflection, debate, and decision-making, or decision-makers with strong personal integrity. Moreover, whilst the introduction of codes of ethics primarily represents an attempt to manage employee conduct, organizations have increasingly found that the management of business ethics also requires them to manage relationships with a wide range of stakeholders, as we shall now discuss.

■ **Think theory**

Think about the notion of a global code of ethics from the perspective of a rights versus a post-modern perspective on ethics. What does each contribute and can they be reconciled?

Managing stakeholder relations

In Chapter 2 (50–55) we introduced stakeholder theory as one of the key theories in the debate on business's role and responsibilities in society. Whilst our main concern there, and in the subsequent chapter, was to highlight the normative basis of stakeholder theory, it is important to also acknowledge the descriptive argument that managers do indeed appear to recognize distinct stakeholder groups and manage their companies accordingly (Clarkson 1995). Whilst in some European countries this is institutionalized in corporate governance, such as in the German two-tier supervisory board, even in more shareholder-focused countries such as the UK, many managers appear to have embraced at least some degree of recognition for stakeholder claims. For example, in a recent survey by the UK's Institute of Directors of its 850 members,[3] almost 90 per cent of respondents claimed that they tried to devise policies which took account of all stakeholders, and although 42 per cent agreed to some extent that shareholders' interests were their first priority, 27 per cent completely disagreed.

The recognition that not only businesses, but organizations of all kinds, including charities, schools, universities, and governments, have a range of stakeholders whose interests might need to be taken into account in making decisions has given rise to a significant body of research dealing with the management of stakeholder relations. Let us look at some of the main themes addressed in this literature.

Assessing stakeholder importance: an instrumental perspective

Much of the stakeholder management literature has tended to focus on the strategic aspects of identifying which stakeholders actually matter to the organization and how they

---

[3] Institute of Directors, *Ethics in Business*, Jan. 1999.

should be dealt with in order for the organization to effectively achieve its goals. Thus, Hill and Jones (2001: 45) in one of the leading Strategic Management textbooks suggest that: 'Stakeholder impact analysis enables a company to identify the stakeholders most critical to its survival and to make sure that the satisfaction of their needs is paramount. Most companies that go through this process quickly reach the conclusion that there are three stakeholder groups the company must satisfy if it is to survive and prosper: customers, employees and shareholders.'

As Donaldson and Preston (1995) suggest, it is important to distinguish this *instrumental* perspective on stakeholder theory from the *normative* perspective we developed in Chapters 2 and 3, and the *descriptive* perspective briefly mentioned above. Hill and Jones's (2001) argument is not so much that organizations have to rate the relative strength of the *ethical* claims of their various stakeholders, but rather that strategic objectives can best be realized by deciding which stakeholders are more likely to be able to *influence* the organization in some way. This is likely to be particularly important when organizations are in a position where they have to decide how to assign relative importance or priority to competing stakeholder claims. For example, we saw in the case study on BMW and Rover at the end of Chapter 2 how BMW was faced with conflicting demands from various stakeholders likely to be affected by any decision they made on the Rover plant.

Following a comprehensive review of the stakeholder management literature, Mitchell et al. (1997) suggest three key relationship attributes likely to determine the perceived importance or *salience* of stakeholders:

• **Power.** The perceived ability of a stakeholder to influence organizational action;

• **Legitimacy.** Whether the organization perceives the stakeholders' actions to be desirable, proper, or appropriate;

• **Urgency.** The degree to which stakeholder claims are perceived to call for immediate attention.

According to Mitchell et al. (1997), managers are likely to assign greater salience to those stakeholders thought to possess greater power, legitimacy, and urgency. Thus stakeholders thought to be in possession of only one of these attributes will be regarded as the least important, and might be regarded as 'latent' stakeholders. Those in possession of two of three qualities are moderately important and hence can be thought of 'expectant' stakeholders. Finally, those in possession of all three will be seen as the most important constituencies and hence are termed 'definitive' stakeholders. For businesses, these definitive stakeholders often require active engagement in order to develop an effective and appropriate working relationship. Indeed, a variety of different relationships might be expected to emerge between businesses and their stakeholders, as we shall now see.

Types of stakeholder relationship

Until relatively recently, it had been generally assumed that relationships between businesses and their stakeholders tended to be somewhat antagonistic, even confrontational in nature. For example, just as companies might exploit consumers or downsize employees, consumers might equally boycott company products, employees could initiate industrial action, suppliers withhold credit, competitors engage in industrial espionage, and pressure groups employ aggressive direct action campaigns against companies. Increasingly, however, it has been recognized that there might also be a place for co-operation between stakeholders. To begin with, the 1990s witnessed an explosion in business–business collaboration, taking the form of joint ventures, strategic alliances, co-marketing initiatives, supplier partnership programmes, and other means of collaborative activity.[4] This was followed by a similarly dramatic increase in collaborations between businesses and other stakeholders such as non-governmental organizations (NGOs), government bodies, and trade unions.

Much of this development in broader stakeholder collaboration was pioneered in the field of environmental management. For example, as we will describe in more detail in Chapter 10, various partnerships between businesses and NGOs emerged across the globe during the 1990s and into the 2000s aimed at tackling environmental problems such as packaging, deforestation, green product innovation, mining, and fishing (Bendell 2000a; Murphy and Bendell 1997). These have involved leading national and multinational companies such as AEG Hausgeräte, the Body Shop, Intergamma, McDonald's, and Unilever, as well as many well-known NGOs including Greenpeace, Friends of the Earth, and WWF. Similarly, the Dutch covenant approach, initially pioneered in the 1980s, and developed extensively since, has involved business and government in jointly setting up voluntary environmental agreements based on consensus and consultation between government and industry bodies (Elkington 1999: 236–7). Increasingly, these extended forms of stakeholder collaboration have also emerged in other areas of business: various charities have joined with corporations in cause-related marketing campaigns; governments have worked with corporations to develop public–private partnerships for tackling social, educational, health, and transportation problems; and NGOs, trade unions, and government organizations have worked with businesses to develop initiatives aimed at improving working conditions and stamping out child labour and other human rights abuses in developing countries.

All of these developments and more we will discuss in greater detail in the second part of the book where we focus on business ethics and specific stakeholder groups. What is immediately clear, however, is that stakeholder relationships can take a variety of different forms, including the following:[5]

• **Challenge**—relationship based on mutual opposition and conflict;

• **Sparring partners**—relationship based on 'healthy conflict' and periodic bouts of conflict;

---

[4] Since the late 1980s and early 1990s numerous articles and books have extolled the virtues of collaborative activity amongst companies, including Hamel et al. (1989) and Jarillo and Stevenson (1991).

[5] Adapted from Elkington and Fennell's (2000) and Hartman and Stafford's (1997) delineation of different forms of business–NGO relationship.

- **One-way support**—relationship based on philanthropy, sponsorship, or other forms of resource contribution from one party to the other;

- **Mutual support**—relationship based on formal or informal two-way support, such as derived from strategic philanthropy, or as formalized through a third party association or body of some kind;

- **Endorsement**—relationship based on paid/unpaid public approval granted from one partner to the other in relation to a specific product or programme, such as in the case of labelling and accreditation schemes;

- **Project dialogue**—relationship based on discussion between partners regarding a specific project or proposal, such as stakeholder dialogue accompanying major regeneration or construction projects;

- **Strategy dialogue**—relationship based on discussion between partners over longer-term issues and the development of overall strategy for organizations, industries, or regulatory regimes;

- **Task force**—relationship based on co-operation to achieve a specific task such as a research project or new product/system development;

- **Joint venture or alliance**—relationship based on formal partnership involving significant mutual resource commitment to achieve specific goals.

Ethics in Action 5.1 presents the example of the Swedish organization The Natural Step, which works with businesses mainly in the areas of strategy and project dialogue. As the example shows, the organization seeks to use dialogue to find solutions that advance its own aims whilst simultaneously satisfying business goals.

> ### ■ Think theory
> What type of stakeholder relationship does The Natural Step have with its industry partners? What are the benefits and limitations of this approach for achieving sustainability?

It would appear that whilst the more confrontational forms of relationship are still very much in evidence, there has certainly been a significant shift towards the more collaborative types of relationship such as stakeholder dialogue and alliances. These can be seen to be emerging means for *managing* business ethics, primarily because closer forms of collaboration can surface stakeholder demands and interests and thereby provide companies with a greater opportunity to satisfy their stakeholders in some way. Moreover, by involving stakeholders more, it can be argued that a greater degree of democratic governance is introduced into corporate decision-making, thus enhancing corporate accountability.

On the reverse side, it is also clear that despite their obvious benefits for the management of business ethics, developments towards closer stakeholder relationships are not without their problems.

Ethics in Action 5.1

The Natural Step

Begun in Sweden in 1989 by Dr Karl-Henrik Robèrt, The Natural Step (TNS) is an international organization that uses a science-based systems framework to help organizations, individuals, and communities take steps towards sustainability. TNS is based on a framework that provides an all-embracing definition of the conditions that must apply in any sustainable society. These four system conditions, developed in collaboration with an international network of scientists, are as follows:

In the sustainable society, nature is not subject to systematically increasing . . .

1) Concentrations of substances extracted from the Earth's crust
This means substituting certain minerals that are scarce in nature with others that are more abundant, using all mined materials efficiently, and systematically reducing dependence on fossil fuels.

2) Concentrations of substances produced by society
This means systematically substituting certain persistent and unnatural compounds with ones that are normally abundant or break down more easily in nature, and using all substances produced by society efficiently.

3) Degradation by physical means
This means drawing resources only from well-managed eco-systems, systematically pursuing the most productive and efficient use both of those resources and land, and exercising caution in all kinds of modification of nature.
And, in that society . . .

4) Human needs are met worldwide.
This means using all of our resources efficiently, fairly and responsibly so that the needs of all people on whom we have an impact, and the future needs of people who are not yet born, stand the best chance of being met.

The main focus of TNS is to initiate change processes within organizations, rather than to develop programmes from outside and then impose 'solutions' on the organization. Their main focus therefore is training and consulting on a more general level, with the goal of enabling managers and staff themselves to identify areas of implementation and concrete steps for improvement.

By 2002 TNS was operating in nine different countries (including the UK, USA, and Japan), and counted among its national directors leading figures in the environmental movement such as Jonathon Porritt (UK) and Paul Hawken (USA). The organization has worked with many large business corporations, and in its home country of Sweden almost all regional municipalities have adopted the initiative.

For example, at IKEA, TNS provided management with the impulse to develop an eco-friendly line of furniture, and to implement a comprehensive staff training scheme on sustainability issues. When TNS started to work with Electrolux in 1998, the Swedish appliance multinational had just faced the loss of a major client for failing to meet key environmental criteria (see Case 10). The results of the collaboration were significant changes in the company's production technology and logistics systems, as well as cutting-edge innovations in products. When TNS started to work with Scandic, a leading hotel chain in northern Europe, the company had just been through a period of huge losses. Within a short time, though, with the help of TNS the company discovered the potential for an eco-friendly positioning in the hotel market that proved to be both an environmental and an economic success. TNS has also worked with the fast food chain McDonald's, first in Sweden, and later in the USA. The company has moved from plastic to paper wrapping, and now supplies many restaurants in Sweden and a few in the USA with alternative power.

In its approach, TNS has adopted an industry-friendly, co-operative style that focuses on win-win situations (for the environment and for the bottom line) rather than meting out criticism and condemnation of business methods. The leap to sustainability is often a daunting prospect for many corporations and TNS has worked towards providing companies with the impetus to get started. As one corporate manager that had worked with TNS put it, there was a need to set 'a vision' and TNS gave the company 'the route map'. Although, in the context of fast food companies or low-cost furniture manufacturers, the whole issue of sustainability might seem to some to be unattainable, TNS has concentrated on practical solutions.

SOURCES

Anon. (1998). 'Sustainable argument takes a step forward'. *Observer* (Business), 22 Mar.: 7.
Bradbury, H., and Clair, J. A. (1999). 'Promoting sustainable organizations with Sweden's Natural Step'.
    Academy of Management Executive, 13/4: 63–74.
www.thenaturalstep.org.

Problems with stakeholder collaboration

Potential problems with stakeholder collaboration can arise at a number of different levels, but can be basically summarized as follows:

1. **Resource intensity.** Stakeholder collaboration can be extremely time-consuming and expensive compared with traditional forms of corporate decision-making. Not only may firms not have sufficient resources to engage in extensive stakeholder collaboration, but by doing so, they may fail to meet the short-term financial goals expected of them by shareholders.

2. **Culture clash.** Companies and their stakeholders often exhibit very different values and goals, and this can lead to significant clashes in beliefs and ways of working, both between and within collaborating organizations (Crane 1998a).

3. **Schizophrenia.** At the same time as they are collaborating on one issue or project, companies and their stakeholders may also often be in conflict over another issue or project. This can result in apparently schizophrenic behaviour on either or both sides, which their partners may find it hard to deal with (Crane and Livesey 2003; Elkington and Fennell 2000).

4. **Uncontrollability.** Even with the best intentions of all parties, there is no guarantee with stakeholder collaboration that a mutually acceptable outcome can always be reached. However, not only can consensus be elusive, but by collaborating with many different partners, companies can lose control of both their strategic direction and their corporate image (Crane and Livesey 2003).

5. **Co-optation.** Some critics have raised the question of whether by involving themselves more closely with corporations, some stakeholder groups are effectively just being co-opted by corporations to embrace a more business-friendly agenda rather than maintaining true independence. The UN's Global Compact initiative described earlier in the chapter was criticized by some NGOs for allowing corporations to 'bluewash' their questionable practices by aligning themselves with the blue flag (and humanitarian ideals) of the UN and thereby weakening the scope for the UN to hold MNCs accountable for environmental, labour, and human rights.[6]

6. **Accountability.** Whilst stakeholder collaboration may partially redress problems with *corporate* accountability, there are also important concerns about the accountability of stakeholder organizations themselves (Bendell 2000*b*). Government bodies, quangos, trade unions, and NGOs, for example, can also be challenged on grounds of accountability to their members or the general public.

Again, we shall revisit some of these questions and problems in more detail in the relevant chapters in the second part of the book. However, our general conclusion regarding the benefits or otherwise of closer business–stakeholder relationships is that whilst the problems noted above need to be effectively thought through and dealt with, such developments should be cautiously welcomed and encouraged given their considerable potential for enhancing the management of business ethics.

Assessing ethical performance

As with any other form of management, the effective management of business ethics relies to some extent on being able to assess and evaluate performance. Low or disappointing performance in business ethics might call for increased attention to ethical issues and problems; high performance might indicate an effective approach to the management of business ethics. Almost immediately, however, it is possible to identify problems with this whole notion of ethical performance. What exactly is ethical performance? How can it possibly be measured? What criteria can we use to determine how good or bad our ethical performance is? What level of ethical performance is expected by, or acceptable to, our stakeholders? These are all vitally important questions to answer if we are to make any progress at all towards the effective management of business ethics. Unfortunately, whilst there are impressive developments currently taking place in this area, we are still a long way from being able to provide a comprehensive response.

At present there is a whole patchwork of initiatives that we might include within the umbrella of assessing ethical performance. These include ethical auditing, social auditing, accounting, and reporting, as well as environmental auditing, accounting, and reporting, and even sustainability reporting. With such a diversity of labels in use, there are obviously problems with distinguishing between different tools, techniques, and approaches. This is not helped by the fact that at times the distinctions between these terms are fairly

---

[6] See, for example, Nader (2000); for more information: **www.corpwatch.org/un**.

illusory and there has been much inconsistency in the way that different terms have been applied and used. For example, whilst the approach developed at Nijenrode Business School with the European Institute for Business Ethics has gone under the label 'ethical auditing', a reasonably similar approach developed by Traidcraft and the New Economics Foundation (NEF) is presented as 'social accounting and auditing' (Zadek 1998). Whilst Shell produces a 'social report', the Body Shop produces a 'values report', and Ben & Jerry's produces a 'social performance assessment'. Here though are some general distinctions which tend to apply in most cases:

- Approaches prefaced 'ethical' often tend to focus on internal management systems, or individual level aspects of the business, such as compliance with codes of ethics, incidences of bribery, legal violations, etc. For example, Ferrell et al. (2002: 196) suggest that an 'ethical compliance audit is a systematic evaluation of an organization's ethics program and/or performance to determine its effectiveness'. A second common use of 'ethical' is found in approaches which tend to focus on stakeholder values such as the 'ethical accounting' technique used by SbN Bank and Wøyen Mølle and the Body Shop's 'ethical audit' technique.[7]

- Approaches prefaced 'environmental' tend to focus exclusively on the organization's impact on the natural environment. Hence an environmental report will typically report on an organization's policies, programmes, and performance in various areas of environmental management, such as air and water pollution, resource efficiency, recycling, etc.

- Approaches prefaced 'social' tend to have a broader remit, covering a range of issues in addition to (or sometimes separate to) the environment, such as employee conditions, health and safety, equal opportunities, human rights, corporate giving, community relations. These approaches often incorporate impacts on a wide range of organizational stakeholders.

- Approaches prefaced 'sustainability' tend to be concerned with the triple bottom line of social, economic, and environmental considerations.

- Differences between the use of the terms 'auditing', 'accounting', and 'reporting' are still less clear-cut, but essentially 'accounting' is an overall process or discipline which includes 'auditing' (i.e. a measurement or checking exercise) and 'reporting' (i.e. a means of communicating data).

Given these distinctions, we shall refer to **social accounting** as the generic term which encapsulates the other tools and approaches. With its first usage dating back to the early 1970s, social accounting is also, according to Gray et al. (1997), the longest established and simplest term with which to work.

Defining social accounting

Probably the key factors that distinguish social accounting from conventional (financial) accounting are:

[7] For descriptions of these approaches, see chapters 5, 7, and 10 in Zadek et al. (1997).

- Its focus on issues other than (but not necessarily excluding) financial data;
- The intended audience being stakeholders other than (but again not excluding) shareholders;
- Unlike financial accounting, social accounting is not (at least as yet) required by law.

Broadly defined then, we regard social accounting as the following:

> Social accounting is the voluntary process concerned with assessing and communicating organizational activities and impacts on social, ethical, and environmental issues relevant to stakeholders.

So what does the process of social accounting involve? Again, there are no clear answers to this question. Unlike financial accounting, there are as yet no formal standards laying down the rules that determine which issues should be included, how performance on particular issues should be assessed, or how the organization should communicate its assessments to its audience. In many ways, this is not surprising. After all, whilst it is reasonably straightforward to calculate how much wages an organization has paid, or how many sales it might have made, this is much more difficult with social, ethical, and environmental issues. True, some of the social activities of an organization can be reasonably accurately determined, such as how much effluent might have been discharged into local rivers, or how much money has been given away to charitable causes. But even here, this does not tell us what the actual impact of these activities has been—how polluted does this make the water and what is the ultimate consequence for fish and other life? Or what were the actual effects of company donations on their recipients and how much happiness did they cause?

Much of the data collected and reported in social accounting is therefore inevitably qualitative in nature, particularly as organizations move away from an emphasis on environmental impacts towards more integrated social or sustainability reports. For example, Shell's 2001 social report *People, Planet, Profits* includes a mixture of quantitative data, such as greenhouse gas emissions, safety statistics, and gender diversity, as well as more qualitative data in the form of case studies of specific projects, quotes from various stakeholders, and outlines of key social issues and Shell's position on them.

The problem though is not only one of how to *assess* social impacts, but also of which impacts to *account for* in the first place. Organizations have different aims, problems, and achievements, their stakeholders have different interests and concerns, and the reasons for even engaging in social accounting at all will vary between different organizations. Inevitably, then, the nature and process of social accounting adopted by any organization is to some extent a function of how the particular organization sees itself and its relationship with its stakeholders (Zadek et al. 1997). As such, the practice of social accounting to date has tended to be evolutionary in nature, with organizations not only developing and refining their techniques over time, but also building in adaptation within the development cycle of a given report or audit. For example, **Figure 5.3** shows the framework established by the Body Shop. This includes **stakeholder consultation** to identify issues regarded as salient or of particular interest to stakeholders, prior to the main collection of data.

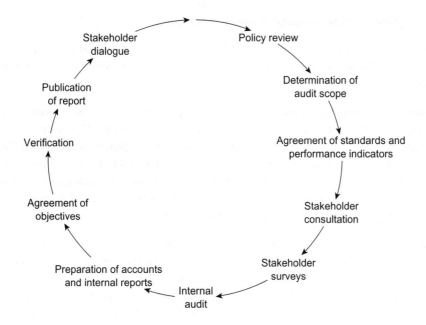

Figure 5.3. Framework for social accounting established by the Body Shop.

Source: Derived from Sillanpää and Wheeler (1997) and Sillanpää (1998).

Similarly, it also includes a process of **stakeholder dialogue** following publication of the report in order to obtain feedback and set priorities for future action.

Much of the activity involved in social accounting has therefore tended to increasingly revolve around communicating with stakeholders and getting their views on what issues matter, and how they regard the organization's impact on areas of concern. **Stakeholder satisfaction surveys**—of employees, customers, and others—have therefore been extensively used, as have focus groups and other methods of communication and data collection.

What is clear then is that in the absence of recognized standards for social accounting, organizations have had to (or been able to) develop their own particular approaches. Although this has resulted in some innovative, impressive, and genuinely useful methodologies and reports, it has also led to the production of some vague, self-serving, and rather disappointing efforts that have been useful neither to stakeholders nor to the organization's management. Thus, whilst some organizations such as Traidcraft, BSO/ Origin, Shell, SbN Bank, the Body Shop, Co-op Bank, Volvo, and others have won awards and plaudits for their social and environmental reports, many other companies (and even some of those we have just mentioned!) have simply been accused of trying to cynically 'greenwash' the public. This raises two important questions:

• Why do organizations take up social accounting in the first place?

• What makes for an effective approach to social accounting?

Why do organizations engage in social accounting?

As with many aspects of business ethics, there are both practical and moral reasons for taking up social accounting, but in essence, we can usefully reduce these to three main issues.

• **Internal and external pressure.** Pressure from competitors, industry associations, governments, shareholders, consumers, and even internal executives can all provide incentives for firms to engage in various aspects of social accounting (Solomon and Lewis 2002). Not only have the FTSE4Good and the Dow Jones Sustainability indices fuelled interest from investors in social accounting, but associations such as the Association of British Insurers and the UK National Association of Pension Funds have also called for companies to report on social and environmental matters (Cowe 2001).

• **Improved stakeholder management.** At the very least, social accounting provides a new channel of communication to stakeholders by which organizations might seek to improve their reputation. Indeed, consumers and other stakeholder tend to believe that concerns for marketing and enhancing the corporate image are the main reasons corporations engage in such processes (Solomon and Lewis 2002). At a more sophisticated level, though, it is evident that in order to manage their relationships with stakeholders effectively, organizations need to know what issues those stakeholders regard as important, and how well they think the organization is performing in those areas (Zadek et al. 1997). Social accounting can therefore give organizations a clearer picture of what they are trying to achieve, what they are actually doing, and what the implications are of their business activities (Zadek 1998).

• **Enhanced accountability and transparency.** Social accounting is not just about more effective management, though. As we saw in Chapter 2, the need for corporations to make evident their social role and impacts (transparency) is a key requirement for ensuring that they are answerable in some way for the consequences of their actions (accountability). Clearly, by reporting on social performance, social accounting can play a significant role in this drive for enhanced accountability and transparency (Gray 1992; Zadek 1998). However, there are also limitations to the approach, particularly as it currently stands. Not only is social accounting voluntary, but also, without adequate standards, organizations can effectively report on anything they want. Moreover, as Livesey (2002a) contends, corporations can utilize the medium of social reports to shape expectations about what corporations can and should do, as well as use them to wrestle greater control over controversial debates regarding the definition of social and environmental justice.

Given these reasons there is a reasonably strong case for suggesting that corporations 'should' engage in social accounting, provided one believes that stakeholders have some intrinsic rights and legitimate claims on the corporation. Clearly though, as yet most corporations do not practise any form of social accounting, suggesting a number of important **disincentives for social accounting**. These include: perceived high costs;

insufficient information; inadequate information systems; lack of standards; secrecy; and an unwillingness to disclose sensitive or confidential data.

■ **Think theory**

Which ethical perspectives appear to be driving the development of social accounting?

What makes for 'good' social accounting?

Clearly the question of what is 'good' social accounting will depend on what the initial purpose is, and which perspective—organizational, stakeholder, or other—you are asking the question from. However, it is evident that as the development of tools and techniques has evolved and been refined over time, there is some consensus emerging about standards of quality. The following eight issues have been proposed by three leading figures in social accounting as the key principles of quality (see Zadek et al. 1997):

• **Inclusivity.** Good social accounting will reflect the views and accounts of all principal stakeholders, and will involve two-way communication *with* them rather than just one-way communication either *to* them or *from* them.

• **Comparability.** In order for assessment of social performance to be meaningful, social accounting should allow for comparisons across different periods, with other organizations, and relative to external standards or benchmarks.

• **Completeness.** All areas of the organization's activities should be included in the assessment, rather than just focusing on areas where a more positive impression might be realized.

• **Evolution.** In order to reflect changing stakeholder expectations, social accounting practices should also demonstrate a commitment to learning and change.

• **Management policies and systems.** To ensure effective institutionalization of the social accounting process, it should be consolidated within systems and procedures that allow for it to be rigorously controlled and evaluated.

• **Disclosure.** The issue of accountability would suggest that good social accounting should involve clear disclosure of accounts and reports to all stakeholders, in a form that is appropriate to their needs.

• **External verification.** The extent to which audiences will have faith and confidence in a social account will depend to some extent on whether it has been verified as a true representation of reality by an external body trusted by that audience. The perceived independence of verifiers from the organization will also be critical in this respect.

• **Continuous improvement.** Finally, a good method of social accounting should be able to actively encourage the organization to continually improve its performance across the areas covered by the process, and to extend the process to areas currently unassessed, or assessed unsatisfactorily.

Existing evidence suggests that many of these principles are not currently integrated particularly well into most companies' social accounting procedures. For example, Belal's (2002) recent analysis of the main social reporters in the UK leads him to conclude that issues of stakeholder inclusiveness, external verification, and completeness are relatively poorly attended to. Nonetheless, the delineation of quality principles does at least represent an initial step in a process towards developing adequate standards for social accounting—a process that is already well under way. Several important schemes are currently in place that seek to tackle specific aspects of social accounting. For example:

• **Auditing and certifying.** The social accountability standard **SA 8000** is a workplace standard launched in 1997 that covers key labour rights such as working hours, forced labour, and discrimination, and, crucially, certifies compliance through independent accredited auditors. SA 8000 has been developed through consultation with a broad range of stakeholders including workers, employers, NGOs, and unions, and continues to do so in order to ensure continuous improvement of the standard, and to shape it according to regional and cultural differences (**www.sa-intl.org**).

• **Reporting.** The **Global Reporting Initiative (GRI)** is an international multi-stakeholder effort to create a common framework for reporting on the social, economic, and environmental triple bottom line of sustainability. Ethics in Action 5.2 describes the challenges and achievements of the GRI in more detail.

• **Reporting assurance.** The **AA1000S Assurance Standard**, launched in 2002, is the first attempt to provide a coherent and robust basis for assuring a public report and its underlying processes, systems, and competencies against a concrete definition and principles of accountability and stakeholder engagement. The standard is specifically designed to be consistent with the GRI sustainability reporting guidelines (**http://www.accountability.org.uk**).

Such programmes are still in relatively early stages of development, yet they clearly offer considerable potential in providing more effective means for assessing, and ultimately improving, the sustainability and accountability of corporations through social accounting. Moreover, the ongoing efforts of the organizations leading the development of AA1000S, GRI, and SA 8000 to integrate their different systems and approaches means that corporations are gradually being offered a range of interlocking standards for some of the many different aspects of business ethics management. As we shall now see, in the next and last main section in this chapter, there are a number of different ways of organizing these various aspects within an overall approach to business ethics management.

Ethics in Action 5.2

The Global Reporting Initiative

At present, over 2,000 companies around the world report information on their economic, environmental, and social policies, practices, and performance. However, this information is generally inconsistent, incomplete, and unverified. Measurement and reporting practices vary widely according to industry, location, and regulatory requirements. One recent study found that seventy-nine of the top hundred UK companies published some information on social performance—but that three-quarters of those companies provided no quantitative data at all to back up their claims. A generally accepted framework for reporting is therefore regarded as vital if stakeholders are to be able to gauge the social performance of organizations and make meaningful comparisons with other organizations.

The Global Reporting Initiative (GRI) was established in 1997 by the Coalition for Environmentally Responsible Economies (CERES) in partnership with the United Nations Environment Programme (UNEP). Its mission was to create just such a common framework for voluntary reporting on economic, environmental, and social performance, i.e. the 'triple bottom line' of sustainability. The GRI is an international multi-stakeholder effort involving dialogue and collaboration between corporations, non-governmental organisations (NGOs), accountancy organizations, business associations, and other stakeholders in order to develop and implement widely applicable sustainability reporting guidelines.

Following a lengthy consultation period and extensive pilot testing in companies such as British Airways, Body Shop, Electrolux, Norvo Nodisk, and Ford, the first GRI guidelines were released in 2000. These represented the first global framework for comprehensive sustainability reporting, and have been referred to, or followed by, more than a hundred companies across the globe since their release. Certainly, then, the GRI guidelines have been an important first step in the ongoing drive towards harmonization of reporting procedures. Clearly, though, the path to widely accepted guidelines for reporting on something as complex and multifaceted as sustainability is likely to be a long and difficult one. The standardization sought by GRI, particularly given the impressive inclusivity of its consultation process, might easily become a recipe for dilution of standards towards the lowest common denominator.

GRI obviously recognizes the enormous challenge presented by its mission and adopts a process of continual learning and revision of its guidelines. Immediately following the release of the 2000 guidelines, the GRI initiated another extensive and wide-ranging consultation process involving hundreds of organizations and individuals, including both reporters and report users. The purpose of this was to develop the next draft of the guidelines, which was subsequently released in 2002.

The GRI still has a long way to go before it succeeds in its vision to elevate sustainability reporting to the status enjoyed by financial reporting and make sustainability reporting 'as routine and credible as financial reporting in terms of comparability, rigour, and verifiability'. Among others, one critical issue is that GRI is only concerned with establishing procedures for *voluntary* reporting and has no explicit aim to promote *mandatory* reporting. Moreover, there are still important questions to be answered about how and whether the GRI guidelines can best accommodate the needs of diverse communities across the globe, particularly in the context of small companies and/or those operating in developing countries where formal company reports typical of MNCs may be excessively burdensome to produce and of little practical use to their relevant stakeholders. Nonetheless, GRI has met with considerable success in taking the critical first steps towards greater harmonization in sustainability reporting, and it represents an important and, in many respects, progressive attempt to wrestle with the enormous challenge of enhancing corporate accountability through social accounting.

SOURCES

www.globalreporting.org.

Line, M. E., and Woodhead, J. P. (1999). 'Global Reporting Initiative draft guidelines and their application in corporate reporting'. In *Business Strategy and the Environment Conference Proceedings*. Shipley: ERP Environment: 199–208.

Cowe, R. (2001). 'Corporate gloss obscures the hard facts'. *Financial Times*, 11 Dec.: 18.

■ **Think theory**

Think about the GRI in terms of Zadek et al.'s (1997) eight principles of quality in social accounting. To what extent would you say it conforms to and contributes to good practice?

Organizing for business ethics management

If businesses are going to directly manage business ethics, then at some stage they are likely to face the question of how best to organize the various components and integrate them into the company in order to achieve their goals. In the USA, it has become commonplace for business ethics specialists and textbooks to advocate formal ethics or compliance programmes, and such an approach has been taken up by many leading US corporations. However, due to a different regulatory environment, as well as significantly different business cultures in Europe, such a formal approach to business ethics management has been much more rarely promoted or adopted here. However, the increasing attention being devoted to ethical codes as well as to various accounting, auditing, and reporting standards in Europe suggests that a more formal approach to ethics management is becoming more widespread, and can be expected to become more so in the future.

Formal ethics programmes

According to Treviño et al. (1999) there are four main ways of approaching the formal organization of business ethics management (see **Figure 5.4**):

• **Compliance orientation.** Under this approach, the main emphasis is on preventing, detecting, and punishing violations of the law. Employees are informed of the law and are motivated to do the right thing through fear of being caught. This is based on the assumption that, regardless of their own values, the competitive environment may encourage employees to do whatever it takes to get a job done, including illegal or unethical activity (Hoffman et al. 2001). However, according to Lynne Sharp Paine (1994), because a compliance

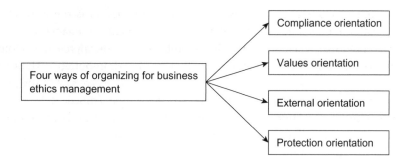

Figure 5.4. Organizing for business ethics management
Source: Treviño et al. (1999).

approach defines ethics in terms of legal compliance rather than ethical aspirations, it implicitly endorses a 'a code of moral mediocrity'.

• **Values orientation.** This approach is based on defining organizational values and encouraging employee commitment to certain ethical aspirations (Paine 1994). According to Treviño et al. (1999: 135), the values approach is 'rooted in personal self-governance' and provides the means for ethical decision-making where no particular rules are in place.

• **External orientation.** An external orientation focuses less on company values, and more on satisfying external stakeholders such as customers, the community, and shareholders (Treviño et al. 1999). Here, what is regarded as right is what is expected by, or at least acceptable to, key external constituencies.

• **Protection orientation.** Finally, Treviño et al. (1999) suggest that some programmes are primarily (or at least perceived to be) oriented towards protecting top management from blame for ethical problems or legal violations. Employees and other stakeholders may see the introduction of ethics management as little more than an attempt to create legal cover for managers in case of accidents or legal infractions of some sort. Indeed, it is not uncommon for regulators to impose lower fines on corporations with some kind of management system in place to prevent ethical, environmental, or legal violations.

In the USA, compliance approaches appear to predominate (Weaver et al. 1999*b*), whereas in Europe, as we have seen, the emergence of ethics management has tended to be driven more by external and values-based approaches. However, the important thing to remember is that these four approaches are not mutually inconsistent, and most organizations are likely to combine two or more approaches (Weaver et al. 1999*b*). For example, earlier in the chapter we explained that many ethical codes are based on core corporate values and principles (a values orientation), whereas the effectiveness of such codes also depended on appropriate implementation and follow-through, such as the disciplining of employees found in breach of them (compliance orientation). Similarly, rigorously policed ethical auditing processes based on stakeholder consultation and engagement might be said to combine values, external, and compliance orientations.

Although research on the effectiveness of different approaches (and combinations of approaches) is fairly scant, Treviño et al.'s (1999) survey of over 10,000 employees in six large American companies suggests that a values orientation is the most effective single orientation for encouraging ethical behaviour, although compliance and external orientations could also, to a lesser degree, be helpful. A protection approach was found to be a clearly harmful approach. Nonetheless, regardless of their importance, these formal elements are only one aspect of business ethics management. As we saw in the previous chapter, many authors suggest that the broader ethical context, embedded in the culture and climate of the organization, is highly influential in shaping ethical decision-making. Hence, in organizing for business ethics management, it is important to also consider the ethical culture of the organization.

Informal ethics management: ethical culture and climate

In Chapter 4 we saw how the culture and norms of an organization could have a profound effect on ethical decision-making. However, this does not necessarily mean that culture can be simply changed or made 'more ethical' to support enhanced business ethics. Nonetheless, this is exactly the argument that has been most commonly advocated in the business ethics literature. Improvements in ethical decision-making have been widely argued to require a managed transformation of the organization's values in order to create a 'more ethical' culture (Chen et al. 1997; Robin and Reidenbach 1987; Treviño and Nelson 1999) Thus, Treviño and Nelson (1999: 204) in their best-selling textbook suggest that 'organizations can proactively develop an ethical organizational culture, and that organizations with "ethics problems" should take a culture change approach to solving them'.

Despite the popularity of the **culture change** approach, there has been rather limited attention focused on establishing how such a transformation might take place, why it might occur, or even if it is possible at all. As the management and organizational studies literatures have so effectively demonstrated, the deliberate management of culture is a difficult, lengthy process, which is rarely successful except at very superficial levels.[8] Indeed, there has been precious little empirical evidence in the literature that provides wholesale support for the claim that culture can indeed be managed in the realm of ethical behaviour. Existing cultural beliefs and values about what is right and wrong tend to be very resistant to change (Crane 2001a; Desmond and Crane 2003).

Accordingly, the use of explicit culture change to improve corporate ethical behaviour has begun to be seriously questioned, particularly among European authors, where such compliance- and control-based approaches are generally afforded a certain degree of scepticism. Amanda Sinclair (1993: 68) for example concludes that: 'the lessons from research are that you meddle with the organizational culture if you've got little choice, lots of resources, and lots of time—a combination of circumstances, some would argue, rare enough to render the approach irrelevant.' Peter Dahler-Larsen (1994) further contends that attempts to create 'ethical cultures' tend to reward conformity rather than the very autonomy that is crucial for a sense of morality to exist.

---

[8] This has been a recurring theme in the organizational and management studies literature. See for example Martin (1985), Nord (1985), Ogbonna (1992), and more recently, Ogbonna and Harris (1998).

A somewhat different approach has therefore been more vigorously advocated in Europe that focuses on **cultural learning**. Rather than seeking conformity to a single set of values, the learning approach focuses on smaller subcultural groups within the firm. By encouraging surveillance, dialogue, and critique between these subcultural groups (and with the firm's stakeholders), 'ethical discourse and dialectic as well as conflict' can be prompted, thus surfacing and challenging commonplace assumptions and behaviours (Sinclair 1993: 69). Ken Starkey (1998) thus contends that moral development in organizations requires factionalism and dissent in order to promote learning. The role of management consequently becomes one of surfacing conflicting values, unleashing the moral commitment of subcultures, and from this promoting *moral imagination* rather than imposing authoritarian *ideological control.*

Clearly both approaches have their merits and problems. The culture change approach may have only limited potential to effect real change, but is considerably more attractive to many firms who not only may desire considerable control over the culture, but may also be worried about the potentially damaging effects of surfacing moral differences through the process of cultural learning. Clearly, though, both pose significant challenges for company leaders in shaping a more appropriate context for ethical decision-making.

Business ethics and leadership

Whatever approach an organization might have to managing business ethics, whether it is formal or informal, compliance-based or values-based, minimal or extensive, the role of the organization's leaders is going to be significant. Leaders are often said to set the ethical tone in organizations. If they are perceived as being ruthless and inconsiderate in their dealings with others, or if they seem to care only about the short-term bottom line, employees are likely to get that message too. When that happens, there would appear to be little prospect for ensuring ethical behaviour lower down the organizational hierarchy. Leaders can thus play a significant role in the contextual factors such as authority, norms, and culture that we have shown to be key influences on ethical and unethical decision-making (Sims and Brinkmann 2002).

Unfortunately, although leadership is one of the most widely discussed and researched areas of organizational behaviour, there is considerable disagreement about even the most elemental aspects of the subject (Gini 1997). However, the main starting point is usually to delineate leadership from management. According to Kotter (1990) whereas management is about *imposing order*—through planning, organizing, budgeting, and controlling—leadership is more about *coping with change*—setting direction and vision, motivating and inspiring people, and facilitating learning. For many writers, then, leadership is an intrinsically moral terrain, for it is fundamentally entwined with a particular set of values or beliefs about what is the right thing to do. As Gini (1997: 325) argues: 'All leadership is value laden. All leadership, whether good or bad, is moral leadership . . . The point is, all leadership claims a particular point of view or philosophical package of ideas it wishes to advocate and advance. All forms of leadership try to establish the guidelines, set the tone and control the manners and morals of the constituency of which they are a part.'

If one accepts this argument then leaders clearly have a profound role in shaping the ethical decisions of their employees. However, as we saw above in relation to the management of culture, it is one thing to say that something—leadership, culture, etc—*shapes* business ethics, but is quite another to then suggest that one can simply *change* the culture or the leadership to ensure ethical behaviour. Nonetheless, it would appear reasonable to conclude that since leaders do appear to influence the actions of their employees, it is important to look at how best to develop ethical leadership.

If we return to our two approaches to managing for an ethical culture—*culture change* and *cultural learning*—it is possible to identify two very different modes of ethical leadership. Under the culture change approach, the leader's role is to articulate and personify the values and standards that the organization aspires to, and then to inspire and motivate employees to follow their lead. For example, Treviño et al. (2000) suggest that there are two pillars to developing a reputation for ethical leadership: to be perceived as a *moral person* and as a *moral manager*. According to the authors, for the executive to be perceived as a moral person employees need to recognize genuine individual traits in them such as honesty and integrity; to be seen as a moral manager entails focusing the organization's attention on ethics and values and infusing the organization with principles that will guide the actions of all employees. This is a well-worn path for commentators on business ethics to go down, but it holds clear dangers if employees perceive a credibility gap between the public pronouncements of senior executives and the reality they experience according to their view 'from the trenches' (Badaracco and Webb 1995). As we saw earlier in the chapter, follow-through is often significantly more important in encouraging ethical behaviour than statements of beliefs or codes of ethics.

From the cultural learning perspective, the role of leadership is more one of participation and empowerment in order to foster moral imagination and autonomy. Thus, employees are encouraged 'to think independently, to be able to make reasoned, responsible evaluations and choices on their own; to be, in short, free moral agents' (Rosenthal and Buchholz 2000: 194). There are resonances here with those advocating both postmodern ethics and discourse ethics. Ethical behaviour is not to be promoted simply through the promulgation of specific beliefs and principles, but through facilitating personal moral engagement, dialogue, and choice. There are dangers here too though—such as shifting from encouraging individual choice to accepting moral relativism, or surrendering control over employees and their decisions.

Ultimately, given the controversy and debate that continues to rage in the leadership literature, there is unlikely to be any real consensus emerging in relation to ethical leadership. Clearly though it is an important area of business ethics management, and without top management support, most of the tools and techniques discussed in this chapter would be unlikely to contribute all that much to improving business ethics. However, there is always a slight danger of focusing too strongly on the few people at the top of the organization when many of the fundamentals of business ethics are about the day-to-day decisions that each and every one of us makes in our organizational lives.

Summary

As this chapter has demonstrated, the area of business ethics management is evolving rapidly, and much of the literature we have covered here has been at the very forefront of contemporary business ethics theory and practice. As a result, much of what we have presented here is, by its very nature, somewhat partial and inconclusive. Nonetheless, we have shown that the nature of business ethics management in Europe emphasizes an external, socially based orientation rather than concentrating mainly on ethical codes to ensure compliance. Indeed, we have shown that the effectiveness of codes of ethics has been seriously questioned, with current thinking stressing the importance of implementation over content. We have also set out a clear picture of developments in stakeholder management, social accounting, and organizing for the management of business ethics.

We will finish the chapter though by addressing a more general criticism that has frequently been raised about business ethics management tools and techniques, particularly in respect to how they have been implemented in business practice. Does the development and use of these practices represent a genuine commitment by companies to accept their social responsibilities, or does it merely represent an increasing sophistication in deflecting criticism through smart public relations?

At one level, dismissing these efforts as 'merely PR' does an injustice to both fields. Many of these techniques share a common goal with public relations in their emphasis on developing and maintaining good relationships with key stakeholder groups (Clark 2000). PR models suggest that sophisticated public relations involves two-way dialogue with relevant publics in order to build mutual understanding and consensus, as well as to understand emerging issues and pressures (Grunig and Hunt 1984). However, the accusation of 'merely PR' is distinctly pejorative, and is meant to suggest that business ethics management is largely a cosmetic exercise to make the company look more responsible than it actually is. Clearly this is a very real concern, and one that is habitually raised by consumers, employees, and others in response to various developments in business ethics management.

Our view is that whilst there may well be little substance behind many impressive-sounding codes of ethics or glossy environmental reports, this doesn't mean that we should denounce *all* business ethics management as just cynical window dressing. Each case should be assessed on its own merits. The key issue to address is how to determine what makes for best practice in each area, and how best to establish widely accepted frameworks and quality standards through which meaningful evaluations and comparisons can be made.

At another level, perhaps one of the reasons why some commentators are so often critical of the application of business ethics management tools and techniques is that those who promote or use them may simply be overstating their benefits. Suggesting that an organization's ethics problems will be solved simply by having an ethical code, an ethics officer, a marketing tie-up with a charity, or any of the other elements we have discussed in this chapter, is never going to stand up to scrutiny. The application of these tools can only ever assist in managing business ethics, and their success or failure rests not so much on the tool itself, but on the motivation for its use, the process of its development, and the manner in which it is implemented and followed up.

STUDY QUESTIONS

1   What are the main elements of business ethics management? Discuss and account for the extent to which they are likely to be used in contemporary European corporations.

2   Can business ethics be taught to current or future business people? Explain with reference to your own experience of studying business ethics.

3   What are codes of ethics and how useful are they for the management of business ethics?

4   Set out the main types of relationship that corporations can have with their stakeholders. Are any of these types preferable? Explain your answer with reference to examples from current business practice.

5   What is social accounting, and why do companies engage in it?

6   Assess the relative benefits and drawbacks of different approaches to ethics management. Would you recommend that an organization emphasized a formal or an informal approach to business ethics management?

RESEARCH EXERCISE

Search on the internet for examples of two companies who produce social reports where the two companies are either:

(a) From different industries but in the same country; or
(b) From the same industry but different countries.

1   What differences are evident between the two companies in terms of the range of issues dealt with in the reports and the depth of coverage on specific issues?

2   To what extent can these differences be explained by the country or industry differences? What other explanations might there be?

3   Assess the apparent quality of the social accounting approach utilized by each company according to Zadek et al.'s (1997) criteria.

4   How appropriate would it be for the two companies to use the same standardized approach?

CASE 5

Shell shocked: has Shell moved towards a new way of managing business ethics?

This case looks at the efforts made by Shell to develop new ways of managing business ethics in the aftermath of major problems in its international operations in the mid-1990s. The case gives an opportunity for examining the benefits and drawbacks of various components of business ethics management discussed in the chapter, and in particular provides for a focus on stakeholder dialogue and social accounting.

Operating in over 135 countries, and employing more than 90,000 people, the British-Dutch group of companies Royal Dutch/Shell is one of the world's largest companies. Known mainly for its Shell brand of petrol and lubricants, the firm is actually involved in various aspects of the energy industry. In recent years, though, the Shell name has become as much associated with business ethics issues as it has with the energy business. The experiences of 1995, when Shell was catapulted to international attention over its battles with Greenpeace over the Brent Spar oil platform, and with its problems in Nigeria, led to the beginning of a significant turnaround in the company that is still being played out today. The new approach has represented an enormous challenge to Shell's previously conservative and inward-looking style of management, with it even becoming a pioneer in developing new ways of engaging and communicating with stakeholders. Whilst the firm has won prizes and plaudits for its actions, not all of its critics have been appeased. For many, the question still remains whether its attempts to marry profits with principles are just window dressing for an essentially unsustainable approach to business.

1995: Shellshock!

For any multinational company, one huge blow to the corporate reputation in a year is a major cause for concern. However, two massive public relations disasters *in the same year* is about as close to out-and-out corporate catastrophe as you can get. That though is exactly what happened to Shell in 1995 when the firm attracted international vilification for actions which, in many respects, were little different from what it had always done. In the event, though, almost overnight Shell found itself turned into a symbol of all that was wrong about multinational companies.

Two key events crystallized Shell's problems in the 1990s. First, Shell UK's plans to dispose of its ageing oil platform Brent Spar in the North Sea became the subject of international news headlines when the platform was dramatically occupied by Greenpeace activists. Playing on the David and Goliath imagery of its fight against the multinational, Greenpeace denounced Shell's 'toxic time-bomb' and mobilized intense protests across Europe, most notably in Germany. This included a major consumer boycott, an intervention by Chancellor Kohl at the G7 summit, a second, more daring occupation of the Spar, and even vandalism, firebombing, and gunfire at Shell service stations. In the wake of such criticism, and despite continuing to have the full support of the UK government, Shell capitulated and abandoned its decision to dump the Spar. Greenpeace hailed the decision as a 'victory for everybody, a victory for common sense and a victory for the environment'. Shell meanwhile continued to maintain that sea disposal was the best environmental solution (as did the UK government), suggesting that the affair was a matter of 'the power of emotion [and] fear' over 'scientific reason and careful judgement'.

More problems surfaced for Shell later in the year when its operations in Nigeria came under fire following the execution of Ken Saro-Wiwa and eight other campaigners for the Ogoni people. The Ogoni had long protested against Shell's drilling activities in their homeland in the Niger delta, arguing that not only had Shell's operations devastated the local environment, but few if any of the benefits of the multinational's lucrative operation in Ogoniland had found their way back to the Ogoni people. International condemnation of Shell's implicit support of the Nigerian military regime exploded when the company declined to use its influence in Nigeria to try and revoke the death sentences passed on the nine environmentalists for their anti-Shell protests.

The road to recovery

Regardless of the rights or wrongs of Shell's actions, these events constituted massive shocks to the firm. In 1996 the Group undertook extensive market research and stakeholder consultation to discover how it was perceived. Stunned by the resulting picture of public antipathy and stung by its image as a corporate villain, Shell sought to change direction. Beginning with a very public acknowledgement that it had erred in its approach to Brent Spar and Nigeria, the company virtually reinvented its strategy. Realizing that it had to operate in a very different world from the past, with radically new expectations and challenges, the Group revised and updated its General Business Principles to take account of a broader range of ethical issues and constituencies—and even committed bosses to report directly on efforts to live up to them. Perhaps more remarkably, though, the once insular company committed itself to a level of stakeholder consultation and engagement unthinkable even a few years previously. Shell argued that reliance on its traditional modes of insular, scientific decision-making and justification was no longer appropriate for dealing with the social and human problems it faced, and the multiple actors and viewpoints involved. Shell, its leaders claimed, had to learn how to listen. In the words of its 1998 report, the company decided it had to move from a 'trust me' world to a 'show me' world.

These changes had significant impact on the Brent Spar decommissioning decision. The cold rationality of cost–benefit analysis and 'best practicable environmental option' was supplemented with a series of stakeholder dialogue meetings where Shell would listen to the views of key stakeholders and opinion formers, including their critics. In 1999, following an extensive consultative process —including even its former nemesis Greenpeace—the Spar was eventually recycled as the base for a quay in Norway—at twice the cost of sea disposal. Stakeholder consultation and engagement was also rolled out to other areas of the firm's operations, including well-publicized programmes in Peru, the Philippines, and Canada. As Shell put it, its decision processes had been transformed from DAD—decide, announce, deliver—to DDD—dialogue, decide, deliver.

In Nigeria, whilst improvements were made, the new approach appeared to have been more difficult to implement. This stemmed from a number of factors, including the legacy of the past, the profusion of factions amongst the Ogoni, and certain differences in management competence and culture in Shell Nigeria. Despite making various commitments, instituting new policies, and activating stakeholder responsiveness strategies, Shell struggled to engage successfully with local communities and establish mutual understanding with the Ogoni. Problems have persisted, and reconciliation has been only partial.

More successful has been Shell's introduction of social accounting. Appearing initially in 1998 under the title 'Profits and Principles: Does There Have to be a Choice?', the Shell Group's annual social report has publicly committed the company to sustainable development. With sections on the triple bottom line of economic, social, and environmental performance, the report includes an impressive array of data and discussion on virtually all issues relevant to the business. Developing a credible approach to social auditing and reporting has, however, not been easy, not least because Shell was moving into virtually uncharted territory for such an immense multinational corporation. The process appears though to have benefited from an ongoing commitment to consultation, learning, and continuous improvement in developing indices and reporting methods. Claiming that to some extent it has had to 'write the book [on social reporting] as it has gone along', Shell has also been involved in multilateral efforts to improve systems and standards, such as the Global Reporting Initiative. Indeed, Shell's progressive approach to reporting has been widely praised and has consistently garnered awards from bodies such as the UK Association of Chartered Certified Accountants (ACCA).

Accompanying the new approach to accounting and engagement has been the Tell Shell programme which gives anyone who is interested an easy means of communicating with the company, either through reply-paid postcard, email, or Shell's uncensored web forum. The latter in particular is a brave attempt by the company to acknowledge, rather than attempting to silence or discredit, its critics. Comments on the web forum are incredibly diverse, both in subject matter and in their level of appreciation for Shell's efforts. A few random quotes taken from the website are illustrative of this diversity:

A word to your marketing department: people will tolerate greed and corruption, but no one will willingly put up with hypocrisy. Disgusted.

Shell, I work for a franchise that consists of you, Texaco and Chevron in Seattle and I think you guys are doing an excellent job. I believe all those tree huggers need to calm down. People like us help keep the world moving. Without gas how would people get around? I am very impressed by your work and it is a pleasure working for your corporation.

Read: Marxism. Plain and simple. What a load of bull****. And this one's for all you 'Global Warming' pundits— Fill a glass with ice and let it melt. I'll bet my paycheck it doesn't flood your city. Idiots.

The Tell Shell programme feeds into the company's social report, with the document liberally sprinkled with quotes, both positive and negative, under the heading 'You Told Shell'. In this way, Shell is able to indicate the breadth of views relevant to a particular issue and to point to how it has listened to its stakeholders and responded to them. Tell Shell has also been linked up with the company's ambitious global advertising campaign that has sought to help rebuild its tarnished corporate image. Launched to a mass market in 1999, the €23m 'Profits and Principles' campaign marked a step change from Shell's initial efforts to open up dialogue with specific publics and influencers. The ads featured employees living Shell's new values through environmental work, and invited audience feedback through the Tell Shell programme. Nonetheless, the campaign drew fire from its critics for glossing over the messy realities of Shell's global business operations. A company with a legacy of environmental destruction whose business model was still almost completely reliant on the extraction of non-renewable fossil fuels was perhaps inevitably going to be met with some degree of cynicism when making so public a declaration of integrity.

For Shell, then, whilst it has clearly triggered a much lauded, and almost unthinkable, sea-change in its approach to managing business ethics, the memories of the past have prevented it from thoroughly winning over all of its critics. The experiences of its main competitors are apposite in this respect. UK oil giant BP, which actually continues to enjoy a rather less hostile relationship with industry critics, provoked something of a storm in 2001 when it rolled out its ambitious, high-profile €100m ethical rebranding campaign complete with a new name, *Beyond Petroleum*, and a new 'green' logo. Still, the critics' main ire in recent years has been reserved for US industry leader ExxonMobil, which trades in Europe under the Esso brand. A major boycott against the company was sparked in 2001 when the company refused to join Shell, BP, and others in supporting the Kyoto Protocol on global warming and making commitments to cut greenhouse gases. Much like the Shell of old, ExxonMobil has stood its ground and, in efforts to undermine its detractors, has persistently lobbied government representatives and financed research and marketing campaigns to cast doubt over the scientific validity of climate change.

Questions

1 How would you describe Shell's overall strategy of business ethics management? To what extent are each of the elements used by the company complementary to this strategy?

2 Describe the different stakeholder relationships revealed in the case. Using the instrumental perspective on stakeholder importance described in this chapter, how would you rate the apparent importance of each of Shell's stakeholders here? In what ways does this differ from their importance from a *normative* perspective?

3 Do you feel that Shell has gone far enough in its attempts to turn around its approach? What more could or should it do—or should it not have even embarked on this course of action in the first place? Will it ever satisfy its critics sufficiently?

Sources

Arnold, Matthew (2001). 'Walking the ethical tightrope'. *Marketing*, 12 July: 17.

Curtis, James (1999). 'Is TV too much for Shell's "ethical" rebuild?' *Marketing*, 7 Oct.: 21.

Hutton, Will (2001). 'Fortune favours brave who join the new world order'. *Observer*, 8 July.

Livesey, Sharon (2001). 'Eco-identity as discursive struggle: Royal Dutch/Shell, Brent Spar, and Nigeria'. *Journal of Business Communication*, 38/1: 58–91.

Wheeler, David, Fabig, Heike, and Boele, Richard (2002). 'Paradoxes and dilemmas for stakeholder responsive firms in the extractive sector: lessons from the case of Shell and the Ogoni'. *Journal of Business Ethics*, 39: 297–318.

Zyglidopoulos, Stelios C. (2002). 'The social and environmental responsibilities of multinationals: evidence from the Brent Spar case'. *Journal of Business Ethics*, 36: 141–51.

www.shell.com.

www.accountability.org.uk.

PART II

Contextualizing Business Ethics

The Corporate Citizen and its Stakeholders

Introduction to Part II

The second part of the book looks in turn at the key individual stakeholder groups faced by the corporation—shareholders, employees, customers, suppliers, competitors, civil society, and government—and addresses business ethics within the specific context represented by each of these groups.

The structure of each chapter breaks down into five main parts reflecting some of the key themes developed in Part I of the book. So, following the introduction of each chapter there is:

(a) A brief explanation of how and why this particular constituency can and should be represented as a *stakeholder* for the corporation;

(b) An overview of the *ethical issues* and problems typically encountered in relation to this particular stakeholder, along with consideration of potential responses and solutions;

(c) A deepening discussion of those issues and problems in the light of *globalization*;

(d) An analysis of how these problems and issues can be reframed or responded to from the viewpoint of *corporate citizenship* thinking;

(e) An examination of the challenges thrown up by notions of *sustainability* in relation to this particular stakeholder group, particularly in the context of competing stakeholder demands and expectations.

As we progress through Part II, we will also continue to raise the question of how ethical theory can be applied to address the business ethics problems faced by corporations with respect to stakeholder groups. To this end, the 'Think theory' comments and questions utilized in the latter part of Part I will be posed at relevant parts of each chapter.

6

Shareholders and Business Ethics

In this chapter we will:

- Discuss the nature of shareholder relations to the corporation;

- Analyse the rights and the duties of shareholders;

- Investigate specific ethical problems and dilemmas arising in the relation between companies and their shareholders;

- Discuss the ethical implications of globalization on shareholder relations;

- Discover the differences in shareholder roles in various parts of the world;

- Explore the notion of shareholder democracy and the accountability of corporations to their shareholders and other stakeholders;

- Develop perspectives on how shareholders can influence corporations towards sustainability

Introduction: reassessing the importance of shareholders as stakeholders

For many people, corporations exist, and indeed act, solely for the benefit of shareholders. The relentless pursuit of profitability in order to provide dividends, as well as the constant drive to increase share prices to appease the financial markets, have been widely cited as crucial contributory factors in causing firms to play fast and loose with business ethics. Other people point to the expansion of ethical investment and the emergence of various indices of 'sustainable' or 'socially responsible' stocks to suggest that shareholders can also be a force for good in society. Whichever way you look at it, the role of shareholders is fundamental to understanding business ethics, and as such, they are the first stakeholder group that we will focus on in this second part of the book.

We first discussed the role of shareholders in the corporation (albeit quite briefly) in Chapter 2. Our argument there was in favour of a broad perspective that acknowledged various constituencies with a stake in the corporation. This suggested that whilst shareholders clearly have an important stake in the corporation, this has to be understood within the range of other stakeholders, such as employees, consumers, and suppliers.

In this chapter we will investigate the finer nuances of this perspective. Whilst maintaining support for a broad stakeholder perspective, we will examine the contention that shareholders in some way have a unique and superior claim upon the corporation. This relationship, as we shall see, confers certain crucial rights on shareholders, as well as imposing some quite important responsibilities in terms of the governance and control of corporations. By examining this relationship in some detail, we will provide the all-important context for discussing the various ethical issues that arise in shareholder relations, including insider trading, executive pay, and money laundering.

As we shall explain, both the impetus and the resolution of these issues and problems are shaped by certain national characteristics of corporate governance. We shall therefore go on to look at how shareholder relations vary quite significantly in a European context, ranging from more Anglo-American-oriented models of shareholder capitalism to continental European variations. This will be followed by a further broadening of perspective to allow for a deepening understanding of the relationship between globalization and shareholder rights and responsibilities. Such issues have received a growing amount of attention through recent protests against 'global capitalism' and the problem of corporate accountability. We shall therefore move on to discuss issues surrounding shareholder and stakeholder accountability before, finally, taking a look at how shareholders can use their unique position to address the question of sustainability of corporations.

Shareholders as stakeholders: understanding corporate governance

At the beginning of modern capitalism, and throughout the nineteenth-century industrial revolution, the common pattern of governing a company was a very simple one. At that time, industrialists such as the Whitbreads or Cadburys in the UK or the Thyssens or Krupps in Germany both owned and managed their companies directly. Today, except in very small businesses, owner-managers are considerably more rare. Some exceptions to this include Luciano Benetton (and family) in Italy or Richard Branson and his Virgin conglomerate in the UK. However, the common pattern in large corporations is a separation of ownership and management functions. In fact, this separation is at the heart of modern capitalism: owners no longer have a personal relationship to 'their' corporation, but rather they buy a 'share' in the corporation and expect the managers and employees of the company to run it in their (and other shareholders') interests.

The debate about the separation of ownership and control dates back at least to the 1930s and the landmark publication by Adolph Berle and Gardiner Means (1932). This debate essentially problematizes the notion of ownership when applied to corporations. In our everyday life, to own a bike or a car or even a house implies that we are able to do with our property pretty much whatever we like, and therefore can exert a considerable amount of control over it. After all, we discussed in Chapter 2 the right to property as one of the fundamental rights of citizens. If I want to paint my bike green, ride it down the street, or even completely destroy it, then I can.

With regard to the ownership of corporations, there are however some crucial differences (see Monks and Minow 2001: 96–9; Parkinson 1993: 56–63):

• **Locus of control.** The control of the owned property no longer lies in the hands of the owner. The actual control lies in the hands of the directors, the board, or another committee. Shareholders thus have at best indirect and impersonal control over their property.

• **Fragmented ownership.** There are so many shareholders of a corporation that one individual could hardly consider themselves to be the owner in the same way that the plumber next door owns her own company.

• **Divided functions and interests.** Shareholders have interests that are not necessarily the same as the interests of those who control the company. Shareholders might seek profits whilst managers seek growth. Furthermore, a shareholder has no real task and responsibility regarding their property apart from keeping a piece of paper that entitles them to a share in the company.

Given this somewhat modified relation between shareholders and directors of corporations we can analyse their relationship a bit more closely. Obviously the primary consideration for *shareholders* is the protection of their right to property which, in the given context, amounts to certain specific *rights* (see Monks and Minow 2001):

• The right to sell their stock
• The right to vote in the general meeting
• The right to certain information about the company
• The right to sue the managers for (alleged) misconduct
• Certain residual rights in case of the corporation's liquidation.

Most notably these rights do not include the right to a certain amount of profit or dividend; this is not only subject to the effort and skill of the management but also—even if the company is profitable—dependent on the decision of the other shareholders in the general meeting.

Managers are entrusted with the duty to run the company in the interest of shareholders (Moore 1999*b*). This general duty breaks down into various more specific duties (Parkinson 1993: 76–100):

• **Duty to act for the benefit of the company.** This obligation can be interpreted in terms of both short-term financial performance and long-term survival of the company. Principally, it is for the shareholders to decide on which level they want the company to perform; however, managers have a considerable amount of discretion in actually implementing this duty.

• **Duty of care and skill.** Living up to this duty implies that managers seek to achieve the most professional and effective way of running the company.

• **Duty of diligence.** This last duty is the most general one and as a rather legally flavoured term 'refers to the expected level of active engagement in company affairs' (Parkinson 1993: 98). Consequently this is the broadest way of establishing pressure on managers to invest every possible effort in running the company in the most successful way.

Clearly then, the duties of managers are rather broadly defined. After all, one of the main tasks of a manager is to manage the property of shareholders in their interests. This involves so many things that it is hard to pin it down to concrete activities and initiatives: which strategies, which products, which international investment projects will add to the success of the corporation? These questions are already hard to tackle for an insider, let alone for a shareholder who has only little knowledge about the internal workings of the corporation and the finer specifics of its products, markets, and competitors.

The relationship between shareholders and the company is therefore defined by relatively narrow but well-defined **rights for the shareholder** and far-reaching but rather ill-defined **duties for managers** or for the firm in general. It is no wonder that this situation has always been a delicate one and that conflicts continue to plague the relationship between managers and shareholders. Such conflicts focus on the key phrase of 'corporate governance'. In the light of the above, this can be defined along the following lines (Parkinson 1993: 157):

> Corporate governance describes the process by which shareholders seek to ensure that 'their' corporation is run according to their intentions. It includes processes of goal definition, supervision, control, and sanctioning. In the narrow sense it includes shareholders and the management of a corporation as the main actors; in a broader sense it includes all actors who contribute to the achievement of stakeholder goals inside and outside the corporation.

Corporate governance: a principal–agent relation

When looking at recent scandals and problems in corporate governance one might ask why the relationship seems to be so delicate. Let us have a look at some examples that have grabbed the headlines recently:

• In November 2002, it was revealed that Jean-Pierre Garnier, the French CEO of the British pharmaceutical giant GlaxoSmithKline (GSK), was seeking a massive increase to his salary of £7m, despite the company's poor performance and dramatic fall in share price. Why should such a demand even be deliberated by shareholders?

• Earlier in 2002, it was revealed that Percy Barnevik, the chairman of the supervisory board of the Swiss-Swedish technology conglomerate ABB, had netted €40m in pensions. Only after enormous public uproar did he agree to hand back most of the money. Why was he able to claim it in the first place?

• When Jürgen Schrempp, the CEO of Daimler-Chrysler, merged Mercedes with Chrysler in order to build a new global player in the automotive industry he labelled it a 'merger of equals'. After a year, when it was revealed that Chrysler was in deep financial trouble, he disclosed in an interview to the *Financial Times* that he had never intended to have

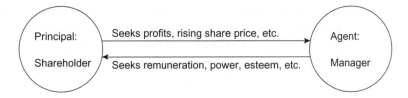

Figure 6.1. Agency relation between the manager and shareholder

Chrysler as an equal partner in the long run but wanted the American company as a part of the German conglomerate Daimler-Benz. Why was it only then that major Chrysler shareholders discovered that they had been partly deceived about the true intentions of the German management?

The problem is obviously that firm–shareholder relations cannot be that easily framed in a contract that neatly states rights and responsibilities. As authors like Jensen and Meckling (1976) have shown, the relation is a so-called *agency relation*. This means that the shareholder is a principal who contracts management as an agent to act in their interest within the boundary of the firm. **Figure 6.1** shows a very basic view of the relationship between firm, manager, and shareholder using this framework.

Shareholders want the managers in the firm to perform a certain task for them. As a principal, they want managers to do certain things with their property. Managers as agents, on the other side, have certain interests as well and the figure gives some examples in a potentially long list of such interests. Agency relations, however, are special relations due to two features that are by no means necessarily common for all other manager–stakeholder relations (Shankman 1999):

1. There is an inherent **conflict of interest** between shareholders and managers. Shareholders want profits and rises in share price, which includes hard effort from managers, and may suggest low salaries. Managers want to have high salaries and might pursue power and prestige to the detriment of shareholder value. For instance, the evidence that acquisition and merger lead to higher returns for shareholders is at best equivocal, and at worst indicates that they often erode shareholder value (Johnson and Scholes 2002: 332–340). Why then do managers continue to create mega-mergers which put them at the head of enormous corporations?

2. The principal has only a limited knowledge and insight into the qualifications, actions, and goals of the agent, something economists refer to as an **informational asymmetry**. GSK shareholders might consider their CEO's pay claim since they rely on him for his leadership skills and detailed knowledge of relevant markets, technologies, etc. Similarly, Chrysler shareholders were not aware what Jürgen Schrempp had in mind when merging the two companies; they could only listen to his plans later when he announced then in public.

It is the combination of these two characteristics that makes shareholder relations with managers, and the whole issue of corporate governance, so precarious. Indeed, conflicts of interest and informational asymmetry can be seen to underlie a host of ethical problems and dilemmas for either side to deal with in the area of corporate governance, as we shall see in a moment. Before we move on to the main ethical issues pertaining to shareholders, though, we need first to clarify the position of shareholders in relation to other stakeholders. Specifically, it is important to recognize that two main models are in operation in Europe.

Shareholders' relations with other stakeholders: different European frameworks of corporate governance

The corporate governance framework 'describes whom the organization is there to serve and how the purposes and priorities of the organization should be decided' (Johnson and Scholes 2002: 195). The role of shareholders in the governance framework varies quite significantly between different European countries (Monks and Minow 2001). In the following, we will generalize in terms of the two major approaches to governance in operation in Europe, which in turn are based on different forms of capitalism. On the one hand, we could identify the **Anglo-Saxon** version of capitalism, and on the other hand, there is a **continental European model**, sometimes also called 'Rhenish Capitalism' (Albert 1991). **Figure 6.2** provides an overview of the relevant differences from the perspective of corporate governance.

Within Europe, the Anglo-Saxon model is predominantly in evidence in the UK and Ireland. Crucially though it is also strongly represented in the USA, and also in Australia. The continental European model is evident throughout most of the rest of Europe, most notably France, Italy, Germany, and Spain as the largest economies on the continent.[1] Whilst simplifying the corporate governance frameworks within Europe along these lines, it is important to take into account a couple of qualifying statements. *First*, there are considerable pressures towards convergence of national business systems, especially on the European continent, so that the continental European model is partly changing towards the Anglo-Saxon model (Hunt 2000). *Second*, this process is even more manifest in smaller countries such as Sweden or the Netherlands, so that the alleged dichotomy of systems is clearly an oversimplification in such cases (Coffee 2001).

The **Anglo-Saxon model** focuses on the stock market as the central element of the system of governance. Most of the larger, publicly owned companies source their capital there, and in these countries, shareholding is largely in the hands of smaller shareholders with the result that shares are broadly dispersed (Becht and Röell 1999). As the goal is short-term maximization of profits—either gains in share price or dividends—ownership is changing frequently. With the stock market being the most important source of capital, corporations have to provide a high degree of transparency and accountability to shareholders and investors. Executives are in turn increasingly remunerated with regard to their corporation's performance on the stock market.

In this model ethical concerns from a shareholder's perspective arise mainly around the proper functioning of the market mechanisms and the market-related patterns of

---

[1] A third approach to governance is represented by the Asian model, most notably in Japan. For a comparison with the Anglo-Saxon and Rhenish models, see Johnson and Scholes (2002).

	Anglo-Saxon model	Continental European model ('Rhenish Capitalism')
Organization	Market capitalism	Network capitalism

Market capitalization
Market capitalization as a
percentage of GDP (1999)[a]
	High
	  UK: 198%
	  USA: 181%
		Low
		  Italy: 62%
		  Germany: 68%
		  Spain: 73%
		  France: 105%

Ownership structure	Dispersed	Concentrated, interlocking pattern of ownership between banks, insurance companies, and corporations
Changes in ownership	Frequent	Rare
Goals of ownership	• Shareholder value • Short-term profits	• Sales, market share, headcount • Long-term ownership
Role of banks	• Marginal role in corporate control • Short-term financing	• Crucial role in corporate control as creditor, owner, and major representation in supervisory boards • Long-term financing
Control of executives by shareholders	• Strong • Emphasis on public accountability	• Weak • Accountability to boards and actors within the network of owners
Executive remuneration	Growing percentage of performance related elements, e.g. stock options, shares	Salary based
Key stakeholders	Shareholder	Owners and employees (trade unions, works councils)

Figure 6.2. Comparison of corporate governance regimes in Europe

[a] *Source*: Coffee (2001: 18).

corporate governance. Typical ethical problems would be insider trading or manipulated accounting statements. In a broader perspective, the Anglo-Saxon model clearly assigns a dominant role to shareholders and, consequently, all major criticisms of the shareholder-oriented model of managerial capitalism discussed in Chapter 2 would apply to this approach.

In the **continental European model** of capitalism, corporations tend to be embedded in a network of a small number of large investors, among which banks play a major role. Within this network of mutually interlocking owners, the central focus is the long-term preservation of influence and power. For the purpose of sourcing capital, banks and their loans, rather than just the market, are still of major importance for continental European corporations. Next to shareholder value, the expansion of market share, retention of employees, and other goals not directly profit oriented are important for owners. Executive pay is less performance related and is regarded as an issue between the boards of corporations without any perceived need to disclose this to the general public (Buck 2002).

Moreover, more significant from an ethical point of view is that within the continental European model, stakeholders other than shareholders also play an important role, sometimes even equivalent to or above that of shareholders. For instance, in German companies up to half of the members of a corporation's supervisory board (which oversees the management of the firm) have to be appointed by the employees of the corporation. In contrast, in the Anglo-Saxon model, employees have no say at all in the control of the firm. From an ethical perspective, then, one could argue that the continental model of capitalism is to some extent a European manifestation of the stakeholder theory of the firm. With the most important stakeholder next to shareholders in this model being employees, a corporation in continental Europe is seen more as a member of a certain community which has to serve wider goals than just those of a small group of investors. From the perspective of a single shareholder, however, major ethical concerns derive from the fact that the system of ownership prefers the interests of big, mostly corporate shareholders and the interests of many other actors who have no direct ownership rights in the corporation. Let us now look then at some of these ethical issues arising from the two models in a little more detail.

Ethical issues in corporate governance

Corporate governance has been a topic high on the agenda of all major western economies in recent years. Partly this has been the result of various scandals that have hit the headlines during the last decade or so. From recent examples of corporate misconduct in the USA, sudden bankruptcy announcements such as those of the German companies Philip Holzmann and Mobilcom, to the spectacular pay rises of 'fat cat' CEOs, interest in the ethical dimensions of corporate governance has never been higher. In the following sections, we will examine the main issues arising here, focusing specifically on those that primarily affect shareholders.

Executive accountability and control

Looking at corporate governance, there are certain core elements that need to be present in order for the principal–agent relationship to be managed effectively. The most important element is a separate body of people that supervises and controls management on behalf of shareholders, namely a board of directors. In practice, this tends to result in a dual structure of the leadership of a publicly owned corporation. On the one hand, there are **executive directors** who are actually responsible for running the corporation. On the other, there are **non-executive directors** who are supposed to ensure that the corporation is being run in the interests of those for whom it is supposed to be run, usually shareholders.

The different governance frameworks in Europe give rise to important differences in how this board is structured and composed. In the Anglo-Saxon model, there is usually a single-tier board that comprises both executive and non-executive directors. In continental Europe, a two-tier board is more common. The upper tier is composed of non-executive directors and the lower tier of executive directors. The upper tier, often also called a **'supervisory board'**, effectively oversees the lower tier that is more concerned with the day-to-day running of the company. As we have already said, the supervisory board commonly includes representatives of stakeholders other than just shareholders, including banks and employees.

Regardless of the structure, the central ethical issue here is clearly the independence of the supervisory, non-executive board members. They will only be able to reasonably act in the shareholders' interest if they have no directly conflicting interests. In order to achieve this, a number of points are important (see Boyd 1996; Nader 1984):

- Non-executive directors should be largely drawn from outside the corporation.

- They should not have a personal financial interest in the corporation other than the interests of shareholders. This includes the fact that the remuneration for the role must not significantly exceed a reasonable compensation for time and other expenses.

- They should be appointed for a limited period in order to prevent them from getting too close to the company.

- They should be competent to judge the business of the company. This would require and allow to some degree a limited number of insiders, such as former executives or even works council members (as in certain parts of Europe).

- They should have sufficient resources to get information or commission research into the corporation.

- They should be appointed independently. This would be either by the shareholders directly in the annual general meeting, or through appointment by the supervisory board.

A further element of supervision comes from an independent auditor who audits the work of the executive board—normally the main aspect of their role—and also of the non-executive board. We will discuss the role of auditors and the ethical issues involved a little later.

Despite the guidelines above, the independence of non-executive directors remains a delicate issue. Often they belong to the same peer group as executive directors, or are themselves in executive roles elsewhere, or have been in such a role in the past. This means that a completely neutral and independent approach will always be quite difficult to reach (Gordon 2002).

Executive remuneration

The issue of executive pay, and in particular accusations that senior managers have enjoyed 'fat cat' salaries at the expense of shareholders, employees, consumers, and other stakeholders, has been a feature of the business press over the past decade, especially in the UK, but also increasingly in other parts of Europe. This has been fuelled by the revitalization of the shareholder value ideology, combined with the massive privatization move in the late 1980s and early 1990s that saw the remuneration enjoyed by bosses of formerly public companies skyrocket.

We have already briefly mentioned the case of Jean-Pierre Garnier, the French Philadelphia-based chairman of the British pharmaceutical company GSK (see Finch and

Treanor 2002). His salary of £7m consisted of a large chunk of share options. These are allocations of shares for senior staff that they can choose to exercise (or 'option') at some time in the future. As such, they are intended to provide incentives for managers to improve the market rating of the company, thereby aligning the interests of managers and shareholders. However, in Garnier's case, a 25 per cent decline in profits at GSK, coupled with a fall in share price of 30 per cent from when he had taken over, had meant that the options had become more or less worthless.

Prior to GSK's annual general meeting, the board sent a letter to major shareholders suggesting a massive £20m pay rise for Garnier, based on a 'restructuring' of his current package, and including various other kinds of benefits and 'incentives'. The main argument was that his peers in the pharmaceutical industry in the USA were all on a similar level and therefore that Garnier may have been under-incentivized. The letter was leaked to the press, causing uproar in the British media, and ultimately resulting in the rejection of Garnier's rise—an outcome that many commentators said would have been unlikely without the press coverage.

This case exemplifies many of the ethical problems with executive pay in firm–shareholder relations:

- First, there is the issue of performance-related pay in a world of reinvigorated shareholder value (Koslowski 2000). In order to tackle the problem of divergent interest, most executive salaries nowadays contain a significant amount of shares and share options to align shareholders' and managers' interest. The first problem here however is that by including these elements, salary levels have exploded, often leading to considerable unrest within companies. Furthermore, as the example of GSK shows, this pay model does not always result in the desired effect on share prices, as these are of course linked to other factors as well.

- Second, this case shows the influence of globalization on executive pay: the market for executive talent is a global one and so the standards of the highest level of pay seem to be applicable across the board. This means that particularly in Europe, where the introduction of performance-related pay is only just entering the executive suite (Buck 2002), significant rises in pay can still be expected. This domination of the Anglo-American shareholder value orientation has also had its influence in newly privatized companies in public transport, telecommunication, and utilities where salaries have rocketed during the last fifteen years (Cannon 1994).

- Third, this case also illustrates that the board often fails to reflect shareholder (or other stakeholder) interests. Why would shareholders want to reward a CEO who had over-seen a period of such poor performance?

Such problems show few, if any, signs of diminishing, and indeed may be expected to occupy shareholders (not to mention the press) for some time yet. Although, as we shall see at the end of this section, corporate governance reforms have been proposed throughout Europe, the issue of executive remuneration touches an ethical cord. This is not actually so much because the public feels sorry for shareholders, but because the pay differentials between those at the top and those at the bottom appear to be so inequitable.

We shall pick up this issue again in the next chapter when we address the question of fair pay for employees.

■ **Think theory**

Assess the pay packages of Jean-Pierre Garnier and other chief executives from the perspective of traditional ethical theories. What are the consequences, rights, and duties here? How do they conflict or align with expectations for fairness and justice?

Ethical aspects of mergers and acquisitions

We have already touched upon some of the ethical issues in mergers and acquisitions when discussing the merger between Daimler-Benz and Chrysler. The central source of ethical concern in this context is that managers often pursue interests that are not congruent with shareholders' interests. Basically the conflict is around executives' prestige on the one hand and profit and share price interests of shareholders on the other. There is in particular a wealth of discussion in the American business ethics literature on this issue, mainly since the US business system very much encourages these types of transaction more than is the case in tightly regulated Europe. However, with an increasing deterritorialization of financial markets, these practices have become more common in Europe as well in recent years, as the recent example of Anglo-German or Franco-German mergers in the telecommunication industry illustrate. In the following, we will have a look at main issues that have arisen, or are likely to arise, in the European context.

Next to 'normal' mergers, there are particular ethical problems involved in so-called **hostile takeovers**. Here, an investor, or a group of investors, intends to purchase a majority stake in a corporation (often secretly) against the wishes of its board. Without going into a detailed philosophical debate, there are basically two lines of arguments (see De George 1999: 462–4). On the one side, one could argue that hostile takeovers are ultimately possible only because shareholders want to sell their stocks, otherwise they would keep them anyway. On the other side, an ethical concern arises with the remaining shareholders that do not want to sell. If the company is taken over by someone who has different ideas about the corporation, for instance, who wants to split the company and sell off certain parts, a hostile takeover might interfere quite significantly with the property rights of those remaining shareholders.

A particularly interesting role is played by the executives of the corporation to be taken over. According to Carroll and Buchholtz (2000: 558–60), they basically have two main options in this situation:

- First, they could be seduced into agreeing to the takeover, for example by being offered what are sometimes called 'golden parachutes', which means a large sum of money which they would be paid once they agree to the merger and their own redundancy. Their 'agreement', of course, does not mean that they actually have an active role in selling or buying shares, but in past cases, the role of the CEO has been quite crucial in recommending the merger to the supervisory board and to shareholders in general. The most recent case of a hostile takeover in Europe when Vodafone bought the German Mannesmann conglomerate is a good example: only when Klaus Esser, the CEO of the German conglomerate, agreed to the merger was the board willing to accept the British offer and to proceed with the merger. As we intimated before, there is at present a court case running in Germany against Esser accusing him of having given this recommendation against the interests of shareholders because of a €30m golden parachute he was paid after the merger went ahead.

- The second type of reaction of management is just the opposite. In order not to lose their job after the takeover, managers could secretly send 'greenmail' (as opposed to blackmail) to the potential hostile party and offer to buy back the shares for the company at a price higher than the present market price. By this, managers secure their jobs using corporate money. This raises a significant ethical problem regarding whether such a move is actually in the company's interest or not. Sometimes it may be, but in other instances, greenmail appears to be primarily used because the CEO does not want to lose their lofty position.

A particular ethical line of conflict opens if we have a look at the intentions and consequences of mergers and acquisitions. The famous former CEO of General Electric (GE) acquired his nickname 'Neutron Jack' because he turned GE into one of the best-performing conglomerates on Wall Street by acquiring all sorts of corporations and significantly **restructuring and downsizing** them immediately after takeover. The buildings and assets remained, only the people had to leave, similar to the effect of a neutron bomb. Very often acquisitions only target the profitable parts of the bought-up corporation while at the same time the other parts will be liquidated. Sometimes these acquisitions even focus only on the brand value or certain patents and technologies of the bought-up firm, with the consequence that other stakeholder interests, such as those of employees or local communities, are seriously disregarded.

The role of financial markets and insider trading

There has been a remarkable silence in the literature on financial markets with regard to ethical issues (Rudolph 1999). A simple justification for this would be the following: financial markets, especially the stock market, are based on shareholders expecting a future dividend and/or a rise in share prices as a basis for their decision to buy or sell stocks. As long as the rules of the market are fairly set and every player plays according to these rules, there is no ethical dilemma to be expected. Issues such as mergers, acquisitions, or executive pay then are not so very much an object of ethical consideration but a simple object of the economic calculation of the shareholder: if she does not agree to the CEO's remuneration demands, she is fully entitled to sell the stock. It might be cheeky to demand more pay, or the merger might be problematic, but ultimately every shareholder can take a fully informed decision and could sell her stocks.

Behind this argument, there is the assumption of a perfect market, and in particular the assumption that ultimately all publicly available information about the company is reflected by the stock price. However, we all know that this simple rationale of 'the stock market never lies' is only part of the truth. Sometimes, this alleged 'information efficiency' of stock markets is quite flawed, as the following issues show.

Speculative 'faith stocks'

An often-discussed problem is the speculative nature of share prices. If we think of the recent 'dot.com' bubble and all the companies that had not made a single euro profit but were worth billions on the market, we have a situation where this speculative element is taken to an extreme. Rather than being built on solidly calculated profit expectations these stocks were more akin to '**faith stocks**' (Gordon 2002) built on little else than blind faith. Even a company such as Amazon.com, which was always cited as one of the more solid candidates in the market, needed more than seven years to make even a dollar in profit. When it finally broke the hurdle in 2002, it had accrued some $2.2bn in long-term debt, despite once being valued at more than $30bn (Hof and Green 2002). Such overblown speculation was even more the case with the great number of dot.coms traded at Nasdaq in New York or the Neuer Markt in Frankfurt, most of which then went spectacularly bust taking the entire stock market into an unprecedented downturn.

One problem here is that many pensioners whose funds had invested in these bonds lost large parts of their income. The ethical issue clearly lies in the fact that while stock prices always contain a solid amount of speculation, stock markets do not fully reveal the amount of uncertainty. This might be somewhat trivial for brokers or other stock market professionals; however, with large institutional investors investing other people's money in these stocks, the fact that these bonds were based entirely on speculation can be said to be close to an abuse of trust. This also questions the role of analysts and accountants (see below) who, among others, are responsible for ensuring *informed* transactions on the stock market.

Insider trading

Slightly the opposite problem exists with the phenomenon of **insider trading**, namely that some investors might have superior knowledge in the market. Insider trading occurs when securities are bought or sold on the basis of material *non-public* information (Moore 1990). The executives of a corporation and other insiders know the company well, and so might easily know about events that are likely to have a significant impact on the company's share price well in advance of other potential traders. Consequently, insiders are privileged over other players in the market in terms of knowledge, a privilege that they could take advantage of to reap a questionable profit. In the long run insider trading could therefore undermine investors' trust in the market—a problem that has led most stock markets to forbid the practice (Carroll and Buchholtz 2000: 560–2; De George 1999: 316–23).

While the ethical assessment of insider trading is still quite controversial (Chryssides and Kaler 1996: 42–3), there appear to be a number of possible routes. Jennifer Moore (1990) for instance, discusses four main ethical arguments that have been used against insider trading:

• **Fairness.** There are inequalities in the access to relevant information about companies leading to a situation where one party has an unfair advantage over the other. Moore (1990) argues that this is the weakest, but most common argument that tends to be used against insider trading.

- **Misappropriation of property.** Insider traders use valuable information that is essentially the property of the firm involved, and which they have no right to have access to. According to Moore (1990), this has become a common basis for legal cases involving insider trading.

- **Harm to investors and the market.** Insider traders might benefit to the cost of 'ordinary' investors, making the market riskier, and threatening confidence in the market.

- **Undermining of fiduciary relationship.** The relationships of trust and dependence among shareholders and corporate managers (and employees) are based on managers acting in the interests of shareholders, yet insider trading is fuelled by self-interest on the part of insiders rather than obligation to their 'principal'. Moore (1990) argues that this is the strongest argument against insider trading.

■ **Think theory**

How do these four arguments correspond to the traditional ethical theories set out in Chapter 3?

Whichever way we look at it, the central problem here seems to lie in the question of where to define the boundaries. After all, every investor tries to receive as much knowledge about a company as possible and analysts of major investment banks would by no means treat their knowledge necessarily as publicly available. A particular problem has arisen from the aforementioned fact that many companies remunerate their executives and staff with share options or shares. These people clearly use their inside knowledge of the company to decide when to exercise their options or sell their shares, and it would be irrational to expect them to do otherwise. As a result, such 'acceptable' incentives are difficult to distinguish from 'unacceptable' insider trading. For this reason, the chairman of Porsche, Wendelin Wiedeking, has for example categorically ruled out shares as part of his employees' packages (Koslowski 2000). **Ethical Dilemma 6** presents a typical situation where the boundaries of insider trading might be difficult to draw very clearly.

The role of accountants

One of the main institutions to bridge the asymmetric distribution of information between shareholders and corporate actors is that of accountants. Their task is to provide a 'true and fair view' of the company's financial situation. However, their role varies from country to country. In the Anglo-American sphere they are most heavily involved in the actual accounting process, whereas in continental Europe they have more of a supervisory role and just check and testify whether the corporation's accounts and annual reports give a realistic picture of the company's actual financial situation.

With shareholder value orientation becoming more and more popular over the last years, the nature of the accounting profession has undergone substantial changes (Mellahi and Wood 2002). Rather than certifying the quality of published accounts, today's audits

Who cares whose shares?

....

These Friday nights out drinking with your friends had become an institution since you started work-ing with MillerGross Elmcham (MGE), one of the biggest pharmaceutical and chemical companies in the world, five years ago. And it had been five great years. Not only had it brought you career suc-cess and a very healthy bank balance, but it had also made you a successful player in the stock market. Since you were promoted to regional marketing director for the north-east, MGE had started to pay most of your bonuses in share options. This had proved to be an extremely lucrative package, given your success in meeting sales targets and, of course, the impressive performance of the shares over the last two and a half years.

But this Friday night, however, you are not feeling so relaxed. Yes, you have an expensive bottle of imported beer in your hand, yes, you have some of your best mates with you, all totally up for a big night out, and yes, Freddie, your best friend from college, will be arriving any minute. However, today at work has been a nightmare. A special meeting had been called by one of the vice presidents for all of the senior managers. In the meeting it was announced that scientists in a leading research lab at SFW University in the USA had discovered some potentially lethal side effects associated with one of MGE's best-selling herbicides. The report had been confidential to the board of MGE but an article containing the research was going to be published in *Big Science* magazine next week on Thursday. The purpose of the meeting was to inform everybody and to discuss potential strategies to tackle the problem. Consequently you were urged to be absolutely silent about the research find-ings, particularly as the likelihood was that this would turn out to be a major news story.

Knowing about this makes you uneasy now. It is pretty sure that this information will have a major effect on the share price of MGE as court cases in the USA with huge damages are a certainty. When digesting the news in your office after lunch you already have decided to sell your shares in MGE next thing on Monday—as it is almost certain that the value of your stocks will never be the same in the foreseeable future once this news is out. However, your are certain that Freddie, your friend from college, is also going to be very much affected by the news once it gets out. He is now an account manager for a major investment bank. And not only has he invested heavily in MGE shares himself but he has also advised many of his clients—among them managers of major funds—to invest in MGE.

You are quite uneasy now about what to do. Freddie is an old mate, and you want to help him. You know he will hear of the news soon anyway, and maybe, given his contacts, even before it is pub-lished next Thursday. But if you tell him now, you are certain that he will not only sell his own shares (which you really would not mind), but, as he is measured by the performance of his advice to his clients, you can be pretty certain that he will also advise his clients to sell. The effect on the share price before the publication of the article could be substantial.

Questions

1 What are the main ethical issues in this case?
2 Who are the main stakeholders here, and how would you compare the relative importance of their stakes?
3 Explain how you would ultimately decide and why.
4 Is there a difference between acting yourself on the information you were given or passing this information on to Freddie?

target the actual or potential shareholder and therefore focus a great deal not only on statements of past periods but on the future potential of the corporation. This process, sometimes pejoratively termed **'creative accounting'** (Pijper 1994), mirrors the demands of a major group of addressees of corporate statements. However, the risk inherent in this process is evident: the discretionary element of auditing existing figures is already quite significant; this is even more the case for projections based on these figures. To take up the expression used above, the ethical challenge for audit firms lies in the fine line between presenting a share as a 'faith stock' or using this term for repackaging what one would normally simply call a dud or a 'lemon' (Gordon 2002).

Given this delicate balancing act, it is therefore no wonder that accountancy firms increasingly find themselves in the ethical spotlight. Ballwieser and Clemm identify five main problematic aspects of the auditor's job:

- **Auditing companies that then go bust:** Auditors necessarily do not make a judgement about the economic viability of a corporation—they simply make a judgement of whether the accounts of the corporation provide a realistic picture of the real situation. This means though that they have to make an assessment of whether the company is legitimately putting a good light on the figures or presenting a deceptive account. If an auditor is too outspoken about a company at present sailing in rougher waters, this might actually have detrimental effects on the firm and thus potentially add to its difficulties. On the other hand, the presentation of a deceptive account is a risk mainly incurred by the auditor itself. Even though there are pretty well-defined rules, regulations, or codes of practice for the auditing process there remains discretion in valuing assets, foreign currency transactions, goodwill assets, etc.

- **Cross-selling of consulting services to audit clients:** An auditing firm necessarily gets a very close insight into the corporation. These auditing firms, especially the big global firms such as PriceWaterhouseCoopers, KPMG, or—until recently—Arthur Andersen, also have large pool of expertise as they get to see so many companies. It is only natural then that they use this insight and experience to develop an extra source of income by providing management consultancy and other business services to their clients. The crucial problem, however, is that this involvement with a corporation puts an end to the necessary neutrality of the auditor. We will discuss the ethical issues involved here in more detail in Chapter 9 (312–14) when we discuss **conflicts of interest** in company–supplier relations.

- **Long-term relationships with clients:** Accounting firms and their individual representatives enter a position of confidentiality with their clients and therefore the tendency is to look for long-term relationships. Although this is restricted by law in some countries, the general problem persists. Having such a confidential position of trust with clients often creates long-term personal relationships that can threaten independence. For example, it has been revealed that Patricia Hewitt, the cabinet Minister for Trade and Industry and former Arthur Andersen manager, has given several audit and consulting jobs to Arthur Andersen in the past. These relationships, lucrative as they are for business, nevertheless put the neutrality of the accounting firm in serious doubt.

• **Size of the accounting firm:** The bigger the accounting firm is, the more economies of scale it can realize in terms of staff training, standardization of auditing procedures, and tools, and the better it can specialize into different branches and tasks. However, the more a firm grows, the more it gets difficult to maintain a constant standard of diligence. Standardized procedures of auditing may also diminish the diligence of the individual auditor who might lose the personal sense of responsibility for the task. This distancing effect of bureaucracy was something we first discussed in Chapter 4 (132–3).

• **Increase in competition between auditing firms:** With intensifying competition between auditors over the last years, there is the inherent danger that corners will be cut to reduce costs, raising the prospect of less diligence and scrutiny in auditing firms.

Reforming governance

Given the weight and significance of many of the problems and issues discussed above, it is clear that there are some important shortcomings in the present system of governance in many countries. It is perhaps not surprising then that various reforms of corporate governance have been proposed and debated over the past few years, both in Europe, the USA, and elsewhere.

Ethics in Action 6.1 provides an overview of recent major reforms of corporate governance across Europe. However, as this overview suggests, one of the key drivers of reform has not so much been an ethical concern over corporate malpractice as the more practical concern that governance failures might detract from investment. As we shall now see, globalization has increased the relevance of global financial markets for the sourcing of corporate capital resources. The more corporations finance themselves via global markets the more questions of corporate governance become an issue of interest for those involved in capital markets. Especially in continental Europe, where financing methods other than the stock markets had been quite popular, the number of shareholders has significantly increased over the last decade (Warren 1999; Whitley 1999). Competition for these investors and for their financial resources has become a feature of global markets—and one good way to attract such investors is to be able to give them a decent guarantee that corporations will act in their interests. Improved systems of governance may help to provide a better framework to effect this, but it would seem that there is no failsafe way of solving principal–agent problems of this kind.

■ **Think theory**

Read Ethics in Action 6.1 and think about the development of corporate governance codes from the perspective of postmodern ethics. Do you think that this is an area where codes of practice are a good way of dealing with ethical problems, or do you agree with those postmodernists who argue that codes tend to squeeze out a sense of morality from our relationships with others? What role do you think such codes can play in ensuring more ethical relations between managers, shareholders, and other stakeholders?

Ethics in Action 6.1

Reforming corporate governance in Europe

....

While corporations are legally bound to publish an annual report or—in certain European countries—to allow their workers a degree of participation on the company's board, most issues in corporate governance are within the discretion of the corporations themselves. However, the limitations in current governance mechanisms have been widely acknowledged, both across Europe and elsewhere. The reform of corporate governance has therefore become a major issue in many European countries over the past decade.

Probably the main way that this reform has been tackled is through the definition and implementation of new corporate governance codes. The idea of codes is to prescribe 'best practice' standards for corporations so as to help ensure that certain minimal standards of corporate behaviour are met. Typical issues dealt with in codes of corporate governance are:

- Size and structure of the board
- Independence of supervisory or non-executive directors
- Frequency of supervisory body meetings
- Rights and influence of employees in corporate governance
- Disclosure of executive remuneration
- General meeting participation and proxy voting
- Role of other supervising and auditing bodies

Between 1991 and 2002, Europe witnessed the issue of thirty-five different national corporate governance codes across thirteen countries. These were:

- Ireland, Italy, Spain, Portugal, Sweden (one each);
- Denmark, Finland, Greece (two each);
- France, Germany, the Netherlands (three each);
- Belgium (four);
- United Kingdom (eleven).

While the UK has the longest tradition in developing and debating various codes, latecomers such as Germany and Denmark only started in 1999. In addition to these national codes, there have also been four codes issued by pan-European organizations such as the OECD.

Not all of these codes have gained the same degree of attention. In the UK, for instance, the most prominent and still most influential code is the Cadbury Report of 1992, which was developed following a number of severe incidents of fraud and corporate misconduct. Another, more recent example is the German code proposed by the Cromme-Commission in 2002. This signified a landmark in German corporate history since it attempted to codify and regulate certain areas of corporate governance hitherto regarded as the pillars of Rhenish network capitalism.

When analysing the main objectives of these codes, the central concern of regulators in fact seems to be enhancing the attractiveness of the local financial markets and their capacity to attract foreign capital. Therefore, although some codes do give passing reference to other stakeholders, it would appear that the main concern is the interest of shareholders (or even future shareholders). Given this orientation, the legal basis and the power of these codes vary significantly: while governments and the general public would ideally like to make codes legally binding, industry takes a more cautious stance. On the one hand, the general implementation and enforcement of codes is desirable, on the other hand extra regulation makes business more inflexible and enhances bureaucracy and 'red tape'.

In practice, then, most of these codes have been voluntary, while some have implemented mandatory frameworks for disclosure that follow the rule 'comply or explain'. Although corporate governance codes are now an established element of every major European national economy, their role is still therefore somewhat ambivalent.

Furthermore, it is also clear that each of the national codes still tends to substantially reflect the different national peculiarities of the stock market that they are concerned with. However, as recent reviews have shown, a growing orientation towards shareholders' interests resulted in a significant convergence of codes in Europe. It remains to be seen whether the European Commission will finally come up with a proposal for an integrated code; up to now it has confined itself to commissioning a comparative study of corporate governance codes.

SOURCES

Boyd, C. (1996). 'Ethics and corporate governance: the issues raised by the Cadbury Report in the United Kingdom'. *Journal of Business Ethics*, 15: 167–82.

Weil Gotshal & Manges (2002). *Comparative Study of Corporate Governance Codes Relevant to the European Union and its Member States (on Behalf of the European Commission, Internal Market Directorate General)*. Brussels: European Commission.

Williamson, H. (2002). 'Germany announces voluntary business code'. *Financial Times*, 21 Feb.: 7.

See also Chapter 5 (148–155) for more on the general role and function of codes of conduct.

....

Shareholders and globalization

Globalization has had a crucial impact on the role of shareholders, the nature of their ownership, and the scope of their activities. With global equity and finance markets being probably the most globalized, or *deterritorialized* markets, the consequences of this reformed role for shareholders is beginning to become increasingly visible. We might think of shareholders becoming players in the global arena in four different ways:

• Shareholders might become **directly** involved abroad by buying shares of companies in other countries. Typically, this would mean, for example, that French or Spanish investors would buy shares at the London Stock Exchange in a British company.

• Shareholders might be involved **indirectly** by buying shares in a domestic (or international) company that operates globally by selling goods and services worldwide. Even the shareholders of a corporation such as Porsche, which avowedly wants to remain a 'German' company (by refusing to invest anywhere else than at home), are nevertheless involved in the globalization process given that the corporation has the majority of its sales abroad. This aspect has particular consequences for many continental European countries where the capital markets are still very nationally focused. The scandal in 2002 about the sacking of Deutsche Telekom chairman Ron Sommer was a typical example of this. Deutsche Telekom, which markets the mobile phone brand 'T-Mobile', was one of the first German privatized utilities to reinvent itself as a publicly owned company. The firm marketed their shares (the 'T-Aktie', as they called it) to the general public as a 'German' share particularly targeting minority shareholders of middle-class people. These shareholders, however, while thinking they had invested in a German company (as the company name proudly proclaimed), did not realize that Sommer was about to put together a global player. His long-term expansion strategy and its inherent risks ultimately were not accepted by shareholders which led to serious discontent and, finally, to a reshuffle of the Telekom board.

- Similar to this indirect involvement, but more pronounced, is the role of shareholders in explicitly **multinational corporations** (MNCs). Investing in such companies makes shareholders indirect players in global capital markets, especially if these companies are heavily involved in foreign direct investment activities in other countries.

- Finally, shareholders may become **direct players** in international capital markets by investing in funds that explicitly direct their money in global capital markets. Significant players in this category are large American and British pension funds which administer something like $32bn in global capital markets, making them very influential players in such markets (Monks and Minow 2001).

This differentiation helps us to recognize the particular effects of globalization on the ethical issues confronting firm relationships with shareholders. The first two instances involve stakeholders as actors in certain well-defined national capital markets. The ethical issues of corporate governance as discussed above are therefore similarly relevant for these instances. The two latter cases, however, are special since they involve shareholders in the context of global financial markets. We would define these markets along the following lines:

> Global financial markets are the total of all physical and virtual (electronic) places where financial titles in the broadest sense (capital, shares, currency, options, etc.) are traded worldwide.

If we just recall our definition of globalization in Chapter 1 (16), global financial markets can perhaps be at present regarded as the most globalized markets since they are the least dependent on a certain territorial basis. The main factors leading to globalization that we mentioned in Chapter 1 are clearly at play here:

- Due to the **technological** advances, especially in telecommunication and electronics, most notably the internet, financial markets today are neither confined to locations nor to certain time slots (Parker 1998). Consequently, trade at these markets takes place around the clock and regardless of the geographical location of supply and demand.

- Financial markets count among the most deregulated. It is only this **political** development which allows us to fully exploit the technological potential of electronic trading.

Financial trade today may take place twenty-four hours without a break, starting from London, to New York, Tokyo, Sydney, Singapore, Delhi, Dubai, and back again to Frankfurt, one hour before trade in London starts again. And though these markets are local markets and regulated by local authorities, these developments make it possible to talk more about one global market rather than many individual places of financial trade.

From an ethical point of view, this development raises some serious issues. Among the most important count the following:

• **Governance and control.** Deterritorialized markets impose the problem that no national government is entitled to govern these markets (Becker and Westbrook 1998). With regard to financial markets this means that the allocation of a fundamentally important resource for modern industrialized economies takes place without any serious normative rules other than the 'laws' of supply and demand (Koch 2000: 189–209). This might not sound too much of a problem but it becomes immediately clear if we have a look at the some-times negative consequences of global financial market transactions, as we will show in a moment. More fundamentally, though, one of the drivers for introducing democracy in Europe and elsewhere during the last 300 years was the idea of giving people a say in how the key resources (usually at that time land) were used and allocated. Therefore, national governments, which govern the national territory, were elected by and accountable to their people. Today, rather than land or territory, one of the key resources is capital, and the mechanisms of allocation in global capital markets are presently beyond the control of any government, let alone the individual citizen.

• **Speculation.** Global financial markets encourage speculation. This is not an ethical problem as such; after all, arbitrage is one of the key reasons why financial markets exist in the first place. However, speculative movement of capital may have quite significant impacts on real-life situations. In the UK, people still remember 'Black Wednesday' in 1995, where the plans of the British government to realign the currency rate of the pound to the European Currency System were undermined by speculative trading on both sides of the Atlantic. The result was serious damage to government finances which, by some accounts, cost every British citizen £12, and contributed to the end of the Tory government (McGrew 1997a).

• **Unfair competition with developing countries.** Economic crises in developing countries during the 1990s such as in Mexico, Brazil, or most notably South-East Asia have been mainly triggered by speculative moves of capital out of these countries. Investors have been attracted to invest there in boom phases; as soon as it turned out that much of the boom was speculative, capital was withdrawn with disastrous effects for local economies and people. These crises however can only be partly blamed on speculation or on the poor institutional structures of these countries (Hauskrecht 1999). A crucial reason lies in the fact that while global financial markets are strongly deregulated and thus capital can flow easily in and out of the countries, this is not the case for the markets for goods and services. While capital for investment from developed countries can enter developing countries freely, the goods produced with that investment do not find markets in those developed countries so easily. As the markets of the European Union and North America are still largely protected by tariffs and other barriers, developing countries cannot build up an even trade balance (Oxfam 2001). The consequence is that every now and again the more promising among developing countries attract large amounts of capital on speculative motives. As the countries are unable to actually live up to those expectations in the short run, the capital is withdrawn after a while, leaving the local economy in turmoil.

• **Space for illegal transactions.** As these markets are not regulated and controlled by national governments, they can easily be used for transactions that would be illegal in most countries. Even the most fervent advocates of liberalization in the USA started to question the consequences of globalization after the terrorist activities in autumn 2001 in New York and Washington. The same applies to international drug trafficking or illegal trade of weapons, all of which are substantially aided by global financial markets in their present shape.

The Tobin Tax

There are several efforts, especially by global financial actors such as the World Bank, the International Monetary Fund, and others, to impose some kind of control on global markets (Koch 2000: 189–209). While many of these initiatives are of a more voluntary nature, the debate has been recently dominated by one particular suggestion, the 'Tobin Tax'. As early as the 1970s, the Nobel Prize winning economist James Tobin (1978) suggested a tax on foreign currency transactions. Originally, this idea was directed towards tackling economic instability on international currency markets after the break-up of the Bretton Woods financial system of fixed currency exchange rates in 1973. Today, it has experienced a miraculous renaissance in the unlikely guise of anti-globalization protesters, and most notably NGOs involved in the anti-globalization movement such as ATTAC.[2] Currency crises due to speculative movements of capital, the proponents argue, lead to undesired economic consequences for the developing world which ultimately hit the poorer parts of the population hardest (International Labour Organization 1998).

The idea of the tax is fairly simple (see Cassimon 2001). The starting point was the observation that most of the instabilities and crises in the developing world of recent years had been initiated by currency speculation. Once the speculative transactions started, often initiated by only very thin margins but involving large amounts of equity, they resulted in a domino effect on global currency markets and finally led to a massive flight of capital out of that particular country and its national currency. In order to prevent traders from triggering these processes, the Tobin Tax proponents argue, it is necessary to put a very marginal tax on all currency transactions, thus making the transactions less attractive to speculative traders. Levels currently discussed range around 0.1 per cent since many speculative transactions are motivated by currency disparities at around this same level. Therefore, the tax would not make international currency transactions impossible but it would 'throw sand in the wheels' of international currency speculation. The other

---

[2] For details see their websites at **www.waronwant.org** or **www.tobintax.org.uk**. ATTAC is the subject of Ethics in Action 10.2 (367–8).

benefit of this 'Robin Hood Tax', as some refer to it, would be that the money generated by the tax could be used to the benefit of these poorer countries which otherwise suffer most from those transactions.

The discussion about the tax, however, is controversial. Commentators have tended to point to two main problems (Cassimon 2001; Davidson 1998):

- The biggest problem is the **global enforcement** of the tax. As the tax intends to avoid instability it would only work if it were enforced on a global level. Given the lack of global political governance structures this seems to be a significant obstacle. However, proponents argue that the majority of speculations take place in only a few countries, at least at the 'top end' of those speculative transactions in the developed world. So it would already make sense if only these few countries started with the tax. This still though carries the risk that these countries would suffer exclusion from certain attractive global financial transactions and that the speculation would be confined to other, even less regulated areas.

- The second group of arguments question the benefit of the tax for international trade since it penalizes all transactions across the board without **differentiating between desirable and undesirable transactions**. In practice, it might be quite difficult to differentiate between speculative and non-speculative transactions. In the end, the tax would increase the cost of foreign capital for these countries thus harming them in a different way. Such arguments focus on the actual construction of the tax. In response, advocates have argued that a 'two-tier' tax with low rates on 'normal' transactions, and the option of putting the tax up once a suspicion of a snowballing avalanche of speculative transaction had arisen, might solve this problem.

Despite these and other technical difficulties of the tax, its popularity has risen significantly over the last years. So, for instance, in November 2001, the French Parliament passed a law committing France to the introduction of the tax when other EU countries adopt it as well. In the UK 147 MPs have signed a motion in favour and the proposal has broad support from various other political wings.

Combating global terrorism and money laundering

One of the lessons of recent incidents of terrorism is that deregulated social spaces are an invitation to all sorts of illegal financial activities. Money laundering for example is the practice whereby the illegal proceeds of criminal activity are 'cleaned' in order to make them appear to be legitimate gains. Although the exact scale of the money laundering problem can, of course, not be easily determined, it is estimated to be anywhere between a staggering $500bn and $1.5 trillion per year (Abel and Gerson 2001). What is immediately clear here is that criminals obviously profit from the features of global financial markets that many shareholders actually prize. Low market entry and exit costs, low transaction costs through absence of all sorts of regulatory 'red tape', anonymity, and flexibility are just some of the features that make the possession and, most notably, the speculative buying and selling of shares, a lucrative way of increasing wealth. They are also, though, exactly the kind of conditions that appeal to criminals seeking to evade scrutiny of their finances.

Ultimately, as the debate on the so-called 'war against terrorism' suggests, the combating of these and other criminal activities might only be achieved when certain civil and economic liberties are curtailed. However, as the interests of very powerful actors would suffer significantly from restricting these liberties (by this we mean the investors, not the criminals!), certain crucial measures have not yet been introduced. The main focus at present seems to concentrate on those actors who are involved in the majority of transactions, namely the banks. Recently, the IMF has come up with some recommendations for how banks could contribute to making life more difficult for money laundering and transferral of money in the context of illegal activities (Aninat et al. 2002; Cocheo 2002):

- 'Know your customer': systematic checks on the identity and legitimacy of clients in combination with extensive record keeping which allows banks to draw analogies and construct profiles of client behaviour and transactions;

- Implementing measures that prevent criminals from getting control of key positions in banks. This would entail systematic and far-reaching checks of the background and life of employees;

- Identifying and reporting unusual or suspicious transactions;

- Training and other initiatives to raise general awareness for regulators and staff.

The IMF sees itself in the role of a mentoring institution, providing expertise, helping in assessing clients and cases, as well as providing technical assistance. It remains to be seen to what extent these measures can really be implemented. Not only do they impose serious curtailments of, for instance, banking secrecy and data protection legislation, in many cases banks would see themselves in serious conflict with issues discussed in this book in the context of ethical management of human resources (see Chapter 7).

> ■ **Think theory**
>
> Think about the role of banks in countering money laundering. Which ethical theories can you draw on to suggest that they have a responsibility to (a) actively participate in or (b) refrain from participating in efforts to curb such practices?

Shareholders as citizens of the corporation

In Chapter 1, we briefly mentioned the fact that globalization weakens national governments while at the same time MNCs are becoming increasingly powerful. This idea was developed in Chapter 2 (55–61) with the broader notion of the firm as a *political actor* replacing some of government's role in administering citizenship rights. We also discussed the growing demand for transparency and accountability to the general public that results from this gradual shift in state–business relations. In this section, we take up these ideas and explore whether the constituency of shareholders could at least be a starting point to regain some control over corporations. The idea is to show that shareholders have a particularly powerful position from which to hold the company accountable on a variety of issues that involve the administration of citizenship rights.

Shareholder democracy

The notion of shareholder democracy is a commonly discussed topic in corporate governance (Parkinson 1993: 160–6). The basic idea behind the term is that a shareholder of a company is entitled to have a say in corporate decisions. Analogous to the political realm, shareholder democracy describes a community of people that own the company and are therefore able to influence it in some way. The tantalizing idea here is that in comparison with other stakeholders, shareholders, by dint of their property rights, have a legally protected claim on the corporation.

Given the vast number of shares, this influence for the single shareholder is rather small; however, with institutional investors or holders of larger share packages, the situation looks considerably different. Nevertheless, the actual ways of influencing the board of the corporation and the institutions of proxy vary across Europe. Therefore, the actual possibilities of acting vary in scope. Furthermore, since the crucial occasion where shareholders vote is the annual meeting, their power is mainly focused retrospectively. They may or may not approve of the company's activities during the last year, whereas their influence on *future* plans is somewhat limited. This is because in most cases management will be reluctant to publish too much of their plans in advance.

Clearly, though, these limitations and qualifications do not exclude corporations from being **accountable** to their shareholders. You may remember that we suggested in Chapter 2 that 'corporate accountability refers to whether a corporation is answerable in some way for the consequences of its actions'. Corporations and their managers are then (at least in principle) answerable to their shareholders, mainly through the AGM but also through the shareholders' representatives on the board of directors. In empowering shareholders to exert power over the corporation, a crucial role also falls to the annual report. This is the main vehicle through which shareholders learn about 'their' company, and is the main resource they have by which to make decisions regarding how they will vote in AGMs.

Now this is all well and good, and our discussion would probably end there if our interest were just in corporations being accountable for the financial performance reported on in their annual reports. However, our concern is more with whether shareholders can be a force for wider *social* accountability and performance. For this, we need to consider three further issues.

• **Scope of activities.** First, we have to consider the scope of activities for which a corporation has to assume accountability to shareholders. It is one thing to say that corporations need to answer for their financial performance, but it is quite another to suggest that they need to also be accountable for all sorts of other ethical decisions and social and environmental impacts. Are shareholders interested in such issues or do they just look for a decent return on their money? **Ethics in Action 6.2** for example describes the tangle that the Norwegian government got itself into when it dispensed with ethical considerations

Ethics in Action 6.2

The Norwegian Petroleum Fund: keeping the Nobel Prize sponsors noble
....

What does Norway, the home of the Nobel Prize, have in common with Saudi Arabia? Well, not too much really apart from the fact that both countries are among the main oil exporters in the world. Oil and gas contributed around 15 per cent of Norway's GDP in 1999 and more than a quarter of the country's annual budget comes from such exports. But perhaps unlike some of their Saudi counter-parts, Norwegians have not tended to invest their oil riches simply in smart cars and shining palaces. In fact the Norwegian government has established a fund where a proportion of the huge income derived from the oil industry can be invested and ultimately reallocated for future generations of Norwegians.

The Norwegian Petroleum Fund (NPF) was set up in 1990 to administer and invest the state's revenues from the oil industry. Rising oil prices, a 78 per cent taxation rate on the oil sector, and investment of the proceeds have rapidly stocked up the Fund. In the first quarter of 2002 it was worth NOK 635bn (€83bn) and conservative estimates expect it to be worth €400–530bn in 2030, thus containing about €106,100 per Norwegian citizen. With those scales, the NPF is one of the major players on a global scale, playing in the same league as the world's biggest investment funds such as CALpers (pension fund for public employees in California, €210bn) or the European Pension Fund (for public employees in the Netherlands, €155bn) as of 2000.

In 2001, however, it was revealed by Norwegian journalists that the fund had invested in a Singaporean company producing antipersonnel mines. Just recently, Norway had been one of the key forces behind the international prohibition of landmines in 1997 and had even awarded the Nobel Peace Price to one of the key figures in the movement, Jody Williams. With public scrutiny stirred up, it turned out that the NPF had also invested in companies condoning or actively supporting nearly everything Norwegians tend to officially disapprove of. This not only included the usual suspects such as rainforest depletion, child and slave labour, genetic engineering, or producers of cluster bombs and nuclear weapons (which non-NATO-member Norway has banned from its territory). Also on the list were companies actively supporting *coups d'état* in Africa, or those closely collaborating with regimes in Burma and Sudan.

These revelations put the Norwegian government and the Norwegian Bank (which administers the fund) under heavy pressure. Jens Stoltenberg and his centre-left government developed what was called 'Uttrekningsmekanisme', a policy of pulling out of those avowedly problematic investments. The debate however was whether one of the richest countries in the world could not afford to operate an overall policy of ethical investment for a fund whose annual profit exceeds the GDP of countries such as Zambia or Mozambique.

Arguments against an ethical investment policy for NPF were manifold and not unconvincing:

• NPF is for future generations and therefore the main ethical consideration for the Norwegian government was risk avoidance; with the scope of investment opportunities radically curtailed by ethical criteria, a fund of this size would be quite heavily exposed to risks without the opportunity of any portfolio risk-sharing.

- Enforcing ethical policies is a task of Norwegian foreign policy. To tackle ethical problems the government should use the proper political and diplomatic tools and avenues. This indeed was an area of international policy where Norway had become one of the leading countries in the world. The NPF serves other purposes, and so both objectives should be tackled by different tools.

- Such a policy of ethical investment is very hard to monitor. It would impose an extremely high burden of administrative cost to trace all activities and interrelations of companies in whose shares NPF invests. It would again be irresponsible to future generation to 'waste' money on these concerns.

- After all, how does a country define ethical investment? There are no internationally agreed standards. For instance, by pulling out of companies investing in the third world, would it not be unethical also to prevent capital from flowing in these regions?

On the other side, the Norwegian public was overall in favour of ethical guidelines for the fund. In a Gallup poll, a full three out of four respondents supported the idea of the NPF including ethical criteria. Furthermore, similar experiences with funds in the Netherlands showed that public pressure towards ethical investment appears irresistible in the long run. However, the Norwegian government seems largely unresolved concerning the issue. With public pressure mounting, though, in June 2002 the Norwegian government finally decided that, as an initial step, they would install a committee to develop ethical guidelines for investment subject to parliamentary evaluation in two years' time.

SOURCES

Andreassen, G. Å. (2002). 'Business Ethics in Scandinavia'. MBA dissertation, University of Wales Swansea.
Ergo, T. (2001). 'Finansierer død og fordervelse'. *Dagladet Magasinet*, 4 May.
Moene, K. (2001). 'Olje og Fattigdom'. *Dagens Næringsliv*, 3 Feb.
Tørres, L. (2002). *Money, money, money. Et Oljefond å Være Stolt Av?* Oslo: Fafo.
Versto, O. (2001). 'Blodpenger'. *Verdens Gang*, 27 Mar.
www.solidaritetshuset.org.

....

■ **Think theory**

Describe the competing explanatory potential of three main ethical theories by using the facts of this case. On which considerations would you finally base your ethical judgement of the situation?

for its hugely successful social fund. However, even if shareholders do have a conscience about where their money goes, are they even able to assess company performance in these areas?

• **Adequate information.** This leads on to the second issue, namely that if shareholders are to decide on the ethical performance of the corporation they have to be provided with adequate information on such issues. This is where *social accounting* comes in. In Chapter 5 (162–170), we discussed different ways of social accounting and outlined some indications of 'good' social accounting. Social accounting usually results in the production of a social report or sustainability report of some kind. This can be used by shareholders for making informed decisions, just as the annual report can. Therefore, this instrument can play

Shareholder activism	Ethical investment
Single-issue focus	Multi-issue concerns
No financial concerns	Strong financial interest
Seeks confrontation	Seeks engagement
Seeks publicity	Avoids publicity

Figure 6.3. Two approaches to 'ethical' shareholding

Source: Sparkes (2001).

an important role in empowering stakeholders to exert their 'democratic' rights over the corporation.

- **Mechanism for change.** Finally, we have to think about the mechanism for change that shareholders can use in order to communicate their ethical choices and influence the corporations they own stock in. One way of doing this is for family owners of corporations to use their powerful position to encourage attention to business ethics. This was actually one of the first ways that ethical criteria were integrated into shareholders' decisions, beginning with the first capitalists such as the Cadburys or Rowntrees in UK who integrated philanthropic and paternalistic elements into the way they invested in their companies (Taylor 2000). However, our interests are mainly with situations characterized by a division of ownership and control. The role of shareholders here with respect to the ethical performance of corporations broadly falls into two categories: **shareholder activism** and **ethical investment** (Sparkes 2001). In the following, we will have a look at both approaches to supposedly 'ethical' shareholding, an overview of which is provided in **Figure 6.3**.

Shareholder activism

One of the potential levers with which to make corporations accountable for their ethical behaviour is to buy shares of that company. The motive for doing so in this case is not so much to make a profit or to speculate on the market, but to make positive use of the rights of shareholder democracy. The most important right here is the right to speak in the AGM and at other occasions where shareholders (and usually *only* shareholders) are allowed to voice their opinions on the company's policies.

Normally, these forums would be used by investors to take on the company on performance issues and other typical shareholder concerns. These rights, however, also open the possibility for other stakeholders to voice their concern and challenge the company on allegedly unethical practices. Perhaps even more importantly, they also open the possibility to get broad media attention for these issues by 'disrupting' the meeting from its usual course of action. In this situation, what we essentially have is a stakeholder group that adopts the role of a shareholder, but does so in a way that potentially provides it with greater leverage.

Shareholder activism was first witnessed in the USA, for instance in the campaign to improve race relations at General Motors in the 1970s (Carroll and Buchholtz 2000: 571).

In the UK it is quite difficult to raise issues in the AGM as this would need the involve-ment of larger institutional investors (Taylor 2000). However, there are a few examples of shareholder activism in recent years where NGOs such as Greenpeace or Partizans, a London-based human rights group, have used shareholdings, or the influence of large institutional investors, to challenge corporations such as Shell, BP, Rio Tinto, and Huntingdon Life Sciences on issues such as treatment of indigenous populations, pollu-tion, or animal testing. Embedded in larger campaigns, the filing of shareholder resolu-tions, talking at annual meetings, or even filing lawsuits as a shareholder can be very effective ways of making corporations change their behaviour.

The critical issue, however, is that in buying shares of a corporation the particular shareholder group gets involved with 'the enemy' and in the long run there might be certain integrity problems involved. Furthermore, this is only an option for reasonably wealthy individuals as—depending on the legal system—a certain amount of shares are necessary to attain visibility and influence.

Ethical investment

The second main mechanism is more removed from the corporation and certainly less active than confronting managers head-on in AGMs. However, with the general public apparently getting increasingly concerned about corporate accountability, a large and rapidly growing body of shareholders has emerged who specifically include ethical con-cerns in their investment decisions (Rivoli 1995; Taylor 2001). This is primarily the case in the UK, but also increasingly in Sweden, France, and Belgium (Anon. 2002).

In contrast to shareholder activism, ethical investors do not *directly* use their investment to make companies listen to their concerns and subsequently change their behaviour. Rather, they rather look for a profitable investment that at the same time complies with certain ethical standards. We could define ethical investment along the following lines (Cowton 1994):

> Ethical investment is the use of ethical, social, and environmental criteria in the selection and management of investment portfolios, generally consisting of company shares.

The criteria for choosing an investment can either be negative or positive. Investors can either exclude certain companies with undesired features (negative screening) or adopt com-panies with certain desired features (positive screening). **Figure 6.4** provides an overview of the most common issues for both types of criteria. Besides investment brokers and portfolio management companies, the key actors in ethical investment are funds that offer investment opportunities in company shares complying with certain defined ethical criteria. In 2002, there were nearly 300 such funds in Europe, although they accounted for less than 1 per cent of the total stocks managed by European funds (Anon. 2002).

In addition to the normative motivations for ethical investment, some commentators (and indeed investors) have argued that choosing according to ethical criteria makes sense from an economic perspective too. The risks of public boycott of products or the risk linked to environmental disasters can also influence the performance of shares, making ostensibly 'ethical' companies less risky investments. In a similar vein, the potential

Negative criteria

- Alcoholic beverages production and retail
- Animal rights violation
- Child labour
- Companies producing or trading with oppressive regimes
- Environmentally hazardous products or processes
- Genetic engineering
- Nuclear power
- Poor employment practices
- Pornography
- Tobacco products
- Weapons

Positive criteria

- Conservation and environmental protection
- Equal opportunities and ethical employment practices
- Public transport
- Inner city renovation and community development programmes
- Environmental performance
- Green technologies

Figure 6.4. Examples of positive and negative criteria for ethical investment

Source: McEwan (2001: 298–300).

market success of ethical products or environmental innovation might prove an ethical investment to be a very profitable one. So, for instance, the shares of the wind power company Vestas have risen by 500 per cent in three years (Mackenzie 2001).

Among ethical funds, there are two broad types (Mackenzie 1998). **Market-led funds** are funds that choose the companies to invest in following the indication of the market. These gather data about the ethical performance of corporations from various research agencies. Among the most reputed institutions here is the London-based Ethical Investment Research Service (EIRIS), which provides a regularly updated list of 300 criteria and an up-to-date database of 1,100 companies. The market though is not to everyone's tastes. For example, **Figure 6.5** lists the companies most commonly held in ethical investment funds in Europe, and these might not necessarily feature on everyone's list of 'ethical' companies.

In contrast to market-led funds, **deliberative funds** base their portfolio decisions on their own ethical criteria. This involves more research and forces the fund's management to regularly assess companies and practices. The difference in practice is that deliberative funds provide investors with detailed ethical criteria whereas market-based funds just provide a list of companies regarded as ethical by the market.

In practice, the choice of the right criteria and companies proves to be not always clear-cut (Cowton 1999*a*; Sparkes 2001). So, for instance, many electronic corporations may well produce components for household appliances as well as military technology. Some investors would also object to investing in bank shares, as banks fund industries across the board including those companies that do not comply with ethical norms of investors. These

Position	Company
1	Nokia
2	Johnson & Johnson
3	Vodafone
4	GlaxoSmithKline
5	ING
6	Vivendi
7	Shell
8	Pfizer
9	BP
10	Home Depot

Figure 6.5. Top ten stocks held in European ethical investment funds 2002

Source: Anon. (2002).

processes involve fund management in constant updating of their criteria and company research, encouraging a more flexible and less bureaucratic approach over time (Cowton 1999*b*).

Ethical investment is quite a striking example of what we referred to at the beginning of this section as shareholder democracy. By allocating their investment to corporations which comply with certain ethical standards, investors not only have some influence on the company's policy but they also set incentives for other companies to review their policies. Increasingly, analysts and investment firms question companies on their ethical policies, as the existence of ethical funds has proven to be not simply a new niche in the market, but has raised attention on a previously ignored issue. As Rob Hardy, an asset manager from the investment banker JP Morgan Fleming in London, puts it: 'we monitor the environmental and social profiles of the companies we invest in and adopt an engagement approach with the worst performers. I like to think we're waking companies up to these issues' (Cowe 2002). Ultimately, ethical investment obviously has an ongoing disciplinary effect on a wide range of companies, mainly because unethical behaviour makes them less attractive for a growing number of investors.

Shareholding for sustainability

With shareholders using their power and ownership rights to encourage companies to live up to their role as corporate citizens they often contribute to one of the major goals of business ethics: the triple bottom line of environmental, economic, and social sustainability. In this last section, we will have a look at two selected aspects under which shareholders become directly involved in contributing to sustainable corporate behaviour. The first area is still closely linked to what we discussed in the previous section and looks at shareholders aligning their investment decisions to the criterion of sustainability. The second part will have a look at alternative concepts of linking ownership, work, and community involvement.

The Dow Jones Sustainability Group Index

During the last decade, there have been several attempts to construct share indexes that rate corporations according to their performance towards the broader goal of sustainability. The more long-standing tradition exists in the USA, where the Dow Jones Sustainability Index (DJSI) has emerged to be the leading index in this respect. Recent developments in Europe led to the launch in October 2001 of the 'FTSE4Good Europe 50' in London. This includes a family of indices embracing companies meeting certain social, environmental, and ethical standards (EIRIS 2000). However, as the DJSI has been in existence the longest—it was launched in 1999—and actually comprises a majority of European companies (at the time of writing), we will focus mainly on this.[3]

The DJSI follows a 'best-in-class approach' comprising those identified as the sustainability leaders in each industry. Companies are assessed in line with general and industry-specific criteria, which means that they are compared against their peers and ranked accordingly. The companies accepted into the index are chosen along the following criteria:

• **Environmental (ecological) sustainability:** for example, environmental reporting, eco-design, environmental management systems, executive commitment to environmental issues;

• **Economic sustainability:** for example, strategic planning, quality and knowledge management, supply chain management, corporate governance mechanisms;

• **Social sustainability:** for example, employment policies, management development, stakeholder dialogue, affirmative action and human rights policies, anti-corruption policies.

The data that form the basis for the judgements is based on questionnaires, submitted documentation, corporate policies, reports, and, finally, public information as far as it is available. In 2002 the index included 310 companies out of 62 industry groups in 26 countries.

According to its proponents, by focusing on sustainability, the index identifies those companies with future-oriented and innovative management. Interestingly, since its inception in 1999, the DJSI has slightly outperformed the mainstream Dow Jones Index, although it should be noted that financial robustness also forms an important part of the DJSI. It has also attracted significant interest from the investment community. As of 2002, it had been sold to 37 fund-managing companies in 14 countries.

There are however a number of criticisms of the index, some of which focus on the technicalities of the index, and some of which actually concentrate on the ethical credentials of the companies chosen.

• The biggest criticism is that the data on which a company is accepted into the index depends largely on data provided by the corporation itself. Although the data is analysed by the Swiss consultancy firm SAM Sustainability Group, and verified by an independent auditor (PriceWaterhouseCoopers), the assessment is basically an inside-out provision of data.

---

[3] This section draws on the following articles, each of which might be referred to for further details and discussion: Barkawi (2002); Knoepfel (2001); Cerin and Dobers (2001a; 2001b).

- This coincides with criticisms over the questionable criteria used by the index. Some critics have asked how it could be that corporations with massive ethical credibility problems, such as Nike, are included in the index. Similarly, the entry of the cigarette manufacturer British American Tobacco into the index in 2002 was greeted with considerable controversy. The index does not however exclude on the basis of industry. Despite the obvious problems for sustainability of the tobacco industry (as well as armaments, alcohol, energy, and others), SAM argues that industry leaders should be identified and rewarded in order to stimulate progress towards sustainability.

- The sustainability assessment focuses mainly on management processes rather than on the actual sustainability of the company or its products. Evidence of policies and management tools features more prominently than concrete emission data or resource consumption figures. Again, SAM argues that the index does not identify sustainable companies, but those making progress towards addressing the issues.

Overall, then, the DJSI has to be regarded as little more than a first attempt to link investors' interest in financial performance with the broader goal of sustainability. However, the development towards sustainable investment rating has only just recently begun and hopefully we will see concerted progress towards more in-depth indices and investment tools in the near future. Nonetheless, while criticisms that it is simply a case of 'greenwashing' without any substantial performance implications are probably a little overwrought, developments such as the DJSI are never likely to be sufficient to encourage firms towards more sustainable practice. Indeed, another rather more fundamental way of addressing sustainability from the perspective of shareholders is to completely rethink the whole notion of corporate ownership. One model, which is sometimes promoted as a possible antidote to the problems of shareholder capitalism, is that of the co-operative.

Rethinking sustainable corporate ownership: corporation or co-operation?

For some advocates of sustainability thinking, one of the crucial limitations of corporations that are effectively 'owned' by shareholders is that whatever their attention to other stakeholders, the ownership model simply precludes an entirely just allocation of rewards. Co-operatives, however, are businesses that are owned neither by investors nor by their managers (such as the first capitalist entrepreneurs) but are owned and democratically controlled by their workers or their customers. Co-operatives are businesses that are not set up to make profit, but to meet the needs of their members.

The reasons for founding co-operatives can be different. For example, consider the following cases (**www.coop.org**):

- Retail co-operatives are set up to meet retailing needs: e.g. in remote parts of Sweden consumers founded the 'Kooperativa Forbundet' to provide them with shopping facilities. 'Crédit Mutuel', nowadays the number four bank in France, was initially founded to supply its members with capital.

Originally established in 1844 by the Rochdale Pioneers (a group of British social reformers who set up the first formal co-operative movement), the principles of co-operation have since been developed into an internationally agreed set of principles governing the co-operative movement across the globe. The principles as set out by the International Co-operative Alliance are as follows (cited in Butcher 1996):

1. Education of the membership, staff and general public;
2. Co-operation among co-operatives;
3. Voluntary and open membership;
4. Democratically based control;
5. Equitable use of profit/surplus;
6. Limits on the participation of capital.

Beyond these basic principles, underlying social ideals have been important in guiding the movement. The biographer of the UK co-operative union Arnold Bonner (1961: 292) described these ideals as 'an economic system based upon common ownership and mutual aid . . . in which equity, individual freedom and a strong sense of fellowship would be the basis of social relations . . . i.e. a system conducive to good character and consequent happiness.'

Figure 6.6. Principles of co-operation

Source: Bonner (1961); Butcher (1996).

- Producer co-operatives are set up to meet production needs: e.g. many agricultural co-operatives, today most notably in developing countries, were founded to share tools, supplies, and know-how.
- Purchasing co-operatives are set up to meet buying needs: e.g. the German 'Dachdeckereinkauf' is a co-operative of small companies in the roof-laying industry that use co-operation to increase purchasing power.

Worldwide, there are some 750,000 co-operatives with 760 million members in 100 countries. They are based on the principles of voluntary membership, democratic control through the members, and concern for the community. **Figure 6.6** provides an overview of the fundamental principles of co-operation.

One of the most remarkable and worldwide unique examples of a co-operative is the Spanish 'Mondragon Corporación Cooperativa' in the Basque region of Spain (see Cheney 1995). It was founded in 1956 by five engineers and a Catholic priest after having been built up over fifteen years prior to that date. Today the co-operative consists of 150 smaller co-operatives, employing around 60,000 people. It includes large companies such as a supermarket chain, and Spain's largest manufacturer of refrigerators, as well as smaller companies in the electronics sector, and a translation service with just eight employees.

Each company has its own general assembly meetings where all workers have the same vote and decide on corporate policies. On top of that, each company has a vote in the general assembly of the Mondragon co-operative as a whole. The co-operative is about twice as profitable as the average company in Spain and has the highest worker productivity in Spain. Up to 70 per cent of the profit flows back to owner-member-workers, 20 per cent is reinvested, and 10 per cent goes into local community projects.

The contribution to sustainability of the Mondragon co-operative is striking:

- **Economic sustainability.** The principle of solidarity between the different parts means that they mutually support each other in years of economic downturn in one industry. This leads to long-term survival and growth of the co-operative as a whole. Furthermore, the workers will always have an interest in the long-term survival of the organization, as they personally own it.

- **Social sustainability.** Tremendous job security, embeddedness in the local communities, and active support for social projects such as education, housing, and drug prevention make Mondragon an active supporter of a socially stable and supportive environment. With workplace democracy as the guiding principle, the individual worker has a relatively high protection of the rights we shall discuss in Chapter 7.

- **Environmental sustainability.** Though the literature is not too explicit about this aspect, it is clear that with local ownership of the corporation, the group of people that would be directly affected by polluted air, water, or soil is at the same time the very constituency to decide about these issues. This at least ensures attention to environmentally friendly working conditions and production processes.

However successful Mondragon has been in the past, it nevertheless faces some challenges in the age of globalization. The typical cultural fabric of the Basque region has increasingly eroded in the last years, and the co-operative faces growing international competition. With greater mobility of workers, wage solidarity in the co-operative has also come under threat. From a ratio of 3 : 1 between the highest and lowest earners, the figure has now doubled to 6 : 1, representing a definite erosion of the initial principles of solidarity. However, this is still remarkable by international standards (for example in the USA the ratio is 200 : 1). Insiders expect further modifications towards more market orientation but there is great optimism that Mondragon will continue to be a successful example of a 'third way' in corporate governance.

Summary

In business ethics texts, shareholders are normally a somewhat neglected species. This is perhaps not surprising given that since they are prioritized so much in virtually all other areas of business thinking, business ethics is usually considered the area where a counterpoint can be developed. However, our view is that since they are such an important corporate constituency, it is simply inappropriate to sideline them in this way. This chapter, then, in a way, has tried to achieve a more balanced view on shareholders, and thereby afford them at least equal status with the other stakeholders discussed in the second part of the book.

We started by looking at the peculiarity of the principal–agent relation that defines the relationship between managers and shareholders, and provides the basis for our understanding of corporate governance. We showed here how divergent interests and an unequal distribution of information between the two parties effectively institutionalizes some fundamental ethical conflicts in governance. This led us to examine the different models of governance evident in Europe, followed by the various ethical issues pertinent to share-holder relations, such as executive control, remuneration, insider trading, etc. Furthermore, the peculiar situation of shareholders also shone through in the three main issues that reframed the contemporary challenge for ethical business—globalization, citizenship, and sustainability.

Globalization, we have shown, has significantly changed the nature of ownership and investment in corporations, and has exposed shareholders to some of the fiercest criticism of the anti-globalization movement. In a more positive vein, we discovered that shareholders also have considerable opportunities to act as something akin to citizens of the corporation by using their power over capital supply to influence corporations to behave more ethically. Finally, we showed how shareholders could also play a role in driving corporations towards enhanced sustainability by their investment decisions at the stock market, as well as examining more unconventional patterns of ownership.

STUDY QUESTIONS

1   Why is the ownership of corporations different from that of other forms of 'property'? What implications does this have for the nature of shareholder rights?

2   Define corporate governance. What are the main ethical problems that arise in the area of corporate governance?

3   'Executive pay is not an ethical issue—it is just a question of paying people a market rate.' Critically evaluate this statement using examples from contemporary business practice.

4   Define insider trading. What are the main ethical arguments against insider trading?

5   What are the effects of globalization on the ethical problems that arise in company–shareholder relations? How can these be addressed?

6   Compare the effectiveness of ethical investment and shareholder activism in ensuring ethical conduct in corporations.

RESEARCH EXERCISE

Go to the university library or check on the web to do some research on the nature of corporate governance in your home country. You might find details in a corporate governance or corporate finance textbook, or on a website dealing with national governance codes or governance reform.

1   Set out as clearly as you can the system of corporate governance that operates in your home country.

2   To what extent is the system you have set out in accordance with the Anglo-Saxon or the continental European governance model? How can you explain any differences?

3   What priority does this system appear to afford to different stakeholders?

4   Do you think that the governance system in your country provides a fair basis for corporate activity?

CASE 6

Derailing privatization: Railtrack, shareholders, and the 'travelling public'

This case examines the decision by the UK government to put Railtrack, the privatized operator of the rail network, back under public administration. The decision resulted in a fierce political and economic debate between the company's shareholders and the 'travelling public'. This case study provides insights into the conflicts of interests between shareholders and other stakeholders of the corporation.

'Expropriation'—the taking of private property by public authorities—is a term that one would have expected to be virtually extinct in modern Europe. The last wave of expropriation in the region happened more than fifty years ago when parts of Eastern Europe fell to the communist bloc. But in autumn 2001, this was exactly what the UK government announced it was going to do to the shareholders of Railtrack plc, the UK company responsible for operating the country's rail network. Following a series of rail disasters and amid mounting criticism of the firm, the government took the unprecedented step of forcing Railtrack into liquidation.

The history that led to this contested decision is long and turbulent. Privatization of public services has been an escalating trend in many European countries during the past decade or two, and nowhere more so than in the UK, where sixteen years of Conservative Party rule had implanted the neo-liberal free market approach into nearly every public utility. The last flagship public service to be privatized was British Rail. The idea was to transform the company into many smaller, competing, privately owned entities that could then supposedly be run more efficiently and deliver better quality of services at lower prices.

In 1996, the privatization took place and British Rail was split up into nearly thirty different regional service operators. The largest new company though was Railtrack. Unlike the other companies, which were primarily responsible for running train services, Railtrack was responsible for running the network itself. This included tracks, stations, signalling, and various other elements of the rail infrastructure.

After five years, however, none of the intended targets for the big sell-off were anywhere near within reach. Rail transport in Britain had become the most expensive in Europe, the quality of trains and tracks was extremely poor, and safety standards appeared to be falling to unacceptable levels.

The rail companies' performance increasingly came under the microscope when the gradual escalation in rail accidents and 'near misses' culminated in a series of devastating crashes. The most shocking incident came in 1999 in west London, when two passenger trains collided head-on after one of the drivers had overlooked a poorly positioned signal. Thirty-one people died in the flames that ripped through one of the packed commuter trains, and many more were injured in the blaze. A year later another derailment of an Intercity train north of London led to a further four deaths.

As the company responsible for signals and tracks, the rail disasters put Railtrack under particular scrutiny. But these were just the major accidents. Headlines such as 'Passengers' nine-hour journey from hell' (describing the fate of passengers on a London to Nottingham train that took nine instead of the scheduled two hours) had become so familiar that the travelling public in the UK had become increasingly outraged, or just deeply contemptuous, about the country's flagging railway system.

The focus of the public and media critique was Railtrack. Despite governmental subsidies and loans of more than £3.3bn (€5bn), the company had not been able to provide a safe and reliable framework for train operators. Moreover, despite offering an apparently deteriorating service, Railtrack had up until 2001 paid out more than £450m (€675m) in dividends to its shareholders.

The government, which had just been re-elected on the promise to improve public services, experienced mounting pressure to deal with the problem—and to deal with Railtrack. The options were in many ways quite simple. With the company reliant on injections of further subsidies from taxpayers' money just to sustain its creaking network at the same deplorable level, the only other plausible option was to take public concerns about safety seriously and acknowledge that private ownership might not be the most effective way to run the rail network Although 'renationaliza- tion' had previously been largely dismissed as a viable policy instrument by the Labour government, on 8 October 2001 Railtrack was finally forced into liquidation and taken back under governmental administration.

The decision, however, sparked the most furious criticism. The main target was the Transport Secretary, Stephen Byers, who had overseen the expropriation (and who later resigned partly because of the furore over the Railtrack decision). Not only were the legions of minority share- holders (many of whom were regular middle-class people or employees of Railtrack) upset about the fact that their investment had been confiscated, and their savings wiped out, but also the big investors in the City of London threatened action. Although everybody knew—even out of personal experience—that something had to be done about Railtrack, such a measure was denounced as a disincentive for private investors to get involved in proposed public–private partnerships such as the renovation of the London Underground.

The general public, however, approved of the move. For many it seemed intolerable that a com- pany that made £1.3m (€2m) profits per day (in 1999) and provided its shareholders with hefty dividends did so at the price of under-investment that threatened people's lives. Finally though, amid threats of legal action by disgruntled shareholders, and after several months of 'consultation', the government made a partial concession to shareholder demands and decided to pay the 'out-of- pocket' investors approximately the price of Railtrack shares when the company was put into administration. And rather than staying under government control, today Railtrack is a not-for-profit trust company under the new name Network-Rail.

The adventures of Railtrack are particularly interesting in the context of experiences elsewhere in Europe. A comparison with other countries in Europe shows that either railways do not neces- sarily have to be privatized (such as in Germany or France) or privatization might be halted due to similarly bad experiences (such as in the Netherlands). German rail passengers are able to travel at prices 15 per cent lower than in the UK, and in France even 60 per cent lower. Nonetheless, these benefits come at a cost to the public purse—for example, in Germany the government paid £1.8m (€2.7m) in subsidies to the railways in 2000—but the public evidently regards it as an acceptable price for relatively cheap, efficient, and safe rail travel.

Questions

1 Who are the stakeholders in this situation?

2 Set out the main interests of the stakeholders involved in this case.

3 To what extent are the various claims of the different stakeholders legitimate? Can shareholders claim any superior rights to property? Give an ethical assessment of the situation.

4 What is your view of the governmental reaction to this situation? Could you think of other options that might have solved the problem?

5 What insight do the experiences in railway management in other European countries provide? Provide an ethical assessment of practices in those countries.

Sources

BBC (2001). 'Railtrack in administration'. **www.bbc.co.uk/news**, 8 Oct.

—— (2002). 'Dutch rail privatisation under fire'. **www.bbc.co.uk/news**, 21 Jan.

Curwen, P. (1997). 'The end of the line for British Rail'. *Public Money & Management*, Oct.–Dec.: 55–67.

Gow, D. (1999). 'Railtrack contrite as profits rise to £236m'. *Guardian*, 5 Nov.: 2.

Morgan, O. (1999). 'The Paddington disaster: the three sell-off millionaires'. *Guardian*, 10 Oct.: 14.

Simokins, E., and Fagan, M. (2002). 'Byers u-turn on Railtrack'. *Sunday Telegraph*, 24 Mar.: 1.

Treanor, J., and Hume, N. (2002). 'Railtrack share bailout'. *Guardian*, 23 Mar.

7

Employees and Business Ethics

In this chapter we will:

- Discuss the specific role of employees among the various stakeholder groups and identify issues of concern for corporations;

- Identify the core ethical topics of employees' rights and duties;

- Outline the ethical issues and problems faced in business–employee relations, by focusing particularly on the different rights of employees;

- Analyse the duties of employees and the company's involvement in enabling employees to live up to their duties;

- Further explore the notion of corporate citizenship in relation to employees by examining the specific European context of employee relations;

- Examine basic issues and problems of managing employees in the different cultural and national contexts necessitated by globalization;

- Discuss the implication of sustainability for workplaces and for specific working conditions.

Introduction

Dealing with employees is probably the area where all of us at some stage are most likely to encounter ethical issues and dilemmas. Whether it is a question of fair wages and conditions, sexual harassment in the workplace, or simply taking advantage of company resources such as the phone or internet for personal use, employee-related ethical problems are unavoidable for most contemporary managers. Such problems can run from the most everyday questions of how to treat other workers fairly to fundamental questions of human rights.

In a certain sense one could argue that ethical issues with regard to employees have been a consideration for corporations long before the topic of 'business ethics' was even on the agenda of business schools, let alone of corporations. When we look to the first wave of the industrial revolution in the nineteenth century, the fair and proper treatment of employees was a controversial issue right from the beginning. Famous writers, such as Charles Dickens in his novel *Oliver Twist*, explored the exploitation and poor working conditions of the masses during this era. In a more positive vein, this time also saw various examples of industrialists setting an example by caring for their workers' housing, healthcare, and diet, just to name a few examples (Cannon 1994: 7–29). As some have argued, this paternalistic involvement of employers with the working and living conditions of their employees was often motivated by what we referred to earlier as 'enlightened' self-interest: only if workers live in halfway decent living circumstances are they likely to be productive and committed to the firm's economic success (Fitzgerald 1999).

One could in fact argue that the big political divide of the twentieth century—between capitalism on the one hand and socialism or even communism on the other—originally focused on the function of employees in the working process. Karl Marx, Lenin, and even Mao developed their ideas ostensibly with the improvement of workers' living conditions in mind. At least on paper, workers in communist systems were the owners of their companies and entitled to govern their own working life. On a smaller scale, the political agendas of traditional 'labour', 'socialist', or 'social democratic' parties throughout Europe were targeted at changing legislation, implementing a so-called 'welfare state', and providing the masses with the entitlement to decent basic working conditions. By the end of the last century, however, with socialism and communism broken down, and even most left-wing governments under heavy budget pressures to cut back on the welfare state and reduce regulation, ethical issues in employment regained their position on the business ethics agenda.

These issues, however, appear on stage these days from quite a different angle. Crucially, there are still problems similar to those faced by workers in the nineteenth century, albeit less so in Europe, but certainly in countries in the so-called third world. European MNCs are confronted with issues such as the protection of workers' human rights in their factories in China or Cambodia, while at home, a variety of different ethical questions arise from the usage of new technologies such as the internet, and the introduction of new work environments such as call centres. One crucial development, however, seems to be that fewer and fewer issues are directly addressed through governmental legislation compared to a hundred, or even fifty years ago. Increasingly, we witness a growing tendency to leave the solution of these issues to corporations themselves. Consequently, the discussion of ethical issues in firm–employee relations is a matter of growing interest and concern.

Employees as stakeholders

Like shareholders, employees occupy a peculiar role among stakeholders as they are closely integrated into the firm. Whereas shareholders basically 'own' all material and immaterial assets of the firm, employees, in many cases even physically, 'constitute' the corporation. They are perhaps the most important production factor or 'resource' of the corporation, they represent the company towards most other stakeholders, and act in the name of the corporation towards them. This essential contribution, as well as the fact that employees are quite clearly affected by the success or otherwise of their company, is widely regarded as giving employees some kind of definable stake in the organization.

Referring back to our definition of stakeholders in Chapter 2, both the legal and the economic sides of the relation between employees and the corporation are worthy of examination. On the *legal* level, there is normally some sort of contract between the corporation and the employee that stipulates rights and duties of the two parties. This legal relationship, furthermore, is quite strongly embedded into a rather dense network of legislation that—especially in Europe—provides a legally codified solution to a large number of issues between companies and employees. Although there are certainly, to a varying degree, a fair amount of legal rules pertinent to all other stakeholder relationships, the relation between corporations and employees is peculiar in that it has traditionally been a subject of governmental regulation in Europe, from the very beginning of the industrial revolution onwards.

This characteristic has strong implication also for the *economic* aspect of firm–stakeholder relationships. The relation between firms and employees is characterized by a huge amount of externalities on both sides—by which we mean that there are costs to each that are not included in the employment contract. These 'hidden' costs can lead to situations of 'asset specificity'—that is, employees 'invest' time and effort in developing 'assets' specific to a particular employer, and vice versa. Such costs of specificity can create what we call a **moral hazard** for both parties, opening up a wide range of ethical issues. Let us think about some examples from the perspective of the *employee*:

- Taking up a job normally requires a considerable commitment or investment from the employee. It might involve a physical move to a new town, a shake-up to their circle of friends, perhaps an investment in education or special training, etc.

- Working for a company for a longer period results in a considerable amount of dependency upon the corporation. The employer can become the financial basis of an employee's existence. Similarly, much of the employee's knowledge might become strongly related to one particular company, meaning that redundancy could be disastrous for their career.

- Another aspect is hidden in the familiar English synonym of 'making a living' for having a job. Much of our waking life is committed to our job. As a result, it is often the place where friends and social relationships are made, and where the human need for self-actualization is met in not only having a 'job', but hopefully also a meaningful 'career'. All this results in a considerable amount of dependence of an employee on his or her employer.

All these aspects (and it would be easy to prolong this list) are not really covered in the contractual side of the firm–employee relation—and so might be regarded as moral hazards. Although there has been considerable effort to improve the legal status of employees, the general situation for employees is that they are heavily dependent for many of the necessities of life on their employer—a situation even worsened by a relatively high unemployment rate throughout most European countries. Generally speaking, employees live in the constant risk that employers might take advantage of this dependency.

Employers, on the other hand, also face similar elements of moral hazard from their employees:

• No employer can control or predict 100 per cent of the activities of its employees. Although a company may well discover the true efficiency, integrity, and reliability of its staff in time, this often could be at a point where considerable damage to the company has already occurred. Therefore, a company has an interest in tightly monitoring and controlling its employees' behaviour.

• In the global marketplace, companies in the industrialized west have increasingly switched from low-skilled, manufacturing-related work to a more knowledge-based service economy. This has led to a situation where a considerable amount of value creation is carried out by highly skilled specialists whose knowledge the company can only partly control. Furthermore, examples from the IT or Biotech industry have repeatedly shown that there is a constant danger that these specialists will be poached by competitors, thereby threatening the company's competitive advantage.

• Even the most clairvoyant personnel managers and the toughest assessment centres are unable to fully disclose the true capabilities of a future employee. From the applicant's real character up to issues like his or her health—these are still uncertain when the corporation hires staff and commits to invest expensive training in them. It is next to impossible to determine whether this investment will ultimately be rewarded.

As mentioned above, many of these moral hazards in the employer–employee relation have been subject to legislation. As the moral hazard is normally greater for the employee (since they are the more dependent and weaker party), most of this legislation focuses around workers' rights. However, as we have discussed in Chapter 1, there are clear limits to the legal trajectory in settling ethical issues. Furthermore, the nature of the relation between employer and employees often makes the sheer application of existing law (and the exploitation or otherwise of legal loopholes) an object of ethical considerations, which is one of the reasons why we discussed 'legal responsibility' as one of the four key elements of corporate social responsibility. In the following, we will have a look at the issues involved in the relations of the company to the stakeholder group of employees.

Ethical issues in the firm–employee relation

Management of human 'resources': an ethical problem between rights and duties

Employees are normally managed by the so-called 'Human Resources' department—a term which already indicates a first problem from an ethical perspective. As it is, the term 'human resource management' and its implications have been a subject of intense debate in business ethics (Barrett 1999; Greenwood 2002; Hart 1993; Torrington 1993). If we recall Kantian theory, the second maxim requires us to treat humanity 'always as an end and never as a means only'. Human resources management (HRM), however, does exactly

Rhetoric	Reality
'New working patterns'	Part-time instead of full-time jobs
'Flexibility'	Management can do what it wants
'Empowerment'	Making someone else take the risk and responsibility
'Training and development'	Manipulation
'Recognizing the contribution of the individual'	Undermining the trade union and collective bargaining
'Teamworking'	Reducing the individual's discretion

Figure 7.1. Rhetoric and reality in HRM

Source: Based on Legge (1998)

this: we as humans are constituted as an important *resource* and, in most cases, the most costly resource as well. Consequently, employees are subject to a strict managerial rationale of minimizing costs and maximizing the efficiency of the 'resource'. In fact, one could argue that the core ethical dilemma in HRM lies in the fact that people in the firm, under economic criteria, are nothing else than a resource, next to and often competing with other resources, most notably new technology, or cheaper resources from overseas.

Nevertheless, the management of human 'resources' implies more than just the application of economic criteria. In other words, human beings within the firm are of course means to an end as they are employed to perform certain functions. However, from an ethical perspective, they should not be treated as a 'means *only*', and it is this restriction that makes all the difference in terms of business ethics. This difference becomes fairly visible when looking at the gap between the rhetoric of HRM policies and the reality often hidden behind it. Some common examples are given in **Figure 7.1**.

According to Kantian thinking, it is human dignity that forbids treating employees as a means only, and it is exactly this duty that posits the main ethical boundary for the management of employees. As we have argued earlier, Kantain duties have their equivalent in the rights of the individual. Human beings deserve respect and, on the other side of the coin, are entitled to certain basic rights. It is therefore no surprise that the central ethical issues in HRM can all be framed around the issue of rights and duties of employees (Rowan 2000; Schwarzer et al. 1995; van Gerwen 1994).

> ■ **Think theory**
>
> Think about what it means to talk about employees in terms of 'human resources'. Compare Kant's theory with the feminist approach to business ethics in relation to human resource management. Do you think the term HRM is adequately chosen? What are the implications of this terminology from both perspectives?

In the following, we will have a look at the basic rights and duties of employees and discuss the major issues involved. **Figure 7.2** provides a selection of the most important rights, duties, and the main ethical problems commonly associated with them in the day-to-day reality of business.

Employee rights	Issues involved
Right to freedom from discrimination	• Equal opportunities • Affirmative action • Reverse discrimination • Sexual and racial harassment
Right to privacy	• Health and drug testing • Work–life balance • Presenteeism • Electronic privacy and data protection
Right to due process	• Promotion • Firing • Disciplinary proceedings
Right to participation and association	• Organization of workers in works councils and trade unions • Participation in the company's decisions
Right to healthy and safe working conditions	• Working conditions • Occupational health and safety
Right to fair wages	• Pay • Industrial action • New forms of work
Right to freedom of conscience and speech	• Whistleblowing
Right to work	• Fair treatment in the interview • Non-discriminatory rules for recruitment

Employee duties	Issues involved
Duty to comply with labour contract	• Acceptable level of performance • Work quality • Loyalty to the firm
Duty to comply with the law	• Bribery
Duty to respect the employer's property	• Working time • Unauthorized use of company resources for private purposes • Fraud, theft, embezzlement

Figure 7.2. Rights and duties of employees as stakeholders of the firm.

We should stress that these rights are all more or less directly deduced from the general notion of human rights, and most of them are in some way or other codified in various acts and laws. The codification of workers' rights is particularly advanced in Europe (Ferner and Hyman 1998) so that corporations in most cases should simply have to obey the existing law in the country. From this perspective, the density of codified employee rights would suggest rather little necessity for ethical reasoning in firm–employee relations. However, such a view would overlook four important aspects:

• First, it is important that the codification of these rights is an ongoing process where in many cases the law leaves a considerable amount of discretion open to individual actors. Very often, the type of law involved is not fully specified in minor details, but rather is left open until certain issues are brought into court proceedings and finally settled by the judges. As corporations might benefit from exploiting loopholes in employment legislation, even codified employees' rights still ask for ethical reasoning when applied in a concrete business situation.

- Second, the legal framework regarding workers' rights still varies quite significantly in Europe, even within the EU. So, for instance, the UK only introduced a statutory minimum wage during the first term of the Blair government (1997–2001) whereas many continental European countries had had this for many years. On the other hand, there is detailed legislation on whistleblowing in the UK whereas this issue is still not particularly regulated in most other EU countries. On a European level, there is therefore still quite some space for corporations to resolve these ethical issues on their own.

- Third, MNCs have their operations outside Europe and, in many such countries, workers' rights tend to be less accepted—let alone codified—than at home. Consequently, MNCs are in a situation where they have to consider carefully how to cope with these ethical issues. This problem becomes even more delicate as many European companies deliberately go abroad in order to circumvent domestic regulation regarding employees' rights. So, for instance, when BMW and Mercedes were looking for a new location for their recently opened new manufacturing plants in the USA, one of their key conditions was that no works councils and union representation of workers should be allowed—a criterion that would not have been permissible at home in Germany. Even though companies are therefore often successful in circumventing these laws and regulations, questions of employee rights not only remain valid, but also are more likely to raise *ethical* dilemmas because of the lack of *legal* protection.

In the following sections, we shall therefore discuss each of the eight employee rights set out in the top part of **Figure 7.2**, before proceeding to examine the three main employee duties to the firm that are depicted in the bottom part of the figure.

Discrimination

Discrimination in the business context occurs when employees receive preferential (or less preferential) treatment on grounds that are not directly related to their qualifications and performance in the job. The most common bases for discrimination in the workplace are race, gender, age, religion, disability, and nationality. However, any factor that is unrelated to job performance might be used to discriminate against employees, including marital status, physical appearance, sexual orientation, or even gender reassignment. Accordingly, many organizations now are having to come to terms with the fact that their employees increasingly come from a range of different religious, racial, national, and cultural groups, making the whole issue of *managing diversity* a prominent feature of contemporary business discourse.

The majority of diversity issues have been subject to extensive legislative efforts in most European countries. Consequently, the mere issue of discrimination in most cases should just involve the application of existing legislation to a particular business situation. However, the question of whether a factor such as one's appearance, ethnic background, or marital status is related to one's job performance is sometimes not as clear as we might suppose.

Discrimination in essence is a violation of the second principle of Rawls's theory of justice as outlined in Chapter 3, that 'social and economic inequalities are to be arranged so that they are attached to offices and positions open to all under conditions of fair equality of opportunity'. There are inequalities between individuals, but the reasons for choosing one person over the other have to be based on qualifications that in principle could be fulfilled by everyone. Making gender or race a criterion for a particular position would exclude certain persons right from the start, and would clearly constitute an act of discrimination. However, say, for instance, the owner of an Indian supermarket in the UK was looking for a manager who spoke Hindi or Urdu fluently, who had a reasonable knowledge of Indian culture, and had knowledge of current consumer preferences in the British Asian products market. Although one might reasonably consider that this would mean that it would be perfectly acceptable to advertise specifically for an Indian manager, this would in fact be discriminatory. Certainly, these criteria might be *most likely* met by a certain ethnic group, but it is in principle possible for *all* potential applicants to attain these qualifications, and so they should have equal opportunity to apply.

Although the most overt forms of discrimination have by now been addressed reasonably successfully through regulation, problems of this nature persist. **Ethics in Action 7.1** shows that racial discrimination is by no means a thing of the past in European countries —and indeed with the issue of immigration currently high on the social and political agenda across much of Europe, is unlikely to recede. Indeed, in recent years a number of major multinationals have also found themselves in the ethical (and legal) spotlight regarding race discrimination.

Ford, for example, has hit the headlines several times over accusations of racism in its UK operations. In 1996, it was revealed that the company had doctored photographs in some of its publicity material in order to change shots of black workers' faces to appear as if they were white—four workers subsequently received compensation. The company also faced strike action at its Dagenham plant in 1999 following complaints by workers of racial abuse. Continued problems led to the company eventually admitting liability for racial abuse directed at one Indian worker at the site, and the firm was forced to agree to an action plan to stamp out racism (BBC 2000a) However, the extent to which race discrimination persists in contemporary business was perhaps most dramatically illustrated in 2001, when Coca-Cola paid the world's largest settlement for racial discrimination, a sum of nearly $200m, for alleged problems in its home town of Atlanta. In an attempt to restore credibility and tackle the problem head-on, the firm took the unusual step of directly linking directors' pay to diversity targets (BBC 2001).

Ethics in Action 7.1

Red lights for black staff at the Moulin Rouge
....

'Le Moulin-Rouge, c'est encore un peu la France.' The Moulin Rouge, it's still like France at its best: these are the words with which the French paper *Le Monde* began its coverage of a court case that illustrated just how much racial discrimination is still a persistent problem in the European workplace.

Moulin Rouge, the racy Parisian cabaret and nightclub, just recently the setting (and title) of a blockbuster movie starring Nicole Kidman and Ewan McGregor, is one of the symbols of decadent Parisian 'red light' nightlife, attracting a constant stream of tourists from all over the world. In autumn 2002 however, the Moulin Rouge hit the headlines in far less glittering circumstances: it was hauled into the courts on allegations of 'racial discrimination' by one of France's leading race watchdogs.

The scandal had started in a rather unglamorous setting on a grey November day in 2000. François Mallet, a young social worker in a church mission in a Paris suburb, had just called the Moulin Rouge and he put down the receiver unable to believe his ears. In front of his desk sat Abdoulaye Marega, a 22-year-old Senegalese man who had just finished training for a certificate as a waiter, and whom Mallet was helping to find work. The ad from the Moulin Rouge had looked like a promising opportunity—'Wanted: Waiter aged 18–22, beginners welcome, to work from 5pm to 1am'—but the answer Mallet received from the famous nightclub took him completely by surprise.

According to Mallet, the recruitment manager at Moulin Rouge had initially been quite interested in the qualified applicant, but the mood changed as soon as the waiter's Senegalese origin was mentioned. 'We don't take foreigners in the front of the house,' the manager was alleged to have said. 'Well, Europeans, yes, but not coloured people. We take coloured people in the kitchen but not in the club.' Stunned by the explicit discrimination, Mallet set the French anti-discrimination pressure group 'SOS Racisme' on the case.

SOS Racisme contacted the Moulin Rouge with further applications from black applicants only to be met with the same response. With hidden microphones and a concealed camera. the organization taped telephone calls and a job interview with a black candidate, before airing the incriminating evidence to the public. When confronted with the evidence, the Moulin Rouge attempted first to play it down as an isolated incident. Interrogated about the fact that all the waiters were white while the entire kitchen staff was black, the manager of the cabaret simply commented that no qualified black applicants had come forward during the last forty years. He even contended that mixing people of different races would pose a threat to the good team spirit among the waiters. However, SOS Racisme saw things differently. As the pressure group's lawyer concluded: '100% white in the front of house, 100% black in the kitchen: this is not simply racism, this is apartheid!'

In November 2002, the case was finally decided in a Parisian court. The director of Moulin Rouge and his recruitment manager were fined €13,000 and ordered to pay damages of €4,500 to Marega. 'I am really very, very content,' the beaming winner said on leaving the court; 'those who say that France is a racist country are wrong. France is a country of liberties, of qualities.'

SOURCES

Chemin, A. (2002). 'Au Moulin-Rouge, les Noirs sont priés des rester aux cuisines'. *Le Monde*, 6 Oct.
Gilson, M. (2002). 'Les Gens de couleur? En cuisine . . .'. Le Nouvel Observateur, 3 Oct., **www.nouvelobs.com**.
Yahoo (2002). 'Le Moulin Rouge condamné pour discrimination raciale à l'embauche'. *Yahoo! Actualités*,
    22 Nov., **fr.news.yahoo.com**.

....

■ **Think theory**

Think about this case from the perspective of the Moulin Rouge management. Is it possible to use ethical theory to construct a defence of their actions? How robust is this defence compared to the competing arguments?

Percentage of female executives by responsibility level

Responsibility level	1990	1995	1996	1997	1998	1999	2000
Director	1.6	3.0	3.3	4.5	3.6	6.1	9.6
Function head	4.4	5.8	6.5	8.3	10.7	11.0	15.0
Dept. head	7.8	9.7	12.2	14.0	16.2	16.6	19.0
Section head	13.3	14.2	14.4	18.2	21.9	24.9	26.5
All	7.9	10.7	12.3	15.2	18.0	19.9	22.1

Figure 7.3. Women in top management positions

Source: UK Institute of Management Report, 2000;
www.inst-mgt.org.uk/institute/press/womeninroads.html.

Another as yet unresolved issue is gender discrimination. Women still on average receive lower wages for the same jobs than their male equivalents. Women are also still severely under-represented in top management positions, despite often outperforming men educationally. **Figure 7.3** sets out some recent statistics underlining the persistence of this problem.

The point is that no matter how good the legislation, many forms of discrimination are deeply embedded in business. Sometimes this is referred to as **institutional discrimination**, namely that the very culture of the organization is prejudiced against certain groups. For example, one could suggest that in a company where there was an informal understanding amongst the staff that in order to get on, one had to stay late at the office and work far in excess of 'normal' office hours, certain groups such as single parents (who might be unable to commit such time over and above their contractual obligations) would face an institutionalized barrier to progression.

■ **Think theory**

Although we have suggested that employees have a *right* to be free from discrimination, it is clear that it still occurs. Is this just because employers haven't recognized that discrimination is wrong, or is it possible to establish a defence of discrimination from the perspective of other ethical theories? Which theory provides the most convincing defence?

Sexual and racial harassment

As well as discrimination occurring in the areas of promotion, pay, and job opportunities, issues of diversity might also be exploited to inflict physical, verbal, or emotional harassment. In the case of sexual harassment, a problem might even be that certain sexual favours are requested for promotion or other rewards that would normally be a result of successful work. 'Mild' forms of harassment would be jokes or comments about a person's gender, race, sexual orientation, etc. that could lead to significant effects on the working climate and working relations of an individual in a company.

Regulation tends to be still quite reluctant to take up these issues. The main reason for this seems to be that the line between harassment on the one hand and 'office romance', 'joking', or other forms of 'harmless' harassment is pretty much blurred and often defined by a number of contextual factors such as character, personality, and national culture. So, for instance, in certain southern European countries men might get away with patterns of behaviour that in other places would be regarded as overtly 'macho', and vice versa. Companies increasingly have introduced codes of practice and diversity programmes in order to tackle these issues and to define for the specific context of the company the borders of harassment (Crain and Heischmidt 1995).

Equal opportunities and affirmative action

So how should organizations respond to problems of discrimination? In one sense, they could simply look to legislation to tackle the problem, particularly as most European countries have a reasonably well-established legal framework of anti-discriminatory laws and statutes. However, as we have already seen, even the existence of clearly specified laws hasn't prevented discrimination from occurring. Moreover, most legal approaches do not specify exactly *how* discrimination should be avoided, leaving many decisions open to the discretion of management. As a result, many companies have sought to tackle discrimination through the introduction of so-called equal opportunity or affirmative action programmes. These programmes establish policies and procedures that aim to avoid discrimination, and may even go so far as to attempt to redress inequity in the workforce.

The most basic and conservative approach is usually referred to as an **equal opportunity programme**. These have been widely introduced in European business, and it is now common to see job adverts and company websites proclaiming that an organization is an 'equal opportunity employer'. Of course, many countries legally require that companies are equal opportunity employers, but the label is usually intended to signify that the organization has gone beyond the normal expectations.

Equal opportunity programmes mainly involve the introduction of procedures that ensure that employees and prospective employees are dealt with equally and fairly. For example, one way of ensuring equal opportunity to jobs is by ensuring that they are advertised in such a way that all potential applicants can reasonably learn of the vacancy and apply—as opposed to, say, simply selecting someone through informal channels. Similarly, by setting out specific criteria for jobs, and ensuring that interview panels use structured assessment of candidates against those criteria, factors unrelated to the job such as gender or race can be excluded from the formal appraisal of candidates. As such, equal opportunities programmes are generally targeted at ensuring that **procedural justice** is promoted, i.e. the key issue is ensuring that the procedures are fair to all.

Some equal opportunities programmes go further than merely introducing non-discriminatory procedures. Often referred to as **affirmative action (AA)** programmes, these approaches deliberately attempt to target those who might be currently under-represented in the workforce, for instance by trying to increase the proportion of women, disabled, or racial minorities in senior management positions. Four main areas of affirmative action can be distinguished (De George 1999: 431–5):

- **Recruitment policies.** In order to enhance the proportion of under-represented groups, AA programmes might look at actively recruiting these groups, for example by deliberately targeting job ads in media with a wide circulation amongst under-represented groups, or dispatching outreach recruitment staff to areas or schools where under-represented groups might predominate.

• **Fair job criteria.** Discrimination can often surface in an ostensibly 'objective' form through the definition of job criteria in such a fashion that they automatically make the job beyond the reach of a great number of potential applicants. In many cases, these job criteria might not necessarily be crucial to the achievement of the job role yet they disadvantage certain parts of the population more than others. For example, those from low-income or immigrant communities may not have had the same educational opportunities as others. This will often mean that regardless of intelligence, experience, or ability for the job, they may be less likely to have the formal qualifications required by potential employers. Similarly, given that it is usually mothers rather than fathers who most frequently take on childcare and other household roles, inflexibility in employees' working times can discriminate against women. Ensuring that job criteria are fair to all is often a major task for AA programmes to tackle. **Ethics in Action 7.2** illustrates some of the ways that the Italian manufacturer Zanussi has set about restructuring some of its working patterns to be more flexible for working parents and others.

• **Training programmes for discriminated minorities.** Even following the revision of job criteria to ensure some degree of fairness, it is very possible that they will still include certain special skills, qualifications, and experience that particular under-represented groups are simply unlikely, from a statistical point of view, to have. This might be because of discrimination earlier in life, historical or cultural precedents, or just the plain realities of certain groups' socio-economic situation. In principle, ethnic Algerians might be accepted by a French *Grande École*, but in practice, the social situation of these families does not encourage the children to pursue such an academic option compared to certain other groups in French society. Not all possible remedies here are within the company's scope of action—no one is expecting them to eradicate discrimination throughout the whole of society—but targeted pre-recruitment training programmes for under-represented groups can boost their eligibility for vacant positions. For example the German automotive company Volkswagen AG provides special information events for female school leavers and graduates, targets women with information on training opportunities, and holds workshops for secretaries and clerical staff.[1]

• **Promotion to senior positions.** The fact that senior management positions in virtually all industries in Europe are dominated by white males might also be tackled by specific leadership training for women and other under-represented groups once they are already within the organization. For example, the Spanish food company Nutrexpa has a programme in place which seeks to improve the training and qualifications of women workers in order to make them eligible for promotion and expanded responsibility.[2]

---

[1] CSR Europe, Full Business Best Practice Case: Volkswagen AG, **www.csreurope.com**.
[2] CSR Europe, Full Business Best Practice Case: Nutrexpa, **www.csreurope.com**.

`Ethics in Action 7.2`

Producing white goods with clean hands at Zanussi

Founded in 1916 by the young Antonio Zanussi, the company still named after its founder is one of Europe's biggest producers of white goods, selling more than five million units a year in sixty countries around the globe. The Italian company, now a wholly owned subsidiary of the Swedish conglomerate Electrolux, has recently attracted attention because of some innovative workplace policies, especially those targeting discrimination and the delicate issue of work–life balance.

With 40 per cent of their labour force being women, Zanussi has launched a telework scheme specifically designed for pregnant women and mothers so that they can work from home. Participation in this project is voluntary and those women participating have to provide the working space at home, while the company provides and installs all necessary equipment and services. Working time then for the employees is completely flexible, with only a few hours where employees have to be available to be contacted by colleagues. Another project, called OIKOS (Greek for 'house'), aims to help those mothers who work in production units where the workplace cannot be located at home. Zanussi provides skilled personnel and space for mothers to drop their children in the corporate nursery school during their shift. Furthermore, the company operates a special scheme of rewarding overtime in a way that gives an over-proportional reward in the form of extra days off.

'We are committed to increase the role of women in the factories,' a senior executive of Zanussi commented. But there are also other reasons for Zanussi's approach: the improved schemes have reduced the level of sick leave among the targeted groups of women, giving Zanussi back almost 150,000 hours of work since the introduction of the scheme in 2000.

This approach to human resource management seems also to have a more long-standing tradition. When the company had to lay off staff in the late 1980s due to massive restructuring Zanussi felt responsible for redundant employees. Particularly critical was the fact that the majority of workers were unskilled and a third of them older than 50—thus normally the classic profile for sliding into long-term unemployment. In a joint effort with trade unions, the company initiated a programme targeted at systematically improving employment chances: paid leave, reimbursement of travel expenses for interviews, training courses, help for employees who wanted to start up an own business, and a number of other measures were granted to facilitate the return to work. As a result, most of these highly critical cases were relocated into new employment.

SOURCES

CSR Europe (2002a). 'Zanussi: comprehensive support programme for relocated staff (Full Business Best Practice Case).' **www.csreurope.org/library**.

—— (2002b). 'Electrolux Zanussi SpA: telework and nursery schools to help women raising a family (Full Business Best Practice Case).' **www.csreurope.org/library**.

www.zanussi.com.

> ■ **Think theory**
>
> Apply the perspective of virtue ethics and feminist approaches to business ethics to this case. Do you think that Zanussi's approach has a particularly Italian flavour?

Reverse discrimination

Affirmative action targets the remediation of long-standing discriminatory tendencies in the workplace: people of a certain gender, sexual orientation, or ethnic background become the subject of policies or regulations that provide supposedly fairer conditions for these groups. In many cases this does not simply intend to provide equal opportunities for these groups but AA in many cases focuses on the correcting of past injustices by, for instance, attempting to enhance the percentage of women in executive positions. However, one side effect of this approach is that at some point AA can itself be deemed discriminatory because it disadvantages those thought to already be in an 'advantaged' position. In some European countries it is deemed acceptable to 'tip the scales' to favour under-represented groups if candidates are thought to be equal on all other criteria. For example, if you are a man applying for a job in a German university, the employment ad might inform you that in the case of equal qualification, a female applicant will be preferred. The situation is taken a step further if minorities are preferred to mainstream candidates when the minority candidate is *less qualified* for the job or promotion. For instance, some jobs might be subject to quotas that specify what proportion of a certain minority group must be selected for interview, or even for the job itself, regardless of whether they are less qualified than over-represented groups. In these cases, people suffer **reverse discrimination** exactly because AA policies prefer certain minorities.

The justification of 'reverse discrimination' is somewhat ambiguous. On the one hand, companies could argue that, for instance, women have been discriminated against for such a long time and are so badly under-represented that it is time to reverse this development and consequently women deserve preferential treatment. This argument could be based on the notion of **retributive justice**—i.e. that past injustices have to be 'paid for'. On the other hand, there is the problem that the individual applicant, say a white male, is not responsible for the misconduct of his race or gender on previous occasions and so should not be made responsible by being the subject of reverse discrimination.

More defensible are arguments based on **distributive justice**—i.e. that rewards such as job and pay should be allocated fairly among all groups (Beauchamp 1997). These arguments tend to be underlined by the observation that many male executives have been promoted not necessarily because of their objective qualifications but because of their membership in 'old boys' networks' or similar groups. Even objective 'merit' can be difficult to determine when certain roles and industries have been for so long dominated by certain genders or races. Women and racial minorities, it might be argued, require role models in professions they have been excluded from, and those professions in turn might need to acquire new ideas about what a 'normal' professional would look or sound like. How many of us, for instance, automatically assume that a company director will be a white man in his fifties or sixties rather than, say, a young black man, or a woman? For most advocates of reverse discrimination, then, cultural arguments such as these suggest that fair outcomes rather than fair procedures should be paramount.

Opponents of reverse discrimination tend to marshal a number of fairly compelling arguments criticizing the practice, not least the basic notion that discrimination is wrong *per se* and that procedural justice should be paramount. Moreover, it can be argued that someone promoted on the basis of their gender or colour may well be discredited amongst their peers, and if they are not the best person for the job, this can even harm business efficiency (Pojman 1997). It has further been shown that decisions made on the basis of race, gender, or any other characteristic unrelated to merit can actually serve to promote stereotyping and reinforce existing prejudices. Burke and Black (1997) go so far as to suggest that reverse discrimination can prompt a 'male backlash' against the perceived injustice.

For reasons such as these, stronger forms of reverse discrimination tend to be illegal in many European countries. For example, whilst it may be acceptable for companies to have 'targets' or 'aims' of how many women or minorities they would like in certain roles or levels, they may be prevented from having an explicit quota that has to be fulfilled.

Employee privacy

Let us begin this next section with a short test:

Answer each of the following questions True or False:

1. I feel sure there is only one true religion
2. My soul sometimes leaves my body
3. I believe in the second coming of Christ
4. I wish I were not bothered by thoughts of sex
5. I am very strongly attracted by members of my own sex
6. I have never indulged in any unusual sexual practices

You may be relieved to know that we're not going to ask you to announce your answers to these questions in class! However, these are actual questions from a pre-employment test administered by Dayton Hudson Corporation for the position of security guard at one of its Target stores in California in 1989 (Boatright 2000: 159). The company eventually conceded in court that asking such intimate questions constituted an invasion of privacy, but the prospect of companies invading employees' privacy has become an increasingly pressing issue in the contemporary workplace. The escalation in health, drug, alcohol, even genetic testing of employees, coupled with the possibilities for more and better surveillance through advances in information and communication technologies, has meant that employee privacy has never been so much under attack.

The fundamental right to privacy consists of an individual's right to control information about oneself, and to control situations where such information could be gleaned (Cranford 1998). According to Michele Simms (1994) there are four different types of privacy we might want to protect:

- **Physical privacy:** physical inaccessibility to others, and the right to 'one's own space'. For example, organizations that place surveillance cameras in employees' private rest areas might be said to compromise physical privacy.

- **Social privacy:** freedom to interact with other people and in whichever way we choose. For instance, some employers will threaten social privacy by suggesting that employees should not bring their firm into 'disrepute' by behaving in an 'unacceptable,' 'immoral', or illegal way during their social lives.

- **Informational privacy:** determining how, when, and to what extent private data about us is released to others. This can be breached, for example, when employers hire private security firms to make investigations about employees without due cause.

- **Psychological privacy:** controlling emotional and cognitive inputs and outputs, and not being compelled to share private thoughts and feelings. For instance, psychological privacy is threatened when retailers introduce programmes aimed at making sure employees smile and appear happy in front of customers.

Obviously, not all social interactions or information about ourselves can be deemed private. Employers have a right to know about our qualifications and work experience, just as they have a right to know if we have had a meeting with one of the company's clients. The key issue is whether some certain aspects of our life are *relevant* to the relationship we have with our employer (Simms 1994). Let us take a look at this question in the main areas where employee privacy appears to be challenged.

Health and drug testing

A long-standing area of conflict has been health and drug testing of potential and present employees. **Ethical Dilemma 7** gives a case of an increasingly common situation in today's business world. Companies argue that knowing about the health of their employees, or whether they have been drinking or taking drugs, is necessary in order to make a judgement about their employability and continuous ability to fulfil the job. This might be quite understandable in the case of jobs where stable health is a key issue, such as pilots or workers on oil rigs. In these cases, knowing about the state of the employee is crucial in order to avoid accidents and ensure the proper fulfilment of the employee's tasks. Other arguments brought forward in favour of these tests focus on the employer's right to know about future costs due to absenteeism and loss of productivity. So, for instance, proponents of drug testing point to the huge costs that drug abuse causes for companies (Cranford 1998). This latter aspect gets a further significance given the ever-increasing scope of information that could be gained by genetic testing in the workplace. This can provide far-reaching insights into an employee's future health prospects.

Health and drug testing, however, remains a highly contested issue in business ethics. The central objection seems to be that these tests make available far more information on the employee than the employer actually needs. Des Jardins and Duska (1997) highlight three main aspects here.

- **Potential to do harm.** There are only a few jobs where information on health and drug use is really vitally important for the safety of the job or for the protection of customers.

Ethical Dilemma 7

A testing time for the high livers?

You are the personnel manager of a London-based investment bank, LSD Investments. Recently, there have been a number of high-profile reports in the media concerning finance executives who have been sacked following the discovery that they had been using illicit drugs out of work.

The reports indicate that UK businesses lose around £3bn every year to drink- and drug-related illness, whilst in the USA, drug use is estimated to cost employers $75–100bn annually in lost time, accidents, healthcare, and workers' compensation costs. Sixty-five per cent of all accidents on the job in the USA are said to be directly related to drugs or alcohol. Drug testing has become common in the USA with around 80 per cent of firms currently using some kind of test. Testing is not nearly so common in the UK, but is apparently on the increase following the introduction of extensive programmes at companies such as Railtrack and London Transport. The hectic, fast-living lifestyle of the London financial district is thought to make traders and other city finance executives increasingly prone to cocaine usage and other illegal drug taking.

In the light of this, your managing director has decided to ask you to consider the case for instituting a programme of drug testing for LSD Investment's employees.

Questions

1 What are the main ethical issues in this case?
2 What are the main ethical arguments for and against drug testing of employees in this situation?
3 Think of companies where you have had a job before. Try to imagine the impact of a drug-testing scheme in a work environment which you are familiar with.
4 How would you respond to your managing director?

An AIDS test conceivably makes sense for a nurse or a chef, but it is certainly not an issue for a software specialist or a lorry driver. The key issue for Des Jardins and Duska is whether the job involves *a clear and present danger to do harm*.

• **Causes of employee's performance.** Des Jardins and Duska also argue that an employer is entitled to information about the employee's performance, but not necessarily about the *causes of that performance*. Given that employees are expected to produce a certain level of performance, employers are well within their rights to determine whether their employees are performing at a satisfactory level. If an employee is found to be underperforming, then equally the employer is entitled to take action against the employee, perhaps by issuing a warning. However, we must question whether the employer has a legitimate right to know about all the factors influencing whether the employee is, or is not, performing at the required level. Suppose we are depressed, or suffering from bereavement, or have just stayed up drinking too much the night before—this may affect our performance, but then again it may not. It would be quite difficult to accept that we should reveal this information on arriving at the office in the morning unless there is a clear, ongoing problem with our performance. The fact is that it is the performance that is at issue, not the reason behind it, at least in the first instance.

- **Level of performance.** Finally, Des Jardins and Duska further claim that an employer is only entitled to an *acceptable* level of performance from their employees, not their *optimal* performance. Most drug, alcohol, and health tests aim to identify factors that *potentially* might prevent the employee from functioning in the most optimal fashion. Again, the key issue is whether we are performing at an acceptable level in the first place, not whether we could be made to perform better. This particularly questions AIDS tests and genetically based tests as in most cases they provide the employer with information about the employee far beyond what is necessary for the day-to-day performance of their job.

Despite these criticisms, such tests have become increasingly common in the modern workplace, particularly in the USA. The particular cultural context of the USA may help to explain this, in particular the strong legalistic approach that makes employers vulnerable to litigation from customers and other employees if members of staff are found to have put them at risk when unfit for work due to sickness, drugs, or alcohol. However, testing programmes are most certainly on the rise in Europe too, occasioned perhaps by the exporting of US business practices to their European operations (Eaglesham 2000). Nonetheless, despite these developments, probably the biggest threat to employee privacy at present comes from the increasing use of electronic surveillance.

Electronic privacy and data protection

Surveillance and control of workers has a long legacy in management practice. However, as Ottensmayer and Heroux (1991) suggest, the escalation in usage of new technologies in business has added a new dimension to the issue of privacy.

First, there is the fact that the computer as a work tool enables new forms of surveillance (Ottensmeyer and Heroux 1991). The computer makes possible detailed overviews about time and pace of work carried out, particularly since every strike of the keyboard can now easily be monitored. This means that the employer is not only in a position to judge the result of the employee's work, but they can also trace in every detail the process of its coming into existence. Similarly, many employers now routinely place cameras and other recording devices in work areas to monitor employees (Hartman 1998). Whilst this might be justified to assess performance or to prevent thefts and other misdemeanours, it is clearly an entry into the physical privacy of employees, particularly when it intrudes on ostensibly private areas such as changing rooms, bathrooms, and staff rooms. It remains a highly contested issue as to how far this breach of privacy is legitimate.

This control does not only extend to the work process but it pertains also to the usage of employees' time for private reasons, such as when using email or the internet. This includes fairly straightforward issues such as the downloading of pornography but also extends to all sorts of other usage of communication technologies for private purpose. Should companies be allowed to monitor and check their employees' email, or their private conversations on the phone? With regard to conventional mail, there are extensive regulations in place safeguarding privacy, which are simply not applicable to electronic mail in the same way. Most companies meanwhile have established codes of conduct that at least provide the employee with some knowledge of the boundaries to privacy established by the firm. However, throughout Europe, there are different standards in legislation that determine the extent to which privacy could be restricted in these areas. The UK at present grants some of the most far-reaching surveillance rights to companies. The Regulation of Investigatory Powers Act 2000 gives employers the power to monitor workers' phone calls, emails, and internet use without consent. As a result there are, for example, German companies that send all their internal email via a server in London so that it can be legally monitored and checked by the company (Inman and Wilson 2001).

While the abuse of company time is a perfectly legitimate complaint of companies, we might ask whether the policing to prevent or identify such an abuse legitimizes such a far-reaching incursion into workers' privacy. As with drug and alcohol tests, the invasion of privacy here is often based on the threat of *potential* harm to the company, rather than *actual* harm. However, the harm to both employees and the firm itself can be very real when implementing such extensive surveillance. After all, for employees such as call centre operatives, who spend most of their work time on the telephone, not only is almost everything they say during the day open to surveillance, but employers often also enforce a way of talking and behaving to clients that potentially threatens psychological privacy also. In the long run, employers may also suffer by eroding trust within the organization and failing to capitalize on employee discretion.

Finally, the issue of privacy occurs in situations where data is saved and processed electronically (De George 1999: 346–53). The relation between an employee and the company's doctor is one of privacy, and if the doctor enters the data of the employee into his PC system this is not a breach of the patient–doctor confidentiality. But as soon as this database could be linked with the company's other systems, the employee's privacy would clearly be broken. The problem here is that it might not be a problem if companies are in possession of their client's or employee's data *per se*. The problem occurs where, for instance, the phone company is taken over by the credit card company and both clients' databases are matched: such an operation suddenly provides access to a wide range of information posing a far more potent breach of privacy.

With advances in information and communication technologies accelerating at an unprecedented rate, we might expect threats to privacy such as these to intensify. However, legislation is often relatively slow to catch up with these changes, and since employee surveillance is so ingrained in management, managers often do not even recognize privacy as an ethical issue (Ottensmeyer and Heroux 1991). Therefore, although it remains to be seen whether Europe goes the same way as the USA in successively eroding employee privacy, we might at the very least question whether 'spying' on employees is counter-productive to fostering trust and integrity in the workplace.

■ **Think theory**

Think about electronic surveillance in terms of utilitarianism. What are the costs and benefits involved? Is this likely to offer a reasonable justification for incursions into employee privacy?

Due process and lay-offs

As anyone who has ever worked in the kitchens, bars, and restaurants of clubs and bars across much of Europe will be able to vouch, many employees are constantly at risk of arbitrarily losing their jobs for relatively minor indiscretions, personality clashes, or simply because their face 'doesn't fit'. The right to due process though has a long history in European working practices and can be deduced from the notion of procedural justice. As we saw with discrimination, this form of justice requires the application of rules and procedures to people in a consistent and even-handed way, avoiding arbitrary decision-making, and without discrimination on bases other than merit (Chryssides and Kaler 1996). Promotion, disciplinary proceedings, and firing are the most common processes where the right to due process is particularly important.

Promotion is typically a decision that is particularly reliant on the discretion of the employer. However, in addition to discrimination issues, an employee can also be said to have a right to be subject to the same promotion criteria as their colleagues, and for criteria to be clearly job related. Some companies, and especially public bodies and authorities, even operate specific codes for promotion, linking criteria to certain positions in order to establish transparency in the process. This is even more necessary in the case of disciplinary procedures. Employees should only be subject to these if a clear and objective neglect of their duties and a breach of their contractual obligations has occurred (van Gerwen 1994).

In cases of firing and redundancies the same procedures have to apply. Normally, the legal framework of most European countries, certainly those of the EU, provides detailed codification of employee and employer rights in these circumstances—even if some industries and countries tend not to respect these as fully as others. This is less clear-cut in the area of redundancies and downsizing of corporations. Following the concept of CSR (corporate social responsibility) as outlined in Chapter 2, the 'economic responsibility' as the first element of CSR might well ask for firms to cut back on labour costs to remain competitive and in business. There are however certain ethical considerations in the process of downsizing.

- A first important area is the information policy of the corporation (Hopkins and Hopkins 1999). It can be contended that employees have a **right to know** well ahead of the actual point of redundancy that their job is on the line. This issue of timing is closely connected to the method of announcement. For example, when the UK firm Rolls-Royce laid off 5,000 of their workers in the aftermath of the 11 September 2001 disaster, the workers only learnt of the decision on the BBC morning news. Furthermore, it is usually contended that employees have a right to know about the exact causes for the downsizing, as this will provide them with the possibility of judging the fairness of the downsizing process (Hopkins and Hopkins 1999).

- A second important area is the **compensation package** employees receive when laid off (Hopkins and Hopkins 1999). These typically should include enough money to bridge the time for finding a new job. Generally, many European firms tend to have quite a generous approach to these issues, and many also provide social schemes for redundant workers including early retirement options for those workers whose chances of finding another job are lower due to advanced age.

With increasing moves towards restructuring and flexibilization, however, the needs of employees in lay-off situations have moved beyond merely involvement and remuneration to retraining and reintegration into the workforce. Over the past decade, European employees have increasingly been exposed to the need for *occupational transitions*—i.e. having to find work in completely new industries rather than just switching employers. This has obviously meant that employees have experienced escalating insecurity, whilst also facing greater challenges for developing their *employability* (Kieselbach and Mader 2002).

Such developments have potentially surfaced new expectations on corporations, particularly in respect to developing 'outplacement' strategies to help employees find work following lay-offs. In the Netherlands, for example, most companies offer employability training, and restructuring is often supported with career counselling; in Belgium and Italy, companies are legally obliged to offer outplacement counselling in the case of lay-offs (Kieselbach and Mader 2002). Although, in other countries such as Spain and the UK, employment is primarily regarded as an individual or governmental responsibility, there is clearly a case for suggesting that some form of outplacement process might be a 'fairer' approach to lay-offs.

■ Think theory

Think about outplacement strategies from the perspective of justice and fairness. See if you can set outplacement in the context of Rawls's theory of justice.

The right to due process is mainly concerned, then, with establishing appropriate procedures for treating workers, particularly in the case of lay-offs and dismissals. Some proponents of employee rights though make a somewhat stronger claim by suggesting that workers should also be involved in all company decisions that affect them. This is called the right to participation.

Employee participation and association

The recognition that employees might be more than just human 'resources' in the production process has given rise to the claim that employees should also have a certain degree of influence on their tasks, their job environments, and their company's goals—i.e. **a right to participation**. There are quite a number of ethical justifications for this claim (see Claydon 2000; Cludts 1999). Apart from references to human rights, a particularly powerful grounding can be derived from Kant's thinking. Specifically, participation implies that people are not treated only as a means to another's end. Employees have their own goals, and their own view of which ends should be served, and so might be said to have some rights to determine the modalities of their involvement in the corporation. Other justifications can be based on egoism, namely that an employee can only freely pursue their own interests or desires with some degree of participation at the workplace.

Questions over the right to participation continue unabated, not least because such a right often clashes with management's duty to determine how best to protect the interests of owners. However, the key issue at a practical level now in Europe is not so much whether employees should at all have a right to participate in decisions, but rather to what degree this should take place. There are two main areas to which a right to participation expands (Kaler 1999*a*):

Financial participation allows employees a share in the ownership or income of the corporation. Some recent initiatives predicated on (partly) remunerating employees with shares or share options have tried to work in this direction. In Chapter 6, we also discussed the example of the co-operative firm, which is the most common pattern of financial participation.

Operational participation occurs at a more practical level, and can include a number of different dimensions:

- **Delegation:** employees might take control of a wider range of individual decisions relevant to their own jobs. Efforts of this kind have often been labelled as 'job enrichment' or 'job enlargement' schemes and have been practised successfully, for instance, in the automotive industry. Several European companies, such as Volvo and Porsche, have in part stopped their line production and reorganized their workforce in semi-autonomous teams. By this, many decisions about how to actually manufacture a car have been taken away from the formal control of line management and into the sphere of the individual employee (Woywode 2002).

- **Information:** employees might also receive information about crucial decisions that have an effect on their work. This concerns particularly information about the actual performance of the corporation, the security of jobs and pensions, etc. This form of participation is in many respects wider than just participation through delegation since it also may pertain to issues that are not directly necessary for the fulfilment of the employee's own immediate task.

- **Consultation:** employees are allowed to express their views on decisions taken by the employer. This form of delegation is stronger again since it opens up the opportunity to potentially influence the decision taken by the employer.

- **Codetermination:** here employees have a full and codified right to determine major decisions in the company. This is the strongest form of participation and would include decisions about the strategic future of the corporation, such as mergers or diversification into new markets (Ferner and Hyman 1998).

In a European context, there is still quite a variety with regard to the degree of participation allocated to employees. Whereas employees in Britain, for instance, mostly learn from the papers if their jobs are on the line, Swedish or French companies usually cannot take these measures without detailed communication, consultation, and agreement with employees. In many such countries, there is a quite extensive body of legislation that focuses on the representative organization of the workforce. Consequently, many of these participatory rights are not practised by employees directly but by their representatives in works councils, trade unions, or other bodies. With converging legislation and the constant extension of the EU, there is reasonable ground for expecting future convergence of legislation regarding worker participation, as the example of European Works Councils illustrates (Ferner and Hyman 1998).

Given the important role for works councils and trade unions in facilitating the right to participation, we must also consider here the underlying question of whether employees have a 'right' to join together in such organizations. This is usually framed in terms of a **right to association**. The crucial factor here is that without a right to associate, employees often lack an effective form of representation of their interests to employers, leaving them in a far weaker position than management in bargaining over pay and conditions. Such rights are in fact enshrined in many parts of continental Europe, especially France, Germany, and the Netherlands, although far less so in countries such as the UK and USA. Still, even where rights to associate are legally protected, companies may seek to obstruct or avoid them. For example, Royle and Towers (2002) vividly illustrate how, in the fast food industry, companies with a strong 'anti-union' stance such as McDonald's have been able to tame, neutralize, or subvert systems of employee representation, especially at a workplace level. In Germany, for instance, they argue that the company successfully managed to avoid collective agreements for eighteen years, and continues to resist works councils.

The rights to participate and associate therefore remain crucial issues for corporations, especially when moving to countries where the legislative framework is different from at home. The motivation, however, does not only have to come from concerns about compliance with legislation or issues of fairness and equity. Increasingly, in modern organizations participation at least has been identified as a means to enhance workers' efficiency, especially when jobs ask for flexibility and creativity on behalf of the employee (Collier and Esteban 1999). Ultimately, though, the rights to participation and association within a company follow a similar line of argument to that concerning participation of citizens in the political process (Ellerman 1999). Corporations have power over one of the most important areas of an employee's life, namely their economic survival. Consequently, the principles of a democratic society necessarily ask for some rights to participation in the firm, usually through a representative body of some kind such as a trade union. Trade unions, however, also play an important role in other employee rights, including those of due process, fair wages, and, as we shall now see, working conditions.

Working conditions

The right to healthy and safe working conditions has been one of the very first ethical concerns for employees, right from the early part of the industrial revolution. Novelists such as Charles Dickens and various social reformers such as Robert Owen, who pioneered the co-operative movement, sought to shed light on the appalling conditions faced by those working in mines, factories, and mills at the time. Consequently, a considerable number of issues concerned with working conditions were initially addressed as far back as the early nineteenth century, either by way of legislation (such as Bismarck's social laws in Germany) or by voluntary initiatives of paternalistic, often religiously motivated entrepreneurs (Fitzgerald 1999).

Today most industrialized countries, most certainly those of the EU, have implemented a dense network of health, safety, and environmental (HSE) regulation that companies have to abide by. Consequently, such issues are either already regulated by existing laws or become an object of court proceedings, rather than necessarily being ethical issues that have to be resolved within the boundaries of the firm. The main issue, however, often becomes the *enforcement and implementation of existing regulation*. In practice, some companies may cut corners on health and safety through negligence or in contempt of regulators. Similarly, many of these regulations, such as wearing a safety helmet or ear plugs, can be disliked by workers themselves. This imposes a responsibility on employers to actually 'police' workers' compliance with regulations. A common example is the signs, typically found in the toilets of pubs and restaurants, which instruct members of staff to wash their hands (or 'wash your hands NOW!') after using the toilet. HSE requirements may also become a more pressing issue in developing countries where corporations are not forced by law to heed tight standards. However, many of these issues, as mentioned earlier, actually occur in their suppliers' operations rather than their own, and as such will be discussed in more detail in Chapter 9.

However advanced protection measures and HSE regulation might be, there will always be certain jobs that include a high risk to health and life. Working on an oil rig, doing research in nuclear technology, or working as a stuntman in action films are all inextricably linked to certain hazards. As a general rule one could adopt the **principle of informed consent**: no worker should be exposed to these factors without precise information about the risks involved. Consequently, any damage to the worker's health is the result of his or her deliberate decisions—perhaps to effectively 'trade' exposure to health risks for the higher compensation that is often linked to such jobs.

HSE issues though become increasingly relevant in the context of new risks, most commonly in the form of *new diseases* and *new technologies*. In fact, some diseases even owe their name to the company where they first occurred, such as 'Pseudo-Krupp', a lung disease first discovered among workers and neighbours of the German steel mill 'Krupp'. More recent examples of new diseases include the rise of the AIDS epidemic (McEwan 2001: 187–9). Employers see themselves in the dilemma that, on the one hand, they want to provide their employees with a reasonable level of protection, but on the other hand a company does not want to discriminate against employees or customers (e.g. patients) infected with the disease.

A similar problem occurs in the context of new technologies. When asbestos was first developed for use as a fire retardant, nobody was yet aware of its inherent health risks. Given that asbestosis—the debilitating, often fatal condition caused by exposure to asbestosis—can take up to twenty or thirty years to surface after exposure, enormous numbers of production and installation workers handling the substance were placed at serious health risk (Treviño and Nelson 1999: 320–30). The long-term consequences of extended computer work for eyes and other parts of the body are also only now beginning to emerge. The dilemma for corporations lies in the fact that the more sophisticated certain technologies are, such as genetic engineering, the bigger their potential benefits, but to the same extent as well, their potential risks. The principle of informed consent we mentioned earlier can only very partially be applied as the very nature of those risks lies in the fact that the potential consequences, let alone their likelihood, are simply not known. Some therefore suggest the necessity for something more akin to the **precautionary principle**, which, in acknowledging scientific uncertainty about many processes and impacts, imposes the *burden of proof of harmlessness* on those introducing a technology.

Some newly emergent HSE issues relate less to new risks and more to changing patterns of work. In particular, ethical issues arise in the context of:

- Excessive working hours and presenteeism;
- Flexible working patterns.

Excessive working hours and presenteeism

An increasing threat to employee health and well-being that is receiving considerable attention now is excessive work hours, and their influence on the employee's overall state of physical and mental health. For example, one recent survey found that 84 per cent of managers claimed to work in excess of their official working hours with the average lying between fifty and sixty hours a week (Simpson 2000). **Case 7** at the end of this chapter looks at some of the issues surrounding excessive working hours in more depth, particularly in the context of the health profession.

'**Presenteeism**', as in the phenomenon of being at work when you should be at home due to illness or even just for rest and recreation (Cooper 1996), is a common cultural force in many organizations. The implicit assumption is that only those putting in long hours will be rewarded with career progression and other company rewards. Presenteeism appears to particularly affect the middle and upper levels of management, and in particular is likely to disadvantage women in career progression since they tend to have more responsibilities for childcare, etc. at home (Simpson 1998). As such, the whole issue of work–life balance has come very much more to the fore in recent years, as we shall discuss in more detail later in the chapter.

Flexible working patterns

Changes in working patterns have also led to more 'flexibility' in working arrangements. Although, as we saw with the Italian manufacturer Zanussi in **Ethics in Action 7.1**, greater flexibility can enhance opportunities for women and other disadvantaged groups, it can also have a major downside for those marginalized from 'standard' work and working conditions. As Karen Legge (1998) suggests in **Figure 7.1**, flexibility can just be another way of saying that management can do what it wants.

Pressure towards the deregulation of labour markets in many parts of Europe brought on by intensification of global competition, and rapid market changes, has led to the emergence of a large constituency of workers on 'non-standard' work relationships, including part-time work, temporary work, self-employment, and teleworking (Stanworth 2000). The legal status of such workers in the 'periphery' of the organization is often less secure than that of those in the 'core', giving rise to the potential for poorer working conditions, increased insecurity, lower pay, exclusion from training and other employment benefits, as well as a whole raft of other possible disadvantages.

These problems are particularly acute in low-skill service industries such as retailing, the hospitality industry, industrial cleaning, and in call centres—areas that have actually seen some of the greatest growth in jobs in recent years. Such workers are often expected to work 'unsocial' hours, with working hours often unpredictable and changed at short notice. Work intensification is common, as are significant levels of surveillance and control. Perhaps the ultimate in flexible working patterns though is exemplified by some retailers that have used 'zero-hours' contracts. These guarantee no minimum hours, no stable level of earnings, and prevent workers from planning even the basic elements of their lives (Stanworth 2000).

Of course, there are good arguments for why flexibility can boost competitiveness and provide for a strong economy, as well as provide new opportunities for women and other groups traditionally excluded from 'standard' working patterns by dint of home respons-ibilities, etc. However, the problem comes when flexibility erodes basic protections for employee rights, and/or where one group of workers on part-time, temporary, or otherwise 'flexible' contracts is treated unfairly compared to the core workforce. Naturally, one of the areas where this becomes most evident is in the area of wages, as we will now discuss.

Fair wages

As with most rights in this section, the right to a fair wage is to some extent protected through regulation in most companies throughout Europe. This certainly applies to lower incomes —for example with the establishment of a statutory minimum wage, which is by now com-mon throughout Europe. However, our assessment of what is a 'fair' wage becomes more complex when we place wage levels of those at the bottom of the organizational hier-archy in comparison with those at the top.

The basis for determining fair wages is commonly the *expectations* placed on the employee and their *performance* towards goals, measured by hours worked, prior training, risks involved, responsibility for assets, meeting of targets, etc. However, jobs are valued very differently in some employment markets compared to others. Let us have a look at a couple of examples:

• Even if you don't support Real Madrid, you might well consider that David Beckham is a pretty hard-working footballer. Not only did he spend much of his youth training and improving his skills, he still today has to dedicate himself to constant fitness work and training, provide on-the-pitch commitment and leadership consummate with being the captain of England, and is even expected to put himself at risk of painful, possibly career-threatening injuries. Certainly, he deserves decent pay for his efforts. On the other hand, if you watch the crew from the municipal waste collection service exerting themselves in collecting rubbish, from running after their trucks in all kinds of weather, to picking up heavy bins of rubbish, and enduring the stench of garbage cans, you might easily see the same necessity of a decent wage. However, David Beckham's reported weekly remuneration of about £90,000 (€120,000) is more than the latter earn in several years.

• Klaus Esser was CEO of Mannesmann, the German conglomerate that owned Orange, when it was taken over in 2000 by the UK mobile giant Vodafone. The takeover brought an increase in value to the company of about DM 397bn (€200bn). As the CEO who helped negotiate the deal, Esser was awarded a bonus of DM 60m (€30m). However, as a result,

Esser and some of his colleagues currently face a court inquiry making serious allegations of abusing the firm's assets and enriching themselves with shareholders' money.

These two examples show very extreme cases where the measure for assigning compensation is related to the consequences of employees' activities on relevant markets: if we put David Beckham's salary in relation to what his club Real Madrid earns from television and other media deals one could potentially argue that his salary is acceptable. Similarly, Klaus Esser's work was valued by the stock market in such a fashion that the €30m he was handed out could almost be regarded as pocket money.

Similar examples can be found throughout the business world. The introduction of the share price of the corporation as a performance measure for executive remuneration has brought about salary increases which have led the media to label these managers as 'fat cats' or similar. And in fact, in some cases executive pay has reached outrageous levels, which is even boosted by the fact that, for instance, cutting costs by firing staff or keeping employees' salaries low might improve the company's share price, and thus increase the salary of top management (see Chapter 6 for more discussion of executive pay).

For corporations, the increasing influence of markets on various aspects of their business (which is the result of the neo-liberal movement of reform in the 1980s that we discussed in Chapter 2) has brought about a difficult dilemma. On the one hand, traditional pay schemes are increasingly under threat with serious consequences for the distribution of income within the firm and the perceived injustice of remuneration within the company. On the other hand, firms have to compete for talent, and if the market for managers is governed by these rules, there are ultimately few alternatives to paying the market rate. After all, it could be argued that in some cases, one of the reasons why public services are so badly run is that capable managerial talent has been siphoned off into private sector jobs with higher levels of payment. A tentative solution of the widening gap between executive and 'normal' staff pay is the effort by some companies to provide part of their salary to *all* their employees in stock options so that all groups can participate to some extent in the company's performance on the stock market.

This, however, leads us on to the broader issue here of **performance-related pay (PRP)** and other contingent systems of reward. It is one thing rewarding those at the top for good performance, but when such procedures are introduced for those at lower levels, further ethical problems can arise. Edmund Heery (2000) suggests that this raises two main problems:

• **Risk.** First, PRP introduces greater risk into remuneration, meaning that salaries and benefits for employees become less secure, and potentially open more to arbitrary and subjective management decision-making.

• **Representation.** Second, PRP also tends to individualize employee pay bargaining, restricting the influence of collective representation of employee interests, and thereby weakening employee power.

Of course, there are also good arguments in support of PRP, but as Heery (2000) indicates, the ethical appeal of such payment systems often depends on how they are developed and implemented. Such arguments typically depend upon notions of justice, in that fair processes and outcomes should accompany pay schemes, regardless of the mechanism used.

■ **Think theory**

Think about PRP from the perspectives of utilitarianism and ethics of justice. How would each approach determine a fair wage? Can the two approaches be reconciled?

Freedom of conscience and freedom of speech in the workplace

Normally, the right to freedom of conscience and speech is guaranteed by governments, and so individuals can usually count on the government to grant this right. However, within the boundaries of the firm there might occur situations where this right, especially the freedom of speech, might face certain restrictions. This is the case with regard to, for example, speaking about 'confidential' matters regarding to the firm's R&D, marketing, or accounting plans that might be of interest for competitors, shareholders, or other stakeholders. In almost all cases, this restriction of the freedom of speech is unproblematic, since most rational employees would find it in their own best interests to comply with company policy, and there is little reason to suggest that most corporate decisions need to be made public.

There are, however, some cases where those restrictions could be regarded as a restriction of employees' rights. Imagine, for example, that a manager asks you to take part in activities that are of contestable moral status, such as some 'creative accounting' for the organization. The problem for you is that you cannot ask third parties outside the organization for help in this situation without risking serious embarrassment, disruption, and even possibly financial harm to your company. As we said in Chapter 4 (123–4), if employees decide to inform third parties about alleged malpractice within the firm, this behaviour is normally called 'whistleblowing'. The main problem for employees with whistleblowing is the fact that it involves a considerable risk for them. As they violate the confidentiality which would normally be part of their duty of loyalty towards the firm, they put their job and thus their economic security at risk. This risk, as the story in **Ethics in Action 4.1** showed, can be very high, and even if the allegations are right, the individual worker might find themselves in a critical situation until finally, for instance through court proceedings, the whistleblowing activity is vindicated.

Again, as we saw in **Ethics in Action 4.1**, as a result of these problems, various regulatory efforts have been undertaken to secure the whistleblower's position, at least when there are issues of public interest at stake. These include efforts of self-regulation where companies work out a code of practice for whistleblowing, up to new legislation such as the UK's 1998 Public Interest Disclosure at Work Act.

The right to work

Established in the Declaration of Human Rights and more recently in the European Charter of Human Rights, the right to work has been codified as a fundamental entitlement of human beings. As such, the right to work is derived from other basic human rights (De George 1999: 359–65), namely: it is linked to the *right to life*, since work normally provides the basis for subsistence; and it reflects the *right to human respect*, as the ability to create goods and services by working represents a major source for self-respect for human beings.

In the context of modern economies, however, there has been considerable debate whether a right to work automatically translates into a right to employment (van Gerwen 1994). On a macroeconomic level, one might argue that governments have the responsibility to create economic conditions that protect the right to work of every citizen. Nevertheless, governments in most (capitalist) economies will normally only ever be able to provide this right indirectly, as they do not take the employment decisions themselves. So does this mean that individuals have a right to demand employment from corporations, since they are the ones who directly provide jobs? Or, in terms of the example in **Case 2**, does this mean that employees in the Rover plant had a right to employment by BMW?

The answer from an ethical perspective would be to ask whether this right of the employee collides with the rights of the employer, and most notably the shareholders of the company. Employing and, most notably, paying people a salary is only possible if the company is able to sell a reasonable amount of goods and services. If this condition is not fulfilled, a one-sided focus on the right to work would clearly violate the right to own property, and the right to free engagement in markets. Therefore, the right to work in a business context cannot mean that every individual has a right to be employed.

Is the right to work then completely irrelevant? Certainly not, but rather than granting everybody employment, the right to work should result in the claim that every individual should face the same equal conditions in exerting this right. If every individual has the same right to be employed, they are all entitled to the same rights in the process of exerting this fundamental right. Consequently, the right to work chiefly results in equal and fair conditions in hiring and firing. Thus, most notably the right to freedom from discrimination particularly has to be applied in the process of employing people as well as making people redundant (Spence 2000).

Relevant duties of employees in a business context

So far in this chapter, we have focused exclusively on employee rights. However, these rights also of course need to be considered in the context of a set of duties that are expected of employees (van Gerwen 1994). You might wonder why we have given so much attention to employees' rights in this section. However, in the context of business ethics, the main focus has to be on the rights of employees as these are the main considerations to determine ethical behaviour towards employees. The rights of employees are more endangered than the rights of employers, primarily since employees are more dependent on the employer and face a greater risk of sacrificing or bargaining away their rights in order to secure or keep a job, or face other undesired consequences. Consequently, even when talking about employee duties, our main focus will be the consequences of those duties for employers.

Among the most important duties of employees are the duty to comply with the labour contract and the duty to respect the employer's property. These include the obligation to provide an acceptable level of performance, make appropriate use of working time and company resources, and refrain from illegal activities such as fraud, theft, and embezzle-ment. As research into employee theft has shown, the propensity of employees to commit crimes is highly dependent on the organizational climate in the organization (Gross-Schaefer et al. 2000). This leads to an important question when discussing employees' duties: what is the employer's responsibility with regard to ensuring that employees live up to their duties? Normally these duties are codified in the employment contract and other legal frameworks. Ethically delicate issues arise when looking at how the employer will enforce these duties and monitor employees' compliance. Is the employer allowed to check emails and phone calls? Should they be allowed to monitor which websites employees are accessing? What measures are allowed to control working time and work quality? Most of these kinds of issues ultimately touch on the employee's right to privacy, which we have discussed already earlier on in this chapter.

There are, however, a few issues where corporations are actually responsible to some degree for ensuring that their employees live up to a specific duty. This is particularly the case with the duty to comply with the law, since this duty often asks for some 'help' from the side of the employer. Earlier on in **Case 4** we discussed the experiences of the so-called 'rogue traders' Nick Leeson and John Rusnak. Leeson, for example, committed fraud and, most notably, broke various laws governing the Singaporean financial market. This incident not only had judicial consequences for Leeson, but also for Barings Bank, his employer. One could very easily argue that the bank did not have sufficient safeguards in place to ensure that its employees actually complied with legal requirements.

Similar issues occur, for instance, in the area of bribery: winning a contract by bribes does not only benefit the individual salesperson, but ultimately the corporation as well. Consequently, corporations might on one hand provide a context that to some extent encourages behaviour that is of dubious legality and, on the other, be expected to ensure that employees fulfil their legal obligations.

The most common tool for corporations to take up this responsibility is codes of con-duct (Gordon and Miyake 2001; Somers 2001). In establishing such a code, a corporation has to make sure that employees know about corporate policy with regard to the legal framework of its operations. However, such codes, and other forms of documenting and establishing policy, do not necessarily ensure that employees actually comply with their duties; from a corporate perspective the main point is often to document that they have done everything they can to prevent illegal actions. In practice then many of these codes of conduct are more symbolic 'red tape' than they are real substance, and have been shown to have had mixed results on the actual ethical and legal behaviour of employees (Higgs-Kleyn and Kapelianis 1999). For further discussion on such codes and their impact, you might want to review Chapter 5 (148–56).

Employing people worldwide: the ethical challenges of globalization

Globalization of business practices has had a significant impact on the question of the eth-ical treatment of employees. Although, as we shall see in the next section, most European countries are characterized by a well-established national framework of legislation and governance systems that ensure that the rights of employees are protected and advanced, one of the most commonly cited fields of corporate misdemeanour in recent years has been the treatment of employees in developing countries by MNCs. Globalization has led to a situation where many corporations in the industrialized world have transferred significant amounts of their manufacturing to low-wage countries of Eastern Europe, South-East Asia, Africa, or South America. While the simple explanation for this is obviously the lower costs associated with production in these countries, these 'favourable' conditions for companies are often accompanied by questionable working conditions for workers: low wages, high risks for health and safety, inhumane working conditions, just to name a few (Legge 2000).

This however is part of a broader question about the universality of employee rights. Issues such as discrimination, fair treatment, acceptable working conditions, fair wages, and the necessity for freedom of speech are interpreted and made meaningful in different ways in different cultures. For example, a conception of racial, sexual, or religious discrimination in Iceland might be different from that in Italy, India, Israel, or Indonesia. Similarly, freedom of speech might be conceived differently in Belgium and in Burma. In the following, we will look at some of the underlying issues involved here, namely:

- National culture and moral values;
- Absolutism vs. relativism;
- The race to the bottom.

National culture and moral values

As we discussed in Chapter 4 there is a connection between national cultures and moral values across the globe. We introduced at that stage the Hofstede (1980) model with its four dimensions characterizing different cultural values: individualism/collectivism, power distance, masculinity/femininity, and uncertainty avoidance. These dimensions implicitly focus on some of the key aspects underpinning the moral values that govern employer–employee relations. For example, consider the dimension of individualism/collectivism, which represents the degree to which people think of themselves as independent autonomous actors or acting for the good of the group. Individualist cultures will tend to regard it as more acceptable for each worker to be individually responsible to their employer whereas collectivist cultures will tend to emphasize the necessity of association and collective participation. Similarly, in collectivist societies, a person's ability to work well with others and make collaborative decisions might be just as much prized as educational and professional qualifications. As Treviño and Nelson (1999: 292) suggest, this might mean that in a collectivist culture, the extent to which an applicant and their family are known, trusted, and liked by the employer will be considered an important qualification, whereas in individualist countries such 'nepotism' may be considered to be biased and discriminatory.

The point is that different cultures will view employee rights and responsibilities differently. This means that managers dealing with employees overseas, or even critics of business who look to business practices overseas, need to first understand the cultural basis of morality in that country. Of course, this then begs the question as to whether it is fair to treat people differently, and to what we in Europe might regard as a 'lower' standard, just because they happen to live in Lagos and not in Lisbon. Do Vietnamese employees not have the same needs for health protection as workers in Venice? This raises the problem of relativism vs absolutism.

■ Think theory

We have just looked at one of Hofstede's four dimensions and its implications for understanding employee–employer relations. Think about the other three dimensions, and set out how each may affect one's view of employee rights and duties. Go back to Chapter 4 (118–19) if you need to review Hofstede's theory.

Absolutism vs. relativism

We first discussed the issue of absolutism vs. relativism in Chapter 3. Absolutism, we suggested, represented the idea that if an ethical principle were to be considered valid, it had to be applicable anywhere. Relativism, by contrast, suggests that no one view of ethics can be said to be right since it must always be relative to the historical, social, and cultural context. We contended in Chapter 3 (76–8) that both extremes of ethical absolutism and relativism do not give a sufficient answer to the different conditions evident in countries across the globe.

Relativists would finish the argument quite easily by dismissing the necessity for moral judgement from Europe about foreign cultural contexts. If Pakistani culture is permissive of a fourteen-hour working day, who are we to judge by imposing our western standards? Relativism ultimately would deny any ethical problem around exploitation and poor working conditions as long as they comply with the standards of the respective country or culture.

At the other end of the spectrum, *absolutists* would say that if our moral standards are right they are right everywhere around the globe. Consequently, companies should respect employee rights equally, wherever it is that they are actually contracted to work.

Obviously, these two sides are never likely to reach a common solution. Therefore, if we are to find a practical way forward, we need to look at this a little differently, and a little more carefully.

Some yardsticks for ethical decision-making

The issues discussed so far in this chapter have led to a varied and ongoing debate in business, the media, and academia. Far from having reached a consensus, the debate has nevertheless surfaced some yardsticks that might be useful for establishing guidelines for behaviour.

The most general rule would be to start with *human rights* as a basic compass for providing direction (Frankental 2002). The Universal Declaration of Human Rights, ratified in 1948 through the UN, is the most widely accepted set of principles pertaining to the rights of others. If a certain practice violates human rights, there is fairly broad acceptance that it is ethically wrong and unacceptable.

Beyond considerations of human rights, ethical considerations circle around the fact that differences in the treatment of employees on a global scale are not necessarily ethically wrong *per se* but depend on the relative *economic development* of the country in which the practice is taking place. The basic ethical question then is to ask whether the differences in wages and labour conditions are due to the economic development of the developing country (Donaldson 1989: 101–6). For example, would the fourteen-hour day that the French MNC imposes on its workers in Pakistan be acceptable if France had the same economic conditions?

The 'race to the bottom'

Apart from adapting or not adapting to *existing* employment standards in foreign cultures, Scherer and Smid (2000) among others argue that MNCs also play a role in *changing* standards in those countries. Globalization clearly enables corporations to have a fairly broad range of choice for the location of plants and offices. The deterritorialization of economic space has meant that when you pick up the phone in London and dial the customer service department of your bank, you could just as well be connected to an operative in Dublin or Delhi, Blackpool or Bombay. Consequently, developing countries compete against each other to attract the foreign investment represented by such relocation decisions.

Many critics of globalization have contended that among the key factors in this competition for investment are the costs incurred by MNCs through environmental regulation, taxes, and tariffs, social welfare for employees, and health and safety regulations. As a result, large investors may well choose the country that offers the most 'preferable' conditions, which often means the lowest level of regulation and social provision for employees. This competition therefore can lead to a 'downward spiral' of protection, or what is often called a 'race to the bottom' in environmental and social standards. MNCs in particular have been accused of being the key actors in propelling this race (Spar and Yoffie 1999).

The logic here is straightforward and compelling. Not surprisingly, though, it has also been hotly contested, not least because of the political and ethical ramifications of such an argument. Those advocating unfettered free trade tend to see the race to the bottom argument as not only fallacious, but opposed in principle to free trade and deregulated global markets. Still, evidence of the reality or otherwise of such a race is difficult to discern, not least because of the complexity of the equation, given the range of variables and motives involved (Spar and Yoffie 1999). What evidence there is does actually tend to dispute the hypothesis, although the logic of the argument, and the very real problems which continue to plague LDCs, suggest that such a phenomenon is still worryingly plausible (Spar and Yoffie 1999). At the very least, many LDCs clearly view their low standards as a competitive advantage with which they market themselves to MNCs—and the MNCs clearly in turn have been fairly relentless in their pursuit of lower-cost areas for production (Scherer and Smid 2000).

This leads to a broader potential responsibility for MNCs in the context of globalization. Rather than being concerned with ethical standards solely within the premises of their own company, MNCs as perhaps the most powerful actors in such countries are also in a position to assume a key role in building up so-called 'background institutions' (Scherer and Smid 2000; Spar and Yoffie 1999). This includes institutions such as trade unions, health and safety standards, and various other rules, regulations, and standards that help to protect workers' rights. Quite simply, given their powerful role in the global economy, MNCs do not have to just take for granted the poor infrastructure protecting employee rights—they often have the possibility of influencing these conditions too (De George 1999: 542–8).

The corporate citizen and employee relations in a varied European context

As we have discussed in some detail earlier in the chapter, ethical issues in employee relations are primarily framed in terms of a collection of rights. As such, these issues have a close relation to the notion of corporate citizenship: corporations administer a good deal of the social and civil rights of citizens in the workplace. They need to protect privacy of information, provide humane working conditions, ensure fair wages, and allocate sufficient pensions and health benefits. Looking across Europe, however, we discover that the extent to which corporations take over this role, as well as the degree to which corporations are held accountable for their administration of these rights, varies quite a lot.

As we have briefly discussed in Chapter 6, there are some differences between the Anglo-American and the European model of capitalism. This latter model has been quite extensively discussed by the French author Michel Albert (1991), who branded the European version as 'Rhenish Capitalism'. This alludes to the fact that the heartland of this approach lies particularly in those countries bordering the river Rhine: France, Germany, the Netherlands, Switzerland, Austria, but in a broader sense also the Scandinavian countries and Italy, Spain, and Portugal. The main difference in the context of this chapter is that capitalism in continental Europe has tended to take into account the interests of employees to a greater degree than the Anglo-American model. This has given rise to a variety of legal, educational, and financial institutions that focus particularly on the rights of employees.

The key concept in this context is the idea 'codetermination', which describes the relationship between labour (employees) and capital (shareholders) in Europe, namely that both parties have an equal say in governing the company (Ferner and Hyman 1998). In Germany and France, in particular, this has resulted in a very strong legal position for workers, works councils, and trade unions. So, for instance, in German companies in the metal industry, half of the supervisory board consists of employee representatives, and the executive board member for personnel has to be appointed by the workers directly. Consequently, the employees and their rights tend to be far better protected than in a capitalist model where shareholders are regarded as the most important group.

The institutionalization of employees' rights across Europe actually differs quite considerably, due in part to different socio-cultural norms and principles. In Scandinavia the institutionalization of employee rights is mainly predicated on the egalitarian principles of society and a strong welfare state (Parkum and Agersnap 1994). In the Netherlands, the strong emphasis of consensus has led to the emergence of a more equal role and say for employees (Garrison and Verveen 1994). In Germany and France, the manifestation is clearly more focused towards laws and regulations, which is also generally the case in southern Europe (Diaz and Miller 1994; Trouvé 1994). In the latter countries, the main forces in assuring employee rights are powerful trade unions and industry associations.

The general consequence for companies in this European context is that a good many issues are not so much a problem of ethical reflection and decision-making in the company but rather a question of compliance with existing codified standards. However, the forces of globalization do not stop with regard to these peculiarities. As recent research has shown, global competition by cheap labour has put these national 'models' under pressure (Schmidt and Williams 2002). The rather strong legal position of employees in Europe might therefore weaken in the coming years (Hyman 2001). Interestingly, it would appear that the more 'soft' institutions of consensus and egalitarianism present in northern Europe and Scandinavia are somewhat fitter for survival than those 'hard', legally oriented, and trade-union focused institutions of middle and southern Europe (Garrison 1994). A particularly good example is the development in the UK where trade unions as the main agents of employee rights have been largely marginalized over the last three decades (Boggis 2002).

A softer approach to institutionalizing employee rights—or, perhaps more aptly in this context, a 'weaker' approach—has also been evident in European firms' relations with their employees in LDCs. As we saw in the previous section, the dangers of a so-called 'race to the bottom' impose greater responsibilities on MNCs to build up better background institutions protecting employee rights, particularly where few such institutions exist, or where their effect is weak. Where firms have taken on such responsibilities—and this is certainly not the case in the majority of instances—the approach taken thus far has very much focused on voluntary self-regulation based on industry standards and other codes of ethics. This is in preference to the alternative that might, for example, involve corporations in contributing to the development of formal employment legislation, strengthening existing regulators, or supporting the development of trade unions. We will discuss this issue at far greater length in Chapter 11 when we come on to discussing the role of government and regulation in business ethics. Finally though, in the context of employees, it is necessary to take a closer look at the issue of sustainability.

Towards sustainable employment

In this chapter, we have talked a great deal about respecting and guaranteeing employees' rights in the workplace. On the one hand, this inevitably suggests certain tensions when we think in terms of sustainability. Sometimes protection of wages and conditions for workers may have to be sacrificed to encourage sustainable economic development and maintain employment. Expansion of environmentally damaging industries such as the airline industry can often be seen to be good for job creation. Looking at it this way, there usually have to be some sacrifices or trade-offs between protecting employees and promoting various aspects of sustainability.

On the other hand, it is also possible to discern certain links between the intention to protect employee rights and the notion of sustainability. Only if we are gainfully employed in useful work, and feel respected as human beings, are we actively contributing to long-term sustainability in the *economic* sense. A workplace that puts us under stress or makes us want to forget the day as soon as possible will have long-term effects on our lifestyles, health, and well-being. This aspect is closely linked to the *social* dimension of sustainability: workplaces should treat the community of workers in a way that stabilizes social relationships and supports employees to maintain meaningful social relationships with their families, neighbours, and friends. Sustainability, finally, is also an issue here in the *ecological* sense. The modern corporation has in many ways created workplaces that are ecologically unsustainable. Employing fewer and fewer people in a highly mechanized and energy-intensive technological environment, while at the same time making no use at all of something like 10 or 15 per cent of the potential workforce, is simply a gigantic waste of material and energy.

In this section we shall look at three main ways in which these problems and tensions have been addressed, both in theory and in practice:

* Re-humanized workplaces;
* Wider employment;
* Work–life balance.

Re-humanized workplaces

The 'alienation' of the individual worker in the era of industrialized mass production has been discussed at least since the time of Karl Marx. The suggestion is that the impact of technology, rationalized work processes, and the division of labour has meant that many employees simply repeat the same monotonous and stupefying actions over and over again, bringing little real meaning, satisfaction, or involvement in their work (Braverman 1974; Schumacher 1974: 122–33). Whether in factories, fast food restaurants, or call centres, much employment has been reduced to a series of meaningless 'McJobs' subject to intense management control and with little chance of real engagement or job satisfaction. Even a shift towards more 'white-collar' work in offices and bureaux can be argued to have created a legion of cubicle dwellers tirelessly tapping away at computers rather than enjoying active, creative, meaningful work.

Therefore although our 'rational' ways of organizing work can, and have, brought us tremendous efficiencies and material wealth, they have also created the prospect of a dehumanized and deskilled workplace. The relationship between technology and the quality of working life is, however, actually a much-contested one (see Buchanan and Huczynski 1997: 549–87). The impacts on the workplace are at the very least contingent on a variety of factors including work organization, managerial motivation, and employee involvement (Wallace 1989).

There have been numerous attempts over the years to re-humanize the workplace in some way, for example by 'empowering' the employee (Lee and Koh 2001). This might include 'job enlargement' (giving employees a wider range of tasks to do) and 'job enrichment' (giving employees a larger scope for deciding how to organize their work). Many of these ideas attempt a completely different pattern of production. Rather than mass production in a Fordist style (after the inventor of the production line, Henry Ford), the idea is to create smaller-scale units where workers can be engaged in more creative and meaningful work utilizing 'human-centred' technology (Schumacher 1974). As mentioned earlier, some car manufacturers (most notably the Swedish firms Saab and Volvo) have experimented with replacing the production line with small, partly autonomous, team-based working groups. Again, though, the success of such schemes has been contested, suggesting that the 'humanized' approach might be more appropriate and effective in some cultures (e.g. Scandinavia) than others (Sandberg 1995).

Wider employment

The mechanization of work has led to the situation where large numbers of unemployed people have become a normality in many countries, threatening not only the right to work, but the social fabric of particular communities. It has been argued that all efforts by politicians to change job markets or reinvigorate their economies will only ever partly solve the problem since the increasing level of mechanization and computerization of working processes has meant that we simply do not require as many workers to provide the population with its needs (Gorz 1975). Authors such as Jeremy Rifkin (1995) have even gone so far as to suggest that new technologies herald the 'end of work'.

From a sustainability perspective, the problem is essentially one of ensuring that what work there is, is shared out more equitably. Modern employment patterns have tended to create a cleavage between those who have the highly skilled jobs which require long hours of work for high returns, and those who are reduced to unemployment or at best a succession of low-skilled, poorly paid, temporary jobs. In recent years, there have been a number of interesting efforts to tackle this problem of creating a society of 'haves' and 'have-nots'. One recent attempt from the French government was the introduction of a thirty-five-hour week. By legally reducing the working time for the individual, the idea was that organizations would be forced to employ more people to maintain the same level of output. Logical as the idea is, it has nevertheless had an ambiguous effect. For certain industries the number of workers employed clearly rose, while in others the relative increase in the cost of labour prompted a tendency to replace labour with technology (Milner 2002).

Another initiative, this time at the corporate level, comes from Germany. In order to maintain a competitive cost structure, Volkswagen was recently faced with the choice of either laying off large numbers of workers in its northern German operations (where Volkswagen was the main employer) or reducing work time and pay for existing employees. After long negotiations, the '5,000 × 5,000' model was set up in early 2000. This allowed Volkswagen to keep 5,000 workers with a reduced working time and fixed pay of DM 5,000. All parties involved saw that it would be more economically and socially sustainable to accept this model rather than exposing an entire region to massive unemployment and economic recession (Schmidt and Williams 2002).

Work–life balance

As we have seen, the increasing threat of unemployment for some has been matched with almost exactly the opposite problems for others, namely the increasing incursion of working hours into social life. As we will discuss in more detail in **Case 7**, there has been a growing pressure for longer hours in (and travelling to) the workplace. This is most notable amongst professionals, such as doctors or accountants, but it has been evident in other jobs too. Low pay and job insecurity, for example, can equally prompt people to exchange social time for employment time in order to guarantee certain standards of living.

Clearly, a 'healthy' balance between work and private life—or 'work–life balance'—is difficult to maintain. Parents may face difficulty with childcare and/or hardly see their children, couples may face the delicate task of maintaining a long-distance or weekend relationship, and many employees might find that their life is completely absorbed by work without any time or energy left to maintain or build up meaningful social relationships (Collier 2001; Simpson 1998). Such problems appear to pose a significant challenge for long-run economic and social sustainability.

This problem is quite difficult to resolve. From the individual's perspective, any demands for less involvement in the workplace may ultimately be counter-productive to one's career aspirations or even a danger to one's job security. Furthermore, some of these jobs, especially where they involve a high level of specialized skill, are not easily reducible or sharable.

Nonetheless, some companies have also discovered that employees with poor work–life balance might not be as effective in the long run, and that different work patterns might need to be encouraged. A popular instrument is the introduction of sabbatical schemes that allow people in highly demanding jobs to take a period of time off to concentrate on all those issues that have been falling by the wayside and thereby restore greater balance. Another widely advocated solution is home-based teleworking. Although, as we discussed previously, this can be used as an excuse for poorer working conditions, teleworking can also, for example, help those with families to carry out their jobs whilst at the same time still being able to look after children and fulfil other important family roles (Sullivan and Lewis 2001). The teleworking scheme run by the Italian manufacturer Zanussi is described in **Ethics in Action 7.2**. Apart from the *social* benefits for the employee that teleworking can potentially bring, there may also be *economic* benefits for the company, and even *ecological* advantages too. For instance, rather than commuting into work and adding to road congestion and air pollution, teleworkers are likely to use far fewer resources by staying at home and communicating remotely.

Summary

In this chapter, we have discussed the specific stake that employees hold in their organizations, and suggested that although this stake is partially regulated by the employment contract, employees are also exposed to further moral hazards as a result of the employee–employer relationship. We have also discovered how deep the involvement of corporations with employees' rights can be. Nearly the entire spectrum of human rights is touched upon by the modern corporation, including issues of discrimination, privacy, fair wages, working conditions, participation, association, due process, and freedom of speech.

The corporate responsibility for protection and facilitation of these rights is particularly complex and contestable when their operations become more globalized, thus committing them to involvement with employees whose expectations and protections for rights may differ considerably. Indeed, we explained that the governmental role of issuing legislation in favour of, and aimed at the protection of, employees' rights has to some extent retracted. With the removal of such certainties, corporations would appear to have gained a good deal more flexibility with respect to employee relations. This has its downside in that corporations are left with a far larger degree of responsibility and discretion regarding the protection of employee rights, making ethical decision-making far more complex and challenging—and more ripe for abuse.

We suggested that European corporations might be said to have some inbuilt advantages for dealing with these developments, as well as some entrenched barriers that will make any transition a difficult one. On the one side, a long tradition of respect for, and protection of, employee rights can place European corporations on a surer footing with regard to some of these problems. Employees have long been regarded as an extremely important stakeholder in European businesses, long before the stakeholder concept even became fashionable. This has led to a quite advanced institutionalization of employee rights in Europe. On the other side, the emerging framework for employee rights in the era of globalization tends to emphasize a much more voluntary and self-regulatory approach than many European companies are used to.

STUDY QUESTIONS

1 What rights do employees have in a business context?

2 To what extent are employee rights protected by:
   (a) The employment contract
   (b) Legislation?

3 What is reverse discrimination? What are the main ethical arguments for and against reverse discrimination?

4 What are the four main types of privacy that employees might expect? Provide examples where each type of privacy might potentially be violated in a business context.

5 To what extent is it possible to accept that a European multinational corporation will offer lower standards of wages and conditions in less developed countries? What implications does your answer have for the proposition that when in Rome, we should do as the Romans do?

6 What responsibility should employers have for ensuring that their employees maintain an appropriate work–life balance? Set out some practical steps that employers could take to improve work–life balance.

RESEARCH EXERCISE

The American sports goods company Nike has been targeted for a number of years regarding its employment practices in less developed countries. Visit one or two of the websites where these criticisms have been set out. You might like to try the following:

• www.saigon.com/~nike/.

• www.caa.org.au/campaigns/nike/.

• http://boycott-nike.8m.com/.

• www.geocities.com/Athens/Acropolis/5232/.

Also, see what Nike has done in response, according to its own website at:

• www.nikebiz.com.

Now answer the following questions:

1 Set out the main ethical criticisms levelled at Nike in the area of employment practices.

2 Do you think these criticisms are justified?

3 To what extent are Nike's critics suggesting the company should employ an absolutist or relativist approach to such issues?

4 What else, if anything, should the company do to appease its critics?

CASE 7

Unhealthy business: junior doctors and excessive working hours

This case study describes the current workplace situation for junior doctors in Europe. It explores the working conditions in the profession, notably in the area of excessive working hours, and illustrates some of the regulatory efforts that have been undertaken to tackle the situation. The case provides the opportunity to reflect on the potential reasons why certain jobs and professions might be particularly vulnerable to unhealthy working conditions, and offers a chance to consider the benefits and limitations of regulatory approaches to protecting employee rights.

If we believe all those hospital dramas that feature so prominently in the programming schedules of television stations, it would seem that the medical profession is pretty much a dream job—intelligent, energetic young people, surrounded by attractive nurses, constantly dealing with exciting crises (both professional and personal), and sorting out the troubles of all who come and seek the doctor's help. Watching George Clooney as the handsome and humane Dr Ross in *ER* reruns, one could think that to work as a junior doctor is about as good as it gets. In reality, though, hospital life for young doctors suggests a somewhat different picture.

In many European countries such as the UK, Ireland, Germany, or France, junior doctors are facing working conditions that are increasingly intolerable for both staff and indeed their patients. For example, in 2002 the average working hours for hospital doctors in Germany was eighty hours a week. In the UK, working hours are limited to fifty-six hours a week, but surveys have shown that one doctor in six works longer than this. One young British doctor, Rachel Armstrong, for instance, explained in a newspaper article how she had worked an average of 100 hours a week during the first five months. Given the extent of the problem, we could easily multiply such examples many times over. Indeed, anyone who is, or knows, a doctor could probably add countless examples of their own of junior doctors working well over a 'normal' thirty-five- or forty-hour week.

Of course, with doctors on an annual salary, these long hours are effectively usually unpaid. Moreover, with the ambiguity about the question of whether time 'on call' counts as 'work time' or 'leisure time' (the latter of which has tended to be the norm in most European countries until recently), shifts of seventy-two hours and more are a normal occurrence in the profession. Research though has shown that twenty-four hours without sleep has the same effect as a blood level of 1.3 pro mille of alcohol. Given that 0.5 pro mille is the limit for driving a car in most European countries, it appears that some doctors are expected to carry out potentially life-threatening operations in the same or worse state as someone who would not be allowed to drive. It is no wonder then that the medical profession is actually getting less and less attractive. In Germany, for example, one-third of trained doctors are at present not working in their original profession, and shortages of doctors are not exactly unknown in other countries as well.

Problems of excessive hours are not of course restricted to junior doctors, as many young professionals, labourers, and various other employees will be all too aware. As a result, there have been several attempts to tackle problems of excessive working hours through legislative means. In Europe, the most important development has been the 1993 EU Working Time Directive (Council Directive 93/104/EC). The directive sought to make a forty-eight-hour week the legal maximum for all workers across Europe, as well as ensuring suitable rest periods during the working day/night.

The directive as initially approved by the EU covered all economic sectors and activities. Political intervention by member states, however, meant that certain industries were excluded from the scope of the directive. The final result was that junior doctors (as well as certain other workers, particularly in the transport industry) were not adequately protected. Whilst the EU recognized that some sectors required individual attention, countries such as the UK and Ireland simply argued that their health services were not yet ready to give junior doctors the protection to which other workers were entitled.

Hence, when the directive was supposed to be adopted by the individual EU countries, the UK successfully lobbied to postpone implementation throughout Europe until 2009 or 2010, while agreeing to a restriction to fifty-eight hours valid from 2004. When the UK Health Secretary Frank Dobson then called for an attempt 'to bring junior doctors inside the forty-eight hour working time directive within a realistic time scale', the move was met with scepticism and considerable outrage in the profession and beyond. Indeed, even forty-eight hours seems to be quite excessive compared to a 'normal' forty-, or, as in France, a thirty-five-hour week. There are however some countries, such as the Netherlands and Denmark, that have successfully reduced their doctors' working hours to forty-six hours a week, but this seems to remain the exception.

What are the reasons for this situation in the medical profession? One group of reasons certainly lies in the nature of the profession. With the 'vocation' to help people and save lives there seems to be some pressure on doctors to put patients first. This aspect becomes particularly tricky when combined with the fact that most hospitals are run by the government. Consequently, with tightening budgets in many European countries, public health institutions have been under constant pressure to reduce staffing budgets whilst seeing no reduction in patient numbers.

Yet another problem lies in the nature of doctors' typical career paths. Most junior doctors see their time in hospitals as the first step in their career, aspiring to stages where they might work as consultants, or in their own practice, or in a private healthcare facility. Since access to these subsequent career steps is administered in most European countries by professional bodies, or chambers of the medical profession, there are major risks for the individual junior doctor to risk conflicts with their superiors.

Finally, with doctors still being seen as relatively affluent members of society, there seems to be little public pressure to change this situation. Only recently, with growing incidents of surgical mishaps and longer waiting times, does the general public seem to have been alerted to the worsening situation.

Questions

1 What are the main ethical conflicts and issues in this case study?

2 Set out the main ethical arguments that might be used to (a) criticize and (b) defend the excessive hours typically imposed on doctors. How convincing is each set of arguments?

3 Reflect on the reasons given to suggest why the problem of excessive working hours might arise in the medical profession. To what extent are these reasons valid for other jobs and professions?

4 Assess the role of legislation in protecting employee rights in the context of working hours. Is it an effective 'solution' to this problem? How does the role of legislation in this situation compare with its role in the context of other employee rights, such as the right to participation and the right to be free from discrimination?

Sources

Anon. (1999). 'Overworked, underpaid, under pressure'. *Guardian*, 10 June: 8.

—— (2002). 'Arbeitsbedingungen im Gesundheitswesen', **www.med2day.de**.

—— (2003). 'Doctors' hours must be slashed'. *Liverpool Post*, 13 Feb. 2003: 11.

Lehnen, A. (2002). 'Die Dauerbaustelle Krankenhaus läßt immer mehr Nachwuchs-Mediziner an ihrem Beruf zweifeln'. *Ärzte Zeitung online*, 2 July: **www.aerztezeitung.de**.

McMahon, D. (2001). 'Reasonable working hours for junior doctors: how much longer must they wait?' *Trinity Student Medical Journal*, 2: 71–5.

Smith, M., and Buckby, S. (1999). 'EU ministers agree to delay junior doctors' hours reform'. *Financial Times*, 26 May: 1.

8

Consumers and Business Ethics

In this chapter we will:

- Discuss the specific stake that consumers have in corporate activity by introducing the notion of consumer rights and stressing the potential for the interests of consumers and businesses to both converge and conflict;

- Outline the ethical issues and problems faced in business–consumer relations, paying particular attention to the criticisms commonly raised against questionable marketing practices;

- Identify the shifts in these issues and problems as globalization progressively deterritiorializes marketing and consumption activities, giving rise to concerns over the impact of the marketing activities of large multinationals from the developed world on consumers in less developed countries, as well as the subsequent emergence of global consumer activism;

- Analyse the arguments for more responsible marketing practices based on voluntarist notions of corporate citizenship where consumers' interests are protected by corporations in order to enhance their reputation;

- Further develop the notion of corporate citizenship in relation to consumers by examining the role of the market and consumer 'purchase votes' in effecting positive social change;

- Examine the challenges posed by sustainability to consumer stakeholders, detailing the problems in progressing towards a sustainable society in the contemporary culture of consumption typical in Europe and much of the rest of the world.

Introduction

Consumers are obviously one of the most important stakeholders for any organization, since without the support of customers of some sort, such as through the demand for or purchase of goods and services, most organizations would be unlikely to survive for very long. By consumers, though, we do not just mean the end consumers who ultimately buy finished products in the shops, but also all of the organizations that purchase or otherwise contract for the provision of goods and services from other organizations. Your university, for example, is just as much a consumer as you or we are, in that it buys furniture, stationery, books, journals, cleaning services, and various other products and services in order to go about its business of providing teaching and research. It has also become increasingly common for people to refer to departments serviced in some way by other departments within the *same* organization as internal customers. Hence, consumers here should be regarded as a broad category including the whole chain of internal and external constituencies that receive goods or services of some kind, usually through some form of exchange.

Given the importance of consumer support for the ongoing success of an organization, it is no surprise that being ethical in dealing with consumers is generally regarded as one of the most crucial areas of business ethics. Moreover, since consumers are primarily outside the organization, ethical problems in this area are often some of the most visible and most difficult to hide of ethical violations. This can lead to potentially damaging public relations problems, media exposés, and other threats to the reputation of the corporation which might be more easily avoided in the context of employees, shareholders, and other stakeholders.

In this chapter, we shall examine the challenges faced by corporations in dealing ethically with consumers in the global economy. The main corporate functions responsible for dealing with consumers are sales and marketing, and it is evident that these professions have long been subjected to a great deal of ethical criticism. Many writers on marketing ethics have highlighted the lack of public trust in the advertising and sales professions (e.g. Laczniak and Murphy 1993; Assael 1995), and marketing is often argued to be perceived as the least ethical of all the business functions (Baumhart 1961; Tsalikis and Fritzsche 1989).

However, although ethics does not appear to have traditionally been a central concern of marketing professionals and academics, there is some evidence of moral considerations entering marketing thought for as long as marketing has existed as a distinct field in its own right (Desmond 1998). After all, it does not take someone with an MBA to work out that there are likely to be certain benefits in having customers that feel they have been treated honestly and ethically rather than just feeling like the victims of a cynical rip-off operation! More recently, though, there has been a surge in interest regarding ethical marketing, ethical consumption, and such issues, from both the public, practitioners, and academics alike. As we shall see, this has led to a fascinating, yet still unresolved debate about the nature of ethical marketing, and in particular about the role of consumers in shaping the social impact of corporations through their purchase decisions. In order to address such questions, though, we first have to establish the nature and scope of the stakeholder role played by consumers.

Consumers as stakeholders

It is by now largely commonplace to hear the argument that businesses are best served by treating their customers well. Indeed, this is essentially one of the core tenets of business strategy—that organizations succeed by outperforming their competitors in providing superior value to their customers. Those companies that prosper in the marketplace are those that pay close and continuous attention to satisfying their customers. Indeed, in many ways it is hard to argue against the logic of this argument. Of course, an organization will seek to satisfy its customers, for if it does not, then those customers will defect to competitors, thus resulting in loss of market share, and ultimately, profitability.

However, one might also ask why is it, if the interests of producers and consumers are so closely aligned, that ethical abuses of consumers continue to hit the headlines and that the reputation of the marketing and sales professions remains so poor? For example, in recent years, there have been numerous examples of firms being accused of treating their customers in a questionable manner:

- Tobacco companies have been accused of knowingly hooking their customers on a product hazardous to their health, whilst denying its addictive properties.

- Multinational drug companies have been accused of exploiting the sick and poor of the world by maintaining high prices for HIV treatments and preventing the sale of cheaper generic drugs in less developed countries.

- Football teams have been accused of exploiting the goodwill of their fans by continually changing their team strips in order to boost sales of expensive replica kits.

- Fashion brands and women's magazines have been accused of exacerbating eating disorders amongst their young readers by featuring idealized images of excessively thin models which only a minority of women can emulate in a physically and emotionally healthy manner.

- Rail, air, and automotive companies have been accused of putting their customers' lives at risk by compromising safety standards in the face of competitive pressures and cost-cutting exercises.

- Financial services companies have been accused of deliberately misleading their customers in order to enhance sales of insurance policies, pensions, and other personal finance products.

- Airlines have been accused of misleading their consumers about the real price of flights by omitting airport tax and other extras from the prices advertised in promotions.

These are just a few of the many examples that are regularly revealed by the media and by consumer groups and other 'watchdog' organizations. Clearly, such incidences are cause for concern, but what does this tell us about the nature of the stake held by consumers? The first point to make here is that we must question whether the satisfaction of consumer stakeholders is necessarily always consistent with the best interests of the firm. Whilst such an assumption of aligned interests may well be legitimate in some contexts, or where certain conditions are met, there may also be situations where the interests of buyers and sellers diverge (Smith 1995).

We shall examine some of these contexts and conditions as we proceed through the chapter, but at the most basic level, the co-alignment of interests between the two groups depends on the availability of alternative choices that the consumer might reasonably be able to switch to. Secondly, though, in the absence of a clear mutual interest in all contexts, we also need a normative conception of the stake held by consumers in order to determine what constitutes (un)ethical behaviour towards them. Typically, this normative basis has been established on notions of **consumer rights**.

Given the notion of rights that was introduced in Chapter 3 (89–90), consumer rights can be regarded as follows:

> Consumer rights rest upon the assumption that consumer dignity should be respected, and that producers have a duty to treat consumers as ends in themselves, and not only as means to the end of the producer. Thus, consumer rights are inalienable entitlements to fair treatment when entering into exchanges with other parties.

What constitutes fair treatment is, however, open to considerable debate. In the past, consumers were adjudged to have few if any clear rights in this respect, and the legal framework for market exchange was largely predicated on the notion of *caveat emptor*, or buyer beware (see Smith 1995). Under caveat emptor, the consumer's sole right was to veto purchase and decide not to purchase something (Boatright 2000: 273). The burden for protecting the consumer's interest should they have wanted to go ahead with purchase lay with the consumer themself, not with the party making the sale. Therefore, under the rule of buyer beware, providing producers abided by the law, it was the consumer's responsibility to show due diligence in avoiding questionable products. If they were subsequently harmed by or dissatisfied with a product or service, it was regarded as their own fault.

The limits of 'caveat emptor'

During the latter part of the twentieth century, this notion of caveat emptor was gradually eroded by changing societal expectations and the introduction of consumer protection laws in most developed countries (Smith 1995). Consequently, protection of various consumer rights, such as the right to safe and efficacious (i.e. effective in doing what they are supposed to do) products and the right to truthful measurements and labelling, are now enshrined in EU regulations as well as in the national and regional legal framework of member countries. As we have restated a number of times in this book, though, business ethics often begins where the law ends. So, it is frequently in the context of the more ill-defined or questionable rights of consumers, and those that are not legally protected, that the most important ethical questions arise.

For example, we might reasonably suggest that consumers have a right to truthful information about products, and legislation usually proscribes the deliberate falsification of product information on packaging and in advertisements. However, certain claims made by manufacturers and advertisers might not be factually untrue, but may end up misleading consumers about potential benefits. For instance, in many European countries, claims that a food product is 'low fat' are permissible providing the product is lower in fat than an alternative, such as a competing product or another of the company's product line. This means that even a product with 80 per cent fat can be labelled 'low fat' providing the company also markets an alternative with 85 per cent fat. For customers seeking a healthy diet, the 'low fat' product may seem attractive, but might not actually provide the genuinely healthy benefits as suggested by the labelling. We might question then whether the consumer purchasing such a product has been treated fairly by the seller. It is in such grey areas of consumers' rights that questionable marketing practices arise. In the following section, we will review the most common and controversial of these ethical problems and issues.

Before we go on to discuss these practices, though, it is important to mention at this stage that the stake consumers hold in corporations does not only provide them with certain rights, but also entrusts them with certain responsibilities too. At one level, we can think of this just in terms of the expectations we might have for consumers themselves to act ethically in dealing with the producers of products. Customers might sometimes be in a position where they can take an unfair advantage of those who supply them with products, particularly if we think about the situation where customers are actually other firms. For instance, powerful retailers may exert excessive pressure on their suppliers in order to squeeze the lowest possible prices out of them for their products. Even at the level of individual consumers like you or us, there are certain expectations placed on us to desist from lying, stealing, or otherwise acting unethically in our dealings with retailers.

At a different level, though, and probably more importantly, various writers have also suggested that there are certain responsibilities placed on us as consumers for controlling corporations in some way, or for avoiding environmental problems, through our purchase decisions. If we don't like the way that Reebok treats its third world labour force, or the way that ExxonMobil has responded to global warming, is it not also up to us to make a stand and avoid buying their products in order to get the message through? If we really want to achieve sustainability, don't we have to accept certain curbs on our own personal consumption? These are vital questions in the context of corporate citizenship and sustainability, and we will discuss these problems in more depth towards the end of the chapter.

Ethical issues and the consumer

The question of dealing ethically with consumers crosses a wide range of issues and problems. Generally speaking, these fall within one or another of the three main areas of marketing activity, as summarized in **Figure 8.1**. We shall look at each of these in turn, and explore the different perspectives typically applied to such problems in order to reach some kind of ethical decision or resolution.

Ethical issues in marketing management

Most ethical issues concerning business–consumer relations refer to the main tools of marketing management, commonly known as the 'marketing mix'—product policies, marketing communications, pricing approaches, and distribution practices.

Ethical issues in product policy

At the most basic level, consumers have a right to—and in most countries, organizations are legally obliged to supply—products and services which are safe, efficacious, and fit for

Area of marketing	Some common ethical problems	Main rights involved
Product policy	Product safety Fitness for purpose	Right to safe and efficacious products
Marketing communications	Deception Misleading claims Intrusiveness	Right to honest and fair communications
	Promotion of materialism Creation of artificial wants Perpetuating dissatisfaction Reinforcing stereotypes	Right to privacy
Pricing	Excessive pricing Price fixing Predatory pricing Deceptive pricing	Right to fair prices
Distribution	Buyer–seller relationships Gifts and bribes Slotting fees	Right to engage in markets Right to make a free choice
Marketing strategy	Targeting vulnerable consumers Consumer exclusion	Right to be free from discrimination Right to basic freedoms and amenities
Market research	Privacy issues	Right to privacy

Figure 8.1. Ethical issues and the consumer

the purpose for which they are intended. In many respects it is in both the buyer's and the seller's interest that this is the case since a producer of shoddy or unsafe products is generally unlikely to prosper in a competitive marketplace. Indeed, the vast majority of exchanges are conducted to the entire satisfaction of both parties. However, many everyday products that are bought or used can potentially harm, injure, or even kill people, especially if they are used improperly. This not only goes for products such as alcohol and cigarettes but also for cars, bicycles, tools, medicines, public transport, investment services, catering services—in fact almost no area of consumption is free from at least the potential to inflict some form of physical, emotional, financial, or psychological harm upon consumers. The questions that arise then are: to what lengths should the producers of these goods and services go to make them safe for our use, and to what extent are they responsible for the consequences of our use of them?

One way in which to look at this is to argue that manufacturers ought to exercise **due care** in establishing that all reasonable steps are taken to ensure that their products are free from defects and safe to use (Boatright 2000: 290). The question of what exactly constitutes due care is of course rather difficult to define, but this assessment tends to rest on some notion of negligence and whether the manufacturer has knowingly, or even unwittingly, been negligent in their efforts to ensure consumer protection. Such presumptions go well beyond the moral minimum typically presented by the notion of caveat emptor. Rather, here we are suggesting that it is the producer's responsibility to ensure that products are fit and safe for use, and if they are not, then producers are liable for any adverse consequences caused by the use of these products.

Ultimately, though, safety is also a function of the consumer and their actions and precautions. Providing a producer has exercised due care in ensuring consumers are protected under expected, perhaps even extreme or emergency conditions, consumers themselves must take some responsibility for acting hazardously or misusing the product. For example, surely we can't blame a manufacturer of ice cream if a consumer eats so many tubs in one go that they make themselves sick from (over)consuming the product (providing at least that such practices haven't been advocated by the firm in adverts for the product). Moreover, if we think about the example of cars, we can see that the consumer's right to a safe product is not an *unlimited right*. Whilst they might certainly expect that a manufacturer has ensured that the vehicle meets 'reasonable' safety standards, all cars can be made safer yet at some cost, and in all likelihood with some compromise on other features such as performance or styling. Because these improvements are possible, it does not mean that consumers have a right to them.

Ethical issues in marketing communications

In all of the areas of business ethics pertaining to consumers, probably no other issue has been discussed in so much depth and for so long as has advertising. Advertising though is just one aspect of marketing communications, and whilst much less attention has been afforded to other aspects, ethical problems and issues also arise in respect to personal selling, sales promotion, direct marketing, public relations, and other means of communicating to consumers (see Smith and Quelch 1993). Criticisms of these practices have been extensive and varied, but can be usefully broken down into two levels: individual and social. At the *individual* level, critics have been mainly concerned with the use of *misleading or deceptive practices* that seek to create false beliefs about specific products or companies in the individual consumer's mind, primarily in order to increase the propensity to purchase. At the *social* level, the main concern is with the *aggregate social and cultural impacts* of marketing communications on everyday life, in particular their role in promoting materialism and reifying consumption.

Looking first at **misleading and deceptive practices** affecting individual consumers, marketing communications are typically said to fulfil two main functions: to *inform* consumers about goods and services, and to *persuade* consumers to actually go ahead and purchase products. If such communications were just about providing consumers with information, then it could be suggested that the question of misleading practices is essentially one of assessing whether a particular claim is factually true or not. However, this perspective suffers from a number of shortcomings, most notably first, that marketing (along with much human communication) does not only deal with straightforward declarative sentences of literal fact; and second, that it is possible to mislead even when making statements of fact (De George 1999: 278).

The first shortcoming is evident if we think about some typical advertisements. Consider, for example, the ad campaign for the soft drink Red Bull which claims 'Red Bull gives you wings.' Obviously, the advertiser is not claiming that by drinking Red Bull the consumer will literally sprout a pair of wings, simply that the high caffeine drink can give you a bit of an energy boost. Similarly, the slogan used for many years by the Dutch brewer Heineken, which claims that 'Heineken refreshes the parts other beers cannot reach', is not meant to deceive us into thinking that Heineken literally flows to different areas of the body from other beers, but is merely meant to suggest that the beer might provide a different taste experience. Such claims are not misleading because we don't expect them to be telling us a literal truth.

The second shortcoming of this perspective is clear if we look at some cases where manufacturers have been criticized for making factually true, yet somewhat misleading claims. For example, in the late 1980s and throughout much of the 1990s, many compan- ies were criticized for making misleading and deceptive claims regarding the environmental features of their products. Terms such as 'biodegradable' and 'recyclable' were shown to have been used to describe essentially true but overly unrealistic product benefits, for example where biodegradation was only actually possible under highly unlikely condi- tions, or when recycling would be practically impossible without the introduction of new collection facilities (see Davis 1992; Kangun and Polonsky 1995).

The situation then is not so clear-cut as to just limit our discussion to factual truth. The persuasive nature of most marketing communications means that we expect them to exaggerate, overclaim, boast, and make playful, if sometimes outlandish, allusions—and indeed often enjoy them for these very same reasons (Levitt 1970). When Air France claims that it 'Fait le ciel le plus bel endroit sur la terre' (Makes heaven the most beautiful place on earth), we are not evaluating this as a factual statement but as a typically exaggerated claim that seeks to convince us of the superior quality of the company's service.

It is important to recognize then that persuasion in itself is not inherently wrong. We all attempt to persuade people to do or believe certain things at various times: your lecturer might try and persuade you about the benefits of reading your Crane and Matten *Business Ethics* text; your friends might try and persuade you to forget about studying and join them for a night of drinking and partying. The problem comes when persuasion involves deception of some sort. Deception is somewhat difficult to define in this respect, but is largely concerned with acts where companies deliberately create false impressions on the part of consumers to satisfy their own ends. It is one thing to put a good gloss on something—after all, much marketing communications activity such as public relations and advertising is intended to show organizations and their products and services in the best possible light. However, when this involves creating or taking advantage of a belief that is actually *untrue*, then we start to move into the field of deception.

The following definition, derived from Boatright (2000: 288), should help us then to clarify the nature of deception in the context of marketing communications:

> Deception occurs when a marketing communication either creates, or takes advantage of, a false belief that substantially interferes with the ability of people to make rational consumer choices.

For example, if your lecturer chose to persuade you to read Crane and Matten's book by suggesting that by doing so you would get better marks in the end of term examination, then we might consider that she had attempted to create a false belief in your mind. If a person of reasonable intelligence would be likely to believe her claim, then it could be suggested that this might impair your rational judgement about whether to read the book or to go out with your friends, and thus would constitute an act of deception. However, it is important to recognize that deception is not just about telling lies, or even just about verbal claims. Consumers can also be deceived by advertisements that appear to intimate that using a certain product will make them more attractive, more popular, more successful, or whatever. By focusing on consumers' ability to make rational choices, then, we are essentially concerned with their right to make independent decisions free from undue influence or coercion.

Potential violations of such rights occur fairly frequently in the field of marketing communications, not least because the line that needs to be drawn between honest persuasion and outright deception becomes somewhat hazy where certain practices are concerned. For instance, some manufacturers have chosen to veil price increases by making small, unannounced reductions in package sizes whilst keeping prices constant, thus creating the impression that prices have remained stable. Should we expect them to issue us with announcements of any size changes, or, given that weights and volumes have to be legally identified on packaging anyway, is it not up to us as consumers to check sizes? **Ethical Dilemma 8** presents another typical situation where questions of deception might arise.

Practices such as these are usually perfectly legal, particularly as the advertising industry continues to push for self-regulation rather than governmental regulation of its members. The European Advertising Standards Alliance (EASA) for example brings together self-regulatory organizations and advertising industry representatives throughout Europe to promote self-regulation and to set and apply ethical rules and guidelines for good practice.[1] Even so, many marketing communications continue to sail close to the wind in ethical terms on the grounds of customer deception. Ultimately, though, it will depend on what degree of interference on consumers' rational decision-making we decide is acceptable, how well consumers can delineate between fact and fiction, and whether, by getting this wrong, they will be significantly harmed. After all, as Boatright (2000: 289) contends: 'claims in life insurance advertising, for example, ought to be held to a higher standard than those for chewing gum.'

The second level at which criticisms of marketing communications have been raised concerns their **social and cultural impact on society**. This argument largely concerns the aggregate impact of marketing communications in society rather than being specifically focused on particular campaigns or techniques. Moreover, these criticisms have again been principally addressed at advertising rather than other forms of communication, but can be seen to be more widely relevant. There are a number of strands to this argument, but the main objections appear to be that marketing communications:

- **Are intrusive and unavoidable.** We are exposed to hundreds of adverts every day, on the television and radio, in newspapers and magazines, on the internet, in stores, on billboards, on the side of buses, at concerts, on tickets and programmes, on athletes and footballers, to the extent that almost no public space is free from the reach of corporate branding, sponsorship, or promotion. In her best-selling book about the ubiquity of branding, *No Logo*, Naomi Klein (2000) highlights the increasing incursion of brands into previously unbranded space including schools, towns, streets, politics, even people (think for example about the popularity of the Nike 'swoosh' logo as a template for tattoos).

---

[1] For more information, click on **www.easa-alliance.org**.

Ethical Dilemma 8

A fitting approach to shoe selling?

You are the manager of an independent high street shoe store, specializing in trendy shoes for both men and women. Your staff comprises a small team of eight salespeople who all take part in selling shoes, checking and maintaining stock, and processing sales and orders. You run a pretty successful operation but there is intense competition in the city where you are located from major shoe store chains as well as one or two other independent stores. To motivate your staff, a couple of years ago you introduced an incentive scheme that gives employees 5 per cent commission on everything they sell. This has worked pretty well—the store has maintained profitability and the employees are all fairly well paid.

You have recently hired a new salesperson, Lola, who has made quite an impact on sales. And she not only seems to be enjoying a great deal of success selling shoes, but she also has proved to be popular with everyone in the store, including the customers. Since she has arrived, though, Lola has also been giving you some cause for concern. Although no one has complained about her, you have noticed that some of her successful sales techniques do not always rely too much on the truth.

For example, on one occasion last week you noticed that she was serving a customer who was plainly unsure whether to purchase a particular pair of shoes. Lola obviously thought the shoes suited the woman, but to create a little more urgency said the model the woman was interested in was the last pair in stock and that she didn't think the store would be able to get any more for another month. However, you knew for certain that there were a good five or six pairs in the stockroom, and that reordering when they were sold out should only take a week. Still, the customer eventually decided to buy the shoes and once she had made the decision, seemed delighted with them.

Then yesterday, Lola was serving a man who obviously wanted a particular pair of shoes that he'd seen in the window. She asked him his size (which was 43) but when she got to the storeroom dis-covered that there was only a 42 and a 44 in stock. She asked you if you knew whether there was a 43 anywhere but you had to tell her no—you'd sold the last one yourself only the day before. Undeterred, Lola picked up both the 42 and the 44 and took the shoes back out to the man. Giving him the 42 first, she said to him that the company didn't sell 'odd' sizes and they only came in 42 and 44. The customer tried on the 42 but obviously found them too small. While he was doing this, though, Lola took out the 44 and carefully placed an additional insole in the bottom of the shoe. 'Give this a go,' she said handing the shoes to the man, 'this should do the trick.' To his delight they fitted fine and he said he'd take them. At this point Lola mentioned that because the manufacturer didn't do 'odd' sizes, she'd put insoles into the shoes, which would cost an additional €3. Still pleased with the shoes, the man said fine and paid for the shoes and the insoles.

You were unsure what to do about the situation. Although the customers seemed pleased with their purchases, Lola was clearly lying to them. Would there be any long-term repercussions of such prac-tices? And what would the rest of the team think about it? Would they start copying Lola's successful sales techniques too?

Questions

1 What are the arguments for and against Lola's actions?

2 Do you think such practices are common in sales situations? What would you think if you were a co-worker or a customer of Lola's?

3 To what extent do you think your incentive scheme has contributed to Lola's actions?

4 How would you approach this situation as Lola's manager?

- **Create artificial wants.** The persuasive nature of advertising has long been argued to make us want things that we do not particularly need (e.g. Packard 1957). The economist John Kenneth Galbraith has perhaps been the most popular advocate of this argument, suggesting that firms generate artificial wants in order to create demand for their products (Galbraith 1974). For example, one might question whether we really felt a need for products such as personal computers, mobile phones, or cars that talk to us before companies developed the technology and set out to create a demand for them. The problem here though is in defining what are 'real' wants and needs and what are 'artificial' or 'false' ones. Jean Baudrillard (1997), for example, condemns Galbraith's 'moralizing idealism' and his depiction of the individual as a passive victim of the system, suggesting instead that the consumer is an active participant seeking to satisfy very real needs for social identity and differentiation through consumption.

- **Reinforce consumerism and materialism.** More broadly, then, the saturation of everyday life under a deluge of marketing communications has been argued to generate and perpetuate an ideology of materialism in society, and to institute in our culture an identification of consumption with happiness (Pollay 1986). Contemporary cultural studies authors as well as the popular press now commonly depict modern western society as being a 'consumer society' where not only is consumption the principal site of meaning and identity, but it also increasingly dominates other arenas of life such as politics, education, health, and personal relations (e.g. Baudrillard 1997; Featherstone 1991). Thus, emotional or psychological ills such as a broken relationship, depression, or low self-esteem might be more readily addressed through 'retail therapy' or 'compensatory consumption' than through other more traditional or professionalized channels (Woodruffe 1997).

- **Create insecurity and perpetual dissatisfaction.** Ashamed of your mobile phone? Embarrassed by your cheap brand of coffee? Guilty that your baby isn't clothed in the most advanced and effective (and expensive) nappies? Worried that your feminine sanitary products will let you down? These are all typical worries and insecurities that ad campaigns identify and perpetuate in order to enhance demand. Hence, critics of advertising have further contended that by presenting glorified, often unattainable images of 'the good life' for us to aspire to, marketing communications create (and indeed rely on creating) constant dissatisfaction with our lives and institute a pervading sense of insecurity and inadequacy (Pollay 1986).

- **Perpetuate social stereotypes.** Finally, marketing communications have also been argued to spread socially undesirable stereotypes of certain categories of person and lifestyle (see Pollay 1986), such that women are always either housewives or sex objects; health, beauty, and happiness are only possible with 'perfect' body shapes; 'nuclear' families become associated with 'normality'; and racial minorities, the disabled, and gays and lesbians become excluded from the picture of 'normal' life. Whilst the usual defence to this argument is that marketers do no more than reflect the social norms of target audiences (Greyser 1972), it is clear that it is in companies' own interests to depict images desired by their customers. However, this still leaves open the question of the extent to which firms should be expected to avoid the use of 'irresponsible' images and stereotypes in their marketing communications. Ethics in Action 8.1 discusses some of the problems associated with the use of very thin female models in fashion industry advertisements.

Such criticisms have been common for at least the last thirty years, yet many social commentators also contend that, as a society, we have never been so informed and educated about the role of advertising, promotion, and branding as we are today. Accordingly, it would appear that consumers now are much more media literate and less likely to be the 'victims' of marketing communications than when these criticisms were first raised. To some extent then, the wider ethical case against marketing communication as a social phenomena is fairly difficult to uphold, not least because many of the criticisms often essentially boil down to criticisms of capitalism (Phillips 1997).

However, this is not to deny that these problems with marketing communications are significant, more that if we accept capitalism, we must also to some extent accept these problems. The question remains, though, given such drawbacks, to what extent should marketers be held responsible for the consequences? Moreover, we must also question how far marketing communications should be allowed to increasingly advance into hitherto ad-free social spaces. As the success of Klein's (2000) book attests, this is perhaps one of the most popular criticisms currently raised against marketing communications today, and, as we will discuss later in the chapter, this is particularly pertinent when considering the global context of marketing and consumption.

■ **Think theory**

Think about the question of whether marketers should be responsible for the aggregate consequences of their actions. Which ethical theories do you think would typically be used to argue either for or against this proposition?

Ethical issues in pricing

It is perhaps unsurprising that issues of pricing are often among the criticisms levelled at companies, for it is in pricing that we most clearly see the potential for the interests of producers and consumers to diverge. Whilst consumers may desire to exchange the goods and services they require for as little cost as possible, producers are likely to want to maximize the amount of revenue they can extract from the consumer. Pricing issues are thus central to the notion of a fair exchange between the two parties, and the **right to a fair price** might typically be regarded as one of the key rights of consumers as stakeholders.

The concept of a fair price is open to a number of different views, but typically is thought of as the result of a mutual agreement by the buyer and seller under competitive conditions. Thus, under neoclassical economics, prices should be set at the market equilibrium

The female body in advertising

The advertising industry has long been criticized for its depiction of the female body, including charges of excessive stereotyping and 'unnecessary' nudity in ads. In May 2000, the British Medical Association (BMA) took the bold step of publicly criticizing the advertising, fashion, and media industries for their overuse of excessively thin women in ads and TV programmes. The BMA report *Eating Disorders, Body Image and the Media* suggested that the image of the female form being projected in the media was so unrealistic that it encouraged vulnerable young women to try for the impossible. 'Young girls try to emulate the very thin women they see on television and in adverts, and it's not possible without starving themselves. Even if they don't die they can cause themselves permanent, irreversible damage,' said a BMA spokesman.

Around 60,000 people in the UK are believed to suffer from eating disorders, the majority of whom are young women (about one in ten are men). Anorexia nervosa affects up to 2 per cent of females between 15 and 30 years old. The report says that up to 20 per cent of these cases are likely to end in death. Research has estimated that most fashion models in the 1990s had 10 to 15 per cent body fat—as opposed to 22 to 26 per cent for a healthy woman. Models and actresses are often dress sizes eight to ten; ordinary healthy women can range up to size sixteen. The gap between the advertising ideal and reality appears to be making eating disorders worse. 'Models are becoming thinner at a time when women are becoming heavier, and the gap between the ideal body shape and the reality is wider than ever,' said the BMA report.

According to the BMA, the result is that women are increasingly pressurized, feeling that their bodies are fat by comparison. Vulnerable adolescents are said to be particularly susceptible. Half of adolescent girls are thought to read fashion- and beauty-related magazines, and at the same time are at their peak exposure to television. Whilst eating disorders have complex causes, low self-esteem caused by excessive exposure to ads depicting extremely thin fashion models is argued by the BMA to be an important contributory factor.

Following the report, the UK government held a number of focus groups with teenage girls and promptly organized a 'Body Image' summit in June, chaired by Tessa Jowell, the Minister for Women. This was attended by BMA representatives, fashion magazine editors, modelling agencies, stylists, fashion writers, other industry representatives, and a number of independent experts. Whilst the BMA agreed to conduct more research on the causes of eating disorders, the summit failed even to set up a proposed self-regulatory code for the fashion industry. With the government suggesting that the meeting was primarily an attempt to initiate discussions, fashion magazine editors were unhappy with proposals for any kind of policing, with the editor of *Elle* condemning the 'wave of body fascism' initiated by the government and the apparent 'slim girl witch hunt in the media'.

SOURCES

Barwick, Sandra (2000). 'Thin stars on TV put pressure on the young: images encourage women to try for the impossible, says the BMA'. *Daily Telegraph*, 31 May.

McIntosh, Fiona (2000). 'It's the thin end of the wedge: the size of models is none of the Government's business'. *Daily Telegraph*, 10 May.

Norton, Cherry (2000). 'Fashion world, claiming to have seen error of its ways, agrees to stop using anorexic models'. *Independent*, 22 June.

Womersley, Tara (2000). 'Magazines ban anorexic models: editors agree on voluntary code to improve women's self-image'. *Daily Telegraph*, 22 June.

■ **Think theory**

Think about this example in terms of stakeholder theory. Consumers are one of the key stake-holders here, but are all consumers equivalent as stakeholders? And which other groups can be legitimately regarded as stakeholders? Use stakeholder theory as a basis for determining where the responsibility should lie for avoiding the problems revealed by the BMA report.

where marginal cost equals marginal revenue. However, the assumption here is that buyers and sellers can leave the market at any time, and that there are a number of competing offerings in the market. Problems of fairness naturally arise then when prevailing market conditions allow companies to exploit an advantageous market position, such as a monopoly, or where consumers are unable to leave the market, perhaps because they have an irrevocable need for a product, such as for housing, food, or medicine.

In Europe, organizations such as the Bundeskartellamt in Germany and the Competition Council in France provide national protection against market distortions of this kind, and the Competition Directorate of the European Commission deals with pan-European issues. However, ethical problems still arise, either because the distortions are opaque, or because market conditions fail to explain the perceived unfairness of prices.

There are four main types of pricing practices where ethical problems are likely to arise:

• **Excessive pricing.** At the most basic level, the problem of consumers being charged a price deemed in some way excessively high is a common source of conflict between consumers and companies. For example, the European Commission recently fined Nintendo a whopping €149m for keeping prices of computer games artificially high in the 1990s by preventing distributors from sourcing from low-cost countries. Prices of Nintendo products were found to have been up to 65 per cent higher in Germany or the Netherlands than in Britain (BBC 2002a). Sometimes known as *price gouging*, the charge of excessive prices rests on the assumption that the fair price for goods and services have been exceeded. Whilst this may well be due to prevailing market conditions, as discussed above, the perceived fairness of a price may also depend on other factors, such as the relative costs of the producer, or the price charged to other consumers. For example, accusations of overcharging of car customers in certain parts of Europe have followed publication of price differentials by the European Commission, a sample of which is given in **Figure 8.2**.

• **Price fixing.** The problem of excessive pricing is probably most difficult to address when, rather than being the action of one single firm, it occurs as a result of collusion between competing firms to fix prices above the market rate. Whilst this is illegal in most European countries, much price fixing appears to be tacit and hence conducted without any explicit discussion or agreements. For example the UK Competition Commission recently announced that it would be investigating claims that the 'big four' mobile phone companies, Orange, Vodafone, T-Mobile, and O$_2$, were overcharging consumers, particularly when talking to people on other networks—a practice which seems to benefit all of the companies yet adds pounds to consumers' phone bills (BBC 2002b).

• **Predatory pricing.** A further problem of anti-competitive practice can occur when a firm adopts the opposite course of action, and rather than charging *above* market rate, sets a

Make and model	Approx. price in euros (000s excluding tax)				
	Germany	Finland	Italy	Denmark	UK
Audi A3	15.0	12.1	14.5	11.2	15.2
Ford Focus	13.8	11.2	11.5	9.8	14.6
Nissan Almera	12.5	10.2	10.5	9.0	14.3
Peugeot 206	10.2	8.5	8.9	7.8	10.2
Renault Laguna	17.0	14.4	16.4	12.0	18.8
VW Golf	12.4	9.5	11.9	9.7	12.3

Figure 8.2. Price differentials in car prices across Europe

Source: European Commission, Competition DG, Car Prices in the European Union, Manufacturer Price Tables, May 2002; http://europa.eu.int/comm/competition/car_sector/price_diffs/.

price significantly *below* the market rate in order to force out competition. Known as predatory pricing, this practice allows firms with a size or other advantage to use their power to eliminate competitors from the market so that more favourable market conditions can be exploited. For example, in 1999 the British Office of Fair Trading (OFT) ruled that News International had pursued a predatory pricing strategy on *The Times* newspaper during 1996–8. With prices of some editions lowered to 10p, the OFT concluded that the firm had deliberately incurred losses on *The Times*, leading to adverse effects on its competitors as a result of being drawn into a costly price war (BBC 1999; Barrie 1998). Whilst at first glance such a lowering of price might seem to have some advantages to consumers, the removal of competitors can give firms the opportunity to subsequently raise prices over the long term.

• **Deceptive pricing.** Finally, unfair pricing can also occur when firms price in such a way that the true cost to consumers is deliberately obscured. For example, 'no frills' airlines in Europe including Ryanair, Buzz, British European, and Bmibaby have all been criticized by advertising watchdogs for misleading consumers over the price of budget air tickets. Advertised prices are often only available for a small percentage of flights and depend upon certain booking restrictions often not made clear to consumers. Given that advertised prices represent a claim on the part of producers, deceptive pricing can be assessed in the same way as deception in marketing communications.

Clearly, the issue of pricing is a crucial one when it comes to assessing and protecting the relative rights and responsibilities of consumers and companies. As we can see here, much of the activity associated with ethical practice in this area actually also concerns and depends upon the relationships between firms and their competitors. This we shall examine in more depth in the next chapter.

■ **Think theory**

Fairness in pricing will obviously depend on how we define fairness. One way we can do this is by using Rawls's theory of justice (93). How would the practices outlined here be assessed according to this theory?

Ethical issues in channels of distribution

In the final area of marketing management, channels of distribution, we are concerned with the ethical issues and problems that occur in the relations between manufacturers and the firms which deliver their products to market such as wholesalers, logistics firms, and retailers, namely the product supply chain. Given that we shall be devoting most of the next chapter to such relationships between firms and their suppliers, we shall do no more than mention here that ethical problems clearly arise in this context—for example when retailers demand 'slotting fees' from manufacturers in order to stock their products, or when assessing the environmental impact of different logistics systems—and reserve a fuller discussion until the following chapter.

Ethical issues in marketing strategy

Marketing strategy is primarily concerned with the decisions of market selection and targeting. The targeting of markets is central to marketing theory and practice, and the choice of specific groups of consumers (or market segments) to target has been carefully refined over the years by companies eager to focus their efforts on 'attractive' segments characterized by factors such as high profitability, low competition, or strong potential for growth. As marketers have become more adept at targeting specific groups of consumers, and even individual consumers, important criticisms of certain aspects of this practice have emerged. In particular, criticisms tend to arise when there is a perceived violation of the consumer's **right to be treated fairly**. This violation can happen in two main ways:

- Those markets selected are composed of consumers who are deemed 'vulnerable' in some way, such as children, the elderly, the poor, or the sick, and marketers take advantage of their vulnerability to satisfy their own ends; or

- Certain groups of consumers are discriminated against and excluded from being able to gain access to products that are necessary for them to achieve a reasonable quality of life.

Targeting vulnerable consumers

If we begin with the targeting of vulnerable consumers, it is evident that this concern rests largely on the perceived right to fair treatment for consumers, which imposes certain duties on sellers. Specifically, arguments criticizing unfair targeting practices are based on the degree of *vulnerability of the target*, and on the *perceived harmfulness of the product* to those consumers (Smith and Cooper-Martin 1997).

Vulnerability of the target is somewhat difficult to determine here, and to some extent will be contextually defined. Clearly though there is a case for saying that some consumers are less capable than others of making an informed, reasoned decision about whether to purchase a product or certain types of products. There are a number of reasons why consumers might be vulnerable, such as because they:

- Lack sufficient education or information to use products safely or to fully understand the consequences of their actions (see **Case 8** at the end of this chapter);

- Are easily confused or manipulated due to old age or senility;

- Are in exceptional physical or emotional need due to illness, bereavement, or some other unfortunate circumstance;
- Lack the necessary income to competently maintain a reasonable quality of life for themselves and their dependants;
- Are too young to make competent independent decisions.

In the case of customers perceived to be vulnerable in some way, the idea that consumers should be treated as ends in themselves is often said to give rise to a **duty of care** on the part of sellers. Where the seller has a possibility for exploiting the vulnerability of a potential customer—for example where a drug company might be in a position to charge an excessively high price for life-saving medications, or an insurance salesperson might consider exploiting the illiteracy of a potential investor by misrepresenting the terms and conditions of the investment—it can be argued that the seller has an inherent duty to act in such a way as to respect the interests of the consumer as well as the interests of themselves and their company.

For example, one of the main groups typically agreed to be vulnerable in some way is young children. A child of 4 or 5 might reasonably be said to lack the cognitive skills necessary to make entirely rational choices. Therefore, it is perhaps not surprising that the direct targeting of young children, especially for toys, has been the subject of much criticism over the years (see Paine 1993). It is not so much that the children themselves purchase the products targeted at them, but that advertisers seek to encourage and take advantage of the 'pester power' that children have towards their parents. Practices such as daytime television advertising for toys, as well as merchandizing tie-ups with children's movies and computer games like *Toy Story*, *Harry Potter*, and *Pokemon* might be said to take advantage of young children who are highly impressionable, incapable of distinguishing the persuasive intent of advertising, and cannot understand the usual limitations of family purchasing budgets. Whilst one could maintain that it is the responsibility of parents as the ultimate purchasers to resist the pestering of their children, this does not detract from the criticism that by directly targeting a vulnerable group, advertisers might be guilty of an invasion of consumer rights by deliberate manipulation and treating children only as means to their own ends (De George 1999: 283).

Still there is the difficulty here in deciding at what age children can be legitimately regarded as able to make a rational, informed decision. Although there is considerable controversy over research results, it is apparent that even very young children tend to recognize and recall advertising very well, but it would appear that they do not have a good understanding of its persuasive intent, at least until they start to reach ages of around 8 to 12 years old (Oates et al. 2001). Many European countries have actually introduced legislation restricting advertising to children. Greece, for example, bans toy advertising on television until after 10 p.m., Norway does not permit advertising during children's programmes, and Sweden bans all advertising to children under 12. In other countries, such as Spain and France, governments have desisted from regulation, insisting not only that exposure to advertising is necessary preparation for life in consumer society, but also that firms have a democratic right to inform potential consumers about products which, in the final analysis, are not likely to pose any real harm to them.

The issue of the **perceived harmfulness of the product** is therefore a critical one in assessing the ethics of particular targeting approaches. Although there is evidence of a general social unease with the targeting of vulnerable groups, whatever the harmfulness of the product, it is perhaps unsurprising that much of the literature dealing with ethics and targeting has focused on products with a clear and present potential to do harm such as cigarettes and alcohol (Smith and Cooper-Martin 1997). By focusing on such products, the ethical arguments shift somewhat from a focus on rights and duties towards a greater focus on consequences. Hence, the argument is less that taking advantage of consumer vulnerability is wrong in and of itself, but that it is primarily wrong only if the consumer might be expected to suffer in some way.

In the early 1990s, for example, RJ Reynolds Tobacco Company (RJR) was forced to cancel plans to launch two new cigarette brands aimed at potentially 'vulnerable' US consumers. A menthol cigarette Uptown designed and marketed to appeal specifically to black smokers, and Dakota, a brand targeted at young blue-collar women, both faced enormous criticism from various pressure groups and the media for attempting to exploit those with limited incomes, poor education, and disproportionately high extant health problems. Whilst RJR made a reasonable case for suggesting that many black and young female smokers might be able to make their own decisions regarding potential health risks, the clear and present potential for the product to do these consumers harm led to strong criticisms of exploitation (see Smith and Cooper-Martin 1997).

Consumer exclusion

Some criticisms of marketing strategy focus not on who *is* targeted but on who *is not* included in the target market. In some cases, this can lead to accidental or even deliberate exclusion of certain groups of consumers from accessing particular goods and services that might be deemed necessary for them to maintain a reasonable quality of life. This problem has become particularly highlighted in recent years with the spread of the practice of 'redlining', especially by financial services companies such as banks, building societies, and credit agencies. Redlining consists of identifying particular areas in towns and cities where the populace predominantly has low incomes and very poor credit ratings and denying anyone from that area the ability to receive products such as bank accounts, credit cards, credit purchase facilities, etc. By effectively drawing a red line around particular geographical no-go zones, critics charge that companies can either be said to be discriminating against consumers (by judging them on their residential location rather than individual merit) or treating them unfairly by preventing them from participating in normal market activity. This practice can be particularly problematic when consumers are subsequently forced to enter into arrangements with unscrupulous, sometimes illegal, substitute providers of these products, such as loan sharks and unregistered moneylenders.

A more benign form of exclusion, but one which similarly attracts charges of unethical practice, is where companies that provide essential goods and services such as food, utilities, postal services, or financial services decide to pull out of unprofitable or remote markets, thus denying or making it extremely difficult for consumers to enjoy a reasonable quality of life. For example, in 2000, the UK high street bank Barclays Bank received a storm of protest from local communities and MPs after announcing the closure of 172 branches deemed no longer viable, thus leaving more than eighty villages without a branch. Again, there appears to be some case here for suggesting that whilst companies have the right to choose which markets they serve and do not serve, consumers also have some rights in relation to being provided with necessary goods and services.

Ethical issues in market research

The final area where we need to examine the rights of consumers is in relation to market research. The main issue here is one of the possible threats posed to the consumer's **right to privacy**. Market research involves the systematic collection and analysis of enormous amounts of data pertaining to individual consumers, including much information that consumers may not know that researchers have in their possession, and much that they might not wish to have shared with a third party. Many of the issues of consumer privacy are related to those of employee privacy discussed in Chapter 7 (237–241), and especially the dangers posed by developments in information and communication technology to maintaining individual privacy.

One major area of pressing concern that has arisen recently is the use of genetic testing results by insurance companies. Whilst there are various advantages to the emergence of tests which can predict the likelihood of an individual's genetic predisposition to certain conditions and illnesses, there are fears that insurance companies might use the information to increase premiums or deny cover altogether for those with high susceptibility. Whilst one might argue that such information is private, particularly if it might be used to create a 'genetic underclass' unable to obtain health or life cover, it can also be argued that premiums are 'fairest' when based on the best available information. The case for such 'genetic discrimination' has yet to be fully resolved, and in the UK, for example, the government announced in 2001 that it had reached agreement with the Association of British Insurers to institute a five-year moratorium on the use of genetic test results in assessing applications for life insurance policies (Cicatti 2002).

Globalization and consumers: the ethical challenges of the global marketplace

Convergence in consumer needs across different countries has been widely identified as one of the key drivers of globalization in business, not least because brands such as Coca-Cola, McDonald's, Microsoft, Kodak, and Sony among others have been able to expand into multiple international markets, often necessitating little if any adaptation in their products to local tastes and preferences.

At one level, these developments have clearly extended many of the issues identified in the previous section to an international context, and indeed have made many of the problems more acute. For example, the problem of targeting 'vulnerable' consumers becomes increasingly problematic with the move into markets where much of the population might be poor, badly educated, and inexperienced in dealing with sophisticated marketing techniques. Tobacco companies for instance have been criticized for targeting cigarettes at customers in LDCs who might have less knowledge and understanding of attendant health problems, be more susceptible to inducements to purchase such as free gifts, and be less likely to have regulations prohibiting advertising and other types of promotion (*Guardian* 1999; BBC 2000*b*; 2000*c*). The problem of 'acceptable' levels of safety is also accentuated where the lack of basic products and services might mean that even partially defective products may be better than none. For example, it might be deemed appropriate for a western pharmaceutical company to supply drugs which tackle dysentery in a country such as India, where the incidence of such a condition is extremely high, even though sale may be banned or delayed in Europe because of side effects (Donaldson 1996).

At another level, globalization has also brought with it a new set of problems and issues relevant to consumer stakeholders. Broadly speaking, these expanded, reframed, and/or new issues can be explained in relation to four main considerations:

• Reproduction of consumerism and dissatisfaction;

• Dislocation of production and consumption;

• Cultural homogenization;

• New forms of resistance.

Reproduction of consumerism and dissatisfaction

As domestic markets for various products have matured in developed countries, many companies have increasingly sought to expand through the development of new international markets. Hence, many multinationals now market their products in hundreds of different countries. This deterritorialization of markets has meant that multinationals have needed to stimulate demand for their products overseas, thus resurrecting and intensifying many of the criticisms typically aimed at marketing, and especially advertising, in the developed world. Expansion in global communications technologies such as satellite TV and the internet has meant that the promotion and reification of consumerist lifestyles now takes place not just within national borders but on a global scale (Sklair 1991). Moreover, by promoting products and brands which are beyond the purchasing possibilities of the majority of consumers in LDCs, multinationals can reproduce dissatisfaction on an even greater scale than previously possible.

These developments raise a number of complex ethical problems, particularly at a time when western modes of consumption are increasingly subject to criticism due to their role in fostering socially and environmentally undesirable consequences. Should LDCs be 'protected' from potentially making the same mistakes or do they also have a right to the same 'opportunities' in terms of raising consumption levels? Are indigenous patterns of consumption inherently better, fairer, or more sustainable than western patterns or are they even more inequitable and destructive? Whose responsibility is it, if anyone's, to police consumption activities? These are thorny issues which are only just beginning to be asked. Crucially, though, in the past, the promotion of materialism and consumerism was often justified on the (consequentialist) economic argument that increasing demand would lead to growth, which would ultimately benefit all. In the global marketplace, however, even this basic relationship between consumption and growth appears to be under threat. This is due to the increasing dislocation of production and consumption occurring under globalization.

Dislocation of production and consumption

If we look to the massive rise in living standards and material wealth that accompanied economic growth in the developed world in the twentieth century, one of the key mechanisms involved in this process was the strong association between those that produced products and those that consumed them. Known as the Fordist mode of economic relations, this worked by employing increasing numbers of workers in factories and other production units, ensuring they were paid decent wages, and thus fuelling realistic demand for ever more products as those workers became better off.

Globalization can be seen to weaken this mechanism by breaking the link between production and consumption through the outsourcing of production of western consumer goods to companies in LDCs. For example, the production of clothing and footwear for consumers in the developed world is now primarily carried out by workers thousands of kilometres away in LDCs. Hence, firms such as Nike, Reebok, and Adidas who market primarily to consumers in the west are subject to no intrinsic link between the wages paid to factory workers and the demand for their products (although, as we shall see, western consumers may choose to create a link). Moreover, even when effective advertising does create a desire for such products in LDCs, the massive gulf between the typical prices being charged for them, and the wages being paid to produce them, means that workers are unlikely to be ever in a position to even dream of actually being able to purchase what they are making. This of course raises further issues of justice in the global marketplace.

■ **Think theory**

Compare arguments based on consequences with arguments based on justice in assessing the impact of marketing on less developed countries. What recommendations do you think proponents of these theories would have for global marketing practice?

Cultural homogenization

A third criticism focuses on the effect of the exporting of global products and brands on local cultures, and the effective homogenization of certain cultural facets (Baughn and Buchanan 2001). Whilst global trade coupled with the imperialistic roots of many European countries has long provided a context for cultural exchange or imposition, the unprecedented international success of high street chains such as fast food companies, coffee shops, and clothing stores, and in particular globalized media and entertainment companies, has led to concerns over increasing standardization and uniformity (Klein 2000). There are few high streets in Europe now without the ubiquitous Blockbuster, McDonald's, KFC, Starbucks, and Gap stores. And although much attention has focused on American multinationals, European stores such as Benetton, H&M Hennes & Mauritz, IKEA, Marks & Spencer, and others have also contributed to this progressive erosion of difference.

In their defence, of course, multinationals point to the fact that they have never forced consumers to buy their products, and that their success is simply based on giving people what they want. However, as we shall examine in more detail in the next chapter, the tactics of many such multinationals are also argued to include the deliberate and aggressive removal of incumbent domestic rivals. Moreover, the fact remains that whatever the intentions or reasons, globalization clearly brings forth problems of homogenization and therefore ultimately places on consumers a new ethical choice about whether to resist or embrace this process and its implications.

New forms of resistance

Finally, then, we come to the issue of consumer resistance to corporate practices in the global marketplace. Just as firms have increasingly sought to exploit convergent consumer preferences for their standardized products across the globe, so too have they had to deal with a convergence in consumer rebellion and resistance to corporate activities deemed unethical or irresponsible. Whereas once a firm engaged in questionable practices may have only have had to deal with a few local protesters, or a small national consumer group, they are now faced with the potential of taking on a global force of protesters who can exchange information and informally 'gather' on the internet wherever they are in the world (Klein 2000). Anti-corporate protests such as the May Day actions in London or the disruptions caused to the annual Davos meetings of world business leaders are organized not in one geographical location, but in the deterritorialized space of the worldwide web. Similarly, brands such as McDonald's, ExxonMobil, Shell, Nestlé, and others have faced not just local actions against them, but international days of action co-ordinated across several continents.

In the global marketplace, it becomes increasingly difficult for firms to hide their misdemeanours, or to use their power to quash protesters. One infamous email that was rapidly forwarded across the globe in 2001 provides an exemplary instance of the power of global communications to unseat unsuspecting corporations. When Jonah Peretti, a student at Massachusetts Institute of Technology in Boston, had his request to have the word *sweatshop* emblazoned on his Nike running shoes (as part of a Nike customization promotion) rejected, he forwarded his comical email conversation with the firm to a few friends. One thing led to another and Peretti's misadventures rapidly became the subject of an international cult phenomenon that saw his email forwarded to millions of in-boxes and write-ups appearing in national newspapers and anti-globalization sites across the world—all to the extreme embarrassment of Nike (see **Figure 8.3** for the text of the email).

Branded 'the poster boy of guerrilla media', Peretti's experiences illustrate how one minor story can quickly undermine a firm's attempts to present themselves as a responsible company. As one addition to the forwarded mail aptly predicted: 'this will go round the world much further and faster than any of the adverts they paid Michael Jordan more than the entire wage packet of all their sweatshop workers in the world to do.'

NIKE: Your **Nike** iD order was cancelled for one or more of the following reasons:
1) Your Personal iD contains another party's trademark or other intellectual property.
2) Your Personal iD contains the name of an athlete or team we do not have the legal right to use.
3) Your Personal iD was left blank. Did you not want any personalization?
4) Your Personal iD contains profanity or inappropriate slang, and besides, your mother would slap us.

PERETTI: Greetings, my order was cancelled but my personal NIKE iD does not violate any of the criteria outlined in your message. The Personal iD on my custom ZOOM XC USA running shoes was the word 'sweatshop.' Sweatshop is not: 1) another's party's trademark, 2) the name of an athlete, 3) blank, or 4) profanity. I choose the iD because I wanted to remember the toil and labor of the children that made my shoes. Could you please ship them to me immediately.
Thanks and Happy New Year,

NIKE: Your NIKE iD order was cancelled because the iD you have chosen contains, as stated in the previous e-mail correspondence, 'inappropriate slang'.

PERETTI: Thank you for your quick response to my inquiry about my custom ZOOM XC USA running shoes. Although I commend you for your prompt customer service, I disagree with the claim that my personal iD was inappropriate slang. After consulting Webster's Dictionary, I discovered that 'sweatshop' is in fact part of standard English, and not slang. The word means: 'a shop or factory in which workers are employed for long hours at low wages and under unhealthy conditions' and its origin dates from 1892. So my personal iD does meet the criteria detailed in your first email.

Your web site advertises that the NIKE iD program is 'about freedom to choose and freedom to express who you are.' I share Nike's love of freedom and personal expression. The site also says that 'If you want it done right . . . build it yourself.' I was thrilled to be able to build my own shoes, and my personal iD was offered as a small token of appreciation for the sweatshop workers poised to help me realize my vision. I hope that you will value my freedom of expression and reconsider your decision to reject my order.

NIKE: Regarding the rules for personalization it also states on the NIKE iD web site that 'Nike reserves the right to cancel any Personal iD up to 24 hours after it has been submitted'.

In addition it further explains: 'While we honor most personal iDs, we cannot honor every one. Some may be (or contain) others' trademarks, or the names of certain professional sports teams, athletes or celebrities that Nike does not have the right to use. Others may contain material that we consider inappropriate or simply do not want to place on our products. Unfortunately, at times this obliges us to decline personal iDs that may otherwise seem unobjectionable. In any event, we will let you know if we decline your personal iD, and we will offer you the chance to submit another.' With these rules in mind we cannot accept your order as submitted.

PERETTI: Thank you for the time and energy you have spent on my request. I have decided to order the shoes with a different iD, but I would like to make one small request. Could you please send me a color snapshot of the ten-year-old Vietnamese girl who makes my shoes?
Thanks, Jonah Peretti

Figure 8.3. Nike gets stitched up.

We will look at the effects of globalization on organized resistance to corporations in more detail in Chapter 10 when we will discuss at some length business ethics in the context of pressure groups. In the meantime, it is important for us to first discuss the process through which consumers might use their resistance to provoke some kind of change in business practice.

Consumers and corporate citizenship: consumer sovereignty and the politics of purchasing

We said at the beginning of this chapter that changing expectations and improved protection of consumer rights had moved us away from the traditional conception of caveat emptor or buyer beware. More now is expected of firms in terms of how they treat their customers. But what exactly would constitute truly ethical marketing in this sense? According to Craig Smith (1995), the most effective way to answer this question is by drawing on the notion of *consumer sovereignty*.

Consumer sovereignty

Consumer sovereignty is a key concept within neoclassical economics. It essentially suggests that under perfect competition, consumers drive the market; they express their needs and desires as a demand, which firms subsequently respond to by supplying them with the goods and services that they require. This gives rise to the idea that the customer is king—or, to put it another way, that consumers are sovereign in the market.

Real markets, however, are rarely characterized by perfect competition: consumers may not know enough about competing offerings to find out exactly where they can get the best deals (what economists call informational asymmetries); there may be very few competitors in some markets, thus limiting consumer choice; some firms may be able to take advantage of monopolistic positions to exploit consumers with high prices; and so on. Hence, in practice, there are clearly some limitations to the power and sovereignty of consumers. In many situations, they simply cannot exercise informed choice.

These limitations in making informed choices are an ethical problem on two counts. First, it may well mean that individual transactions will be unfair in some way to certain consumers. And second, that without consumer sovereignty, the economic system itself does not work efficiently and allocate resources fairly (see Smith 1990). In basic terms, this would imply that the economy serves business interests rather than those of consumers. By the same token then, enhanced consumer sovereignty would therefore shift the balance of power *away* from business and *towards* the consumer. It is for this reason that Smith (1995) argues that consumer sovereignty represents a suitable ideal for marketing ethics to aspire to, and to be evaluated against. According to this argument, the greater the degree of sovereignty in a specific exchange or market, the more ethical the transaction should be regarded as. But how is consumer sovereignty to be assessed? For this, Smith (1995) proposes the **consumer sovereignty test (CST)**.

According to Smith (1995), consumer sovereignty is comprised of three factors:

- **Consumer capability:** the degree of freedom from limitations on rational decision-making enjoyed by the consumer, e.g. freedom from vulnerability or coercion.

- **Information:** the availability and quality of relevant data pertaining to a purchase decision.

- **Choice:** the extent of the opportunity available to freely switch to another supplier.

	Dimension	Definition	Sample criteria for establishing adequacy
Consumer sovereignty test	Consumer capability	Freedom from limitations in rational decision-making	Vulnerability factors, e.g. age, education, health
	Information	Availability and quality of relevant data	Quantity, comparability, and complexity of information; degree of bias or deception
	Choice	Opportunity for switching	Number of competitors and level of competition; switching costs

Figure 8.4. Consumer sovereignty test

Source: Derived from Smith (1995).

The CST therefore is a test of the extent to which consumers are capable, informed, and free to choose when confronted with a potential purchase situation. If sovereignty is substantially restricted—say, if the consumer's capability is reduced through vulnerability, or the option of switching is precluded due to high switching costs—then we might suggest that any exchange that happens may well be, at the very least, open to ethical question.

How exactly one defines what is an adequate level of sovereignty is of course rather hard to decide. Sovereignty is a relative, rather than an absolute, concept. However, some of the ways in which adequacy can be established for each factor in the CST are presented in **Figure 8.4** along with a summary of the main elements of the CST.

Ultimately, as with many business ethics tools, the CST cannot really be expected to tell us exactly in which situations consumers have been treated unethically. However, it does provide us with a relatively simple and practical framework with which to identify possible ethics violations, and even to suggest potential areas for remediation. This is particularly important from the corporate citizenship perspective. If, as we have argued, corporations just as much as governments and other social actors have come to be responsible for protecting consumers' rights, then they need clear ways of assessing ethical situations. Nonetheless, as Smith (1995) suggests, the application of the CST by managers not only requires some kind of moral impulse or conscience on their part, but also leaves consumers relying on the marketer's paternalism for their protection.

Finally, consumer sovereignty also has a yet more profound role to play in the citizenship perspective on consumer stakeholders. This relates to the emergence of what has become known as ethical consumption.

Ethical consumption

Whilst forms of ethical consumption of one sort or another have been around for centuries, the phenomenon has risen to considerable prominence in the last ten or fifteen years. Ethical consumption covers a range of different activities, including boycotting certain companies in response to a poor social, ethical, or environmental record, buying non-animal-tested products, avoiding products made by sweatshop or child labour, choosing fair trade or organic products, reusing or recycling products, etc. It is difficult to sum up the full range of activities that could potentially be included under the umbrella of ethical consumption, but a reasonable definition that captures the main essence of the concept might be as follows:

> Ethical consumption is the conscious and deliberate decision to make certain consumption choices due to personal moral beliefs and values.

The main form of ethical consumption we are concerned with is that where the consumers' personal moral beliefs and values refer to the specific actions of businesses, such as a decision to deliberately boycott Esso over its approach to global warming, or a decision to deliberately seek out detergents low in bleach because of environmental considerations.

There is much evidence to suggest that many consumers do indeed include ethical considerations in their evaluations of businesses and the products they sell. For example one recent UK survey suggested that a third of consumers were 'seriously concerned' with ethical issues, whilst just over half had bought a product and recommended a company because of its responsible reputation in the last year (Cowe and Williams 2000). Such findings imply that ethical consumerism can no longer be dismissed as simply a few disparate pockets of extremists—in fact, as the report suggests, most studies of ethical consumers reveal that they cross most socio-political boundaries, and are not easily defined by party politics, social class, age, or gender. Taken together, the market for ethical products is now said to be worth something like €9bn in the UK, which although representing a market share of less than 2 per cent, appears to be growing more than six times faster than the overall market (Brock et al. 2001). Similar findings have appeared across much of Europe. Significantly, the results of the first-ever Europe-wide survey on consumers' attitudes to corporate social responsibility[2], which covered 12,000 consumers across twelve countries, revealed that:

- Seventy per cent of consumers said that a company's commitment to social responsibility was important when buying a product or service;

- In all of the twelve countries surveyed over half the population believed a company's commitment to social responsibility was an important factor when making a purchase. This was particularly prominent in Spain (89 per cent agree) and the Netherlands (81 per cent agree);

- One in five said they would be very willing to pay more for products that were environmentally and socially responsible. This proportion was highest in Denmark (56 per cent) and lowest in Italy (24 per cent).

- Almost 60 per cent believed businesses did not pay enough attention to their social responsibilities at present. This was highest in Finland (75 per cent) and the UK (71 per cent), and lowest in the Netherlands (40 per cent), Denmark (44 per cent), and Sweden (46 per cent).

---

[2] MORI (2000). See **www.csreurope.org**.

Such findings obviously have significant implications for businesses. Evidence suggests that enhancing or maintaining a good corporate reputation is one of the main motivations for businesses to take an interest in business ethics—a finding ironically revealed by the auditor implicated in the Worldcom and Enron accounting scandals, Arthur Andersen (2000)![3] In addition, ethical consumers have been increasingly seen as playing an important role in prompting businesses to address ethics more enthusiastically, either through marketing specifically ethical products, or through developing a more ethical approach to business in general (Crane 2001*b*).

If we draw the connection here with consumer sovereignty, what this means is that consumers to some extent can act as a social control of business (Smith 1990). If consumers demand improved business ethics through the market, then business might be expected to listen and respond. Hence, the consumer is effectively using their purchases as 'votes' to support or criticize certain business practices rather than using the ballot box to vote for political solutions through government and regulation. This, as we initially mentioned in Chapter 2 (67–70), is hugely significant for the notion of corporate citizenship since the corporation then begins to act as a conduit for the exercise of consumers' political rights as a citizen.

As Noreena Hertz (2001*a*) has noted, increased political apathy has taken hold in many European countries, the USA, and elsewhere, yet consumer activism appears to be on the increase. As she contends (Hertz 2001*a*: 190), 'instead of showing up at the voting booth to register their demands and wants, people are turning to corporations. The most effective way to be political today is not to cast your vote at the ballot box but to do so at the supermarket or at a shareholders' meeting. Why? Because corporations respond.' For example:

- When the public registered their concerns about the health value of GM foods, governments across Europe did little, yet many major supermarkets soon removed the products from their shelves.

- As concerns about child labour in the clothing and footwear industry have escalated, it is corporations and not governments that have stepped in to deal with the problem.

- While governments across the world stalled on applying sanctions to Burma, consumers applied their own sanctions—the threat of consumer boycott orchestrated by the Free Burma Coalition encouraged major multinationals such as Philips, Heineken, C&A, and Carlsberg to pull out of the country.

Food safety regulation, child welfare, and oppressive regimes have traditionally been issues dealt with by politicians. In Hertz's words, such issues have undergone a 'silent takeover' by corporations, with consumers using the lever of the all-important corporate reputation to effect social change. These developments take ethical consumption away from merely being a way for consumers to assuage their consciences, towards active participation in making social and political choices.

In the absence of better ways to make their views heard, ethical consumption is certainly a positive phenomenon. However, it does have its downside. For example:

[3] See **Ethics in Action 9.1** in the next chapter for more on Arthur Andersen's involvement in these events.

- However socially responsible they may be, the motives of corporations will always be primarily economic rather than moral. Hence, their attention to social concerns will always be driven by market appeal. Minority interests or unattractive causes are likely to be ignored or pushed aside.

- Market choices are predicated on an ability and willingness to pay. If consumers decide they no longer want to pay extra for these ethical 'accessories', or if they can no longer afford them, will they just be dropped?

- If purchases are 'votes' then the rich get far more voting power than the poor. The market is hardly democratic in the same way that elections are.

For all its benefits, then, ethical consumption is never going to be an adequate replacement for political action—even if the latter appears to be falling out of favour as the former becomes more mainstream. It does however show us that consumers are now important actors in the regulation and shaping of business ethics—and that, whether we like it or not, corporations are increasingly becoming the most viable channel through which moral choices can be expressed. And if the value of ethical consumption is subject to challenge, the question of sustainability contests the whole practice of consumption itself.

Sustainable consumption

As we noted earlier in the chapter, it is now commonplace to refer to Europe and much of the rest of the developed and developing world as a consumer society. Not only are levels of consumption ever increasing, but we increasingly define ourselves by what and how we consume; we use consumption as a site for social, cultural, and, as we saw above, political activity; and consumption of products and services increasingly pervades new areas of our lives, such as the movement away from active participation in sporting activities to consumption of sports products such as TV programmes, computer games, and replica shirts, or the replacement of home cooking with pre-packaged 'ready meals'.

Consumption is ultimately the reason why anything gets produced. Even since 1980, per capita private consumption in Western Europe has grown by over 50 per cent and is set to continue unabated (OECD 2002). Without doubt, then, the massive growth in consumption in the latter part of the twentieth century and the beginning of the twenty-first has placed enormous strains on the natural environment. After all, consumer society is built on two very problematic assumptions: that consumption can continue to increase because there are no finite resource limits, and that the by-products and wastes created by consumption can be disposed of indefinitely. Hence, it is not unreasonable to suggest that high (and ever-increasing) levels of consumption pose enormous barriers to the development of sustainable business (Kilbourne et al. 1997)—and that consumers can be held responsible for much of the social and environmental degradation that their spiralling demands for products and services inevitably seem to bring (Heiskanen and Pantzar 1997). This is particularly true in the developed world, where, for example, the average American today consumes seventeen times more resources than his or her Mexican counterpart, and hundreds of times more than the average Ethiopian (Hart 1997).

What is sustainable consumption?

Whilst current levels of consumption may indeed be unsustainable, the question of how to move towards a more sustainable form of consumption is a vexed one, but also a vital one. What indeed would constitute a sustainable level of consumption? One reasonable definition which is used by the OECD in a recent report (OECD 2002) comes from a 1994 Norwegian Ministry of Environment paper:

> Sustainable consumption is: 'the use of goods and services that respond to basic needs and bring a better quality of life, while minimising the use of natural resources, toxic materials and emissions of waste and pollutants over the life-cycle, so as not to jeopardise the needs of future generations.'

However, it would be a mistake to assume that people can, or will, readily give up current levels of consumption, given that it is widely regarded as an enjoyable, liberatory, and expressive activity in modern society (Borgmann 2000). Indeed, the whole notion of ensuring that the satisfaction of needs does not compromise the satisfaction of future generations' needs is extremely problematic if the 'needs' satisfied by contemporary consumption are those of sustaining our self-image, our identity, and even our social relationships and culture (Dolan 2002). This goes back to Galbraith and Baudrillard's debate about 'real' versus 'artificial' needs that we raised on p. 275. Nevertheless, whatever our normative position on whether people *should* have needs for products simply for social status or self-image, it is clear that consumption *does* serve such functions in con- temporary society. Let us look a little more closely at what kind of challenge this presents for sustainability.

The challenge of sustainable consumption

Rogene Buchholz (1998) suggests that a move towards more sustainable consumption needs to be seen in the light of changes in the ethics governing our societies (see **Figure 8.5**). Returning to the work of Max Weber, Buchholz argues that the Protestant ethic of self- discipline and moral sense of duty that held sway during the establishment of market systems in much of Europe encouraged people to engage in productive labour for the pur- suit of gain, but to desist from immediate pleasure in order to accumulate capital and wealth[4]. However, the advancement of secularization, and in particular the ethic of consumerism that has gradually replaced these traditional values, have served to promote instant grati- fication and hedonism, and have downgraded the value of saving and durability.

   To move towards sustainability, Buchholz suggests, we need a new environmental ethic that again provides moral limits to consumption. Of course, reducing consumption is problematic, both politically and practically, for it also has serious implications for employment, income, investment, and other aspects crucial to economic well-being and growth. The ideology of consumption is deeply embedded in the dominant social paradigm of modern societies—a paradigm which is beneficial to, and sustained by,

---

[4] Ostensibly, this was for the glory of God. See Chapter 1 (29–30) for a fuller explanation.

Ethic	Imposes limits to	Promotes
Protestant ethic	Consumption	Investment in productive capacity
Consumerism ethic	Saving	Instant gratification and consumption
Environmental ethic	Consumption	Alternative meanings of growth and investment in the environment

Figure 8.5. Changing social ethics and consumption

Source: Derived from Buchholz (1998).

powerful social, economic, and political actors (Kilbourne et al. 1997). However, as we said in Chapter 7, by redirecting growth towards more socially beneficial ends—such as environmental products, civil society work, etc.—growth *could* still occur. Ultimately, though, the real challenge of sustainable consumption is to introduce alternative meanings of growth into society so that we can learn to cultivate deeper non-material sources of fulfilment. You don't need us to tell you that this is an immense challenge in the consumer culture of Europe in the twenty-first century.

Such changes in values can only ever happen gradually, and usually imperceptibly. In terms of real actions to promote more sustainable consumption on a day-to-day level, we need to look at the more practical solutions that are emerging from businesses, government, and consumers.

■ **Think theory**

Think about the challenge of sustainable consumption from a consequentialist point of view. This is the main approach to justifying increased consumption, but can it also provide the basis for moving towards a more sustainable level of consumption?

Steps towards sustainable consumption

On a practical level, there is much that business, government, and consumers *could* do to seek more sustainable modes of consumption. As yet, progress has been very limited, but some signs of change are emerging, primarily in the following areas.

Product recapture

Current business systems of production tend to operate on a linear model where materials are used to make products, which are then consumed and disposed of (see **Figure 8.6**). And that is the last that we see of them. However, by moving towards a circular use of resources—ensuring that so-called 'waste' is recaptured and brought back into productive use—can not only minimize waste, but also means that less 'virgin' material is needed at source (Fuller 1999). As we shall see in the next chapter, this often relies on close collaboration between businesses to be truly effective, but product recapture can also be introduced within a single company.

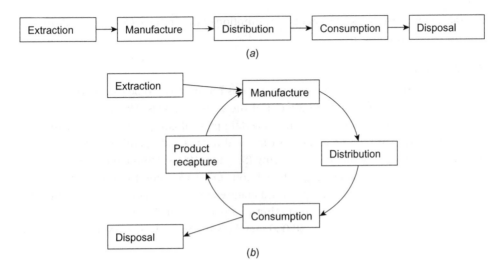

Figure 8.6. From a linear to a circular flow of resources
(a) Linear flow of resources
(b) Circular flow of resources

For example, the German company Grammer AG guarantees to take back and reuse its 'Natura' brand of office chairs with no cost to the customer. The returned chairs are then disassembled, the parts are tested, and up to 90 per cent of the old chair is reused in the manufacture of new ones (Belz 1999). The challenge for companies is to design for recycling, reuse, and repair and to establish channels that facilitate the flow product recapture. Such considerations will be brought into sharp focus with the EC Directive on Waste Electrical and Electronic Equipment (WEEE), due to come into force in 2002/3. This will make producers directly responsible for taking back and recycling electrical and electronic equipment, at no cost to the consumer.

Service replacements for products

If this thinking is taken a little further, there is no reason for the consumer to own the product in the first place. After all, what we are often seeking when we buy products is their performance—the ability to wash clothes for example—not necessarily the ownership of the physical product—a washing machine, say—itself. What we have seen in recent years then are companies experimenting with product leasing, where the company maintains ownership, but conducts servicing, replacement of worn parts, upgrading of obsolete elements, and ultimately replacement and/or redistribution.

This has been most common in industrial contexts—for example, Xerox typically rents and leases most of its commercial photocopiers—because customers are larger and easier to service. An Electrolux pilot project of fifty households on the Gotland Island in Sweden has taken this one step further, and introduced service replacements for products directly into the home. Instead of buying a washing machine, the customer borrows a new 'intelligent' energy-efficient washing machine, and pays a €50 fee for installation. The washing machine connects to a household electricity meter that is linked via the internet to a central database that tracks the energy consumption of the product. Customers pay for the function of washing alone.

Product sharing

Another similar way of reducing consumption is for products to be shared by groups of consumers, thereby getting more use out of the same resources. This way of increasing eco-efficiency has been fairly successful in certain parts of Europe, such as Germany and the Netherlands, with products such as cars, washing machines, and certain tools being found to be particularly suitable for sharing (Schrader 1999). Although inconvenience is a major disadvantage, studies suggest that consumers welcome the savings in storage space, money, and the hassle of repairs and maintenance—not to mention benefiting the environment. Europe's largest car-sharing company is the Swiss company Mobility, which by 2002 had an impressive 48,000 members sharing over 1,500 vehicles at nearly 1,000 locations.

Reducing demand

Ultimately though, the challenge of sustainability can only really be met if society accepts that people simply have to buy less stuff. It doesn't take much intelligence to work out that this idea tends not to be too popular with business—nor for that matter with customers or governments either! However, there are some areas where deliberate reduction of demand can benefit all constituencies. For example, in 2002 the Republic of Ireland saw the introduction of mandatory pricing for carrier bags (which had previously tended to be given away free) in order to reduce the number of bags used by consumers—which, because they were free, tended to end up either as unsightly litter or ultimately finding their way into landfill. Where excessive consumption can even mar consumer enjoyment and threaten business—such as in the tourism industry—demand reduction can be particularly pertinent. **Ethics in Action 8.2** looks at the issue of sustainable tourism—currently a major challenge facing the travel industry, where much controversy has arisen in recent years.

Demand reduction can also come from consumers themselves. As a slightly different form of ethical consumption (as described earlier in the chapter), consumers choosing to go the route of 'voluntary simplicity' or 'downshifting' go beyond registering their approval or disapproval of certain companies or practices and actively attempt to consume less overall. Indeed, as Shaw and Newholm's (2001) study of voluntary simplifiers makes clear, some degree of reflection on restraint is almost inevitable once consumers begin to take ethical stances on consumption. Instead of buying a shirt guaranteed to be sweatshop free, why not do without completely? Just as car sharing might seem more sustainable than owning your own, the decision to cut down on making journeys altogether may well represent a yet more sustainable option. For many people, such decisions will probably be taking things just a step too far. But if modern society is to tackle sustainability seriously, we may just find that reducing consumption is simply a bitter pill that just has to be swallowed.

Ethics in Action 8.2

Sustainable tourism? A taxing question for the Balearics

With international air tourist travel projected to triple by 2020, rapidly growing numbers of people are flocking to tourist destinations across the globe. The social, ethical, and environmental impacts of this are becoming evident almost everywhere. Whether it is a Thai fishing village, a Mediterranean beach, or a London monument, concerns regarding over-development of all kinds of tourist destinations have become very real. Air and road traffic have mounted, local resources such as water and sanitation have been overstretched, natural attractions have become blighted by overcrowding and littering, and local communities have seen few of the rewards being reaped by what is now the world's largest industry.

At the same time, consumers, the hotel and leisure industry, airlines, travel agents, as well as local and national governments are pressing for yet more expansion of the tourist trade. In defence of their negative impact on local habitats, proponents of the tourist industry stress the importance of the revenues generated by tourism for economic development. Countries in the developed world, just as much as in the developing world, are keen to enjoy the benefits that a growing influx of tourists brings.

The debate is a very controversial one, and both sides have been quick to denounce the other. However, various moves are now under way to develop what is known as 'sustainable tourism', that is, tourism that aims for the triple bottom line of economic, social, and environmental benefits. This means that whilst developments in tourism should remain profitable for industry operators, guidelines should be in place to ensure that: there is minimal harm to the natural environment; local workers and communities are not exploited; adequate employment and income for local people is provided, etc. Perhaps the most far-reaching of the demands of sustainable tourism however is that destinations should limit their number of visitors. Friends of the Earth have even gone so far as to demonstrate at major airports, waving placards and demanding that travellers should think about whether their trip is really necessary.

Clearly, many critics still have their doubts, particularly given the projected growth in the tourism industry over the next few decades. As one journalist from *The Times* warned: 'the truth is that there is a fatal flaw in the notion of "sustainable" tourism. No country has found a magic formula for attracting millions of visitors yet somehow preserving its ecology and landscape. From Goa to Galway, tourism has been like the "worm that flies in the night" in William Blake's poem The Sick Rose. It eats into the very heart of that which it loves.'

The government of the Balearic Islands in Spain—which includes three of Europe's most popular holiday destinations: Mallorca, Ibiza, and Menorca—sparked enormous controversy in 2001 when they announced the introduction of Europe's first tourist tax, specifically aimed at tackling the sustainability issue. The tax, of between 1 and 2 euros per person per night, is intended to provide revenue for environmental protection and to repair some of the damage that mass tourism has brought to the area. Its introduction followed massive protests by local people aimed at halting development on the islands. At one protest, some 30,000 people—one in ten of the indigenous population—marched on the Mallorcan capital of Palma.

However, the tax has attracted considerable criticism, even leading to a court action questioning its legality. With around 84 per cent of the islands' GDP dependent on tourism, price rises threaten many people's livelihood. Many island hoteliers were dismayed by the possible knock-on effects on visitor numbers. And tourists in Britain and Germany (where most of the area's estimated eleven million visitors originate) threatened to revolt by taking their business elsewhere.

SOURCES

BBC (2002). 'Tourists taxed on Spanish islands'. BBC News On-line, 1 May.

Morrison, Richard (1999). 'Why it's unwise to let the army of tourists walk all over us'. *The Times*, 20 July: 15.

OECD (2002). *Towards Sustainable Household Consumption? Trends and Policies in OECD Countries*, OECD Policy Brief, **www.oecd.org/publications/Pol_brief**.

Wilkinson, Isambard, and Cadwalladr, Carole (2001). 'Sunbed truce as Britons fight Majorca tourist tax'. *Daily Telegraph*, 13 Apr.

··

■ **Think theory**

Compare a traditional consequentialist-based assessment of the tourist tax with a postmodern perspective. It may help to think about the postmodern view of the need for a localized, pragmatic response to ethical problems. Do you consider the tourist tax to be such a response? Explain your answer.

Summary

In this chapter, we have discussed the specific stake held by consumers and outlined some of the main rights of consumers, including rights to safe products, honest and truthful communications, fair prices, fair treatment, and privacy. That firms still sometimes fail to respect these rights suggests that the interests of producers and consumers are not always seen by firms to be as harmonized as stakeholder theory might imply. These problems simply wouldn't occur if firms really saw their own interests to be best served by looking after their consumers' best interests. Of course, in many of the problems and examples we have traced in this chapter, there are quite complex ethical arguments at stake. And doing the right thing by customers and potential customers may not always seem particularly attractive when one thinks that they are, for most companies, the single source of revenue to keep the business going. Still, consumers appear to be demanding better treatment, and we suggested that tools such as the consumer sovereignty test might at least provide some guidance on what should constitute ethical practice.

What we have also shown in this chapter though is that, as the expectations placed on business have grown, so too have the possibilities for consumers to assume certain responsibilities in the control of business. The rise of ethical consumption places consumers in the role of policing companies, and even exercising their political rights as citizens through corporations. Notwithstanding the problems and dangers of such a situation, the challenge of sustainability pushes this yet further. In the consumer society that we currently live in, it appears that consumers might be expected to shoulder increased responsibilities as well being afforded certain rights.

STUDY QUESTIONS

1 'Of course, corporations should avoid treating their customers in an unethical manner. After all, in the long run, unethical behaviour towards customers only serves to harm firms' own interests.' Critically evaluate this statement with reference to examples from the following:

   (a) Telephone companies
   (b) Holiday companies
   (c) Chemical companies

   How does your answer differ for each type of company? Explain your answer.

2 What is deception in marketing communications? Give examples of marketing practices that you believe are deceptive.

3 Set out and explain the four main pricing practices where ethical problems are likely to arise.

4 How is it possible to determine consumer vulnerability? Whose responsibility is it to prevent exploitation of vulnerable consumers? Explain using examples from contemporary business practice.

5 What are the contributions and limitations of ethical consumption for providing some kind of social control of corporations in the global marketplace?

6 What is sustainable consumption? What practical steps can corporations introduce to move towards sustainable consumption?

RESEARCH EXERCISE

Many football teams, such as Manchester United, have been accused of exploiting the goodwill of their fans by continually changing their team strips in order to boost sales of expensive replica kits. Select one of the top football teams in your country and conduct some research to find out the current prices of the club's replica kits, and the frequency with which the kit has been changed over the last five years. Now do some similar research at Manchester United.

1 Assess the veracity of the accusations of exploitation at both clubs. On what basis are you making this assessment?

2 To what extent would you say that consumers of replica kits are 'sovereign' consumers? Explain your reasoning.

CASE 8

Boycotting the 'baby killers'? Nestlé and the ongoing infant formula controversy

This case discusses the controversy surrounding Nestlé's marketing of infant formula, and in particular looks at how the campaign against Nestlé has been sustained over thirty years despite attempts by the company to appease its critics. The case provides the opportunity to examine the ethics of marketing practices, as well as to discuss the role of ethical consumption in curbing perceived ethical violations.

'Nestlé kills babies,' or at least that is what the leaflets, stickers, and placards proclaim about the world's largest food company. And this is what they have been saying now for thirty years, ever since the controversy over Nestlé's marketing of infant formula in developing countries first went public in 1973. Amazingly, Nestlé continues to face intense opposition to its practices, and has the dubious distinction of having endured the world's longest consumer boycott. Has Nestlé failed to listen properly to its critics? Does it simply not care? Or is it that the critics will never be satisfied? In what has been one of the most remarkable, and probably the best-known, campaign against a single company over just one main issue, the truth of the matter remains thoroughly contested.

The details of the Nestlé infant formula controversy (or in truth a series of related campaigns from several parties) have been extensively discussed, almost to the point of becoming business ethics folklore. There have been three major books about the events; various academic and media articles; numerous reports from research institutes, development agencies, non-government organizations (NGOs), the World Health Organization (WHO), and others; and nearly all of the major business ethics textbooks seem to include a case on the subject.

Unfortunately, all this discussion hasn't brought a whole lot of agreement. However, in a nutshell, these are the basic details of the criticisms against the company. Nestlé, the Swiss-based multinational behind global brands such as Nescafé, Kit-Kat, Perrier, Maggi, Milo, and Buitoni pasta, is one of the leading suppliers of infant formula (powdered baby milk) across the globe. There have never been any major criticisms of infant formula as a product, but problems can arise when it is used or marketed inappropriately. For example, before being fed to babies, infant formula needs to be mixed with water, and all utensils need to be thoroughly sterilized. In many countries, though, high levels of illiteracy can mean that mothers are unable to read the necessary instructions, and poor sanitation can lead to babies being accidentally fed formula mixed with contaminated water. Similarly, mothers in poor countries may try to save money by 'economizing' on the formula by using less than the recommended dose or replacing it with other inferior alternatives such as cow's milk, rice water, or cornstarch with water.

Many of the initial problems for Nestlé, and one of the main reasons why it has continued to spark hostility, arose from the claim that it has 'aggressively' promoted infant formula. Ironically, the product is actually a vital health resource for mothers who *cannot* for one reason or another breastfeed. Infant formula is clearly a preferred alternative to other 'traditional' substitutes such as those mentioned above. But critics argued that Nestlé actively promoted the product to mothers who *could* breastfeed. This included practices such as:

- Free samples to mothers;
- Free supplies to hospitals and clinics;
- Advertisements encouraging mothers to adopt 'modern' bottle feeding in place of 'old-fashioned' and 'inconvenient' breastfeeding;
- Posters and pamphlets announcing the benefits of formula in hospitals;
- Promotional booklets ignoring or downplaying the benefits of breastfeeding;
- Incentives to milk nurses and health workers to endorse bottle feeding.

With breastfeeding in decline and sales of infant formula on the rise, many saw the actions of Nestlé (and the rest of the industry) as a direct cause of infant mortality in the developing world. Widespread condemnation ensued and boycott action was initiated against the company during the 1970s. Although there was much debate about the causal relationships involved, criticisms of such aggressive marketing practices eventually led to the WHO introducing a code of conduct governing the marketing of infant formula in 1981.

Virtually all of the above practices were effectively banned by the code (and its subsequent resolutions), which also eliminated all direct company contact with consumers, and called on producers to ensure that products contained appropriate health warnings, and used languages understood by local users. Although a voluntary agreement, and only legally enforceable once adopted by national governments, Nestlé announced it would comply fully with the code.

That should have been the end of the story. However, in many ways it was only the beginning. Although the first boycott of Nestlé was effectively called off in 1984, various groups initiated further campaigns throughout the 1980s, 1990s, and 2000s, usually as a result of new allegations surfacing of apparent non-compliance with the WHO code, or lobbying by Nestlé to prevent governments translating the code into legislation. Baby Milk Action, a UK pressure group involved in the global campaign against Nestlé, argues: 'worldwide independent monitoring consistently shows that Nestlé, more than any other company, systematically violates the *International Code* and *Resolutions*, promoting its products in many ways which damage infant health. The few limited changes Nestlé has made do not counterbalance the harm caused by its marketing and its persistent undermining of legislation and trading standards.' In a 2001 report, the group claimed to have identified 'hundreds' of violations of the code from fourteen different countries.

Nestlé's response to the alleged violations has tended to rely on denial, arguments about different 'interpretations' of the code, and blaming of miscreant employees. Although it has admitted making mistakes in the distant past, the company maintains that it has always abided by the WHO code. Its own charter further claims that Nestlé 'does encourage and support exclusive breastfeeding as the best choice for babies during the first months of life', 'does not advertise infant formula to the public', and 'will take disciplinary measures against any Nestlé personnel who deliberately violates this policy'. Aware that campaigners remained unconvinced, though, in 2002 the company introduced an 'ombudsman system' to encourage employees to report violations of the code without fear of retribution.

Whichever way you look at it, the boycotters of Nestlé have certainly made considerable progress in forcing the company to change its ways. Although there seems to be little chance of any staunching of the steady flow of criticism and exposés about its marketing practices, Nestlé has clearly done much to respond to its critics. Nonetheless, one might wonder why, if the company is so committed to the WHO code, not to mention its own charter, it is seemingly so easy for its critics to uncover further examples of violations. You would have thought that a thirty-year boycott would have helped stop *all* such problems before now. After all, the infant formula business makes only a minor contribution (about 1 per cent) to the multinational's profits, yet has generated vast amounts of adverse publicity for the company. It is difficult to determine whether the ongoing boycott actions have harmed the firm's profitability, but it remains a resolutely solid 'cash cow' that has provided a total shareholder return of 16.6 per cent over the last ten years.

Ultimately, though, despite its protestations that it is doing no wrong, Nestlé still remains among the handful of companies universally condemned by anti-corporate activists, student unions, and pressure groups. Recently the infant formula issue even led to widely publicized boycott action by comedians at the 2001 Edinburgh Festival (for its sponsorship of the Perrier Comedy Awards), and by authors at the 2002 Hay Literary Festival in the UK (another event it sponsors). And in 2003, the company faced another PR disaster following public outrage over its attempt to claim €6m 'compensation' from the famine-stricken Ethiopian government. Seemingly unaware that the public might baulk at demands for money from a country in such a desperate situation, the chief executive of Nestlé, Peter Brabeck, said the company had been 'shocked and surprised' by the response. In a bid to avoid further action, the company was forced into an embarrassing U-turn, which saw the firm hand over a reduced settlement of €1.5m straight to the famine relief effort.

Questions

1 Set out the main ethical criticisms of Nestlé's marketing of infant formula. Which consumer rights are these practices failing to respect?

2 Many of the criticisms of Nestlé's practices stem from the argument that consumers in the developing world are 'vulnerable'. To what extent is this a valid argument, and do you think it justifies a separate code of practice for developed and less developed countries?

3 What are the arguments for and against continuing the Nestlé boycott? Do you think that consumers are right to continue boycotting the company?

4 How would you explain Nestlé's apparent failure in pacifying its critics?

Sources

Betts, P., and Hall, W. (2002). 'Swiss cash cow in search of richer pastures'. *Financial Times*, 8 Apr.: 12.

Clark, A. (2002). 'Nestlé appeases critics'. *Guardian*, 29 Mar.: 21.

Denny, C. (2002). 'Nestlé to plough debt money back into Ethiopia'. *Guardian*, 23 Dec.: 12.

—— (2003). 'Nestlé u-turn on Ethiopia debt'. *Guardian*, 24 Jan.: 2.

Morrison, J. (2002). 'Nestlé sends in lawyers as Hay controversy grows'. *Independent on Sunday*, 2 June: 5.

Newton, L. H. (1999). 'Truth is the daughter of time: the real story of the Nestlé case'. *Business and Society Review*, 104/4: 367–98.

www.babymilkaction.org.

www.nestle.com

Suppliers, Competitors, and Business Ethics

In this chapter we will:

- Show how other businesses—notably suppliers and competitors—exist in mutual interdependence with a given organization, raising the prospect that these organizations too can legitimately claim a stake in the firm;

- Describe the ethical issues and problems that arise in an organization's dealings with its suppliers and competitors, including bribery and gift giving, negotiation, intelligence gathering, and abuses of power;

- Outline how globalization reframes these problems, and in particular examine the effect of MNC actions on overseas suppliers and competitors;

- Discuss whether corporations should assume some degree of responsibility for the ethics of their suppliers, and analyse the role of corporations in influencing the social and environmental choices of suppliers and competitors through their business relationships. From here we will examine the prospects for corporations to act as proxy regulators of other organizations;

- Assess the arguments suggesting that attention to business interrelationships and the network economy may contribute to more sustainable business models.

Introduction

The relationships between different businesses—as opposed to relationships between a firm and its non-business stakeholders—are probably one of the most commonly overlooked aspects of business ethics. This is perhaps not so very surprising when we stop to consider that ethical problems in dealing with consumers, employees, pressure groups, or the local community tend to be quite public and visible, and frequently enjoy the spotlight of media attention. Ethical problems between businesses however tend to stay relatively hidden from public view, and violations of one sort or another are rather less easy to uncover and scrutinize when they do not emerge from behind the screen of the business world. Clearly, though, the relationships between different businesses are very much relevant to a study of business ethics, not least because it is an aspect of business that ordinarily confronts many of us in our working lives.

In this chapter, we shall examine these relationships in the context of two types of businesses—suppliers and competitors. The issue of other businesses that are customers of a particular organization we have already dealt with at length in the previous chapter. What though of an organization's behaviour or responsibilities towards those who supply it with the goods and services necessary to conduct its day-to-day business? And there are clearly many, many of these suppliers, whether they are providing raw materials for making products, stationery for administering the firm's operations, cleaning services for its offices, or consultancy services to help it improve its competitiveness—just to name a few examples. Contracts between businesses and their suppliers often involve substantial sums of money, which can even mean the difference between business survival and failure. Hence there is always the possibility for relationships with suppliers to give rise to ethical problems, whether it is procurement staff being offered bribes or kickbacks to encourage them to select a particular supplier, or whether the purchasing staff are using the buying power of their company to exploit their suppliers with unfair trading agreements. Likewise, we have already seen that relationships between competitors in the same industry can lead to ethical problems if consumers get short-changed—for example because of collusion over pricing. Such anti-competitive practices are only half the story though. Some of the main ethical problems that arise in relations with competitors are as a result of arch-rivals employing 'dirty tricks' tactics in order to outdo one another.

What will soon become clear then as we go through this chapter is that the relationships between businesses can raise ethical problems both by being too adversarial as well as by being too cosy. Ultimately, though, whatever the nature of a specific relationship between two businesses, our interests in business ethics among suppliers and competitors are best framed in a somewhat broader context that takes account of the network of relationships and interdependencies that constitute the business community. It is, after all, membership in this wider community that not only helps give credence to a notion of the corporation as a citizen of some sort, but also serves as a launch pad to explore the possibilities of addressing sustainability through business–business relationships. It is also, as we shall now see, the basis for defining other businesses such as suppliers and competitors as stakeholders of an organization.

Suppliers and competitors as stakeholders

Models of organizational stakeholders, from Freeman's (1984) original formulation onwards, have tended to vary somewhat in their definitions of what constitutes a stakeholder and what does not. Many conceptualizations even discriminate between primary (mainly economic) stakeholders and secondary (non-economic) stakeholders (see Carroll and Buchholtz 2000: 66–70). All formulations however tend to include suppliers and most, if not all, tend to exclude competitors (Spence et al. 2001). Although there are very good reasons for this, in our view such a distinction is not entirely useful or appropriate. Let us briefly have a look at some of the arguments.

Suppliers as stakeholders

In Chapter 2 (50–55), we used Evan and Freeman's (1993) definition as a way of clarifying what a stakeholder was. A stakeholder of a corporation is an individual or a group that either is *harmed by or benefits from the corporation* or whose *rights can be violated*, or *have to be respected*, by the corporation.

It is clear without much further argument that suppliers are stakeholders—they can benefit from the success of the corporation by receiving orders for products and services and they can be harmed by losing orders. Similarly, we might easily suggest that suppliers have certain rights that might need to be respected by corporations, such as the right to a contract, to a fair deal, or to some level of fair treatment or loyalty. Indeed, organizations and their suppliers can be seen to be *mutually dependent* on each other for their own success: just as suppliers rely on their customers for the orders which keep them in business, so too do the purchasing firms rely on their suppliers to provide them with the products and services they need to carry on their operations. Just as we saw with consumers in the previous chapter, though, by saying that organizations and their suppliers are interdependent does not necessarily imply that their interests are always convergent. For example, whilst the buying company may wish to reduce costs by sourcing cheaper products, the supplier will usually seek to obtain the best possible deal and maximize revenue. We shall examine a number of such problems in the next section.

Competitors as stakeholders

Competitors on the other hand are rarely referred to as stakeholders—certainly not in academic treatments of business ethics, nor, it would seem, in most business communications by corporations and their leaders. As Spence et al. (2001) suggest, competitors are very much the forgotten stakeholders. Why? Well, competitors are, to begin with, typically seen as being in an ongoing, zero-sum battle with each other for customers, resources, and other rewards. Why should organizations accord their competitors any specific ethical claim when these are the very businesses that they are vying with for such rewards? What rights could, say, Nokia possibly have in its competition for mobile phone customers with Ericsson?

This is not actually as simple, or as redundant, a question as it might at first seem. Nokia certainly has a number of **legal rights** that are more or less protected by national and international trade agreements, and which Ericsson must respect. These include the right to freely enter and leave the market, the right to set their own prices free from influence or coercion, and the right to inform potential customers about their products. In 2001, for example, over-the-counter drugs manufacturers in the UK finally capitulated to demands to remove retail price agreements that had prevented retailers from setting their own prices rather than those set by manufacturers (Meikle 2001).

It is a relatively short step from these legal rights to claim that a competitor also has some form of **moral claims** on an organization which go beyond those codified in law—for example some form of right to privacy, or a right to 'fair play'. Certainly, it is open to debate whether the mere fact of a competitive situation bestows upon an organization

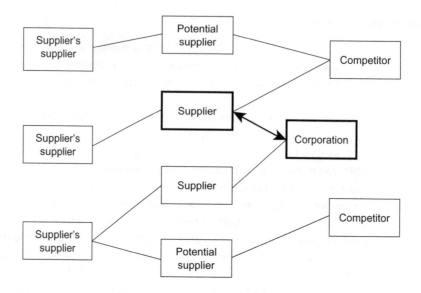

Figure 9.1. Supplier relationship as part of an industrial network

carte blanche to act in whatever way is necessary to beat their competitors, including lying, deception, providing false information about competitors to consumers, poaching staff, and other such questionable practices that we shall examine as we proceed through the chapter.

In addition to that, if we look to the first condition of being a stakeholder given above there is little doubt that competitors most certainly can be *harmed by* or *benefit from* the organization (Spence et al. 2001). Competitors can experience a loss or gain of market share as a result of the actions of their rivals, they can experience a change in trading conditions (for example, their suppliers might switch to a competitor offering higher prices), or they can face changes in the perception of their industry by customers, regulators, or other stakeholders as a result of the behaviour of their competitors.

To sum up, then, businesses should not be seen as isolated islands of economic activity, but as actors operating within a web of other businesses, bound by mutual interests and interlinked flows of resources and rewards. This suggests that firms are probably best understood as part of an **industrial network**, rather than just as part of a simple exchange between two parties (Easton 1992). An illustration of such a network is shown in **Figure 9.1** with the focal relationship between a corporation and its supplier highlighted, and put into context with other relationships amongst competing companies, suppliers, and their suppliers.

According to the industrial network model, notable decisions about how the firm deals with any single other firm (such as one of its suppliers) can have a significant effect on numerous other members of the business network including other suppliers, potential suppliers, and competitors. Whilst the ethical obligations the firm has to these other network members might vary, this does not deny the fact that they all have some form of stake in the decisions made—and may act upon that stake in ways that are of consequence to the organization.

These interrelationships give rise to a number of potential ethical problems. In the following two sections we shall look at the specific issues that arise with respect to dealings with suppliers and then respectively competitors, before moving on to examine the impact of globalization on the ethics of business relationships.

Ethical issues and suppliers

Ethical issues in dealing with suppliers can arise at two levels:

- The organizational level;

- The individual level.

At the *organizational* level, ethical issues arise from the relationships between the businesses themselves. That said, on reading a typical contemporary European commentary or textbook on supply management, one might wonder how ethical problems could possibly arise at the organizational level. Due in part to the influence of Japanese business, firms appear to be moving away from their traditional adversarial relationships with suppliers, based upon short-termist, transactional arrangements with large numbers of supply firms, to be replaced by more partnership-based approaches which emphasize long-term relationships with a few core supply firms based upon mutual trust and collaboration (Durán and Sánchez 1999).

The attention afforded to partnership sourcing is significant for our understanding of business ethics because it very much reinforces the notion of suppliers as stakeholders in the firm. In fact, though, the partnership approach is certainly not representative of all, or probably even the majority, of business–supplier relationships involving European firms. Evidence suggests that whilst many progressive firms have indeed moved towards more collaborative approaches, much so-called 'partnership' sourcing actually involves problematic power relations and troublesome intra-firm tensions (New 1998). These, as we shall see, can quite easily surface a number of ethical problems and issues.

It is also important to recognize that, regardless of the overall approach to business –suppliers relations undertaken by the organizations themselves, the *individuals* who actually conduct these relationships—namely the purchasing and sales staff—are often confronted with a whole host of ethical dilemmas on a day-to-day level. This can include the giving and acceptance of gifts, bribes, hospitality, and other potential inducements which might lead to decisions being made which are not necessarily in one's employer's interest, as well as the use of questionable tactics in business-to-business negotiations. These individual level issues are just as important as the broader organizational level issues, and, because they largely rest upon conflicts of interest, are often in fact very much shaped by them. We shall examine each in turn, but before we do, it might be helpful to think through **Ethical Dilemma 9**, which presents a typical ethical problem occurring in supplier relations.

Ethical Dilemma 9

A beautiful deal?

You work as a purchasing manager for a large European retailing company that is in the process of revamping its line of own-label cosmetics. This line is important to your business, but as your company has expanded, own-label cosmetics have gradually occupied an increasingly less important role in the product mix in stores.

Your existing supplier, Beauty To Go, has supplied your company for ten years and over two-thirds of their business is accounted for by your company's own-label cosmetics orders. You have a good relationship with the Account Manager of Beauty To Go who, like yourself, has been in her role for a number of years. However, in the time that you have known each other, your relationship has never strayed from its strictly professional footing.

As you are considering how to proceed with the revamp, a competing supplier Real Cosmetics also contacts you, offering virtually identical products to Beauty To Go, with equivalent supply arrangements, but at a slightly lower price per unit. Over a year this would work out to approximately €200,000 savings p.a.—not a huge sum for your company, but quite a substantial saving of about 7 per cent on your costs. In addition, Real Cosmetics also highlights in its sales pitch that they go well beyond the industry standard for non-animal testing of their products' ingredients—again, a significant improvement over what Beauty To Go has been offering you.

Questions

1 What are the ethical issues at stake in this situation?
2 Which ethical theories do you think might be of help in deciding an appropriate course of action?
3 What are the main considerations that these theories raise?
4 How would you proceed in this situation?

Organizational level issues

Misuse of power

The issue of power in buyer–supplier relationships has received much attention over the years, not least because the relative power of the two parties can be extremely influential in determining industry profitability (Porter 1980). Clearly, though, imbalances in power can also lead to the emergence of ethical problems, particularly when any imbalance is misused to create unfair terms and conditions for one or the other party.

   One useful way of looking at the relative power of buyers and sellers is using resource dependence theory (Pfeffer and Salancik 1978). According to this theory, power derives from the degree of dependence that each actor has for the other's resources. This dependence is a function of how scarce an organization's resources are—i.e. the level of *resource scarcity*—and how useful they are to the other party—i.e. the *resource utility* (Cox et al. 2000).

Therefore, the buyer is likely to be able to wield considerable power over the supplier when:

(*a*) The supplier's resources are relatively plentiful and not highly important to the buyer; and/or

(*b*) The buyer's resources are relatively scarce and highly important to the supplier.

This situation has been a major feature of the relationship between major European supermarkets and their suppliers. With a handful of very large supermarket chains dominating each national market—Metro, Aldi, or KarstadtQuelle in Germany, Intermarché, Carrefour, and Promodés in France, and Tesco and Sainsbury in the UK—their resources in terms of purchase potential and access to markets have become relatively scarce but extremely important for food suppliers. At the same time, the suppliers' resources have become less scarce and important to the supermarkets since they increasingly source on a global basis from a vast array of suppliers and manage to stock an impressive range of products which, except in a very few cases, would hardly suffer from the removal of one supplier's products. It is perhaps not surprising then that Europe's supermarkets have often been criticized for abusing their power over suppliers.

Such practices can be criticized from a **deontological** perspective—in that those with power might be said to have a duty not to abuse it. More interesting however is a **consequentialist** position: the problems caused by abuse of supply chain power are not just of consequence to the weaker partner. Using the example of the suppliers of UK clothing retailers, Jones and Pollitt (1998) show that an opportunistic abuse of power by retailers can lead to reductions in quality, lack of investment, lack of innovation, and even job losses and industry decline. In this case, the overexposure to risk may result in an underperformance of suppliers. Ultimately, excessive abuse of power may eventually even harm the powerful partner, particularly if their supplier relations become so dysfunctional as to jeopardize product quality and industry growth—thereby reducing long-term profitability.

Given such a set of possible negative outcomes, one might wonder why abuse of power will ever happen. Jones and Pollitt (1998) suggest that:

• In the short term, there may well be profit advantages to be gained by exercising excess power.

• Also, it is evident that many firms will view the situation from a relatively narrow perspective and fail to see the broader cumulative industry effects that may ultimately harm them.

• Finally, abuse of market power may well be subtler and far less destructive at the macro level than envisaged by Jones and Pollitt (1998). Although market conditions may disadvantage suppliers, their customers may choose to exploit their power differentials in some areas of business—e.g. by forcing down prices—but offer support and investment in others—e.g. by contributing market knowledge, financial support, and other management resources. This more variegated picture may well offer a more realistic picture of some industries (Ogbonna and Wilkinson 1996; Bloom and Perry 2001), but it makes any conclusive ethical evaluation difficult. Whilst individual actions may seem unethical, when put in the context of a longer-term interaction, the action may be more acceptable.

The question of loyalty

Related to the issue of power is the question of loyalty. The fair treatment expected by suppliers can be viewed in terms of a given deal struck between the two parties, but as we have just intimated, where those parties have been involved in a long series of exchanges over some time, we might also include further considerations. In particular, one might start to consider whether such an arrangement also confers some kind of expectation for loyalty on the part of the organizations. For example, in October 1999 the British high street retailer Marks & Spencer suddenly dropped one of its long-term clothing suppliers, the UK-based William Baird textiles group, thereby ending a thirty-year business relationship. The dramatic loss of sales suffered by Baird resulted in the closure of sixteen factories and 4,500 redundancies. Should Marks & Spencer have shown more loyalty to its business partner? Was it, in part, also responsible for the job losses? The courts certainly thought not, and Baird subsequently failed in its bid to sue the retailer for £56m damages for breach of contract. Indeed, continued problems stemming from this devastating loss of business led to the resignation of Baird's CEO in 2001.[1] Is it possible therefore to suggest that firms have some kind of obligation of loyalty to their suppliers—and, if so, how do we determine which suppliers can legitimately expect loyalty, and what exactly does an obligation of loyalty entail?

Loyalty is one of the virtues often prized in business, but loyalty to suppliers does not easily fit with an **economic view of the firm** that stresses the importance of free competition in order to achieve the most beneficial outcomes. According to this view, if a retailer such as Marks & Spencer is 'encumbered' by loyalty from selecting new suppliers which offer higher quality or lower costs then the retailer will become less competitive and its final consumers will have to face higher prices and/or poorer-quality products.

It is possible to question these assumptions on a number of grounds.

- First, loyalty does not necessarily imply slavish acceptance of any conditions offered by the supplier. It can perhaps be better interpreted as the establishment of a long-term commitment, from which the two partners can potentially seek mutually beneficial outcomes. So rather than accepting a poorer deal from its supplier, the firm might work with their supplier to ensure that it remains as competitive as its rivals.

- Second, a long-term commitment can provide the opportunity to take advantage of reduced transaction costs through less switching of suppliers and contracts, as well as enable the fashioning of more complex and customized ways of working together which are better for both partners, but are not easily replicable by other industry players (Artz 1999).

These arguments can be used to construct a fairly robust defence of intra-organizational loyalty from a consequentialist point of view, provided the area of business involved is one in which benefits can be accrued through longer-term working relationships. Some industries, however, appear to rely almost exclusively on a short-term transactional basis, particularly where products being exchanged are commodities with little potential for adding value

---

[1] See Kilgreen (2001); Jackson-Proes (2001).

through the supply arrangement, such as basic manufacturing components or simple foodstuffs like rice and sugar. In this case, the ethical case for loyalty to suppliers would have to rely on deontological or virtue-based reasoning.

■ **Think theory**

How would you apply deontological reasoning to the question of supplier loyalty? Does this offer, in conjunction with the consequentialist argument above, a sufficient rationale for judging the actions of companies such as Marks & Spencer to be unethical?

A common situation where the presumption of the need for loyalty is perhaps strongest is where business with a single purchasing company comprises a large proportion of the supplying company's total trading—and, hence, is effectively keeping them in business. In an era of long-term partnership supplying, this is not exactly an unusual situation, but clearly creates a situation ripe for exploitation, and might be said to place a heftier responsibility on the purchasing company. For example, Tim Eagles (2001) discusses how the British stairlift manufacturer Stannah Stairlifts was faced with a thorny ethical dilemma in 2000 when it was discovered during routine benchmarking that a 20 per cent cost reduction in upholstery components could be achieved by resourcing to a new supplier—but that it would mean ending a twenty-year relationship with one of Stannah's top ten suppliers (by annual spend), 98 per cent of whose turnover was accounted for by Stannah. In this case, the influence of an ethical stance from the company's family owners was credited by those involved with creating a culture where the suppliers were automatically offered considerable time (in fact, over a year) to adapt and respond before termination was even considered.

The issue of supplier loyalty also becomes considerably more complex when we look at the situation from the point of view of other potential suppliers. What may seem like loyalty to the two partners involved may seem more like unfair preferential treatment to other suppliers.

Preferential treatment

The giving of preferential treatment to favoured suppliers is widely identified as one of the main ethical issues faced by purchasing staff—and one of the most complex challenges (Rudelius and Buchholz 1979). Where does an obligation to be loyal end, and the granting of an unfair advantage begin? For example, is it acceptable for a firm to give a valued supplier information about its competitors' quotations so that the supplier can have a better chance of offering the best quotation?

One way of addressing the problem of preferential treatment is to apply the notion of **procedural justice**. Procedural justice is concerned with the fairness of the processes through which decisions are made. You may remember that in Chapter 7 (233–6) we discussed equal opportunities policies in relation to procedural justice. In the context of avoiding unduly preferential treatment for suppliers, we would be concerned with whether the contracting processes applied to different suppliers were equitable, such that all suppliers had equal opportunity to bid for business, their bids were assessed in the same way, and the assessment criteria used were non-discriminatory. As we have already said, it may very well be that a long-standing supply relationship is a pertinent criterion to the awarding of a contract, and this can legitimately be used to assess relative bids. But according to the tenets of procedural justice, this does not mean that valued suppliers can be advantaged by going through a process that discriminates against their competitors. This however is the case in the example given above because only the valued supplier gets to glean information about their opponents' quotes.

Of course, many cases of preferential treatment of suppliers occur when the individual purchasing officer is offered personal gifts or other inducements to sway their opinion. This can interject a **conflict of interest** into the supply relationship since the interests of the purchasing officer might diverge from the interests of their company. As we shall see in a moment, this is one of the main individual level ethical problems facing business–supplier relations. Before we look at this, though, we shall first briefly consider the issue of conflict of interest at the broader organizational level.

Conflicts of interest

Conflicts of interest are critical factors in causing various ethical problems, not just in relation to suppliers. However, this is probably the area where conflict of interest is most likely to surface. A conflict of interest occurs when a decision has to be made about whose interests to advance (Ferrell et al. 2002). However, the key element in a conflict of interest situation that distinguishes it from a normal decision about whose interests to advance— for example where a decision has to be made about which employee to promote—is that it involves an explicit obligation to act in another's interest (Boatright 2000). Using this as a starting point, we can define conflict of interest (whether at the individual or organizational level) as follows:

> A conflict of interest occurs when a person's or organization's obligation to act in the interests of another is interfered with by a competing interest that may obstruct the fulfilment of that obligation.

Organizational conflicts of interest typically occur when a firm is employed as a supplier of professional services of one sort or another—and hence would be expected to act in their client's interest—but this arrangement clashes with another interest of the supplier—perhaps an arrangement with a competitor to the first client, or even a desire to gain more work from the same client. Accounting firms, marketing agencies, law firms, and investment bankers are all organizations that might face conflicts of interest of this sort (Boatright 2000). For example, a market research agency might be employed to do a pilot study for a consumer products company to investigate the market potential for a new product. In expectation that positive results will lead to the client contracting further, more lucrative, market analysis, the market research company might be tempted to put an overly optimistic spin on its findings and thereby commit its client to an imprudent course of action.

One of the most prominent examples of supplier conflict of interest in recent years involved the accounting firm Arthur Andersen and its part in the downfall of US giants Enron and WorldCom in 2002. This is outlined in **Ethics in Action 9.1**. Whilst conflicts

Ethics in Action 9.1

Arthur Andersen: there's no accounting for one's friends

Until 2002, Arthur Andersen was one of the largest accountancy firms in the world. Employing more than 85,000 people worldwide, the US-based firm was one of the 'Big Five' accounting firms that dominated the industry. By the end of that year, though, the company was in ruins. Many of its high-profile clients had defected, it had been found guilty of obstructing justice, the US arm of the company had shed nearly two-thirds of its workforce, and the regional Andersen partnerships in eighty-three other countries in which it operated had decided to abandon their colleagues in the USA and merge with rival companies. Perhaps most significantly of all, Andersen completely closed down its core business of auditing publicly listed companies. All in all, Andersen's downfall was one of the most astonishing business collapses of all time.

The main cause of the collapse was the accounting scandals that accompanied the dramatic failure of the US firms Enron and WorldCom during 2001 and 2002. Both companies were discovered to have massively overstated their earnings over a number of years. And both firms' accounts were audited by Andersen. For example, in 2002, despite having its accounts signed off by Andersen, WorldCom was forced to restate its earnings by a massive $7.7bn—the biggest accounting swindle in Wall Street history. Similarly, just months after Andersen signed off on Enron's last annual report, the firm admitted it concealed a huge $586m loss.

At best, Andersen's critics have said that their auditing services were incompetent. However, at worst, there are suggestions that they deliberately overlooked accounting irregularities in order not to lose the lucrative stream of consulting and other work that the auditing relationship brought them. Although Andersen had already separated from its main consultancy division, Accenture, the firm had continued to provide such high-value services itself in order to enrich its revenue stream. The problem was, could Andersen really be regarded as fully able to fulfil its role as an 'external', independent verifier of its clients' accounts when it was also an 'insider' providing management services?

Perhaps notably, the Enron case was not the first time that Andersen's potential conflict of interest had been under the microscope. In 2001, it was convicted of 'improper professional conduct' by the US Securities & Exchange Commission and given a $7m fine. This related to auditing work for a waste management firm that involved some $1.4bn in overstated earnings—and was also accompanied by cross-selling of consultancy services. Perhaps predictably, then, revelations that Anderson executives were actually involved in shredding documents to cover up the Enron scandal led to a conviction of the US arm of Andersen of obstructing justice. Many Enron investors have also claimed that Andersen is responsible for the massive losses they incurred as a result of the collapse. This has led to further lawsuits against the firm that could bankrupt what remains of the embattled auditor.

The fallout from the WorldCom and Enron affairs has however been far wider than just the collapse of Andersen. Concerns about the conflicts of interest engendered by auditing firms providing consultancy services to their clients has led to other members of what is now a 'Big Four' hiving off their consultancy divisions. And other suppliers of financial services to Enron and WorldCom, especially those providing loans to bolster their massive losses, have been implicated in lawsuits including

Barclays, Deutsche Bank, Citigroup, Merrill Lynch, Crédit Suisse First Boston, Lehman Brothers, Bank of America, and JP Morgan.

SOURCES

BBC (2002a). 'Enron suit implicates nine US banks'. BBC News On-line, 8 Apr.
—— (2002b). 'Audit giants called to account'. BBC News On-line, 2 May.
—— (2002c). 'Andersen guilty in Enron case'. BBC News On-line, 15 June.
English, Simon (2002). 'Citigroup faces lawsuit over loan to WorldCom: allegations of "corporate cosiness" mire bank deeper in scandal'. *Daily Telegraph*, 15 Oct.: 33.
Foremski, Tom, and Skapinker, Michael (2002). 'Bigger Blue: technology companies are taking over from accountants as providers of consultancy services'. *Financial Times* (Comment & Analysis), 2 Aug.: 16.

■ **Think theory**

Think about the Andersen case in terms of the conflicting duties that the company had to its various stakeholders. Who were these stakeholders and how would you assess the strength of their rights in this situation?

of interest such as that experienced by Arthur Andersen are clearly of major importance, most problems of this type actually pertain to conflicts of interest between an individual purchasing officer and their organization. Let us then turn our attention now to this and a few other individual level ethical problems with suppliers.

Individual level issues

Gifts, bribes, and hospitality

Gifts, gratuities, hospitality, bribes, kickbacks, bungs, sweeteners—there is seemingly no end to the variety of terms that are used to describe the official and unofficial 'perks' that purchasing staff might be offered in the course of their interactions with salespeople. Some of these offers might be innocent and quite genuine expressions of gratitude; some might be part and parcel of maintaining a decent buyer–seller relationship; some however will simply be inducements to get business that would not otherwise have been earned by more legitimate means. The offering of personal inducements is regularly identified by purchasing staff as one of the main ethical issues confronting their profession (Rudelius and Buchholz 1979; Cooper et al. 2000). The key question is where to draw the line between acceptable and unacceptable practice.

We have already discussed some of the main issues involved in this problem in the section above on organizational level issues. Inducements usually are made in order to secure some form of **preferential treatment** for the supplying company, and typically involve purchasing staff in a **conflict of interest** between their own personal gain and the best interests of their firm. As employees of the firm, purchasers are expected to fulfil an obligation to act in the firm's interest—namely getting the best deal, whether in terms of price, quality, support services, or whatever else best achieves the company's goals. When a purchaser receives a personal benefit from the seller—such as a bottle of whisky, a trip to a football game, or an envelope stuffed with money—the problem is that the purchaser may be swayed to make a decision that does not fulfil this obligation to their employer.

Of course, many of us could probably quite easily rationalize that the gift did not affect our decision, particularly if it was unsolicited, or it was received after the actual transaction took place. How could one be influenced by something that hadn't even happened when the decision was made? There are a number of ways of looking at this.

- One is to consider the **intention of the gift giver**. If their intention is to gain an additional advantage (as opposed to merely offering thanks for a job well done) then we might question the action.

- Another way is to look at the **impact on the receiver**. If their evaluation of the gift giver is enhanced after receiving the gift, then again we might start to raise some doubts about its ethicality. This is pertinent even when the gift is received after a deal has been concluded since it might be seen to prejudice future evaluations.

- Finally, we might focus on the **perception of other parties**. If a competing supplier might interpret the giving of the gift as a deliberate bribe, then again we should probably question the action.

The raising of the issue of perception by others is significant here because it suggests that the resolution of ethical dilemmas does not just depend on those who are directly involved in them. Bribery in particular is a problem that, when its occurrence is perceived by others, can erode trust and reinforce a culture of dishonesty. For instance, imagine that you heard that your class professor had received a nice Christmas present of an expensive bottle of cognac from one of your class members. Regardless of the intention of the student, or its impact on the professor, if the student's grades were anything other than terrible then you might well start questioning the integrity of your professor, and even maybe consider the possibility of purchasing a small gift yourself.

As we saw in Chapter 4 (esp. 131–7), once a culture of dishonesty has been created, the prevailing ethic in the workplace can be both difficult to dislodge, and profoundly influential on subsequent behaviour. Although many large organizations have a formal **purchasing code of ethics** in place, and guidelines for appropriate behaviour on issues such as gifts and hospitality are provided by professional bodies such as the International Chartered Institute of Purchasing and Supply (see **Figure 9.2**), the purchasing function is widely regarded (by other company personnel and outsiders) to be largely unconcerned with ethics and very commercially minded (Drumwright 1994). Indeed, the purchasing environment seems to suffer more than most other organizational functions in relation to the conditions that might foster ethical abuse. As Badenhorst (1994: 741) argues:

The purchasing environment creates a climate which promotes unethical behaviour. . . . Often sales representatives have little concern for ethical behaviour, and purchasers are tempted to obtain some personal gain from a transaction, often with the approval of the representative's employer. The management often encourages its sales representatives to act in a manner which they would find entirely unacceptable in their purchasing department. These double standards create a climate of dishonesty in a company, and tempt everyone, especially the purchaser.

Given this pervading influence of culture, it is not surprising that some industries are more prone to problems of bribes, gifts, and hospitality than others. The construction

Introduction

1. Members of the Institute undertake to work to exceed the expectations of the following Code and will regard the Code as the basis of best conduct in the Purchasing and Supply profession.

2. Members should seek the commitment of their employer to the Code and seek to achieve widespread acceptance of it amongst their fellow employees.

3. Members should raise any matter of concern of an ethical nature with their immediate supervisor or another senior colleague if appropriate, irrespective of whether it is explicitly addressed in the Code.

Principles

4. Members shall always seek to uphold and enhance the standing of the Purchasing and Supply profession and will always act professionally and selflessly by:

   a) maintaining the highest possible standard of integrity in all their business relationships both inside and outside the organisations where they work;

   b) rejecting any business practice which might reasonably be deemed improper and never using their authority for personal gain;

   c) enhancing the proficiency and stature of the profession by acquiring and maintaining current technical knowledge and the highest standards of ethical behaviour;

   d) fostering the highest possible standards of professional competence amongst those for whom they are responsible;

   e) optimising the use of resources which they influence and for which they are responsible to provide the maximum benefit to their employing organisation;

   f) complying both with the letter and the spirit of:

      i) the law of the country in which they practise;

      ii) Institute guidance on professional practice;

      iii) contractual obligations;

5. Members should never allow themselves to be deflected from these principles.

Guidance

6. In applying these principles, members should follow the guidance set out below:

   a) Declaration of interest—Any personal interest which may affect or be seen by others to affect a member's impartiality in any matter relevant to his or her duties should be declared.

   b) Confidentiality and accuracy of information—The confidentiality of information received in the course of duty should be respected and should never be used for personal gain. Information given in the course of duty should be honest and clear.

   c) Competition—The nature and length of contracts and business relationships with suppliers can vary according to circumstances. These should always be constructed to ensure deliverables and benefits. Arrangements which might in the long term prevent the effective operation of fair competition should be avoided.

   d) Business gifts—Business gifts, other than items of very small intrinsic value such as business diaries or calendars, should not be accepted.

   e) Hospitality—The recipient should not allow him or herself to be influenced or be perceived by others to have been influenced in making a business decision as a consequence of accepting hospitality. The frequency and scale of hospitality accepted should be managed openly and with care and should not be greater than the member's employer is able to reciprocate.

Decisions and Advice

7. When it is not easy to decide between what is and is not acceptable, advice should be sought from the member's supervisor, another senior colleague or the Institute as appropriate. Advice on any aspect of the Code is available from the Institute.

Figure 9.2. Chartered Institute of Purchasing and Supply Code of Ethics

industry for example has a long history of sanctioning the use of unofficial inducements, and in recent years professional sport has been rocked by a number of scandals involving bribes and kickbacks, including the revelation that officials in the USA paid over €1m in bribes to various International Olympic Committee members to secure the 2002 winter games for Salt Lake City (Mackay 2002).

Ethics in negotiation

Finally, any discussion of ethics in supplier relationships is not complete without addressing the issue of business–supplier negotiation. As we said at the outset of this section, many commentators have identified a shift away from adversarial supplier relationships towards a more partnership model, suggesting that negotiation might be less subject to questionable ethics than in the past. Although to some extent this may well be true, the whole process of negotiation between buyer and supplier inevitably raises some ethical tensions, given that the situation itself is often characterized as one of two combatants coming together to do battle (Badenhorst 1994). As Reitz et al. (1998) suggest, to many people ethics and negotiation are like oil and water: they just don't mix. To illustrate their point they list ten popular negotiating tactics, all of which they contend can be challenged on ethical grounds:

- Lies—about something material to the negotiation.
- Puffery—i.e. exaggerating the value of something.
- Deception—including misleading promises or threats and misstatements of facts.
- Weakening the opponent—by directly undermining the strengths or alliances of the opponent.
- Strengthening one's own position—for example by means not available to the opponent.
- Non-disclosure—deliberately withholding pertinent information that would be of benefit to the opponent.
- Information exploitation—misusing information provided by the opponent in ways not intended by them.
- Change of mind—engaging in behaviours contrary to previous statements or positions.
- Distraction—deliberately attempting to lure an opponent into ignoring information or alternatives that might benefit them.
- Maximization—exploiting a situation to one's own fullest possible benefit without concern for the effects on the other.

According to Reitz et al. (1998), although there are certain risks in doing so, a more ethical approach to negotiation can, and should, steer clear of such tactics. This is not only because it is the right thing to do, but also because such practices can incur costs for the negotiator. Specifically, these costs are:

- **Rigid negotiating.** Unethical tactics can draw negotiators into a narrow view of the tactics available to them, especially if they are perceived as having been successful in the past. However, in longer-term relationships, a more flexible and open approach may help to yield more advantageous win-win solutions.

- **Damaged relationships.** Customers and suppliers rarely cease to rely on each other once a deal has been negotiated. Even when the negotiation is a single event, implementation of the deal may be marred as a result of perceived ethical infractions. Where negotiations are part of a longer-term cycle, the costs of unethical negotiation may mount as negotiators turn into embittered enemies rather than mutually supportive partners.

- **Sullied reputation.** Unethical negotiation can have a negative influence on the individual's or their company's image, making future bargaining more troublesome.

- **Lost opportunities.** Unethical negotiation not only undermines the negotiators' capabilities to reach mutually beneficial win-win agreements, but it also tends to prevent any progressive discussions which could bring new, profitable issues to the table.

Whilst this undoubtedly presents an overly positive perspective on ethics in negotiation between buyers and sellers, it is useful in helping us to view negotiation not so much as a zero-sum game, but as a chance to build towards a more mutually beneficial relationship. Firms' dealings with their suppliers do not always have to be characterised as a tussle between warring combatants. Somewhat more challenging, however, is the idea that this can also be true of their relationships with their competitors. Let us look at this now in more detail.

Ethical issues and competitors

As we have already mentioned, whilst there is some disagreement in the literature as to whether competitors are actually legitimate stakeholders in an organization, there does seem to be a reasonable case for suggesting that they in fact are, and that it is reasonable to expect a certain level of ethical behaviour in a firm's dealings with its competitors. Of course, this certainly does not preclude active, or even quite aggressive, competitive behaviour between rivals. In fact, as we saw in the previous chapter (and shall elucidate on below), the deliberate avoidance of competitive behaviour is itself a cause for ethical concern should consumers and other stakeholders be disadvantaged as a result.

The point is then that there appears to be a need to establish some kind of parameters regarding the limits to competition at either end of the scale. This means that ethical issues in dealing with competitors can relate to two distinct problems:

- Overly aggressive competition;
- Insufficient competition.

In the following, we shall examine the main issues and dilemmas that arise in both areas.

Problems of overly aggressive competition

Intelligence gathering and industrial espionage

All organizations collect and make use of some kind of information about their competitors. Just as your university or college will typically investigate which courses are offered by their main competitors, so too will companies take a keen interest in the products, policies, and processes undertaken by their rivals. Indeed, such intelligence gathering activities are very much a standard aspect of conventional market research and competitor benchmarking, and make for effective competitive behaviour. Ethical questions arise, though, when one or both of the following are deemed to have occurred:

(*a*) The tactics used to secure information about competitors are questionable since they appear to go beyond what might be deemed acceptable, ethical, or legal business practice;

(*b*) The nature of the information sought can itself be regarded as in some way private or confidential.

Questionable tactics may take many forms, from the clearly illegal, such as breaking and entering a competitor's offices to steal information and installing tapping devices, to rather more grey areas. This includes searching through a competitor's rubbish, hiring private detectives, infiltrating competitors' organizations with industrial 'spies', covert surveillance through spy cameras, contacting competitors in a fake guise such as a potential customer or supplier, interviewing competitors' employees for a bogus job vacancy, and pressuring the customers or suppliers of competitors to reveal sensitive information about their operations (Hallaq and Steinhorst 1994). See **Case 9** at the end of this chapter for some actual examples and illustrations from current business practice of some of these activities and their implications.

Such tactics are of dubious ethicality primarily because they violate a duty to be honest and truthful in business dealings (Boatright 2000: 141), and might easily be criticized from the perspective of deontological precepts such as the 'golden rule'—do unto others as you would have them do unto you—or Kant's categorical imperative. Moreover, once such methods become accepted—or, to use Kant's words, they become 'universal law'— into business practice, all firms tend to lose out: (*a*) because the industry is likely to suffer from a loss of trust; and (*b*) because it becomes necessary for all industry players to commit resources to institute procedures guarding against the loss of trade secrets to unscrupulous competitors (Boatright 2000: 141).

Private or confidential information may refer to any kind of information which the organization feels should not be freely available to outsiders and which therefore should be under some kind of moral or legal protection. Whilst in principle this seems quite reasonable, it is rather more difficult to establish a corporation's right to privacy than it is an individual's—and certainly, the enforcement of privacy is considerably trickier. Specifically:

• Corporations are to some extent 'boundary-less'—they have fewer clear boundaries to define the private 'corporate space' compared with private individuals.

• Corporations consist of, and deal with, multiple individuals, making control of information difficult.

• Much corporate activity takes place in public and quasi-public spaces such as shops, offices, hospitals, colleges, etc., and via shared infrastructure such as roads, railways, seas, telephone lines, fibre optic cables, etc.: these are easily and usually quite legitimately observed, infiltrated, or tracked.

However, even if it is difficult to fully ascribe a right to privacy to corporations, it is relatively more straightforward to suggest that certain information that corporations have is a form of property and is thus subject to **property rights** (Boatright 2000: 132). This particularly tends to apply to trade secrets, patents, copyrights, and trademarks—all of which are to some extent legally enforceable *intellectual property* that is said to belong to the organization. Intellectual property rights can be assigned to many intangible forms of property, including product formulations, theories, inventions, software, music, formulae, recipes, processing techniques, designs, and so on. The development of such 'information' frequently involves organizations in millions of euros investment in R&D costs. Unsurprisingly then, corporations often go to great lengths and invest substantial resources in trying to keep this information secret from their competitors so that they may reap the rewards of their investment.

With improvements in information and communication technologies, the ease of replication of digital information, as well as the refinement of 'reverse engineering' techniques (where competitors' products are stripped down and analysed in order to copy them), the unauthorized accessing and exploitation of intellectual property has been on the rise (Shapiro 1998). Intellectual property infringements have subsequently been the subject of numerous recent cases, including the record industry's battle against Napster, the internet music-swapping service. These are essentially cases for the courts to settle— as indeed they did with Napster, siding with the record industry in a series of settlements that ultimately condemned Napster to bankruptcy (Grimes 2002). However, the emergence of new technologies will continue to spark new ethical debates about what constitutes intellectual property and what restrictions can and should be put on different forms of property, including human and plant genes, and digital information.

'Dirty tricks'

Overly intense competition can also lead to questionable tactics beyond just stealing secrets and spying on competitors. A more generic term often used in the business world to describe the range of morally dubious practices that competitors occasionally revert to in order to outdo their rivals is 'dirty tricks'. In addition to industrial espionage, dirty tricks can include various tactics including:

• **Negative advertising:** where the firm deliberately sets out to publicly criticize their competitors, their products, or any product or performance claims the competitor may have made.

• **Stealing customers:** where a rival's customers are specifically approached in order to encourage them to switch suppliers, often using underhand methods such as misrepresentation, providing false information, bribery, or impersonating the competitor's staff.

• **Predatory pricing:** as we saw in the previous chapter, this involves the deliberate setting of prices below cost in order to initiate a price war and force weaker competitors out of the market.

• **Sabotage:** this can take many forms but basically involves direct interference in a competitor's business in order to obstruct, slow down, or otherwise derail their plans.

While some of these tactics may seem a little extreme, they are not entirely uncommon in contemporary business practice. Perhaps the most striking example in recent years was the campaign waged by British Airways against Virgin Atlantic in the 1990s. The campaign, which ultimately resulted in BA chairman Lord King issuing a public apology to Virgin in court, was alleged to have involved the accessing of confidential Virgin passenger information, impersonating Virgin staff, poaching of customers as they queued for Virgin tickets, theft of documents, a hostile smear campaign in the press, as well as aggressive predatory pricing aimed at putting Virgin out of business (*The Economist* 1993).

Anti-competitive behaviour

Putting rival firms out of business can be about more than just intense competition between two industry rivals. In many cases, the stakes are considerably higher since the action can signal an attempt to deliberately restrict competition in an industry in order to reap longer-term profitability. As we argued in the previous chapter, such anti-competitive practices usually contravene competition law, which is in place to ensure fair competition and protect consumers from monopolistic behaviour. However, such charges can be extremely difficult to prove. And many smaller competitors may well be forced out of business before a truly monopolistic position is reached.

Naomi Klein (2000) for example criticizes the aggressive market expansion strategy of high street brands such as Starbucks, Gap, and McDonald's which involves the saturation of a geographical area through 'clustering'. By increasingly saturating an area with more and more individual stores, overall company sales increase even though the returns from individual stores may be reduced through 'cannibalization' (poaching customers from one part of a business by another). The effect of such a strategy has been to squeeze out smaller competitors like independent cafés, coffee shops, and boutiques who, unlike the high street giants, cannot afford the loss of sales from individual stores. Hence, although it could be claimed that they are not necessarily motivated by a deliberate intention to do so, such strategies can result in the development of a monopolistic position in a particular geographical area.

Problems of insufficient competition

Anti-competitive behaviour can obviously also hurt consumers, particularly when it results in companies being able to abuse their dominance in a market to exploit customers through higher prices. Sometimes, though, ethical problems arise here not so much because competitors are overly competitive with each other, but because competition is reduced by competitors being insufficiently competitive with each other. Most such behaviours are precluded by competition law, but the problems of determining when firms have colluded or abused a position can be difficult to resolve.

Collusion and cartels

At the other end of the scale from such intense rivalry, then, is where select groups of competitors band together in a cartel or trading group to fix prices and other trading arrangements for their own mutual benefit. Again, we briefly discussed this issue of collusion in the previous chapter, since it mainly results in a potential threat to consumer interests.

Abuse of dominant position

Finally, some markets may already be dominated by a single large competitor, which then has the opportunity to use its extra muscle to disadvantage consumers and smaller competitors alike. The European Commission, for example, is currently investigating whether Microsoft's move into the market for low-end servers (i.e. the hubs of computer networks) abused the dominant position of its Windows operating system. Competition Commissioner Mario Monti also is looking at whether Microsoft's bundling of its Media Player software with Windows has given it an unfair advantage over competing audio and video software. This follows antitrust rulings in the USA that criticized Microsoft's abuse of its position by bundling its Explorer internet browser software, thereby disadvantaging competing browsers such as Netscape (*Los Angeles Times* 2002).

Globalization, suppliers, and competitors: the ethical challenges of global business networks

Deterritorialization of the corporate value chain can be identified as an important influence contributing to the process of globalization. George Yip (1995) for example identifies the key forces driving globalization in business to be:

- Convergence of markets;
- Global competition;
- Cost advantages;
- Government influence.

Convergence of markets has meant that firms increasingly have sold their products across the world, thereby bringing them into direct competition with firms in, and from, different countries. This move towards *global competition* means that competitors may now hail from cultures with different understandings and expectations of business and of the nature of competition. Moreover, the impact of foreign competition in many countries might well have significant effects on the local economy.

The potential for *cost advantages* overseas has involved business in a fundamental restructuring of supply chains in the pursuit of lower-cost sites for production. This has seen vast numbers of European corporations (as well as their counterparts in North America, Asia, and Australia) increasingly shifting the sourcing and production of their products, components, and labour to less developed countries—a move that has been expedited by *government influence* in these countries. Again, this has involved corporations in business relationships with organizations operating under a different set of cultural practices and assumptions, and where standards of working practices and health, safety, and environmental protection may differ markedly from at home.

What we have seen then is a dramatic reshaping of ethical considerations and problems when dealing with suppliers and competitors in a global, as opposed to a purely locally based, business network. This reshaping brings to the fore four main considerations:

- Different ways of doing business;

- Impacts on indigenous businesses;

- Differing labour and environmental standards;

- Extended chain of responsibility.

Different ways of doing business

By coming into contact with overseas suppliers and competitors, corporate managers are often confronted with very different ways of thinking about and evaluating business ethics. As we have already seen in earlier chapters dealing with employees and consumers, it is clear that certain practices which may be morally questionable at home might be seen as perfectly legitimate in a different cultural environment, as will some practices which are perfectly acceptable in one's own country raise questions overseas. For example, Jerold Muskin (2000) suggests that for *competitors*, differences in national culture and law give rise to different notions of *intellectual property*. Whilst European, and even more so US, companies might expect the granting of exclusive rights to any novel technologies they develop, in Asia innovation is often seen as a public good to be used for the advance of technology by all.

In the main, though, different ways of doing business are primarily important for corporations' dealings with their suppliers, particularly in relation to **gift giving, bribery, and corruption**. Different countries tend to exhibit differing attitudes towards the appropriateness of gift giving between customers and suppliers. Thomas Donaldson (1996) explains that in countries such as Japan people doing business together often exchange gifts—sometimes quite expensive ones—as part of a long-standing cultural tradition. Still, a European purchasing officer might easily interpret the gift as an attempt at bribery rather than simple courtesy. However, if they chose to refuse to accept the gift, they might risk giving offence, thus harming the business relationship or jeopardizing the deal. Donaldson (1996) suggests that, as a consequence, as western firms have become more familiar with such traditions, they have increasingly tolerated the practice and even applied different limits on gift giving and receiving in countries such as Japan from elsewhere. This, he argues, is not so much a matter of *ethical relativism* (which, he claims, as we too have, can be a highly problematic approach to business ethics), but is simply a matter of respect for local tradition.

Going back to our different ways of evaluating gift giving above (314–317), if the act is without an *intent* to gain undeserved favour, if it does not have the *effect* of doing so, and if it is not *perceived* as doing so, then probably it should be regarded as acceptable when consistent with a broader social norm. This is especially the case when the norm also dictates that the giving is an *exchange*. There is, it would seem to us, a significant difference between a buyer and a seller exchanging gifts, and a salesperson simply offering the buyer a long line of presents with the expectation that the reciprocity would come in the form of extra business rather than a gift in return. The latter offers a lot more potential for conflict of interest than the former.

Country	Score
Australia	8.5
Sweden	8.4
Switzerland	8.4
Austria	8.2
Canada	8.1
The Netherlands	7.8
Belgium	7.8
United Kingdom	6.9
Singapore	6.3
Germany	6.3
Spain	5.8
France	5.5
USA	5.3
Japan	5.3
Malaysia	4.3
Hong Kong	4.3
Italy	4.1
South Korea	3.9
Taiwan	3.8
People's Republic of China	3.5
Russia	3.2

Figure 9.3. Bribe paying by multinational companies according to country of origin

Notes: Scores based on 0 to 10, where a perfect score, indicating zero perceived propensity to pay bribes, is 10. Thus, those countries with a lower score have a higher perceived propensity to bribe.

Source: www.transparency.org.

The main problem here though is that people all too often take this kind of respect for tradition as a signal that all local customs should be accepted and adapted to, regardless of their ethical implications. If we accept gifts from suppliers, then why should we blanch at taking or giving bribes to oil the wheels of business? The issue of corruption is a major problem in many countries, especially in less developed or developing economies. However, the problem is not simply with those accepting bribes, but also with those willing to pay them.

For example, the *Bribe Payers Index* produced by the not-for-profit organization Transparency International provides an illuminating picture of the propensity for bribe paying by MNCs from various countries. The 2002 index, based on responses from over 800 business experts in fifteen leading emerging market countries, shows that companies from Russia, China, South Korea, Taiwan, and Italy are widely seen as likely to use bribery to gain business in developing countries. At the other end of the scale, Australian, Swiss, and Swedish companies are seen as the least likely (see **Figure 9.3**). The Index also shows that the most flagrant corruption is seen in the construction and defence sectors, which Transparency International claims are 'plagued by endemic bribery by foreign firms' (see **Figure 9.4**).

Why is bribery so endemic to international business? The answer to some extent seems to be that multinational businesses are promulgating the practice because it is 'normal,' 'expected', or 'customary' in the host country. Unless we are going to slip into relativism,

Business sector	Score
Public works/construction	1.3
Arms and defence	1.9
Oil and gas	2.7
Telecommunications	3.7
Pharmaceuticals/medical care	4.3
Heavy manufacturing	4.5
Banking and finance	4.7
Information technology	5.1
Light manufacturing	5.9
Agriculture	5.9

Figure 9.4. Bribe paying by multinational firms according to sector

Note: The scores are mean averages on a 0 to 10 basis where 0 represents very high perceived levels of corruption, and 10 represents extremely low perceived levels of corruption.

Source: **www.transparency.org**.

though, this does not necessarily condone the practice. Just to say something is 'normal' does not imply that it is 'right'. Thirty-five states across the world, predominantly from Europe, have now signed up to the OECD Anti-Bribery Convention. The convention is aimed at stamping out corruption in international business, and the broad range of signatories suggests a gathering international consensus over the undesirability of corruption, and a commitment to dealing with it. However, these good intentions have yet to manifest themselves very significantly in practice, with only one in five of Transparency International's respondents signifying knowledge of the accord (**www.transparency.org**).

In fact, for the individual manager, the question is not always one of whether bribery is right or wrong, but whether doing business in certain countries is even *possible* without such practices. Regardless of whether an individual firm has a code prohibiting bribery, or whether one's country has signed up to the OECD convention, if a reasonable level of business cannot go ahead without bribery how is the individual going to proceed? Many MNC staff seem to be caught between the ethical commitments of their code, and the realities of everyday business. One way that some firms have responded to this problem is to amend their codes of conduct so that employees are not penalized for any loss of business due to avoidance of bribery. For instance, if you go back to Unilever's code of business principles in **Figure 5.2**, this categorically states that 'the Board of Unilever will not criticise management for any loss of business resulting from adherence to these principles'.

Impacts on indigenous businesses

The role of MNCs in corruption is often one of perpetuating extant problems. However they can often bring new problems too. The size, power, and political influence of MNCs often means that they enjoy considerable cost and other advantages compared to local competitors. This can mean that the exposure to the competition of a major multinational such as Starbucks, IKEA, Microsoft, or Monsanto can severely threaten the business of indigenous competitors (Klein 2000). Of course, the introduction of more and better competition can often be a force for innovation, better products, lower prices, and economic growth. This is why international organizations such as the WTO exist to establish the global rules of trade, and why even humanitarian organizations such as the UN promote the desirability of market development for underdeveloped countries. However, such competition can also result in the matching of unequal rivals where the ultimate consequence can be the elimination of local competition and, as we saw in the previous chapter, a homogenization of the high street.

The key point here is that MNCs may often be able to negotiate far more attractive trading arrangements than their weaker indigenous competitors; they may bring specialized management knowledge, economies of scale, advanced technology, powerful brands, and a host of other advantages (Dawar and Frost 1999). Similarly, they may be able to force local suppliers into accepting terms and conditions which barely keep them in business. There are clearly issues of fairness to be considered here, as well as questions of whether local competitors should be protected in some way—particularly if MNCs themselves are benefiting from certain protections. For example, the interests of large MNCs are often promoted by their own national governments (because their success is vital to economic growth), and even by host governments overseas (since the influx of jobs and investment can be highly beneficial).

This problem of unfair competition from MNCs is particularly a cause for concern when it threatens the viability of an entire local industry, as this can lead to more fundamental social and economic decay. For example, the eight-year 'banana war' between the EU and the USA over import duties on bananas was caused by European attempts to protect small-scale Caribbean banana growers against cheaper imports from US MNCs such as Dole foods, Delmonte, and Chiquita International. Many Caribbean countries are reliant on the banana industry, but with costs up to double those of Latin American-based MNCs, the sustainability of the Caribbean industry was dependent on EU import restrictions introduced in 1993. The US administration, driven by lobbying from the MNCs, logged a formal complaint against the EU's 'discriminatory' system with the WTO. When the WTO instructions to the EU to amend its policies were refused, the USA launched devastating retaliatory action by imposing sanctions valued at nearly €200m on random European imports. The war was finally resolved in 2001 when the EU agreed to change its rules, providing for the phasing out of protection for Caribbean bananas by 2006 (Lister 2001a; 2001b).

■ **Think theory**

To what extent is it appropriate to protect local businesses from 'unfair' competition from MNCs? Consider this situation from the perspectives of theories of justice and utilitarianism.

Differing labour and environmental standards

As western firms have increasingly sourced through global supply chains, probably the most prominent ethical problem to have come under the spotlight concerns the labour and environmental conditions under which their suppliers operate. You may remember that back in Chapter 7 (255) we looked at the 'race to the bottom' occasioned by the demand by MNCs for lower-cost production in developing countries such as China, Indonesia, Vietnam, and India. This raises substantial ethical problems for European companies that source their products in lower-cost countries, for it is the case that the lower costs are often accompanied by poorer labour conditions, less environmental protection, and lower attention to health and safety protection. These, as we have already mentioned a number of times in the book so far, can, and frequently have, led to human rights and other abuses.

The number of high-profile media exposés of such incidents since the beginning of the 1990s has been phenomenal. Clothing and sportswear producers have frequently been the most affected, with accusations of sweatshop conditions being launched at major European brands such as Adidas-Salomon, C&A, Marks & Spencer, and Reebok, as well as high-profile US brands such as Disney, Gap, Levi's, Nike, Tommy Hilfiger, and Wal-Mart.[2] Other industries that have been the subject of media, trade union, and pressure group attention include toy assembly, rug and carpet making, and food production.

Typically, the debate has mainly centred on pay, working conditions, and child labour. The fundamental conventions of the International Labour Organization (ILO), however (which are probably the most widely recognized and influential agreement on labour rights), also refer to broader issues, such as freedom of association, equality, abolition of forced labour, etc. Many companies have discovered (or their critics have discovered for them) that in their suppliers' factories, workers have been paid below a living wage, they have been subjected to physical and verbal abuse, overtime has been compulsory, statutory rights to time off have been denied, children as young as 10 or 12 years old have been employed, and so on.

We have seen in Chapter 3 that different ethical theories provide a range of arguments for and against issues such as child labour. However, these conditions have been seen as all the more inequitable because of the startling comparison that they make with the prices paid by consumers in Europe and the USA for the products they make, as well as the pay and conditions earned by staff in the company's head office—in particular the stellar remuneration packages of the companies' CEOs. For example, one widely quoted statistic is that while Disney CEO Michael Eisner was earning $9,783 an hour, a Haitian worker sewing Disney pyjamas earned just 28 cents an hour. This means it would have taken a Haitian worker 16.8 years to earn Eisner's hourly income! Plus, the $181m in stock options that Eisner received in 1996 would have been enough to take care of the 19,000 Haitian workers working on Disney products, and their families, for fourteen years! (Klein 2000: 352). Such disparities are alarming, and to many appear unjustifiable when the total cost of labour in producing, for example, clothes typically only amounts to something like 1 per cent of the final retail price (compared to 25 per cent for brand profit, overheads, and promotion) (Robins and Humphrey 2000).

---

[2] Naomi Klein's (2000) *No Logo* covers many of these accounts and provides a good, if somewhat sensationalist, overview of the issues.

■ **Think theory**

In Chapter 7, we discussed Thomas Donaldson's argument that many problems of poor wages and conditions were problems of relative development rather than simply differences in ethics (see pp. 252–6). How would you compare Donaldson's argument with that of the justice-based argument above?

Different environmental and health and safety standards in suppliers' countries can also provide a loophole through which MNCs can potentially secure lower-cost supplies by bypassing the stringent standards in their country of origin. For example, in November 2002, the ageing oil tanker *Prestige* sank off the coast of Spain, despoiling the coastal waters with thousands of tonnes of oil. However, responsibility for its poor state of repair, and ultimately for the disaster itself, was muddied by the complex of international bodies and standards involved. As Will Hutton (2002) commentated at the time: 'this was a vessel chartered by the Swiss-based subsidiary of a Russian conglomerate registered in the Bahamas, owned by a Greek through Liberia and given a certificate of seaworthiness by the Americans. When it refuelled, it stood off the port of Gibraltar to avoid the chance of inspection. Every aspect of its operations was calculated to avoid tax, ownership obligations and regulatory scrutiny.'

Extended chain of responsibility

Ultimately, the implication of these shifts towards global supply and competition is that individual firms appear to be faced with the prospect of an **extended chain of responsibility**. Where once it may have been perfectly acceptable to argue that the ethics of a firm's suppliers, or a firm's impact on its competitors, was simply not any of its business, this no longer seems to be the case (see Emmelhainz and Adams 1999). The different social and economic conditions present in other countries, as well as the sheer inequalities surfaced by international trade, have meant that the relatively level playing field constituted by national business has been replaced with the sloping and bumpy playing surface of globalization. Relations with other businesses are no longer conducted within a national community with legislation and broadly agreed rules of the game that are considered to be fair to all. Hence, corporations now increasingly have to consider their ethical responsibilities much more broadly, not least because pressure groups have discovered that the best way to focus attention on practices and conditions in anonymous factories in far-off places is not to target the factory itself, but to target the big brand multinational which sources its products from them. This, as we shall now see, has led to the supply chain being used as a conduit for ethics management and regulation.

The corporate citizen in the business community: ethical sourcing and fair trade

We stated in Chapter 2 (67–70) that one of the most crucial areas where corporations enter the realm of citizenship and begin to take over the role of governments is in the regulation and control of other businesses. This can be mainly seen to happen through the supply chain, via a process known as *ethical sourcing*.

Ethical sourcing

Ethical sourcing occurs when a supply chain member introduces social and environmental criteria into their purchase decisions in order to support certain practices and/or suppliers. Therefore, whilst it can actually take a variety of forms, ethical sourcing can be broadly defined as follows:

> Ethical sourcing is the inclusion of explicit social, ethical, and/or environmental criteria into supply chain management policies, procedures, and programmes.

Although far from comprehensive, increasing numbers of European companies now include some type of criteria of this kind into their purchasing policies and agreements, although most tend to focus almost exclusively on environmental issues (Young and Kielkiewicz-Young 2001). One of the forerunners of this practice was the UK DIY retailer B&Q. Since 1991, B&Q has required all of its suppliers to provide information on environmental performance as part of its Supplier Environmental Audit. In 1995, this initiative was subsequently integrated into a more comprehensive supplier audit, QUEST (QUality, Ethics, SafeTy). More recently, various firms such as Nike, Reebok, and Puma have introduced ethical codes of conduct intended to prevent labour and human rights abuses in their suppliers' operations (Emmelhainz and Adams 1999).

Of course, the mere inclusion of ethical sourcing criteria into supply chain management is no guarantee that they will be especially germane to the continuation of supply relationships. However, studies have shown that supply chain pressure has been a key factor in prompting firms to seek various social and environmental certifications of one sort or another, even if they are not necessarily perceived as intrinsically valuable. These include accreditations such as the staff training and development award, Investors in People (Ram 2000) and the environmental quality standard ISO 14001. For example, Volvo required all of its suppliers to have ISO 14001 by the year 2000, whilst Ford had a similar expectation for 2002 (Young and Kielkiewicz-Young 2001). Moreover, a handful of firms, such as the Danish life sciences company Novo, have announced supply chain regimes that elevate the social and environmental performance of suppliers on a par with price and quality considerations—making compliance with ethical sourcing criteria essential for doing business with the firm.

Ethical sourcing as intra-business regulation

In the absence of specific or insufficient legislation in suppliers' countries, or, more usually, where there is simply weak enforcement of existing legislation, this kind of supply chain pressure can be the most effective form of regulation on these companies. Although this is not regulation in the formal sense of ensuring compliance with government legislation, the pressure exerted by powerful corporate customers to comply with ethical sourcing guidelines and criteria does constitute strong and indeed often very effective regulation of supply chain members (Cashore 2002). The threat of losing business or being de-listed by a major customer can act as a powerful force for change, particularly when the threat is shown to be more than just an idle one. In particular, when *competitors* within an industry collaborate to introduce ethical guidelines for suppliers, it is often difficult for the suppliers to avoid compliance.

This kind of pressure on suppliers can effect further change through the supply chain, and even into the wider business network. This is because not only are suppliers' own suppliers often involved in any progress towards compliance with ethical sourcing guidelines (and in turn *their* suppliers, and so on), but competing suppliers also have a chance to gain business if they have the right ethical policies or accreditations. Hence, a purchasing 'multiplier effect' can be set in motion which has the potential to achieve social change more quickly and thoroughly than any other single activity that a particular firm could undertake (Preuss 2000).

The mechanism by which ethical sourcing works is very much the same as the process of ethical consumption discussed in the previous chapter (289–292)—except here it is a corporation (or group of corporations) that is the customer, not an individual person. This obviously constitutes a concentration of buying power far in excess of that wielded by individual consumers, implying that ethical sourcing is a very potent source of corporate citizenship. This is particularly pronounced when it is not just solo firms introducing ethical sourcing criteria, but whole groups of competing firms joining together in a coalition to address the problem. Such industry alliances can take a number of forms, from setting up supplier codes of conduct, to systems of supplier auditing and evaluation. Frequently, they also involve pressure groups or government agencies as advisers or even managers of the programme.

For example, the WWF 95 Plus Group is a coalition between the pressure group Worldwide Fund for Nature and more than seventy companies involved in the production and sale of wood, paper, and pulp products in the UK. The group was set up to improve and certify forest management practices at source, and works by leveraging the combined buying power of major retailers such as B&Q, Body Shop, Boots, Sainsbury, and Tesco to create an impetus for change throughout industry, from forest to final consumer (see Crane 1998*b*). Alliances such as these are examples of the stakeholder partnership approach to business ethics management that we introduced in Chapter 5 (156–162). We will look at these in more depth when we discuss pressure groups in more detail in Chapter 10.

Strategies of intra-business regulation

There appear to be two main ways in which firms can effect regulation through the supply chain (see Winstanley et al. 2002):

• **Disengagement:** this involves the setting of clear standards for suppliers (e.g. a code of conduct) coupled with a means for assessing compliance with those standards (such as an ethics audit). Failure to meet standards in the short to medium term will result in disengagement by the company in order to do business elsewhere. Reebok's 'zero tolerance' policy on child labour is illustrative of this approach (Winstanley et al. 2002).

• **Engagement:** this too involves setting standards and compliance procedures, but tends to rely on longer-term 'aims' together with incremental 'targets' in order to foster a step-by-step approach to improving standards. Here, the firm is likely to work with their suppliers to achieve improvements, as illustrated by the approach of the Dutch clothing retailer C&A in **Ethics in Action 9.2**.

Whichever strategy an organization adopts, an ethics code or supplier code of conduct is likely to play an important role. We saw in Chapter 5 (148–156) that there were four types of codes, any of which might be used in this context. This includes corporate codes (such as the one used by C&A in **Ethics in Action 9.2**), a professional code (such as the UK Institute of Purchasing code of conduct in **Figure 9.2**), industry codes (e.g. the Apparel Industry Partnership's Workplace Code of Conduct—see van Tulder and Kolk 2001), or a programme code (such as the WWF 95 Plus Group code mentioned above).

However, we also noted in Chapter 5 that simply having a code was insufficient for ensuring ethical behaviour. According to Emmelhainz and Adams (1999), to be successful in practice, ethical sourcing of this kind actually requires three things:

• A workable code of conduct;

• A system of monitoring supplier compliance with the code;

• Enforcement policies which establish the penalties for violation.

Whilst many companies have been relatively quick to introduce supplier codes of conduct, the introduction of effective monitoring and enforcement has proved to be less common (Emmelhainz and Adams 1999). This no doubt is at least partially due to the complexity and expense of doing so. However, one area where a more comprehensive system has been successfully introduced is in the fair trade industry.

Fair trade

So far, we have discussed ethical sourcing as a form of regulation through the supply chain. This tends to give the impression that ethical sourcing is always a way of controlling suppliers. However, in some cases, ethical sourcing can actually be a way of protecting or rewarding certain suppliers that are seen to be socially beneficial in some way. For example, we saw earlier in the chapter (326) how the so-called 'banana wars' represented an attempt to apply a form of ethical sourcing to protect the interests of Caribbean farmers. Similarly, the Body Shop has for some years operated a 'Trade Not Aid' programme which seeks to assist small-scale, indigenous communities in enhancing their standard of living through supposedly 'fair' supply contracts with the retailer.

Approaches to ethical sourcing that seek to improve the prospects of suppliers are usually referred to as *fair trade*. Many of the growers for products such as coffee, tea, and cocoa live in poverty, and are faced with poor working conditions, exploitation, and limited health, safety, and environmental protection (McIntosh et al. 1998). At the heart of this problem are international commodity markets, which often set prices that fail to provide the growers even with a living wage. The aim of the fair trade movement is to foster the protection

Ethics in Action 9.2

An unfashionable approach to ethical sourcing at C&A?

For many years, the Dutch high street clothing store C&A was associated with no-nonsense, practical clothing at reasonable prices. This formula made the store a favourite with cost-conscious consumers, but its staid image could sometimes make it unpopular with trendy teenagers and young people. As a result, many 20- and 30-something adults across Europe still bear the emotional scars from their childhood of being dragged around their local C&A store by their mothers in search of a nice new jacket or pair of trousers that could ultimately put them at risk of ridicule by their friends!

During the 1990s, the firm suffered a loss of market share in a number of its European markets, especially in the UK and Germany. This prompted C&A to implement a fairly drastic retrenchment strategy that saw it downsize its operations and pull out of the UK altogether in 2001. However, it retained a strong presence in the rest of Europe, with 577 stores still operating in twelve countries, and it remains the Netherlands' biggest clothes retailer.

While things have not been going entirely smoothly for C&A commercially, they have, perhaps surprisingly, become one of the European clothing retailers most respected for their sourcing ethics. Following a media exposé revealing the use of child labour in a factory supplying C&A merchandise in 1995, the company, guided by its family owners the Brenninkmeijers, introduced a code of conduct for suppliers in 1996. The Code of Conduct for the Supply of Merchandise requires suppliers to respect the ethical standards of C&A in the context of their own particular culture. Specifically, the code lays out detailed requirements for labour conditions, covering issues such as child labour, wages, safety standards, and forced labour.

What is unusual about the C&A approach is that rather than either conducting their own in-house auditing, or contracting a third party auditor such as PriceWaterhouseCoopers, the firm accompanied the introduction of the code with the founding of a stand-alone auditing organization of its own named SOCAM (Service Organization for Compliance Audit Management). Although SOCAM is funded by C&A (with a budget of approximately €3m), it is independent of C&A's commercial activities and is accountable only to the C&A board. With a staff of some thirteen employees, SOCAM can focus exclusively on auditing with the full authority to monitor the standards defined by the code.

Each year SOCAM demands information about the location of all production units used by C&A's almost 1,300 suppliers. The organization makes over 1,000 unannounced visits to audit employment conditions, paying particular attention to suppliers in countries with a poor reputation for labour standards. Following visits, any suppliers found in breach of the code are likely to be approached directly by SOCAM to discuss problems. All information is treated as confidential in order to build relationships of trust between SOCAM and suppliers. However, SOCAM can make recommendations to C&A's sourcing department based on their findings. These recommendations can include suggestions to send warning letters, cancellation of orders, or suspension of business pending the introduction of a corrective plan.

As the results for 1999 show, SOCAM is an auditor with teeth. Following unannounced visits to 1,459 production facilities, almost a full two-thirds showed shortcomings. Eight hundred letters were sent out asking suppliers to improve and C&A stopped doing business with forty-nine suppliers—

twenty-eight of which were subsequently reinstated following the acceptance of a corrective plan. Such figures show the very real problems of ensuring acceptable labour standards in the textiles industry, even when firms implement codes of conduct and auditing procedures.

The establishment of SOCAM is seen by many as a positive step in the right direction. One 2000 report for example showed that among high street clothing retailers in the UK (a market it has now pulled out of), C&A was the first to introduce a code of conduct, and was the only firm at the time to monitor compliance. However, the firm still faces criticism from a number of NGOs, especially for failing to introduce truly independent auditing. However, while such a move could improve the firm's reputation with some stakeholders, it might also harm the fragile relationships of trust, transparency, and reliability that SOCAM has been able to build with suppliers. Moreover, independent auditing could also include costs at a time when C&A is struggling financially. As the recent decision by the firm to halt ISO 14001 environmental certification in several European countries attests, the burden of cost imposed by accreditation programmes can sharply focus attention on appropriate priorities when times are hard.

SOURCES

BBC (2001). 'C&A closes UK doors for the last time'. BBC News On-line, 31 May.
Graafland, J. J. (2002). 'Sourcing ethics in the textile sector: the case of C&A'. *Business Ethics: A European Review*, 11/3: 282–94.

■ Think theory

Think about the problems of conflict of interest discussed in this chapter with respect to C&A's relationship with SOCAM. To what extent do you consider the approach adopted by C&A to be an adequate response to conflict of interest problems in dealing with SOCAM as a supplier of auditing services?

and empowerment of growers as well as to encourage community development by guaranteeing minimum prices and conditions (Brown 1993). This is effected through the application, monitoring, and enforcement of a fair trade supply agreement and code of conduct typically verified by an independent social auditing system operated by a national body such as the FairTrade Foundation (in the UK), Max Havelaar (in The Netherlands), or Reilun Kaupan (in Finland).

The systems put in place by these fair trade bodies ensure that whatever price the market may allocate to goods such as cocoa and tea, the growers involved are guaranteed a minimum price by the purchaser. As a result, growers are prevented from sinking into poverty at the whim of commodity markets. Products such as filter coffee, chocolate bars, and bananas sourced and produced according to the strict fair trade conditions are permitted to use a fair trade label, indicating to consumers that growers have received a fair price and been afforded decent conditions and community support. Many growers involved in the fair trade system organize into local co-ops in order to ensure that the benefits are shared appropriately and so that community development can be promoted (Brown 1993).

The fair trade movement initially operated through charitable organizations such as Oxfam and alternative trade organizations (ATOs) such as Traidcraft. For a number of years now, certain fair trade products have also been sold through mainstream supermarkets (Strong 1997), although firms such as the Body Shop and others have also introduced their own operations outside the established international framework for fair trade accreditation. Moreover, in recent years there has been a move within the established fair trade movement away from its charity-supported background towards a more commercial position (Davies and Crane 2003). This has given rise to the emergence of private sector for-profit fair trade companies, such as the Day Chocolate Company, which markets the Dubble and Divine chocolate brands in the UK. This greater commercialization has been accompanied by a steady growth in penetration of fair trade products. For example, in Denmark where fair trade is relatively new, the net retail value of labelled products exceeds €8m, and market share for fair trade products such as coffee, tea, and bananas is about 2 per cent (**www.salam.dk**). In the UK, where fair trade has a longer history, the value of labelled products at the checkout is approaching €70m, compared with €4m in 1994—a staggering seventeen-fold increase. Fair trade ground coffee now has more than 7 per cent of the UK ground coffee market (**www.fairtrade.org.uk**).

Such successes of course can also have their drawbacks. The increasing commercialization of the fair trade movement could potentially put pressure on its ethical standards. Research by Davies and Crane (2003) suggests that the strict regulations, for instance of the national fair trade body in the UK, can effectively impose what they call a 'moral curtain' on ethical decision-making. This means that all activities in the early stages of the chain of supply tend to be regarded as virtually sacrosanct, whereas those on the other side of the moral curtain—marketing, sales, and retailing for example—are more vulnerable to ethically dubious practices. For the growers at least, then, the continued success of fair trade seems still to be providing a positive force for change—and even appears to be generating increasing interest from more mainstream industry players.

■ **Think theory**

Fair trade is presented as a fairer means of doing business—benefits are distributed more equally, and basic rights are protected. However, some critics have argued that such schemes might be deemed unethical. What arguments might there be against fair trade practices and which theoretical bases do you think they are derived from?

Sustainability and business relationships: towards industrial ecosystems?

Finally, then, we need to look at the corporation's relationships with other companies in the context of sustainability. Approaches such as **fair trade** are certainly one way in which notions of sustainability can be addressed through business–business relationships. The mixture of economic, social, and environmental goals associated with fair trade programmes is very much within the spirit of sustainability thinking. For example, fair trade standards stipulate that traders must:

- Pay a price to producers that covers the costs of sustainable production and living;
- Pay a 'premium' that producers can invest in development;
- Make partial advance payments when requested by producers;
- Sign contracts that allow for long-term planning and sustainable production practices.[3]

Fair trade is therefore concerned with more than just the fairness of exchange relationships, in a narrow economic sense. Fair trade, though, still only considers one type of exchange between a relatively small set of businesses. A somewhat different, and perhaps even greater, challenge posed by sustainability for intra-firm relationships concerns the exchange of various kinds of resources between a wider community of organizations.

From supply chains to supply loops

As we proposed in Chapter 1 (20–26), sustainability encourages us to think about the long-term maintenance of systems, raising, among other things, issues of resource efficiency and waste minimization. In the previous chapter (294), we introduced the notion of product recapture—i.e. bringing 'waste' products back into the supply chain as resources—as a way of developing more sustainable consumption. As we suggested, such a development shifts our thinking about supply relationships away from a linear view towards a more circular perspective. If wastes are to be recaptured and brought back into productive use, we need to think not of supply chains, but of **supply loops** that create a circular flow of resources (we illustrated this in **Figure 8.6** in the last chapter; 295). To their proponents, such closed loop models have been promoted as not only waste reducing, but even eliminating the very concept of waste (Lovins et al. 1999).

   Using supply loops to increase resource efficiency and minimize waste places a considerably larger burden on inter-firm relationships than is the case with more traditional modes of supply. Effective stewardship of a product requires attention throughout its entire life cycle, thus necessitating active collaboration between value chain participants (Roy and Whelan 1992). To effect ongoing product recapture, reuse, recycling, and remanufacture, firms have to communicate, exchange information, develop joint proposals, co-design, and conclude stable exchange relationships. For example, the EU End of Life Vehicle Directive, signed in September 2000, will make car makers responsible for the disposal of all end of life vehicles they subsequently produce. It also stipulates that car makers must reuse or recover 85 per cent of cars by weight, and that at least 80 per cent of that weight must be reused or recycled. Such a proposal poses a significant headache for car supply chains, and is ultimately likely to cost the industry some €45bn. However, by integrating considerations about recovery and recycling into the design stage of cars, the burden of the legislation can be reduced. For instance, over 80 per cent of the Smart Car is designed for recyclability, making recovery much less costly.

---

[3] See **www.fairtrade.org.uk**.

Industrial ecosystems

Supply loops begin to shift our way of conceiving organizations away from an atomistic view, where each organization is seen as a separate entity with its own inputs and outputs, towards a more system-oriented view, where groups of firms are seen as interdependent entities that share resources and produce a shared environmental burden. Sustainability urges us to take such thinking still further though. Taken beyond the context of a single product supply and recapture loop, we can begin to also conceive of wider communities of organizations bound by interdependence of all kinds of resources and wastes. These are called **industrial ecosystems** (Allenby 1993).

According to Paul Shrivastava (1995), the concept of industrial ecosystems parallels that of natural ecosystems: just as natural ecosystems comprise a balanced network of interdependent organisms and their environments which feed off each other and give and take resources of each other to maintain equilibrium and survive, so too can businesses use each other's waste and by-products to minimize the use of natural resources.

Shrivastava (1995) uses the example of a much-cited network of companies in Kalundborg in Denmark to illustrate the concept of an industrial ecosystem (see **Figure 9.5**). It consists of a power plant, an enzyme plant, a refinery, a chemical plant, a cement plant, a wallboard plant, and some farms. These different companies all use one another's wastes and by-products as raw materials, co-ordinating their use of energy, water, raw materials, and waste management. For example, instead of dumping it, the power plant sells its used steam to the enzyme plant and refinery, offloads its waste ash to the cement factory, and its surplus heat to the city for domestic heating. It also warms a fishery—which

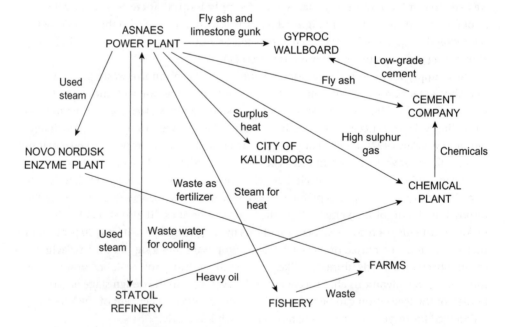

Figure 9.5. Kalundborg industrial ecosystem
Source: Shrivastava (1995).

in turn provides its waste to local farms as fertilizer. Additional fertilizer comes from the enzyme plant's waste.

Industrial ecosystems such as the one in Kalundborg are relatively rare, but there are numerous projects across and beyond Europe, often to be found in so-called 'eco-parks'. Perhaps the most complex and diverse example yet uncovered though is the 'industrial recycling network' in the Austrian province of Styria, which includes a network of exchanges among over fifty facilities.

Whether industrial ecosystems will ever become more than an interesting, perhaps even utopian, vision of how industry could be organized remains to be seen. Much will no doubt rest on local and national government support, encouragement, and planning. However with the general shift towards more collaborative business activity identified at the outset of this chapter, and the potential for considerable cost savings represented by closed loop business models, the conditions for further development appear to be reasonably good at present.

Summary

In this chapter, we have discussed the stake held by other companies in a corporation, focusing both on suppliers and the somewhat more contestable role of competitors. Our argument was that there were certainly issues of an ethical nature that arose in both groups of companies that went well beyond the legal protections of fair competition. These included: misuse of power, loyalty, preferential treatment, conflicts of interest, bribery, and negotiation with suppliers; and intelligence gathering, industrial espionage, dirty tricks, anti-competitive behaviour, and abuse of a dominant position in the context of competitors. Globalization appears to have substantially increased the scope of these problems, suggesting expanded responsibilities for corporations over their operations.

Despite these problems, developments in our understanding of the relationships between businesses appear to increasingly emphasize the importance of interdependence and co-operation. This is both in terms of our descriptive understandings (how businesses *do* relate) and our normative assessments (how they *should* relate). Nonetheless, ethical problems persist, and we are left to wonder if all parties can ever benefit equally from business interdependence. Many of the apparent problems are mainly raised simply by the highly competitive nature of contemporary industries and markets, particularly when the basic rules of the game do not favour all companies equally. Hence, it would appear that in the global economy, there will always be winners and losers—and justice, even within the so-called business 'community', can be elusive. Indeed, as the scope of business operations expands, the ethical problems actually become more wide-ranging and complex, and so the stakes inevitably increase.

That said, business relationships are also increasingly seen as one of the main levers for effecting greater attention to social and environmental problems. In this chapter, we have mainly looked at intra-organizational pressure through the supply chain. However, such self-regulation from business can also happen amongst competitors. For example, competing companies have often developed specific industry programmes aimed at addressing social or environmental issues, such as the chemical industry's Responsible Care Programme. Here, competing firms including ICI, Aventis, or Bayer via their global association ICCA (International Council of Chemical Associations) have banded together to develop a common response to environmental issues in the industry. Failure to meet specified standards or targets can result in pressure from competitors to comply, or even the issuing of sanctions. There are numerous other examples of self-regulation amongst groups of companies, ranging from those with little or no power to those that are able to wield considerable influence. The point is that government is certainly not the only source of business regulation, and that much informal and formal control actually takes place within the business community itself. As we shall see in the next chapter, we should not even stop there. In addition to government and business, we also need to think about another sector involved in business regulation, namely pressure groups, or what have become known as 'third sector' or 'civil society' organizations.

STUDY QUESTIONS

1 Compare the case for (a) suppliers and (b) competitors to be regarded as stakeholders of a corporation. How convincing are the arguments proposing that each group is a legitimate stakeholder?

2 What is a conflict of interest? Outline the conflicts of interest that might typically arise in firm–supplier relations.

3 How might we assess whether a gift received from a potential supplier is acceptable? Explain how this assessment might be affected by cultural context.

4 'Competition between rival firms is like a battle. You play to win and anything goes.' Critically assess this statement using examples.

5 What is ethical sourcing? What factors are likely to influence the success of ethical sourcing in changing supplier practices?

6 Explain the following:
   (a) The industrial network model;
   (b) Industrial ecosystems.
   What are the main differences between the two concepts?

RESEARCH EXERCISE

In Ethics in Action 9.2, we discussed the experiences of C&A in developing an ethical sourcing approach. Select another company in the clothing industry and do some research so that you can write your own ethics in action feature outlining the company's particular approach to ethical sourcing.

1 How does your selected company's approach vary from that of C&A?

2 Which company has the most ethical and/or appropriate system?

3 Which criteria are you using to compare the two approaches?

The spying game: allegations of industrial espionage at Unilever, Canal Plus, and Ericsson

This case looks at the experiences of industrial espionage among some leading European companies. The case provides the opportunity to discuss the appropriate boundaries of competitor intelligence gathering, and the problems of maintaining security in contemporary business.

Espionage is a word that brings to mind James Bond movies, or the spy stories of John Le Carré. But in recent years, espionage has also become widely associated with business practice. Industrial espionage is essentially a form of competitive intelligence gathering. With global competition intensifying, finding out about rivals' products and processes has become big business—and competitive intelligence gathering is increasingly seen as an important and largely acceptable form of market research. Although industry representatives, such as the Society for Competitive Intelligence Professionals, argue that industrial espionage, or spying, is both unethical and illegal, there is sometimes a fine line between the 'legitimate' tactics of competitive intelligence gathering and the 'illegitimate' practice of industrial espionage. In this case, we shall look at some examples where allegations of industrial espionage involving some of Europe's top companies have hit the headlines, and in so doing explore some of these grey areas between acceptable and unacceptable intelligence gathering practices.

Unilever falls victim to 'dumpster diving'

Cases of industrial espionage actually only very rarely make it to the attention of the world's media, not least because they often remain completely undiscovered. Probably the best-known incident of recent years involved the arch-rival branded-goods companies Procter & Gamble and Unilever. Known for their often fierce competition, the espionage scandal exploded in 2001 when it came to light that private investigators hired by Procter & Gamble to find out more about its competitor's hair care business in the USA had sifted through rubbish bins outside Unilever's offices.

The investigators succeeded in gathering piles of unshredded documents relating to Unilever's plans for the shampoo market. Although not necessarily illegal (different countries, and even different states, have differing rules on the legal status of rubbish), the practice commonly known as 'dumpster diving' broke Procter & Gamble's own internal guidelines on intelligence gathering. Alerted to the breach, Procter & Gamble bosses decided to come clean to Unilever about the supposedly 'rogue operators' having overstepped the mark.

Although the public details of the case remain sketchy, it has been suggested that it was the timing of the covert operations that would have been of particular concern to Unilever, coming as they did when the two companies were involved in an auction for the Clairol hair care brand—which Procter & Gamble ultimately won. Moreover, some industry insiders have expressed scepticism at the 'rogue operator' explanation offered by Procter & Gamble. For instance, it can be argued that companies who want to engage in dubious practices simply contract the work out to independent operators to 'do the dirty work' whilst providing 'plausible deniability' for the company in case the operation is exposed or goes wrong.

Following their own internal review of the breach, Unilever responded by threatening legal action against their rivals seeking a reported 'tens of millions of dollars' in restitution. The case was finally resolved when Procter & Gamble made an out of court settlement of some \$10m (€10m).

Canal Plus claims 'piracy' by rival

Another case of alleged espionage between bitter rivals that this time did end up with a massive $1bn (€1bn) lawsuit concerned the two huge media corporations News Corporation and Vivendi Universal, and their combative chief executives, Rupert Murdoch and Jean-Marie Messier. Although the two media tycoons were not named in the suit itself, the dispute centred on allegations made by Vivendi's subsidiary the French pay-TV company Canal Plus Technologies in March 2002 against NDS, a UK-based technology firm 80 per cent owned by News Corporation.

NDS is responsible for providing the encryption services used by satellite television companies to prevent people viewing programmes they haven't paid for. Canal Plus used a rival security technology, which it claimed NDS employees deliberately cracked, and then sent to hackers on the west coast of the USA, to be published on a website used by software pirates. According to Canal Plus, NDS employed a 'sophisticated and well-funded' team of scientists to crack the codes on smart cards that protected the company's pay TV systems. Following the publication of its smart card codes on the web, pirates were able to watch pay channels for free, depriving the French company of millions in lost revenues. The failed UK company ITV Digital, a user of Canal Plus cards, also blamed such piracy for the loss of some £100m (€150m) revenue, which ultimately contributed to the firm's collapse in 2002.

The case, one among many suits and counter-suits in the ultra-competitive digital TV industry, also underlines the murky world of anti-piracy. NDS, for example, is known to have financially supported a UK hackers' website, supposedly to attract illegal counterfeiters in order to prosecute them. Similarly, 'reverse engineering' of competitors' products in order to unravel the technology behind them is common practice in this and other high tech industries. However, NDS vehemently refuted the allegation that it was involved in any way in actually sending the codes to pirates or placing them on hackers' websites. As the company's chief executive claimed, the allegations were 'outrageous and baseless' and merely served to cover up Canal Plus's 'inferior' technology and 'poor performance'.

At the time of writing, the case hadn't actually reached the courts—and increasingly looked like it might not. Whilst NDS revealed that it had already spent over €2m in legal costs fighting the lawsuit, just in the first three months, it had also subsequently been presented with a lawsuit by another rival, Echostar Communications, based on similar allegations. However, in a surprise twist, in June 2002 Canal Plus suspended the lawsuit, and looked set to drop it completely. The move came as part of a deal between the two parent companies Vivendi and News Corporation that was set to see the latter take over an Italian pay television company from Canal Plus for €1bn.

Ericsson involved in spy scandal

If the two previous cases illustrated the tensions caused by intense competition between rivals, our final example shows that industrial espionage can also escalate to national security concerns.

Ericsson, the Swedish telecommunications company best known for its mobile phones, was the surprise subject of a major diplomatic incident in 2002. What many people probably don't know about Ericsson is that in addition to being one of the leading suppliers of mobile phones, it is also involved in developing highly sophisticated radar and missile guidance systems for Sweden's Gripen fighter plane, the country's main strike aircraft.

The events surrounded the alleged leaking of company information from Ericsson to a foreign intelligence service. Two Ericsson employees and one former employee were taken into custody suspected of passing on secret documents, and two further employees were suspended on suspicion of breaking company security rules. However, the employees were not particularly senior, and the company was quick to suggest that they had been caught quickly before a serious security breach could have occurred.

Nonetheless, the implications certainly became more serious when Sweden expelled two Russian diplomats who were said to be 'directly linked' to the industrial espionage case at Ericsson. Although the Swedish authorities and Ericsson were reluctant to disclose too many details, such developments gave clear indication that they believed that the Ericsson employees had been passing sensitive information to the Russians. Incensed at the expulsions, the Russians subsequently announced tit-for-tat expulsions of two Swedish diplomats, drawing accusations from Stockholm that they were returning to 'Soviet-era foreign policy'. Whichever way you look at it, then, Ericsson had clearly got itself embroiled in a case of industrial espionage that not only threatened its own reputation for information security, but even had major implications for diplomatic relations.

Questions

1 What are the main ethical issues raised by each case? Are these issues the same or different in each case? Why?

2 What role does the law play in each of these cases?

3 What level of competitive intelligence gathering is acceptable for:

    (a) Procter & Gamble

    (b) NDS

4 To what extent is it possible to safeguard against the practices revealed here? How would you advise the managers of Unilever, Canal Plus, and Ericsson to protect against further acts of espionage?

Sources

Anon. (2002a). 'Echostar begins piracy lawsuit against NDS'. *Independent*, 1 Oct.: 22.

—— (2002b). 'Two Ericsson spy case suspects freed from custody'. **www.reuters.com**, 5 Dec.

Burns, J. (2002). 'Bribes and trash archaeology'. *Financial Times*, 11 Apr.: 5.

Cassey, J. (2002). 'Top Murdoch lawyer to fight hacking claim'. *The Guardian*, 18 Mar.: 7.

Edgecliffe-Johnson, A. (2001). 'P&G admits spying on Unilever'. *Financial Times*, 31 Aug.: 17.

Godson, R. (2002). 'TV deal to end piracy action'. *Sunday Times*, 9 June.

Osborn, A. (2002). 'Sweden expels Russian jet "spies"'. *Guardian*, 12 Nov.

Skapinker, M., and Edgecliffe-Johnson, A. (2001). 'Tricks of the corporate spying game'. *Financial Times*, 1 Sept.: 9.

Snoddy, R. (2002). 'Personal friction at heart of media battle'. *The Times*, 20 Mar.

10

Civil Society and Business Ethics

In this chapter we will:

- Show how the role played by various types of civil society organizations in society constitutes them as important stakeholders of corporations, both directly and indirectly.

- Examine the tactics that such groups might employ towards corporations to achieve their purposes, as well as the ethical problems and issues that typically accompany civil society action.

- Discuss the impacts of globalization on the nature and extent of the role played by civil society towards corporations.

- Discuss the appropriate relationships between business and civil society, identifying a significant shift from a conflictual mode of engagement to a more collaborative approach.

- Assess the role of civil society in providing for enhanced corporate sustainability.

Introduction: what is civil society?

So far in this book, we have looked at business ethics in relation to the corporation's four main economic stakeholders—i.e. those vital constituencies that provide firms with the resources they need merely to exist. Shareholders supply capital, employees provide labour, consumers provide income, and suppliers provide the resources necessary to produce products and services. In the next two chapters we shall broaden our scope to consider other stakeholders outside the immediate economic realm of the corporation—in this chapter, civil society, and in the next, government. These constituencies, as we shall see, also have important stakes in the corporation, and various ethical problems and issues can arise in the corporation's dealings with such actors.

To some readers though, the notion of civil society might be unfamiliar. Although **civil society** as a concept has long been in use, it has only returned to popular use in the last decade or so (Bendell 2000c; Reece 2001). Previous to this resurgence, social and political theorists tended to believe that we lived in a two-sector world, comprising the market or economic sector (business) and the state sector (government). Therefore, it was assumed

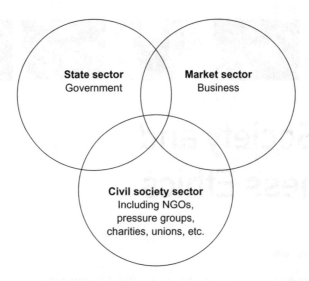

Figure 10.1. Civil society as the 'third sector'

that issues such as social welfare and environmental protection would be looked after either through labour and product markets, state provision, or else corporate philanthropy. More recently, though, considerable attention has focused on the role of other types of organizations such as pressure groups, charities, non-government organizations (NGOs), local community groups, religious organizations, etc. in attending to these issues. There are a number of reasons to explain this renewed attention, including a failure of the state or corporations to ensure effective provision of social welfare, and a disillusionment among certain sectors of the public that the traditional two-sector institutions actively listened to and served their interests (see Beck 1992).

This has opened up space to consider a third type of institutional actor in society, namely what has become known as civil society. As such, civil society is often said to comprise a **third sector** after the market and the state. This is illustrated in **Figure 10.1**. As a third sector, civil society is usually regarded to be a counterbalance to the state (and more recently also to business) guarding against the abuse of power and ensuring that the people's best interests are served (Reece 2001). Hence, the supposed role of civil society is to ensure a degree of social and political pluralism that provides for a more civilized society.

Civil society is made concrete and meaningful for corporations through specific **civil society organizations** (CSOs). Only very rarely do corporations actually deal with individual citizens who are not their workers or customers. It is therefore CSOs as the tangible manifestation of civil society that we shall mainly be concerned with in this chapter. However, there is considerable confusion, contradiction, and overlap in the definition of CSOs and related organizational types such as NGOs, pressure groups, and the like (McIntosh and Thomas 2002). We shall use CSO as an umbrella term for the different types of organization that might be considered to be civil society actors. Although NGOs tend to be the most visible actors in the literature dealing with business and civil society, organizations such as labour unions, consumer associations, religious groups, community groups, etc. are also important CSOs, yet are typically not thought of as NGOs.

Essentially, then, we are using the term CSO to describe all of these voluntary, not-for-profit bodies outside business and government that represent a particular group or cause which brings them into contact with corporations. As such, for the sake of simplicity we might reasonably suggest the following basic definition:[1]

> Civil society organizations include a plethora of pressure groups, non-governmental organizations, charities, religious groups, and other actors that are neither business nor government organizations, but which are involved in the promotion of certain interests, causes, and/or goals.

Clearly, there are any number of interests, causes, and goals that CSOs might be involved with, from environmental protection, to animal rights, social welfare, regeneration, child protection, development, famine relief, or health promotion—all of which, it would appear, are likely to pertain to business ethics in some way.

Many of the larger international CSOs are at least as well known as large multinational corporations: Greenpeace, Friends of the Earth, WWF, Amnesty International, and Oxfam for example are just some of the most widely recognized civil society organizations. However, although many of us may only be aware of little more than a handful of the major CSO actors, the number and scope of CSOs is actually quite staggering. For example, in the USA alone, there are by some estimates around two million domestic NGOs (*The Economist* 2000), whilst in the UK over 180,000 registered 'non-governmental charities' were identified in 1998 (Bendell 2000c). These can range from local neighbourhood associations and church groups to powerful national level lobbying groups. At the international level too, there has been an explosion of CSOs working across borders on issues as diverse as climate protection, international development, and anti-globalization. For example, a 1995 UN report suggested that nearly 29,000 international NGOs existed (*The Economist* 2000), and this figure is now estimated to be about 50,000 (McIntosh and Thomas 2002). Indeed, overall estimations of the scale of NGO activity propose something like €1 trillion in trade worldwide, coupled with the employment of over nineteen million people across the globe (Salamon et al. 1999).

It is evident then that there is an enormous heterogeneity and diversity amongst these thousands of CSOs. Not only might they be different in terms of the issues they focus on and their scope of operations, but they also take different forms and structures and are involved in a varied mixture of activities. **Figure 10.2** illustrates this breadth of diversity in more detail.

In this chapter, we shall examine the relationships that CSOs have with corporations, exploring the specific stake that they have and the ways in which they seek to influence corporate action. Whether through media campaigns, boycotts, or actively working together with corporations and governments, it is clear that now, perhaps more than ever, CSOs have a vital role to play in enhancing and ensuring ethical behaviour in business. Indeed, as we shall see as the chapter progresses, the global reach of many CSOs coupled with their

[1] For a further look at some of this definitional debate, see Candler (2000).

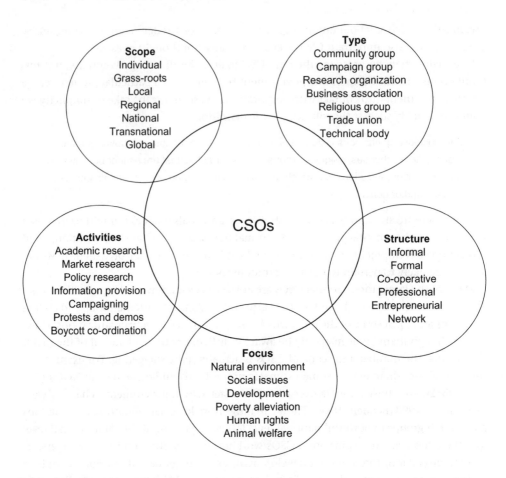

Figure 10.2. Diversity in CSO characteristics

Source: Adapted from McIntosh and Thomas (2002: 31).

successes in working with businesses and governments has meant that they are now often seen as an integral part of the global governance regime that shapes and regulates corporate practice.

Civil society organizations as stakeholders

It is clear that CSOs of one sort or another have long been involved in the activities of corporations. Whether it is receiving corporate donations, organizing employee resistance to labour practices, leading consumer boycotts of particular products, or more violent action such as firebombing animal testing laboratories, various CSOs have over the years been very much involved in the business ethics field. We need only look at some of the cases covered in this book, from the battles of McDonald's with Jose Bové's farmer's union, to Nestlé's tussles with Baby Milk Action, and Shell's problems with Greenpeace and Ogoni community groups, to see that CSOs can certainly affect, or be affected by, the performance of a corporation.

In many respects, though, the stake held by CSOs is quite different from that held by other stakeholder groups. Employees, consumers, or shareholders for example all contribute something directly to the corporation in the form of labour, income, and capital. Likewise, as we will see in the next chapter, governments provide corporations with a licence to operate in a particular territory.

CSOs on the other hand only very rarely contribute any resources directly to corporations. Hence, while consumers may have been able to retract their purchases of Shell petrol if they disagreed with the company's decision to dump the Brent Spar oil platform, Greenpeace had nothing tangible to retract since it did not directly contribute to the company in the first place. However, this is not to say that Greenpeace was not a stakeholder in this situation. As an organization with a mission to protect the environment on behalf of its members, Greenpeace certainly did have a stake in the decision contemplated by Shell. And as the actor organizing the consumer boycott and other action against Shell, Greenpeace had an important role to play on behalf of those consumers and other citizens who disagreed with Shell's decision.

Looking at it this way, the stake held by CSOs is largely one of **representing the interests of individual stakeholders**. By organizing together into a CSO, individual stakeholders of whatever kind can gain greater voice and influence than they have alone. If a local resident of Heathrow wanted to voice their concern about the development of a new runway, they would have little effect alone. However, by joining a local association, or even a national or international lobby group dedicated to preventing air and noise pollution from air traffic, they would be much more likely to have their views heard. Similarly, we can also see this illustrated by trade unions and other labour organizations: they represent the interests of individual employee stakeholders, both inside the workplace and on the political stage.

If we look at the Shell–Greenpeace situation another way, though, a slightly different form of representation effected by CSOs becomes evident. Rather than its members, or the wider public, Greenpeace could be argued to be representing the environment itself. As a non-human entity, the environment clearly cannot speak for itself—and therefore Greenpeace and other CSOs step in essentially as proxy stakeholders. A similar case can be made for animal welfare CSOs such as the RSPCA (Royal Society for the Protection of Animals) or PETA (People for the Ethical Treatment of Animals). Hence another potential CSO role is **representing the interests of non-human stakeholders**.

Whichever of these two ways of conceptualizing the stakeholder role of CSOs is relevant, it is clear that the stake of CSOs is *indirect* and *representative*. CSOs are mainly delineated as stakeholders on the grounds that they represent some broader if less tangible constituency of civil society itself. Corporations tend not to deal with civil society as a group of innumerable individual citizens, but as a more discrete collection of representative CSOs.

The literature on pressure groups suggests that, depending on who exactly they are representing, CSOs tend as a result to fall into two main types (see Smith 1990: 105–13; Whawell 1998), summarized in **Figure 10.3**:

	Sectional groups	Promotional groups
Membership	Closed	Open
Represent	Specific section of society	Issues or causes
Aims	Self-interest	Social goals
Traditional status	Insider	Outsider
Main approach	Consultation	Argument
Pressure exerted through	Threat of withdrawal	Mass media publicity

Figure 10.3. Different types of CSOs

• **Sectional groups** include trade unions, professional associations, student bodies, neighbourhood groups, parent associations, etc. They are member based and primarily seek to represent the interests of their members (who are deemed to be a particular 'section' of society). The membership of sectional CSOs is only open to those fulfilling certain objective criteria that put them within the specific section to be represented, e.g. that they are part of a particular workplace, profession, or geographical region. The CSO will above all else pursue the self-interest of this membership.

• **Promotional groups** in contrast are focused on promoting specific causes or issues. Environmental groups, anti-smoking groups, and pro-life groups are all examples of promotional CSOs. These organizations represent those with a common ideology or shared attitudes about an issue. Membership is usually open to all, although only those with similar subjective viewpoints are effectively represented. These groups are less concerned with the self-interest of their members and more focused on seeking to achieve wider social aims.

Traditionally, sectional groups have been said to enjoy insider status whilst promotional groups have largely been outsiders (Whawell 1998). What this means is that because sectional groups are regarded as the legitimate representative of a specific, identifiable constituency—say, electricians, farmers, Muslims, or students—their views are actively solicited (or at least readily accepted as legitimate) on issues relevant to the constituency. For example, if the government were developing agricultural policies, then it would typically engage in some kind of consultation with farming unions.

Promotional groups, however, have tended to have less easy access to governmental or corporate policy-making. Since they do not represent a readily identifiable constituency, it is not obvious whom exactly they are speaking for. As a result, promotional groups have tended to need to mobilize mass public opinion before they are heard or involved in any kind of decision-making. For this reason, promotional groups have needed to very actively and visibly promote the issues they are concerned with (hence the label promotional group). This has typically involved them in articulating vigorous arguments, demonstrations, and/or provocative media stunts in order to get their message across. One need only think of Greenpeace's dramatic confrontations over the years with its adversaries in the whaling, oil, and nuclear industries to see the importance of a provocative and media-friendly argument to many promotional groups.

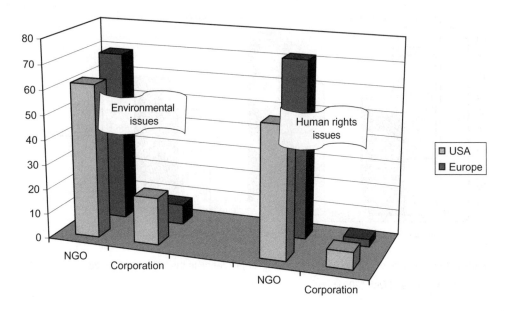

Figure 10.4. Perceived credibility of corporations and NGOs regarding specific issues
Source: Wootliff and Deri (2001).

More recently, the various successes of promotional CSOs such as Greenpeace, Amnesty, WWF, Friends of the Earth, etc. in establishing themselves as credible and legitimate contributors to major social and environmental debates in society have given them much more of an insider status than they were once afforded (Whawell 1998). As Wootliff and Deri (2001) show, NGOs and pressure groups such as these have begun to enjoy considerably more trust from the public than business, the government, or the media on issues related to the environment, human rights, health, and social policy (see **Figure 10.4**). Their evidence also suggests that this is particularly the case in Europe where, in marked contrast to the USA, CSOs are now seen in a more favourable light than corporations overall. For example, whilst, in the USA, 44 per cent of opinion leaders were found to trust business to do what is right over government (27 per cent) and NGOs (26 per cent), in Europe this was reversed with NGOs (48 per cent) apparently enjoying more trust than government (36 per cent) or business (32 per cent) (see Wootliff and Deri 2001). However, this picture also varies between particular organizations and between particular countries in Europe. For example, French opinion leaders appear to have a far more favourable view of NGOs (55 per cent) than do their counterparts in the UK (26 per cent). **Figures 10.5, 10.6**, and **10.7** illustrate this picture in more detail with further results from Wootliff and Deri's (2001) survey.

Although survey evidence of this type—based on the opinions of relatively small samples of key informants—does not provide conclusive evidence, the favourability and trust apparently enjoyed by CSOs on certain issues, particularly in Europe, gives a clear indication that they demand some degree of attention from corporations. In the past, this attention was typically gained through a situation of often quite intense conflict—CSOs

CONTEXTUALIZING BUSINESS ETHICS

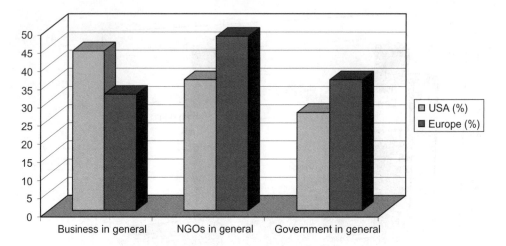

Figure 10.5. Degree of trust in different types of organization in the USA and Europe
Source: Wootliff and Deri (2001).

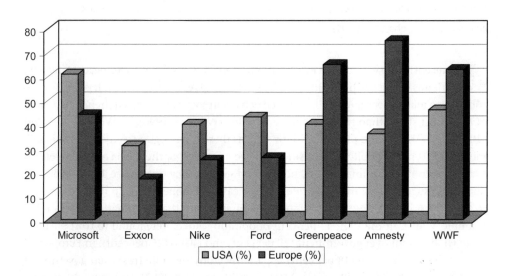

Figure 10.6. Degree of trust in specific organizations in the USA and Europe
Source: Wootliff and Deri (2001).

would exert pressure on companies through strikes, boycotts, demonstrations, media campaigns, etc. in order to achieve their ends. Whilst this was particularly true of promotional groups, this was often the case even with sectional groups such as unions whose most potent weapon has often been the threat of disruption and withdrawal. More recently, though, as the insider status of CSOs has expanded to include previous adversaries of corporations, we have also seen a move towards a more consensual and collaborative approach

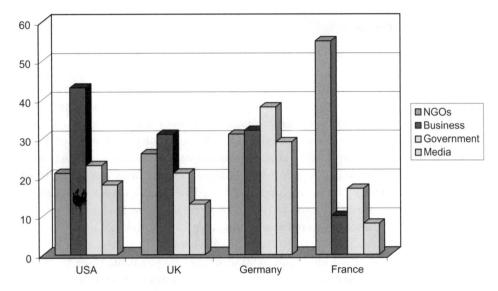

Figure 10.7. Favourability differences between countries

Source: Wootliff and Deri (2001).

in business–CSO relations (Hartman and Stafford 1997; Murphy and Bendell 1997)—a point we first introduced in Chapter 5 (156–162) and one that we shall develop further later on in this chapter.

It is clear then that in many ways they have become just as much an accepted part of the debate over business ethics as other more conventional 'economic' or 'primary' stakeholders. Although their claim is often an indirect one, being as it is a claim to represent individual stakeholders or even causes themselves, it would be hard to refute the argument that CSOs are legitimate claimants of stakeholder status—albeit less clear-cut ones. Indeed, questions of exactly *which* CSOs are legitimate stakeholders of a corporation, and *how* exactly they should go about claiming or exercising their stake, are certainly not straightforward. As we shall now see, such questions are in fact at the root of a bundle of interrelated ethical problems and issues that underlie the emergence of CSOs as significant stakeholders in the corporation.

Ethical issues and CSOs

Given the growing importance of CSOs to the business ethics field, it is perhaps surprising that only very limited attention has yet been paid in the literature to the ethical issues surrounding corporate engagement with them. However, there are a number of significant issues that arise from the somewhat less tangible stake held by CSOs. Chief among these are the decisions by corporations about which CSOs might be recognized as worthy of attention, the tactics used by CSOs to gain attention, and the degree to which CSOs are genuinely representative of, and accountable to, their intended beneficiaries.

Recognizing CSO stakes

If we take any given corporation—say, BP—it is fairly straightforward to objectively determine who their consumers, suppliers, employees, shareholders, and competitors are. Once we acknowledge that inclusion within any of these groups confers some kind of stake in the company, it is a short step to very clearly defining who BP's main stakeholders are. With civil society stakeholders, however, this question is considerably more muddied. With BP's diverse interests in the energy sector, it is possible to think of hundreds, probably even thousands of CSOs that might potentially claim a stake in the company's activities. From Azerbaijan educational groups, to British transport organizations, to Saharan desert communities, or fishing community groups in Trinidad, BP has been involved in debates about its operations with an extensive array of CSOs across the globe. But how does a company such as BP determine which of these groups are legitimate stakeholders and which are not? And who is to determine legitimacy here? Just because, hypothetically speaking, BP may decide that a radical Inuit land rights group has no legitimate cause to pursue regarding the company's drilling operations in Alaska, does this necessarily mean that it is not a stakeholder?

These are taxing problems to resolve, but they go to the heart of what it means to be a stakeholder. If we look back to Chapter 5 (156–162) when we discussed how corporations might manage their stakeholders, we suggested that one way of assessing which stakeholders were worthy of attention that was popular in the strategy literature was the *instrumental* approach. Here, the *relative salience* of stakeholders would be assessed according to, for example, their power, influence, and urgency (Mitchell et al. 1997). However, we also suggested that such an approach ignores the fact that even though some stakeholders might lack much salience to the corporation, they might reasonably claim to have an *ethical right* to be involved in a particular decision or process (Hummels 1998).

What this comes down to is that in any given company (or any other organization for that matter), the definition of 'who our stakeholders are' is not simply a matter of objective observation. Rather, this decision is influenced by the *subjective interpretations* of managers and their value judgements of what constitutes a legitimate claim (Fineman and Clarke 1996). This issue is particularly pronounced in the case of promotional CSOs, since they cannot usually call on any specific constituency as the source of their inherent rights to claim stakeholder status. Of course, many of these groups tend to **'self-declare'** themselves as stakeholders in a particular issue (Wheeler et al. 2002). This they accomplish by issuing statements, launching campaigns, or initiating some kind of action towards the corporation. For example, in 2002 Coca-Cola suddenly found itself confronted by an international coalition of AIDS activists and CSOs, including ACT UP, the European AIDS Treatment Group, and the Thai Network of People Living with HIV (TNP+), who all self-declared themselves as stakeholders in demanding that Coca-Cola provide free medical treatment for its workers living with AIDS.

Self-declaring does not however necessarily lead to *recognition*. For instance, Wheeler et al. (2002) illustrate how, for a number of years, Shell failed to recognize the CSO called the Movement for the Survival of the Ogoni People (MOSOP) as a legitimate stakeholder in its Nigerian operations. Initially the company referred to 'the Ogoni community' in its literature on the issue without identifying specific stakeholder CSOs. Then as the situation intensified, and MOSOP's figurehead Ken Saro-Wiwa starting gaining greater attention, Shell sought to represent MOSOP as illegitimate, and questioned the CSO's authority to represent the Ogoni. Instead the company began dealing with what became known as 'Shell Chiefs'. These were conservative Ogoni leaders that the company found more compliant, but who had little mandate to represent the majority of the Ogoni. As Wheeler et al. (2002) show, it was only when Saro-Wiwa and MOSOP gained third party legitimization through international NGOs such as Amnesty International and Greenpeace that MOSOP was granted stakeholder status by Shell. By this time, however, a gulf had opened up between the company and the Ogoni nation in general (and MOSOP in particular), leading to persistent problems in achieving subsequent reconciliation. This is not to say that MOSOP was the only CSO that Shell should or could have recognized as a stakeholder in Ogoniland, but it does illustrate quite powerfully some of the complexities involved in identifying CSOs as stakeholders.

So the question remains: which CSOs should corporations recognize as legitimate stakeholders? On the one side, there is certainly a case for arguing that companies cannot be expected to listen and engage with every organization that decides to take issue with their policies. Simon Zadek (2001: 156), the founder of the influential Institute of Social and Ethical AccountAbility, for example, reports the following discussion with one exasperated British utility manager:

As a water utility we are a major landowner. We have been approached by representatives from the anti-hunting league and asked to stop renting out a parcel of land for use by sports-hunters. To be honest, we don't particularly have a corporate view on hunting, and do not particularly want to have one. Where does this all end? If there is a church but no mosque on our land, will we eventually have to have a view on God?

However, even though many CSOs and their demands may seem peripheral, illegitimate, or just simply unrelated to the corporate sphere of activity, this does not mean they can merely be ignored. As soon as a CSO starts to direct its attentions towards a corporation, the stakes begin to rise, and the potential impact on the corporation and its reputation becomes more hazardous. Whilst ignoring ostensibly 'irrelevant' CSOs and hoping they go away may be a typical corporate response to such 'irritants', it may have detrimental long-term consequences. Zadek (2001: 163) therefore goes so far as to say that 'it is simply not really the company's choice who is and is not a stakeholder'. Clearly, as he suggests, the boundaries defining which CSOs can reasonably be defined as stakeholders are permeable and evolving rather than concrete and fixed.

Certainly, though, managers have to make important decisions as to how to best respond to CSO demands for inclusion, and where to draw the boundaries of their responsibilities to such groups (Zadek 2001). After all, there is usually only a limited allocation of time and resources available for managing relations with CSOs. At present, it would appear that there is typically, though not unsurprisingly, still a strong element of instrumental logic embedded in such decisions within corporations (Cragg and Greenbaum 2002). Firms are more likely to recognize and respond to CSOs that are known, trusted, and not too critical. Typically they will distinguish between campaigners who are regarded as 'reasonable' and those deemed 'unreasonable', and between those who are thought to have 'sound' or supposedly 'suspect' intentions in raising an issue (Fineman and Clarke 1996).

Normative stakeholder theory is not at its most helpful in determining specific boundaries of responsibility to civil society groups (Banerjee 2000). Although it may help us to identify that most affected groups have *some* claim on the firm, the nature of this claim is difficult to determine very precisely. Ultimately, though, there would seem a reasonable case to be made for at least *listening* to all those who feel they have a stake in the firm—even the critics. Harry Hummels (1998) suggests that managers have much to gain from listening to the alternative realities of critical voices—and in a complex, multifaceted, global economy there are likely to be many sides to any major corporate action which impacts significantly on society. Listening to critics can raise awareness of potential problems, help to define priorities, and aid in setting out more informed visions of the future. Of course, simply listening to what CSOs have to say is not always going to be a sufficient level of involvement, but it represents a good place to start. And perhaps more importantly, there appear to be both instrumental and ethical arguments to support such an acknowledgement of at least this limited stake in the company. **Ethical Dilemma 10** gives you the opportunity to think about and apply some of these ideas in a more particular example.

CSO tactics

Obviously CSOs are not passive actors in the process through which corporations ascribe (or do not ascribe) legitimacy to their stake in a situation or issue. CSOs are frequently very active in promoting their causes and in seeking corporate recognition, engagement, and response. However, some of the tactics used by CSOs to do this can be challenged on ethical grounds (Whawell 1998). Is it acceptable, for example, for animal rights activists to break into animal testing labs to release animals, or even to threaten the staff of testing companies? Is it possible to defend the occupation of oil platforms, the vandalism of fast food restaurants, or the deliberate destruction of GM crops?

There is in fact a whole range of tactics that CSOs might call on in seeking to achieve their aims. One set of tactics is through **indirect** forms of action, such as provision of data, research reports, and policy briefings (Smith 1990). At a more advanced level, though, we must also question how exactly CSOs pressure corporations in more **direct** forms of action. Craig Smith (1990) classifies the main approaches as violent direct action and non-violent direct action.

Indirect action

At the most basic level indirect action will tend to involve research and communication about the issues of relevance to the organization. For promotional groups in particular, the need to compete for public attention and approval often requires that they first establish a sound basis of research in order to develop credible arguments (Smith 1990: 123). Sometimes, though, the need to raise interest and convince a sceptical or apathetic public can lead CSOs into misrepresentation and overclaiming on the basis of their evidence. One area where CSOs have typically been open to ethical criticism is therefore in relation to the **provision of misleading information** (Whawell 1998). Greenpeace, for example,

Ethical Dilemma 10

Where's the beef?

As the public affairs manager of U-Buy, the country's leading supermarket chain, things have been fairly busy the last year. Still, having successfully dealt with the media response to the company's plans to close a number of unprofitable rural branches, you feel that the latest incident shouldn't be causing you quite as much trouble as it is.

It all started when you received a letter from Gay Men for Equality (GAME), an activist group in the USA. Although you had never even heard of GAME before, the group wrote to you asking about your company's position on BigBeef Corporation, a large US food company that supplies much of your processed meat products. Thinking it a strange request, but having no idea of any problems that GAME might be concerned about, you replied by saying simply that U-Buy had always enjoyed a good commercial relationship with BigBeef.

Thinking that this would be the last you would hear of GAME, you were surprised then to get by return post a much more stridently worded letter that asked why U-Buy was supporting a company that had recently been convicted after a string of accusations about discrimination and harassment of gay employees, and whose chief executive Buck Leghorn was an outspoken critic of the gay and lesbian equality movement.

You decided to do some research on the accusations, and it appeared that GAME was pretty accurate in its claims about BigBeef and Leghorn. And from the press coverage in the States, it looked as if BigBeef wasn't going to back down too much on this one. It appeared that GAME had been campaigning for some time against the company, but had yet to force a change of policy.

Although you could have done without the association between discrimination and U-Buy, this was BigBeef's business, and you felt it did not have much to do with your company. In the meantime, though, you had started receiving several emails a day from GAME demanding a response, so you decided to write to them again. This time you reiterated that U-Buy had always enjoyed a good working relationship with BigBeef, but added that U-Buy deplored discrimination of any kind and itself actively complied with all relevant legislation.

GAME refused to be pacified by your response and started intensifying its demands, claiming that U-Buy should demand a complete apology and change of policy at BigBeef or else cease trading with them. When you got this email from GAME you almost laughed, thinking what a crazy suggestion this seemed to be. What did this have to do with you and U-Buy? It wasn't your fault that BigBeef had been prosecuted. And it certainly wasn't up to you what their chief executive Buck Leghorn decided to pronounce upon in the papers.

Still, you thought you'd mention the problem to the Head of Purchasing and let him know what was happening. When you did so, he made it extremely clear that there was no way he was willing to risk the good relations that U-Buy had with BigBeef. The company was one of U-Buy's most important suppliers, and the company had a lot of influence on the global food industry. 'This will soon blow over,' he told you, 'just lie low and don't say anything that will get us into trouble.'

Despite the Head of Purchasing's forecast, GAME's campaign seemed to be gaining a bit of steam, and even your own national press had somehow got hold of the story. It looked like GAME had turned its attention onto some of BigBeef's main customers in the public eye (such as U-Buy) to try and force some changes at the company. And to your dismay, it now appeared that a local chapter of GAME had even been set up specifically to target U-Buy—and were said to be planning a demonstration outside your flagship store in the capital. Things were certainly escalating to a level that needed dealing with. You didn't want to risk threatening U-Buy's good relations with your powerful American supplier, but at the same time, you didn't want to be associated with discrimination, however indirectly. You could just see the placards now: 'U-Buy supports gay harassment' or some such thing. How come this minor problem was causing you such a major headache?

Questions

1 Which are the legitimate stakeholders in this situation? Give reasons as to why you think they are legitimate and establish some kind of priority ranking.
2 How would you proceed in this situation?
3 How would you try and prevent similar problems from occurring in the future?

---

was found to have massively overestimated the quantities of toxic sludge contained on the Brent Spar oil platform when it was campaigning against Shell's plans for sea disposal of the structure. Although the NGO later apologized, it was criticized for attempting to mislead the media and the public (Whawell 1998).

Overall, though, the provision of misleading information does not seem to be as much of an ethical problem for CSOs as it does for corporations (see Chapter 8; 271–6). As we have already said, many CSOs, especially the mainstream NGOs, consumer associations, and charities, have been extremely successful in establishing themselves as credible and authoritative institutions, and many are now more trusted sources of information on social issues in business than the businesses themselves. More marginal CSOs involved in anti-business communication, as well as certain religious groups and other clearly partisan civil society actors, may not of course enjoy the same degree of overall trust from the public. However, their specific slant is usually reasonably well understood, with the result that their information is often seen more as subjective interpretation than objective fact.

Violent direct action

Violent direct action is often illegal, although, as Smith (1990) notes, it often generates the most publicity. Because of the publicity it raises, violent action frequently raises awareness of the issues that the CSO is promoting very quickly. For example, it was when the 1999 anti-globalization protests at Seattle degenerated into street riots that the issue of anti-globalization was assured front-page coverage across much of the world. Similarly, the often violent campaign against animal cruelty at the UK's Huntingdon Life Sciences, led by SHAC (Stop Huntingdon Animal Cruelty) and others, has led to extensive media publicity and a series of damaging setbacks for the company. This case is described more fully in **Ethics in Action 10.1**.

Huntingdon Life Sciences: a corporate killing for animal rights activists?

Huntingdon Life Sciences (HLS), the UK-based drug testing company, has faced probably more intensive and more devastating direct action campaigning from CSOs than any other corporation. The company, which is the largest of about ten contract research organizations that carries out animal testing in Britain, became the main focus of the anti-vivisection movement in 1997 following a television documentary that showed staff mistreating animals. The revelations that the company oversees the death of most of the 70,000 animals tested each year, as well as other accusations of torture and abuse, brought an avalanche of criticism against the company from animal rights activists.

In 1999, Stop Huntingdon Animal Cruelty (SHAC) was set up by a group of seasoned animal rights campaigners to lead the campaign to force HLS to close down. SHAC is an international coalition of CSOs, with SHAC groups in the UK, USA, the Netherlands, Germany, Italy, and many other countries uniting to target HLS and the various companies it works with. Unusually for such a coalition, the intention from the start was not simply to raise awareness, or seek changes in practices, but to deliberately put HLS out of business. Within two years they had virtually succeeded in doing so.

SHAC has been unapologetic in its use of what it calls 'ferocious' direct action methods to attack HLS and its supporters—although it maintains that all of its actions have remained within the law. Nonetheless, HLS and their employees (and companies connected to them) have suffered broken windows, rescued animals, paint-stripped cars, glued-up locks, office occupations, rooftop demos, and blockades. More seriously, employees, investors, local residents, and others connected to HLS have been verbally abused, issued with threats, and even at times physically assaulted. Indeed, although SHAC itself identifies underground activist groups such as the Animal Liberation Front (ALF) as the perpetrators of violence against HLS, the SHAC website actively encourages occupations and other potentially illegal activities.

Despite the questionable nature of some of the methods advocated by SHAC, its aggressive strategy for attacking HLS has not been without considerable sophistication. One particularly successful avenue has been the targeting of HLS investors. Following SHAC's procurement and release of a list of HLS's largest investors, a series of direct attacks were made against each of the company's financial backers. This rapidly led banks such as Barclays, HSBC, Merrill Lynch, TD Waterhouse, Crédit Suisse First Boston, and others to sell off their shares in the company rather than face further action.

Faced with an almost complete loss of confidence from the investment community, in January 2001 HLS were ready to go into receivership. A last-gasp rescue package from two US backers saved them, with the Royal Bank of Scotland allegedly writing off a £12m debt for just £1.

Undeterred, SHAC also turned its attentions to the company's customers. Giant pharmaceutical companies such as GlaxoSmithKline, Pharmacia, Eli Lilly, and Novartis (all of which contracted tests from HLS), experienced aggressive campaigning during 2001 aimed at encouraging them to dispense with HLS's services. The company's stock price continued to deteriorate.

The decisive moment came in early 2002 when the embattled testing company's backers finally moved their financial listing out of the UK altogether and began trading exclusively in the USA. Hailed as a victory by SHAC, the move saw HLS incorporate themselves into a shell company, Life Science Research, located in Maryland, USA. Crucially, local law in Maryland requires no public declaration of shareholders, thereby protecting the identities of investors. However, SHAC continued attacks on traders dealing with the shares of the newly formed company. Staff, their families, and neighbours were threatened, and offices sabotaged with 'autodial' computer programs that ring target numbers hundreds of times a day to jam up the telephone system. In September 2002, SHAC claimed another success when one of the main dealers targeted by the group allegedly released sensitive shareholder information in a bid to stem the barrage of direct action aimed at it. HLS, it seems, remains unable to ignore the attentions of its fierce opponent.

SOURCES

Finn, David, and Guerrera, Francesco (2001). 'Huntingdon chief calls for squad to target activists', *FT.com*, 23 Feb.

Jenkins, Patrick (2002). 'Animal activists extract shareholder details', *FT.com*, 15 Sept.

Mackintosh, James (2001). 'Huntingdon clients to be next protest targets', *FT.com*, 21 Jan.

www.shac.net.

> **■ Think theory**
>
> Consider this example from the perspective of stakeholder theory. Who are the legitimate stakeholders of Huntingdon and what intrinsic rights do they have? Do SHAC have any right to try and put the company out of business?

Nonetheless, it is difficult to condone the more violent protests by CSOs—although the destruction of property and violence towards people would seem to be on somewhat different moral planes. For one thing, this calls into question whether such action can really be deemed 'civil' at all. Perhaps in the interests of attempting to create a more civil society in the long run (for example, one where animals were not used for tests of cosmetic ingredients), we could begin to see a defence of violent action on consequentialist grounds. However, the perceived illegitimacy of such tactics by the public, government, and business tends to make them largely unsuccessful at gaining CSO members access to decision-makers and the decision-making process—which is often a major goal of such campaigns. Sometimes, even fairly legitimate protests can be denigrated when associated with violent protest. Overall then, violent direct action remains an important, if controversial, tactic for CSOs. We would suggest that it seems to be particularly attractive for those who are (or who feel they are) largely excluded from any other means of engagement with decision-makers, and who feel that their ends justify their means. In a liberal, pluralistic society, though, such means can be highly contestable.

Non-violent direct action

Non-violent direct action is a far more common approach for CSOs to use (Smith 1990). This can include, but is not limited to:

- Demonstrations and marches;
- Protests;
- Boycotts;
- Occupations;
- Non-violent sabotage and disruption;
- Stunts;
- Picketing.

Sometimes these may cross the line into illegality, such as when road protesters trespass on private land in order to prevent clearing and construction work from commencing on infrastructure projects. In the main, though, direct action of this sort tends to remain quite legal. As a result there are often considerably fewer ethical problems arising with non-violent direct action. However, as we saw in Ethics in Action 10.1, supposedly non-violent actions can lead to intimidation of the subjects of the demonstration, and can even tacitly encourage more violent action. Moreover, even tactics such as boycotts can raise some concerns, and sometimes the very choice of companies to target can be a point of contention. We won't go into detail on all of the non-violent direct action tactics open to CSOs, but it seems worthwhile to focus a little more attention on these two latter points.

Boycotts

Boycotts are probably the most commonly recognized and most widely used form of non-violent direct action. Research suggests that something like 20 per cent of people claim to have boycotted, or are willing to boycott, a product for ethical reasons (Brock et al. 2001). As such, they represent an organized form of *ethical consumption*—a subject we first discussed in Chapter 8. Essentially, whilst ethical consumption is often an individual activity or choice, a boycott is usually a co-ordinated endeavour that seeks to achieve some impact on corporations through *collective action* (Smith 1990). Boycotts can thus be defined as follows (from Friedman 1999: 4):

> A boycott is an attempt by one or more parties to achieve certain objectives by urging individual consumers to refrain from making selected purchases in the marketplace.

CSOs of one sort or another are usually the parties behind most boycotts of corporations and products. Some CSOs in fact even come into existence simply to organize boycott activity, such as the various organizations that have sprung up to support and co-ordinate efforts to boycott Nike, including the Oregon-based Justice–Do it Nike! and the Alberta-based Just Do It! Boycott Nike!

Consumer boycotts have been targeted at numerous companies over the years. Some of the more high-profile ones in Europe are set out in **Figure 10.8**. According to one survey conducted by the UK-based *Ethical Consumer* magazine in the mid–late 1990s, by far the most widely boycotted company amongst its readership was Nestlé, with a staggering 78 per cent of respondents having boycotted the company. The next most boycotted companies were McDonald's with 34 per cent and Shell with 26 per cent. Perhaps unsurprisingly, all of these companies feature as cases in this book, but, as we hope these cases

Target company	Organized by	Occurrence	Main issues	Outcomes
DIY retailers (UK)	Friends of the Earth	Early 1990s	Stocking of 'unsustainably sourced' tropical timber The campaign eventually became a consumer boycott and proved tremendously successful.	All six major UK DIY companies agreed to stop selling mahogany in 1994. Led by B&Q, the firms went on to join the WWF-co-ordinated sustainable timber project which accredits wood according to internationally agreed criteria determined by the Forest Stewardship Council (FSC). Mahogany imports fell by 68% 1992–6.
ExxonMobil (Esso)	Greenpeace, Friends of the Earth and People & Planet	Ongoing since 2001	Company's active lobbying against Kyoto global warming treaty, political donations to US Republican Party (which has pulled the USA out of the treaty), and lack of investment in renewable energy.	None to date.
Nestlé	IBFAN (International Baby Food Action Network) and various church groups, student unions, politicians, etc.	Ongoing since the 1970s	Nestlé's aggressive promotion of breast milk substitute in developing countries and breaches of WHO code regulating the marketing of infant formula.	The introduction of the WHO code was a major achievement and Nestlé claims to have eradicated the practices identified by boycotters. However, accusations (and boycotts) have continued.
Shell	Greenpeace	1995	Sea disposal of the Brent Spar oil platform.	Sales of Shell petrol shot down by 70% in some German outlets. The company halted the disposal and eventually agreed to land dismantling and reuse after review process and stakeholder consultation.
Triumph International	Burma Campaign	2001–2	Manufacturing operations in Burma.	Announced withdrawal from the country in 2002.
WH Smith	Campaign Against Pornography	Mid-1990s	Sale of soft porn magazines in high street stores.	Products removed from high street in 1997, but were continued at its railway station and airport stores and so the boycott continued.

Figure 10.8. Some well-known boycotts in Europe

Sources: www.ethicalconsumer.org; www.stopesso.org; www.ibfan.org.

make clear, the arguments for and against whether to boycott them are not always as clear as the CSO organizers suggest.

Some boycotts are clearly more controversial than others. The questions of **which companies should be targeted** (and the reasons why) are critical ethical choices for CSOs to make. For a start, whilst CSOs often try to occupy the moral high ground, the values and causes they promote are obviously not going to be to everyone's taste. For example, many liberal commentators were critical of the boycott of Disney organized by the Southern Baptist Convention and the Catholic League during the 1990s that criticized the company's position on homosexuality, including its policy of extending health benefits to partners of homosexual employees.

Slightly less controversial perhaps was the boycotting of the lingerie firm Triumph International mentioned in **Figure 10.8**. This was part of a broader set of actions against companies operating in Burma, whose repressive regime has been implicated in human rights abuses. Protesters argue that firms investing in Burma provide support for the country's military dictatorship, and a number of companies have even been argued to have utilized forced labour provided by the authorities. In addition to Triumph, boycotts have also been initiated against firms such as Pepsico, Arco, and Texaco, all of which have now left the country. However, many companies retain business links with the country, and a 2002 publication by the International Confederation of Free Trade Unions (ICFTU) listed a total of over 325 multinational companies that currently had business links with the Burmese dictatorship.[2] Some of the latest additions to this list included:

- British American Tobacco (BAT) subsidiary Rothmans Pall Mall Myanmar Private Ltd. which, in a joint venture with Burmese company UMEH, was found to own a cigarette factory in a military-owned industrial estate.
- Pinault-Printemps-Redouté, the French retailer and catalogue operator, which was found to import clothes made in Burma.
- Suzuki, the Japanese automotive company, which was revealed to have a sizeable investment in Burma making cars and motorcycles.

However, not everyone is in agreement about the morality of boycotting firms with links to Burma. For example, some companies targeted by campaigners have argued that by remaining in Burma, and abiding by established codes of ethics, they can raise awareness about human rights and protect workers from forced labour and other such abuses. If they left the country, the companies argue, these problems would only worsen. Similar debates arose in the past about the presence of multinationals in South Africa during the apartheid era (De George 1999: 542–8). Such issues illustrate that arguments can be made both for and against corporations having a more positive role in promoting civil rights in countries with poor human rights records. However, boycotts against firms remaining in both South Africa and Burma have already shown that organized campaigns can put firms in the ethical spotlight, leading to potentially major (and costly) publicity problems.

---

[2] See **www.icftu.org** for more details.

■ **Think theory**

Think about the arguments for and against the presence of companies in Burma. Which ethical principles and theories would you say these arguments primarily rely on?

Of course, the reasons for boycotts can vary. Friedman (1999) in fact suggests that CSOs might actually have four different purposes for boycotts:

• **Instrumental boycotts** aim to force the target to change a specific policy. Goals may be very clear, such as the repudiation of the challenged policy, the introduction of better conditions, etc.

• **Catalytic boycotts** seek to raise awareness about the company's actions and policies. The boycott itself is more of a means to generate publicity, either for the CSO or for a broader campaign of action against the company.

• **Expressive boycotts** are more general forms of protest that effectively just communicate a general displeasure about the target company. This form tends to be characterized by more vague goals since their focus is more on the CSO and consumers registering their disapproval.

• **Punitive boycotts** seek to punish the target company for its actions. Therefore, rather than communicating displeasure, the boycotters actively seek to cause the firm harm, usually by aiming for significant erosions of sales.

Regardless of the purpose of CSOs in calling a boycott, it is often the extent and intensity of consumer participation that determines whether such goals are met. Clearly a number of factors can affect whether consumers join and maintain boycotts, including the degree of effort involved in switching to an alternative, the appeal of the boycotted product to the consumer, social pressure, and the likelihood of success (Sen et al. 2001). In practice, many, many more boycotts are called than are successful. For every highly publicized success story there are likely to be a host of fairly unsuccessful attempts. Any given issue of *Ethical Consumer* magazine for example lists somewhere between twenty and forty current boycott actions in the UK alone, only a few of which are ever brought to the notice of the general public.[3] This then of course starts to raise the question of which constituencies exactly are CSOs supposed to be representing—and perhaps more importantly in what way are they answerable to those whose interests they are supposed to be advancing? These are essentially questions of CSO accountability, the last of our main ethical issues confronting business relations with CSOs.

CSO accountability

In recent years, the issue of CSO accountability has been raised with increasing regularity (Hilhorst 2002). This is perhaps not surprising when one considers that they have often been the parties most vociferously questioning the accountability of corporations. We might

---

[3] For the current list of boycotts, see **www.ethicalconsumer.org/boycotts/boycotts_list.htm**.

reasonably expect critics of corporate accountability to 'have their own house in order' first (Hilhorst 2002).

Indeed, it is interesting to note that questions about CSO accountability have largely mirrored the same questions that have been raised in relation to corporations. For example, who exactly is an organization such as Greenpeace supposed to be serving? Are the interests of its managers aligned with those of its principal constituents? To what extent and to whom are Greenpeace responsible for the consequences of their actions? We have asked almost exactly the same questions in discussing issues of corporate responsibility and accountability in Chapter 2 (55–61), and issues of ownership, control, and governance in Chapter 6 (184–91; 207–10). This suggests that we can conceptualize CSO managers as 'agents' for a broader collective of civil society 'principals' in the same way that we do for corporate managers and shareholders (see Doh and Teegen 2002). Likewise, we can model CSOs as representative of different stakeholder interests just as we can with corporations (e.g. Hilhorst 2002).

Specifically, **CSO stakeholders** might be said to include:

- Beneficiaries;
- Donors;
- Members;
- Employees;
- Governmental organizations;
- Other CSOs;
- General public (especially those who support their ideals).

Significantly, though, there is also very clearly a case for saying that CSOs represent some notion of *civil society itself*—a largely indefinable stakeholder but one that is nonetheless central to the notion of the third sector. Increasingly, we might also suggest that *corporations* are in some situations relevant stakeholders of CSOs.

Given such a range of stakeholders, issues of accountability and responsibility are clearly quite complex. Different stakeholders might have different expectations of CSO performance, and of how that performance is reported. Similarly, different stakeholders might have very different expectations about how much say they should have in the affairs of the organization. Whilst we might as the general public support the work of Oxfam in providing famine relief, we do not expect to have much meaningful input into how they go about providing this. Perhaps our interest in this respect grows if we donate significant sums of money to the organization, but even so, we would generally be less concerned about how they spent our money than the intended beneficiaries would be.

Still, it is in fact the **accountability of CSOs to their supposed beneficiaries** that tends to raise the most debate. A number of problems are evident here (see Ali 2000; Bendell 2000*b*; Hilhorst 2002), including:

- CSOs in developed countries purporting to represent the interests of those in LDCs have been accused of imposing their own agendas on local people without adequately understanding their situation and needs.

- The involvement of beneficiaries in agenda setting, defining priorities, and making strategic decisions is often limited.
- The need for financial support and other resources can focus CSOs' interests on donors' priorities rather than those of their intended beneficiaries.
- Beneficiaries typically lack effective mechanisms to voice approval or disapproval of CSO performance.

In some ways then it would appear that many CSOs have tended to be equally as inattentive to issues of accountability and democracy as many corporations have. Given their largely positive impact on society, as well as their avowedly moral emphasis, it could be argued that perhaps the issue of accountability is less crucial in respect to CSOs. However, given the growing importance of their role in society in general, as well as their involvement in business specifically, the question of CSO accountability is only really likely to gain in significance.

For corporations, the main problem then is how to assess the legitimacy of any CSO contribution to the debate about business ethics and to decide what such an assessment implies for how they should respond to CSO challenges. At one extreme, they could choose to play CSOs at their own game and refuse to take seriously the views of unelected, unaccountable ideologues. At the other, they could seek to work together to develop enhanced mechanisms of governance and accountability for both types of organizations. The reality, however, is likely to be somewhere in the middle—with all the ambiguity and ambivalence that such a situation brings.

■ Think theory

Think about the relevance of stakeholder theory for CSOs compared with corporations. In which aspects is it more or less relevant or applicable for either category of organization?

Globalization and civil society organizations

Globalization has brought a number of significant changes to CSOs that are relevant for our understanding of business ethics. First, globalization has also brought MNCs into confrontation with an extended community of CSOs, including a whole new set of local CSOs in other countries that they did not have to deal with before. Second, we have seen the emergence of new global issues for CSOs to engage with. Indeed, even the very contestability of the benefits or otherwise of globalization has led to the formation of new 'anti-globalization' CSOs. Finally, we have also seen CSOs themselves increasingly globalize in terms of scale and/or scope. Clearly it is not only corporations that organize across borders, and CSOs have often been extremely effective at galvanizing a transnational community of constituents to support their campaigns aimed at corporations.

In summary, it is possible to discern three main areas where globalization is reshaping the relations between corporations and CSOs.

- Engagement with overseas CSOs;
- Global issues and causes;
- Globalization of CSOs.

Let us look at each of these in a little more detail.

Engagement with overseas CSOs

For corporations acting solely within the domestic sphere, the notion of civil society tends to be quite naturally framed simply in terms of national or even regional constituencies. Just as an Italian corporation such as the construction giant Impregilo might have typically been mainly involved in dealing with Italian labour and environmental groups (such as Campagna per la Riforma della Banca Mondiale) so might an Indian corporation such as Tata Tea, the largest tea company in the subcontinent, have typically dealt with just Indian CSOs. However, the increasingly deterritorialized nature of business activity inevitably puts corporations with international operations into a number of different civil societies across the globe. MNCs are therefore confronted with a whole new set of unfamiliar CSOs in overseas countries.

For example, Impregilo's involvement in constructing more than 160 hydroelectric projects around the world in countries such as Argentina, China, Honduras, Nigeria, and Pakistan has brought it to the attention of various local environmental and community groups in those countries, as well as CSOs from countries represented by some of Impregilo's consortia partners. See end of chapter **Case 12** for a fuller discussion of Impregilo's experiences with the controversial Ilisu Dam in Turkey.

Global issues and causes

In addition to bringing corporations into contact with an extended community of CSOs overseas, it is evident that many of the problems now dealt with by CSOs in their relations with corporations are global in nature and/or emerging as a consequence of globalization in other areas of business. We need only look back at **Figure 10.8** (which describes some CSO-led boycotts) to see that many of the issues championed by CSOs, such as global warming, tropical deforestation, marine conservation, labour conditions in the supply chain, and international marketing practices, are **problems that transcend national boundaries**. We won't go into these in any more detail here, as most of these issues are covered elsewhere in the chapters dealing with the specific stakeholders involved.

Given this attention to global problems, though, it is perhaps unsurprising that much of the currently popular **critique of globalization** itself has been initiated, sustained, and popularized by civil society actors. At one level this has involved existing CSOs incorporating messages of anti-globalization into their campaigns. For example, Friends of the Earth, which is mainly known for its environmental activism, has recently initiated a campaign targeting 'corporate globalization'.[4] Similarly, another more radical group initially

---

[4] For more information see **www.foe.org.uk**.

formed to support environmental action, the US-based Ruckus Society, has more recently broadened its remit. The group's mission to train activists for tree-sits, banner-hangs, and barricades (it even has its own training camp) has led to it, for example, training activists who helped close down the WTO in Seattle in 1999.[5] Moreover, many groups with a more directly political orientation such as anarchist cells and Marxist action groups have maintained a position of resistance to global capitalism for many years—although many of these might be more correctly regarded as political organizations rather than CSOs.

On another level, there have been the new groups that have sprung up specifically to protest against globalization. Most notable in their demonstrations at the various meetings of economic and political leaders including the World Economic Forum, WTO, and G8 summits, the civil society challenge to globalization has seen the emergence of a myriad of new groups dedicated to a range of causes which mainly relate to the taming of global corporations, global capitalism, and various other aspects of globalization. Again, which of these groups and organizations should actually be regarded as civil society actors is somewhat debatable, but certainly those which advance a specific cause primarily outside the political or market sector would seem to count within a broad definition of civil society.

The CSOs tackling globalization have taken many forms—and it is evident that some of them are more civil than others! **Ethics in Action 10.2** provides an overview of ATTAC, one of the main European CSOs involved in the anti-globalization movement. Although ATTAC is arguably at the more intellectual end of the scale, much of the emphasis among protesters has been one of resistance and civil disobedience. Although this has certainly at times led to violence, some groups claim to focus more on pranks and spectacle. This includes the Biotic Baking Brigade, whose approach relies on throwing pies at leading advocates of globalization (including Microsoft CEO Bill Gates and the right-wing economist Milton Friedman whom we first discussed in Chapter 2), and the UK-based Reclaim the Streets who organize dance parties and 'guerrilla' tree plantings on public roads (see Klein 2000: 311–26).

We can see here echoes of a **postmodern** take on ethics: individuals forming loose, fragmented coalitions in order to stake out temporary zones of autonomy where they can challenge the 'grand narratives' of society (capitalism, globalization, progress, etc.) and make active choices about how to act (Desmond et al. 2000). There is much to be said for such tactics, not least because they can result in tremendous publicity for the 'cause' (Higgins and Tadajewski 2002). Clearly, though, there is the danger that as a consequence serious questioning may be dismissed as mere media stunt, devoid of commitment and moral force (Gabriel and Lang 1995: 196).

This leads us on to perhaps one of the most interesting aspects of the protests: the way that the CSOs involved have tended to make use of many of the phenomena that they themselves criticize (Higgins and Tadajewski 2002). For example, consider Adbusters, the Canadian organization which seeks to promote an 'anti-marketing', 'anti-corporate' agenda through creative media and advertising, or even the popularizer of the anti-globalization movement Naomi Klein herself, who not only registered the 'No Logo' logo on the front of her book as a trademark, but even published the book in the UK through

---

[5] See **http://ruckus.org**. Also: Harding (2001a).

Ethics in Action 10.2

Attacking globalization at ATTAC

The anti-globalization movement consists of thousands of different organizations espousing a range of different ideologies and convictions. In fact, to call it a movement is probably not even entirely appropriate, since it involves such a diverse and inchoate activism with no unifying agenda or leaders. One of the most passionate and coherent critics of globalization though is ATTAC, a counter-capitalist group founded in France in 1998, which has expanded to become probably Europe's largest anti-globalization CSO.

ATTAC stands for the **A**ssociation for the **T**axation of Financial **T**ransactions for the **A**id of **C**itizens. It consists of a network of independent national and local groups in thirty-three countries, and claims a membership of some 80,000 members worldwide. The main aims of the group are to promote the idea of an international tax on currency speculation (the Tobin Tax, which we described in Chapter 6; 204) and campaigns to 'outlaw tax havens, replace pension funds with state pensions, cancel Third World debt, reform or abolish the World Trade Organisation (WTO) and, more generally, recapture the democratic space that has been lost to the financial world'.

Clearly this agenda represents quite an undertaking, but the leaders of ATTAC are both well versed in the economic arguments, as well as relatively well funded. The director of ATTAC is Bernard Cassen, one of the top editors of the French journal *Le Monde diplomatique*, which has been an enthusiastic critic of liberalization and corporate-led globalization for nearly two decades. Their funding comes partly from the extensive membership, but the biggest single donor to ATTAC so far is actually the European Commission, which gave the organization around €120,000 over two years. Interestingly this has not exempted the Commission from the ire of ATTAC. As Cassen says: 'We regard the European Commission as the spearhead of neo-liberalism in Europe.'

Unlike much of the anti-globalization movement, though, ATTAC doesn't just critique existing policies, but proposes what it claims are 'specific, practical alternatives that governments could implement now'. Moreover, it also goes a considerable way to practising what it preaches. The group's approach is announced on its website:

Membership equals participation, and participation equals decision-making power. There is no elite group of lobbyists supported by passive members, and no bureaucracy to deal with. Members of local groups organise whatever events and campaigns they'd like to see happen, as long as the topic is consistent with ATTAC's platform.

ATTAC isn't run by experts; experts participate as equals. A lot of what we do is self-education: doing our own research, and organising discussions and debates to compare different analyses and proposals.

The impact of ATTAC is difficult to determine. However, it took part in the demonstrations at Seattle in 1999 against the WTO, and estimates that it sent nearly 5,000 people to the protest against the G8 in Genoa in July 2001. The group in its many guises organizes a constant stream of events, talks, educational seminars, protests, briefings, and other actions. Whatever else it may or may not achieve, ATTAC has been remarkably successful in helping to engender lively discussion about seemingly dull and impenetrable ethical issues—such as financial markets, taxation, and institutions of governance—which are often overlooked in favour of more accessible issues such as labour conditions, environmental protection, and consumer exploitation.

SOURCES

www.attac.org.

Harding, James (2001*a*). 'Globalisation's children strike back'. *FT.com*, 10 Sept.

—— (2001*b*). 'Feeding the hands that bite'. *FT.com*, 15 Oct.

■ **Think theory**

Think about ATTAC in terms of globalization. Which aspects of globalization does the group condemn and which aspects does it take advantage of? Do you feel that attacking globalization is a tenable proposition for a CSO such as ATTAC?

---

an arm of Rupert Murdoch's global publishing empire (Higgins and Tadajewski 2002). Similarly a number of protest groups, including the Ruckus Society, have received financial support from the Anglo-Dutch multinational Unilever as part of its endowment to a fund operated by Ben & Jerry's, the 'socially responsible' ice cream company it bought in 2000 (Harding 2001*a*). Whichever way we look at it, there are a number of intriguing parallels, interlinkages, and commonalities between the anti-globalization protesters and their targets. Perhaps the most visible aspect of these, though, is the increasingly globalized nature of civil society itself.

Globalization of CSOs

'The resistance will be as transnational as capital.' So goes one of the main rallying calls of the protest movement. And as this suggests, the so-called anti-globalization movement is as much reliant on, and a by-product of, globalization as are Gap stores in every high street and the ubiquity of McDonald's hamburgers. In particular, the mobilization of anti-corporate sentiment across the world has only been realized on such a scale because of the supraterritorial scope of the internet (Harding 2001*c*). With the ability to co-ordinate international protests and boycotts, to use sophisticated technology to transmit media-friendly images into the world press, not to mention the possibility of travelling across the globe as a result of cheaper air fares—it is clear that the travelling circus of protesters has been considerably expedited by certain aspects of globalization (Harding 2001*c*; 2001*b*).

Significantly, though, this is not only true of the anti-globalization protesters, but of much of contemporary civil society. Rather than just engaging with multiple local civil societies (as we suggested on p. 365) some corporations have been faced with something more akin to a *global civil society*. Talk of a global civil society to describe such developments first began to spread in the 1990s and has now become fairly commonplace in social and political debates (Scholte 2000: 277). From giant NGOs such as Greenpeace and Friends of the Earth, to international union bodies such as the International Confederation of Free Trade Unions (ICFTU), and fringe activist outfits such as Reclaim the Streets and SHAC (Stop Huntingdon Animal Cruelty), there are innumerable civil actors engaged in the debate about corporate practices which are organized on a transnational basis. Just as corporations have increasingly gone global, so too have CSOs.

However, this position as global institutions on a similar (de)territorialized basis as corporations potentially brings with it new roles and responsibilities for CSOs. Given that most regulation of business activity was formerly in the province of local and national governments, the movement of both corporations and CSOs (but less so governments) to a global level means that CSOs might be expected to take on some of these responsibilities that were formerly held by government. As we have said a number of times, business ethics tends to begin where the law ends. And with a dearth of global laws, global CSOs have found themselves involved in (and at times pushed themselves into) the process whereby global regulation of business is debated, decided, and implemented (Doh and Teegen 2002; Zadek 2001). As we shall discuss in more detail in the next section, this potentially has significant implications for our understanding of corporate citizenship with respect to civil society.

■ **Think theory**

Think about the notion of globalization as deterritorialization. Which aspects of CSOs are, or could be, deterritorialized? How does the degree of deterritorialization of CSOs and CSO protests compare with that of corporations?

Corporate citizenship and civil society: charity, collaboration, or regulation?

So far in this chapter we have mainly discussed corporate and civil society actors as though they were dedicated adversaries in a perpetual state of conflict. However, recognition by firms that 'good' citizenship might entail a positive response to civil society challenges has for some time now brought them into more constructive contact with civil actors. Traditionally, this has mainly centred on **charitable giving** and other philanthropic acts intended to benefit community groups and other civil actors. More recently, though, we have also witnessed an increasing number of more intensive **business–CSO collaborations** seeking to provide more partnership-based solutions to social and environmental problems (Hartman and Stafford 1997; McIntosh and Thomas 2002; Murphy and Bendell 1997). Looking at the nature and purpose of CSO involvement in the business sector, a number of authors have also advanced the proposition raised in the previous section that CSOs might even go beyond simply collaborating with business to actually forming some kind of **'civil regulation'** of corporate action (e.g. Bendell 2000*b*; Zadek 2001).

These tighter interrelationships should come as no surprise, particularly when we stop to think about the implications of talking about citizenship in the context of corporations. After all, civil society is typically thought of as an important arena where individual citizens can express and pursue their particular values and interests. Whether we think of corporations as fellow citizens in this society (as the *limited* and *equivalent* views of CC suggest) or as administrators of citizenship for individuals (as our preferred *extended view* proposes) corporations must almost inevitably at some time become involved in civil society. In this section we will look at these ways in which corporations and civil society have become more tightly interrelated, and consider the question of what role CSOs can play in making corporations more responsible and accountable within society.

■ **Think theory**

Think about our competing definitions of CC in Chapter 2 (61–70; go back and read the chapter if you are unsure of them). Which of these definitions do you think would be most acceptable to the CSOs that we have discussed in this chapter? Why do you think this is?

Charity and community giving

The main starting point for a consideration of business involvement in civil society is inevitably charitable giving and other forms of corporate philanthropy and community participation. As we have suggested a number of times already in the book, corporations have long been involved in philanthropic behaviour towards local communities, charities, the arts, and various other aspects of civil society. Based on the notion of 'putting something back', many large corporations have now set up a separate unit or foundation that oversees charitable giving. Employees are also often involved in philanthropy schemes, such as through the granting of sabbaticals for workers to pursue voluntary work. The Dutch ING Bank for example has charitable foundations in Europe, the USA, and Australia, offers support for employee volunteering, and on the occasion of its tenth anniversary in 2001 made €1m available for donations to ten different charities chosen by employees. Asked to select the charitable goals that would best fit the theme 'investing in the future', the charities chosen by employees included WWF, UNICEF, Stop Aids Now, and SOS Villages for Children. See **Ethics in Action 2.1** in Chapter 2 (45) for more examples of corporate giving.

Many firms tend to regard charitable donations and the like as the mainstay of their 'corporate citizenship' programmes, and clearly some corporations have made enormous contributions to civic life through such activities. The scale of corporate giving is significantly larger in the USA than in Europe, with American corporations giving, for example, something like five times more to charity than UK companies.[6] According to Reingold (1993), there are a number of reasons for this, including:

- US corporations usually enjoy more generous tax breaks on charitable donations than European corporations;

- US corporations tend to pay less in terms of taxation to support social welfare than in Europe—where the state has traditionally been expected to take responsibility for such things;

- American companies give much more than their European counterparts to organized religion, with nearly 50 per cent of US corporate giving going to church groups.

[6] See *Guardian* (2002).

Authors such as Friedman (1970) initially criticized charitable giving for effectively stealing from shareholders. More recently attention has turned to 'strategic philanthropy' (Smith 1994) and 'cause-related marketing' (Varadarajan and Menon 1988) as a means of aligning charitable giving with firm self-interest. Under such initiatives, firms select suitable recipients of funding not so much according to need, but according to their potential for adding brand value, improving firm reputation, and other instrumental ends. Although this is a logical response to doubts about the business value of community involvement, it does suggest certain limitations to philanthropy as a means of satisfying broader civic roles and responsibilities. As we said in Chapter 2 (64–66), this form of community involvement is very much within a limited view of corporate citizenship. Although it benefits communities and civil society, it does not usually allow them much voice in shaping corporate action. Essentially, according to our depiction of different modes of stakeholder engagement in Chapter 5 (157–161), this is a form of **one-way support** from business to civil society.

Business–CSO collaboration

In addition to these one-way philanthropic gestures, closer and more interactive relations between civil society and corporations have also risen to prominence in recent years. This move towards **business–CSO collaboration** has included dialogue between business and civil society actors, such as when major regeneration or construction projects are planned, and even strategic alliances between business and civil partners on matters such as supply chain management and certification. These developments have included various civil society actors, including environmental NGOs such as Greenpeace, aid charities such as Oxfam, labour organizations such as the ILO (International Labour Organization), and various local and community groups. Some examples involving European companies and/or CSOs are described in **Figure 10.9** (see also **Case 10** at the end of this chapter).

Whilst reliable figures on the number of collaborations between CSOs and corporations are not readily available, there is considerable case study and anecdotal evidence to suggest that the incidence has increased quite dramatically over the last ten years or so. For instance, authors such as Bendell (2000a) and Murphy and Bendell (1997) both provide details of numerous recent cases of business co-operation with civil society. There is considerable evidence to suggest that the degree of interaction between commercial and civil organizations has intensified. Both Hartman and Stafford (1997) and Murphy and Bendell (1997) for example set out examples where CSOs have not merely been the passive recipients of the philanthropic gestures of PR-smart companies, or the 'brand-for-hire' endorsers of existing company products, but have played a critical role in developing corporate policy and shaping the strategic development of their commercial partners.

Sometimes these types of collaborations are included under the umbrella term of **social partnerships** (Nelson and Zadek 2000; Waddock 1988). However, this can cause some confusion, particularly in Europe where this label has been more commonly used in the area of industrial relations (Ackers and Payne 1998).[7] Given that we have already discussed

---

[7] For further discussion of the term social partnership and its ramifications in Europe, see Kjærgaard and Westphalen (2001).

Name of initiative	Country	Main CSO(s) involved	Main corporation(s) involved	Launch	Aims and objectives
Hart voor Hout (Heart for Wood)	The Netherlands	Novib, Milieudefensie (Friends of the Earth, NL), and WWF-NL	3 DIY companies, incl. Intergamma, and 72 real estate developers	1992	To cease the sale of unsustainably produced tropical timber.
Greenfreeze	Germany	Greenpeace	Foron	1992	Development of a viable alternative to ozone-depleting refrigerants.
Marine Stewardship Council (MSC)	UK	WWF-UK	Unilever	1997	Establishment of principles and criteria for certification and promotion of sustainable fisheries practices.
Atlanta Alliance	Pakistan/ International	Save the Children-UK, UNICEF, Pakistani NGOs, ILO, and Sialkot Chamber of Commerce and Industry	World Federation of Sporting Goods Industry (WFSGI) and various local manufacturers	1997	To prevent and eliminate the use of child labour in the production of hand-stitched footballs in Pakistan.
Ethical Trade Initiative	UK	15 NGOs and 3 trade unions incl. International Confederation of Free Trade Unions, Anti-Slavery International, and Christian Aid	30+ companies, incl. Body Shop, Levi Strauss, Mothercare, and Tesco	1998	To share experience and promote learning about implementing international labour standards in international supply chains.
West–East Pipeline Project	China	United Nations Development Programme (UNDP)	Shell	2002	Assess the social impact of China's West–East Pipeline project through a consultation programme with local people and community organizations.

Figure 10.9. Some examples of business–CSO collaborations

Drivers for business engagement with CSOs	Drivers for CSO engagement with business
Consumer expectations	Growing interest in markets
NGO credibility with public	Disenchantment with government as provider of solutions
Need for an external challenge	Need for more resources
Cross-fertilization of thinking	Credibility of business with government
Greater efficiency in resource allocation	Cross-fertilization of thinking
Desire to head off negative public confrontation and protect image	Access to supply chains
Desire to engage stakeholders	Greater leverage

Figure 10.10. Drivers towards business-CSO partnerships

Source: Adapted from Elkington and Fennell (2000).

employment issues in some depth in Chapter 7, we will focus here more on business collaborations with other CSOs.

Given the history of boycotts, strikes, occupations, protests, and other conflicts, businesses and CSOs might seem at first to be rather strange, and somewhat uneasy, bedfellows. However, Elkington and Fennell (2000) report on a survey of business and NGO leaders by the consultancy SustainAbility that suggests there are a number of reasons why the two have sought to work more closely together, including a need for better resources and better access to markets for NGOs, and an interest in leveraging NGO credibility for businesses (see Figure 10.10). Accordingly, some 85 per cent of the survey's respondents indicated that they expected there to be growth in partnerships over the next few years.

In many respects, such collaborations appear to be very welcome, and certainly were afforded a very positive response in the academic literature, as well as the business press, when they first began to draw attention towards the end of the 1990s (e.g. Hartman and Stafford 1997; Murphy and Bendell 1997). We can see in such developments the potential for greater discussion, debate, and reflection on business ethics by the different partners. This raises the prospect of those from different sectors gaining greater understanding of the different facets of problems and learning to engage with competing, even conflicting, perspectives in order to build mutually acceptable solutions. Clearly this has strong resonance with a **discourse ethics** approach to resolving ethical problems. However, as we shall now see, the value of this approach will depend on a number of other factors.

Limitations of business–CSO collaboration

Several authors have suggested potential limitations to business–CSO collaboration. Possible drawbacks include the difficulties of *managing relations* between such culturally diverse organizations (Crane 1998*a*) and the difficulties of *ensuring consistency and commitment* (Elkington and Fennell 2000). Similarly, Ackers and Payne (1998) reveal a strong element of critique of the rhetoric of social partnerships in the industrial relations literature, particularly where notions of partnership appear to mask *continuing hostility* and/or *power imbalances* between the 'partners'.

The question of power imbalance is a crucial one here in addressing the potential for a discourse ethics approach to bring benefits to the two parties. Typically, one would expect business partners to be considerably more powerful than CSOs in terms of size, capital, political influence, and other key power resources. However, such a perspective tends to overlook the important power that CSOs wield in terms of specific knowledge, communications expertise, and public credibility (Arts 2002). Certainly, though, where large companies and small CSOs work together there is the danger that the relative influence of the two parties will be skewed towards corporate interests, and rewards may be unevenly shared. In addition, it has been argued that business–CSO alliances might favour the interests of large companies and CSOs in developing countries over those in less developed countries (Bendell and Murphy 2000).

We might also look to the **distribution of the benefits** of partnerships. Darcy Ashman (2001) for example suggests that the benefits of many CSO–business partnerships are garnered more by the partners than they are by the constituencies they are supposed to be aiding. Examining ten cases of collaboration in Brazil, India, and South Africa, Ashman (2001) reveals that, although both businesses and CSOs tended to reap benefits in terms of improved public images, better external relations, gains in resources, and organizational capacity-building, the development impacts on community beneficiaries were less predictable and considerably less emphatic. In a similar vein, Pearson and Seyfang (2001) argue that the benefits of international labour codes agreed by businesses and CSOs have tended to do more for the public image of western MNCs than they do for the pay and conditions of workforces in LDCs.

Finally, probably the main potential limitation of business–CSO collaboration is the prospect it raises of CSOs being co-opted by business and losing some of the independence that makes the civil sector such an important balance to corporate (and government) power. Through working with business, CSOs lay themselves open to the accusation of 'sleeping with the enemy' and thereby forfeiting some of their legitimacy and public credibility (Zadek 2001: 47–50). This in fact is part of a broader ethical problem of **CSO independence** that requires further elaboration.

CSO independence

For the relations between CSOs and businesses to function effectively, whether those relations are adversarial or collaborative, requires that the parties remain independent from one another. On the one hand, CSOs are unlikely to be able to occupy the moral high ground and pose a credible challenge to corporate abuses unless they are, and are seen as, sufficiently distant from the corporate protagonists. On the other hand, if CSOs become too closely involved in working with corporations, they might lose the public credibility that made them attractive partners for business in the first place. Simon Zadek (2001: 47–50) for example discusses a number of cases where companies' 'borrowing trust' from CSOs has led to criticism. These include the implicit endorsement by Amnesty International of Rio Tinto and Shell's new business principles, and Oxfam and Christian Aid's involvement in the Ethical Trade Initiative.

In many ways, though, the issue of CSO independence goes yet deeper. If we return to our earlier categorization of civil society as the 'third sector', the idea that CSOs provide social and political pluralism in order to create and sustain a civilized society is clearly compromised if the third sector loses its independence from the other sectors (market and government). The very purpose of CSOs as representatives of the diversity of interests in society is potentially weakened once they begin to lose their unique position outside the market sector. This is particularly problematic in a society where the power of corporations and of the market is so substantial that working with them can often be the most effective way of achieving real change. As many CSOs have found, if you want to improve the working conditions of workers in LDCs, or prevent the destruction of tropical rainforests, the best way to do so is to leverage the purchasing power of corporations in the west. But what happens when the former 'poacher' becomes the 'gamekeeper' (Zadek 2001: 80)?

There is clearly a certain degree of ambivalence here. Whilst CSOs might want to harness the power of the market (usually through corporations) to achieve social ends, the market can be seen to 'contaminate' the primarily moral orientation of the civil sector. As Kaler (2000) suggests, the power of many campaigning groups to tap into public opinion and influence business is in itself derived from the avowedly moral stance that they take—and in particular their ability to relate to people as moral agents rather than just as consumers. The criticism that followed the announcement of the UN's collaboration with multinational corporations to forge the Global Compact is illustrative of these tensions that underlie any significant step by civil sector organizations such as the UN into the corporate sector. The ethical challenge for CSOs then is to retain their distinctly moral orientation whilst making a positive and constructive contribution to business practice— a delicate balance by any standards.

Thus far, most CSOs appear to have been relatively successful at doing this. Sometimes they will do so by setting up a separate 'business' unit within the organization, such as Amnesty's Business Group, or by forming specific task forces charged with developing business relations whilst the rest of the organization gets on with its usual campaigning role. Clearly, though, such a development involves CSOs (and for that matter corporations) in a certain degree of schizophrenia, i.e. they often need to be both friends and foes to corporations, sometimes even at the same time (Elkington and Fennell 2000). Perhaps the most fundamental problem here though is one of **CSO accountability**, a problem that we discussed in some depth earlier in the chapter. After all, the proposition that CSOs should remain to some extent independent from corporations is based on an assumption that they have a specific task to fulfil on behalf of a certain constituency—and that this task is compromised by a loss of independence. This has perhaps even greater significance in the last of the modes of business–CSO engagement we will consider in this section—civil regulation.

Civil regulation

In the last chapter we saw how the regulation of business could be effected outside government. At that juncture we looked mainly at self-regulation by business, corporations 'policing' their suppliers, and even competitors regulating each other through industry partnerships and programmes. As we have already seen in the current chapter, civil society can also be a source of regulation of corporations. Whether through protests and boycotts or various forms of collaboration, CSOs increasingly appear to have the power to shape,

1. **Employment is freely chosen**
    1.1. There is no forced, bonded or involuntary prison labour
    1.2. Workers are not required to lodge 'deposits' or their identity papers with their employer and are free to leave their employer after reasonable notice.
2. **Freedom of association and the right to collective bargaining are respected**
    2.1. Workers, without distinction, have the right to join or form trade unions of their own choosing and to bargain collectively.
    2.2. The employer adopts an open attitude towards the activities of trade unions and their organisational activities.
    2.3. Workers representatives are not discriminated against and have access to carry out their representative functions in the workplace.
    2.4. Where the right to freedom of association and collective bargaining is restricted under law, the employer facilitates, and does not hinder, the development of parallel means for independent and free association and bargaining.
3. **Working conditions are safe and hygienic**
    3.1. A safe and hygienic working environment shall be provided, bearing in mind the prevailing knowledge of the industry and of any specific hazards. Adequate steps shall be taken to prevent accidents and injury to health arising out of, associated with, or occurring in the course of work, by minimising, so far as is reasonably practicable, the causes of hazards inherent in the working environment.
    3.2. Workers shall receive regular and recorded health and safety training, and such training shall be repeated for new or reassigned workers.
    3.3. Access to clean toilet facilities and to potable water, and, if appropriate, sanitary facilities for food storage shall be provided.
    3.4. Accommodation, where provided, shall be clean, safe, and meet the basic needs of the workers.
    3.5. The company observing the code shall assign responsibility for health and safety to a senior management representative.
4. **Child labour shall not be used**
    4.1. There shall be no new recruitment of child labour.
    4.2. Companies shall develop or participate in and contribute to policies and programmes which provide for the transition of any child found to be performing child labour to enable her or him to attend and remain in quality education until no longer a child; 'child' and 'child labour' being defined in the appendices.
    4.3. Children and young persons under 18 shall not be employed at night or in hazardous conditions.
    4.4. These policies and procedures shall conform to the provisions of the relevant ILO standards.
5. **Living wages are paid**
    5.1. Wages and benefits paid for a standard working week meet, at a minimum, national legal standards or industry benchmark standards, whichever is higher. In any event wages should always be enough to meet basic needs and to provide some discretionary income.
    5.2. All workers shall be provided with written and understandable Information about their employment conditions in respect to wages before they enter employment and about the particulars of their wages for the pay period concerned each time that they are paid.
    5.3. Deductions from wages as a disciplinary measure shall not be permitted nor shall any deductions from wages not provided for by national law be permitted without the expressed permission of the worker concerned. All disciplinary measures should be recorded.
6. **Working hours are not excessive**
    6.1. Working hours comply with national laws and benchmark industry standards, whichever affords greater protection.
    6.2. In any event, workers shall not on a regular basis be required to work in excess of 48 hours per week and shall be provided with at least one day off for every 7 day period on average. Overtime shall be voluntary, shall not exceed 12 hours per week, shall not be demanded on a regular basis and shall always be compensated at a premium rate.

Figure 10.11. Ethical Trading Initiative base code of workplace standards

Source: www.ethicaltrade.org.

7. No discrimination is practised

    7.1. There is no discrimination in hiring, compensation, access to training, promotion, termination or retirement based on race, caste, national origin, religion, age, disability, gender, marital status, sexual orientation, union membership or political affiliation.

8. Regular employment is provided

    8.1. To every extent possible work performed must be on the basis of recognised employment relationship established through national law and practice.

    8.2. Obligations to employees under labour or social security laws and regulations arising from the regular employment relationship shall not be avoided through the use of labour-only contracting, sub-contracting, or home-working arrangements, or through apprenticeship schemes where there is no real intent to impart skills or provide regular employment, nor shall any such obligations be avoided through the excessive use of fixed-term contracts of employment.

9. No harsh or inhumane treatment is allowed

    9.1. Physical abuse or discipline, the threat of physical abuse, sexual or other harassment and verbal abuse or other forms of intimidation shall be prohibited.

10. The provisions of this code constitute minimum and not maximum standards, and this code should not be used to prevent companies from exceeding these standards. Companies applying this code are expected to comply with national and other applicable law and, where the provisions of law and this Base Code address the same subject, to apply that provision which affords the greater protection.

Figure 10.11. (*continued*)

influence, or curb business practice. A number of authors have referred to this as 'civil regulation' (Bendell 2000*b*; Zadek 2001). As Bendell (2000*b*) argues, civil society effects regulation by creating norms for business and then enforcing them in some way.

Civil regulation then goes somewhat further than just the *relations* that CSOs have with business. Rather, we also have to look at the *outcomes* of these processes. Sometimes these outcomes are company or project specific, sometimes they have more lasting impact. For example, it is evident that many of these conflicts and collaborations have led to the establishment of codes of conduct intended to govern corporate action. Such codes clearly encompass aspects of norm creation and enforcement that are more institutionalized and lasting than say a single change in corporate policy made as a result of boycott action. As Schneidewind and Petersen (1998) suggest, business collaboration with civil society can help to build social and political structures that might even change the rules for other business actors.

The *Ethical Trade Initiative* (ETI) for example (see **Figure 10.9** for an overview) commits its members to adopting or incorporating its internationally agreed code of practice on workplace standards, and requires that members' suppliers meet the provisions of the code within a reasonable time frame. The code of the initiative, based on conventions of the International Labour Organization (ILO), is shown in **Figure 10.11**. The membership requirements further commit partners to 'demonstrable implementation of their codes' and 'collaborating actively in developing means for such effective and transparent implementation, particularly in relation to monitoring and independent verification'. These commitments essentially act as regulatory forces on member organizations since failure to abide by them would, at least in principle, lead to them being thrown out of the initiative.

Of course, as we explained back in Chapter 5 (148–156), codes of conduct are open to considerable criticism. However, the involvement of civil actors here clearly helps to overcome some of the limitations of individual company codes. In the case of the ETI, the code itself is widely agreed upon among different constituencies. Perhaps more importantly, though, membership also commits companies to effective *implementation* of the code. Probably the main drawback though of this and other examples of civil regulation is their **voluntary** nature. Whereas state regulation is obligatory and usually includes some form of punishment for non-compliance, such as a fine, civil regulation relies on the voluntary commitments of companies. Many companies will not choose to join, and even among those that do, there is always the option to leave if their priorities change. For example, in 2003 the UK clothing retailer Littlewoods, which was a founding member of the ETI, pulled out of the initiative following a change in the firm's ownership. The announcement signalled the shutting down of the company's entire ten-person ethical trading team (Bowers and Finch 2003). Although some form of censure is available for civil actors in these kinds of circumstances—they can publicize the incidents, create bad publicity, and even initiate protests, boycotts, and other direct actions—this constitutes a relatively 'soft' form of regulation compared to traditional government modes.

Despite such limitations, civil society has certainly taken an increasingly important role in forming codes of practice and even other more formal elements of rule setting and regulation (Zadek 2001). As we intimated in the previous section on globalization, given the apparent absence of effective global government, this is especially the case of transnational regulations, such as those dealing with environmental management or labour conditions. Although the business literature has been fairly slow in acknowledging this development, even here the growing influence of civil society in the institutional arrangements facing international business has been recognized (e.g. Doh and Teegen 2002). Certainly CSOs can now at the least be considered to be part of the group of actors shaping the rules, norms, and practices of international business—assigning them a place in what writers in the politics literature tend to call systems or regimes of 'global governance' (e.g. Nickel 2002). We shall examine the implications of this further in the next chapter when we move on to discuss the role of government and regulation more generally in shaping the context of business ethics.

The key point to take away from this section is that civil society can act as a conduit through which individual citizens can exert some kind of leverage on, or gain a form of participation in, corporate decision-making and action. When we speak of corporate citizenship in its extended sense, the idea that corporations are increasingly involved in administering various citizen rights suggests that those citizens might need a way of registering their desires and wishes in some way. Voting and consumer choices are two avenues; participation in civil society is another. As we shall see in the final section, this issue of participation also has important ramifications for notions of sustainability.

Civil society, business, and sustainability

Civil society has been at the forefront of the development of sustainability theory and practice. This is hardly surprising when we consider that each of the three elements of sustainability—social, environmental, and economic—have been typical foci for CSOs of various kinds, from humanitarian NGOs (social issues), to development agencies (economic and social issues), and environmental activists (environmental issues). More-over, many environmental and other CSOs are now actually dedicating themselves to advancing the cause of sustainability itself, rather than focusing on specific issues. For example, the mission of Friends of the Earth International is to 'campaign on the most urgent environmental and social issues of our day, while simultaneously catalyzing a shift toward sustainable societies'.

It is then the representative nature of the stake held by CSOs that makes them so integral to sustainability in business. At best, corporations can only really claim to repres-ent economic interests. However, progress towards sustainability requires that a wider set of interests are also represented and incorporated in business decisions. Certainly government is one actor that can do this, but given the retraction of the state and the growth in civil society influence, CSOs also increasingly fulfil this role for social, environmental and—to a lesser extent—economic interests. As we saw with some of our examples of business–CSO collaboration in the previous section, diverse social, environmental, and economic interests can be brought together in a single project in order to develop solutions that are more balanced on the sustainability scorecard. Of course, it is contestable whether busi-ness has to necessarily work *with* civil society to achieve sustainable solutions, but at the very least civil actors have a role to play in encouraging business to take notice of and ad-dress particular dimensions of sustainability.

The problem here, though, is that because CSOs are advancing particular interests, they cannot necessarily be expected to agree on what actions are likely to be the most appro-priate for corporations to take. Sustainability remains thoroughly contested in most if not all areas where corporations might be expected to act. Hence, if corporations are serious about addressing sustainability, the principal challenge is inevitably going to be how best to **balance the competing interests** of different civil actors. For example, in recent years civil interests have clashed in a number of key European industries. Let us look at a couple of examples: North Sea fishing and the energy industry.

North Sea fishing

Overfishing in the North Sea has led to dwindling fish stocks of many popular species, especially cod. Over the years, various scientists and civil actors such as Greenpeace and WWF have produced evidence of an impending fishing crisis and advocated the need for intervention (Fowler and Heap 2000). However, any restrictions on fishing quotas pose a major threat to jobs and the local economies in fishing areas. This is especially a problem for the North Sea fishing industry since it is concentrated in isolated regions where the industry is at the hub of local communities and provides either directly or indirectly a significant proportion of local jobs.

Although not necessarily rejecting the evidence against depleting stocks, civil organiza-tions representing local communities and fishworkers have sought to protect their interests, with governments in many European countries such as the UK, Spain, Ireland, and France backing their calls to reject proposals to impose restrictions (Mortishead 2002). As a result, the price of cod and other endangered species has rocketed. However, some governments such as those in Iceland and Norway have long imposed more rigorous management systems to ensure more sustainable stocks. Similarly, Unilever, one of the world's biggest fish buyers, has collaborated with WWF to set up the (now independent) Marine Stewardship Council to establish and certify sustainable fish supplies, thereby creating further sustainable alternatives to North Sea fish (Fowler and Heap 2000).

As a result of these developments, in countries such as the UK, where fish and chips is perhaps the best-known national dish, most cod is now imported from Iceland and other more sustainable sources. In fact, one of Unilever's brands, Birds Eye, provoked controversy in UK fishing communities when it ran an ad in 2002 saying the company would no longer be taking any cod from the North Sea in line with its policy of sourcing from sustainable fisheries (Mortishead 2002). And with the announcement late in 2002 that the EU was finally going to impose a 45 per cent reduction in the North Sea cod quota, thereby limiting fishing vessels to just fifteen days a month at sea, fishing industry and community groups argued that they were being crippled by insensitive and blunt instruments of policy (Macleod 2003).

Energy industry

The energy industry has also been the scene of contestation between civil groups for many years, involving a range of issues around oil extraction, power station location, nuclear power, and more recently even wind power. If we just take the example of wind power, a number of competing civil interests are evident. Many governments and national and international environmental NGOs, for example, actively promote investment in wind power technologies because they offer clean renewable energy. Similarly, local governments, development agencies, farming groups, and landowners have generally been supportive of wind farm development because of the financial rewards, jobs, and investment that it brings. However, some local environmental organizations, community groups, and tourism promoters have opposed the erection of wind turbines, arguing that they despoil the countryside.

In some parts of Europe this has therefore led to wind farm developments arousing much controversy, and many of them have been blocked. In the UK, for example, nearly 90 per cent of wind farm projects between 1995 and 1999 were rejected after planning inquiries (Nuttall 1999). Various anti-wind farm protest groups have recently emerged in Scotland, where groups such as the Skye Wind Farm Action Group (SWAG) have lobbied against development on Scottish islands (Macaskill 2002). Similarly, moves to escalate the development of wind farming in Wales has led to protest from virtually all Welsh environmental and local community groups, yet the area already has the largest concentration of on-shore turbines in Europe (Jenkins 2002).

In some other parts of Europe, civil society has been much more supportive of wind farming. In Germany, the world's leading wind energy producer, Schleswig-Holstein, produces 15 per cent of its energy from wind power (Houlder 1999). In Spain, wind turbines have also generally been welcomed, with Navarra in north-east Spain now producing 20 per cent of its electricity from wind power (Macaskill 2002). And Denmark has such a dominant position in the wind generator market that Danish companies account for about 55 per cent of the world's wind power manufacturing industry and employ over 12,000 people (Houlder 1999; Nuttall 1999). Significantly, Denmark appears to have avoided planning protests by developing wind power through a modest step-by-step approach which has seen four out of five Danish turbines being erected by individuals on their own land rather than in large concentrated wind farms (Houlder 1999).

■ Think theory

Think about the triple bottom line of sustainability and set out the various stakeholders that represent the different interests involved in wind power and in North Sea fishing. Is it possible to determine which of the elements of sustainability are deemed more legitimate or are the most strongly represented from the stakeholders involved?

Towards participation and empowerment

These are just two of the industries in Europe that have experienced civil contestation (as well as varying degrees of government and business support) regarding sustainability issues in business. As our examples show, the range of interests represented by different civil actors often puts them at odds with each other, especially when different facets of the triple bottom line of sustainability are at issue. We have focused mainly on 'downstream' activities—i.e. those involved primarily in resource extraction and utilization—since it is often here where different interests are most evident, and where local communities in particular tend to be involved. However, we could easily have also referred to the various other areas where different civil actors have fought over specific business issues, including plant closures, gene technology applications, retail park or housing developments, road building, mining, and dam construction.

In some ways, though, the key issue for sustainability in business–civil society relations is not so much that civil groups agree but that they are able to actively **participate** in decisions that affect them. Many authors writing about sustainability in business stress the need for greater democracy in corporations through community participation. As Bendell (2000*b*: 249) contends:

Organizations . . . that affect you and your community, especially when they affect the material foundations of your self-determination, must be able to be influenced by you and your community . . . What are required are new forms of democratic governance so that people can determine their own futures in a sustainable environment.

CSOs clearly have a crucial role to play in enabling individuals to participate, at least in some way, in the corporate decisions that affect them. Although evidence suggests that corporations tend to limit the degree of participation that civil groups and other stakeholders can exercise—often concentrating more on simply consulting or placating them (Banerjee 2000; Cumming 2001)—this does at least provide a possible mechanism for participation. Moreover, whilst arguments about the accountability and representativeness of CSOs themselves are likely to persist, their role in bringing a plurality of interests to bear on corporations would appear to make them important actors in the evolving sustainability agenda.

Summary

In this chapter we have discussed the role that civil society has played in business ethics. We have taken a fairly broad definition of what constitutes civil society in order to include the whole gamut of organizations outside business and government that have confronted corporations over various aspects of business ethics. These civil society organizations or CSOs have been shown to have a somewhat different stake in the corporation compared with the other stakeholders we have looked at so far. Specifically, the representational nature of CSO stakes makes their claim rather more indirect than for other constituencies.

In examining the ethical issues arising in business–CSO relations and the attempts by business to deal more responsibly with civil society, we have charted a gradual shift in the nature of these relations. Business and civil society appear to have moved from a primarily confrontational engagement to a more complex, multifaceted relationship that still involves confrontation but also includes charitable giving, collaboration, and aspects of civil regulation. Regardless of the nature of this interaction, though, we argued that for citizens, local communities, and other groups typically excluded from the decision processes of business, CSOs can act as important conduits through which their interests can be expressed and advanced within business. Although civil groups themselves may not even always agree with each other, the contribution they make to engendering a pluralistic context for business decision-making and action appears to be a vital one in our understanding of business ethics.

STUDY QUESTIONS

1 What is a civil society organization?

2 Select three civil society organizations that you have some knowledge of. Who or what do these organizations purport to represent? Would you say they are promotional or sectional groups?

3 'It is simply not really the company's choice who is and is not a stakeholder' (Zadek 2001: 163). Evaluate this statement in the context of civil society organizations as stakeholders.

4 Reread Ethics in Action 10.1 about Huntington Life Sciences. Provide an assessment of the campaign against the firm from the following perspectives:

　　(a) Huntington Life Sciences;
　　(b) An investor in the firm;
　　(c) The government;
　　(d) An animal rights activist.

　　Are there other CSO protest approaches that might have been more acceptable to each of these actors?

5 Explain the concept of civil regulation. How appropriate is this term for describing the nature of civil society activities?

6 What role do civil society organizations play in enhancing business sustainability?

RESEARCH EXERCISE

Select a CSO with which you are familiar and conduct some research on its main activities with and/or against business.

1 What are the main tactics and approaches used by the CSO in its relations with business?

2 Would you say its approach has shifted at all over time? Explain your answer.

3 How effective and ethical do you think the CSO's approach has been?

CASE 10

From conflict to collaboration? Greenpeace's Greenfreeze campaign

This case examines Greenpeace's attempts to develop a solutions-oriented approach to introducing more sustainable technologies in the refrigerants industry. The case details the NGO's initial collaboration with the former East German manufacturer Foron to develop the 'climate-friendly' Greenfreeze refrigerant, and their subsequent negotiations with companies such as Bosch-Siemens, Electrolux, Hotpoint, Sainsbury, and even Coca-Cola to diffuse the technology in Europe and further afield. The case provides the opportunity to examine the approaches open to civil society organizations in attempting to influence corporate policy, and in particular their roles and responsibilities in shaping the rules and norms of global business practice.

When Coca-Cola announced in 2000 that it would convert all of its refrigeration appliances such as fridges and dispensing machines to climate-friendly 'Greenfreeze' technology by 2004, and would pressurize all of its distributors to do likewise, Greenpeace scored a major success in its international campaign to eliminate climate-damaging refrigerants. And what's more, given Coca-Cola's global market clout, it showed just how far Greenpeace had come in its Greenfreeze campaign from its initial beginnings in 1992 when the organization developed a partnership with a former East German company on the brink of bankruptcy.

The very first steps in the Greenfreeze campaign actually started a few years before Greenpeace itself got involved. Greenfreeze is a refrigerant, i.e. a type of coolant used in fridges, freezers, air conditioners, and other types of cooling appliances. It was first developed in 1989 by the Dortmund Institute of Hygiene in Germany as an alternative to existing industrial refrigerants, many of which were ozone-depleting, and all of which contributed to global warming.

At the time it was developed, most of the refrigeration industry was starting to move from refrigerants using CFCs (which contributed to ozone depletion) to HCFCs (which still contributed to ozone depletion, but less so) and ultimately to HFCs (which did not contribute to ozone depletion). All however contributed significantly to global warming. The benefit of Greenfreeze then was that since it was based on hydrocarbons, it succeeded in avoiding both of the main environmental problems of existing refrigerants and their supposed replacements—and what is more, it was economically viable. Despite winning an environmental prize, however, the refrigeration industry took almost no notice at all of the new technology, and the Dortmund project was abandoned.

It was at this point that Greenpeace became involved in the story. The organization is probably best known for its dramatic campaigning activities on the high seas—saving whales, attempting to block nuclear tests, and storming oil platforms, among other things. But in 1992 when Greenpeace entered the Greenfreeze story, it decided to take a different approach from its usual confrontational, protest-based methods. Seeing the significant potential of the new technology, it decided to take it upon itself to champion hydrocarbons to refrigerator manufacturers. So, it was Greenpeace that gave Greenfreeze its distinctive name, and it was Greenpeace that attempted to resurrect the stalled development programme of the new technology.

The task of converting the refrigeration industry however was a daunting one. Most of the industry infrastructure, including the manufacturers and their suppliers, was set up for the existing refrigerants and so the major players refused to 'leapfrog' to an entirely new technology. Moreover, the powerful chemical industry, which supplied refrigerants to the fridge and air-conditioner manufacturers, was actively pushing HFCs as the replacement of choice for CFCs. And the chemical manufacturers had little interest in developing Greenfreeze commercially since the mixture could not be patented (because it consisted of two common gases) and the technology was free.

In the end, only the former East German manufacturer Foron Household Appliances was willing to experiment with the new technology. Like many former East German firms after reunification, Foron was close to bankruptcy. The firm was under the administration of the German privatization agent the Treuhand, which needed to find investors for the ailing company, else it would be dissolved. Foron agreed to work with the Greenfreeze technology as a last resort.

In May 1992, Greenpeace secured an arrangement between Foron and the Dortmund Institute, and commissioned ten prototype Greenfreeze refrigerators. Before work could be completed, though, the Treuhand announced that Foron would be liquidated. Greenpeace and Foron rapidly organized a press conference, and almost overnight produced the first Greenfreeze fridge to present at the conference. Although the Treuhand attempted to halt the conference (believing that Greenfreeze was a ploy by 'ex-communist' Foron employees to save 'their unreformed skins'!), the partners ignored their demands and went ahead. Greenpeace launched a grass-roots campaign to persuade the media and consumers, and after public debate, the Treuhand relented and ended up supporting the venture to the tune of DM 5m (€2.5m).

But the Treuhand was not the only adversary that the alliance faced. To begin with, Greenpeace faced its own internal revolt over the collaboration with Foron. Endorsing any kind of company was a significant departure from Greenpeace's usual confrontational style, and was viewed by many inside the organization as a 'sell-out'. One member referred to the response as a 'bloody internal battle', illustrating the depth of feeling underlying the change of approach. While Greenpeace International, based in Amsterdam, wanted to attack the chemical producers themselves, Greenpeace Germany, which was spearheading the Foron alliance, wanted to focus attention on the refrigerator manufacturers who merely used rather than made the damaging substances. This represented the first main attempt by Greenpeace to use the market to try and create positive change in industry.

The main resistance however came from the chemical and refrigerator industries. During 1992 they launched a disinformation press campaign, and sent letters to manufacturers and retailers warning that the technology was unproven, unfeasible, inefficient, and potentially dangerous—'a potential bomb' no less! However, Greenpeace's publicity machine generated over 70,000 advance orders from consumers, and eventually the claims against Greenfreeze were dropped as Greenpeace managed to persuade the government and scientists to test (successfully) for product safety. By the end of the year Greenfreeze was certified by the German safety standards authority, and the following February, Foron's 'Green Cooler' fridge, using Greenfreeze technology, was awarded the prestigious 'Blue Angel' eco-label.

By the time Foron's fridge actually made it into the shops in March of 1993, several of the German manufacturers such as Bosch-Siemens and Miele, which had so vociferously criticized

Greenfreeze, had already developed their own Greenfreeze prototypes. And by 1994, all German manufacturers declared that they would abandon HCFCs and HFCs for Greenfreeze. Greenpeace of course heralded this as a major success, but for Foron, the wider adoption meant that the company rapidly lost its competitive advantage. As the more sophisticated rival Greenfreeze fridges entered the market, Foron's precarious financial position and lack of marketing clout left it in an extremely weak market position. The company eventually declared bankruptcy in 1996, and its refrigerator division was purchased by the Dutch firm ATAG.

Greenpeace meanwhile took its Greenfreeze campaign into the rest of Europe, and ultimately worldwide. Despite campaigns that saw Greenfreeze fridges (made in Germany) sold throughout Europe, most manufacturers outside Germany initially resisted the technology. A major success was gained though when the UK supplier Calor Gas approached Greenpeace anonymously through a third party, and after extensive negotiation, eventually became a major industrial supplier of Greenfreeze. The major Swedish manufacturer Electrolux, however, remained critical of the technology. But after Greenpeace revealed that the company was actually selling Greenfreeze models in Germany under the 'Privileg' brand, the firm eventually switched.

Greenpeace also sought to leverage other players in the supply chain. In the UK, Greenpeace collaborated with Calor to target supermarkets—one of the biggest users of refrigerants. Sainsbury became the first UK supermarket to use all Greenfreeze technologies in one of its stores, and when Tesco appeared to be backtracking out of a commitment to phase out HFCs, Greenpeace toured a truck fitted with Greenfreeze freezers and emblazoned with the slogan 'Tesco freezers wreck the planet' around the country. Greenpeace also worked with Iceland, a major UK appliance retailer, to launch its own line of Greenpeace-endorsed fridges and freezers. In fact, Iceland became so proactive in its support that it even dropped the prominent Hotpoint brand from its stores when the brand's owner General Electric refused to convert from HFCs.

In the rest of the world, too, Greenpeace has been active in promoting Greenfreeze. Developing countries have posed a particular problem since western chemical and refrigerator multinationals have been dumping CFC- and HCFC-based technologies in countries such as China and India. Nonetheless, by 2000 approximately half of all fridges sold in China (which now has the world's largest domestic refrigeration industry) were based on hydrocarbons. Inroads had also been made into other developing countries, such as Argentina, Belarus, Cuba, Indonesia, and India—although progress has been hampered by various factors including technical challenges, industry resistance, and government inertia. In the USA, Japan, and Australia, though, despite significant efforts, Greenpeace has met with almost complete failure—mainly due to either apathetic markets or powerful lobbying by existing industry players.

The organization had hoped that such resistance would be weakened when it showcased Greenfreeze as part of the 2000 Sydney Olympic Games' 'Green Games' initiative. However, following pressure from manufacturers and chemical suppliers the Games' organizing committee backtracked from the draft environmental guidelines that had been drawn up with Greenpeace, and which stipulated against the use of CFCs, HCFCs, and HFCs in Olympic venues. In response, Greenpeace targeted the Games' sponsors including Coca-Cola and McDonald's, branding them 'dirty Olympic sponsors'. The organization even set up a website CokeSpotlight modelled on the anti-McDonald's McSpotlight site (see **Case 1**) and released postcards and badges aping the style of the famous 'Enjoy Coca-Cola' slogan with the acerbic 'Enjoy Climate Change'.

Still, it was a surprise to many when Coca-Cola announced its new refrigeration policy. Even the Greenpeace international director was impressed—in a letter to the Coca-Cola CEO, he commended his 'decisive leadership role' on the issue and proclaimed that it 'could be perhaps one of the most important legacies' of Sydney's 'Green' Olympic Games.

Questions

1 Set out the tactics used by Greenpeace in the Greenfreeze campaign. Can you discern an overall strategy used by the organization?

2 To what extent would you say that Greenpeace had changed from a conflict-based approach to a more collaborative mode of engagement?

3 Who are Greenpeace's stakeholders in this case? What responsibilities, if any, would you say that they had to these stakeholders?

4 How would you assess Greenpeace's relative advantages in pursuing the Greenfreeze campaign compared to a company attempting to diffuse an innovation?

5 In what ways, and in which industries (if any), is the notion of a 'civil regulator' a useful way of describing Greenpeace's role in this case?

Sources

Stafford, E. R., and Hartman, C. L. (2001). 'Greenpeace's "greenfreeze campaign": hurdling competitive forces in the diffusion of environmental technology innovation'. In K. Green, P. Groenewegen, and P. S. Hofman (eds.), *Ahead of the Curve*. Dordrecht: Kluwer: 107–31.

—— , Polonsky, M. J., and Hartman, C. L. (2000). 'Environmental NGO–business collaboration and strategic bridging: a case analysis of the Greenpeace–Foron alliance'. *Business Strategy and the Environment*, 9: 122–35.

www.greenpeace.org.

11

Government, Regulation, and Business Ethics

In this chapter we will:

- Discuss the specific stake that governments have in corporate activity by discussing the double agency that governments assume;

- Outline the ethical issues and problems faced in business–government relations, paying particular attention to practices commonly criticized in the media and public discourse;

- Identify the shifts in these issues and problems as globalization progressively deterritorializes social activities, resulting in limited scope and power of national, territorial governments;

- Further develop the notion of corporate citizenship by analysing the changing role of business and CSOs in the regulatory process and discuss various alternative routes of regulating corporate behaviour, especially in a globalized world;

- Examine the challenges posed by sustainability to business–government relations and show the importance of strong governmental regulation for achieving potentially sustainable solutions.

Introduction

With the growth in corporate attempts to influence government policy through lobbying, political donations, and even bribery, the issue of business relations with government has increasingly become a key issue of business ethics. Is it acceptable for corporations to use their considerable power to shape government policy? Is the government jeopardizing its role in protecting the public interest when politicians sit on the board of corporations? Should powerful business interest groups such as the oil industry or the food industry actively contribute to the development of regulation that is supposed to ensure they operate in society's best interest? These are all crucial questions for business ethics when looking at relations with the government. And, as we shall see, they represent some of the most pressing problems confronting us in an era of globalization, where the lack of a 'global government' makes the 'policing' of multinational corporations increasingly problematic.

In this chapter, we will analyse in more depth some of these ideas that have been bub-
bling up throughout this book—the increasingly political role taken up by corporations,
the involvement of private actors in the regulation of business ethics, the weakening of
the state in protecting our social, political, and civil rights, etc.—as well as examining some
new (but related) issues that arise when looking at the business–government relation,
such as corporate lobbying and party financing. Government has a crucial role to play in
establishing the 'rules of the game' by which we judge business ethics. However, as we shall
see in this chapter, in the era of globalization, the traditional boundaries between business and government have blurred to such an extent that defining these rules has become
a matter of ethical concern in itself.

Government as a stakeholder

Before we proceed, though, it is important that we define a few terms that will be used
throughout this chapter a little more precisely.

Defining government, laws, and regulation

We have actually come across government several times already in this book. For a start,
government is involved in issuing laws regulating business practice. Back in Chapter 1 (9),
for example, when we made our initial definition of business ethics, we pointed out that
business ethics tended to begin where the law ended. This would suggest that government
takes on the role of setting at least the baseline of acceptable practice in business. As we
shall see shortly, government also effectively provides business with a 'licence to operate'
in its jurisdiction.

When talking about 'the government' in this context, though, we have to be aware
that we are actually talking about a whole group of different actors, institutions, and
processes. In democratic societies, such as in most European countries, the government
would include all legislative and executive bodies that act on the basis of parliamentary
consent. Furthermore, the incorporation of those functions pertains to various *levels*: it would
start with the legislative bodies on the *European level* in Brussels, Luxembourg, and, most
notably, Strasbourg; it would then include the *national government*, but also in many cases
regional governments, such as the Welsh Assembly, or the government of a French *départe-
ment* or a German *Bundesland*; finally, it would also relate to *local or municipal authorities*.

In short, we can define 'government' as follows:

> The government consists of a variety of institutions and actors at different levels that share
> a common power to issue laws.

By laws, you should remember that in the context of business ethics we are basically
concerned with the codification of what society deems are appropriate and inappropriate
actions. This suggests the following definition:

> Laws serve as a codification into explicit rules of the social consensus about what a society
> regards as right and wrong.

Looking specifically at laws codifying right and wrong *business* practices, it is important to recognize that the law is only one aspect of the broader area of **regulation of business**. Although laws are of some relevance to business ethics, it is the role of regulation that is most vital to understand. This is because it is regulation more generally, rather than the law specifically, which tends to operate in the *grey areas* of business ethics. After all, once we have a clear legal ruling on certain business practices, they are no longer really matters of business ethics. But those still open to other forms of non-legally binding regulation certainly are. So what exactly do we mean by regulation here then?

Regulation is all about the *rules* governing business behaviour. It includes laws and acts, but also pertains to other forms of formal or informal **rule-making and enforcement**. This includes broader governmental policies, concepts, goals, and strategies, all of which ultimately enable or restrict the activities of business actors. For example, in the UK there are specific *laws* dealing with issues of discrimination in the workplace, including the Sex Discrimination Act 1975 and the Race Relations Act 1976. In addition to these legally binding rules, though, there are also other *regulatory instruments* such as the Anti-Ageism voluntary code introduced in 1999, which are intended to encourage compliance with non-discrimination through non-legally binding (hence 'weaker') modes of influence. Not all regulation is therefore enforced through the law; sometimes it operates by creating norms that define 'acceptable' behaviour, but which essentially only operate through social enforcement or encouragement.

Originally, most regulation would be issued and enforced by governmental bodies in the narrow sense such as parliament, ministries, and public authorities. However, if we look at the London Stock Exchange, we find that the majority of rules that govern the actors in this and similar markets are not in fact issued by the government at all, but by a *private* body, in this case the Financial Services Authority. In a similar vein, in the last two chapters we have raised the prospect of corporations and civil society organizations becoming involved in regulatory activity. Later in this chapter, we will discuss in more detail the role of *private actors* in regulatory processes. To begin with, though, it is important to clearly state that regulation is no longer the solitary prerogative of the government: it can be *delegated* to other parties.

These two clarifications—that regulation is about certain types of rules, and that it operates through governmental and non-governmental actors, leads us to the following definition:

> Regulation can be defined as rules that are issued by governmental actors and other delegated authorities to constrain, enable, or encourage particular business behaviours. Regulation includes rule definitions, laws, mechanisms, processes, sanctions, and incentives.

This leads us to one final clarification about the relationship between business and government. When talking about government, the terms 'political' and 'politics' typically arise. Originally, these terms described the governance of the Greek people, the 'polis', and consequently included issuing laws, running the economy, (international) diplomacy, etc. In the course of time, however, 'politics' has become a somewhat ambiguous concept, with all sorts of connotations, such as in 'office politics' or 'political correctness', etc. In this chapter, however, we will use the word 'politics' in its original sense. Therefore, when we discuss how companies are getting more and more involved in 'politics', we mean that they increasingly act in areas that have traditionally been the prerogative of governments.

Let us start then by clarifying the nature of the relationship between business and government, and, in particular, the specific stake held by the government in corporations.

Basic roles of government as a stakeholder

When talking with managers about the government, or even simply skimming through the business press, it does not take long to realize that people in business tend to have a very ambiguous attitude towards the government. On the one hand, business likes to complain about an over-active government, perhaps because it demands 'excessive' taxes, or because it restricts their activities, for example by blocking mergers or raising new standards for product safety. On the other hand, business also expects the government to be constantly active in protecting their interests, such as improving the infrastructure, or keeping foreign competitors out of the market.

If we look at this relation from the government's perspective, the situation is by no means any more straightforward. While politicians like to surround themselves with powerful business leaders and are quite aware of the fact that a booming economy helps their chances at the ballot box, they also have to consider the interests of their electorate who expect governments to 'police' business and to make sure that they act for the benefit of society.

We could go on and find numerous examples of the rather complex, interwoven, and often quite contradicting ties between business and government. However, when discussing stakeholder theory in Chapter 2 (50–55), we determined that a stakeholder of a corporation could be defined by the fact that it benefits or is harmed by the corporation, and/or that its rights were affected by the corporation. Applying this to government we have to ask the question, how is government affected by business and how are certain governmental rights influenced by corporate action?

In order to sort out this slightly complicated relationship we have to differentiate the two basic roles of government, which are shown in **Figure 11.1**. These are government as an elected representative of citizens' interests and government as an actor (or group of actors) with interests of its own.

Government as an elected representative of citizens' interests

Unlike many other stakeholders, such as shareholders, employees, or suppliers, government in principle represents an *entire community*, since it is elected by the citizens of a certain town, region, country, or even continent (such as the European Parliament).[1] In this respect, governments are similar to CSOs, which we discussed in the previous chapter, in that they administer and represent the interest of a wider community. In this role as the

---

[1] We should just add that in this chapter we mainly talk about democracies such as those in most European countries. The situation of course changes dramatically if we move out of this context (see also pp. 412–13 in this chapter).

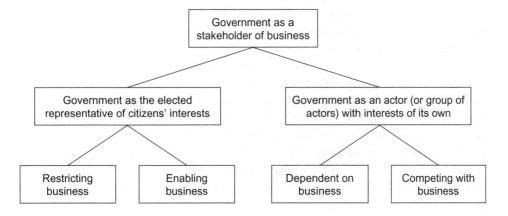

Figure 11.1. Government as a stakeholder of business

elected representative of citizens' interests, government mainly defines the conditions for the **licence to operate** of business.

In practice, this definition of the licence to operate normally becomes most visible in areas where governments—in their fulfilment of the electorate's mandate—try to **restrict business**. For example: they issue environmental regulation that forces companies to install filters or to recycle rather than dump waste; they impose taxes on corporate profits; and they investigate whether a merger bid is in the public interest. All this is done because society wants business to operate in a way that, to stick with these examples: does not threaten the health of present or future generations; contributes to the maintenance of the infrastructure in a country; or maintains free and fair competition for the benefit of consumers (Thorne McAlister et al. 2003: 97–120).

The latter aspect, however, is closely linked to the positive side of the government's role towards business (Carroll and Buchholtz 2000: 208–15). In forbidding a merger or regulating the behaviour of traders at the stock market, governments in fact take over a key role in **enabling business** activities in the first place. For instance, if the EU Commissioner for Competition forbids a merger and thus avoids the gradual emergence of monopolies he or she makes sure that there is still competition and—ultimately—still a free market as such. In fact, if we look to most of the regulatory functions of governments with regard to business they in fact have an enabling role more than anything else: markets can only function if basic rules are established and an appropriate regulatory framework exists.

This enabling role of the government, however, is by no means confined to markets and other directly economic issues. It also pertains to a number of broader rules in society, such as a reliable and fair legal system, and efficient sanctioning mechanisms for illegal behaviour. Economic transactions rely heavily on safe expectations about the behaviour of the transaction partners. One of the problems of so-called less developed countries is that a weak government does not tend to provide the stability that encourages foreign investors to enter these markets. Striking examples are the economies in Eastern Europe, most notably some parts of the former Soviet Union. Here, the implosion of the communist regime has resulted in a political and legal vacuum that (among many other problems) has led to poorly enforced regulation and escalating corruption, which together make it increasingly diffi-cult to attract foreign investment to foster economic growth.

There is of course some debate about the *degree* of governmental responsibility for a func-tioning economy (Carroll and Buchholtz 2000: 218–21). The options range from a passive, 'laissez-faire' hands-off approach where government just sets the rules and controls the compliance of economic actors, to the other extreme where government assumes a force-ful role in 'industrial policy' by actively interfering with the economy. In Europe, the United Kingdom tends towards the first type of governmental role, whereas Germany and France are examples of approaches more towards the second type. For instance, the French government still owns considerable parts of French industry, and the German government still actively steps in with support and financial aid when large employers are at the brink of bankruptcy.

Government as an actor (or group of actors) with interests of its own

The motivations for government to take an active role in the economy might be quite strong at times, but it is important to understand that this is not only because they are acting directly in the interests of their electorate. Government can also be seen as *an actor (or group of actors) with interests of its own*. One reason for this is that governments normally have a self-interest to be re-elected. One could also argue that in most democracies the control of the government by the electorate is somewhat indirect. This certainly applies to the EU level of government but is increasingly an issue in most European countries as well. As a result of this situation, we have to assume that government's stake in business is not only as a (indirect) representative of its electorate but also as a (direct) stakeholder with its own rights and interests.

As such, governments are first and foremost interested in a booming economy. Bill Clinton's successful election slogan 'It's the economy, stupid!'—meaning that govern-ment success should simply be judged in terms of competence in running the economy— could be said to be largely true now for many countries. This actually makes governments very **dependent on business**. On the one hand, their electoral success depends on main-taining high employment, increasing incomes, and expanding business activities. On the other hand, none of these things are *directly* influenced, let alone achieved, by government alone. This situation makes government a rather weak and dependent stakeholder, which businesses are often only too aware of. The 'race to the bottom', which we discussed back in Chapter 7 (255), is clearly indicative of this government dependence. **Case 3** on Rover/ BMW and **Case 11** on Elf's relations with politicians at the end of this chapter also both explore some of the ethical problems governments face in their dependency on business with regard to attracting or maintaining employment in certain regions.

Government in this role, however, is not only *dependent* on business, but also **competes with business**. If we think about the privatization of telecommunications, the ownership of television companies, or the growing usage of private companies in national health-care provision, we can see that business increasingly has also either taken over from, co-operated with, or competed with public organizations in certain industries. Just looking at television companies, it is obvious that in many European countries, publicly funded television companies such as the BBC in the UK or ARD in Germany compete with privately owned operators.

One could argue that, in this context, governments are similar to those stakeholders described in Chapter 9, especially competitors. However, the delicate nature of the relation of business and governments when they collaborate or compete in the same industry comes from the fact that they are often working from different and unequal positions of power. Government enjoys a surfeit of authority or institutional power since it can define industry rules and exercise legislative power. Corporations on the other hand might sometimes enjoy economic advantages since they have potentially recourse to additional sources of finance for investment that government is sometimes unable or unwilling to generate through taxation.

Having now set out in some detail the two main aspects of the stake held by government, we shall proceed to look at the ethical issues and problems this complex relation inevitably raises.

Ethical issues in the relation between business and government

From the discussion above it should already be fairly obvious that the stake (or stakes) held by government puts it in a precarious position regarding its relation with business, especially given its competing roles as a self-interested actor, and as a representative of its citizens' interests. However, most of the ethical issues that arise in this relation pertain to the *closeness* of business–government relations. In particular, critics have questioned whether cosy relations between business and government can jeopardize the government's ability to fulfil its role of protecting the public's interest. **Ethical Dilemma 11** gives you an opportunity to think about some of these problems in a specific example of 'close' business–government relations.

We will start with the basic issues here—essentially problems of legitimacy and accountability—and as we proceed through this section, we will examine the ethical case for different types and levels of business–government interaction. Towards the end of the section, we will then turn our attention to some further ethical issues that arise from government attempts at privatization and deregulation of industry.

Identifying the basic problems and issues: legitimacy, accountability, and modes of influence

Probably the main source of ethical problems in business–government relations lies in the fact that government has a fiduciary relation to society in general. What this means is that government is entrusted with the responsibility to act in society's best interests. As **Figure 11.2** shows, government here is in a somewhat bipolar situation (Mitchell 1990; Stigler 1971). First, government is in a mutually dependent relation with *society*: government receives consent from society and acts upon this to enact a regulatory environment

Ethical Dilemma 11

Always good to have friends in politics?

Business deals have always been fairly casual in this little Greek town just south of Thessalonica. Since Costas started his construction business fifteen years ago, he has won a lot of contracts from the municipal authority: redecoration of the town hall, a new kindergarten, even a nice chunk of the new circular road around town—all of which kept his twenty employees busy, and helped Costas and his family of four to enjoy a fairly decent lifestyle. Sitting on the patio of his eighteenth-century farmhouse and slowly watching the fumes of his Cohiba Cigar vanishing into the Mediterranean sunset he feels quite at ease—if only there had not been this meeting with Dionisis this afternoon.

Dionisis is an old friend of Costas from his childhood days. But while Costas had to start working at 15 years old, building houses with his father, Dionisis had become a teacher. However, he had soon got bored and before long, he went into politics. For ten years now Dionisis has been the mayor of the town—but despite his lofty position, the two friends continued to get on very well.

They normally meet once a month in the backroom of a local café, share some ouzo, and exchange gossip. Of course, they also talk about business, and knowing what is coming up in the mayoral office has always helped Costas to tailor his bids to what the council just had in mind. Not that Dionisis had directly pushed things for him—but among friends they talked about projects and Costas was clever enough to integrate this information into his bids. Of course he had known how to show his old mate some gratitude: when Dionisis needs something fixed at his house, it never takes one of Costas's employees more than half an hour to turn up and sort it out. And when Dionisis gave a party for his fiftieth birthday last year Costas took over the entire catering for 200 people including drinks—but this was just a 'birthday present' for his mate.

But today things were different. Dionisis knew that Costas urgently needs new contracts to keep his company running; and so he mentioned the new municipal swimming pool that is about to be built. Dionisis also mentioned that the project manager from another construction company, whom he had met last Sunday after church, had offered to build him a swimming pool in his own house, if his company won the contract. Now Costas knows all too well that this has been Dionisis's dream for years. Not that Dionisis had asked for anything, but there was a funny tone about him telling Costas of his little chat about the pool.

Costas could easily fiddle the bills for work and material in such a way that a small swimming pool in a private house could be 'hidden' in the accounting of a project of the dimension of the tendered municipal one. But after all—isn't that taking things a bit too far? On the one hand, there are his employees and their families: there is not much other work in the pipeline. And doing a favour for an old mate here and there can't be a crime. Dionisis is ultimately in charge of a lot more future projects. On the other hand, renewing Dionisis's roof after last year's storms is an important thing he's done for him. But building a swimming pool is clearly a bigger investment than any favours before. What will his employees say? And if they don't say anything, what will they think? Let alone the people in the village. The more he thinks about it, the more angry he gets—at his competitor, offering the swimming pool; at Dionisis for being so cheeky; and at himself for having gradually allowed himself to be dragged into this somewhat puzzling relationship. He decides to discuss the matter with his lovely wife Cassandra as soon as she returns from her shopping trip to Thessalonica later that night.

Questions

1 What are the main ethical issues in this case?
2 What are the main ethical arguments for and against building the swimming pool for Dionisis?
3 Would the situation be different if Dionisis were a regular business customer rather than the mayor?
4 How would you respond to Dionisis's 'suggestion'?

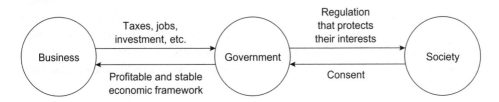

Figure 11.2. Government between business's and society's interests

that protects society's interests. But government also has a relation with *business* where both partners are mutually dependent on each other for certain things: government is expected to provide a profitable and stable economic environment for business to act in; business is expected to provide taxes, jobs, and economic investment in return.

For government, the main ethical issue here lies in the necessity of carrying out the mandate society has given it (in a democracy this would be established through the electoral process) and living up to what it has promised to its constituents. One aspect of this of course is its constraint and enabling of business. However, sometimes the relation that government has with business can threaten its ability to live up to its duty to society.

Let us consider some recent examples:

• When the French government under Lionel Jospin promised to introduce the thirty-five-hour week, there were considerable threats and lobbying from French industry to try and halt the introduction of the policy, arguing that it would be 'bad for business'.

• One of the key issues in the German election of 1998, which led to the shift from the sixteen-year reign of Helmut Kohl to a Social Democrat/Green coalition, was the coalition's promise to deliver Germany's immediate exit out of nuclear power. In the period following the election, the powerful nuclear industry lobby managed to negotiate this 'exit' in such a fashion that the German people will have to wait no less than thirty-five years until the last nuclear power station is closed down.

• When the UK Prime Minister Tony Blair won his second term in government in 2001, one of his key pledges was to improve the quality of Britain's hospitals, schools, and transport while refraining from enhancing the level of personal taxes. In delivering this plan, the government subsequently became heavily dependent on private involvement and finance for boosting some of these public services.

We could extend this list with numerous further examples. What it boils down to though is that business obviously has a significant influence on the implementation and direction of governmental policies. The main ethical consideration arising from this situation is twofold: first, there is the problem of *legitimacy* of business influence; and second, the issue of *accountability*.

Legitimacy of business influence

Looking at our examples above, one might ask if the lobbying of French industry was the legitimate expression of concern about inflated cost structures or an unwarranted attempt to try and block a political decision. Or one might suggest that rather than being a simple case of business obstruction of German policy, the German energy industry should be perfectly entitled to rely on existing agreements and guarantees issued by preceding governments. Either way, the question is one of legitimacy—namely, to what degree is business influence acceptable?

Accountability to the public

We might further contend that since the government acts as a representative of society's interests, the public has a right to be informed about governmental decisions with other constituencies (such as business), and to be able to determine whether it is acting in its interests or not. The relationship between business and government therefore has also to answer the criterion of accountability. In our examples above, the public could be said to have a right to know what exactly shaped the implementation of the thirty-five-hour week in France, or why the German government deems such a long-term exit period for nuclear power more socially beneficial.

Although not the same, both aspects are fairly closely related to each other. Accountability will always be a problem when the influence of business on government is perceived as potentially illegitimate. We discussed the issue of accountability of corporations earlier in Chapter 2 (55–61), and, to a certain degree, this is an issue in all business relations with stakeholders. However, the difference in accountability in business–government relations is that the problem is not just business accountability to its stakeholders, but also the accountability of both parties to society about their relationship.

In the following, we will analyse some of the more common practices where these concerns of legitimacy and accountability arise from the relationship between business and government. Although both partners are able to influence the other, the main concerns for business ethics are where **business has influence on government**. This can happen in a variety of ways.

Modes of business influence on government

There are numerous ways that business can influence government. William Oberman (cited in Getz 1997: 59) distinguishes among different ways according to the following criteria:

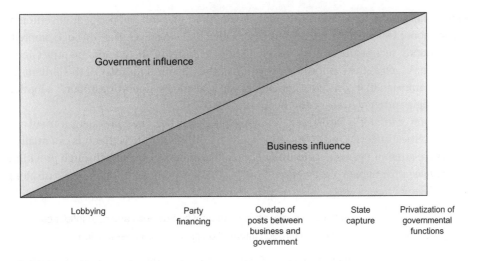

Government influence

Business influence

| Lobbying | Party financing | Overlap of posts between business and government | State capture | Privatization of governmental functions |

Figure 11.3. Types of business influence on government

- **Avenue of approach to decision-maker.** Business influence can range from very *direct* approaches to political decision-makers in person to more *indirect* forms of influence such as advocacy advertising or media editorial that support or challenge political decisions.

- **Breadth of transmission.** Influence can also be *public* (and therefore visible to all), or *private*, where politicians are approached behind closed doors.

- **Content of communication.** Finally, influence can either be *information oriented*, that is, focusing more on communication of information to persuade decision-makers, or *pressure oriented*, which would involve more coercive types of approaches.

Ethical problems of accountability and legitimacy tend to arise primarily in *direct* forms of *private* influence. Beginning with the weakest form of such influence—lobbying—we will explore progressively stronger influences that involve more pressure-oriented content, such as party donations, until we arrive at state capture, where government policy is virtually dictated (or 'captured') by business through illicit payments and other forms of corruption. Beyond state capture, we go on to discuss the problems of privatization and deregulation, which see business not so much merely *influencing* government as actually *replacing* it entirely. These different levels of influence that we will be examining are represented in **Figure 11.3**. As we shall see, these various modes bring with them a range of ethical problems and issues.

Lobbying

The weakest form of direct, private business influence on government is normally called 'lobbying'. For corporations, this area has become increasingly important, and today many major corporations employ professional lobbyists, or have what is called a 'PA expert', a person or even a unit that is responsible for 'public affairs' (van Schendelen 2002), which manages the corporation's attempts to communicate with and persuade government officials about issues relevant to the business.[2] Other lobbying takes place through umbrella organizations, such as the Confederation of British Industry (CBI), or trade and professional associations such as the European Association of the Chemical Industry or the 'Britain-in-Europe' campaign that consists of companies and individuals supporting Britain's adoption of the single currency (Carroll and Buchholtz 2000: 249).

In whatever form it is carried out, lobbying has clearly become a prevalent form of corporate political action (Lord 2000). Its key distinguishing feature is that it is essentially a persuasive attempt by business to influence legislators and their staffs through providing *information* rather than explicit *pressure* (Lord 2000). We can therefore define the term along the following lines:

> Lobbying represents a direct, usually private, attempt by business actors to influence governmental decision-making through information provision and persuasion.

This 'information' can be in the form of specific data, analyses, or opinions on business-related public policy issues. However, the persuasive nature of this provision of information often also introduces considerable pressure on government decision-makers. For this reason, lobbying has often been regarded as a somewhat questionable activity. However, the practice occurs in various guises, some more questionable than others, and includes a broad range of instruments and processes. To get a more concrete picture, then (and a more comprehensive idea of the ethical implications of lobbying), we might consider the different types of lobbying (see McGrath 2002).

• **Atmosphere setting.** This is essentially an awareness raising process intended to enhance government appreciation for industry issues and products, and to create a climate or 'atmosphere' amenable to further influence. This may include events, dinners, or information rallies that create visibility for the interests of industry in the government sphere.

• **Monitoring.** With an ever-increasing amount of regulation, especially at the EU level, an important part of lobbying consists of building up relations with politicians to receive reasonably detailed and up-to-date or 'advance' information about ongoing legislative trends and processes.

• **Provision of information to policy-makers.** Government actors involved in policy-making cannot hope to know everything about the industries they are dealing with. As a result, they often seek out detailed, first-hand information from the very companies that are the subjects of proposed regulation. Strong relations between lobbyists and policy-makers frequently mean that lobbyists are involved in the provision of this information.

• **Advocacy and influencing.** The ultimate influence of lobbying of course is not only informing but ultimately having an influence on decision-makers. Business might attempt

---

[2] Public affairs is not to be confused with PR (public relations), which is primarily a promotional activity for the corporation. In contrast, public affairs usually focuses on the management of government and community relations more broadly. This may well include PR, but public affairs is distinguished by its focus on government relations. See Carroll and Buchholtz (2000: 637).

to do this by offering policy-oriented expertise and 'consultancy', often through industry associations, since they tend to have expert knowledge on certain issues.

- **Application of pressure.** Finally, business lobbying may use the opportunity to communicate with government actors to provide 'information' that is intended to put pressure on them to act in a certain way. This may include implicit or explicit 'warnings' about the potential consequences of particular policies, such as the likelihood of job losses or other politically sensitive outcomes.

In the case of these last three aspects of lobbying, it is not always entirely clear where relatively harmless information provision turns into advocacy, or even more questionable forms of pressurization. In order to clarify this, we often have to examine specific examples in a particular context. Let us take a look then at a couple of illustrations of successful lobbying in action.

- During the UK foot-and-mouth epidemic in 2001, the British government, backed by key players in the retail and tourism industries, was willing to introduce vaccination to stop the spread of the disease. However, the food giant Nestlé lobbied the government to desist from vaccination because of its potential threat to food exports (and ultimately jobs), especially for companies such as Nestlé with major operations in key areas of the epidemic. Finally, the government capitulated and forwent the introduction of vaccination that would have saved much livestock from slaughter (Vidal and Hetherington 2001).

- Germany has typically been known as one of the most progressive countries in introducing environmental legislation, yet in 1999, when the EU End-of-Life Vehicle Directive was about to be issued, it was the German Chancellor who ordered his Minister for the Environment to substantially water down the final document. It has been suggested that the reason for this was the influence of the German car lobby, which urged the German government to consider the directive's potential consequences for job losses in the auto industry. Certainly a strong relation existed between the German Chancellor and the industry, since he had been a long-time non-executive director at Volkswagen (*Financial Times* 1999).

These forms of lobbying are quite frequent and industry appears to be especially keen on using 'information' such as estimates or opinions on possible job losses or threats to competitiveness to encourage governments to withdraw or substantially revise regulation.

But how should we assess lobbying from an ethical perspective? It is obvious that weaker forms of lobbying such as monitoring of legislative processes or communication with decision-makers in government are fairly unproblematic. In a certain sense, they could even be argued to improve regulatory outcomes, and may indeed be desirable. However, there is a case to be made about the relative ease of ability of business interest groups to gain access to political decision-makers compared with other interest groups such as civil society organizations who may lack the resources or presumed *legitimacy* to exercise influence.

The main ethical problem however probably consists of the fact that the involvement of corporations is not 'for free' and may suggest, especially over the long term, a reciprocal arrangement along the lines of 'I'll scratch your back and you scratch mine'. One could suggest then that lobbying threatens the relations of *trust* between governments as supposed 'agents' and representatives of their electorate. The example of the German government's attempt to block the End-of-Life Vehicle Directive is significant in this respect since it meant that one of the first actions of the Green Party Minister of the Environment was to fall short of exactly one of those promises to the electorate that had brought him and his party into government less than a year before! In this sense, the German government gave priority to an agenda that was clearly more attuned to corporate interests than to those of its electorate.

There is however still a further aspect. Many regulatory processes are fairly invisible to outsiders, and lobbying is often based on close personal ties between politicians and business. Consider for example when Tony Blair and his wife are invited to spend their holidays in Richard Branson's (founder and CEO of the Virgin conglomerate) resort on the Maldives. Whilst this may have certain desirable outcomes, such as the Prime Minister gaining first-hand information about key challenges and problems of major business leaders, on the downside, these relations are as it were 'fuelled' and sponsored by industry and there is a fine line between having a close relationship with 'befriended' business leaders and actually taking 'inducements' in the form of holidays and 'gifts'.

One has to add as well that the relations established by corporate lobbyists are not only used in the context of legislative processes. These relations can also impact upon other government activities, such as governmental purchasing decisions, most notoriously in the area of defence technology (Andrews 1996). If BAE Systems, a major defence contractor, 'advises' the British government on which technological option might be the most viable for a certain defence issue, this is hardly neutral advice. As we saw in Chapter 9 (312–314), such **conflicts of interest** are a common problem affecting supplier relations of one sort or another, and lobbying clearly raises the potential for business–government relations to be exposed to similar dilemmas.

■ **Think theory**

Which ethical theory would you find to be best suited to judge whether the lobbying activity of a corporation or industry association is morally right or wrong?

Party financing

A similar situation occurs when industry makes donations to political parties. Like lobbying, donations to parties by business can raise **conflict of interest** problems. For instance in 2002 the British pharmaceutical company Powderject donated £50,000 to the UK Labour Party while still in negotiation about a £2m tax cut for their massive R&D expenditures. When the tax cut was then subsequently approved, the media unsurprisingly suggested the Labour Party was compromised by the donation.[3] A similar case made the

---

[3] *Observer*, 28 Apr. 2002.

headlines when the Blair government exempted motor racing from a proposed ban on tobacco advertising in 1998. It was only when the exemption was announced that it came to light that Formula 1 boss Bernie Ecclestone had donated £1m to the New Labour campaign a year before.[4]

Scandals such as these have led to widespread resentment and cynicism about business donations to political parties. Again, the key issue is the legitimacy of these donations: even if parties are perfectly accountable for these donations—and most European countries are forced to disclose party donations—the temptation to link political decisions to financial support is substantial. Ultimately, some of these party 'donations' could easily be seen as a 'fee' to obtain a certain political decision—which of course raises the prospect of **preferential treatment**, and might even go so far as to threaten the very notion of democratic process. As **Case 11** at the end of this chapter shows, party donations by business can even amount to outright bribery if they are ultimately tied to governmental purchasing orders that directly benefit the donating company.

Again, as we saw in Chapter 9 (314–317), there are a number of ways we can look at such 'gifts' to try and determine whether they are acceptable, including the intention of the gift giver, the impact on the receiver, and the perception of other parties. For business too, though, this situation is clearly a dilemma: while having good relations with political parties seems to be a necessity in many industries, the instrument of party financing can be a double-edged sword. It grants influence—but it could also severely harm the company's image and perhaps encourage questionable behaviour on the part of employees.

The ethical dilemma for corporations becomes even more complicated given that they are not the only ones who work hard at gaining influence on political parties: in an attempt to professionalize their strategies, CSOs have also increasingly sponsored political parties and events (Harris and Lock 2002). This partly brightens the moral terrain of party financing since corporations then are more or less part of a general trend in society—although again the problem of the differential resources available to business actors compared with civil actors needs to be raised.

Of course, one possible way of dealing with these problems is for corporations to simply introduce rules that forbid political donations. This indeed has been the response of BP, one of the world's largest oil companies, which has completely banned any funding of political parties in Europe and—more delicately—in the USA (Ghua and McNulty 2002). Although such a move is certainly to be commended for making a stand on an issue of increasing contestability, there might be said to be more to BP's decision than first meets the eye. With its tax contributions, spending power, and over 100,000 employees worldwide, BP is a typical representative of a group of MNCs that do not necessarily need to do extra party financing in order to be worthy of governmental attention. In addition, BP has skilfully developed a far more effective strategy to secure its influence at top levels of the UK government. Over the years the company has pursued a policy of sending their more senior staff for a couple of years to work in key governmental departments, and vice versa for government staff. By this, there are close informal ties between this company and the government. And of course, these ties conceivably allow the same kind of lobbying

---

[4] See Bogdanor (2002).

efforts that we mentioned earlier without actually needing to particularly invest in formal 'lobbying'. It is perhaps not surprising then that the media sometimes labels the company 'Blair Petroleum' because of its close links with the government. But this, as we shall now see, raises a different kind of conflict of interest problem at the individual level.

Overlap of posts between business and government: individual conflicts of interest

When BP managers go to work in the government, we might reasonably ask whether they as individuals are truly acting for the government (as an agent of the general public) or for BP (as an agent for its shareholders). Clearly this overlapping of posts raises quite substantial individual level conflicts of interest when the two agency relations conflict.

It is not only business people working for the government that is the problem though. The overlap works both ways. Many senior politicians also tend to find themselves on the (supervisory) boards of large companies. How does Kenneth Clarke, deputy chairman of British American Tobacco (BAT) and former British Chancellor of the Exchequer, balance the interests of the company with the interests of his constituents? For example, in 2002, when Clarke wrote to a constituent outlining his discomfort with companies investing in Burma, the human rights pressure group the Burma Campaign used his comments to launch a campaign to force BAT to withdraw from the country (Eaglesham and Maitland 2002). Similarly, during his campaign in 1998, Gerhard Schröder, then board member of Volkswagen, was asked, whilst on a visit to a Mercedes plant, whose interests he would pursue as the German head of state. His joke, 'I will be the chancellor of all cars,' exposes a fundamental conflict of interest which occurs when senior business people get involved in politics and vice versa.

Probably the most extreme, and in many ways troubling, case in Europe is that of Silvio Berlusconi in Italy. Since coming into power in 2000, Berlusconi, as the owner of Italy's three major television stations and largest publishing house, has been able to virtually dominate the media and thereby marginalize any criticism of his government (Jones 2002). **Ethics in Action 11.1** explores this recent trend in European business–government relations in more detail.

The ethics of occupying a dual role in business and politics at the same time is somewhat questionable. On the one hand, one could argue that it has certain advantages if politicians have had the experience of the business world and vice versa. It certainly makes politicians more aware of the economic realities underlying many of the issues on which they have to decide. It might be suggested even that industry experience would provide politicians with a more professional style of work and decision-making compared to what normally dominates the rather bureaucratic structures of the public domain. All these factors could enable a more professional approach to political work and therefore might be argued to be in the best interests of society. Close links between business and politics might also be an advantage in industries and projects whose success is strongly relying on political factors. Examples could be the entry into foreign markets where the principle 'the flag goes and the trade follows' seems to have been a successful approach for some

```
Ethics in Action 11.1
```

Berlusconi and Murdoch: bringing the news about business influence on the government

··

When Silvio Berlusconi won the Italian parliamentary elections in 2001, nobody expected him to become Italy's longest-serving conservative head of state since the war. His first term in government back in 1994 lasted just seven months until he had to resign due to allegations of corruption. But by the time of his second term, Berlusconi had learnt his lessons: during his first hundred days in office he issued legislation that decriminalized some of the activities he had been accused of in the past, and which he was still having to defend himself against in the Italian courts.

The list of accusations he faced was long: money laundering, tax evasion, bribery of judges and officials, even complicity with the Mafia were among the charges. However, during his three-decade rise to become Italy's richest individual, he has become the most powerful person in Italian business and—recently—politics. Mr Berlusconi has a near monopoly of commercial TV in Italy, as Prime Minister he also controls the state TV, he owns the largest proportion of Italy's print media, and has stakes in many major businesses in Italy as well. Buying the football club AC Milan, together with his ability to finance personality-driven election campaigns, paved his entrance into Italian politics. In what is now a double role as politician and industrialist, he enjoys a virtually unprecedented influence on public opinion in Italy.

Although during his election campaign Berlusconi promised to step back from the management of the Fininvest holding company that oversees much of his business empire, there was little sign of any retreat from his commercial involvements even after nearly two years in power. During this time, various contestable bills were debated in parliament without major media coverage. 'If I, taking care of everyone's interests, also take care of my own you can't talk about a conflict of interest,' he is reported to have replied to questions about his dubious role as industrialist turned politician.

Berlusconi represents about as clear a case of overlap between business and government as you could get. A more indirect, but by no means less powerful, illustration of business influence on the political landscape is provided by another media tycoon, Rupert Murdoch. Through his conglomerate News Corporation, Murdoch owns a global media empire including Fox TV, the movie studio Twentieth Century Fox, the publisher Harper & Row, Sky TV, Astra TV, and has recently entered the Chinese TV market as well. In the UK, News Corporation's subsidiary News International owns the biggest selling newspaper, the *Sun*, as well as other major titles such as the *News of the World*, *The Times*, the *Sunday Times*, and the *Times Higher Education Supplement*.

Such control of the media provides Murdoch with a pretty strong influence on public opinion. 'I elected them. And incidentally, I'm not happy with them. I may remove them,' Murdoch claimed back in 1979 about the Australian government and the role of his newspapers in Australian politics. Although there are clearly many other important factors influencing the outcome of elections, the pattern does not seem to have changed. When Murdoch's UK tabloid the *Sun* backed Tony Blair in the 1997 election, Labour subsequently won with a landslide majority. Five years before, when the *Sun* still backed the conservative government, Labour had lost, prompting the newspaper to boast it was the *Sun* 'wot won it'.

Some commentators have suggested that if Murdoch does not approve of a certain political view, he will not hesitate to use his powerful influence on the media to effect a certain degree of censorship. For instance, when Chris Patten, the last British governor of Hong Kong, completed his memoirs, his publisher Harper & Row (owned by News Corporation) promptly dropped its plans to publish the book. Patten's critical views on the Chinese regime in the book were seen by many to have been the critical factor in this decision, especially given that Murdoch was at the time attempting to smooth his entry into the potentially lucrative Chinese TV market.

It has not all been smooth sailing though for the Australian media tycoon in his relations with government. In 1998, when Murdoch announced his plans to buy the football club Manchester United, the Blair government refused permission on grounds that it might have detrimental effects on competition. However, more recently in 2003, the Blair government facilitated new legislation to deregulate the TV industry, which many saw as a boost to Murdoch's empire. Dubbed 'the Murdoch clause' in the media, the legislation removed certain barriers to ownership of the media and paved the way for Murdoch's company to be able at last to buy another major TV channel in the UK.

While Berlusconi seems to maximize a direct influence on the national level, Murdoch's more indirect influence has an extended global range. For instance, while the UN was deeply divided over a potential war against Iraq in mid-February 2003, there was at least one global organization which apparently stood unified behind George W. Bush. All 175 titles of Murdoch's newspaper branch of News Corporation, together publishing 40 million papers a week and dominating the British, Australian, and New Zealand markets, simultaneously ran pro-war headlines. There was one exception though: the Papua New Guinea *Courier Mail* defected with a passionate anti-war message—but whether this was proof of Murdoch easing the brakes on business influence on politics remains to be seen . . .

SOURCES

Carroll, R. (2001). 'Berlusconi bill to take his firm out of the dock: law change will axe three charges against Italian PM'. *Guardian*, 19 Sept.: 14.

—— (2002). 'Yes, Prime Minister'. *Guardian* (Media), 1 Apr.: 2.

Cohen, N. (2003). 'Without prejudice: mortal synergy'. *Observer*, 9 Feb.: 31.

Doward, J. (2003). 'Sun king rising in the East'. *Observer* (Business), 12 Jan.: 16.

Fox, J. (2002). 'First among billionaires: Silvio Berlusconi'. *Guardian* (Weekend), 28 Sept.: 43.

Greenslade, R. (1997). 'Nice one Sun, says Tony'. *Guardian*, 19 May: T2.

—— (2003). 'Their master's voice'. *Guardian* (Media), 17 Feb.: 2–3.

Willan, P. (2002). 'Berlusconi told to leave courts alone'. *Guardian*, 18 Jan.: 14.

■ **Think theory**

Think about the role of Silvio Berlusconi and Rupert Murdoch in European politics from the perspective of stakeholder theory. Whose interests are they, or should they, be representing in their roles as media executives and, in the case of Berlusconi, in his role as Prime Minister? How can we determine whether this clash of roles and responsibilities is acceptable?

countries and industries. This more **utilitarian argument** would in fact see some benefit in a closer overlap between business and politics.

On the other hand, there are also quite significant ethical problems linked to such a close amalgamation of business and politics. When Lord Wakeham, a senior conservative politician, was implicated in the collapse of Enron in 2002 as one of the company's board members, he had to resign from his job as chair of the Press Complaints Commission, a British media watchdog. This incident makes obvious the problems of having a politician who is, as it were, entitled to set the rules of the economic game and, at the same time, is also a player in the game. If a company or an industry is able to influence and manipulate the rules towards its own interests, this clearly violates the principle of justice, most notably the notion of **procedural justice**. This particular type of justice underlies the set-up of modern democracies, since it focuses particularly on fairness and equality in the treatment of all parties involved in political processes. Democratic institutions are tailored towards the representation and the pursuit of the interests of all members of society and not just towards those with the most economic power.

State capture by business

So far, we have been discussing forms of business influence on government that, although they may be in the grey areas of business ethics, are pretty much legal across Europe. However, a more extreme form of business influence that occurs quite widely, but tends to be more often classified as illegal within European countries, is the direct payment of bribes to government officials by businesses. Where this is intended to 'buy' an influence on regulation, we refer to this as 'state capture'.

> By state capture, we understand a situation where private firms shape the formulation of regulation by payments to public officials and politicians.

In a certain sense, state capture is the most direct, private, and straightforward way of influencing governments. The offer of bribes and other forms of corruption to gain influence over politicians is a major problem in many parts of the world. The international anti-corruption pressure group Transparency International produces an annual *Corruption Perception Index*, a listing of different states, and the degree to which their government officials are perceived to be susceptible to corruption. The 2002 Index is shown in **Figure 11.4**.

As the Corruption Perception Index shows, whilst government officials in countries such as Finland, Denmark, Iceland, and Sweden are among those perceived to be least susceptible to corruption, state capture in Europe appears to be a particular problem in the transitional economies of Eastern Europe, such as Bulgaria, Croatia, Latvia, Russia, the Slovak Republic, and the Ukraine. A recent study by the World Bank provides striking evidence of parliamentary legislation, presidential decrees, and even court decisions in such countries being strongly influenced by corruption from private businesses (Hellman et al. 2000).

In the light of the above, the ethics of such practices probably should be beyond much doubt. However, the dilemma for corporations in these countries is that this situation seems to be largely unavoidable. One might argue that given the fact that so many economic actors are effectively 'buying' politicians, to do so has become a necessity for all businesses.

Rank	Country	Score	Rank	Country	Score
1	Finland	9.7	33	Hungary	4.9
2	Denmark	9.5		Malaysia	4.9
	New Zealand	9.5	36	Belarus	4.8
4	Iceland	9.4		Lithuania	4.8
5	Singapore	9.3		South Africa	4.8
	Sweden	9.3	40	South Korea	4.5
7	Canada	9.0	44	Greece	4.2
	Luxembourg	9.0	45	Brazil	4.0
	The Netherlands	9.0		Bulgaria	4.0
10	United Kingdom	8.7		Poland	4.0
11	Australia	8.6	51	Croatia	3.8
12	Norway	8.5	52	Czech Republic	3.7
	Switzerland	8.5		Latvia	3.7
14	Hong Kong	8.2		Morocco	3.7
15	Austria	7.8		Slovak Republic	3.7
16	USA	7.7	57	Colombia	3.6
18	Germany	7.3		Mexico	3.6
	Israel	7.3	59	China	3.5
20	Belgium	7.1	64	Thailand	3.2
	Japan	7.1		Turkey	3.2
	Spain	7.1	71	India	2.7
23	Ireland	6.9		Russia	2.7
25	France	6.3		Zimbabwe	2.7
	Portugal	6.3	77	Pakistan	2.6
27	Slovenia	6.0		Philippines	2.6
29	Estonia	5.6	81	Albania	2.5
	Taiwan	5.6	96	Indonesia	1.9
31	Italy	5.2	101	Nigeria	1.6
			102	Bangladesh	1.2

Figure 11.4. 2002 Corruption Perception Index for selected countries

Note: Score relates to perceptions of the degree of corruption among government officials as seen by business people and risk analysts, and ranges between 10 (highly clean) and 0 (highly corrupt).

Source: Taken from *Transparency International Corruption Perception Index*, Berlin, 2002. www.transparency.org.

This argument, however, leads us directly into the controversy about ethical absolutism and relativism we introduced back in Chapter 3 (76), and which has arisen a number of times throughout this book. Ultimately, from the perspective of western democracies, this situation is beyond what we would regard as an ethically desirable situation. This certainly would question the adoption of such practices by European MNCs when acting in those countries. Furthermore and most interestingly, if instead of the rule of law there is the rule of the most powerful corporations, then individual business is subject to governmental arbitrariness and despotism. When property rights are not granted, and contracts are not reliable, business ultimately becomes very difficult and uncertain (Hellman and Schankerman 2000). From an ethical theory perspective this is a good example of Kant's theory, most notably the first maxim of the categorical imperative: if state capture becomes a 'universal law', a normally functioning economy becomes nearly impossible.

■ **Think theory**

Corruption has also been addressed from the perspective of consequentialist theories. How would these apply to state capture as discussed here?

Ethical issues in the context of privatization and deregulation

If state capture represents a situation where business effectively can dictate certain aspects of government policy, then privatization takes us into a situation where government effectively cedes responsibility for the provision of certain goods and services to business completely. Although we certainly wouldn't want to suggest that privatization raises the same kind of fundamental ethical problems as state capture, there are a number of issues and dilemmas that we need to address.

Starting in the UK during the 1980s Europe has experienced a strong move towards privatization of public industries such as public transport, postal services, telecommunications, and utility supply. This development coincided with, and was partly due to, quite substantial deregulation of certain industries and markets. This deregulation led to a situation where private businesses were allowed to enter industries that formerly were dominated, if not totally controlled, by public organizations. While this process was particularly driven by the Thatcher government in the UK, similar developments took place later in the rest of Europe and are still ongoing in countries such as Germany and France (*The Economist* 2002; Lane 2002). In a similar vein, the fall of the iron curtain propelled the major state-owned companies of Eastern Europe into the privately owned capitalist system, entailing more or less similar consequences.

Given the collectivist nature of the European business system, it is perhaps not surprising that a significant percentage of large employers, public services, and utilities were originally state owned. The downside of this situation was that these large monopolies tended to be inflexible, bureaucratic, and often delivered average quality at high costs. So, for instance, the owner of Capita, one of the major players in the privatized public services industry in the UK, recently boasted that it takes his company seven hours to reach a decision that would take seven weeks in the civil service (*Guardian* 2003).

The results of the process of privatization have been mixed: while some of the newly privatized companies and industries, especially in the area of telecommunication and utilities, have been quite successful, other privatized corporations struggle and have not been able to provide reasonable quality and profitability. The picture is even more mixed from an ethical point of view (Jones 2001). Let's consider some of the typical issues:

• **Privatization profits.** An issue of extensive debate has been the price at which formerly public companies should be 'sold' to private owners. If too high a price is charged, the new owners may feel exploited if their investment subsequently attracts a far lower valuation than their initial investment. For example, when Deutsche Telekom was privatized, the share price immediately sank dramatically below the price of the initial public offering (IPO), thereby infuriating shareholders. If too low a price is charged, a small group of investors taking over a former public utility might end up making huge profits on what were essentially public assets that ultimately belonged to the taxpayer. One example of this is the group that took over British Rail in a management buy-out, and then subsequently split it up for sale in more than twenty different companies, netting a profit of £1.5bn (€2.25bn) in only two years (Morgan 1999). Apart from the fact that stock market prices ultimately are not predictable, the ethical challenge in privatizing state-owned companies is to find a **fair price**.

- **Citizens turned consumers.** Postal services or public transport—just to name two examples—were originally under the care of governments because these services were considered a component of the social rights of citizens. One reason the state became involved in such services was to ensure that provision of basic services was supplied to all, regardless of where they lived, or the cost of providing the service. However, a privatized postal service might argue that it cannot run a post office in rural Lapland or Andalusia just because of five families in the village. They have to take these decisions following a profit rationale—which will mean that these five families will no longer have a post office or bus service. In the absence of regulation, these issues typically cause public outrage and confront corporations with difficult ethical dilemmas.

- **Natural monopolies.** Telecommunications, railways, and other utilities that deliver their services via networks—be it cables, rails, or tubes—cannot easily be privatized and opened up to competition because of the degree of integration that is necessary for them to function effectively. To give a simple example, it is technically and economically infeasible for a new rail company to build a new rail network next to a competitor's. For this reason, such industries are sometimes called *natural monopolies*. Generally, under the privatization of natural monopolies, access to and prices for using such networks are part of more or less complex governmental regulation. However, experience shows that corporations may exploit this situation by either overcharging customers or delivering poor quality. The example of the British rail network operator Railtrack in **Case 6** illustrates some of these problems quite vividly.

Next to full-on privatization, there has recently been considerable debate on so-called '**public-private partnerships**' (PPP). This is partly a reaction to unsuccessful privatization, which sometimes resulted in the opposite of the desired goals of better-quality services and lower prices. The central idea of PPPs is that the government is still responsible for a considerable part of the project while private companies bring in the investment. Again, it is in the UK where PPPs have been most extensively introduced, while the rest of Europe seems rather reluctant to take up these initiatives. Recent UK examples are in the area of public transport, most notably the reform of the London Underground (Shaoul 2002), in civil services, and in healthcare (Grimshaw et al. 2002).

The analysis of both planned and realized PPP projects though is not overly impressive. The general result seems to be that the profit-maximization rationale of the private sector appears to dominate PPPs at the expense of quality and effectiveness for consumers and citizens. Probably the most striking example of a PPP that fell into the same ethical traps as those identified above is the PPP bridge project between the Isle of Skye and the British mainland (Monbiot 2000). While normal, publicly run toll bridges in Scotland would charge around 80p (€1.20), the price for using the Skye bridge in the late 1990s was £11.60 (€18) return! The estimated profits for the private investors were more than 300 per cent—on a PPP in one of the poorest regions of the UK. While this example still might be regarded as an extreme case, the literature on PPP suggests that underlying ethical problems remain with such an approach.

Regardless of the possibility of raising ethical problems, it would appear that privatization, deregulation, and public–private partnerships are likely to continue to be a major feature of the European economic landscape. As we shall now see, such developments are in fact part of a broader shift in relations between the state and business that has arisen from the process of globalization.

Globalization and business–government relations

Back in Chapter 1 (16), we defined globalization as 'the progressive eroding of the relevance of territorial bases for social, economic, and political activities, processes, and relations'. The erosion of the territorial base has some specific consequences for the role of governments in the age of globalization. The British political scientist Anthony McGrew has described this in terms of a transition from a traditional to a global context, which he calls 'the post-Westphalian' setting (Held and McGrew 2000; McGrew 1997*a*; 1997*b*). In the following, we will use McGrew's analysis of this transition in order to set out the implications of globalization for business relations with government.

From the traditional to the global context

McGrew argues that since the Westphalian peace treaties in the seventeenth century, the identity of nation, society, and state has been the leading pattern of political organization of the 'civilized' world. Hence, for the last 400 years or so, we have tended to think of ourselves as being part of nation states, and if we were talking about 'society' in a certain part of the world, we could equally talk about 'the French', 'the Swedes', or 'the Chinese', etc. As Ulrich Beck (1997: 49–55) contends, society and social life mainly took place within the 'container of the nation state'.

However, as we have seen throughout this book, when globalization deterritorializes social, economic, and political action, the significance of these nation states is weakened. This fundamentally challenges the traditional context of the 'Westphalian setting' and in some areas, and for some issues, moves us into a global context, or 'post-Westphalian' setting. This transition is summarized in **Figure 11.5 (*a*)**.

• **Society.** McGrew's argument is basically that the traditional and the globalized world orders coexist. In many respects, we still think of ourselves as 'the French', 'the British', or 'the Japanese', but in others our society is viewed in a transnational context. For example, a French person may also think of himself or herself as 'a Sony employee', a British person as 'a Peugeot owner', or a Japanese person as 'a Greenpeace member'. These latter identities are distinctly transnational rather than being tied to a nation state. Hence, when we consider issues in a globalized context, the notion of 'society' is no longer an entity confined simply to national borders. It is rather a more or less worldwide community conceptualized by authors like Luhmann as a 'world society.'

(*a*)

	Traditional context (Westphalian setting) ←——→	**Globalized context (post-Westphalian setting)**
Society	Nation	World society
Holder of political power	Monopoly by national governments	Multitude of governmental, non-governmental, and private actors
Manifestation of political activity	National regulation (laws)	Systems of transnational negotiations (e.g. EU directives, codes of conduct)
Addressee of regulation	Social actors (e.g. domestic companies, citizens)	Nation states (e.g. EU member states) Private transnational actors (e.g. MNCs)
Intensity of regulation	Decreasing (e.g. deregulation, privatization)	Increasing
Democratic control of political power	Higher	Lower

(*b*)

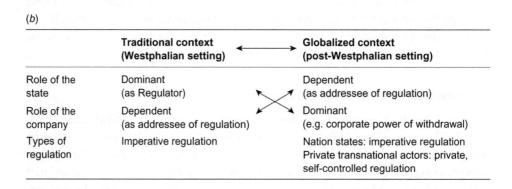

	Traditional context (Westphalian setting) ←——→	**Globalized context (post-Westphalian setting)**
Role of the state	Dominant (as Regulator)	Dependent (as addressee of regulation)
Role of the company	Dependent (as addressee of regulation)	Dominant (e.g. corporate power of withdrawal)
Types of regulation	Imperative regulation	Nation states: imperative regulation Private transnational actors: private, self-controlled regulation

Figure 11.5. Globalization, government, and business: changing context and roles
(*a*) Changing context
(*b*) Changing roles

- **Holder of political power.** This change entails certain consequences for the political control of society. In the traditional context, governments of states possessed the monopoly of political power since they were the only authority that could set rules by issuing regulation. This is radically altered through globalization since society and social interaction can transcend the territorial boundaries of the state and might thus escape the scope of national governments. Political power beyond the nation state is rather broadly distributed and loosely shared. As we saw in the last chapter, it is often MNCs and CSOs that are the main organizations that wield influence on a global level. Therefore there are a *multitude of governmental, non-governmental, and private actors* holding political power.

- **Manifestation of political activity.** What this means is that we still have national regulation, but we also find national governments setting up *systems of transnational negotiations*

—the European Union, or the North American Free Trade Agreement (NAFTA) for example—and we also see CSOs and MNCs involved in setting up regulatory efforts such as international codes of conduct.

- **Addressee of regulation.** Given such transnational negotiations, it is not only social actors such as citizens and domestic companies who are subject to regulation (as we see in the case of national regulation), but also *nation states and private transnational actors* such as MNCs. Indeed, one of the reasons why European countries such as the UK or Denmark are rather suspicious of the European Union is that it involves them in being subject to regulation from another level of government. Significantly for us, this often applies to regulation targeted at environmental protection, human rights, and various other issues of consequence to business ethics.

- **Intensity of regulation.** If we look to individual countries, there have been strong moves towards deregulation and, by this, efforts to decrease the level of regulation on the national level. We have discussed above the reasons and ethical implications on the national level. At the same time, however, we also see that the level of regulation on the transnational and global level is *increasing*, not only for nation states (for instance by EU regulation) but also for private actors (for instance by codes of conducts of the OECD).

- **Democratic control of political power.** The decreasing power and relevance of national governments in the globalized context leads to a central, yet frequently overlooked, problem: the principles of democratic control of political power are eroded. As soon as political actors like CSOs, MNCs, or supranational bodies act beyond the scope of the nation state, where in most industrialized countries political power is controlled by the electorate, these actors are no longer directly accountable to those over whom they exert their power.

These then are essentially the main aspects of the shift identified by McGrew. As we have already mentioned, one of the key things to remember here is that both contexts continue to coexist; it is simply that in the global context, the role and nature of regulation is substantially different from that at the national level. Let us now go on to see how these differences reshape the roles and relations between business and government.

Shifting roles for business and government in a global context

The main consequence of globalization is that it begins to reverse the roles of government and corporations (see **Figure 11.5 (b)**). In the traditional context, states are in the politically dominant position, since they are regulators of economic actors (the 'addressees' of regulation). In the global context, though, nation states also become addressees of all kinds of transnational regulation—a development that is especially visible in the area of regulating global environmental issues such as biological diversity (Görg and Brand 2000).

Companies, on the other hand, seem to gain a specific increase in political power through globalization. The main reason for this is not predominantly that they find themselves in a position where they could wilfully discard or violate national regulation.

Rather, it is based on a phenomenon that Beck (1998) has described as the 'corporate power of transnational withdrawal', namely that in a global economy corporations can quite easily threaten governments that they will relocate to another country if certain 'undesirable' regulations—such as health and safety standards—are enforced. As national governments depend on corporations in terms of employment and tax payments, this situation puts companies in a position of relative power.

Another source of political power of companies, however, is based on the fact that many MNCs have considerable *economic* power of their own. Given that fifty-one of the world's largest economies are corporations, they can have a substantial influence on global developments simply because of their size, scope, and resources.

The consequence of these changing contexts and changing roles is that business finds itself in a situation where it still operates within the traditional national context, as well as being a key actor at the global level. Let us now look at the types of regulation this exposes it to.

Business as an actor within the traditional context (Westphalian setting)

Businesses are still located within nation states and they are therefore still subject to national law, which we have called *imperative regulation* in **Figure 11.5 (b)**. By imperative regulation, we mean that the regulation is mandatory and imposed from above. The ability of governments to use this traditional element of politics remains powerful in areas where companies do not dispose of strong internationalization options (Rugman and Verbeke 2000). Furthermore, the increase in transnational regulation still results in a considerable increase in imperative regulation on the national level. Governments are responsible for the national implementation of, for instance, the Kyoto Protocol or certain EU directives. Since these treaties apply to many countries simultaneously, the power of transnational withdrawal for companies is certainly limited.

As we have discussed previously in section 11.3, there are numerous ethical issues in these relations between businesses and government. Most of what we mentioned there was particularly relevant for *democratic regimes*. While we discussed numerous ways that business tries to influence government, we should also mention that in these countries business also increasingly faces *demands* from the side of government to take part in, and assume an active role in, regulatory processes. We will discuss these issues in the next section as they are closely linked to business in its role as corporate citizen.

Talking about the business–government relations in the context of globalization, though, we should also however mention situations where business becomes an actor in **authoritarian and oppressive regimes**. Recent discussions of this issue have focused on countries such as Zimbabwe, Nigeria, China, and especially Burma. The crucial ethical dilemma here is that MNCs who want to become involved under these political conditions have to collaborate to a certain degree with the regime. This is shown quite visibly with the case of Shell in Nigeria, or British American Tobacco's involvement in Burma, both of which we have mentioned several times already. Next to collaborating, MNC presence in these countries also can be said to contribute to the economic stability and wealth of the existing regime. Therefore, even without directly collaborating with the regime, the presence of western companies can be deemed to be contributing to their support. This argument was used specifically in the case of MNCs in apartheid South Africa in the 1970s and 1980s. There is some evidence to suggest that the eventual withdrawal of major MNCs such as General Motors might at least have contributed to the final collapse of the regime (De George 1999: 542–8).

Business as an actor in the global context (post-Westphalian setting)

On a global level, we argued earlier that corporations assume a more dominant role while governments—bound by their confinement to territorial boundaries—have only limited influence beyond national boundaries. The central ethical problem here is that business can find it easier than in western democracies to negotiate with less developed countries about tax levels, environmental, health, and safety standards, or human rights. The result of this process is the so-called 'race to the bottom' between developing countries, trying to attract foreign investment by offering lower and lower levels of standards (Scherer and Smid 2000). While we have discussed several of these issues throughout the book as being in the firm's discretion we would underline here that many of the local practices and standards which governments in developing countries maintain are not a given but often a result of the influence of corporate activities.

It should be mentioned, however, that this view of business and government in the developing world is by no means received wisdom in the management literature. As these deals between business and government are often negotiated secretly, violations of standards are often hidden, and the precise measuring and monitoring of pollution data is ambiguous (just to name a few reasons), there is quite a mixed array of claims and counter-claims regarding the realities or otherwise of the race to the bottom.

While the general public seems to have quite generally accepted that these ethical issues exist and that the deterioration in standards is a real issue (e.g. Hertz 2001a; Korten 1995) there are a several authors who contest this evidence (e.g. Rugman 2000). While some argue along the lines of decreased levels of pollution in the developing countries during the last decades (e.g. Wheeler 2001), others point at the fact that MNCs in developing countries have a positive influence on environmental standards. So, for instance, Christmann and Taylor (2001) argue that MNCs in China actually improve environmental performance, since they introduce their environmental management systems (such as ISO 14000) in their Chinese subsidiaries.

While this argument in itself is only partly convincing (environmental management systems tend to be process standards rather than performance measures) it nevertheless leads in a far more interesting direction. Although governments in developing countries may be unlikely to provide 'imperative' regulation that *forces* companies into more ethical behaviour—either because they do not dare or do not care—we increasingly witness that business *itself* assumes an active role in setting up certain types of regulation. While imperative regulation does not exist on the global level (since the only actors able to issue such regulation are confined to territorial boundaries), new forms of regulation involving business are indeed the dominant pattern. *Self-regulation* by companies, or rule-setting from other forms of private organizations such as CSOs (often in collaboration with business and governments), is at present the most rapidly developing field of corporate regulation on the global level.

We will have a closer look at these regulatory innovations in the next section as they are very closely linked to the corporate role as a citizen in civil society. Finally, though, before we move on to consider the question of citizenship in the context of government relations, we should mention that within a European context, business also has to deal with another level of government and regulation, a meso level if you will, between the national and the global. This is the European Union.

Business–government relations in the European Union

For business in the European Union (EU), there is still an extra layer of government that influences business decisions. In addition to national government legislation and global regulation, there is the layer of EU government that has an increasing influence on business behaviour.

Generally speaking, the European Union is structured similarly to any other democratic government (see Baron 2000: 447–75; Mercado et al. 2001: 37–80). It has:

- An *executive* body (or bodies), namely the European Commission and Council of Ministers;

- A *legislative* function, in the form of the European Parliament;

- *Judicial* powers, through the European Court of Justice.

However, as the double nature of the executive already shows, structures are more complex than on a national level. In practice, the European Parliament is a rather weak institution while the executive bodies still depend quite heavily on national governmental institutions (Holland 1993: 77–82). The main reason for this is that national governments are still reluctant to delegate too much power into the hands of the European Union. Consequently, every law and every decision has to follow a complicated way through various institutions until every party *and* country involved is happy with the outcome.

From an ethical perspective, we would like to highlight a few issues that are particularly important here in the relation between business and government:

- **Subsidiarity principle.** The EU legislative process follows the subsidiarity principle according to which laws should be made on the *lowest possible level*. Accordingly, most EU laws are *directives* that give guidelines for member states to implement, but it is up to the states themselves to convert these directives into national law. If business ethics starts where lawmaking ends, then this line can become blurred by lawmaking processes in the EU since many of the directives are quite vague and are often more symbolic in nature (Matten 2003). Hence, they do not really codify decisions about right and wrong for individual managers or companies. Furthermore, as with regulation in the global context, EU legislation also increasingly focuses on encouraging *self-regulation*, which again involves business in a very different role from just being the recipient of rules.

- **Direct intervention.** Contrary to the subsidiarity principle, and partly as a response to prolonged and complex decision processes at the national level, there have recently been efforts to provide greater powers of direct intervention to certain actors of the EU executive, most notably the Commissioners. One of the most contested areas for business is the work of the Commissioner for the Directorate-General of Competition (DG IV). Whenever there is a merger between larger companies—even if their headquarters are not based in Europe—DG IV will check whether the outcome is likely to lead to a monopolistic situation in the respective European market. Given the relatively loose definition of laws in this area, however, it is clear that companies have considerable flexibility and discretion in arguing their case to the Commissioner.

• **Subsidies.** In order to help struggling industries, or to encourage economic development in poor regions, the EU pays substantial amounts of subsidies to companies. Based on certain criteria predefined by the European Commission, companies investing in these areas might be eligible for substantial amounts of cash. The central ethical challenge to companies here lies in the fact that the temptation to manipulate data and to 'streamline' reports might secure this aid without the company really being eligible. Fraud in the context of subsidies is a major area of economic crime on the European level.

• **The euro.** While some countries in Europe have already introduced the new currency, other European countries, such as the UK and the accession countries in the former eastern bloc, still have to implement this stage of integration. One of the main ethical issues for business in introducing the new currency is the temptation to profit from consumers' lack of familiarity with the new currency by raising prices. The debate in Europe on this issue has been fierce and diverse with evidence of rip-offs uncovered by critics being quickly denied by companies. Regardless of the truth of the situation, though, perceived unfairness has led to broad cynicism about the new currency: in Germany, for instance, the euro is frequently referred to as the 'Teuro' (a pun on 'teuer' meaning expensive).

■ **Think theory**

Think about the role of the EU from the perspective of globalization—to what extent is the EU a part of, or a resistance to, forces of deterritorialization?

Corporate citizenship and regulation: business as key player in the regulatory game

As we have seen in this chapter, the situation for European companies is that imperative regulation at the national level remains important, but has decreased in intensity, whilst European level and transnational regulation is still limited but has intensified. These transitions, coupled with concerns about 'over-regulation' stifling business innovation, have led to a fertile debate about how to improve the rule-making process governing environmental and social issues in business.

As a result, various innovations and new styles of regulation have emerged. These innovations pose a significant challenge to corporations in terms of how they might think about the notion of corporate citizenship. Specifically, the new regulatory approach usually includes business (next to other actors) in the regulatory process itself. And because regulation is essentially about creating rules to benefit society, this inevitably involves corporations more heavily in the **administration and protection of citizen rights**. In Chapter 2, we likened this to a *political role* for corporations in the era of globalization.

There is a plethora of different labels by which this new trend in regulation is described. The most common one would be **self-regulation** (Doyle 1997), sometimes known as 'reflexive regulation' (Orts 1995). Here, the central idea is that the actors are involved in setting up the very regulation that they themselves will be subsequently affected by. A typical example here is the regulation of financial markets in the UK, which is handled by the Financial Services Authority—a self-regulating industry body rather than a government organization.

This then is closely related to the idea of *privatization*, since regulation is no longer a task only for public (government) actors, but for private actors such as industry associations and CSOs (Knill and Lehmkuhl 2002; Ronit 2001). Moreover, much of this regulation is *voluntary* in that business gets involved in these regulatory processes not because it is forced to by government, but because it sees it as being in its own self-interest (Van Calster and Deketelaere 2001). Regulation might therefore be regarded as 'softer' and more flexible, since it can adjust reasonably easily to new circumstances, issues, and actors (Martínez Lucio and Weston 2000). Accordingly, some authors have suggested that these regulatory processes allow the actors to embark on *learning legislation*, which incorporates past experiences and feeds these into the ongoing rule-making process (Wagner and Haffner 1999).

As Orts and Deketelaere (2001) point out, this innovative approach to regulation is first and foremost a European approach, and one that has only fairly recently been adopted in other parts of the world and, most notably, on the global level. As we argued earlier in Chapter 1 (see Figure 1.6; 22), Europe is characterized by business–society relations that include a variety of stakeholders and focus more on a negotiation-based approach that sees companies as embedded in society. In particular, then, it has been countries such as France, Germany, and the Netherlands that have been among the early adopters of this approach since the 1970s.

There are a number of reasons why these new forms of regulation have emerged. According to Van Calster and Deketelaere, the main goals for those trying to introduce new types of rule-making in this area are:

• **Encouragement of a proactive approach from industry.** Industry as an addressee of regulation (and hence the one that has to adapt to it) has typically been integrated rather late into the rule-making process—if at all. This means that governmental regulation has not always offered much encouragement for business and has not usually been very enthusiastically welcomed by corporations. Self-regulation therefore has tried to encourage earlier and more proactive engagement from industry in the rule-making process, and has tried to make more use of the market to encourage ethical behaviour.

- **Cost-effectiveness.** Another goal of self-regulation is to cut down on bureaucracy and costs by co-operating more closely with business. To give a recent example: rather than telling companies which technology to use, or to measure the emissions at every single chimney, the introduction of a limited amount of tradable emission certificates for a certain industry has the same result without the costly administration and compliance control (Smalley Bowen 2003).

- **Faster achievement of objectives.** The average time for a proposal to be adopted by the EU is two years followed by another two years for transposition by the member states. One reason behind the desire to change the regulatory process is to shorten this time lag. When engaging industry in regulation the assumption is that the aims are attained faster since it shortcuts the long way through the different institutions.

Figure 11.6 provides an overview of the changing field of regulation affecting business. It is based on **Figure 10.1** in the previous chapter (344), which depicts the three main

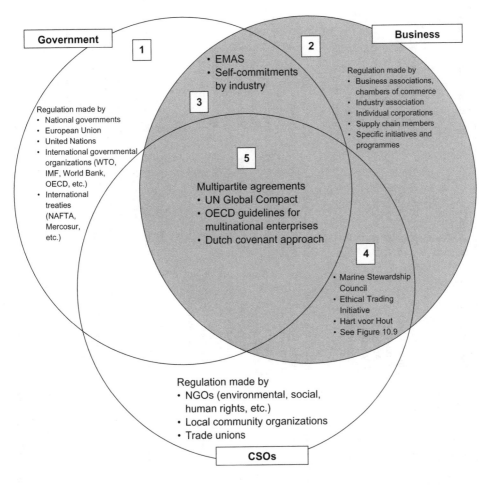

Figure 11.6. Players in the regulatory game and selected examples of private regulatory efforts

Regulatory actor group involved (Segment in Fig. 11.4)	Government (1)	Business (2)	Business + government (3)	Business + CSO (4)	Business + government + CSO (5)
Local/regional level	Regional 'imperative' regulation, e.g. • Anti-pollution • Waste management	Codes of conduct for SMEs or local subsidiaries of corporations, etc.	Regional agreements with government, e.g. • Environmental alliance in Bavaria ('Umweltallianz Bayern') • Industrial symbiosis Kalundborg, Denmark	Regional agreements with CSOs, e.g. • Local Agenda 21 projects • Mediation projects, e.g. noise reduction Frankfurt airport	Regional multipartite agreements and projects, e.g. • Business in the Community (BITC) initiatives • Local development projects
National level	National 'imperative' regulation, e.g. • 35-hr week in France • Dual waste management in Germany (Green Dot) • Closure of nuclear power stations in Sweden	Country-wide self regulation, e.g. • BDI (Confederation of German Industry) commitment to reduce greenhouse gases • Financial market regulation by the FSA in UK	Country-wide agreements with government, e.g. • Irish farm plastic recycling scheme • Various voluntary environmental agreements in nearly all EU countries	Country-wide agreements with CSOs, e.g. • Trade union agreements in France, Germany, and other European countries • Marine Stewardship Council	Country-wide multipartite agreements and projects, e.g. • Covenant for Work in Germany • Dutch covenant approach in environmental management
International/ global level	International 'imperative' regulation, e.g. • GATT • EU regulation on European works councils	Global industry codes of conduct, e.g. • Chemical industry: Responsible Care Programme • ISO 14000	Global industry codes, negotiated with governmental organizations, e.g. • EMAS (environmental management system standard) • Sporting goods industry codes of conduct	Global industry codes of conduct, self-commitments, or agreements, negotiated with CSOs, e.g. • Forest Stewardship Council • Ethical Trading Initiative	Global industry multipartite projects, codes, self-commitments, or agreements, e.g. • UN Global Compact • OECD, ILO codes of conduct for multinational corporations

Figure 11.7. Examples of regulatory outcomes on different levels in a multi-actor setting

institutional sectors in society—government, business, and civil society. **Figure 11.6** shows the relevant actors in each sector and gives some typical examples of the regulatory processes they are involved in. We have shaded the business sphere because this is the area that relates specifically to business *self-regulation*.

While this figure shows the different actors, **Figure 11.7** provides a closer view of the *combinations* of actors, and at different *levels* of regulatory behaviour. Specifically, we look at regulation that involves the following combinations:

- Government;
- Business;
- Business and government;
- Business and civil society;
- Business, government, and civil society;

at the following levels:

- Local/regional level;
- National level;
- International/global level.

Further details on the various approaches and examples are mainly provided in the sections following.

Governments as regulators (segment 1)

First of all, we find governmental bodies as key actors in regulation. As we indicated earlier in this chapter, imperative regulation by government is still quite widely practised. This certainly applies to *national* governments and also to *regional* legislation. Within the growing relevancy of a 'Europe of the regions' and notions of subsidiarity and devolution, we indeed might even suggest that the local or regional level might become of greater importance in the future in Europe (Mercado et al. 2001: 188–92).

Beyond the national level there is growing importance for bodies above the national level (sometimes called the 'supranational' level) such as the EU or treaty systems such as NAFTA. There is still quite some debate about the power and future of nation states but there is certainly evidence that the regulatory power of nation states, although diminished by globalization, will continue to be a significant influence on business (Taplin 2002). **Figure 11.7** shows some of the recent examples where national governments in Europe have issued legislation that has had significant influence on business activities.

However, if we analyse the role of international governmental organizations with global scope, such as the UN or the OECD, we see that their approach to regulation gets increasingly innovative in the sense described above. There are certainly strong 'reflexive' elements, since they tend to integrate business and NGOs in their regulation. Furthermore, as these organizations lack efficient mechanisms of sanctioning non-compliance with their regulation, much of it is voluntary. An exception though is the World Bank and the IMF (International Monetary Fund), since they have the power to either grant or withdraw considerable amounts of money to developing nations (Woods 2001), and, by this, also have considerable leverage on companies doing business in these countries.

Self-regulation by business (segment 2)

In discussing the roles of various actors in the field of regulation, it is apparent that the roles of business and government have increasingly become inseparable. The amount of regulation exclusively set by government is shrinking, as is the share of regulation that is exclusively set by business.

However, at the *local* level, there are still a considerable number of rules and norms that corporations set for themselves (and for other corporations), such as the codes of conduct introduced by small and medium-sized enterprises (SMEs), or the social and environmental rules imposed on local subsidiaries and suppliers by large corporations.

Typical examples for *national* level efforts of self-regulation can be found with regard to environmental issues: so, for instance, in order to avoid costly and restrictive regulation in the realization of the national goals for carbon dioxide reduction, the Confederation of German Industry (BDI) committed itself to the reduction of greenhouse gases far beyond the level originally requested by the government (Van Calster and Deketelaere 2001). Apart from those commitments with regard to environmental goals (see further examples in ten Brink 2002), self-regulation of business practices is also very common in the financial industry (Doyle 1997) and in the area of corporate governance (see Chapter 6).

On the *global* level, there have been numerous initiatives where industry has been involved as a key actor among others. As the table in **Figure 11.7** shows, most of those global initiatives are stimulated by CSOs and/or by governments. There are, however, a few initiatives that have been driven primarily by industry and where the enforcement and implementation of regulation is primarily the responsibility of business.

The most long-standing example is probably the **Responsible Care Programme**.[5] This programme was initiated by the International Council of Chemical Association (ICCA), which is the global industry confederation of all major national chemical industry confederations. Responsible Care was begun as a response to the devastating chemical-related disasters in Bhopal, Basle, and Seveso in the 1980s, and was adopted by the ICCA in 1991. The programme prescribes in quite some detail a large array of measures, practices, and policies intended to ensure responsible management in the industry. Member firms of the industry's national associations have to adopt these measures in order to be allowed to use the Responsible Care logo. As of 2001, the chemical industry associations of forty-five countries worldwide had adopted the programme, thereby making its implementation for member firms mandatory.

An equally important standard that has been developed by industry is the **ISO 14000** standard series of the International Standard Organization in Switzerland.[6] These standards basically accredit environmental management systems for business as a way of setting rules for good practice in environmental management (Gibson 1999; Stenzel 1999). This is the

---

[5] For more details go to the website of the initiative: **www.icca-chem.org**.
[6] For more details go to the website of the initiative: **www.iso.ch**.

most widely implemented standard on a global level, mainly due to the fact that many corporations, especially MNCs, specify ISO 14000 certification for their suppliers (Corbett and Kirsch 2001). There is quite a debate in literature about the actual value of this standard, since it basically defines the nature of an environmental management system rather than ensuring actual improvements in environmental performance (Rondinelli and Vastag 2000; Stenzel 1999).

In fact, where business engages in pure self-regulation such as this, the literature remains somewhat ambivalent about the likely benefits (e.g. King and Lenox 2000; Tapper 1997). These approaches seem to have worked primarily in situations where corporate self-interest would suggest these measures anyway. So, for instance, the self-commitment of the German industry to reduce carbon dioxide emissions was easy to fulfil because large producers of these gases in East Germany were about to close down anyway in the early 1990s (Schrader 2002).

Regulation involving business, governmental actors, and CSOs (segments 3, 4, and 5)

Voluntary environmental agreements and other regulatory approaches between business and government have become quite a common tool in most European countries on a regional (e.g. Wagner and Haffner 1999), national (e.g. Flynn 2002; Schrader 2002), and European level (e.g. Orts and Deketelaere 2001; ten Brink 2002). Increasingly, business also co-operates with CSOs in these areas, although the majority of these collaborations are chiefly project based.

More generally, at the *regional* level, we have previously discussed initiatives such as Business in the Community (**Ethics in Action 2.2**), which often combines business and local civil society or government partners in community programmes. We have also discussed regional co-operations such as the Kalundborg industrial ecosystem in Denmark (**Figure 9.5**; 336), which involves business collaboration with the municipal authority to develop effective resource exchange. Other typical examples of these kinds of local collaborations are 'mediation projects' (see **Ethics in Action 3.2**). These are programmes that seek to develop rules to manage the social and environmental impacts of large projects, such as airport extensions in densely populated areas in places like London, Amsterdam, or Frankfurt (Sack 2001).

On the *national* level, some of the more powerful CSOs are trade unions, which often take a key role in negotiating national pay conditions and—if necessary—initiate industrial action. Several other examples have been discussed in Chapter 10 (see **Figure 10.9**; 372). A specific and in many respects unique approach to national environmental regulation has been developed in the Netherlands. Often called the **covenant approach**, it aims to involve business, government, and other stakeholders in the specification, implementation, and monitoring of environmental regulation (Orts and Deketelaere 2001). Sometimes also referred to as the 'polder model' (after the land reclamation areas where the approach has often been used) (Glasbergen 2002), covenants focus on bringing relevant stakeholders together to find a consensus on acceptable processes and outcomes. There is some debate about the long-term success and the transferability of this approach, especially as some of the outcomes have not been overly satisfactory. There seems to be something of a trade-off between a rather smooth and quick way of regulating on the one hand, and the risk that the consensus comes with the price of watered-down standards on the other.

Finally, on the *global* level, the main instrument of regulation for social, ethical, and environmental impacts of business is **codes of conduct**. We have already discussed these at some length in Chapter 5 (148–156), including questions of effectiveness and the plausibility of developing worthwhile global codes of ethics. Nearly all large global governmental and multipartite organizations, such as the UN, the OECD, the ILO (International Labour Organization), the FAO (Food and Agriculture Organization), or the WHO (World Health Organization), have issued codes intended to provide some degree of rule-setting for corporations in areas beyond the control of the nation state (Christmann and Taylor 2002; Kolk et al. 1999).

Indeed, there is such a rapidly expanding number of codes that it is hardly possible to provide a complete overview of this mushrooming field of regulation. In a recent study on codes relevant to MNCs, Kolk and van Tulder found no less than eleven codes from international organizations, thirteen codes from CSOs, twenty-four from business associations, and eighty-four issued by large MNCs themselves! **Figure 11.8** is taken from a recent study of the ethical behaviour of MNCs in the sporting goods industry by two of the same authors (van Tulder and Kolk 2001). What it shows quite strikingly is that there has not been a shortage of attempts to fill the gap in transnational regulation.

International codes of conduct are quite varied in nature and content (Simma and Heinemann 1999). A growing number of codes focus on the **institution** of the MNC, issued either by *specific corporations* themselves or by other bodies, the best known probably being the 'OECD Guidelines for Multinational Enterprises' of 1994. Others focus on **industries or products**, such as the 'International Code of Marketing of Breastmilk Substitutes' by the WHO in 1981 (see also **Case 8**) or the 'International Code of Conduct on the Distribution and Use of Pesticides' by the FAO in 1985. Finally, some codes target certain undesired **practices**, such as the 'Tripartite Declaration of Principles concerning Multinational Enterprises and Social Policy' by the ILO in 1977, focusing on labour rights issues, or the 'UN Declaration against Corruption and Bribery in International Commercial Transactions' of 1996.

As we have argued throughout this book, the usefulness and effectiveness of codes of all varieties remains contested. Their main weakness as regulatory instruments lies in their non-mandatory, non-legally binding character. Codes do however provide a signal for corporations, as well as for CSOs, about what could be regarded as a consensus on ethical behaviour on a global level. Certainly, the guidelines issued by the OECD and the UN serve these purposes—and companies violating these codes can be subjected to considerable public pressure. They therefore provide a clear yardstick that corporations can refer to in order to prevent or deflect allegations of unethical conduct. However, given the growth and proliferation of codes in the last ten years—and the example in **Figure 11.8** shows the codes for just one industry—there are recent initiatives to move away from these codified attempts at global regulation towards more local, interaction-based approaches. **Ethics in Action 11.2** discusses the UN Global Compact as a recent attempt to explore a different trajectory to fill the lack of regulatory bodies on the global level.

Year	Name of the code of conduct	Actor	Reason for adoption
1979	ILO's Tripartite Declaration of Principles concerning Multinational Enterprise and Social Policy	CSO	To regulate the conduct of MNCs
1992	Nike's Code of Conduct and Memorandum of Understanding	Company	A combination of external pressure of CSOs and the media, and internal willingness to accept responsibility
1992	Reebok's Human Rights Production Standards	Company	A combination of external pressure of CSOs and the media, internal commitment to human rights, and follow-up to Nike's initiative
1993	Athletic Footwear Association: AFA's Statement of Guidelines on Practices of Business Partners	Business association	Out of concern for the practices of business partners, and political and social issues in host countries
1995	Puma's Human Rights Undertaking to Observe Universal Standards	Company	To maintain its present international standing and business reputation
Undated	Mizuno's Code of Business Ethics	Company	To express responsibility towards society
Undated	American Apparel Manufacturers Association: AAMA's Statement of Guidelines:	Business association	To express commitment to fair and rational practice of business
1996	Fédération Internationale de Football: FIFA's Code of Labor Practice	Business association	To recognize the responsibilities to consumers and workers
1997	World Federation of the Sporting Goods Industry; WFSGI's Model Code of Conduct	Business association	To ensure that member companies satisfy the highest ethical standards in the global marketplace
1997	Clean Clothes Campaign; CCC's Code of Labor Practices	CSO	To improve the working conditions in the garment industry
1997	Council on Economics Priorities Accreditation Agency: CEPAA's SA 8000	CSO	To provide a standardized, global system for companies interested in assessing, monitoring, and influencing the social accountability of their suppliers and vendors, as well as their own facilities
1997	Nike's revised Code of Conduct	Company	To incorporate AIP standards in its code
1998	Nike's revised Code of Conduct	Company	To incorporate Nike's new labour initiatives
1998	Asian Human Rights Commission: AHRC's Human Rights Charter	CSO	To promote awareness and realization of human rights in the Asian region

Figure 11.8. Codes of conduct relevant to the sporting goods industry

Source: van Tulder and Kolk (2001: 269).

Ethics in Action 11.2

The UN Global Compact: talking about global regulation
....

The UN has been a player in the global regulation of companies for quite some time. Though backed by national governments as an institution, the codes and regulations of the UN itself have never been able to tackle effectively the various ethical, social, and environmental problems caused by corporations, particularly in the developing world. The UN simply lacks the power, the institutional infrastructure, and the global acceptance by all national governments in order to be an effective 'ethics police' on a global level. Most of the regulatory efforts of the main UN agency for these types of issues, the UN Centre on Transnational Corporations, were not able to get consent from all UN members. As a result, the agency was eventually closed down in 1993.

In a new attempt to address the ethical problems linked to corporate activities on a global scale, in 2000 the UN launched a new initiative called 'the Global Compact'. Rather than pursuing the top-down approach of earlier regulatory efforts, the Global Compact starts bottom up by working directly with corporations. The Global Compact is based on nine principles.

- Human Rights
  Business is asked to:
  1. Support and respect the protection of international human rights within its sphere of influence; and
  2. Make sure its own corporations are not complicit in human rights abuses.

- Labour
  Business is asked to uphold:
  3. Freedom of association and the effective recognition of the right to collective bargaining;
  4. The elimination of all forms of forced and compulsory labour;
  5. The effective abolition of child labour; and
  6. The elimination of discrimination in respect of employment and occupation.

- Environment
  Business is asked to:
  7. Support a precautionary approach to environmental challenges;
  8. Undertake initiatives to promote greater environmental responsibility;
  9. Encourage the development and diffusion of environmentally friendly technologies.

Companies that are willing to join have to (a) provide a letter from their CEO indicating a commitment to these nine principles; and (b) share at least one example per year of how they have translated one or more of these principles into practice. In return, the companies are allowed to use the UN's Global Compact logo for their corporate publicity.

The UN considers the Global Compact to be a facilitator of dialogue and learning between business, government, and CSOs. It achieves this by establishing *learning forums* on a global, national, and local level. Furthermore, in 2001 the Global Compact organized two large *policy dialogues* on the role of business in conflict zones (which took place in Geneva) and on business and sustainable development (in London). Here, multipartite participants engaged in building working groups to further discuss and break down the issues on a concrete business level. The third initiative consists of *partnership projects* where business, public sector actors, and CSOs get involved in specific projects to tackle ethical problems in business

More than 700 companies from over forty countries have signed up to the Global Compact so far, and there are numerous projects, learning groups, and dialogue workshops currently in operation. Much of its impact and acceptance is credited to the personal backing of the UN Secretary-General Kofi Annan, who initially proposed the compact at the 1999 World Economic Forum in Davos. 'Never has the UN achieved so much leverage with so few resources,' says Georg Kell, the executive head of the compact. Kell here is indicating that as a voluntary, facilitating initiative rather than a mandatory, 'imperative' form of regulation, the compact has proven to be far more success-ful at gaining corporate 'buy-in' than any preceding initiatives by the UN.

There are however critics of the compact and its voluntary approach to the problems of global business. Several CSO groups have argued that signing up to the nine principles does not commit corporations to very much, since compliance is not monitored and defection is not sanctioned in any way. Ultimately the critics see the Global Compact as a cheap 'bluewash' for corporations (meaning they cover up or 'wash' their problems with the blue of the UN flag), and a rather naive approach to globalization that ignores the compelling economic rationalities of liberalized world markets.

SOURCES

Kell, G., and Levin, D. (2002). 'The evolution of the Global Compact network: an historic experiment in learning and action'. Paper presented at the 2002 Academy of Management Conference in Denver.
Monbiot, G. (2000). 'Getting into bed with business: the UN is no longer just a joke'. *Guardian*, 31 Aug.: 18.
Willamson, H. (2003). 'Signing up to corporate citizenship'. *Financial Times*, 12 Feb.: 12.
Website of the Global Compact is **www.unglobalcompact.org**.

■ **Think theory**

Relate the UN Global Compact to the concepts of business–society relations as outlined in Chapter 2. Where does the Global Compact fit into these concepts? Which areas does it not cover? By using these concepts, try to give a critical assessment of the future potential and chances of the Global Compact.

In the final analysis, then, it would appear that the whole area of business involvement in self-regulation is multifaceted, multi-level, and highly dynamic. That business *is* involved in regulation is clear—thereby providing support for the argument that corporations have increasingly become involved in the protection (or otherwise) of citizens' rights. What remains unclear, though, is whether voluntary initiatives by corporations can ever succeed in providing suitable and sufficient protection for citizens. In the final section, we shall address this question in the specific context of sustainability.

Governments, business, and sustainability

Back in Chapter 1 (24), we defined sustainability as 'the long-term maintenance of systems according to environmental, economic, and social considerations'. This definition certainly captures the broad understanding of the concept in business, politics, and wider parts of society. Reaching towards the end of the book, however, we should add that this definition by no means satisfies everybody, nor is it how it was originally thought of. Sustainability was certainly first considered a pre-eminently *ecological concept* prescribing rules and principles for the usage of natural resources in a way which allows future generation to survive on this planet (see Pearce and Turner 1990).

The central idea of sustainability is to prescribe and implement new usage of natural resources (Turner 1993). With regard to *renewable resources*, such as wood, agricultural products, water, or air, the key principle would be not to use those resources beyond their capacity of regeneration. The more critical issue, though, are the so-called *non-renewable resources*, such as coal, oil, minerals, metals, and other key resources of modern industry. Here the original rules of 'strict' sustainability would suggest that none of these resources should be used if they would put future generations at a lower level of ability to meet their needs than the present generation. In the case of metals and other recyclables this would result in fairly strict rules for circulating these resources in the economy; with regard to oil or coal, the consequences are more severe. Since resources such as these will ultimately be depleted, we have to be extremely cautious about their use. While some have argued that sustainability does not allow their usage at all, others have proposed that we might use them only if we provide future generations with new technologies that would allow them to have the same level of welfare that we at present enjoy.

Without going into too much detail, sustainability in this sense is quite a tough and —from a business perspective—somewhat threatening concept. This applies particularly to industries that rely on non-renewable resources, such as the mining, oil, or chemical industries. There has been some research that shows that the mutation of the sustainability concept from the original ecological view towards a 'softer' concept has been particularly driven by industry. For example, Mayhew (1997) showed how the World Business Council of Sustainable Development—a key player at the Rio Summit—introduced a systematically watered-down definition of sustainable development and by this gave a new, more industry-friendly meaning to the concept. By linking sustainability not only to ecological, but also to social and economic criteria, the strict rules for using resources are loosened and the concept becomes far more open to deliberation and discretion.

Some authors therefore argue that the original agenda of sustainability has been 'hijacked' by industry and made less threatening and more ready to serve as a buzzword for corporate public relations (Welford 1997). Dirk Matten (1998: 8–10) for instance showed how the German chemical industry association (VCI) introduced the industry-friendly rendition of sustainable development into its discourse through a series of conferences throughout the mid-1990s. The VCI skilfully broadened the agenda for sustainability, defining it as a 'persistent, enduring, severe, intensive, incisive and effective development' —which ultimately allows for all kind of interpretations! This result proved to be quite successful for industry PR though. To give just one example, in a brochure about its implementation of sustainability, the German chemical company Hoechst (today Aventis) even represented its corporate fire brigade—a mandatory legal requirement—as a contribution to sustainability!

Given this more or less subtle resistance of industry to sustainability it is no wonder that the strongest impulse towards regulating for sustainability has come from governments. Mainly as a result of the Rio Summit in 1992 (the forerunner to the 2002 Johannesburg Summit), the industrialized world witnessed an avalanche of legislation in the 1990s aimed at tightening environmental standards for industry. In the following, we will have a look at two examples of regulatory actions aimed specifically at sustainability, first on the global and second on the European level. In so doing, we will discuss the different roles that industry has played in the formulation and implementation of this regulation. In the former, we will show the extreme positions that industry can take (active support and active obstruction); in the latter we will explore more of a middle ground.

Global climate change legislation and business responses: support versus obstruction

One of the political consequences of sustainability has been the debate on regulating global climate change. From an ecological viewpoint, the potentially irreversible destruction of the ozone layer has to be classified as one of most worryingly unsustainable behaviours. Therefore, global warming and changes in the global climate were centre stage at the Rio Summit 1992. Levy and Egan (2000) suggest that by this time, the World Business Council of Sustainable Development (a coalition of 160 international companies) had already subtly lobbied against any concrete measures to be implemented on a global level. However, as the political debate moved on, the Kyoto Protocol was ultimately signed in 1997 by nearly 200 countries. The protocol foresaw significant reductions in the emission of greenhouse gases, most notably carbon dioxide.

Reductions in carbon dioxide, however, represented a severe threat for some industries. Kolk and Levy (2001) illustrate that among the fiercest opponents was the oil industry, which is fundamentally implicated in greenhouse gas emissions through the burning of fossil fuels. As a result, the industry founded the 'Global Climate Coalition' (GCC) in 1989 in order to lobby against governmental regulation to cut back on greenhouse gas emissions. As Kolk and Levy reveal, among the main goals of the GCC were to lobby on the global level for weaker legislation, and on the national level to lobby their governments not to sign, ratify, or implement the Kyoto Protocol.

Counting among the main members of the GCC were the European companies BP and Shell, as well as the American companies ExxonMobil and Texaco. In the course of time, their strategies differed quite significantly and can be discussed as typical reactions to governments embarking on a sustainability agenda. The European companies left the GCC, first BP in 1996, and later Shell in 1998. Despite their industry's profound scepticism towards regulating against greenhouse emissions, both companies had to face the fact that their governments, and most notably the EU, were bound to implement Kyoto at some stage. Moreover, they faced considerable stakeholder pressure from CSOs and others to step back from the obstructive position of the GCC. Ultimately, BP in particular used its withdrawal from the anti-Kyoto camp as an occasion to rebrand itself as a 'green' company whose business was 'energy' rather than just oil. From being plain old 'British Petroleum', the company renamed itself 'Beyond Petroleum'.

The strategy of the US companies was quite different, since they saw considerable mileage in lobbying the US government to refrain from implementing climate protection legislation. The company placed advocacy advertisements in the US press that questioned the 'uncertain' science of global warming, warned that regulation would 'restrict life itself', and argued that technological innovation and the market could meet any 'potential risks' of climate change (Livesey 2002b). Moreover, with ExxonMobil (together with former energy giant Enron) counting among the top sponsors of (former oilman) George W. Bush's presidential campaign in 2000, it was perhaps unsurprising that one of the first acts of the Bush administration was to pull the USA out of the Kyoto agreement. Here, then, we can see ExxonMobil using various direct and indirect government influence strategies to counter sustainability regulation, whilst BP and Shell provided active support since it buttressed a broader organizational change programme.

Public support versus private pressure: a middle ground?

The oil industry corporations in the example above appear to exhibit reasonably clear and consistent stances regarding sustainability regulation. However, between these two extreme stances—active support and active obstruction—there seems to be a somewhat more delicate position in the middle. In some situations, we can see that corporations *publicly support* and endorse a sustainability agenda whilst simultaneously putting *private pressure* on governments to refrain from tighter regulation through covert lobbying.

In the case of climate policy, BP in Europe took the proactive and 'environmentally friendly' stance as early as 1996, while the same company BP (Amoco) in the USA still lobbied strongly against the Kyoto Protocol in 2000—even coming in as third largest donor to the Bush campaign. This attitude underlines that ultimately sustainability, if implemented properly, will face resistance from industry and needs strong and rigid implementation. If the latter is the case—as it was with the European climate policy—companies react proactively and adapt to the changing framework. Indeed, there are strong arguments to suggest that government encouragement for innovation in sustainability technologies can ultimately benefit corporations in international markets since they may become globally pre-eminent in competences that firms from other countries will eventually have to learn (Porter and van der Linde 1995). We only have to look at Danish companies' leadership in wind farm technologies (which we discussed in the last chapter) to see that anticipatory government encouragement can lead to international leadership in emerging industries. However, if governments are weak, or unwilling to implement regulation to encourage more sustainable practices, corporations often tend to preserve the status quo.

Earlier in the book, we made a brief mention of another piece of regulation that was designed to foster enhanced sustainability on the European level: the EU End-of-Life

Vehicle Directive. As briefly mentioned above, sustainability requires an extremely careful use of non-renewable resources, making circular material flows through reuse and recycling a crucial replacement for simple extraction, use, and disposal. The End-of-Life Vehicle Directive, which came into force in 2002 and has to be fully implemented by member countries by 2007, seeks to achieve such a circular flow by making car manufacturers responsible for the take-back and recycling of their cars.

The directive obviously has enormous implications for the automotive industry across Europe. Taking just one example, it has been estimated that the directive will cost the vast German car industry something like €10bn. As a result, the industry has fiercely opposed the directive behind the scenes, exerting considerable pressure on the German government to soften its potential impacts. Ultimately, the German Secretary for the Environment—a member of the Green Party, no less—had to block an earlier, stricter draft of the directive in 1999, having been instructed to directly by the German Chancellor (an ex-board member of Volkswagen) (*Financial Times* 1999).

Whilst this incident is indicative of 'private' pressure on the government, it is interesting to note here the simultaneous 'public' stance of the German car industry. Indeed, with environmental concerns prominent among German consumers, the car industry has for some time branded itself as one of the most proactive in terms of environmental protection. Notably, the association of German car manufacturers (VDA) had already issued a voluntary self-commitment to environmentally friendly car disposal in 1998 (Orsato et al. 2002). This case of the German automotive industry shows then, as it were, a 'middle ground' response to governmental implementation of sustainability: while maintaining an environmentally friendly 'face' on the outside, behind closed doors corporations may lever whatever power they have to obstruct tougher legislation.

Achieving sustainability: a necessary role for government?

So what can we learn from these three stances? The key issue to recognize is that businesses usually focus on short-term success, particularly in economies that are more strongly geared towards the shareholder value ideology. Sustainability however is looking at intergenerational equity and thus assumes a much, much longer time period. There is nothing wrong with industry looking at shorter periods for judging certain aspects of financial success, since this is one of the features of markets. A logical consequence though is that business itself will never have a full long-term interest in implementing sustainability in the kinds of radical ways that we have set out at the end of each of the last five chapters.

The logical conclusion would be that other actors, most notably government as a representative of society, *have* to act in favour of future generations. Although self-regulation and voluntary agreements may well be the most fertile area of regulatory activity in this area at present, we would suggest that the role of government in setting and enforcing rules aimed at promoting sustainability will always be crucial. And ultimately, the success of this regulatory activity will depend upon how much strength governmental institutions can maintain within a rapidly globalizing and deterritorializing economy.

Summary

In this chapter, we have looked in some depth at the stake held by government in business, and set out how the role of government, and its central task of issuing regulation for business, affects this stakeholder relationship. We have seen that 'government' today is quite a complex set of actors and institutions that act on various levels, from a local or regional level to a transnational or even global stage.

During the course of the chapter, we have discussed the complex role of governments and the interdependencies and mutual interests that they have with business. For an actor that is primarily obliged to pursue the interest of the electorate, or society, the dominant ethical challenges in business–government relations are the issues of legitimacy and accountability. This particularly focuses on the question of how much influence business should be allowed on governmental actors, and by what means this influence is engendered. We discussed various forms of business intervention in governmental decision-making, from lobbying, to party financing, up to far stronger forms of state capture and corruption.

We then had a closer look at the way globalization shifts the roles of business and government in regulating issues of relevance to business ethics. We discussed the notion of the 'post-Westphalian' context, which conceptualizes the impact of globalization on the power of nation state governments to shape business behaviour. We linked these shifts particularly to the new role of corporations as active players in the regulatory game, and discussed the various options and innovations in regulation open to business and other players. We concluded that in terms of corporate citizenship, business was actually placed in a *political* role that in certain respects was akin to that of governments. We qualified this new role, though, when analysing the role of government in initiating sustainable practices in business. We stated that sustainable development can clash too strongly with short-term profit goals of business to be left to merely voluntary approaches. So, the last part of our discussion reiterated the importance of governments in encouraging and enforcing ethical behaviour in business.

STUDY QUESTIONS

1 What is regulation? What does it mean to say that actors other than government engage in regulation?

2 Explain the two basic roles of government that determine its stakeholder relationship with corporations.

3 What are the potential ethical problems associated with corporate lobbying of government?

4 To what extent is it desirable or feasible to maintain a clear differentiation between business and government actors, roles, and processes?

5 Set out the main impacts of globalization on business–government relations.

6 Are strong governments necessary to achieve sustainability? Explain using examples from contemporary business practice.

RESEARCH EXERCISE

Conduct some research on the Responsible Care Programme of the chemical industry (**www.icca-chem.org**).

1 Explain the main details of the programme.

2 To what extent is the programme illustrative of self-regulation?

3 What are the advantages and disadvantages of self-regulation compared to government regulation for ensuring ethical conduct in the chemical industry?

4 Would you say the programme is likely to be sufficient to ensure ethical conduct in the chemical industry? If not, what else is necessary?

CASE 11

Mixing oil and Kohl: Elf, Leuna, and allegations of political corruption in France and Germany

This case study is concerned with one of the biggest party financing scandals in recent European history. It involves the alleged financing of the German Christian Democratic Party by the French oil company Elf, and highlights the densely interwoven relationships between business and government in both Germany and France. The case provides the opportunity to examine the ethics of close business–government relations, and offers the chance to explore the difficulty of changing long-standing patterns of interaction between business and government.

'Flourishing landscapes' was the promise of Helmut Kohl when, as the so-called 'architect of German unification' in 1990, he became the first post-war head of an all-German government. Delivering his promise, however, was no easy task. After all, the rapid integration of the currency and economic system of the former East Germany (or GDR for German Democratic Republic) quickly devastated much of the east's now largely uncompetitive industrial infrastructure.

A typical example of this situation was the former 'chemical triangle' near the town of Halle in Saxony-Anhalt. Formerly the centre of the GDR chemical industry, with massive export markets in the former communist bloc, the four big 'Kombinate' of the industry employed more than 80,000 people in 1989. One year later, though, 70 per cent of these jobs were already gone. One of the largest chemical companies in the region, Leuna, was particularly hard hit by the cuts, and by the early 1990s, the majority of its huge premises were largely deserted and abandoned.

If Kohl and his party, the CDU (Christian Democratic Union), were to remain in power, this growing source of discontent and frustration had to be dealt with. Since the industry in the former GDR had been nationalized under the previous regime, it was ultimately the task of the newly unified German government to look after the existing companies and (hopefully) find potential buyers for them. After the wall came down, all the property of the former GDR was pooled in a newly founded company called 'Treuhandanstalt' ('fiduciary agency'). This then sold one state-owned enterprise after another to private investors.

While some companies were hot stock, others were quite hard to sell. Leuna certainly seemed to belong to the latter category. The location of the area, far away from the nearest port, was not very advantageous for chemical production, and with most companies in the chemical industry struggling with overcapacity anyway, it was not easy to find investors for the crumbling enterprises of the chemical triangle.

In the case of Leuna, however, the French oil multinational Elf Acquitaine had an interest in the site. Indeed, in 1992 Elf finally took over Leuna and committed itself to a €2.15bn investment in a brand new refinery. The deal was primarily attractive to Elf though because the German government also included the lucrative network of gas stations of the former GDR state gas retailer Minol in the package to Elf. In May 1994, with considerable ceremony, construction of the refinery finally began, giving rise to hope and optimism for many in the region.

The project however had never been free from doubts. To many in the industry it had always appeared a bit strange that Elf had invested in this particular project. The new management board and the new CEO of Elf (who actually took over after the deal was signed) are said to have been rather doubtful as to whether to pursue the project. Indeed, from hindsight, and judged by the mere economic data, the project did not look to be an obvious investment to make for Elf.

And as time went by, rumours began to surface about doubtful or even illegal deals being made in connection with the sale. Ultimately, by the end of the 1990s, the Elf-Leuna case had grown to an outright scandal, leading to court proceedings in Germany and France, some of them involving high-profile politicians in both countries, and ultimately the imprisonment of some (but by no means all) of the key actors.

For a start, there were massive doubts about the price of the transaction. While the German government had invested a total of €2.4bn to develop the property and provide other investments to make the deal attractive to the French multinational, Elf ultimately paid only €275m to the Treuhandanstalt. Moreover, allegations of side deals and secret agreements sprang up, with the main allegation being that Elf, in order to get the contract, had given a secret donation to the German CDU of about €16m. This was subsequently argued to have helped the party leader Kohl to gain the narrow margin he needed to win the 1994 election.

Amongst the strongest indications of overly close business–government relations was evidence that François Mitterrand, the then French President, had strongly intervened and encouraged the involvement of Elf in Germany. Additionally, there were rumours that he had personally urged Elf to make the party donation to Kohl's party. The argument was that in addition to looking after the interests of Elf, Mitterrand had wanted Kohl to stay in power in Germany in order to accomplish crucial further steps in European unification, most notably monetary union. As the CDU was quite notoriously short of cash, and as public opinion in Germany seemingly turned against Kohl and his party, they needed a massive injection of cash in order to finance the 1994 election campaign.

So why would a multinational like Elf even become involved in such a delicate situation? The first thing we need to understand is the role of the company in the political landscape of France. At that time, the company—now privatized and merged to form TotalElfFina—was a conglomerate owned by the French state. In many ways, the ties between Elf and the government could not have been closer. Sometimes even regarded by some as part of the French diplomatic corps, Elf did not only pursue its own business interest but often served as leverage for the interests of the French government throughout the world. So, for instance, when France decolonized the African continent, Elf still remained in those countries and secured the French government crucial influence on local politicians. And the influence allegedly went both ways: so whilst the French government made use of Elf's commercial power and financial strength to secure political influence, Elf could to some extent rely on the French government to help with crucial deals. In the case of the Leuna acquisition, for instance, it was regarded as reasonably clear that around €40m had been paid out of Elf's accounts to foster the deal.

With so much interconnectedness the road was quite open to all sorts of doubtful practices. Politicians were frequent users of Elf's private fleet of aircraft—often called 'Air Elf'. And allegedly, many of Elf's own senior executives who were supposed to be involved in the payment of so-called 'commissions' to governments, also secured substantial sums of cash themselves out of the deals. Of course, the facts here are difficult to discern. Still, besides the Leuna scandal, Elf found itself in the line of fire for another major scandal that made the headlines in 2001. Roland Dumas, France's Foreign Secretary from 1989 to 1992, and his former mistress were handed prison sentences and high fines for misusing Elf's company funds. Dumas had used his influence to get his mistress a job at Elf, while Elf had readily accepted the deal in order to get a direct line into the Foreign Office. The court regarded it as proven that Dumas had accepted various favours from Elf (via his mistress), probably the least of which was a €1,500 pair of tailor-made shoes bought with his mistress's company credit card. Furthermore, in 2002, after a huge and far-ranging investigation, forty-two members of the French political and business elite were charged with accepting or abusing up to €500m cash in the early 1990s. The trial is still pending.

Obviously there were suspicions that Mitterrand had applied the same pattern of influence between the government and Elf to further his political goals in the Leuna case. This did not only involve Elf in what looked like a poorly conceived business venture, but significantly it also potentially involved the company in the funding of wider political interests. At the time of writing, it has never been proven which amounts of money, coming from which sources, were directed at which final recipients. The German, French, and Swiss judicial systems (as many of the deals were technically carried out in Switzerland or via Swiss bank accounts) were partly reluctant, partly incompetent, and in parts allegedly even unwilling to properly pursue the flows of money. The only certain thing so far is that there were payments involved from Elf and the only people successfully taken to court and sentenced were the minor 'wheeler dealers' who actually dealt with managing, laundering, and delivering the money.

What made the situation especially complicated on the German side of the deal is the fact that the CDU already had quite a legacy of questionable party financing. The series of scandals began in the early 1970s and continued even until 2003, when the party was heavily fined by the Federal Constitutional Court for its funding of an anti-immigration campaign that led to Roland Koch's electoral victory in Hessen in 1998. Similarly, around the time of the Leuna acquisition, the German company Thyssen secured a major contract to supply tanks to the Saudi government that, in gaining the German government's approval, allegedly involved substantial cash injections to the CDU. Like so many such allegations, the exact details of the Thyssen deal remain unproven, but it is clear that significant donations were made to the CDU, some of them in cash. Significantly, perhaps, the former party chairman has since admitted that he accepted cash from the key arms dealer involved in the Thyssen deal, thereby furthering suspicions of corruption, and providing the impetus for continued investigations.

Faced with the specific allegations about Leuna, though, Mr Kohl and the CDU have always vehemently denied all charges against them. Nonetheless, many of the actors said to be involved in the Leuna case were the same as those associated with the Thyssen scandal. Moreover, it emerged that over the course of Kohl's sixteen-year term he had established, and had personal access to, a complicated web of accounts administering about €1m undeclared campaign donations. Although he admitted after he left office that this was a 'mistake', Kohl refused to name the donors and has as yet never been forced to do so by the courts.

Little is certain about the flows of money and influence that occurred between corporations and political parties in France and Germany, either during the Leuna events, or for that matter during the various other scandals that have surfaced over the past decade or so. What is certain though is that some of the relations are both deeply embedded, and deeply hidden.

Questions

1 What types of business–government relations are alluded to in this case?

2 Set out the main issues of ethical concerns in this case study. What difference does it make that many of the allegations referred to in the case remain unproven?

3 Would you describe the strategy of the companies involved as successful? In which ways?

4 What could be done to avoid similar problems in the future?

Sources (selected)

Anon. (2000). 'Greasing the wheels: allegations of high-level international influence peddling have shattered Germany's complacency'. *Time International*, 7 Feb.

—— (2001). 'Germany "paid billions to sell plant"'. **www.bbc.co.uk/news**, 6 Aug.

Fenby, J. (2002). 'Last week, 42 members of the French business elite received a hand delivered packet'. *Business*, 10 Feb.

Keil, G. (1994). 'Ein Spatenstich weckt viele Hoffnungen'. *Berliner Zeitung*, 10 May.

Kleine-Brockhoff, T., and Schirra, B. (2001). 'Genfer Ermittlungsdokumente—Die Spur der Millionen'. *Die Zeit*, 4 July.

12

Conclusions and Future Perspectives

In this chapter we will:

- Reiterate the role, meaning, and importance of business ethics;

- Summarize the influence of globalization on business ethics;

- Assess the value of the notion of sustainability;

- Summarize and extrapolate the specific European aspects of business ethics;

- Discuss the role and significance of stakeholders as a whole for ethical management;

- Review the implications of corporate citizenship thinking for business ethics;

- Summarize the contribution of normative ethical theories to business ethics;

- Consider the benefits of thinking about ethical decision-making;

- Assess the role of specific tools for managing business ethics.

Introduction

We hope by now that you have a pretty good idea of what business ethics is all about, and what some of the main issues, controversies, concepts, and theories are that make business ethics such a fascinating subject to study. There is always a danger, though, that in reading a book such as this, you are left at the end thinking something like: 'fine, each individual chapter makes sense, but how does it all fit together?' In this last chapter, we will therefore attempt to remedy this by setting out a brief overview of the key topics of the book, and providing a round-up of our discussions during the preceding eleven chapters. We will in particular return to the subjects introduced in Part I of the book—such as globalization, sustainability, stakeholder theory, corporate citizenship, ethical theory, and management tools—and provide a summarization of how we have applied, developed, examined, and critiqued them in the context of individual stakeholders in Part II of the book. This final chapter should therefore help you to apply an overall perspective to your revision of the book.

The nature and scope of business ethics

By now you should be quite aware that the simple question of 'what is business ethics?' does not exactly lend itself to a simple answer. In Chapter 1, we defined the subject of business ethics as 'the study of business situations, activities, and decisions where issues of right and wrong are addressed'. Clearly, the range of such situations, activities, and decisions here is immense. We have certainly discussed most of the main ones, but existing problems sometimes go away, or become more a matter of legislation, and new problems continue to arise, either because of new technologies, changes in business practices or markets, exposure to different cultures, changing expectations, or simply the arising of new opportunities for ethical abuse. Consequently, it is never possible to determine the exact extent of the business ethics subject—and nor indeed should it be.

The question of business ethics and the law that we first introduced in Chapter 1 has been substantially expanded upon throughout the book. In particular, we would like to reiterate the importance of seeing business ethics as largely, but by no means exclusively, starting where the law ends. We have actually showed this relation to be an increasingly complex one, with corporations sometimes supplementing or replacing the lawmaking process with self-regulation, and sometimes challenging, resisting, and subverting legalistic approaches to enforcing ethical behaviour. Whichever way we look at it, then, the relationship between business ethics and the law would appear to be an area for continued change and evolution in the years to come. This, if anything, is likely to make the whole issue of business ethics even more important, particularly given the increasing scope for European businesses to act in a range of contexts where state influence over ethical behaviour is limited or on the wane.

Globalization as a new context for business ethics

Our second main subject in Chapter 1 was the new context for business ethics provided by globalization. We quite carefully worked towards a definition of the 'G-word' at the beginning of the book—and the subsequent chapters vividly illustrated that 'deterritorialized' economic, social, and political activities dramatically reshape the role and context of business ethics. As we particularly emphasized in each of the stakeholder chapters in Part II, globalization results in a very specific demand for innovation in all firm–stakeholder relations.

The first aspect of globalization is that much corporate activity takes place in multiple national contexts. We have explained how shareholders, employees, consumers, suppliers, competitors, CSOs, and governments might all conceivably be located in other continents. This, as we said in Chapter 1, typically exposes companies to different *cultural* and *legal* environments that leave considerable discretion to managers in determining and upholding ethical standards. A particular focus for us in discussing the consequences of globalization has therefore been developing countries, since these appear to be particularly keen to attract a globally available capital in the form of direct investment. Throughout the book, we have quite extensively discussed ethical issues in the context of developing countries, and it is fairly reasonable to expect them to remain towards the top of the business ethics agenda for the foreseeable future.

On a second level, we suggested at the outset that globalization creates a social space beyond the power of single nation states. We particularly reiterated this in the context of global financial markets in Chapter 6 and the global regulation of corporations in Chapters 10 and 11. For many business ethics problems, no single nation state is able to regulate and control corporate actors, especially in contexts such as global financial markets. We have argued that an increased governmental grip on such spaces is somewhat unlikely to happen in the near future. We also revealed and explored some of the mechanisms that lead to a situation where many other corporate activities escape the direct control of nation states. This 'transnational space' (Morgan 2001) creates an interesting arena where corporate actors currently appear to dominate the scene. This does not mean that ethical norms are not present here, but these spaces lack governmental authorities to organize and control corporate action. We have, especially in Chapters 10 and 11, discussed ways of filling this gap, by self-regulation, by selected initiatives of global CSOs, or even by initiatives driven by the UN. The latter arena, however, still leaves ample space for corporations, and further challenges them from an ethical point of view. The initiatives discussed in the book, and even more so their limits, show that there still remains much to be desired in terms of the global regulation and enforcement of business ethics. This, again, will no doubt be an area of increasing activity and interest in the future.

Sustainability as a new goal for business ethics

Our next major issue in Chapter 1 was that of sustainability as a new goal for business ethics. Throughout the chapters of the second half of the book, we have discussed the nature of this goal, its challenges, and suggested some of the steps that corporations might take in order to enhance sustainability in the context of different stakeholder relations. We have found that, in different contexts, contributions can be made in the different 'corners', as it were, of the sustainability triangle (**Figure 1.5**), as well as in providing a more even balancing of the triple bottom line of sustainability. Initial but significant progress in sustainability reporting, sustainability share indexes, industrial ecosystems, work–life balance, and civil and intergovernmental regulation has been made, and bodes reasonably well for the future.

However one looks at it, though, the challenge posed by sustainability for business ethics is a huge one. An appropriate balance of the triple bottom line is extremely difficult to engineer, even when (as is quite rare) corporations have the will to attempt it. Many of our suggestions for sustainability in the area of employees, consumers, suppliers, etc. have been quite speculative and potentially threatening to existing corporate ways of thinking, organizing, and behaving. Ultimately, sustainability implies goals that lie beyond the time horizons of business, and which might be thought to jeopardize traditional bottom-line goals. Progress towards sustainable solutions therefore appears to be possible, but slow, tentative, and, at present, often merely exploratory.

What remains to be said then of the goal of sustainability? Our reflections in Chapter 11 have already been rather critical on the role of corporations in the sustainability area. This leaves us to reiterate chiefly two conclusions. First, the triple bottom line definition of sustainability obfuscates the fact that corporations tend to focus primarily on *economic* aspects, and even the majority of those actors pressing for greater sustainability tend to mainly emphasize *environmental* dimensions, at the expense of *social* interests. There is often a trade-off between the different elements, and in the context of developing countries especially, many of those likely to be affected lack sufficient power and influence to have their interests effectively heard and represented.

Second, without strong governments issuing legislation with regard to sustainability goals, it would appear to be unlikely to feature any time soon as a high priority on the business agenda. As much as we have identified the eroding effects of globalization and increasing corporate power on governmental authority, sustainability is likely to demand that governmental actors—perhaps in concert with CSOs and corporations—retain a significant degree of influence over the globalizing economy.

Business ethics in a European context

The final issue that we introduced in Chapter 1 was the need for a European perspective on business ethics. Throughout the subsequent chapters, we have focused on Europe as a particular geographical region where business ethics is shaped by, and has to adapt to, certain expectations and characteristics. We initially showed that the specific movement of business ethics started in the USA, and although we have certainly revealed considerable convergence in some issues, the two sides of the Atlantic appear to have maintained something of a different agenda.

In Europe, major differences come from a more densely regulated environment in certain areas, especially regarding employee rights. This focus on the regulation of ethical issues in business is still quite dominant in Europe, particularly given that the ongoing unification process transfers and perpetuates this approach on the transnational, Europe-wide level. Similarly, the role of CSOs in Europe is perceived as stronger than in the USA, and European companies have tended to adopt rather different approaches to business ethics management from their American counterparts.

The question remains, however, whether Europe will continue to be a distinct entity that differs substantially from other economic regions of the world, or whether the globalization process will continue to reshape business ethics in Europe towards a more homogeneous international approach. Indeed, it is evident that many of the ethical issues discussed in this book such as corporate governance, wages and conditions, employee surveillance, and corporate lobbying are increasingly as much of a concern for European corporations as they have been for US corporations.

On the other hand, especially with the increasing influence of political actors on the European level, there is reason to believe that Europe will pursue its own trajectory in addressing ethical issues in business. Recent prominent examples are efforts from the

European Commission (Commission of the European Communities 2001; 2002) to issue a common framework for corporate social responsibility. To what extent these developments will gain momentum remains to be seen. Another factor, though, which certainly makes prognosis slightly speculative, is the role of the accession countries in Eastern Europe. The fact that they do not share the same institutional heritage as the rest of Europe might result in another idiosyncratic way of dealing with ethical issues in business in a European context.

The role of different stakeholder constituencies in business ethics

In Chapter 2, we introduced a number of important concepts that help us to frame business ethics. Perhaps the most important of these was stakeholder theory, especially given that the major stakeholder constituencies of the corporation provided the structure for Part II of the book. Notwithstanding the fact that many managers will in practice probably deal with stakeholders on a much more instrumental basis, in the main, we have primarily developed a *normative* approach to stakeholder theory, namely the idea that certain groups have certain intrinsic rights and interests that need to be considered by managers. This has been an important element of the discussion in the second part of the book, not least because stakeholder rights often form the basis of many ethical issues and problems faced by business.

In Chapters 6 to 11, we discussed each individual stakeholder group separately, and it might appear as if they were all equally important to the corporation. Although in a certain sense they are, their significance certainly varies in different contexts, issues, and topics. *Shareholders* certainly remain a key stakeholder group for the corporation, especially in a time where globalized financial markets confront companies with the necessity to source their capital on a global level. With Europe more and more adopting the shareholder value ideology, the prospects of assigning a dominant role for shareholders might in fact be imminent. Another challenging area here is the topic of shareholder activism. As **Case 12** at the end of this chapter shows, the leverage of shareholding might be quite an effective tool to foster greater attention to business ethics in corporations. Certainly, the field of ethical investment is an area of growing importance for corporations, and major institutional investors are increasingly responding to demands to add ethical criteria to their investment decisions.

Employees count among the most long-standing stakeholder groups of every business operation. In a European context, there is still considerable ground for expecting employees to be a dominant stakeholder group, especially given the strong legal position this group generally has. However, new working practices, increased flexibilization, and challenges to legally codified protections all appear to have weakened the stake of employees somewhat in recent years. In other cultural contexts too, particularly in the developing world, employee rights might be yet more open to contestation and abuse, requiring considerable attention to new practices and protections.

The role of *consumers* is particularly interesting since, although they have always been of utmost *instrumental* importance to business, their *normative* claims would seem to be somewhat weaker than certain other constituencies. Whilst consumers might easily simply transfer their attention to another product or supplier, groups such as employees, suppliers, and local communities are more 'locked in' to the corporation and cannot so easily switch to an alternative. Nonetheless, it is easy to miss the fact that although the satisfaction of consumers appears to be in the self-interest of corporations, there is still much scope for exploitation and abuse of consumer rights. That said, the power of (some) consumers to exercise ethical purchasing is likely to sustain corporations' attention to consumers' ethical concerns.

The stake of *suppliers* appears to be one that, although it can be quite strong in certain contexts and industries, often has little legal protection, and will in practice often be seen to depend on the relative power balance with the corporation. *Competitors* meanwhile have one of the more contestable stakes in a firm, and although they have certain inbuilt rights that need to be considered, will often be one of the lowest priorities for corporations. Interestingly, in environmentally exposed industries, competitors might be more strongly considered, because of their role in setting up take-back and recycling schemes, just as suppliers might play a major role where integrated networks of recovery are intended. With an increasing trend towards just-in-time production and specialization, as well as strategic alliances and joint ventures, certain industries are more closely tied to their competitors and suppliers than others—a tendency that may also vary across different cultures and countries.

The stake of *CSOs* and *governments* is certainly the most complex and dynamic at the current time. CSOs on the one hand have heralded and pushed crucial ethical issues in the past, even initiating long-term processes of change on the part of corporations to respond, adopt, and incorporate the issues at stake. Over the course of time, CSOs have contributed to mainstreaming business ethics, especially in Europe, but the legitimacy of their stake remains open to contestation in specific cases. The relation of business with government meanwhile seems to develop in an even more controversial direction. While governments seem to be losing some of their traditional power in issuing and enforcing regulation, they have by no means decreased in importance as a stakeholder. The crucial innovation, though, is that the relationship develops more into a partnership rather than the previously dependent role of business. This applies to the national level, but increasingly to the global level as well, as the UN Global Compact for example, illustrates quite well.

One final point that should be made clear at this stage is that one of the most challenging tasks for ethical management is to achieve an effective and appropriate balance between *competing* stakeholder expectations and claims. As we saw even just in the case of CSOs in Chapter 10, different stakeholders are likely to diverge in the demands they place on corporations, making even a supposedly 'ethical' response a matter of some disagreement. Moreover, as we saw in Chapter 5, companies may well make their assessments based on largely instrumental grounds, meaning that those unable or unwilling to influence the corporation may be neglected regardless of any intrinsic rights they might have.

Corporate citizenship as a new concept in business ethics

Back in Chapter 2, we also introduced the concept of corporate citizenship (CC) as the latest step in a number of developments in conceptual frameworks for ethical behaviour in business. Indeed, the subtitle of this book suggests that much of the content is about how to manage CC in an era of globalization. When first talking about the concept, two major points were evident. On the one side, CC in the 'extended' view identifies the corporate involvement in the administration of *citizenship rights*, most notably social, civil, and political rights. On the other hand, we have reiterated throughout the book that alongside this role, the question of accountability automatically surfaces. We have discussed these issues throughout the book, especially in Part II, raising a number of serious issues for consideration.

With regard to the first claim—that corporations take over a governmental function in administering citizenship rights—Chapters 6 to 11 have provided a convincing though nonetheless varied impression. When discussing the relationship to shareholders, we identified quite a substantial influence of corporations over civil rights, most notably the right to property of this constituency. We then had an extensive survey of the various rights corporations have to administer for their employees, many of which touched on their social and civil rights.

In the area of consumers and CSOs, corporations often provide a channel through which the public expresses its political choices rather than going to the ballot box. Corporate involvement in lobbying, as well as self-regulation and voluntary codes of conduct, further underlines their role in areas of politics traditionally occupied predominantly by governments.

In the context of competitors and suppliers, corporations might like to use practices that ultimately focus on infringing or circumventing the mechanisms of the market. In so doing they can determine prices and the range of choices we as citizens ultimately have. Corporations, in this area, assume responsibility over the way markets operate and remain functioning. Large corporations in particular have significant influence over their suppliers, and by this can dictate the way in which products are manufactured. If a large corporation requires certain ethical standards from its suppliers, such as environmental quality or human rights protections, they have considerable power to shape the manner in which citizenship rights of third parties are actually enacted.

On the side of accountability, the picture developed over the previous eleven chapters of this book is not so very bright. We have identified considerable power of shareholders by their right to vote and initiate shareholder activism. In continental Europe at least, employees too can exert a reasonable amount of influence on corporations. Such 'industrial democracy', however, tends to remain limited to a rather narrow scope of societal interest that is closely linked to the interest of the corporation as a whole.

Consumers too have some, albeit quite limited, influence on corporations, since their approval or disapproval of the company's stance on certain ethical issues can be expressed through the market. But certainly the most direct control of corporations in this respect requires the involvement of CSOs and formal campaigns of action. Indeed, it is exactly this sector that will probably play a central role in holding corporations accountable for the way in which they administer citizenship rights in the future. Nonetheless, the lack of accountability and legitimacy of CSOs themselves remains one of the weaker foundations of CSO power to act as proxy for citizens.

Consequently, the relation between companies and governments seems to be the most problematic one. It is apparent that under-resourced governments have ceded increasing influence and power to corporations, even in terms of their own party funding! If anything, the discussion of this book highlights the gaping abyss between the influence of corporations on citizenship rights and the subsequent control and accountability issues involved for citizens. This book clearly identifies this institutional void; however, it also shows potential trajectories for each stakeholder group to use existing links in order to partially fill this gap.

The contribution of normative ethical theories to business ethics

In Chapter 3, we introduced normative ethical theories, suggesting that in a pluralistic perspective they can provide a number of important considerations for ethical decision-making in business. In so doing, we had already watered down a little the inherent claim of traditional ethical theories—that they provide codified rational solutions to most problems. Indeed, as we have progressed through the book, it should have become extremely clear that these theories rarely provide us with a clear-cut, unambiguous, and non-controversial solution. As such, this book could be argued to be closer to a postmodern perspective than anything else: ethical theories are at best tools to inform the 'moral sentiment' of the decision-maker and as such cannot replace, let alone predetermine, solutions from an abstract, theoretical, or 'objective' point of view. Ultimately, ethical decisions are taken by actors in everyday business situations. Ethical theories might help to structure and rationalize some of the key aspects of those decisions, but their status can never be one that allows a moral judgement or decision to be made without effectively immersing into the real situation.

By positioning the role of ethical theory on this level, we by no means intend to play down the role of normative ethical theory though (as a postmodernist would). These theories first of all help the individual actor to rationalize moral sentiments, and to verbalize moral considerations in concrete business situations. Thus, we have emphasized the important role of ethical theory throughout the book, yet at the same time we have tried to encourage you to develop a critical perspective on theory. When discussing cases, ethics in action vignettes, and ethical dilemmas, our hope is that you will have discovered the value of ethical theories for communicating your views, and also for understanding the views and perspective of others. Here, perhaps the main value of ethical theories lies in the fact that they help to rationalize and enable a discourse about ethical considerations in business decisions.

Influences on ethical decision-making

In Chapter 4, we examined descriptive ethical theories. This helped us to understand the way in which people in organizations actually made decisions about business ethics. In the subsequent chapters, we have made evident the enormous range and complexity of ethical problems that continue to occur in business, suggesting that the factors influencing unethical decision-making continue to have a substantial role to play.

Given the increasing internationalization of business discussed throughout the book, we might first suggest that the national and cultural influences on decision-making, both at the individual and situational level, will become more important, but less clear-cut. Personal religious and cultural factors are increasingly challenged and reshaped by global business practices, and the influence of a specific, local, national context also shifts in the context of 'foreign' MNCs with global codes of practice.

Indeed, many of the more important influences identified in Chapter 4 were context based, and were often informal and cultural aspects, such as the moral framing of ethical issues in the workplace, organizational norms, and work roles. This suggests that more formal efforts to target improved ethical decision-making, such as codes of conduct and voluntary regulation, might ultimately have fairly limited impact unless they presage a more profound culture shift in business organizations. Some prospects for hope might be evident here when we consider that the mere fact of actively taking part in designing codes and rules could conceivably lead businesses to a deeper consideration of values in the longer term. Perhaps this is a little optimistic, but the opportunities for doing so would be enhanced if corporations continue to open themselves up to discourse with stakeholders—especially those that might challenge the dominant corporate mindset.

The role of management tools in business ethics

In Chapter 5, the last chapter in the first part of the book, we discussed the management of business ethics. Therefore, unlike, for instance, a book on finance or marketing, Crane and Matten has just one chapter dedicated to what we would traditionally call management instruments and tools. This might strike you as odd, especially if you are a business or management student, but it shows that business ethics is about more than just managing with tools and techniques. To our mind, it is much more about expanding horizons, deepening understandings, and developing critical thinking about business practices. The single chapter on tools also suggests that business ethics is not really a separate branch of management at all. After all, it should be pretty clear by now that business ethics pertains to every traditional branch or aspect of management, such as marketing, finance, strategy, etc., and rather constitutes an additional set of criteria for typical decisions, and a different way of looking at 'normal' business situations.

This is not to say that the explicit management of business ethics is not important, and we have traced some of the potential for tools and techniques in the second part of the book. A crucial role for example is likely to be played by new forms of social auditing and reporting, particularly in helping customers, CSOs, and shareholders evaluate the corporation's performance against ethical criteria. This is closely linked to new forms of stakeholder dialogue that we discussed in Chapter 5. Employee participation, shareholder democracy, or business–CSO partnership, among other things that we discussed in Part II, clearly require active engagement by corporations with their stakeholders.

Another of the tools that we have made frequent reference to throughout Chapters 6 to 11 is codes of ethics. These are certainly one of the most commonly used tools of business ethics, and, as we have discussed, the general lack of governmental regulation in a growing number of business areas means that codes are necessary to fill the rule-making gap. Certainly in industry at the moment, codes of various sorts have been the subject of enormous effort and interest. As we have discussed throughout the book, though, it remains to be seen where this development might lead, and what real impact it might actually have on business practice. Indeed, the multiplication and proliferation of more and more codes might actually be counter-productive to the original purpose of making decision-making more clear, and companies more transparent and accountable.

Summary

In this chapter, we have reviewed the main themes that were introduced in Part I of the book, and have synthesized and summarized the main contributions subsequently made to these themes in Part II. We have concluded that the nature and scope of business ethics is likely to remain complex and ever evolving, with the prospect that the subject will be increasingly important in the years to come. We explained how globalization has dramatically reshaped the role and context of business ethics, whilst sustainability has presented an important yet extremely challenging goal for business ethics to contend with. We then questioned and reiterated the continued significance of a European perspective on business ethics, indicating some of the shifts and nuances that would be necessary to maintain a regional perspective in an age of globalization. Following this, we turned to stakeholder theory, and analysed the relative importance and relevance of each of the different stakeholder groups discussed in Part II. Here, we further emphasized the profound problems of balancing competing stakeholder interests. This then led on to a summary of the different stakeholder contributions to our understanding of corporate citizenship thinking. In the remainder of the chapter, we assessed the contribution of ethical theory, ethical decision-making, and business ethics management to our discussions in Part II. Here, we highlighted the need for a pragmatic, pluralistic approach that was both sensitive to the variety of contexts that corporations and managers are involved in, and went beyond mere adherence to codified laws and procedures. Ultimately, our hope is that by reading this book, and thinking and talking about the issues and concepts raised, you will be better equipped to respond to the complex, yet fascinating problems of business ethics with empathy, imagination, and good judgement.

STUDY QUESTIONS

1 What do you think will be the major new ethical issues and problems that businesses will have to face over the next decade?

2 Compare the challenges posed by globalization and sustainability to business ethics thinking and practice. Which do you think will prove to be the greatest challenge?

3 What are the particular ethical problems and issues that are likely to be faced by Eastern European companies? What approaches to business ethics management are likely to be appealing and suitable for such companies?

4 What are the major implications of corporate citizenship thinking for each major stakeholder group? How well placed is each group to influence the decisions and actions of corporations?

5 What are the benefits and drawbacks of adopting a pluralistic approach to normative ethical theory in business ethics?

6 Account for the prevalence of ethical codes in global business. To what extent do you consider such a development to be beneficial to the improvement of business ethics?

RESEARCH EXERCISE

Case 12 describes the events around the controversial Ilisu Dam in Turkey. Read through the case and select one of the following dam projects to conduct some comparative research on:

- Three Gorges Dam in China;
- Narmada Dams in India;
- San Roque Dam in the Philippines;
- Bujugali Dam in Uganda.

1 Set out the main stakeholders in the case.

2 Which companies are involved in the construction project? Which countries do they come from?

3 What are the main differences between this project and the Ilisu Dam project?

4 Have events unfolded in a similar way in the two projects? Account for any similarities or differences.

CASE 12

No laughing matter: the Ilisu Dam project in Turkey

This case study describes the events surrounding the controversial Ilisu Dam project in Turkey and sets out the relationships between corporations—including the construction firms Balfour Beatty (UK), Impregilo (Italy), and Skanska (Sweden)—and governmental and civil society actors in the initiative. The case sheds light on the divergent roles, responsibilities, interests, and goals that may be involved in a major international construction project and provides an opportunity to explore many of the issues covered in the book, and in particular those of globalization, sustainability, corporate citizenship, and various stakeholder relationships.

Imagine, a large multinational corporation that has been accused of a number of dubious business practices in the past suddenly abandons a controversial dam scheme likely to cause severe environmental and social harm. Is this a case of a sinner turning into a saint? Well, perhaps not exactly. But there was certainly something funny going on when a campaign headed by the unlikely figure of a stand-up comedian succeeded in forcing the UK construction company Balfour Beatty out of the international consortium set to build the Ilisu Dam in east Turkey.

The Ilisu Dam project was actually a long-standing plan held by the Turkish government, and had been mooted for nearly twenty years before finally getting off the ground in 1997. At the centre of the project was the proposal to construct a huge dam on the river Tigris in the east of Turkey, 65 km north of the Iraqi border. The dam would create a lake of 320 km²—roughly the size of Greater Manchester—and would facilitate the establishment of a huge 1,200 megawatt power station, able to provide the entire region with electricity. Its proponents argued that it would also help to irrigate agriculture, mitigate flooding in winter, and offset drought in the summer.

The UK company Balfour Beatty won the Ilisu Dam contract in 1997, as part of a consortium led by the Swiss engineering company Sulzer Hydro, and including the Swiss turbine manufacturer ABB, the Swedish construction company Skanska, the Italian construction company Impregilo, and the Swiss Bank UBS. However, it faced considerable public criticism from the very first day.

For instance, environmentalists argued that if the dam went ahead, water quality would deteriorate, populations downstream would face a lack of water, and precious wetlands in northern Iraq that served as special wildlife habitat to many endangered species would be wiped out. Moreover, once flooded, the buried biomass would deteriorate under water, releasing huge quantities of the greenhouse gas methane.

The impacts of the dam would not only be environmental, though. The project was expected to affect 80,000 people, most of them ethnic minority Kurds, and looked set to make almost 30,000 people homeless. It would also bury eighty-two towns and villages, and would submerge several historic sites, some of them more than 10,000 years old. Furthermore, it was also set to flood the city of Hasakeyf, which for centuries has been the cultural capital of the Kurds.

Because of these likely impacts on the region, critics of the dam argued that it was a well-targeted act from the Turkish government to dissipate and weaken the identity of the Kurdish people, and to crack down on the Kurdish liberation movement, the PKK. The PKK had increasingly been seen as a thorn in the side of the Turkish government, mainly because of their demands for an independent state in the area. Some critics even went so far as to suggest that the Ilisu Dam (and other dam projects in the region) was part of a wider attempt to ethnically cleanse a rebellious minority.

On a social level, then, critics described the dam as a major attempt by the Turkish government to almost literally 'drown' the Kurds' claim to an independent state and defeat the Kurdish liberation movement PKK once and for all. Furthermore, since the dam would be built in a politically sensitive area, Turkey's southern neighbours would be heavily affected by the measures. Notably, it was argued that the dam would virtually give Turkey power over the water supply to northern Syria and Iraq—a form of power that even rivals military supremacy in such a location.

Unsurprisingly then, the protest against the dam included various groups and interests. Not only did the 'usual suspects' among CSO groups such as Friends of the Earth join the protest, but so did the Kurdish Human Rights Project and even the Arab League. Gradually the UK-based Ilisu Dam Campaign emerged as an umbrella organization orchestrating the protest, led by the campaigning British stand-up comedian and writer Mark Thomas.

The campaign faced a major battle, in that their opponents included not just the Turkish government and the construction consortium, but also the national governments of the consortium members. With projects of such dimensions—the total value of the dam was around $2bn (€2bn)

—companies normally seek insurance cover from their governments via export credit agencies to protect themselves against the political and commercial risks of the project. Where the French government uses the insurance company Coface to deal with such issues, the Italian institute for foreign trade insurance is SACE, and the UK has the Export Credit Guarantee Department (ECGD), a branch of the Department of Trade and Industry (DTI). So whilst Impregilo dealt with SACE, it was to the ECGD that Balfour Beatty applied for cover for its £220m (€315m) share in the project.

This move put the UK government in a somewhat delicate position. Although the government had widely touted an 'ethical foreign policy', the ECGD in line with most export credit agencies lacked mandatory social, environmental, and human rights criteria in its decision-making. Tony Blair, the UK Prime Minister, was reported to be in favour of the project—but ultimately, the government did not take any final stance on the dam—and was probably lucky not to have done so.

Meanwhile, as the campaign went on, things seemed not to develop very much in favour of the project. Balfour Beatty, though, did commission an independent report on the environmental impacts of the dam—but refused to publish it until Friends of the Earth threatened to force disclosure in the courts. It also surfaced that, as of September 2000, the Turkish authorities had neither consulted the Kurdish people living on site, nor had they offered any compensation or even come up with any resettlement plans. The main experience of the company officially in charge of such tasks was actually organizing package holidays and business conferences! It also became clear that Turkey had not consulted any of their downstream neighbours, a move which potentially put the country in breach of international law.

Throughout this time, Balfour Beatty, despite the bad publicity the project was generating, appeared to be firmly resolved to continue with the dam. The company was not new to controversy: it had been accused of bribing a state official in Lesotho; had incurred a substantial fine following its involvement in a tunnel collapse at Heathrow; and had been raided by the FBI in the USA concerning an alleged misappropriation of some $280m (€280m).

In the Ilisu campaign, the first big blow to Balfour Beatty's stance came at its annual general meeting in May 2001. Friends of the Earth had bought £30,000 (€45,000) worth of shares in the company, giving them the right to propose a resolution calling on the company to adopt the guidelines on dam building laid out by the World Commission on Dams. These guidelines, if passed, would have ruled out any further pursuit of the Ilisu project. In addition to Friends of the Earth, a hundred other shareholding activists turned up to the meeting—however, the result was a meagre 2 per cent in favour of the resolution. The crucial outcome, though, was that a hefty 40 per cent of Balfour Beatty shareholders decided to abstain from the vote, suggesting that they were unwilling to actively approve the company's stance. This was regarded as a small revolution (in the financial community at least) and was presented as a major PR victory for the campaigners. Friends of the Earth then sold their shares for £13,000 (€20,000) profit and recycled the money back into the campaign.

Amid growing protest, an equivocal government stance, and substantial pressure from campaigners, in November 2001 Balfour Beatty announced that it had pulled out of the project, together with its Italian construction partner Impregilo. As the CEO of the company put it, the decision was not based on changed company values but simply on the insight that 'we have clearly reached a point where no further action nor any further expenditure by Balfour Beatty on this project is likely to resolve the issues in a reasonable timescale'. A year before, the Swedish Skanska had already left the consortium on similar grounds. Balfour Beatty was particularly keen on stating that their decision was in no way influenced by the British government: 'we were not party to or intimate with anything the government was doing. We were separately carrying out our own professional review. . . . I don't believe we have had any direct contact with the DTI for a while.'

The reactions to the decision were quite mixed. On the side of the campaigners, of course, there was triumph and joy. The Turkish government exercised stoic defiance: they had already declared at earlier threats of fallouts in the consortium, 'we can build this dam without the British'. And as one commentator added: 'the Koreans, the Argentines, the Chinese—they are all lined up waiting', suggesting that the loss of the western multinationals might not be terminal to the dam project. The British government appeared to be off the hook for once but it does not seem to have changed its tactical attitude significantly since. By 2002 it was considering a £68m (€90m) guarantee for another dam close to Ilisu, this time built by Spie Batignolle, the French subsidiary of the British firm Amec. And other controversial projects are in the waiting: the Three Gorges Dam in China, the Narmada Dams in India, the San Roque Dam in the Philippines, and the Bujugali Dam in Uganda, just to name a few. The temptation of cheap and clean energy together with control over an increasingly more scarce resource of water will secure the 'dam issue' a lasting place on the agenda for business, governments, and CSOs in the era of globalization.

Questions

1 Who are Balfour Beatty's stakeholders in this situation and what rights do they have that the company should respect? Can you prioritize these stakeholders or rights in any way?

2 State and explain the key ethical issues that arise for each stakeholder group in this case.

3 Put yourself in the role of the different parties involved. Try to argue and defend their particular ethical stance. If you are working in a group, assign different roles to different members and argue the case for each stakeholder constituency.

4 How does the phenomenon of globalization shape and influence the ethical problems in this particular case?

5 Assess the project from the goal of 'sustainability'. Which trade-offs does this goal involve in the particular situation of the Ilisu Dam?

6 Thinking about the 'extended' view of corporate citizenship, how would you assess the role of Balfour Beatty in this case? Compare this role to that of the governmental and civil society actors. Are you satisfied with such a situation? If not, think creatively about how it could possibly be improved.

Sources

Anon. (2000). 'Turkey's latest controversial dam'. *The Economist* (US Version), 29 Apr.
——— . (2001). 'Balfour Beatty denies dam credits warning'. *Financial Times*, 15 Nov.: 3.
Juniper, T. (2000). 'Stuffing Turkey'. *Ecologist*, 30/6: 52–8.
Lean, G., and Dillon, J. (1999). 'Blair plans to drown Kurd town'. *Independent*, 12 Dec.: 1.
Monbiot, G. (2002). 'They're all dammed: Britain is trying to fund a Turkish project to flood thousands of homes'. *Guardian*, 26 Feb.: 17.
Thomas, M. (2001). 'Some very strange business in the City'. *New Statesman*, 14 May.

■ REFERENCES

ABEL, A. S., and GERSON, J. S. (2001). 'The CPA's role in fighting money laundering'. *Journal of Accountancy*, 191/6: 26–31.

ACKERS, P., and PAYNE, J. (1998). 'British trade unions and social partnership: rhetoric, reality and strategy'. *International Journal of Human Resource Management*, 9/3: 529–50.

ALBERT, M. (1991). *Capitalisme contre capitalisme*. Paris: LeSeuil.

ALI, S. H. (2000). 'Shades of green: NGO coalitions, mining companies and the pursuit of negotiating power'. In J. Bendell (ed.), *Terms for Endearment: Business, NGOs and Sustainable Development*. Sheffield: Greenleaf: 79–95.

ALLENBY, B. R. (1993). *Industrial Ecology*. New York: Prentice Hall.

ALTMAN, B. W. (1998). 'Corporate community relations in 1990s: a study in transformation (dissertation abstract)'. *Business & Society*, 37/2: 221–7.

—— and VIDAVER-COHEN, D. (2000). 'A framework for understanding corporate citizenship. Introduction to the special edition of *Business and Society Review* "corporate citizenship and the new millennium" '. *Business and Society Review*, 105/1: 1–7.

ANDREWS, L. (1996). 'The relationship of political marketing to political lobbying'. *European Journal of Marketing*, 30/10–11: 68–91.

ANINAT, E., HARDY, D., and JOHNSTON, R. B. (2002). 'Combating money laundering'. *Finance & Development*, Sept.: 44–7.

Anon. (2002). 'Nokia tops SRI league table'. *Ethical Performance*, 4/7 Dec.: 2.

ARROW, K. J., and HURWICZ, L. (1977). *Studies in Resource Allocation Processes*. Cambridge: Cambridge University Press.

ARTHUR ANDERSEN. (2000). *Ethical Concerns and Reputation Risk management: A Study of Leading UK Companies*. London: Arthur Andersen.

ARTS, B. (2002). ' "Green alliances" of business and NGOs: new styles of self-regulation or "dead-end roads"?' *Corporate Social Responsibility and Environmental Management*, 9: 26–36.

ARTZ, K. W. (1999). 'Buyer–supplier performance: the role of asset specificity, reciprocal investments and relational exchange'. *British Journal of Management*, 10/2: 113–26.

ASHMAN, D. (2001). 'Civil society collaboration with business: bringing empowerment back in'. *World Development*, 29/7: 1097–113.

ASSAEL, H. (1995). *Consumer Behaviour and Marketing Action*, 5th edn. Cincinnati: South-Western College.

BADARACCO, J. L., Jr., and WEBB, A. P. (1995). 'Business ethics: a view from the trenches'. *California Management Review*, 37/2: 8–29.

BADENHORST, J. A. (1994). 'Unethical behaviour in procurement: a perspective on causes and solutions'. *Journal of Business Ethics*, 13/9: 739–45.

BANERJEE, S. B. (2000). 'Whose land is it anyway? National interest, indigenous stakeholders, and colonial discourses'. *Organization & Environment*, 13/1: 3–38.

BARKAWI, A. (2002). 'Benchmarking Sustainability Investments am Beispiel der Dow Jones Sustainability Indexes'. In R. von Rosen (ed.), *Ethisch orientierte Aktienanlage—Nische oder Wachstumsmarkt?* Frankfurt: Deutsches Aktieninstitut: 88–98.

BARON, D. P. (2000). *Business and its Environment*, 3rd edn. Upper Saddle River, NJ: Prentice Hall.

BARRETT, E. (1999). 'Justice in the workplace? Normative ethics and the critique of human resource management'. *Personnel Review*, 28/4: 307–18.

BARRIE, CHRIS (1998). '*Times* defends "predatory pricing" '. *Guardian*, 11 Feb.: 8.

BART, C. K. (1997). 'Sex, lies and mission statements'. *Business Horizons*, Nov.–Dec.: 9–18.

BAUDRILLARD, J. (1997). *The Consumer Society*. London: Sage.

BAUGHN, C. C., and BUCHANAN, M. A. (2001). 'Cultural protectionism'. *Business Horizons*, 44/6: 5–15.

BAUMAN, Z. (1989). *Modernity and the Holocaust*. Cambridge: Polity Press.

—— (1991). 'The social manipulation of morality'. *Theory, Culture and Society*, 8/1: 137–52.

—— (1993). *Postmodern Ethics*. Oxford: Blackwell.

BAUMHART, R. C. (1961). 'How ethical are businesses?' *Harvard Business Review*, July–Aug.: 6.

BBC (1999). 'OFT rules *Times* price cut "predatory" '. BBC News On-line, 21 May.

—— (2000a). 'Warning to Ford over racism'. BBC News On-line, 24 Aug.

—— (2000b). 'UK tobacco firm targets African youth'. BBC News On-line, 20 Sept.

—— (2000c). 'A global smoking battle'. BBC News On-line, 2 Aug.

—— (2001). 'Coke race suit nears settlement'. BBC News On-line, 31 May.

—— (2002a). 'Nintendo fined for price fixing'. BBC News On-line, 30 Oct.

—— (2002b). 'Watchdog probes mobile phone firms'. BBC News On-line, 2 Apr.

BEAUCHAMP, T. L. (1997). 'Goals and quotas in hiring and promotion'. In T. L. Beauchamp and N. E. Bowie (eds.), *Ethical Theory and Business*. Upper Saddle River, NJ: Prentice Hall: 379–87.

—— and BOWIE, N. E. (1997). *Ethical Theory and Business*, 5th edn. Upper Saddle River, NJ: Prentice Hall.

BECHT, M., and RÖELL, A. (1999). 'Blockholdings in Europe: an international comparison'. *European Economic Review*, 43: 1049–56.

BECK, U. (1992). *Risk Society: Towards a New Modernity*. London: Sage.

—— (1997). *Was ist Globalisierung?* Frankfurt am Main: Suhrkamp.

—— (ed.) (1998). *Politik der Globalisierung*. Frankfurt am Main: Suhrkamp.

—— (1999). *What is Globalisation?* Cambridge: Polity Press.

BECKER, B., and WESTBROOK, D. A. (1998). 'Confronting asymmetry: global financial markets and national regulation'. *International Finance*, 1/2: 339–55.

BECKER, H., and FRITZSCHE, D. J. (1987). 'Business ethics: a cross-cultural comparison of managers' attitudes'. *Journal of Business Ethics*, 6: 289–95.

BELAL, A. R. (2002). 'Stakeholder accountability or stakeholder management: a review of UK firms' social and ethical accounting, auditing and reporting (SEAAR) practices'. *Corporate Social Responsibility and Environmental Management*, 9: 8–25.

BELZ, F. (1999). 'Eco-marketing 2005: performance sales instead of product sales'. In M. Charter and M. J. Polonsky (eds.), *Greener Marketing: A Global Perspective on Greening Marketing Practice*. Sheffield: Greenleaf: 84–94.

BENDELL, J. (ed.) (2000a). *Terms for Endearment: Business, NGOs and Sustainable Development*. Sheffield: Greenleaf.

—— (2000b). 'Civil regulation: a new form of democratic governance for the global economy?' In J. Bendell (ed.), *Terms for Endearment: Business, NGOs and Sustainable Development*. Sheffield: Greenleaf: 239–54.

—— (2000c). 'Introduction: working with stakeholder pressure for sustainable development'. In J. Bendell (ed.), *Terms for Endearment: Business, NGOs and Sustainable Development*. Sheffield: Greenleaf: 145–50.

—— and MURPHY, D. F. (2000). 'Planting the seeds of change: business–NGO relations on tropical deforestation'. In J. Bendell (ed.), *Terms for Endearment: Business, NGOs and Sustainable Development*. Sheffield: Greenleaf: 65–78.

BERLE, A. A., and MEANS, G. C. (1932). *The Modern Corporation and Private Property*. New York: Transaction.

BERNSTEIN, A. (2000). 'Too much corporate power?' *Business Week*, 11 Sept.: 52–60.

BIRD, F. B., and WATERS, J. A. (1989). 'The moral muteness of managers'. *California Management Review*, Fall: 73–88.

BLOOM, P. N., and PERRY, V. G. (2001). 'Retailer power and supplier welfare: the case of Wal-Mart'. *Journal of Retailing*, 77/3: 379–97.

BOATRIGHT, J. R. (2000). *Ethics and the Conduct of Business*, 3rd edn. Upper Saddle River, NJ: Prentice Hall.

BOELE, R., FABIG, H., and WHEELER, D. (2000). 'The story of Shell, Nigeria and the Ogoni people— a study in unsustainable development. I—Economy, environment and social relationships'. Paper presented at the Academy of Management Conference, Toronto.

BOGDANOR, V. (2002). 'Paying for politics: a public funding structure would rejuvenate parties and end allegations of sleaze'. *Financial Times*, 15 Feb.: 17.

BOGGIS, J. (2002). 'Global market pressures in a regional context: experiences from field research in the industrial region of South Wales'. In M. Geppert, D. Matten, and K. Williams (eds.), *Challenges for European Managment in a Global Context: Experiences from Britain and Germany*. Basingstoke: Palgrave: 215–36.

BONNER, A. (1961). *British Co-operation*, Stockport: Co-operation Union Ltd.

BORGMANN, A. (2000). 'The moral complexion of consumption'. *Journal of Consumer Research*, 26 (Mar.): 418–22.

BOWERS, S., and FINCH, J. (2003). 'Littlewoods drops ethical code'. *Guardian*, 1 Feb.: 25.

BOWIE, N. E. (1991). 'New directions in corporate social responsibility'. *Business Horizons*, 34 (July–Aug.): 56–65.

BOYD, C. (1996). 'Ethics and corporate governance: the issues raised by the Cadbury Report in the United Kingdom'. *Journal of Business Ethics*, 15: 167–82.

BRAVERMAN, H. (1974). *Labor and Monopoly Capital: The Degradation of Work in the Twentieth Century*. New York: Monthly Review Press.

BROCK, G., CLAVIN, B., and DOANE, D. (2001). *Ethical Purchasing Index 2001*. Manchester: Co-operative Bank.

BROWN, M. B. (1993). *Fair Trade*. London: Zed Books.

BUCHANAN, D., and HUCZYNSKI, A. (1997). *Organizational Behaviour*, 3rd edn. London: Prentice-Hall.

BUCHHOLZ, R. A. (1998). 'The ethics of consumption activities: a future paradigm?' *Journal of Business Ethics*, 17/8: 871–82.

BUCK, T. (2002). 'Corporate governance, path dependence and neo-institutionalism: business history and modern Germany'. Paper presented to the Research Seminar of the International Business History Institute, Nottingham University Business School, Nov.

BUCKLEY, N., and OWEN, D. (1997). 'Belgium attacks "brutal" Renault'. *Financial Times*, 1 Mar.

BURKE, R. J., and BLACK, S. (1997). 'Save the males: backlash in organizations'. *Journal of Business Ethics*, 16: 933–42.

BUTCHER, M. (1996). 'The co-operative movement: business relic or a model for the future?' *Business Studies*, Dec.: 25–8.

CANDLER, G. G. (2000). 'The professions and public policy: expanding the third sector'. *International Political Science Review*, 21/1: 43–58.

CANNON, T. (1994). *Corporate Responsibility*. London: Pearson.

CARR, A. (1968). 'Is business bluffing ethical?' *Harvard Business Review*, 46 (Jan.–Feb.), 143–53.

CARROLL, A. B. (1979). 'A three dimensional model of corporate social performance'. *Academy of Management Review*, 4: 497–505.

—— (1991). 'The pyramid of corporate social responsibility: toward the moral management of organizational stakeholders'. *Business Horizons*, July–Aug.: 39–48.

—— (1998). 'The four faces of corporate citizenship'. *Business and Society Review*, 100/1: 1–7.

—— (1999). 'Corporate social responsibility: evolution of a definitional construct'. *Business & Society*, 38/3: 268–95.

—— and BUCHHOLTZ, A. K. (2000). *Business and Society: Ethics and Stakeholder Management*, 4th edn. Cincinnati: South-Western College.

CASHORE, B. (2002). 'Legitimacy and the privatization of environmental governance: how non-state market-driven (NSMD) governance systems gain rule-making authority'. *Governance*, 15/4: 503–29.

CASSELL, C., JOHNSON, P., and SMITH, K. (1997). 'Opening the black box: corporate codes of ethics in their organizational context'. *Journal of Business Ethics*, 16: 1077–93.

CASSIMON, D. (2001). 'Financing sustainable development using a feasible Tobin Tax'. *Journal of International Relations and Development*, 4/2: 157–73.

CERIN, P., and DOBERS, P. (2001a). 'What does the performance of the Dow Jones Sustainability Group Index tell us?' *Eco-Management and Auditing*, 8: 123–33.

—— —— (2001b). 'Who is rating the raters?' *Corporate Environmental Strategy*, 8/2: 1–3.

CHEN, A. Y. S., SAWYERS, R. B., and WILLIAMS, P. F. (1997). 'Reinforcing ethical decision making through corporate culture'. *Journal of Business Ethics*, 16: 855–65.

CHENEY, G. (1995). 'Democracy in the workplace: theory and practice from the perspective of communication'. *Journal of Applied Communication*, 23: 167–200.

CHILD, J. (2000). 'Theorizing about organizations cross-nationally'. In J. L. C. Cheng and R. B. Peterson (eds.), *Advances in International Comparative Management*. Stamford: JAI Press. xiii. 27–75.

CHRISTMANN, P., and TAYLOR, G. (2001). 'Globalization and the environment: determinants of firm self-regulation in China'. *Journal of International Business Studies*, 32/3: 439–58.

CHRISTMANN, P., and TAYLOR, G. (2002). 'Globalization and the environment: strategies for international voluntary environmental initiatives'. *Academy of Management Executive*, 16/3: 121–37.

CHRYSSIDES, G., and KALER, J. (1996). *Essentials of Business Ethics*. London: McGraw-Hill.

CICUTTI, NIC (2001). 'The appliance of science has been put on hold'. *Financial Times*, 3 Nov.: 5.

CLARK, C. E. (2000). 'Differences between public relations and corporate social responsibility: an analysis'. *Public Relations Review*, 26/3: 363–80.

CLARKSON, M. B. E. (1995). 'A stakeholder framework for analyzing and evaluating corporate social performance'. *Academy of Management Review*, 20/1: 92–117.

CLAYDON, T. (2000). 'Employee participation and involvement'. In D. Winstanley and J. Woodall (eds.), *Ethical Issues in Contemporary Human Resource Management*. Basingstoke: Macmillan: 208–23.

CLEEK, M. A., and LEONARD, S. L. (1998). 'Can corporate codes of ethics influence behavior?' *Journal of Business Ethics*, 17/6: 619–30.

CLUDTS, S. (1999). 'Organization theory and the ethics of participation'. *Journal of Business Ethics*, 21: 157–71.

COCHEO, S. (2002). 'Dousing terrorist funding: mission impossible?' *ABA Banking Journal*, Aug.: 39–44.

COFFEE, J. C., Jr. (2001). 'The rise of dispersed ownership: the roles of law and the state in the separation of ownership and control'. *Yale Law Journal*, 111/1: 1–82.

COLLIER, J. (1995). 'The virtuous organization'. *Business Ethics: A European Review*, 4/3: 143–9.

—— and ESTEBAN, R. (1999). 'Governance in the participative organization: freedom, creativity and ethics'. *Journal of Business Ethics*, 21: 173–88.

COLLIER, R. (2001). 'A hard time to be a father? Reassessing the relationship between law, policy, and family (practices)'. *Journal of Law and Society*, 28/4: 520–45.

COLLINS, D. (2000). 'The quest to improve the human condition: the first 1500 articles published in *Journal of Business Ethics*'. *Journal of Business Ethics*, 26: 1–73.

COLLINS, J. W. (1994). 'Is business ethics an oxymoron?' *Business Horizons*, Sept.–Oct.: 1–8.

Commission of the European Communities (2001). *Promoting a European Framework for Corporate Social Responsibility*. Brussels: EU Commission.

—— (2002). *Communication from the Commission Concerning Corporate Social Responsibility: A Business Contribution to Sustainable Development*. Brussels: EU Commission.

COOPER, C. (1996). 'Hot under the collar'. *Times Higher Education Supplement*, 21 (June): 12–16.

COOPER, R. W., FRANK, G. L., and KEMP, R. A. (2000). 'A multinational comparison of key ethical issues, helps and challenges in the purchasing and supply management profession: the key implications for business and the professions'. *Journal of Business Ethics*, 23 (1/1): 83–100.

CORBETT, C. J., and KIRSCH, D. A. (2001). 'International diffusion of ISO 14000 certification'. *Production and Operations Management*, 10/3: 327–42.

COWE, R. (2001). 'Corporate gloss obscures the hard facts'. *Financial Times*, 11 Dec.: 18.

—— (2002). 'Wanted: shareholders with a global conscience'. *Observer* (Business), 24 Nov.: 6.

—— and WILLIAMS, S. (2000). *Who are the Ethical Consumers?* Manchester: Co-operative Bank.

COWTON, C. J. (1994). 'The development of ethical investment products'. In A. R. Prindl and B. Prodhan (eds.), *Ethical Conflicts in Finance*. Oxford: Blackwell: 213–32.

—— (1999a). 'Accounting and financial ethics: from margin to mainstream'. *Business Ethics: A European Review*, 8/2: 99–107.

—— (1999b). 'Playing by the rules: ethical criteria at an ethical investment fund'. *Business Ethics: A European Review*, 8/1: 60–9.

COX, A., SANDERSON, J., and WATSON, G. (2000). *Power Regimes: Mapping the DNA of Business and Supply Chain Relationships*. Peterborough: Earlsgate Press.

CRAGG, W., and GREENBAUM, A. (2002). 'Reasoning about responsibilities: mining company managers on what stakeholders are owed'. *Journal of Business Ethics*, 39: 319–35.

CRAIN, K. A. and HEISCHMIDT, K. A. (1995). 'Implementing business ethics: sexual harassment'. *Journal of Business Ethics*, 14: 299–308.

CRANE, A. (1998a). 'Culture clash and mediation: exploring the cultural dynamics of business–NGO collaboration'. *Greener Management International*, 24: 61–76.

—— (1998b). 'Exploring green alliances'. *Journal of Marketing Management*, 14/6: 559–79.

—— (2000). *Marketing, Morality and the Natural Environment*. London: Routledge.

—— (2001*a*). 'Corporate greening as amoralization'. *Organization Studies*, 21/4: 673–96.

—— (2001*b*). 'Unpacking the ethical product'. *Journal of Business Ethics*, 30: 361–73.

—— and LIVESEY, S. (2003). 'Are you talking to me? Stakeholder communication and the risks and rewards of dialogue'. In J. Andriof, S. Waddock, S. Rahman, and B. Husted (eds.), *Unfolding Stakeholder Thinking*, 2: Relationships, Communication, Reporting and Performance. Sheffield: Greenleaf: 39–52.

CRANFORD, M. (1998). 'Drug testing and the right to privacy: arguing the ethics of workplace drug testing'. *Journal of Business Ethics*, 17: 1805–15.

CUMMING, J. F. (2001). 'Engaging stakeholders in corporate accountability programmes: a cross-sectoral analysis of UK and transnational experience'. *Business Ethics: A European Review*, 10/1: 45–52.

DAHLER-LARSEN, P. (1994). 'Corporate culture and morality: Durkheim-inspired reflections on the limits of corporate culture'. *Journal of Management Studies*, 31/1: 1–18.

DALY, H. E. (1991). *Steady State Economics*, 2nd edn. Washington, DC: Island Press.

—— and COBB, J. B. J. (1989). *For the Common Good: Redirecting the Economy towards Community, the Environment, and a Sustainable Future*, 1st edn. Boston: Beacon Press.

DAVID, F. R. (1989). 'How companies define their mission'. *Long Range Planning*, 22/1: 90–7.

DAVIDSON, P. (1998). 'Efficiency and fragile speculative financial markets: against a Tobin Tax and for a creditable market maker'. *Journal of Economics and Sociology*, 57/4: 639–62.

DAVIES, I. A., and CRANE, A. (2003). 'Ethical decision-making in fair trade companies'. *Journal of Business Ethics*, 45 (1/2): 79–92.

DAVIS, J. J. (1992). 'Ethics and environmental marketing'. *Journal of Business Ethics*, 11: 81–7.

DAVIS, K. (1973). 'The case for and against business assumption of social responsibilities'. *Academy of Management Journal*, June: 312–22.

DAWAR, N., and FROST, T. (1999). 'Competing with giants'. *Harvard Business Review*, 77 (Mar.–Apr.): 119–29.

DE GEORGE, R. T. (1999). *Business Ethics*, 5th edn. Upper Saddle River, NJ: Prentice Hall.

DERRY, R. (1987). 'Moral reasoning in work related contexts'. In W. C. Frederick (ed.), *Research in Corporate Social Performance*. Greenwich, Conn.: JAI Press: 25–49.

DES JARDINS, J. R., and DUSKA, R. (1997). 'Drug testing in employment'. In T. L. Beauchamp and N. E. Bowie (eds.), *Ethical Theory and Business*, 5th edn. Upper Saddle River, NJ: Prentice-Hall: 309–19.

DESMOND, J. (1998). 'Marketing and moral indifference'. In M. Parker (ed.), *Ethics and Organizations*. London: Sage: 173–96.

—— and CRANE, A. (2003). 'Morality and the consequences of marketing action'. *Journal of Business Research*, forthcoming.

—— McDONAGH, P., and O'DONOHOE, S. (2000). 'Counter-culture and consumer society'. *Consumption, Markets and Culture*, 4/3: 241–79.

DIAZ, A., and MILLER, P. (1994). 'Managing people in Spain'. In T. Garrison and D. Rees (eds.), *Managing People across Europe*. Oxford: Butterworth-Heinemann: 140–62.

DINGWALL, R. (1999). ' "Risk society": the cult of theory and the millennium?' *Social Policy & Administration*, 33/4: 474–91.

DOBSON, A. (1996). 'Environmental sustainabilities: an analysis and typology'. *Environmental Politics*, 5/3: 401–28.

DOH, J. P., and TEEGEN, H. (2002). 'Nongovernmental organizations as institutional actors in international business: theory and implications'. *International Business Review*, 11: 665–84.

DOLAN, P. (2002). 'The sustainability of "sustainable consumption" '. *Journal of Macromarketing*, 22/2: 170–81.

DONALDSON, T. (1989). *The Ethics of International Business*. New York: Oxford University Press.

—— (1996). 'Values in tension: ethics away from home'. *Harvard Business Review*, Sept.–Oct.: 48–62.

—— and PRESTON, L. E. (1995). 'The stakeholder theory of the corporation: concepts, evidence, and implications'. *Academy of Management Review*, 20/1: 65–91.

DOYLE, C. (1997). 'Self regulation and statutory regulation'. *Business Strategy Review*, 8/3: 35–42.

DRUMWRIGHT, M. (1994). 'Socially responsible organizational buying'. *Journal of Marketing*, 58 (July): 1–19.

DU GAY, P. (2000). *In Praise of Bureaucracy*. London: Sage.

DURÁN, J. L., and SÁNCHEZ, F. (1999). 'The relationships between the companies and their suppliers'. *Journal of Business Ethics*, 22/3: 273–80.

DURKHEIM, E. (1993). *The Division of Labour in Society*. Glencoe, Ill.: Free Press.

EAGLES, T. A. (2001). 'Ethics in Purchasing: A Case of a Private Limited Company'. Unpublished MBA dissertation, University of Nottingham.

EAGLESHAM, J. (2000). 'Staff privacy in the spotlight: workplace surveillance'. *Financial Times*, 9 Oct.: 22.

—— and MAITLAND, A. (2002). 'Clarke facing embarrassment over Burma link'. *Financial Times*, 12 Nov.: 3.

EASTON, G. (1992). 'Industrial networks: a review'. In B. Axelsson and G. Easton (eds.), *Industrial Networks: A New View of Reality*. London: Routledge: 3–27.

The Economist (1993). 'Tactics and dirty tricks'. *The Economist*, 16 Jan.: 21–2.

—— (2000). 'NGOs: sins of the secular missionaries'. *The Economist*, 354/8155 (29 Jan.): 25–7.

—— (2002). 'Europe: is Margaret Thatcher winning in Europe?' *The Economist*, 1 June: 55–7.

EDWARDS, V., and LAWRENCE, P. (2000). *Management in Eastern Europe*. Basingstoke: Palgrave.

EIRIS (2000). *Annual Review 2000*. London: EIRIS.

ELKINGTON, J. (1999). *Cannibals with Forks: The Triple Bottom Line of 21st Century Business*. Oxford: Capstone.

—— and FENNELL, S. (2000). 'Partners for sustainability'. In J. Bendell (ed.), *Terms for Endearment: Business, NGOs and Sustainable Development*. Sheffield: Greenleaf: 150–62.

ELLERMAN, D. (1999). 'The democratic firm: an argument based on ordinary jurisprudence'. *Journal of Business Ethics*, 21: 111–24.

EMMELHAINZ, M. A., and ADAMS, R. J. (1999). 'The apparel industry response to "sweatshop" concerns: a review and analysis of codes of conduct'. *Journal of Supply Chain Management*, Summer: 51–7.

ENDERLE, G. (1996). 'A comparison of business ethics in North America and continental Europe'. *Business Ethics: A European Review*, 5/1: 33–46.

EVAN, W. M., and FREEMAN, R. E. (1993). 'A stakeholder theory of the modern corporation: Kantian capitalism'. In W. M. Hoffman and R. E. Frederick (eds.), *Business Ethics: Readings and Cases in Corporate Morality*, 3rd edn. New York: McGraw-Hill: 145–54.

FAULKS, K. (2000). *Citizenship*. London: Routledge.

FEATHERSTONE, M. (1991). *Consumer Culture and Postmodernism*. London: Sage.

FERNER, A., and HYMAN, R. (1998). *Changing Industrial Relations in Europe*. Oxford: Blackwell.

FERRELL, O. C., and GRESHAM, L. G. (1985). 'A contingency framework for understanding ethical decision-making in marketing'. *Journal of Marketing*, 49: 87–96.

—— —— and FRAEDRICH, J. (1989). 'A synthesis of ethical decision models for marketing'. *Journal of Macromarketing*, 9/2: 55–64.

—— FRAEDRICH, J., and FERRELL, L. (2000). *Business Ethics: Ethical Decision Making and Cases*, 4th edn. Boston: Houghton Mifflin.

—— —— —— (2002). *Business Ethics: Ethical Decision Making and Cases*, 5th edn. Boston: Houghton Mifflin.

Financial Times (1999). 'End-of-Life Vehicle Directive blocked again'. *Financial Times*, 1 July.

FINCH, J., and TREANOR, J. (2002). Various articles. *Guardian*, 18/21 Nov.

FINEMAN, S., and CLARKE, K. (1996). 'Green stakeholders: industry interpretations and response'. *Journal of Management Studies*, 33/6: 715–30.

FITZGERALD, R. (1999). 'Employment relations and industrial welfare in Britain: business ethics versus labour markets'. *Business and Economic History*, 28/2: 167–79.

FLYNN, B. (2002). 'Voluntary environmental policy instruments: two Irish success stories?' *European Environment*, 12: 49–60.

FORD, R. C., and RICHARDSON, W. D. (1994). 'Ethical decision making: a review of the empirical literature'. *Journal of Business Ethics*, 13/3: 205–21.

FOWLER, P., and HEAP, S. (2000). 'Bridging troubled waters: the Marine Stewardship Council'. In J. Bendell (ed.), *Terms for Endearment: Business, NGOs and Sustainable Development*. Sheffield: Greenleaf: 135–49.

FRAEDRICH, J., and FERRELL, O. C. (1992). 'Cognitive consistency of marketing managers in ethical situations'. *Journal of the Academy of Marketing Science*, 20/3: 245–52.

—— THORNE, D. M., and FERRELL, O. C. (1994). 'Assessing the application of cognitive moral development to business ethics'. *Journal of Business Ethics*, 13/10: 829–38.

FRANKENTAL, P. (2002). 'The UN Universal Declaration of Human Rights as a corporate code of conduct'. *Business Ethics: A European Review*, 11/2: 129–33.

FREDERICK, W. C. (1994). 'From CSR$_1$ to CSR$_2$: the maturing of business-and-society thought'. *Business & Society*, 33/2: 150–64.

FREEMAN, R. E. (1984). *Strategic Management: A Stakeholder Approach*. Boston: Pitman.

FRENCH, P. (1979). 'The corporation as a moral person'. *American Philosophical Quarterly*, 16: 207–15.

FREY, B. F. (2000). 'The impact of moral intensity on decision making in a business context'. *Journal of Business Ethics*, 26: 181–95.

FRIEDMAN, M. (1970). 'The social responsibility of business is to increase its profits'. *New York Times Magazine*, 13 Sept.

FRIEDMAN, M. (1999). *Consumer Boycotts*. New York: Routledge.

FULLER, D. A. (1999). *Sustainable Marketing: Managerial-Ecological Issues*. Thousand Oaks, Calif.: Sage.

FURMAN, F. K. (1990). 'Teaching business ethics: questioning the assumptions, seeking new directions'. *Journal of Business Ethics*, 9: 31–8.

GABRIEL, Y., and LANG, T. (eds.) (1995). *The Unmanageable Consumer: Contemporary Consumption and its Fragmentations*. London: Sage.

GALBRAITH, J. K. (1974). *The New Industrial State*, 2nd edn. Harmondsworth: Penguin.

GARRISON, T. (1994). 'Managing people across Europe: an introductory framework'. In T. Garrison and D. Rees (eds.), *Managing People across Europe*. Oxford: Butterworth-Heinemann: 1–24.

—— and VERVEEN, P. (1994). 'Managing pepole in the Netherlands'. In T. Garrison and D. Rees (eds.), *Managing People across Europe*. Oxford: Butterworth-Heinemann: 163–73.

GELLERMAN, S.W. (1986). Why 'good' managers make bad ethical choices. *Harvard Business Review*, July–August: 85–90.

GETZ, K. A. (1997). 'Research in corporate political action: integration and assessment'. *Business & Society*, 36/1: 32–72.

GHUA, K., and McNULTY, S. (2002). 'Lord Browne: the inside story'. *Financial Times*, 2 Aug.: 23.

GIBSON, R. B. (ed.) (1999). *Voluntary Initiatives and the New Politics of Corporate Greening*. Peterborough, Ont.: Broadview Press.

GIDDENS, A. (1999). *Runaway World: How Globalisation is Reshaping our Lives*. London: Profile.

GILLIGAN, C. (1982). *In a Different Voice*. Cambridge, Mass.: Harvard University Press.

GINI, A. (1997). 'Moral leadership: an overview'. *Journal of Business Ethics*, 16/3: 323–30.

GLADWIN, T. N., KENNELLY, J. J., and KRAUSE, T. S. (1995). 'Shifting paradigms for sustainable development: implications for management theory and research'. *Academy of Management Review*, 20/4: 874–907.

GLASBERGEN, P. (2002). 'The green polder model: institutionalizing multi-stakeholder processes in strategic environmental decision-making'. *European Environment*, 12: 303–15.

GOOLSBY, J. R., and HUNT, S. D. (1992). 'Cognitive moral development and marketing'. *Journal of Marketing*, 56/1: 55–68.

GORDON, J. N. (2002). 'What Enron means for the management and control of the modern business corporation: some initial reflections'. *University of Chicago Law Review*, 69: 1233–50.

GORDON, K., and MIYAKE, M. (2001). 'Business approaches to combating bribery: a study of codes of conduct'. *Journal of Business Ethics*, 34: 161–73.

GÖRG, C., and BRAND, U. (2000). 'Global environmental politics and competition between nation-states: on the regulation of biological diversity'. *Review of International Political Economy*, 7/3: 371–98.

GORZ, A. (1975). *Écologie et politique*. Paris: Éditions Galilée.

GRAHAM, G. (1990). *Living the Good Life: An Introduction to Moral Philosophy*. New York: Paragon.

GRAY, R., DEY, C., OWEN, D., EVANS, R., and ZADEK, S. (1997). 'Struggling with the praxis of social accounting: stakeholders, accountability, audits and procedures'. *Accounting, Auditing and Accountability Journal*, 10/3: 325–64.

GRAY, R. H. (1992). 'Accounting and environmentalism: an exploration of the challenge of gently accounting for accountability, transparency and sustainability'. *Accounting, Organizations and Society*, 17/5: 399–426.

GREENING, D. W., and TURBAN, D. B. (2000). 'Corporate social performance as a competitive advantage in attracting a quality workforce'. *Business & Society*, 39/3: 254–80.

GREENWOOD, M. R. (2002). 'Ethics and HRM: a review and conceptual analysis'. *Journal of Business Ethics*, 36: 261–78.

GREYSER, S. A. (1972). 'Advertising: attacks and counters'. *Harvard Business Review*, 50 (Mar.–Apr.): 22–36.

GRIFFIN, J. J., and MAHON, J. F. (1997). 'The corporate social performance and corporate financial performance debate: twenty-five years of incomparable research'. *Business & Society*, 36/1: 5–31.

GRIMES, CHRISTOPHER (2002). 'Napster sell-off is quiet finale'. *Financial Times*, 5 Sept.: 23.

GRIMSHAW, D., VINCENT, S., and WILLMOTT, H. (2002). 'Going privately: partnership and outsourcing in UK public services'. *Public Administration*, 80/3: 475–502.

GROSS-SCHAEFER, A., TRIGILIO, J., NEGUS, J., and RO, C.-S. (2000). 'Ethics education in the workplace: an effective tool to combat employee theft'. *Journal of Business Ethics*, 26: 89–100.

GRUNIG, J. E., and HUNT, C. (1984). *Managing Public Relations*. New York: Holt, Rinehart, & Winston.

Guardian (1999). 'Exporting addiction'. *Guardian*, 13 Jan.: 17.

—— (2002). 'Mean Britain: our companies give too little to charity'. *Guardian Unlimited*, 8 June.

—— (2003). 'Fiascos that haunt "can do" company'. *Guardian*, 15 Feb.: 13.

GUSTAFSON, A. (2000). 'Making sense of postmodern business ethics'. *Business Ethics Quarterly*, 10/3: 645–58.

HABERMAS, J. (1983). 'Diskursethik. Notizen zu einem Begründungsprogramm'. In J. Habermas (ed.), *Moralbewusstsein und kommunikatives Handeln*. Frankfurt am Main: Suhrkamp: 53–125.

HALLAQ, J. H., and STEINHORST, K. (1994). 'Business intelligence methods: how ethical'. *Journal of Business Ethics*, 13: 787–94.

HAMEL, G., DOZ, Y. L., and PRAHALAD, C. K. (1989). 'Collaborate with your competitors—and win'. *Harvard Business Review*, Jan.–Feb.: 133–9.

HARDING, J. (2001*a*). 'Feeding the hands that bite'. *FT.com*, 15 Oct.

—— (2001*b*). 'Globalization's children strike back'. *FT.com*, 10 Sept.

—— (2001*c*). 'The by-product of globalization'. *FT.com*, 12 Oct.

HARRIS, P., and LOCK, A. (2002). 'Sleaze or clear blue water? The evolution of corporate and pressure group representation at the major UK party conferences'. *Journal of Public Affairs*, 2/2: 136–51.

HART, S. L. (1997). 'Beyond greening: strategies for a sustainable world'. *Harvard Business Review*, Jan.–Feb.: 67–76.

HART, T. J. (1993). 'Human resource management: time to exorcise the militant tendency'. *Employee Relations*, 15/3: 29–36.

HARTMAN, C. L., and STAFFORD, E. R. (1997). 'Green alliances: building new business with environmental groups'. *Long Range Planning*, 30/2: 184–96.

HARTMAN, L. P. (1998). 'The rights and wrongs of workplace snooping'. *Journal of Business Strategy*, 19/3: 16–20.

HAUSKRECHT, A. (1999). 'Die asiatische Währungs- und Finanzkrise'. In Landeszentrale für Politische Bildung (ed.), *Globalisierung als Chance*. Stuttgart: Landeszentrale für Politische Bildung: 35–40.

HEDIGER, W. (1999). 'Reconciling "weak" and "strong" sustainability'. *International Journal of Social Economics*, 26/7–8–9: 1120–43.

HEERY, E. (2000). 'The new pay: risk and representation at work'. In D. Winstanley and J. Woodall (eds.), *Ethical Issues in Contemporary Human Resource Management*. Basingstoke: Macmillan: 172–88.

HEISKANEN, E., and PANTZAR, M. (1997). 'Toward sustainable consumption: two new perspectives'. *Journal of Consumer Policy*, 20: 409–42.

HELD, D., and MCGREW, A. G. (2000). *The Global Transformations Reader: An Introduction to the Globalization Debate*. Cambridge: Polity Press.

HELLMAN, J. S., and SCHANKERMAN, M. (2000). 'Intervention, corruption and capture'. *Economics of Transition*, 8/3: 545–76.

—— JONES, G., and KAUFMANN, D. (2000). ' "Seize the day, seize the state": state capture, corruption and influence in transition'. Policy research working paper 2444. Washington: World Bank.

HERTZ, N. (2001*a*). 'Better to shop than to vote?' *Business Ethics: A European Review*, 10/3: 190–3.

—— (2001*b*). *The Silent Takeover*. London: Heinemann.

HETTNE, B. (2000). 'The fate of citizenship in Post-Westphalia'. *Citizenship Studies*, 4/1: 35–46.

HIGGINS, M., and TADAJEWSKI, M. (2002). 'Anti-corporate protest as consumer spectacle'. *Marketing Intelligence and Planning*, 40/4: 363–71.

HIGGS-KLEYN, N., and KAPELIANIS, D. (1999). 'The role of professional codes in regulating ethical conduct'. *Journal of Business Ethics*, 19: 363–74.

HILHORST, D. (2002). 'Being good at doing good? Quality and accountability of humanitarian NGOs'. *Disasters*, 26/3: 193–212.

HILL, C. W. L., and JONES, G. R. (2001). *Strategic Management: An Integrated Approach*, 5th edn. Boston: Houghton Mifflin.

HOF, R. D., and GREEN, H. (2002). 'How Amazon cleared the profitability hurdle'. *Business Week On-line*, 4 Feb.

HOFFMAN, W. M., DRISCOLL, D.-M., and PAINTER-MORLAND, M. (2001). 'Integrating ethics'. In C. Moon and C. Bonny (eds.), *Business Ethics: Facing up to the Issues*. London: The Economist Books: 38–54.

HOFSTEDE, G. (1980). *Culture's Consequences: International Differences in Work Related Values*. Beverly Hills: Sage.

—— (1994). *Cultures and Organizations: Software of the Mind*. London: Harper Collins.

HOLLAND, M. (1993). *European Integration: From Community to Union*. London: Pinter.

HOPKINS, W. E., and HOPKINS, S. A. (1999). 'The ethics of downsizing: perceptions of rights and responsibilities'. *Journal of Business Ethics*, 18: 145–56.

HOSMER, L. T. (1987). *The Ethics of Management*. Homewood, Ill.: Irwin Press.

HOULDER, V. (1999). 'Wind power's zephyr builds to gale force'. *Financial Times*, 25 June: 13.

HUMMELS, H. (1998). 'Organizing ethics: a stakeholder debate'. *Journal of Business Ethics*, 17: 1403–19.

HUNT, B. (2000). 'The new battleground for capitalism'. *Financial Times* (Mastering management), 9 Oct.

HUNT, S. D., and VITELL, S. J. (1986). 'A general theory of marketing ethics'. *Journal of Macromarketing*, 6 (Spring): 5–16.

HUTTON, W. (2002). 'Comment: capitalism must put its house in order: the Prestige disaster is yet another example of how unregulated business practices can have a calamitous effect'. *Observer*, 24 Nov.: 30.

HYMAN, R. (2001). 'The Europeanization—or the erosion—of industrial relations?' *Industrial Relations Journal*, 32/4: 280–94.

IMMERZEEL-BRAND, E. (2002). 'Assessing the performance of negotiated environmental agreements in the Netherlands'. In P. ten Brink (ed.), *Voluntary Environmental Agreements*. Sheffield: Greenleaf: 384–98.

INMAN, P., and WILSON, J. (2001). 'Why that joke email could get you the sack'. *Guardian*, 2 Aug.

Institute of Directors (1999). *Ethics in Business*. London: Institute of Directors.

International Labour Organization (1998). *World Employment Outlook*. Geneva: ILO.

JACKALL, R. (1988). *Moral Mazes*. Oxford: Oxford University Press.

JACKSON, T. (2001). 'Cultural values and management ethics: a 10 nation study'. *Human Relations*, 54/10: 1267–302.

—— and ARTOLA, M. C. (1997). 'Ethical beliefs and management behaviour: a cross-cultural comparison'. *Journal of Business Ethics*, 16/11: 1163–73.

JACKSON-PROES, ALEX (2001). 'Suddens quits as chief of Wm Baird'. *Daily Telegraph*, 2 Aug.: 29.

JARILLO, J. C., and STEVENSON, H. H. (1991). 'Cooperative strategies—the payoffs and the pitfalls'. *Long Range Planning*, 24/1: 64–70.

JENKINS, S. (2002). 'The ill wind blowing through energy policy'. *The Times*, 15 Feb.

JENSEN, M., and MECKLING, W. (1976). 'Theory of the firm: managerial behaviour, agency costs and ownership structure'. *Journal of Financial Economics*, 3: 305–60.

JOHNSON, G., and SCHOLES, K. (2002). *Exploring Corporate Strategy*, 6th edn. Harlow: Pearson Education Ltd.

JOHNSON, P., and SMITH, K. (1999). 'Contextualising business ethics: anomie and social life'. *Human Relations*, 52/11: 1351–75.

JONES, A. (2001). 'Social responsibility and the utilities'. *Journal of Business Ethics*, 34: 219–29.

JONES, G. (2002). 'Conflicts continue: pressure mounts on prime minister to sell his TV stations'. *Financial Times*, 22 July: 4.

JONES, I. W., and POLLITT, M. G. (1998). 'Ethical and unethical competition: establishing the rules of engagement'. *Long Range Planning*, 31/5: 703–10.

JONES, T. M. (1991). 'Ethical decision making by individuals in organizations: an issue-contingent model'. *Academy of Management Review*, 16: 366–95.

KALER, J. (1999a). 'Understanding participation'. *Journal of Business Ethics*, 21: 125–35.

—— (1999b). 'What's the good of ethical theory?' *Business Ethics: A European Review*, 8/4: 206–13.

KALER, J. (2000). 'Reasons to be ethical: self-interest and ethical business'. *Journal of Business Ethics*, 27: 161–73.

KANGUN, N., and POLONSKY, M. J. (1995). 'Regulation of environmental marketing claims: a comparative perspective'. *International Journal of Advertising*, 14/1: 1–24.

KELEMEN, M., and PELTONEN, T. (2001). 'Ethics, morality and the subject: the contribution of Zygmunt Bauman and Michel Foucault to "postmodern" business ethics'. *Scandinavian Journal of Management*, 17/2: 151–66.

KIESELBACH, T., and MADER, S. (2002). 'Occupational transitions and corporate responsibility in layoffs: a European research project (SOCOSE)'. *Journal of Business Ethics*, 39: 13–20.

KILBOURNE, W., McDONAGH, P., and PROTHERO, A. (1997). 'Sustainable consumption and the quality of life: a macromarketing challenge to the dominant social paradigm'. *Journal of Macromarketing*, 17/1: 4–24.

KILGREEN, LUCY (2001). 'Lords to rule on Baird's M&S claim'. *Financial Times*, 21 Mar.: 28.

KING, A. A., and LENOX, M. J. (2000). 'Industry self-regulation without sanctions: the chemical industry's Responsible Care Program'. *Academy of Management Journal*, 43/4: 698–716.

KIRRANE, D. E. (1990). 'Managing values: a systematic approach to business ethics'. *Training and Development Journal*, Nov.: 53–60.

KJÆRGAARD, C., and WESTPHALEN, S.-Å. (eds.) (2001). *From Collective Bargaining to Social Partnerships: New Roles of the Social Partners in Europe*. Copenhagen: The Copenhagen Centre.

KLEIN, N. (2000). *No Logo: Taking Aim at the Brand Bullies*. London: Flamingo.

KNILL, C., and LEHMKUHL, D. (2002). 'Private actors and the state: internationalization and changing patterns of governance'. *Governance: An International Journal of Policy, Administration, and Institutions*, 15/1: 41–63.

KNOEPFEL, I. (2001). 'Dow Jones Sustainability Group Index: a global benchmark for corporate sustainability'. *Corporate Environmental Strategy*, 8/1: 6–15.

KOCH, E. (2000). *Globalisierung der Wirtschaft*. Munich: Vahlen.

KOHLBERG, L. (1969). 'Stage and sequence: the cognitive development approach to socialization'. In D. Goslin (ed.), *Handbook of Socialization Theory and Research*. Chicago: Rand McNally: 347–480.

KOLK, A., and LEVY, D. (2001). 'Winds of change: corporate strategy, climate change and oil multinationals'. *European Management Journal*, 19/5: 501–9.

—— VAN TULDER, R., and WELTERS, C. (1999). 'International codes of conduct and corporate social responsibility: can transnational corporations regulate themselves?' *Transnational Corporations*, 8/1: 143–80.

KORTEN, D. C. (1995). *When Corporations Rule the World*. London: Earthscan.

KOSLOWSKI, P. (2000). 'The limits of shareholder value'. *Journal of Business Ethics*, 27: 137–48.

KOTTER, J. P. (1990). 'What leaders really do'. *Harvard Business Review*, 68 (May–June): 103–11.

KUMAR, B. N., and STEINMANN, H. (eds.) (1998). *Ethics in International Management*. Berlin: Walter de Gruyter.

LACZNIAK, G. R., and MURPHY, P. E. (1993). *Ethical Marketing Decisions: The Higher Road*. Boston: Allyn & Bacon.

LANE, J.-E. (2002). 'Transformation and future of public enterprises in continental Western Europe'. *Public Finance and Management*, 2/1: 56–80.

LANG, R. (ed.) (2001). *Wirtschaftsethik in Mittel- und Osteuropa*. Munich: Rainer Hampp.

LEE, M., and KOH, J. (2001). 'Is empowerment really a new concept'. *International Journal of Human Resource Management*, 12/4: 684–95.

LEGGE, K. (1998). 'Is HRM ethical? Can HRM be ethical?' In M. Parker (ed.), *Ethics and Organization*. London: Sage: 150–72.

—— (2000). 'The ethical context of HRM: the ethical organization in the boundaryless world'. In D. Winstanley and J. Woodall (eds.), *Ethical Issues in Contemporary Human Resource Management*. Basingstoke: Macmillan: 23–40.

LEVITT, T. (1970). 'The morality (?) of advertising'. *Harvard Business Review*, 48 (July–Aug.): 84–92.

LEVY, D., and EGAN, D. (2000). 'Corporate politics and climate change'. In R. A. Higgott, G. R. D. Underhill, and A. Bieler (eds.), *Non-state Actors and Authority in the Global System*. London: Routledge: 138–53.

LINE, M., HAWLEY, H., and KRUT, R. (2002). 'The development of global environmental and social reporting'. *Corporate Environmental Strategy*, 9/1: 69–78.

LISTER, DAVID (2001*a*). 'US group sues European Union over banana war'. *The Times*, 26 Jan.

—— (2001*b*). 'Europe and the US end 8-year war over bananas'. *The Times*, 12 Apr.

LIVESEY, S. (2002*a*). 'The discourse of the middle ground: citizen Shell commits to sustainable development'. *Management Communication Quarterly*, 15/3: 313–49.

—— (2002*b*). 'Global warming wars: rhetorical and discourse analytic approaches to ExxonMobil's corporate public discourse'. *Journal of Business Communication*, 39/1: 118–49.

LOE, T. W., FERRELL, L., and MANSFIELD, P. (2000). 'A review of empirical studies assessing ethical decision making in business'. *Journal of Business Ethics*, 25/3: 185–204.

LORD, M. D. (2000). 'Corporate political strategy and legislative decision making'. *Business & Society*, 39/1: 76–93.

Los Angeles Times (2002). 'The Microsoft decision: antitrust talks in EU may resume'. *Los Angeles Times*, 4 Nov., part 3: 5.

LOVINS, A. B., LOVINS, L. H., and HAWKEN, P. (1999). 'A road map for natural capitalism'. *Harvard Business Review*, May–June: 145–58.

LYOTARD, J.-F. (1984). *The Postmodern Condition: A Report on Knowledge*, trans. G. Bennington and B. Massumi. Manchester: Manchester University Press.

LYSONSKI, S., and GAIDIS, W. (1991). 'A cross-cultural comparison of the ethics of business students'. *Journal of Business Ethics*, 10: 141–50.

MACASKILL, M. (2002). 'Green power'. *Sunday Times*, 9 June.

McCABE, D. L., and TREVIÑO, L. K. (1993). 'Academic dishonesty: honor codes and other situational influences'. *Journal of Higher Education*, 64: 522–38.

—— DUKERICH, J. M., and DUTTON, J. E. (1991). 'Context, values and moral dilemmas: comparing the choices of business and law school students'. *Journal of Business Ethics*, 10/2: 951–60.

McEWAN, T. (2001). *Managing Values and Beliefs in Organisations*. Harlow: Pearson Education.

McGRATH, C. (2002). 'Comparative lobbying practices: Washington, London, Brussels'. Paper presented at the Political Studies Association annual conference, University of Aberdeen.

McGREW, A. G. (1997*a*). 'Globalization and territorial democracy: an introduction'. In A. G. McGrew (ed.), *The Transformation of Democracy? Globalization and Territorial Democracy*. Cambridge: Polity Press: 1–24.

—— (1997*b*). 'Democracy beyond borders? Globalization and the reconstruction of democratic theory and practice'. In A. G. McGrew (ed.), *The Transformation of Democracy? Globalization and Territorial Democracy*. Cambridge: Polity Press: 231–66.

McINTOSH, M., and THOMAS, R. (2002). *Corporate Citizenship and the Evolving Relationship between Non-governmental Organisations and Corporations*. London: British-North American Committee.

—— LEIPZIGER, D., JONES, K., and COLEMAN, G. (1998). *Corporate Citizenship: Successful Strategies for Responsible Companies*. London: Financial Times/Pitman.

MACINTYRE, A. (1984). *After Virtue: A Study in Moral Theory*, 2nd edn. Notre Dame, Ind.: University of Notre Dame Press.

MACKAY, DUNCAN (2002). 'Olympic Games: Rogge gamble pays off as IOC back ban on site visits'. *Guardian*, 30 Nov.: 14.

MACKENZIE, C. (1998). 'The choice of criteria in ethical investment'. *Business Ethics: A European Review*, 7/2: 81–6.

—— (2001). 'An evolutionary model for ethics in investment'. *Journal of Pension Management*, 6/2: 165–70.

MACLEOD, A. (2003). 'Deal "will cripple and emaciate" fishing industry'. *The Times*, 29 Jan.: 2.

McPHAIL, K. (2001). 'The *other* objective of ethics education: re-humanising the accounting profession—a study of ethics education in law, engineering, medicine and accountancy'. *Journal of Business Ethics*, 34: 279–98.

McWILLIAMS, A., and SIEGEL, D. (2000). 'Corporate social responsibility and financial performance: correlation or misspecification?' *Strategic Management Journal*, 21/5: 603–9.

MAIER, M. (1997). 'Gender equity, organizational transformation and Challenger'. *Journal of Business Ethics*, 16: 943–62.

MAIGNAN, I. (2001). 'Consumers' perceptions of corporate social responsibilities: a cross-cultural comparison'. *Journal of Business Ethics*, 30 (1/1): 57–72.

—— and FERRELL, O. C. (2000). 'Measuring corporate citizenship in two countries: the case of the United States and France'. *Journal of Business Ethics*, 23: 283–97.

—— —— (2001). 'Antecedents and benefits of corporate citizenship: an investigation of French businesses'. *Journal of Business Research*, 51: 37–51.

MAIGNAN, I., FERRELL, O. C. and HULT, G. T. M. (1999). 'Corporate citizenship: cultural antecedents and business benefits'. *Journal of the Academy of Marketing Science*, 27/4: 455–69.

MARSHALL, T. H. (1965). *Class, Citizenship and Social Development*. New York: Anchor Books.

MARTIN, J. (1985). 'Can organizational culture be managed?' In P. J. Frost, L. F. Moore, M. R. Louis, C. Lundberg, and J. Martin (eds.), *Organizational Culture*. Newbury Park, Calif.: Sage: 95–8.

MARTÍNEZ LUCIO, M., and WESTON, S. (2000). 'European works councils and "flexible regulation": the politics of intervention'. *European Journal of Industrial Relations*, 6/2: 203–16.

MATTEN, D. (1998). 'Sustainable Development als betriebswirtschaftliches Leitbild. Hintergründe—Abgrenzungen—Perspektiven'. In H. Albach and M. Steven (eds.), *Betriebliches Umweltmanagement*. Wiesbaden: Gabler: 1–23.

—— (2003). 'Symbolic politics in environmental regulation: corporate strategic responses'. *Business Strategy and the Environment*, 12: 26–37.

—— CRANE, A., and CHAPPLE, W. (2003). 'Behind the mask: revealing the true face of corporate citizenship'. *Journal of Business Ethics*, 44/1–2: 109–20.

MAYHEW, N. (1997). 'Fading to grey: the use and abuse of corporate executives' "representational power" '. In R. J. Welford (ed.), *Hijacking Environmentalism: Corporate Responses to Sustainable Development*. London: Routledge: 63–95.

MEADOWS, D. H., MEADOWS, D. L., RANDERS, J., and BEHRENS, W. W. (1974). *The Limits to Growth*. London: Pan.

MEIKLE, JAMES (2001). '£300m slashed off drugs as price fixing abandoned: chemists warn of closures as supermarkets cut costs of medicines'. *Guardian*, 16 May: 3.

MELLAHI, K., and WOOD, G. (2002). *The Ethical Business*. Basingstoke: Palgrave.

MERCADO, S., WELFORD, R., and PRESCOTT, K. (2001). *European Business*. Harlow: Pearson.

MICHALOS, A. C. (1988). 'Editorial'. *Journal of Business Ethics*, 7: 1.

MILNER, S. (2002). 'An ambiguous reform: the Jospin government and the 35-hour-week laws'. *Modern & Contemporary France*, 10/3: 339–51.

MINTZBERG, H. (1983). 'The case for corporate social responsibility'. *Journal of Business Strategy*, 4/2: 3–15.

MITCHELL, R. K., AGLE, B. R., and WOOD, D. J. (1997). 'Toward a theory of stakeholder identification and salience: defining the principle of who and what really counts'. *Academy of Management Review*, 22/4: 853–86.

MITCHELL, W. C. (1990). 'Interest groups: economic perspectives and contribution'. *Journal of Theoretical Politics*, 2: 85–108.

MONBIOT, G. (2000). *The Captive State*. London: Macmillan.

MONKS, R. A. G., and MINOW, N. (2001). *Corporate Governance*, 2nd edn. Malden, Mass.: Blackwell.

MOORE, G. (1999a). 'Corporate moral agency: review and implications'. *Journal of Business Ethics*, 21: 329–43.

—— (1999b). 'Tinged shareholder theory: or what's so special about stakeholders?' *Business Ethics: A European Review*, 8/2: 117–27.

MOORE, J. (1990). 'What is really unethical about insider trading?' *Journal of Business Ethics*, 9: 171–82.

MOORE, K., and LEWIS, D. (1999). *Birth of the Multinational Enterprise: 2000 Years of Business History—from Assur to Augustus*. Copenhagen: Copenhagen Business School Press.

MORGAN, G. (2001). 'Transnational communities and business systems'. *Global Networks*, 1/2: 113–30.

MORGAN, O. (1999). 'The Paddington disaster: the three sell-off millionaires'. *Guardian*, 10 Oct.: 14.

MORI (2000). *The First Ever European Survey of Consumers' Attitudes towards Corporate Social Responsibility and Country Profiles*. London: MORI and CSR Europe.

MORIN, E. (1987). *Penser l'Europe*. Paris: Gallimard.

MORRIS, S. A., and MCDONALD, R. A. (1995). 'The role of moral intensity in moral judgements: an empirical investigation'. *Journal of Business Ethics*, 14: 715–26.

MORTISHEAD, C. (2002). 'Birds Eye view raises question of survival'. *The Times* (Business), 21 Dec.: 42.

MURPHY, D. F., and BENDELL, J. (1997). *In the Company of Partners: Business, Environmental*

Groups and Sustainable Development Post-Rio. Bristol: Policy Press.

MUSKIN, J. B. (2000). 'Interorganizational ethics: standards of behavior'. *Journal of Business Ethics*, 24: 283–97.

NADER, R. (1984). 'Reforming corporate governance'. *California Management Review*, 26/4: 126–32.

—— (2000). 'Corporations and the UN: Nike and others "bluewash" their images'. *San Francisco Bay Guardian*, 18 Sept.

NELSON, J., and ZADEK, S. (2000). *Partnership Alchemy: New Social Partnerships in Europe.* Copenhagen: The Copenhagen Centre.

NEW, S. (1998). 'The implications and reality of partnership'. In B. Burnes and B. G. Dale (eds.), *Working in Partnership: Best Practice in Customer–Supplier Relations.* Aldershot: Gower Publishing: 9–20.

NEWTON, L. H. (1992). *The Many Faces of the Corporate Code.* Paper presented at the Conference on Corporate Visions and Values.

NICKEL, J. W. (2002). 'Is today's international human rights system a global governance regime?' *Journal of Ethics*, 6/4: 353–72.

NORD, W. R. (1985). 'Can organizational culture be managed? A synthesis'. In P. J. Frost, L. F. Moore, M. R. Louis, C. Lundberg, and J. Martin (eds.), *Organizational Culture.* Newbury Park, Calif.: Sage: 187–96.

NUTTALL, N. (1999). 'Greens savage greens in the fight to save the planet and keep the lights on'. *The Times*, 9 Jan.

NYAW, M.-K., and NG, I. (1994). 'A comparative analysis of ethical beliefs: a four country study'. *Journal of Business Ethics*, 13/7: 543–55.

OATES, C., BLADES, M., and GUNTER, B. (2001). 'Children and Television Advertising: When do they Understand Persuasive Intent?' Paper presented at the Academy of Marketing, Cardiff.

OECD (2002). *Towards Sustainable Household Consumption? Trends and Policies in OECD Countries.* Paris: OECD.

OGBONNA, E. (1992). 'Managing organizational culture: fantasy or reality?' *Human Resource Management Journal*, 3/2: 42–54.

—— and HARRIS, L. C. (1998). 'Managing organizational culture: compliance or genuine change?' *British Journal of Management*, 9: 273–88.

—— and WILKINSON, B. (1996). 'Inter-organizational power relations in the UK grocery industry: contradictions and developments'. *International Review of Retail, Distribution & Consumer Research*, 6/4: 395–414.

ORSATO, R. J., DEN HOND, F., and CLEGG, S. R. (2002). 'The political ecology of automobile recycling in Europe'. *Organization Studies*, 23/4: 639–65.

ORTS, E. W. (1995). 'A reflexive model of environmental regulation'. *Business Ethics Quarterly*, 5/4: 779–94.

—— and DEKETELAERE, K. (2001). 'Environmental contracts and regulatory innovation'. In E. W. Orts and K. Deketelaere (eds.), *Environmental Contracts.* Dordrecht: Kluwer: 1–35.

OTTENSMEYER, E. J., and HEROUX, M. A. (1991). 'Ethics, public policy, and managing advanced technologies: the case of electronic surveillance'. *Journal of Business Ethics*, 10: 519–26.

Oxfam (2001). *Eight Broken Promises: Why the WTO isn't Working for the World's Poor*, vol. ix. Washington, DC: Oxfam.

PACKARD, V. (1957). *The Hidden Persuaders.* New York: Pocket Books.

PAINE, L. S. (1993). 'Children as consumers: the ethics of children's television advertising'. In N. C. Smith and J. A. Quelch (eds.), *Ethics in Marketing.* Homewood, Ill.: Irwin: 672–86.

—— (1994). 'Managing for organizational integrity'. *Harvard Business Review*, Mar.–Apr.: 106–17.

PALAZZO, B. (2000). *Interkulturelle Unternehemensethik. Deutsche und Amerikanische Ansätze im Vergleich.* Wiesbaden: Deutscher Universitätsverlag.

PARKER, B. (1998). *Globalization and Business Practice: Managing across Boundaries.* London: Sage.

PARKER, M. (1998). 'Business ethics and social theory: postmodernizing the ethical'. *British Journal of Management*, 9 (special issue): S27–S36.

PARKIN, F. (1982). *Max Weber.* London: Routledge.

PARKINSON, J. E. (1993). *Corporate Power and Responsibility.* Oxford: Oxford University Press.

PARKUM, K. H., and AGERSNAP, F. (1994). 'Managing pepole in Scandinavia'. In T. Garrison and D. Rees (eds.), *Managing People across Europe.* Oxford: Butterworth-Heinemann: 111–21.

PAULSON, H. (2001). 'The gospel of globalisation'. *Financial Times*, 13 Nov.: 25.

PEARCE, D. (1999). *Economics and Environment: Essays on Ecological Economics and Sustainable Development.* Cheltenham: Edward Elgar.

—— and TURNER, K. (1990). *Economics of Natural Resources and the Environment*. New York: Harvester Wheatsheaf.

PEARSON, R., and SEYFANG, G. (2001). 'New hope or false dawn? Voluntary codes of conduct, labour regulation and social policy in a globalizing world'. *Global Social Policy*, 1/1: 49–78.

PFEFFER, J., and SALANCIK, G. R. (1978). *The External Control of Organizations: A Resource Dependence Perspective*. New York: Harper & Row.

PHILLIPS, B. J. (1997). 'In defense of advertising: a social perspective'. *Journal of Business Ethics*, 16: 109–18.

PIERCY, N. F. (1999). *Tales from the Marketplace*. Oxford: Butterworth-Heinemann.

PIJPER, P. (1994). *Creative Accounting: The Effectiveness of Financial Reporting in the UK*. London: Macmillan.

POJMAN, L. P. (1997). 'The moral status of affirmative action'. In T. L. Beauchamp and N. E. Bowie (eds.), *Ethical Theory and Business*, 5th edn. Upper Saddle River, NJ: Prentice Hall: 374–9.

POLLAY, R. W. (1986). 'The distorted mirror: reflections on the unintended consequences of advertising'. *Journal of Marketing*, 50 (Apr.): 18–36.

PORTER, M. E. (1980). *Competitive Strategy: Techniques for Analysing Industries and Competitors*. New York: Free Press.

—— and VAN DER LINDE, C. (1995). 'Green and competitive'. *Harvard Business Review*, Sept.–Oct.: 120–34.

POSNER, B. Z., and SCHMIDT, W. H. (1992). 'Values and the American manager: an update updated'. *California Management Review*, 34/3: 80–94.

PREMEAUX, S. R., and MONDY, R. W. (1993). 'Linking management behavior to ethical philosophy'. *Journal of Business Ethics*, 12: 349–57.

PREUSS, L. (1999). 'Ethical theory in German business ethics research'. *Journal of Business Ethics*, 18: 407–19.

—— (2000). 'Should you buy your customer's values? On the transfer of moral values in industrial purchasing'. *International Journal of Value-Based Management*, 13: 141–58.

RABOUIN, M. (1997). 'Lyin' T(*)gers, and "Cares," oh my: the case of feminist integration of business ethics'. *Journal of Business Ethics*, 16: 247–61.

RAM, M. (2000). 'Investors in People in small firms: case study evidence from the business services sector'. *Personnel Review*, 29/1: 69–91.

RAWLS, J. (1971). *A Theory of Justice*. Cambridge, Mass.: Harvard University Press.

REECE, J. W. (2001). 'Business and the civil society: the missing dialectic'. *Thunderbird International Business Review*, 43/5: 651–67.

REINGOLD, J. (1993). 'A continent of givers'. *Financial World*, 162/16 (3 Aug.): 69.

REITZ, H. J., WALL, J. A., Jr., and LOVE, M. S. (1998). 'Ethics in negotiation: oil and water or good lubrication?' *Business Horizons*, May–June: 5–14.

RENN, O., WEBLER, T., and WIEDEMANN, P. M. (eds.) (1995). *Fairness and Competence in Citizen Participation*. Dordrecht: Kluwer.

REST, J. R. (1986). *Moral Development: Advances in Research and Theory*. New York: Praeger.

RIFKIN, J. (1995). *The End of Work*. New York: Tarcher Putnam.

RIVOLI, P. (1995). 'Ethical aspects of investor behaviour'. *Journal of Business Ethics*, 14: 265–77.

ROBIN, D. P., and REIDENBACH, R. E. (1987). 'Social responsibility, ethics and marketing strategy: closing the gap between concept and application'. *Journal of Marketing*, 51 (Jan.): 44–58.

ROBINS, N., and HUMPHREY, L. (2000). *Sustaining the rag trade*. London: International Institute for Environment and Development.

RONDINELLI, D., and VASTAG, G. (2000). 'Panacea, common sense, or just a label? The value of ISO 14001 environmental management systems'. *European Management Journal*, 18/5: 499–510.

RONIT, K. (2001). 'Institutions of private authority in global governance'. *Administration & Society*, 33/5: 555–78.

ROSENTHAL, S. B., and BUCHHOLZ, R. A. (2000). *Rethinking Business Ethics: A Pragmatic Approach*. New York: Oxford University Press.

ROTHSCHILD, J., and MIETHE, T. D. (1999). 'Whistle blower disclosures and management retaliation: the battle to control information about organization corruption'. *Work and Occupations*, 26/1: 107–28.

ROWAN, J. R. (2000). 'The moral foundation of employee rights'. *Journal of Business Ethics*, 24: 355–61.

ROWLEY, T. J. (1997). 'Moving beyond dyadic ties: a network theory of stakeholder influences'. *Academy of Management Review*, 22/4: 887–910.

Roy, R., and Whelan, R. C. (1992). 'Successful recycling through value-chain collaboration'. *Long Range Planning*, 25/4: 62–71.

Royle, T., and Towers, B. (2002). 'Summary and conclusions: MNCs, regulatory systems and employment rights'. In T. Royle and B. Towers (eds.), *Labour Relations in the Global Fast-Food Industry*. London: Routledge: 192–203.

Rudelius, W., and Buchholz, R. A. (1979). 'Ethical problems of purchasing managers'. *Harvard Business Review*, Mar.–Apr.: 8–14.

Rudolph, B. (1999). 'Finanzmärkte'. In W. Korff (ed.), *Handbuch der Wirtschaftsethik*. Gütersloh: Gütersloher Verlagshaus: iii. 274–92.

Rugman, A. M. (2000). *The End of Globalisation*. London: Random House.

—— and Verbeke, A. (2000). 'Six cases of corporate strategic responses to environmental regulation'. *European Management Journal*, 18/4: 377–85.

Sack, D. (2001). 'Jobs, Lärm, Mediation: Zur demokratischen Partizipation bei glokalen Großprojekten'. In M. Berndt and D. Sack (eds.), *Glocal Governance?* Opladen: Westdeutscher Verlag: 219–37.

Salamon, L. M., Anheier, H. K., List, R., Toepler, S., Sokolowski, S. W., and Associates (1999). *Global Civil Society: Dimensions of the Non-profit Sector*. Baltimore: The Johns Hopkins University Centre for Civil Society Studies.

Sandberg, A. (ed.) (1995). *Enriching Production: Perspectives on Volvo's Uddevalla Plant as an Alternative to Lean Production*. Aldershot: Avebury.

Scherer, A. G., and Smid, M. (2000). 'The downward spiral and the U.S. model business principles: why MNEs should take responsibility for improvement of worldwide social and environmental conditions'. *Management International Review*, 40/4: 351–71.

Schlegelmilch, B. B., and Houston, J. E. (1989). 'Corporate codes of ethics in large UK companies: an empirical investigation of use, content and attitudes'. *European Journal of Marketing*, 23/6: 7–24.

Schmidt, G., and Williams, K. (2002). 'German management facing globalization: the "German model" on trial'. In M. Geppert, D. Matten, and K. Williams (eds.), *Challenges for European Managment in a Global Context: Experiences from Britain and Germany*. Basingstoke: Palgrave: 281–93.

Schneidewind, U., and Petersen, H. (1998). 'Changing the rules: business–NGO partnerships and structuration theory'. *Greener Management International*, 24: 105–14.

Scholte, J. A. (2000). *Globalization: A Critical Introduction*. Basingstoke: Palgrave.

Schrader, B. (2002). 'Greenhouse gas emission policies in the UK and Germany: influences and responses'. *Business Strategy and the Environment*, 12: 173–84.

Schrader, U. (1999). 'Consumer acceptance of eco-efficient services'. *Greener Management International*, 25: 105–21.

Schumacher, E. F. (1974). *Small is Beautiful: A Study of Economics as if People Mattered*. London: Abacus.

Schwartz, M. (2000). 'Why ethical codes constitute an unconscionable regression'. *Journal of Business Ethics*, 23: 173–84.

Schwarzer, C. E., May, D. R., and Rosen, B. (1995). 'Organizational characteristics and HRM policies on rights: exploring the patterns of connections'. *Journal of Business Ethics*, 14: 531–49.

Scott, K., Park, J., and Cocklin, C. (2000). 'From "sustainable rural communities" to "social sustainability": giving voice to diversity in Mangakahia Valley, New Zealand'. *Journal of Rural Studies*, 16: 443–6.

Sen, S., Gurhan-Canli, Z., and Morwitz, V. (2001). 'Withholding consumption: a social dilemma perspective on consumer boycotts'. *Journal of Consumer Research*, 28/3: 399–417.

Shankman, N. A. (1999). 'Reframing the debate between agency and stakeholder theories of the firm'. *Journal of Business Ethics*, 19: 319–34.

Shaoul, J. (2002). 'A financial appraisal of the London Underground Public-Private Partnership'. *Public Money & Management*, Apr.–June: 53–60.

Shapiro, B. R. (1998). 'Economic espionage'. *Marketing Management*, 7/1: 56–8.

Shaw, B. (1995). 'Virtues for a postmodern world'. *Business Ethics Quarterly*, 5/4: 843–63.

Shaw, D., and Newholm, T. (2001). 'Voluntary simplicity and the ethics of consumption'. *Psychology and Marketing*, 19/2: 167–85.

Shrivastava, P. (1995). 'Ecocentric management for a risk society'. *Academy of Management Review*, 20/1: 118–37.

Sillanpää, M., and Wheeler, D. (1997). Integrated ethical auditing: The Body Shop International. In S. Zadek, P. Pruzan and R. Evans (eds.), *Building corporate accountability: emerging practices in social and ethical accounting, auditing and reporting*: 102–28. London: Earthscan.

SILLANPÄÄ, M. (1998). The Body Shop values report: towards integrated stakeholder auditing. *Journal of Business Ethics*, 17: 1443–56.

SIMMA, B., and HEINEMANN, A. (1999). 'Codes of conduct'. In W. Korff et al. (eds.), *Handbuch der Wirtschaftsethik*. Gütersloh: Gütersloher Verlagshaus: i. 403–18.

SIMMS, M. (1994). 'Defining privacy in employee health screening cases: ethical ramifications concerning the employee/employer relationship'. *Journal of Business Ethics*, 13: 315–25.

SIMPSON, R. (1998). 'Presenteeism, power and organizational change: long hours as a career barrier and the impact on the working lives of women managers'. *British Journal of Management*, 9 (special issue): 37–50.

—— (2000). 'Presenteeism and the impact of long hours on managers'. In D. Winstanley and J. Woodall (eds.), *Ethical Issues in Contemporary Human Resource Management*. Basingstoke: Macmillan: 156–71.

SIMS, R. R., and BRINKMANN, J. (2002). 'Leaders as moral role models: the case of John Gutfreund at Salomon Brothers'. *Journal of Business Ethics*, 35/4: 327–39.

SINCLAIR, A. (1993). 'Approaches to organizational culture and ethics'. *Journal of Business Ethics*, 12: 63–73.

SINGHAPAKDI, A., and VITELL, S. J. (1990). 'Marketing ethics: factors influencing perceptions of ethical problems and alternatives'. *Journal of Macromarketing*, 10/1: 4–18.

SKLAIR, L. (1991). *Sociology of the Global System*. Baltimore: Johns Hopkins University Press.

SMALLEY BOWEN, T. (2003). 'Reducing pollution: it's a bargain'. *Financial Times*, 2 Feb.: 16.

SMITH, A. (1793). *An Inquiry into the Nature and Causes of the Wealth of Nations*, vol. i, 7th edn. London: A. Sraten & T. Cadell.

SMITH, C. (1994). 'The new corporate philanthropy'. *Harvard Business Review*, May–June: 105–16.

SMITH, N. C. (1990). *Morality and the Market: Consumer Pressure for Corporate Accountability*. London: Routledge.

—— (1995). 'Marketing strategies for the ethics era'. *Sloan Management Review*, 36/4: 85–97.

—— and COOPER-MARTIN, E. (1997). 'Ethics and target marketing: the role of product harm and consumer vulnerability'. *Journal of Marketing*, 61 (July): 1–20.

—— and QUELCH, J. A. (1993). *Ethics in Marketing*. Homewood, Ill.: Irwin.

SOLOMON, A., and LEWIS, L. (2002). 'Incentives and disincentives for corporate environmental disclosure'. *Business Strategy and the Environment*, 11 (3): 154–69.

SOLOMON, R. C. (1999). *A Better Way to Think about Business: How Personal Integrity Leads to Corporate Success*. New York: Oxford University Press.

SOMERS, M. J. (2001). 'Ethical codes of conduct and organizational context: a study of the relationship between codes of conduct, employee behaviour and organizational values'. *Journal of Business Ethics*, 30: 185–95.

SORGE, A. (2000). 'The diabolical dialectics of societal effects'. In M. Maurice and A. Sorge (eds.), *Embedding Organizations: Societal Analysis of Actors, Organizations, and Socio-economic Content*. Amsterdam: John Benjamins: 37–56.

SORRELL, T. (1998). 'Beyond the fringe? The strange state of business ethics'. In M. Parker (ed.), *Ethics and Organizations*. London: Sage: 15–29.

SPAR, D., and YOFFIE, D. (1999). 'Multinational enterprises and the prospects for justice'. *Journal of International Affairs*, 52/2: 557–81.

SPARKES, R. (2001). 'Ethical investment: whose ethics, which investment?' *Business Ethics: A European Review*, 10/3: 194–205.

SPENCE, L. J. (2000). 'What ethics in the employment interview?' In D. Winstanley and J. Woodall (eds.), *Ethical Issues in Contemporary Human Resource Management*. Basingstoke: Macmillan: 43–58.

—— (2002). 'Is Europe distinctive from America? An overview of business ethics in Europe'. In H. von Weltzien Hoivik (ed.), *Moral Leadership in Action*. Cheltenham: Edward Elgar: 9–25.

—— and LOZANO, J. F. (2000). 'Communicating about ethics with small firms: experiences from the U.K. and Spain'. *Journal of Business Ethics*, 27/1–2: 43–53.

—— COLES, A., and HARRIS, L. (2001). 'The forgotten stakeholder? Ethics and social responsibility in relation to competitors'. *Business and Society Review*, 106/4: 331–52.

STANWORTH, C. (2000). 'Flexible working patterns'. In D. Winstanley and J. Woodall (eds.), *Ethical Issues in Contemporary Human Resource Management*. Basingstoke: Macmillan: 137–55.

STARK, A. (1994). 'What's the matter with business ethics?' *Harvard Business Review*, May–June: 38–48.

STARKEY, K. (1998). 'Durkheim and the limits of corporate culture: whose culture? Which Durkheim?' *Journal of Management Studies*, 35/2: 125–36.

STEINMANN, H., and LÖHR, A. (1994). *Grundlagen der Unternehmensethik*, 2nd edn. Stultgart: Schäffer-Poeschel.

STENZEL, P. L. (1999). 'Can the ISO 14000 series environmental management standards provide a viable alternative to government regulation?' *American Business Law Journal*, 37: 238–98.

STIGLER, G. J. (1971). 'The theory of economic regulation'. *Bell Journal of Economics and Management Science*, 2: 3–21.

STONEY, C., and WINSTANLEY, D. (2001). 'Stakeholding: confusion or utopia? Mapping the conceptual terrain'. *Journal of Management Studies*, 38/5: 603–26.

STRONG, C. (1997). 'The problems of translating fair trade principles into consumer purchase behaviour'. *Marketing Intelligence and Planning*, 15: 27–35.

SULLIVAN, C., and LEWIS, S. (2001). 'Home-based telework, gender, and the synchronization of work and family: perspectives of teleworkers and their co-residents'. *Gender, Work and Organizations*, 8/2: 123–45.

TAPLIN, I. (2002). 'The effects of globalization on the state–business relationships: a conceptual framework'. In M. Geppert, D. Matten, and K. Williams (eds.), *Challenges for European Management in a Global Context*. Basingstoke: Palgrave: 239–59.

TAPPER, R. (1997). 'Voluntary agreements for environmental performance improvement: perspectives on the chemical industry's Responsible Care Programme'. *Business Strategy and the Environment*, 8: 287–92.

TAYLOR, R. (2000). 'How new is socially responsible investment?' *Business Ethics: A European Review*, 9/3: 174–9.

—— (2001). 'Putting ethics into investment'. *Business Ethics: A European Review*, 10/1: 53–60.

TEN BOS, R. (1997). 'Business ethics and Bauman ethics'. *Organization Studies*, 18/6: 997–1014.

—— and WILLMOTT, H. (2001). 'Towards a post-dualistic business ethics: interweaving reason and emotion in working life'. *Journal of Management Studies*, 38/6: 769–93.

TEN BRINK, P. (ed.) (2002). *Voluntary Environmental Agreements*. Sheffield: Greenleaf.

THOMPSON, C. J. (1995). 'A contextualist proposal for the conceptualization and study of marketing ethics'. *Public Policy and Marketing*, 14/2: 177–91.

THOMPSON, P., and MCHUGH, D. (2002). *Work Organizations*, 3rd edn. Basingstoke: Palgrave.

THORNE LECLAIR, D., and FERRELL, L. (2000). 'Innovation in experiential business ethics training'. *Journal of Business Ethics*, 23 (3/1): 313–22.

THORNE MCALISTER, D., FERRELL, O. C., and FERRELL, L. (2003). *Business and Society: A Strategic Approach to Corporate Citizenship*. Boston: Houghton Mifflin.

TOBIN, J. (1978). 'A proposal for international monetary reform'. *Eastern Economic Journal*, 4: 153–9.

TORRINGTON, D. (1993). 'How dangerous is human resource management? A reply to Tim Hart'. *Employee Relations*, 15/5: 40–53.

TREVIÑO, L. K. (1986). 'Ethical decision making in organizations: a person–situation interactionist model'. *Academy of Management Review*, 11/3: 601–17.

—— and NELSON, K. A. (1999). *Managing Business Ethics: Straight Talk about How to do it Right*, 2nd edn. New York: John Wiley.

—— and YOUNGBLOOD, S. A. (1990). 'Bad apples in bad barrels: a causal analysis of ethical decision making behavior'. *Journal of Applied Psychology*, 75/4: 378–85.

—— WEAVER, G. R., GIBSON, D. G., and TOFFLER, B. L. (1999). 'Managing ethics and legal compliance: what works and what hurts'. *California Management Review*, 41/2: 131–51.

—— HARTMAN, L. P., and BROWN, M. (2000). 'Moral person and moral manager: how executives develop a reputation for ethical leadership'. *California Management Review*, 42/4: 128–42.

TROUVÉ, P. (1994). 'Managing people in France'. In T. Garrison and D. Rees (eds.), *Managing People across Europe*. Oxford: Butterworth-Heinemann: 40–62.

TSALIKIS, J., and FRITZSCHE, D. J. (1989). 'Business ethics: a Literature review with a focus on marketing ethics'. *Journal of Business Ethics*, 8: 695–743.

TURNER, K. (ed.) (1993). *Sustainable Environmental Economics and Management: Principles and Practice*. London: Belhaven Press.

UN (2001). *2001 Report on the World Situation.* New York: United Nations Publications.

VAN CALSTER, G., and DEKETELAERE, K. (2001). 'The use of voluntary agreements in the European Community's environmental policy'. In K. Deketelaere (ed.), *Environmental Contracts*. Dordrecht: Kluwer: 199–246.

VAN GERWEN, J. (1994). 'Employers' and employees' rights and duties'. In B. Harvey (ed.), *Business Ethics: A European Approach*. London: Prentice Hall: 56–87.

VAN LUIJK, H. J. L. (1990). 'Recent developments in European business ethics'. *Journal of Business Ethics*, 9: 537–44.

—— (2001). 'Business ethics in Europe: a tale of two efforts'. In R. Lang (ed.), *Wirtschaftsethik in Mittel- und Osteuropa*. Munich: Rainer Hampp: 9–18.

VAN PARIJS, P. (2000). 'Must Europe be Belgian? On democratic citizenship in multilingual polities'. In C. McKinnon and I. Hampsher-Monk (eds.), *The Demands of Citizenship*. London: Continuum: 235–56.

VAN SCHENDELEN, R. (2002). 'The ideal profile of the PA expert at the EU level'. *Journal of Public Affairs*, 2/2: 85–9.

VAN TULDER, R., and KOLK, A. (2001). 'Multinationality and corporate ethics: codes of conduct in the sporting goods industry'. *Journal of International Business Studies*, 32/2: 267–83.

VARADARAJAN, P. R., and MENON, A. (1988). 'Cause-related marketing: a coalignment of marketing strategy and corporate philanthropy'. *Journal of Marketing*, 52 (July): 58–74.

VIDAL, J., and HETHERINGTON, P. (2001). 'Foot and mouth crisis: food lobby forced PM into u-turn on plan for vaccination: Nestle chief believed £8bn export market would be compromised'. *Guardian*, 8 Sept.

VOGEL, D. (1992). 'The globalization of business ethics: why America remains different'. *California Management Review*, 35/1: 30–49.

—— (1998). 'Is U.S. business obsessed with ethics?' *Across the Board*, Nov.–Dec.: 31–3.

VON WELTZIEN HOIVIK, H. (ed.) (2002). *Moral Leadership in Action*. Cheltenham: Edward Elgar.

WADDELL, S. (2000). 'New institutions for the practice of corporate citizenship: historical, intersectoral, and developmental perspectives'. *Business and Society Review*, 105/1: 107–26.

WADDOCK, S. A. (1988). 'Building successful social partnerships'. *Sloan Management Review*, 29/4: 17–23.

—— and GRAVES, S. B. (1997). 'The corporate social performance–financial performance link'. *Strategic Management Journal*, 18/4: 303–19.

WAGNER, G. R., and HAFFNER, F. (1999). 'Ökonomische Würdigung des umweltrechtlichen Instrumentariums'. In M. Schröder (ed.), *Rückzug des Ordnungsrechtes im Umweltschutz*. Berlin: Erich Schmidt: 83–127.

WALLACE, M. (1989). 'Brave new workplace: technology and work in the new economy'. *Work and Occupations*, 16/4: 363–92.

WARREN, R. C. (1999). 'Company legitimacy in the new millenium'. *Business Ethics: A European Review*, 8/4: 214–24.

WARTICK, S. L., and COCHRAN, P. L. (1985). 'The evolution of the corporate social performance model'. *Academy of Management Review*, 10: 758–69.

WATSON, T. J. (1994). *In Search of Management: Culture, Chaos and Control in Managerial Work*. London: Routledge.

—— (1998). 'Ethical codes and moral communities: the gunlaw temptation, the Simon solution and the David dilemma'. In M. Parker (ed.), *Ethics and Organizations*. London: Sage: 253–68.

WEAVER, G., TREVINO, L. K., and COCHRAN, P. L. (1999a). 'Corporate ethics practices in the mid-1990s: an empirical study of the Fortune 1000'. *Journal of Business Ethics*, 18: 283–94.

—— —— —— (1999b). 'Corporate ethics programs as control systems: influences of executive commitment and environmental factors'. *Academy of Management Journal*, 42/1: 41–57.

WEBER, J. (1990). 'Managers' moral reasoning: assessing their responses to three moral dilemmas'. *Human Relations*, 43/7: 687–702.

WEBER, M. (1905). *Die protestantische Ethik und der 'Geist' des Kapitalismus*, vols. xxi and xxii. Tübingen: Archiv für Sozialwissenschaft und Sozialpolitik.

—— (1947). *The Theory of Social and Economic Organization*, trans. A. M. Henderson and T. Parsons. Oxford: Oxford University Press.

WEBLEY, S. (1997). *Codes of Ethics and International Business*. London: Institute of Business Ethics.

—— (2001). 'Values-based codes'. In C. Moon and C. Bonny (eds.), *Business Ethics: Facing up to the Issues*. London: The Economist Books: 159–69.

WELFORD, R. J. (1997). *Hijacking Environmentalism: Corporate Responses to Sustainable Development*. London: Routledge.

WERHANE, P. H. (1998). 'Moral imagination and the search for ethical decision-making in management'. *Business Ethics Quarterly*, Ruffin Series (1): 75–98.

WHAWELL, P. (1998). 'The ethics of pressure groups'. *Business Ethics: A European Review*, 7/3: 178–81.

WHEELER, D. (2001). 'Racing to the bottom? Foreign investment and air pollution in developing countries'. *Journal of Environment & Development*, 10/3: 225–45.

—— FABIG, H., and BOELE, R. (2002). 'Paradoxes and dilemmas for stakeholder responsive firms in the extractive sector: lessons from the case of Shell and the Ogoni'. *Journal of Business Ethics*, 39: 297–318.

WHITLEY, R. (ed.) (1992). *European Business Systems*. London: Sage.

—— (1999). *Divergent Capitalisms: The Social Structuring and Change of Business Systems*. Oxford: Oxford University Press.

WHITTINGTON, R., and MAYER, M. (2002). 'The evolving European corporation: strategy, structure and social science'. In M. Geppert, D. Matten, and K. Williams (eds.), *Challenges for European Management in a Global Context*. Basingstoke: Palgrave: 19–41.

WINDSOR, D. (2001). 'Corporate citizenship: evolution and interpretation'. In J. Andriof and M. McIntosh (eds.), *Perspectives on Corporate Citizenship*. Sheffield: Greenleaf: 39–52.

WINSTANLEY, D., CLARK, J., and LEESON, H. (2002). 'Approaches to child labour in the supply chain'. *Business Ethics: A European Review*, 11/3: 210–23.

WOOD, D. J. (1991). 'Corporate social performance revisited'. *Academy of Management Review*, 16: 691–718.

—— and LOGSDON, J. M. (2001). 'Theorising business citizenship'. In J. Andriof and M. McIntosh (eds.), *Perspectives on Corporate Citizenship*. Sheffield: Greenleaf: 83–103.

WOODRUFFE, H. (1997). 'Compensatory consumption: why women go shopping when they're fed up and other stories'. *Marketing Intelligence and Planning*, 15/7: 325–34.

WOODS, N. (2001). 'Making the IMF and the World Bank more accountable'. *International Affairs*, 77/1: 83–100.

WOOTLIFF, J., and DERI, C. (2001). 'NGOs: the new super brands'. *Corporate Reputation Review*, 4/2: 157–65.

World Commission on Environment and Development (1987). *Our Common Future*. Oxford: Oxford University Press.

World Economic Forum (2002). *Global Corporate Citizenship: The Leadership Challenge for CEOs and Boards*. Geneva: World Economic Forum and The Prince of Wales Business Leaders Forum.

WOYWODE, M. (2002). 'Global management concepts and local adaptations: working groups in the French and German car manufacturing industry'. *Organization Studies*, 23/4: 497–524.

YIP, G. (1995). *Total Global Strategies*. London: Prentice Hall.

YOUNG, A., and KIELKIEWICZ-YOUNG, A. (2001). 'Sustainable supply network management'. *Corporate Environmental Management*, 8/3: 260–8.

ZADEK, S. (1998). 'Balancing performance, ethics and accountability'. *Journal of Business Ethics*, 17: 1421–41.

—— (2001). *The Civil Corporation: The New Economy of Corporate Citizenship*. London: Earthscan.

ZADEK, S., PRUZAN, P., and EVANS, R. (eds.) (1997). *Building Corporate Accountability: Emerging Practices in Social and Ethical Accounting, Auditing and Reporting*. London: Earthscan.

SUBJECT INDEX

■ AUTHORS INDEX

■ COUNTRIES AND REGIONS INDEX

■ COMPANIES, ORGANIZATIONS, AND BRANDS INDEX